Assessment and Control
of Software Risks

ANDREWS AND LEVENTHAL   Fusion: Integrating IE, CASE, and JAD
AUGUST   Joint Application Design
BLOCK   The Politics of Projects
BODDIE   The Information Asset: Rational DP Funding and Other Radical Notions
BOULDIN   Agents of Change: Managing the Introduction of Automated Tools
BRILL   Building Controls into Structured Systems
CHANG   Principles of Visual Programming Systems
COAD AND NICOLA   Object-Oriented Programming
COAD AND YOURDON   Object-Oriented Analysis, 2/E
COAD AND YOURDON   Object-Oriented Design
CONNELL AND SHAFER   Structured Rapid Prototyping
CONSTANTINE AND YOURDON   Structured Design
CRAWFORD   Advancing Business Concepts in a JAD Workshop Setting
DeGRACE AND STAHL   The Olduvai Imperative: CASE and the State of Software Engineering Practice
DeGRACE AND STAHL   Wicked Problems, Righteous Solutions
DeMARCO   Controlling Software Projects
DeMARCO   Structured Analysis and System Specification
EMBLEY, KURTZ, AND WOODFIELD   Object-Oriented Systems Analysis
FOURNIER   Practical Guide to Structured System Development and Maintenance
GLASS   Software Conflict: Essays on the Art and Science of Software Engineering
JONES   Assessment and Control of Software Risks
KING   Current Practices in Software Development: A Guide to Successful Systems
KING   Project Management Made Simple
LARSON   Interactive Software: Tools for Building Interactive User Interfaces
MARTIN   Transaction Processing Facility: A Guide for Application Programmers
McMENAMIN AND PALMER   Essential System Design
MOSLEY   The Handbook of MIS Application Software Testing
PAGE-JONES   Practical Guide to Structured Systems Design, 2/E
PINSON   Designing Screen Interfaces in C
PUTNAM AND MYERS   Measures for Excellence: Reliable Software on Time, within Budget
RIPPS   An Implementation Guide to Real-Time Programming
RODGERS   ORACLE®: A Database Developer's Guide
RODGERS   UNIX®: Database Management Systems
SERBANATI   Integrating Tools for Software Development
SHLAER AND MELLOR   Object Lifecycles: Modeling the World in States
SHLAER AND MELLOR   Object-Oriented Systems Analysis: Modeling the World in Data
SHILLER   Software Excellence
THOMSETT   Third Wave Project Management
TOIGO   Disaster Recovery Planning: Managing Risk and Catastrophe in Information Systems
WANG (ed.)   Information Technology in Action
WARD   System Development Without Pain
WARD AND MELLOR   Structured Development for Real-Time Systems
YOURDON   Decline and Fall of the American Programmer
YOURDON   Managing the Structured Techniques, 4/E
YOURDON   Managing the System Life Cycle, 2/E
YOURDON   Modern Structured Analysis
YOURDON   Object-Oriented Systems Design
YOURDON   Structured Walkthroughs, 4/E
YOURDON   Techniques of Program Structure and Design
YOURDON INC.   YOURDON™ Systems Method: Model-Driven Systems Development

Assessment and Control of Software Risks

Capers Jones

YOURDON PRESS
Prentice Hall Building
Englewood Cliffs, New Jersey 07632

Library of Congress Cataloging-in-Publication Data

Jones, Capers.
    Assessment & control of software risks / Capers Jones.
      p.   cm. — (Yourdon Press computing series)
    Includes index.
    ISBN 0-13-741406-4
    1. Computer software—Quality control.   2. Software engineering—
Management.   3. Risk management.   I. Title.   II. Title: Assessment
and control of software risks.   III. Series.
QA76.76.Q35J67   1994
005.1'068—dc20   93-36816
                                         CIP

Editorial/production supervision: *The Wheetley Company, Inc.*
Acquisitions editor: *Paul W. Becker*
Buyer: *Alexis R. Heydt*
Jacket photo: *The Bettmann Archives*
Jacket design: *Tweet Graphics*

 © 1994 by PTR Prentice Hall
Prentice-Hall, Inc.
A Paramount Communications Company
Englewood Cliffs, New Jersey 07632

The publisher offers discounts on this book when ordered
in bulk quantities. For more information, contact:

    Corporate Sales Department
    PTR Prentice Hall
    113 Sylvan Avenue
    Englewood Cliffs, NJ 07632

    Phone: 201-592-2863
    Fax: 201-592-2249

Printed in the United States of America
10 9 8 7 6 5 4 3 2 1

ISBN 0-13-741406-4

Prentice-Hall International (UK) Limited, *London*
Prentice-Hall of Australia Pty. Limited, *Sydney*
Prentice-Hall Canada Inc., *Toronto*
Prentice-Hall Hispanoamericana, S.A., *Mexico*
Prentice-Hall of India Private Limited, *New Delhi*
Prentice-Hall of Japan, Inc., *Tokyo*
Simon & Schuster Asia Pte. Ltd., *Singapore*
Editora Prentice-Hall do Brasil, Ltda., *Rio de Janeiro*

Contents

Preface

This book is a cross-disciplinary effort which applies a format used in medical writing to software engineering. Many years ago in the 1960's as a young programmer working for the Office of the Surgeon General, I became familiar with a book called *Control of Communicable Diseases in Man*. This book was produced annually by the American Public Health Association and published by the U.S. Public Health Service.

This book was very useful to me in clarifying some of the medical terms and concepts which were the background of much of the work carried out by the Public Health Service and the Office of the Surgeon General.

The book, *Control of Communicable Diseases in Man,* was organized alphabetically, and listed all known communicable diseases starting with actinomycosis and ending with yellow fever. The book used the following format for each disease:

1. Identification
2. Occurrence
3. Infectious agent
4. Reservoir and source of infection
5. Mode of transmission
6. Incubation period
7. Period of communicability
8. Susceptibility and resistance
9. Methods of control
   a) Preventive measure
   b) Control of patient, contacts, and immediate environment
   ♦ Report to local health authority
   ♦ Isolation, concurrent disinfection, terminal disinfection, quarantine, immunization, investigation of contacts and source of infection, specific treatment
   c) Epidemic measures
   d) International measures

The book filled a useful niche. Medical terminology is quite extensive, and unlike standard medical dictionaries, *Control of Communicable Diseases in Man* offered background and context to its defined terms.

The book assumed that the reader was in the medical or public health professions, but might need a quick summary of an unusual condition, such as a case of schistosomiasis in a returning traveler. The book casually assumed the existence of substantial medical reference facilities, and did not use much space on detailed citations to the other literature dealing with the conditions. Since the book was organized alphabetically and used a standard format for all topics, it did not need an index. The glossary of terms provided within the book were primarily those dealing with control of communicable conditions—knowledge of basic medical terms was assumed. Therefore terms such as "quarantine" and "isolation" were defined since they were associated with controlling many communicable diseases.

The format and idea of *Control of Communicable Diseases in Man* is the basis for this book. Obviously the contents and structure for this book are not identical to the former, since software engineering is not medicine. However, we have used a similar method of presentation:

1. Definition	11. Product support
2. Severity	12. Consulting support
3. Frequency	13. Education support
4. Occurrence	14. Publication support
5. Susceptibility and resistance	15. Periodical support
6. Root causes	16. Standards support
7. Associated problems	17. Professional associations
8. Cost impact	18. Effectiveness of known therapies
9. Methods of prevention	19. Costs of known therapies
10. Methods of control	20. Long-range prognosis

Medical conditions range from fairly minor to very serious. Even minor conditions may become serious if they are not corrected in time.

The same kind of thinking is appropriate for software. Software problems also range from fairly minor to very serious. But even minor conditions should not be ignored.

With both medicine and software, it is not safe to assume that problems will go away by themselves. The human body at least has an immune system, which offers active resistance to many bacterial and viral infections.

Software groups lack an immune system. The only thing that even approaches an immune system in business or government operations are bright, intelligent people who can understand and solve problems. From time to time, the phrase "white knight" is used in business to describe an individual or company who protects an enterprise against a hostile takeover.

The term is not totally appropriate, but capable problem solvers might be considered as a kind of "white corpuscle" that attacks and sometimes eliminates technical business problems. There are not very many of them and they don't always succeed. But any company that has them as executives, managers, employees, or consultants should consider itself fortunate.

This book assumes that the reader is already familiar with the basic terminology of software and has access to a good source of books and journals. Although this book has a large glossary, the terms defined are primarily those which arise during assessment sessions and are troublesome or ambiguous.

This book is aimed at software managers and software professionals in domains such as software engineering, software quality assurance, and related software topics. The philosophy of this book is similar to that of the authors of *Control of Communicable Diseases in Man:* problems do not go away by themselves. If you wish to control serious problems, you must find the causes and take steps toward curing the problems in those already afflicted. Then you must move toward prevention of future problems.

Another aspect of the two books is also similar. From time to time, new diseases occur or are identified and need to be added to medical references. For example, Lyme disease, the more virulent forms of the herpes simplex virus, and AIDS were not discussed in U.S. medical literature prior to the 1980's.

For software, new problems occur from time to time also. For instance the advent of client-server applications is showing signs of greatly increasing the difficulty of testing applications. Neural-net applications will also introduce new problems, as well as new solutions. As expert system applications become more common, it may be that new kinds of knowledge-acquisition problems may occur. These are only the tips of the icebergs. Neither medicine nor software can assume static conditions. Both must deal with dynamic problems and changing conditions.

It would be highly unprofessional for a medical doctor to prescribe medicine for a patient without an accurate diagnosis of the condition, or an exploration of possible counter indications or reactions to the recommended medicine or therapy. We need that same concept in software engineering. Far too often, companies jump into some kind of a half-baked therapy mode without properly diagnosing or assessing what is right and wrong with the way they build software.

It is very common for software managers to do things which, if it were medicine, would be considered to be malpractice. For instance, buying CASE tools without regard for associated methodologies, training, and office environment is one example. Another might be the assertion that the enterprise "uses Total Quality Management" when in fact the senior managers have only a hazy idea what that phrase means, and have adopted only the name, not the substance.

As of 1993, there are more than half a dozen variations on software process assessments that are used in the United States. The two most common methods, due to the availability of published books which describe the approaches, are those of Software Productivity Research (SPR) and the Software Engineering Institute (SEI).

These two methods might be viewed as separate diagnostic procedures aimed at identifying and isolating software problems. The SPR method is somewhat older than the SEI method, and used more widely by domestic and international companies. The SEI method, since SEI is funded by the Department of Defense, is used primarily with defense contractors, although its usage is now moving into non-defense enterprises.

The SPR assessments attempt to study almost every factor that can affect the outcome of software: cultural factors, methodological factors, technology factors, tools, and even compensation plans, capital investment, and financial factors. Also, the SPR assessments capture substantial amounts of quantitative data on productivity, quality, and volumes of software deliverables. This data is used for comparisons to U.S. national averages and in many cases to industry averages as well.

The use of multiple assessment approaches is sound and practical. Certainly a complete medical examination does not depend upon only a single test for a condition. When multiple assessments are used and when they all point out the same condition, the results are usually conclusive and highly convincing.

Both SPR and SEI assessments are normally followed by a therapy phase. The set of therapies which follow an SPR assessment derive from the diagnosed problems.

Some of the frequent problems which the SPR or SEI assessments uncover (the "common colds" of the software world) include excessive schedule pressure, inadequate software quality control, and inaccurate software cost and schedule estimation.

The first problem, schedule pressure, is purely cultural, and requires therapy that deals with sociological issues.

The second problem, poor quality, is technically a methodological problem but also has a cultural aspect. Effective therapies require new methods in measurement, defect prevention and removal, plus cultural awareness of the true value of quality to business.

The third problem, inaccurate estimation, is essentially a technological problem, and also has a cultural aspect. Inaccurate estimation can be aided by acquiring one or more software estimation and planning tools. However, to determine accuracy, measurement is needed, and here there are cultural and methodological implications to be faced.

The fundamental point is that an accurate assessment or diagnostic approach for software problems must be multi-faceted and deal with cultural, methodological, and tool-related problems. It must also precede the selection of effective therapies. Jumping into therapy acquisition without an accurate diagnosis leads to wasted money and time. Even more serious, hasty solutions ignore problems that were not visible to software management. In addition, acquiring new tools, methods, or technologies without cultural acceptance cannot be totally successful.

There are a number of medical conditions for which therapies either do not exist or are generally ineffective. As of 1993, both Alzheimer's disease and AIDS are examples of medical conditions which lack effective therapies.

In performing software assessments, there may be problems encountered which have no available therapies. For example, enterprises which have been severely damaged by the economic downturn and are hemorrhaging cash and performing emergency surgery on their organizations and staffing levels, are not in a position to do much except perhaps survive. These enterprises certainly cannot make large investments in new tools and methods or afford the expense of climbing the SEI maturity ladder.

Another example of a condition that is difficult to treat is a large portfolio of aging software or legacy systems in low-level language such as assembly. Often such software is without adequate specifications or supporting documentation and the original developers are no longer available. Although a host of restructuring and reverse engineering tools are entering the market, assembly language is seldom supported by such tools. Thus geriatric care is difficult, and there may be no truly effective therapy as of 1993. Even so, it is better to be aware of such conditions.

When medical doctors become sick, they normally seek medical advice from colleagues and other doctors, rather than treating themselves. There is a similar concept in the assessment domain. Indeed, it would be an interesting approach for SEI and SPR to assess one another, and perhaps for all of the assessment providers to receive assessments themselves.

Self-assessments by software managers and software engineers tend to have unconscious bias and are seldom complete or accurate. For example, few of us will admit to our own cultural problems such as inflicting excessive schedule pressure on our subordinates. Many such problems are difficult to detect via self assessments since most humans are blind to their own shortcomings. Fortunately, as of 1993, there is a wide variety of consulting support that can perform independent assessments.

As of 1993, neither the SPR nor the SEI assessment methods even approach medical diagnosis in completeness, accuracy, and diagnostic rigor. This statement is also true of other software assessment methods including those of SDC, Roger Pressman Associates and Hewlett-Packard. However medical diagnosis itself is not perfect either. Both professions must constantly strive toward continued improvements in both diagnostic rigor and therapeutic methods. If we assess or diagnose to the best of our abilities and prescribe therapies which are supported by empirical evidence, then we are moving toward true professionalism.

Acknowledgments

As always, special thanks to my wife, Eileen Jones, for her support during the writing of this book and for her patience when I get wrapped up on our computer. Thanks also for her coordination of my various book and magazine publishing activities.

Great appreciation is due to my colleagues at Software Productivity Research for their aid in gathering the data, assisting our clients, building the tools that we use, and for making SPR an enjoyable environment. Thanks to Lynne Caramanica, Debbie Chapman, Mike Cunnane, Charles Douglis, Rich Gazoorian, Jane Greene, Wayne Hadlock, Bill Harmon, Shane Hartman, David Herron, Fred Jacobsen, Debi Malone, Scott McLeod, Heather MacPhee, Mark Pinis, Diane Scozzari, Christine Siler, Richard Ward, and John Zimmerman. Special thanks to the families of the SPR staff, who have put up with lots of travel and far too much overtime.

Many other colleagues work with us at SPR on special projects or as consultants. Special thanks to Allan Albrecht, the inventor of Function Points, for his invaluable contribution to the industry and for his work with SPR. Thanks to Dave Garmus, the editor of the IFPUG counting practices handbook, for his long association with SPR. Thanks also to Michael Bragen and Ken Foster. Thanks also to Dale

Hedrick and Susan Turner also for their support in their various specialties and also to Kelly Faford and to Judith Vanderkay.

Appreciation is also due to Ronna Alintuck, Shelby Capers Hypes, Paula Mae, Ajit Maira, and the others who have supported SPR in making its research visible.

Thanks also to Jim Dittmar, Rich Stein, and Rich Yurko for their contributions to SPR during our long association.

Appreciation to the external members of the SPR board for their advice: Thanks to Gene Robinson and Dick Spann. Thanks also to Ken Bowes, a former director, for his long service to SPR and the excellence of his counsels. Thanks also to Christine Bowes for her advice in sales and marketing topics.

Much appreciation is due to the client organizations whose interest in software assessments, measurement, and process improvements have let us work together. There are too many groups to name them all, but many thanks to our colleagues and clients at Amdahl, AT&T, Bell Northern Research, Bachman, Bendix, Church of the Latter Day Saints, CODEX, DEC, Dunn & Bradstreet, DuPont, EDS, Fidelity Investments, Ford Motors, General Electric, GTE, Hartford Insurance, Hewlett-Packard, IBM, Informix, Inland Steel, ISSC, JC Penney, Mead Data Central, Motorola, NCR, Northern Telecom, Nynex, Pacific Bell, Ralston Purina, Sears Roebuck, Siemens-Nixdorf, Sun Life Insurance, Tandem, UNISYS, U.S. Navy Surface Weapons groups, US West, Wang, and Westinghouse.

Since this book deals primarily with problem and risk conditions, it is best not to identify the specific enterprises which constitute the set where problems were noted, even if that were possible. Most of the data SPR collects is under nondisclosure agreements, and the specific groups providing it cannot be identified. Suffice it to say that the organizations assessed by SPR include public and private corporations, government agencies, and military services.

The book is based on observations and assessments from several hundred companies and several thousand projects. New data is being gathered at a rate of about 300 projects per year.

Although U.S. companies are in the majority, SPR and the author also work internationally. Over 20 countries have been visited in the course of performing SPR assessments. As an example of the international flavor of software assessment work, the basic SPR assessment questionnaire exists in English, Japanese, German, French, and Portuguese versions.

Although we are business competitors as well as colleagues, appreciation is due to Watts Humphrey, Bill Curtis and Ron Radice of the Software Engineering Institute (SEI) for making software process assessments so well known.

Alphabetical Listing of Tool Citations

The total quantity of commercially available software tools as of 1993 probably exceeds 5,000 in the United States alone and 8,500 on a global basis. New tools and new versions of tools are appearing at a rate of perhaps 50 to 75 a month. The tools cited in this book are used only as representative examples of various kinds of tool capabilities. The listing is not intended to be complete, and constitutes only about a 5% sample of the thousands of commercially available software tools. Tools are also disappearing at frequent intervals, and the number of tools withdrawn by vendors, or where the vendors themselves go out of business, approaches a rate of three to five tools a month.

Since there are only 26 letters in the English alphabet, many tool acronyms and even product names are used by more than a single vendor. This alphabetic listing identifies the products and vendors used in the citations. For example, the name MODEL is used for two different products. The tool named MODEL marketed by Ross Systems, Inc. is a financial management tool. The tool named MODEL marketed by Computer Command & Control Company is an application development tool. When this situation occurs, the context of the discussion should make clear which choice is appropriate.

The author is chairman of Software Productivity Research, Inc. (SPR). This company produces and markets two software cost estimating tools. SPQR/20™ is a trademark of Software Productivity Research, Inc. CHECKPOINT® and CHECKMARK® are both registered trademarks of Software Productivity Research, Inc. CHECKPOINT® is used in the United States. CHECKMARK® is used in the United Kingdom for the same product.

Some product names and services identified throughout this book are trademarks or registered trademarks of their respective companies. They are used throughout this book in editorial fashion only and for the benefit of such companies. No such uses, or the use of any trade name, is intended to convey endorsement or other affiliation with the book. Use of a term in this book should not be regarded as affecting the validity of any trademark or service mark.

2167A Tool Set; Advanced System Technology Corporation.

ABLE (Applications Building Language and Environment); Geac Computers International, Inc.
ABSTRACT; Advanced Systems Concepts, Inc.
ACCENT VUE; National Information Systems, Inc.
ACCESS.204; Computer Corporation of America.
ACT (Analysis of Complexity Tool); McCabe & Associates.
ACT/1; Certified Software Specialists.

AD/VANCE; KnowledgeWare.
Ada Software Development Toolset; AETECH, Inc.
ADABAS; Software AG of North America, Inc.
AdaQuest; General Research Corporation.
ADB (Active Dictionary Builder); Accelerated Methods Group.
ADDERS; Allen Systems Group, Inc.
Adobe Illustrator™ is a trademark of Adobe Systems.
ADS (Advanced Debugging System); Interactive Solutions, Inc.
ADS (Automatic Documentation System); A+ Software, Inc.
ADW/ADS (Application Development Workbench); Knowledgeware, Inc.
(ADC) Aide-De-Camp; Software Development & Management Systems.
Aldus® is a registered trademark of Aldus Corporation.
Aldus Persuasion® is a registered trademark of Aldus Corporation.
ALL™ (Application Language Liberator) is a trademark of Novadyne Computer Systems, Inc.
Ami Pro® is a registered trademark of Lotus Corporation.
AMPLIFY® CONTROL is a registered trademark of CaseWare.
APECS 8000™ is a trademark of Project Software & Development, Inc.
APPGEN (Application Generator); APPGEN Business Software.
APS; Intersolv, Inc.
Artemis; Lucas Management Systems.
Artessa/3000; Quality Consultants, Inc.
AS/400 QUERY; IBM Corporation.
AS/SET™ is a trademark of System Software Association.
ASSET-R; Reifer Consultants.
AutoDoc; Stockholder Systems, Inc.
AutoFlow; AutoCASE Technology.
Automator; Interactive Solutions, Inc.

BACHMAN/Analyst™ is a trademark of Bachman Information Systems, Inc.
BACHMAN/Re-Engineering Product Set™ is a trademark of Bachman Information Systems, Inc.
BAT (Battlemap Analysis Tool™) is a trademark of McCabe & Associates, Inc.
BIBLOS; BIBLOS.
BLACKSMITH; Stauffer Information Systems.
BLACKSMITH INTERCHANGE; Stauffer Information Systems.
Bridge; Applied Business Technology Corporation.

CA-Advisor; Computer Associates International, Inc.
CA-Datadictionary; Computer Associates International, Inc.
CA-Estimacs™ is a trademark of Computer Associates International, Inc.
CA-IDMS; Computer Assoicates International, Inc.
CA-Librarian; Computer Associates International, Inc.
CA-Planmacs™ is a trademark of Computer Associates International, Inc.
CA-Tellaplan; Computer Associates International, Inc.
CADRE Teamwork® is a registered trademark of CADRE Technologies, Inc.
CASE Dictionary; Oracle Corporation.
CASE-PM; CASEWORKS, Inc.
CASEWorks/RT™ is a trademark of Multiprocessor Toolsmiths, Inc.

CCC/DM™ is a trademark of Softool Corporation.
CCC/Manager™ is a trademark of Softool Corporation.
CCC/Resolve-IT™ is a trademark of Softool Corporation.
Change Man; Optima Software, Inc.
CHARM; Worldwide Software, Inc.
CHECKMARK® is a registered trademark of Software Productivity Research, Inc.
CHECKPOINT® is a registered trademark of Software Productivity Research, Inc.
CISLE-C (Integrated Software Lifecycle Environment); Software Systems Design, Inc.
CMF (Configuration Management Facility); GEC Marconi Software Systems.
COCOMO (Constructive Cost Model); TRW Corporation.
COGEN™ is a trademark of Bytel Corporation.
COGNOS; COGNOS Inc.
COHESION; Digital Equipment Corporation.
COMPARE, Aldon Computer Group.
COMPAREX, Sterling Software.
CONDOR, Phoenix Software International.
CorelDraw™ is a trademark of Corel Systems.
CorVision; Cortex Corporation.
COSTAR; Softstar Systems.
Cradle™ is a trademark of Yourdon, Inc.
CREATABASE; NDX Corporation.

DATABASIC II; Consumer System Corporation.
DATAMANAGER, Manager Software Products, Inc.
DB2™ (Data Base 2) is a trademark of IBM Corporation.
DB2 Catalog Manager; BMC Software.
DB2 Xpert; XA Systems Corporation.
DBOL (Data Base On Line); Allen Systems Group, Inc.
DEC/Test; Digital Equipment Corporation.
Deft; SQL Solutions.
DELTA; Corporate Computer Systems, Inc.
Design Aid; CGI Systems, Inc.
DEVELOPER® is a registered trademark of Sterling Software.
DICTONARY MANAGER® is a registered trademark of Manager Software Products, Inc.
Dictonary/204; Computer Corporation of America.
DMS II (Data Management System II); UNISYS Corporation.
DOC (Document Publishing System); Mentor Graphics.
DocEXPRESS; ATA, Inc.
DOCGEN; Software Systems Design, Inc.
DOCPAK; ALR Systems and Software.
Docu-Mint™ is a trademark of Business Computer Design.
DOCU/MANAGER; Application Development Services.
DOCU/TEXT; Diversified Software Systems.
DOME (Distributed Object Management Environment); Dome Software Corporation.
DOSSIER; Systemware Laboratories, Inc.

EasyPath; Panoramic, Inc.
EasySAA™ is a trademark of Multi Soft, Inc.

ENDEAVOR; LEGENT.

Entry Point 90; Datalex.

EPOS (Engineering and Project Management Oriented Development Support System); Software Products and Services (SPS).

ER-Designer; Chen & Associates.

ESTIMACS™ is a trademark of Computer Associates International, Inc. (See also CA-ESTIMACS™).

Estimator; Helix Corporation.

Estiplan; AGS Management Systems.

Excelerator; INTERSOLV.

EXDIFF (Extended Difference Analyzer); Software Research, Inc.

EXPRESS; Information Resources, Inc.

FALCON; Phoenix Software, Inc.

FAST; Database Systems Corporation.

FILECOMP; Computer Task Group.

First CASE™ is a trademark of AGS Management Systems.

FLEE; Goal Systems International, Inc.

FOCUS; Information Builders, Inc.

FOUNDATION™ is a trademark of Andersen Consulting.

FrameMaker; Frame Technology.

Function Point Workbench™ is a trademark of Charismatek.

GECOMO; GEC Marconi Software Systems.

GeneXus™ is a trademark of ARTech.

GEODE; VERILOG.

Grammatik™ is a trademark of Reference Software.

Harvard Project Manager; Software Publishing Corporation.

Hi-Jaak; Inset Systems, Inc.

Historian Plus™ is a trademark of Opcode, Inc.

IBM® is a registered trademark of International Business Machines Corporation.

IDEAL; Applied Data Research, Inc.

IEF™ (Information Engineering Facility) is a trademark of Texas Instruments.

IEW (Information Engineering Workbench); KnowledgeWare.

IMPACT; Project Management Solutions.

IMS (Information Management System); IBM Corporation.

IMSXREF; Logic Engineering, Inc.

Informix®-4GL is a registered trademark of Informix Software, Inc.

Informix-QuickStep™ is a trademark of Informix Software, Inc.

Infront; Multi Soft, Inc.

INGRES (Interactive Graphics and Retrieval System); Ingres Corporation.

Inspector™ is a trademark of KnowledgeWare.

INTACT; Carolian Systems International, Inc.

IPF (Information Processing Family); Control Data Corporation.

ISPF (Interactive System Productivity Facility); IBM Corporation.

KEE® (Knowledge Engineering Environment) is a trademark of IntelliCorp, Inc.
KEY/MASTER; TSI International.

LCS/CMF (Library Control System/Change Management System); Pansophic Systems, Inc.
LIBRARIAN; IBM Corporation.
LINC (Logic and Information Network Compiler); Unisys Corporation.
LINC II (Logic and Information Network Compiler II); Unisys Corporation.
LOOKAT; EDP Management, Inc.

MAESTRO II; Softlab, Inc.
MAGEC™ (Mask and Application Generator and Environment Controller) is a trademark of
    MAGEC Software.
MAGNA 8; Bull HN Information Systems, Inc.
MANAGER; MANAGER SOFTWARE PRODUCTS, INC.
MANTIS; Cincom Systems.
MAPPER; Unisys Corporation.
MARS (Measurement and Reporting System); Computer Power Group.
MI-Project™ is a trademark of Palmer Lake Enterprises, Inc.
Micro Focus Workbench; Micro Focus, Inc.
MicroMan II; (POC-IT Management Services, Inc.)
Microsoft® is a registered trademark of Microsoft corporation.
Microsoft Project; Microsoft Corporation.
Microsoft Word; Microsoft Corporation.
MIL/SOFTQUAL; The Carman Group, Inc.
Millennium; Dun & Bradstreet Software
Mini-ASYST™ is a trademark of Sterling Software.
MISTER (Management Information System for Time Expenses and Resources); Shirley
    Software Systems.
MITROL; Mitrol, Inc.
MODEL, Computer Command & Control Company.
MODEL, Ross Systems, Inc.
MULTITRAK; Multitrak Software Development Corporation.

N5500; Nichols & Company, Inc.
NAPER-DOC; NAPERSOFT, Inc.
NATURAL; Software AG of North America, Inc.
NES (Nichols Extended Scheduler); Nichols & Company.
NETRON/CAP; Netron, Inc.
NOMAD; MUST Software International.
NOVA; Nova Graphics International.

Object Plus™ is a trademark of Easyspec, Inc.
ODE (On-Line Data Entry™) is a trademark of International Software Technology.
OMNI; Haverly Systems, Inc.
ONTOS; Ontos, Inc.
ORACLE® is a registered trademark of Oracle Corporation.

PACBASE; CGI Systems, Inc.
PACE (Professional Application Creation Environment); Want Laboratories, Inc.
PADS® (Productivity Analysis Database System) is a registered trademark of Quantitative Software Management, Inc.
PANVALET® is a registered trademark of Pansophic Systems, Inc.
PARITY; LEGENT.
PASSPORT; The Indus Group.
Pathfinder; A+ Software, Inc.
Pathfinder, Hawkeye Information Systems.
Pathvu, Compuware Corporation.
Pathvu, Bull HN Information Systems, Inc.
PM/SS (Programming Maintenance/Standard Solutions); ADPAC Corporation.
PMS-II® is a registered trademark of North America MICA, Inc.
PMW (Project Managers Workbench); Applied Business Technology.
PolyDoc; INTERSOLV.
PolyLibrarian; INTERSOLV.
POSE (Picture Oriented Software Engineering); Computer Systems Advisers, Inc.
POWER (Project Observation Workbench & Evaluation Reporter); Expertware, Inc.
Power Builder™ is a trademark of Powersoft Corporation.
PowerCASE; Cognos, Inc.
PowerHouse® is a registered trademark of Cognos, Inc.
PowerPoint® is a registered trademark of Microsoft Corporation.
PREDICT CASE; Software AG of North America.
Prestige; Lucas Management Systems.
PRICE-S; General Electric Corporation.
PRIDE; M. Bryce & Associates.
PRODOC™ is a trademark of Scandura Intelligent Systems.
PROJECT/2; Project Software & Development, Inc.
Project/BASE™ is a trademark of the Center for Project Management.
Project/GUIDE; Center for Project Management.
ProKit Workbench™ is a trademark of McDonnel Douglas Systems Integration Company.
ProMod; Promod Support Services.
PS4 (Project Scheduler 4); Scitor Corporation.
PSL/PSA (Problem Statement Language/Problem Statement Analyzer); META Systems Ltd.

QQA™ (Quick Quality Analysis) is a trademark of Unlimited Software Association, Inc.
QUEO™ is a trademark of Computer Techniques.

RA-Metrics™ is a trademark of Howard Rubin Associates.
RAMIS® is a registered trademark of On-Line Software International, Inc.
Recoder™ is a trademark of KnowledgeWare.
Reliance; Concurrent Computer Software.
Retrofit; Compuware, Inc.
Retrofit; XA Systems Corporation.
Retrofit COBOL; Bull HN Information Systems, Inc.
REVIC; U.S Air Force Cost Analysis Agency.
ROBOT/3000™ is a trademark of Productive Software Systems.

SAS™ is a trademark of the SAS Institute, Inc.

SCONS; Corporate Computer Systems, Inc.

Sculptor; MPD International.

SEE (Software Engineering Environment); The Delphi Group.

SEER™ is a trademark of Galorath Associates Inc.

SIMPLE™ is a trademark of Prime Computer, Inc.

Size Planner™ is a trademark of Quantitative Software Management, Inc.

SIZE Plus; GEC Marconi Software Systems.

SLEUTH; CDSI.

SLIM® (Software Lifecycle Management) is a registered trademark of Quantitative Software Management, Inc.

SMARTS (Software Maintenance and Regression Test System); Software Research, Inc.

SMARTsystem; PROCASE Corporation.

SMU (Source Management Utility); COSMIC.

SNAP; Software Architecture & Engineering, Inc.

SOFTCOST; COSMIC.

SOFTQUAL; The Carman Group.

Software Backplane; Atherton Technology.

Software Through Pictures® is a registered trademark of Interactive Development Environments.

SOLOMAN (Source & Object Library Online); Information System Consultants.

SOURCEBANK™ is a trademark of BlueLine Software.

SPECTRUM; Spectrum International.

SPMT (Structured Project Managers Toolbox); W.H. Roetzheim & Associates.

SPQR/20™ (Software Productivity, Quality, & Reliability) is a trademark of Software Productivity Research, Inc.

SQA: MANAGER™ is a trademark of Software Quality Automation.

STAR; Century Analysis Incorporated (CAI).

STAR/PRO; Design Consultants, Inc.

STRADIS (Structed Analysis, Design, and Inplementation of Information Systems); Electronic Data Systems.

SUPER-C; IBM Corporation.

superCASE™ is a trademark of Advanced Technology International, Inc.

SUPERSEARCH; Software Engineering of America.

SUPERSTRUCTURE; Group Operations.

SUPRA™ is a trademark of CINCOM Systems, Inc.

SURE (Software Update Retrieval);Software Clearing House.

Synchrony™ is a trademark of Telepartner International.

Synchrony™ is a trademark of Henco Software.

Synon/2E; Synon, Inc.

Sys/PLAN; System Research Services.

System 1032® is a registered trademark of CompuServe Data Technologies.

System Developer II; CADWARE, Inc.

SYSTEMS ENGINEER™ is a trademark of Learmonth & Burchett Management Systems.

T-Scope; Software Research, Inc.

TAOS; Basis International.

TCAT (Test Coverage Analysis Tool); Software Research, Inc.

TEAMWORK/various suffixes®™ is both a trademark and a registered trademark of Cadre
  Technologies, Inc. depending upon the specific suffix employed.
TELON; Pansophic Systems.
TestGen; Software Systems Design, Inc.
TIE(Q) (Tandem Inspect Extension); Unlimited Software Associates, Inc.
TIGRE™ is a trademark of Tigre Object Systems, Inc.
Timeline; Symantec.
TODAY; Computer Power Group.
TRAK; Marcon & Associates.
Transform; Transform Logic Corporation.

UFO® is a registered trademark of On-Line Software International, Inc.
UniPress; UniPress Software.
UniPress Emacs; UniPress Software.
UNIX™ System V is a trademark of AT&T.

VAW (Visible Analyst Workbench); Visible Systems Corporation.
VAX CDD/Plus (Common Data Dictionary); Digital Equipment Corporation.
VAX DEC/CMS (Code Management System); Digital Equipment Corporation.
VAX DEC/MMS (Module Management Systeem); Digital Equipment Corporation.
VAX Document; Digital Equipment Corporation.
VAX Software Project Manager; Digital Equipment Corporation.
VERIFY® is a trademark of On-Line Software International, Inc.
VIA/SmartDoc™ is a trademark of VIASOFT, Inc.
VIA/SmartTest™ is a trademark of VIASOFT, Inc.
Visible Analyst Workbench; Visible Systems Corporation.
VMLIB™ is a trademark of Pansophic Systems.

WordPerfect® is a registered trademark of WordPerfect Corporation.
WordStar® is a registered trademark of WordStar International.
WORKSHOP/204; Computer Corporation of America.

XPM; XPM, Inc.

CHAPTER 1

Introduction

The year 1993 marks the approximate 50th anniversary of the software and computing professions (the contract to build the ENIAC computer is dated June 5, 1943). At 50 years of age, neither the industry nor the people within it are young any more. The 50-year mark is often a time of mid-life crisis for people. It is also a time of mid-life crisis for industries too, and software is now in the midst of one.

To date, the computing and software industries have been great economic and intellectual triumphs for the United States. Software Productivity Research works internationally in more than 20 countries. From observations through the start of 1993, the author estimates that about 40% of all the software that is operating in the world originated in the United States. In the U.S., which is the world's largest software market, over 85% of all installed software originated here.

However, many United States industries have followed an alarming path. Consider automobiles, cameras, stereo equipment, farm equipment, trucks, motorcycles, and television sets. All of these products were important enough to form significant industries which involved manufacturing and marketing. These primary industries also formed numerous sub-industries which supported and augmented them, in terms of raw materials, sub-assemblies, and after-market add-ons.

For the first 30 to 50 years of industry growth, the United States was the world's major manufacturer of all of the products just cited. But as the industries matured, U.S. leadership began to fade. Overseas companies began to pull ahead of the U.S. in terms of key business factors such as time to market, quality levels, manufacturing costs, and sometimes even in product innovations. Overseas companies began to increase their market shares, even in the United States, while U.S. companies faced declining market shares. Sometimes the U.S. companies could recover and turn the situation around, but often the U.S. presence in the industry would drop to negligible levels.

The factors which fuel success for a new industry include a fairly unsophisticated consumer appetite for the new kinds of products which the industry is providing and a temporary suspension of the importance of manufacturing costs and quality control. For new fast-growth industries, the demand for new products is so high that almost anything can and will be sold.

During the start up phase of an industry, consumers tend to buy almost anything that is new and exciting and have insatiable appetites. Consider how many

1

of us paid more than $100 for a basic four-function electronic calculator with an eight digit display only 20 years ago. Consider how many of us have boxes of obsolete calculators, which mark both the progress of that technology and increasing consumer sophistication. (A quick check of the author's study and desk noted two pocket computers, two electronic organizers, two scientific and two general-purpose calculators that work, six obsolete calculators which no longer operate, and a Post Versalog slide rule circa 1958.)

Would we spend $100 today for a basic four-function calculator? Certainly not. Today basic calculators are given away as door prizes, and we expect to get full statistical and engineering functions and quite a lot more for $100.

The U.S. software industry is now reaching the end of the start-up phase where consumers will buy almost anything just because it is new, different, and exciting. In the next, mature phase the software industry will be dealing with sophisticated and educated clients who are going to demand high quality, low costs, and full support after delivery. Once a purchase is made, consumers will also want continuous improvements in functionality and a non-predatory upgrade policy that makes good business sense to them, rather than a one-sided arrangement that benefits the vendor and penalizes the user.

Will the U.S. software industry be able to make the transition from a start-up industry to a mature industry? No one truly knows the answer to this basic question, but all of us who are players in the software game or students of international competition, find the question extremely important.

One basic fact is certain: in every U.S. industry that has lost market share or suffered significant damage from overseas competition, the United States itself is largely to blame. The causes include failure to control quality, complacency and smugness, lack of satisfactory customer support, inadequate or marginal investments in new technologies, and having expenses rise faster than productivity.

If the United States intends to be the world's most successful software provider in the 21st century, as it has been in the 20th, then we must avoid complacency and approach software engineering with energy, rigor, and effective methods and tools.

Software process assessments are important components of software engineering rigor. They open our eyes to hidden problems, and allow us to focus our energies on problems that need to be corrected.

In a sense, software process assessments and software risk analysis are similar in concept to annual physical examinations. They point out what is right, and what is wrong. Any company that expects to compete internationally must have up-to-date and accurate facts on whether their software development and maintenance methods are excellent, good, average, marginal, or poor. Formal process assessments at one- or two-year intervals should be standard activities within major software producing organizations.

However, software process assessments are only the first step. Diagnosing problems is not the same as curing them. Any notable deficiencies which are revealed in a process assessment must be isolated and remedied by appropriate therapy programs.

A full-scale process assessment using one of the current methods such as that of Software Productivity Research (SPR) or the Software Engineering Institute (SEI) typically requires from one to three months, based on the size of the enterprise and the geographic dispersal of its operating units. Therapies, on the other hand, may require from one to five years before they can be deployed and demonstrate effectiveness.

Jumping into therapy mode without a prior assessment is essentially like trying to cure a serious illness with over-the-counter, non-prescription medicines. It usually doesn't work, it may cause harm, and it delays a serious and effective therapy program.

Process assessments and therapy programs are both only steps on the path to software excellence. The best chance of keeping the U.S. software industry strong, dynamic, and globally successful in the face of competition is to strive for excellence in tools, methods, skills and technologies.

Figure 1.1 illustrates the basic sequence of an assessment followed by therapy selection and deployment.

Note that the assessment itself must be followed by therapy selection and deployment to be fully successful. Assessments by themselves are useful only to find problems. Therapy selection and deployment are the activities which take the most energy and effort.

ORIGINS OF THE SPR ASSESSMENT METHODOLOGY

The ultimate origin of the SPR assessment methodology is based on the paradigm of medical practice and clinical diagnostic studies. When first starting out in software in the 1960's as programmer/analyst, the author worked for the Office of the Surgeon General of the U.S. Public Health Service in Washington, D.C. Some of the first applications dealt with were in the domain of medical software.

Concepts similar to medical diagnostic studies appear useful as the basis for software assessments. The fundamental rationale of the SPR assessment methodology is that accurate diagnosis of software problems is a mandatory step that must be taken before it is safe to prescribe effective therapies.

For both medicine and software, prescribing therapies without an accurate diagnosis of conditions and counter indications is dangerous and unprofessional, and can be viewed as professional malpractice.

IBM's SOFTWARE ASSESSMENTS IN
THE 1960's AND 1970's

Although IBM has been receiving negative publicity of late, few companies have carried out so much research or made so many significant inventions and discoveries. In the 1960's, executives within IBM noted that software was growing rapidly

3

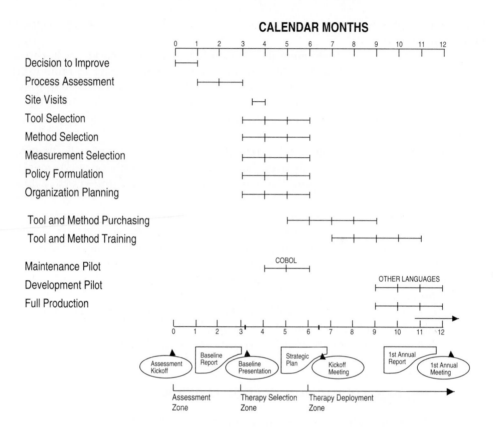

Figure 1.1 *Chronology of Assessment, Therapy Selection, and Therapy Deployment*

in terms of personnel, number of projects, importance, time to market impacts, and criticality to corporate operations. IBM management commissioned a number of studies of software processes, and indeed created permanent process assessment departments in major development laboratories.

It is an interesting historical footnote that two of the most widely used forms of software process assessment both originated within IBM during the same time frame. Watts Humphrey, the originator of the Software Engineering Institute (SEI) method, and the author, the originator of the Software Productivity Research (SPR) method, were both employed by IBM during the explosive software growth decades of the 1960's and 1970's. IBM also had yet another assessment pioneer, Ron Radice of IBM's Kingston laboratories, who is now heading the assessment program at the Software Engineering Institute.

Humphrey and Radice were employed in IBM's East Coast development laboratories, and the author was employed in IBM's West Coast development laboratories. Both the SEI and SPR assessment methods have characteristics that can be traced back to this early work within IBM. In particular, some of the terminology used originated within IBM. Also, both methods were initially applied to large main-frame software development, and then were modified to meet the differing criteria of software on other platforms.

A significant aspect of working at IBM became part of the SEI capability model. In the 1970's and 1980's, IBM was an extraordinarily wealthy and profitable company which had a large staff and many support personnel. In fact, about 10% of IBM's software personnel were in quality assurance. IBM also had both specialists and formal departments including project planning, project measurement, testing, integration, technical documentation, maintenance. Roughly 50% of IBM's software population (about 25,000 in those days) were specialists rather than generalists.

During the 1970's and 1980's, software development in IBM was done primarily in 26 major software development laboratories such as Boeblingen, Boulder, Endicott, Hursley, Kingston, Lidingo, Poughkeepsie, Raleigh, Rochester, San Jose, Santa Teresa, Toronto and Vienna. These large software laboratories, whose sizes ranged from about 300 to more than 1000 technical staff members, were adequately staffed in all technical specialties. They were also amply funded in terms of capital equipment, communication facilities, office space, and conference rooms.

Many technologies were invented and perfected in these laboratories: HIPO diagrams (Poughkeepsie), Joint Application Design (Toronto), formal inspections (Kingston), structured walkthroughs (Poughkeepsie), integrated cost and quality estimation tools (San Jose), formal specifications (Vienna) and of course several varieties of software assessment with the West Coast and East Coast IBM locations pursuing somewhat different approaches.

The best of these large and well-equipped IBM software laboratories provide the fundamental picture of what the SEI capability model means when discussing levels 3 and 4. The IBM pattern is also why achieving SEI levels 3 and 4 has such a significant overhead in terms of special departments and formal organizations. That is how IBM developed large main-frame software during the 1970's and 1980's. In that context, for large main-frame applications, the results and the SEI model should be fairly effective. Certainly the original IBM laboratories were effective, and indeed were often at state of the art levels during the 1970's.

ITT's SOFTWARE ASSESSMENTS IN THE 1980's

At the same time IBM was dealing with explosive growth of software, so were most other large corporations. ITT under its former Chairman, Harold Geneen, had grown from a mid-sized telecommunications company to a large and highly diverse conglomerate.

By the late 1970's, Geneen had noted that software was on the critical path for all major telecommunication projects and for most other high-technology products as well. Geneen was gravely troubled by missed schedules, cost overruns, and the other problems which were endemic to large main-frame applications.

Although ITT had many thousands of software engineers and hundreds of managers and executives with software responsibilities, there was no senior executive with overall responsibility for software methods, assessments or improvements. Geneen decided that a new executive position, focusing on ITT's software methods and processes, might not only solve some of the problems with software but give ITT a notable competitive advantage.

After a national search, the Director of IBM's West Coast software labs, J.H. Frame, moved to ITT. (Note: Frame was director of the IBM labs at Boulder, San Jose, Palo Alto, Santa Teresa, and Hursley.) As ITT's Vice President of Programming, Frame created ITT's well-known Programming Technology Center in Stratford, Connecticut. At its peak in 1982 and 1983, this laboratory had a staff of about 150 and was one of the world leaders in software engineering tool development, CASE, methods development, object-oriented language development, process assessments and baselining, among other aspects of software research.

Unlike IBM, which was comparatively homogeneous in both corporate organization and the kinds of software developed, ITT was very heterogeneous. Indeed, in the late 1970's and early 1980's ITT was perhaps the most diverse conglomerate in history.

Some of the well-known companies owned by ITT in this era of maximum diversity included: AVIS rental cars, Bell Telephone Manufacturing, Bobbs Merrill Publishing, Burpee Seeds, Continental Baking, Courier printers, Defense Communications, Eason Oil, Hartford Insurance, Howard Sams Publishing, ITT education centers, ITT Financial Services, Johnson Controls, Koni shock absorbers, Morton frozen foods, QUME, Rayonier paper, Scotts fertilizer, Sheraton Hotels, Standard Electric Lorenz, and Standard Telephone and Cables. Although the acquisitions did not occur, ITT was also interested in acquiring American Airlines and Electronic Data Systems (EDS) during this same expansive period.

At its peak in 1983, ITT owned more than 200 corporations and had about 8,500 software professionals throughout the world. As a conglomerate, there was essentially no consistency in organization, staffing levels, tools, or any other tangible factor among the ITT companies which produced software.

For example, ITT software was being created for more than 20 different computer platforms including Amdahl, Data General, DEC, IBM, Hewlett Packard, ICL, ITT's own proprietary switching computers, Nixdorf, Nord, Prime, and Wang.

ITT used over a dozen operating systems, more than 50 programming languages (including the world's first CHILL compiler), over 25 varieties of design, and about a dozen system development methodologies.

About 50 of ITT's 200 corporations produced software. The largest in terms of staffing was Hartford Insurance with about 1,500 software personnel. The smallest was Jennings Division in San Jose, with a single professional programmer.

Within ITT, the software assessment methods which evolved into the later SEI and SPR approaches were historically connected. Both the author and Dr. Bill Curtis, who succeeded Watts Humphrey as head of the SEI assessment group, were at the ITT Programming Technology Center during the 1980–1983 expansion era. Also at the ITT Programming Technology Center was Dr. John Manley, who was present at the founding of the Software Engineering Institute.

Although not full time employees, a number of other prominent researchers in software process assessments were consultants to the ITT Programming Technology Center, or visited the laboratory to discuss software technology issues: Dr. Victor Basili, Dr. Barry Boehm, Dr. Fred Brooks, Dr. Tom Gilb, Dr. James Martin, Dr. Alan Perlis, Dr. Roger Pressman, Dr. Larry Putnam, and Dr. Gerald Weinberg, to cite but a few.

The ITT experience had a beneficial impact on software process assessment methods because it expanded the range of projects for which assessments are useful. Software is not homogeneous. Different factors become important depending on whether the software is military or civilian, systems or MIS, mainframe or micro-based.

The need for gathering data from within a multi-national conglomerate tremendously increases the kinds of factors that need to be explored. Indeed, a conglomerate as diverse as ITT at its peak of diversity was very close to being a microcosm of all industry.

In addition to creating more generalized assessment methods than those used by IBM, ITT also developed some significant software engineering technologies at its programming laboratories in the United States, Belgium, England, Germany, and Norway.

Some topics being explored by ITT in the early 1980's are now starting to become important in the 1990's. For instance, groupware and communication methods for geographically distributed project teams was obviously a major topic. Some of ITT's software projects, such as the System/12 switch, had developers in six European countries and several geographically dispersed U.S. labs as well all working concurrently on the same system.

ITT was also exploring CASE technologies, and built a prototype CASE workstation circa 1981 that is actually more advanced than any available today. One of its key features was a secondary display for all reference information and documentation, so that paper manuals would not be required. A secondary display was used because windows within a single display tend to cover and conceal the work that is being performed. A secondary display device allows work to proceed without interruption.

The ITT secondary display was a portable, flat screen device that could be picked up and handled like a book. (The ITT display was somewhat similar in appearance to the Sony Data Diskman.) ITT also had a patent on a keyboard with fiber-optic key tops that could automatically change to match the varying requirements of national languages, and the specific function key needs of any application.

To cite a few other examples, the ITT research on object-oriented languages led to the creation of the Objective-C language and to the foundation of the Stepstone Corporation by Dr. Tom Love, Dr. Brad Cox, and several other ex-ITT personnel.

The ITT research on software reusability was at state of the art levels in the early 1980's. After the sale of the ITT telecommunications groups, this research on software reuse migrated originally to the MCC corporation in Austin, Texas, under Dr. Ted Biggerstaff. More recently, the ITT thread of reusability research has moved to Microsoft's reusability laboratory where it is still expanding.

The court-ordered divestiture of AT&T seemed to give ITT executives a golden opportunity to enter the United States telecommunication business. In 1983, ITT's Programming Technology Center was remissioned to focus on assisting migration of ITT's System/12 switching system from Europe to the United States. This was planned as a temporary mission, and advanced software technologies would not be terminated but merely suspended until the System/12 migration was complete.

Unfortunately the window of opportunity passed before the System/12 was ready for the domestic market. As a result, ITT sold most of its telecommunications business to Alcatel. Included in the acquisition were ITT's two major U.S. research laboratories, the Programming Technology Center in Stratford, Connecticut and the adjacent Advanced Technology Center in Shelton, Connecticut. Alcatel executives decided that these U.S. laboratories were redundant to its existing research facilities in France, and they were both closed.

More than 1000 personnel from the two ITT research laboratories scattered to other companies or founded companies of their own. As already stated, both SPR and SEI have key employees who were formerly connected with the ITT Programming Technology Center.

The diversity of ITT made an impact on all who worked there, and also explains some of the differences between the SEI and SPR assessment methods. The SEI approach is drawn primarily from Watts Humphrey's experiences within IBM in analyzing the methods and approaches used on large main-frame software systems developed within a company that was more or less monolithic and homogeneous in its structure and operations.

Although the author was also at IBM for 12 years in the main-frame systems software era, his four-year tenure at ITT awakened the need to be able to explore diverse software approaches in a very heterogeneous environment where different methods, tools, languages, and philosophies were the norm rather than the exception.

Faced with this kind of diversity, an assessment method that assumes that there is only one correct way of developing software cannot be truly successful. Indeed, there is no one perfect way of either building software or assessing it. A variety of diagnostic approaches, and a variety of design, development, and maintenance methods tailored to the size, nature, and types of software projects are necessary for success.

Medical doctors do not use a single diagnostic approach or a single medicine for all conditions. When exploring or assessing software, it is potentially harmful to prescribe the same therapy for every project. As with medical practice, it is necessary to begin with an accurate diagnosis. Then, after the diagnosis is made, an effective course of therapy can be prescribed to match the specific needs and conditions of the enterprise and its projects.

This approach based on medical practice requires greater sophistication on the part of the assessment personnel to be successful, but this is the direction we should be pursuing if we wish to become true professionals.

KINDS OF SOFTWARE PROJECTS ASSESSED USING THE SPR APPROACH

The SPR assessment method can be and has been utilized on military software, systems software, real-time and embedded software, expert systems, commercial software, and management information systems projects and organizations.

The size ranges of enterprises assessed via the SPR method range from small organizations whose total software staff is less than 25, to some of the largest corporations in the world. Military service projects and civilian government projects have also been assessed.

Specific project sizes have ranged from small applications developed by a single programmer, to very large systems in excess of 25,000 Function Points where the total software staff exceeded 1000 professionals. The mode of projects assessed via the SPR method is in the range of 300 to 5000 Function Points, and three to 100 staff members. There is a bias in the SPR data, since larger enterprises and larger projects are much more likely to have formal assessments than small enterprises and small projects.

When assessments are carried out by profit-making corporations such as SPR as opposed to university research, bias is unavoidable. SPR assessments are used only with corporations and government agencies that commission them and pay for the consulting time, not on random groups. It has been fairly obvious that the organizations which commission software assessments are often fairly advanced and innovative.

After SPR commenced operations in 1985, the SPR assessment approach took five different forms. First, SPR itself carried out assessments using its own consulting staff. This form has been used with about 75 enterprises in the U.S. and abroad, and many more are planned. Second, members of SPR's Enterprise Software Planning (ESP) consortium were licensed to use the SPR methods and performed SPR assessments using their own staff with some assistance by SPR's consultants. This form has also been used with about 40 international enterprises. Third, the SPR assessment method and basic questionnaire is embedded in the CHECKPOINT® tool so many tool clients have done self-assessments. Several hundred enterprises have taken this approach. Fourth, two companies, DMR and Hewlett Packard, were trained and licensed to use SPR's assessment methods with their external clients. Fifth, enough information on SPR assessments has been published in book, monograph, and journal article form so that some companies have attempted SPR-style assessments from published materials alone. The total number is unknown, and only the fact that SPR has been contacted by about 20 of these corporations makes the situation visible. Overseas corporations and government groups constitute the majority of these cases.

This book is not about how to perform assessments using SPR, SEI or any other methodology. The book is about the major problems of building software which assessments have uncovered, and what are the available therapies to prevent these problems and control them. Only enough information is included on how the assessments are performed to illustrate nature of the process.

Some of the problems discovered by assessments are so obvious that many companies know about them without an assessment—poor estimating accuracy and poor quality control, for example, are often painfully obvious.

Other problems are not so obvious, and would probably have escaped notice without the rigor of the assessment process. Crowded office conditions, lack of adequate reference facilities, and lack of rigor in package acquisition are examples of problems which usually escape notice unless pointed out by an assessment.

Some problems are not only difficult to spot, but have seldom been discussed at all. Inadequate standards, inadequate curricula for management and staff, and the topic of friction between the software organization and senior management are instances of problems which lack plentiful citations in the software literature.

The Goals of the SPR Assessment Methodology

An SPR assessment is intended to be similar to a medical diagnostic study. Every factor that can influence the outcome of a software project by as much as 1% is evaluated. The total quantity of factors used in an SPR assessment is about 400. However, the factors are organized into related sets and not every factor is used for every assessment. For example, military software factors differ from civilian software factors. The factors that deal with "enhancements" are not used for studying new projects. The factors that deal with "organization structure" are not used for one-person projects, and so forth. The SPR question sets are divided into several questionnaires, with strategic, tactical, and user satisfaction components.

The SPR questionnaires have been updated once or twice a year since the methodology was formalized. Such updates are necessary to stay current with evolving software engineering and management advances. For example, new approaches such as Quality Function Deployment (QFD) need to be included in assessments.

Strategic Factors That Impact the Entire Enterprise

The SPR strategic factors are corporate or enterprise-wide factors which are global within the enterprise, and which influence *all* software projects and personnel. Examples of strategic factors include compensation plans, the use of merit systems, corporate goals, corporate culture, corporate politics, hiring practices, appraisal practices, and promotion practices. The full set of SPR strategic topics amounts to more than 100 questions. An example of an SPR strategic factor question follows:

Enterprise Compensation Policy?

1) Pay is much higher than competitors
2) Pay is somewhat higher than competitors
3) Pay is at competitive average
4) Pay is somewhat below competitors
5) Pay is much lower than competitors

Several aspects of the SPR strategic topics are aimed at identifying "hardening of the arteries" of an organization's business processes. For example, the SPR strategic questions deal with how long it takes, and how many signatures are required to: A) Create a new department; B) Acquire new software tools; C) Acquire new methodologies; D) Send an employee to an outside seminar; E) Hire a new employee; F) Complete negotiations for a contract; G) Procure capital equipment.

From time to time, jarring inconsistencies between corporate goals and corporate operations are noted. For example, the CEO of one company being assessed was anxious to "make rapid improvements in our software productivity." That same company required four signatures to buy a book for their library and five signatures to send an employee to an external seminar. Any major tool acquisition, methodological change, or process improvement could require up to a dozen signatures and an approval cycle that averaged more than six months and peaked at more than 12 months. It had to be pointed out to the CEO and senior management that their goal of making rapid progress would require streamlining of the approval cycle, and transfer of some spending authority to operating units and subordinate management. The corporation's purchasing and contract policies had become so control-oriented that rapid change was close to being impossible.

Tactical Factors That Influence Specific Projects

The tactical factors are those which influence specific projects. Examples of tactical factors include methods and tools, design, programming languages, specific tasks and activities performed, documents produced, the project's organization structure, and both office space and communication methods for project team members. An SPR assessment includes nearly 200 tactical topics. An example of a tactical factor question follows:

Pre-Test Defect Removal Training?

1) Excellent training for reviews/inspections
2) Adequate training for reviews/inspections
3) Some training or references available for reviews/inspections
4) Very limited material or training on reviews/inspections
5) No training or material on reviews/inspections

While strategic factors are normally discussed with senior management and executives, tactical factors are normally discussed with project personnel and project managers. Usually the project manager and up to half a dozen key technical personnel are interviewed simultaneously during a three- to four-hour assessment session. These joint interview sessions are useful for gathering basic assessment information, and also for correcting errors and gaps in corporate cost and resource tracking systems due to things like unpaid, untracked overtime.

The SPR assessment method deals with a wide variety of ergonomic and environmental topics, such as office space and noise levels. It is a somewhat poignant observation that prior to the assessment sessions, most software professionals state than no one ever asked how they liked their office arrangements. Office ergonomics are almost as important as software process improvements when it comes to software productivity gains, and so this kind of data is highly valuable for correcting instances of overcrowding.

The following is an example of one of the SPR ergonomic questions:

Individual Office Environment?

1) More than 100 square feet of enclosed space per worker
2) 80 to 100 square feet of enclosed space per worker
3) 60 to 80 square feet of enclosed space per worker
4) Less than 60 square feet of enclosed space per worker
5) Open office environment

Questions dealing with ergonomics illustrate why assessments are valuable. It is folly to spend money on CASE tools or other technologies if the software staff is crowded together in small and noisy cubicles or in random open offices. (The mean time to interrupt in crowded office conditions appears to average about 11 minutes.) These arrangements disrupt concentration by creating interruptions, and tend to degrade productivity significantly.

User Satisfaction Factors

Not every SPR assessment includes interviews with software users. In some cases, such as embedded software in a fuel-injection system, the actual users are probably unaware that the software even exists. For the most part, user satisfaction interviews occur with MIS applications, and occasionally with commercially marketed applications. There are about 50 factors evaluated in an SPR user satisfaction assessment. An example of an SPR user satisfaction questions include:

Importance of the Software Product to Your Job

1) Product is mandatory for your job function
2) Product is of major importance to your job
3) Product is of some importance to your job

4) Product is of minor importance to your job

5) Product is of no importance to your job

One of the emerging aspects of assessments that overlaps user satisfaction is to explore the nature and usage patterns of software in business. As it turns out, the quantity, quality, and functionality of available software for knowledge workers exerts a considerable impact on their performance.

The Structure of the SPR Assessment Process

When an SPR assessment begins, the client organization names a senior representative to act as the sponsor and coordinator for activities such as project selection, timing, and presentation of intermediate results.

In order to explain the nature of the assessment process and to alleviate the natural fear that the assessments are some kind of punitive exercise, a kick-off session followed by questions and answers will normally occur, before the assessment session begins.

SPR assessments begin with the selection of a representative sample of software *projects*. A software project can be a stand-alone program, a component within a system, or a complete system. Normally from 10 to 50 projects will be analyzed within a site. The sample of projects should reflect the kinds and types of software which concern the organization being assessed—a mix of new projects, enhancements, package acquisitions, and contract projects would be typical. Both unfinished and completed projects are analyzed.

Figure 1.2 is a general schematic of the SPR assessment process. Coincidentally, the same schematic would probably serve as a fair representation of most other kinds of assessments as well, such as the SEI approach, the Hewlett Packard approach, or the Pressman approach.

A sample of representative projects is necessary because few if any enterprises are homogeneous in their methods, tools, and approaches. A large multi-national corporation can have a thousand or more projects underway at once, can be using more than 250 programming languages, more than 50 design methods, more than 50 different CASE tools, and both hardware and software from literally hundreds of vendors. The same company can have processes and methods that range from state of the art on some projects to 15 years out of date on others, while still others will have no processes at all. To deal with so much diversity, many different data points must be examined.

The SPR approach uses multiple models, and does not assume that military and civilian projects, large systems and small applications, internal projects or externally marketed packages, real-time and batch applications, must follow the same activities and process steps. With the SPR approach, the state of the art is analyzed separately for various software classes, types, and size ranges.

For each project in the assessment, either the full project team or selected team members (up to six) will be interviewed in a structured manner, utilizing the

13

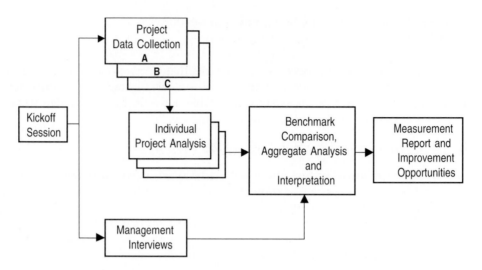

Figure 1.2 *Basic Sequence of SPR Assessment Activities*

SPR assessment questionnaires. The interview sessions average three to four hours and five project team members including the project manager.

Until the assessment sessions begin, there is typically a lot of apprehension and alarm. After the first few sessions, it becomes apparent from the nature of the topics that assessments can be beneficial. After all, how often can employees express their views about topics such as noise, space, usefulness of tools, schedule pressure, and most other factors which influence their jobs daily?

In addition, separate interviews are conducted with executives and senior management on various issues of concern to them. It is an interesting observation that managerial and executive responses are often (but not always) strikingly different from technical staff responses. When directors, vice presidents, and senior managers are queried about technology factors, such as "Does your organization use formal inspections?" the answer is likely to be "Yes." Yet when a dozen project teams are interviewed, it may be discovered that only one project out of 12 used inspections, and they were not adequately trained in the approach.

An SPR assessment in a large enterprise will therefore involve structured interviews with perhaps 50 to 250 technical personnel, 10 to 50 managers, and perhaps 10 executives and senior managers. For smaller enterprises, the project samples are smaller as are the number of people interviewed.

Each project is analyzed separately, and when all project interviews and data collections are complete, the projects are aggregated and analyzed statistically for significant trends. Examples of trends would be situations where all projects were notably better or worse than U.S. norms. Also significant would be situations with severe scatter, where projects varied widely in their usage of tools, methods, and approaches.

Occasionally, topics will arise for which no actual question exists on the questionnaire. A company may have developed proprietary tools and methods which they alone use, for example. When this occurs, the information is recorded and kept available for future analysis and reuse with subsequent assessment sessions.

The SPR Assessment Scale for Influential Factors

Readers have no doubt noticed that the SPR "soft" factor questions use a five-point weighting scale. Over the years, other question formats have been used experimentally: binary "yes/no" questions similar to SEI's; three-point scales, and seven-point scales. On the whole, the five-point scale has given the best results and is the most popular with clients.

The SPR five-point scale is calibrated so that each level has the following approximate meaning:

1	**Excellent**	(Upper 10% of all projects)
2	**Good**	(Upper 25% of all projects)
3	**Average**	(Middle 30% of all projects)
4	**Mediocre**	(Lower 25% of all projects)
5	**Poor**	(Lower 10% of all projects)

To allow fine tuning of responses, decimal points may be used in answering soft-factor assessment questions. Responses such as "2.5" or "3.25" are perfectly acceptable. When averaging all factors, results are normally expressed to two decimal places.

SPR Hard Data for Staffing, Schedules, Resources and Costs

The SPR assessment methodology also collects "hard" data as well as "soft" influential factors. Examples of the hard data collected with the SPR assessment method include:

- Sizes of all specifications and paper documents
  (Pages, words, tables, graphs, etc.)
- Quantities of source code in all languages utilized
  (More than 400 languages supported)
- Function Point or Feature Point totals for the project
  (With automatic conversion between various metrics)
- Activities and tasks performed from requirements to delivery
  (8 phases, 25 activities, and 140 tasks supported)
- Activities and tasks performed for maintenance and enhancement
  (Up to 20 years)
- Schedules, costs, and resources for all activities and tasks

- Special costs such as legal fees, translation into foreign languages, overseas travel, capital equipment, packaging, etc.
- User involvement and costs

Most enterprises do not have this kind of data available from their tracking systems. For example, many tracking systems do not record unpaid overtime, but this phenomenon is very important in understanding true productivity levels. You cannot ignore 5 to 15 hours of unpaid overtime per staff week and understand what is really going on. Even fewer tracking systems record the sizes of deliverables, and yet this kind of information is quite valuable for productivity studies and economic analysis. The SPR approach is to ask the project team to reconstruct the missing elements from memory. This is not very accurate of course, but the alternative is to have null data for many important topics, and that would be far worse.

SPR Hard Data for Quality and Defect Removal

The SPR assessment methodology is particularly rigorous in dealing with quality and defect removal methods. The SPR assessment method deals with defects that originate from five key sources:

- Requirements
- Design
- Source Code
- Documents
- Bad Fixes (secondary defects created during defect repairs)

The SPR assessment method examines the defect prevention methods used to minimize defect potentials and severity levels. Examples of defect prevention methods include prototypes, Joint Application Design (JAD), Quality Function Deployment (QFD), and Total Quality Management (TQM).

The SPR assessment methodology also examines the nature of the defect removal techniques used on software projects. The specific defect removal efficiencies of up to 21 different review, inspection, audit, and test steps are examined during an SPR assessment.

Outputs from the SPR Assessment Method

The full set of input responses and output reports from the SPR assessment tools can total about 150 pages of reports, graphs, and tables per project if all questions are asked and all measurements are taken. A more typical volume, however, would be about 30 pages per project. This information is boiled down to produce the overall assessment report based on aggregation and analysis of all projects explored. Key highlights from the SPR assessments include:

- **Strength and Weakness Reports**
  Detailed diagnostic reports of factors where an enterprise or project is either better than or worse than U.S. norms.

- **Therapy Recommendations**
  Suggested therapies (methods, tools, organization changes, etc.) that can improve weaknesses identified during the assessment.

- **Productivity Baseline**
  How specific projects compare to U.S. norms in terms of productivity, schedules, staffing, etc. For some industries, comparisons against industry data is also available.

- **Quality Baseline**
  How specific projects compare to U.S. norms in terms of defect potentials, defect removal methods, quality assurance methods, etc. It should be noted that the quality baseline is the most difficult to construct. Many people can reconstruct work patterns, such as unpaid overtime, from memory. However, it is almost impossible to reconstruct quality data from memory alone. The solution which SPR uses is to supplement the missing quality data by constructing a quality process model. This may or may not be accurate (in the absence of true historical data there is no way of being sure) but it is a starting point.

Automation of the SPR Assessment Method

The SPR tactical assessment factors are supported by a commercial tool called CHECKPOINT® in the United States and CHECKMARK® in the United Kingdom. This tool also has project estimation, measurement, assessment, and risk analysis capabilities. It also includes a statistical processor for aggregating and averaging both hard and software data. This tool is very useful for processing assessment data and it also is used as a stand-alone estimating and measurement tool.

It is possible to perform an SPR assessment without this tool, or without any tools for that matter, but it is much more convenient to have automation readily at hand.

PUBLICATIONS DESCRIBING THE SPR ASSESSMENT METHOD

Aspects of the SPR assessment process have been discussed in four monographs, four books, and many articles by the author and others.

Monographs

The first monograph was published as IBM Technical Report 02.764 in January of 1977 by the IBM Programming Laboratory at San Jose, California. The title was *Program and Quality and Programmer Productivity*. It discussed the author's internal assessment findings for IBM. The monograph demonstrated the strong correlation of high quality levels and high productivity levels on IBM's system software.

The second monograph is *A 10 Year Retrospective of Software Engineering Within ITT* (Software Productivity Research, 1988). This monograph commemorated the tenth anniversary of the founding of ITT's Programming Technology Center and discussed a number of the technologies, including process assessments, in which ITT was conducting research.

The third monograph is *Critical Problems in Software Measurement* (IS Management Group, 1993). This monograph discusses a number of technical problems associated with collecting large volumes of data from multiple projects within multiple industries. In particular, it is necessary to capture very detailed information on the nature, class, and type of software project, and the standard industry classification (SIC) code of the development organization. This data allows construction of templates derived from similar projects. A controversial feature of this monograph is the assertion that the usage of "Lines of Code" metrics for large-scale software quality or productivity studies including many programming languages constitutes professional malpractice.

The fourth monograph is *International Software Productivity and Quality—The Worldwide Perspective* (IS Management Group, 1993). This monograph discusses the framework and preliminary results of using the SPR assessment approach in many different countries. (The basic SPR assessment questionnaire has been translated into Japanese, German, French, and Portuguese versions.) International software studies require the inclusion of new factors which may not be needed within a single country. For example, the Canadian mandate to produce documentation in both French and English is a fairly unique situation, and one which is important enough to record when carrying out process assessments in Canada.

Books

The first book was *Programming Productivity—Issues for the Eighties*. This was published by the IEEE Press (Catalog Number EH0239-4) in 1981, and revised in 1986. This book expanded the topics discussed in the author's first monograph, and includes supplemental findings by 30 other authors.

The second book is *Programming Productivity* (McGraw-Hill, 1986). This book illustrates the basic SPR assessment questionnaire, and records the findings from a number of early software assessments. It also includes the subsequent analysis of their results. This book covers topics such as the causal relationship of quality and productivity; the impact of structured methods; how high-level languages impact productivity; how structured methods affect productivity, and similar topics. This book was also translated into Japanese, German, French, and Portuguese and has introduced some of the concepts of SPR assessments to a wide international audience.

The third book dealing with SPR assessments is *Applied Software Measurement* (McGraw-Hill, 1991). This book contains preliminary U.S. national averages for software quality and productivity using both direct SPR assessment hard-data results, and secondary data from SPR clients and associates. This book also illustrates the SPR assessment output reports. A Japanese translation of this book was published in 1993.

This fourth book, *Assessment and Control of Software Risks,* is concerned with more than 60 of the major problems which the SPR assessments have uncovered to date.

These four books are not intended to be read in sequence and each delivers its primary message independently of the others.

Articles

Other authors have also described the SPR approach. An interesting short monograph was published by Sharon Miller and George Tucker of AT&T on the concurrent usage of the SPR and SEI assessment approaches. (These two assessment methods are often used concurrently.) The monograph is *Software Development Process Benchmarking* (IEEE Communications Society; 1991).

An interesting but superficial discussion of various assessment methods has been published, but is not widely available. In 1992 DARPA (Defense Advanced Research Projects Agency) commissioned a study of software assessment methods by the Institute of Defense Analysis (IDA). This study evaluated several software process assessment methods including both the SPR approach and the SEI approach as well as the SDC approach.

When the report was finished, its publication was delayed because it was initially classified (apparently because it cited gaps with the SEI method) and comparatively few copies have circulated. A summary of the report, IDA Document D-1202 is dated August 1992 and the cover notes it was cleared for distribution on October 27, 1992.

There has been a move by groups within the Department of Defense (DoD) to mandate assessments in order to do business with the Department of Defense, to mandate maturity level 3, and possibly to mandate the exclusive usage of the SEI assessment approach. Given the state of the art of assessment technology, this is premature. It would certainly be premature to select only the SEI approach.

There are some potentially hazardous repercussions which neither the DoD nor SEI itself have yet considered. For example, there are about 32,000 U.S. companies that produce software in 1993, but less than 50 are currently at SEI maturity level 3. A mandate that would disenfranchise 99.9% of U.S. software companies appears to be unwise, given the fact that there is little or no empirical data which demonstrates that level 3 organizations are actually better than level 2 organizations in quality, and no data at all in terms of costs. Indeed, a mandate to be at level 3 would appear to be likely to be challenged and perhaps result in litigation or appeals. Since about half of military procurements are challenged, it appears foolish to add a burdensome requirement that lacks proof of effectiveness.

Even more alarming, India and other countries have several large software groups already approaching or achieving SEI maturity level 3, whose labor costs are less than one-fifth of U.S. norms. A requirement to achieve SEI maturity level 3 in order to do software business with the Department of Defense or with the military services may well move substantial volumes of software contracting business out of the United States entirely.

As of early 1993, current military procurement protocols are recommending the use of process assessments, but not the specific usage of the SEI assessment approach. Even this may be premature, but it is better than a restrictive mandate locked onto the SEI approach.

What SPR recommends for large enterprises would be the usage of multiple assessment approaches, since each approach tends to emphasize particular aspects. Even if multiple approaches are not used concurrently, it would be desirable to have them available so the most suitable method for each situation can be selected.

For small organizations with a total staff of less than about 50 software professionals, a caution should be given that the current SEI assessment approach may not be suitable. The SEI approach is keyed to very large enterprises and mainframe software, and makes a tacit assumption that enough staff personnel exists to create and staff a number of specialized departments such as quality assurance.

The implicit SEI assumption of available specialists is reasonable for large companies and government agencies, but not really appropriate for small businesses. For example, as mentioned there are about 32,000 businesses in the United States as of 1993 that develop at least some of their own software, or software for other companies. If each of these were to attempt to establish a formal quality assurance department, there are not currently enough trained or experienced software QA personnel in the United States to go around.

RESULTS OF THE SPR ASSESSMENT METHODS TO DATE

Assessments are not an end in themselves. They are only the first step, and must be followed by an active therapy program. Assessments and therapies together are not the end point either: the true goal is software excellence.

However, now that SPR, SEI, and other assessment approaches have been in use for some eight years, a number of findings have occurred that were not visible earlier since it took longitudinal analysis over several years to note the trends. For example, it is only now possible to calculate the Return on Investment (ROI) of a number of technologies. Interestingly, it is even possible to calculate the ROI of assessments themselves now that eight years of history exists.

Among the most significant findings to date are the differences between industries. For example, in the domain of quality, several industries stand out as achieving quality levels much better than average: computer manufacturers, telecommunication manufacturers, medical instrument producers, and defense companies typically have the highest rates of overall quality for their software. These same industries have the highest defect removal efficiency levels, and average more than 95%. Critical projects may exceed 99% in defect removal efficiency. These industries average about 20% higher than U.S. averages overall. Further, these industries are also among the leaders in measuring defect levels and removal efficiency.

There are equally striking differences in productivity, although the industries are not the same. The industries leading the productivity race include the pure software houses, the outsourcing contractors, and contract development shops.

Two of the industries that are tops in quality are near the bottom in productivity: defense and telecommunications manufacturing. For defense projects, assessments immediately point out why productivity is low: military standards such as DoD 2167A create such enormous quantities of paperwork that high productivity is essentially impossible. Defense projects create about 400 English words for every Ada statement, and some 52% of the total cost of military software goes to paperwork.

For telecommunications manufacturing, paperwork is also a problem (this industry is number 2 in paperwork volume). In addition, much of the software must operate continuously at very high rates of throughput. Often the hardware on which the software will operate is also being developed, so stable platforms are not always available. These two problems tend to bring productivity to rather low levels. By contrast, telecommunications operating companies tend to be in the upper third of U.S. companies in terms of productivity.

Another finding of note is that the differences between "industry leaders" and "industry laggards" within any given industry is rather extreme. Within a given industry, such as banking, insurance, telecommunications, or software, there are variances of more than 10 to 1 in both productivity and quality between the top and bottom performers.

When specific project classes are assessed, the range is even broader. For common application types such as insurance claims handling, banking applications, inventory systems, compilers, and many others, ranges of more than 20 to 1 can occur between the most and least productive projects within a set of similar projects.

One might think that leaders are visibly better in all respects than laggards, but this is surprisingly not the case. Both leaders and laggards are "average" in many of the activities and factors assessed.

However, the leaders are much better than average in about one third of all factors, while the laggards trail in about one third of all factors. Industry leaders tend to be far ahead of laggards in measurements, methodologies, technology transfer, and morale.

Figure 1.3 illustrates the patterns that separate leaders, laggards, and average enterprises.

Another important topic based on longitudinal data collected over more than five years is the rate at which companies can improve once an assessment is carried out and therapy programs commence.

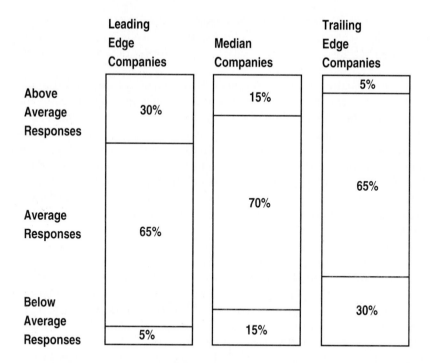

Figure 1.3 *Variance Patterns in Leading, Average, and Lagging Enterprises*

Long-range analysis of the results of SPR assessments and annual follow-ups with past clients reveal that enterprises which are fairly healthy initially can improve more rapidly than lagging enterprises.

Why this striking differential occurs can be revealed by the assessment data itself—lagging companies generally lack the infrastructure necessary to make rapid improvements. Their purchasing and technology transfer abilities tend to be clogged, so there is no way of rapidly acquiring new approaches and making them available to managers and staff. Indeed, for some lagging enterprises, even the approval cycle required to commence an assessment may run over 12 months. Also, lagging enterprises have a distressingly high probability of succumbing to the "silver bullet syndrome." That is, managers in such enterprises tend to succumb to false productivity claims or vendor blandishments that major improvements can occur from a single CASE tools or new language. Thus, instead of a parallel approach that deals concurrently with methods, tools, and social issues the laggards tend to pursue improvements serially, one step at a time.

Figure 1.4 illustrates the rates of improvement correlated with the initial starting position on the SPR assessment scale.

To summarize, the SPR assessment methodology is based on the paradigm of medical diagnosis. The SPR assessments themselves are usually accurate in their

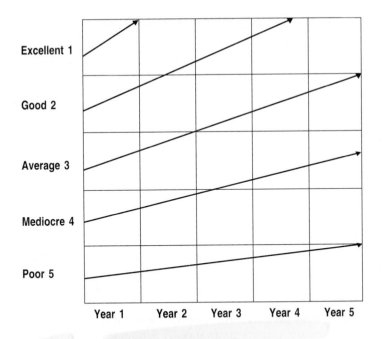

Figure 1.4 *Correlation of Initial Assessment Position and Process Improvement Speed*

diagnoses. They are also fairly quick and easy to carry out, since they have been done so often. However, post-assessment therapy selection, like medical therapy, may require time to be effective. It also requires considerable knowledge on the part of the practitioners.

The best post-assessment results are very encouraging: quality improvements of over 30% per year and productivity improvements in excess of 15% annually for several consecutive years, with the prognosis of continued improvement.

CORRELATING THE SPR ASSESSMENTS AND SEI ASSESSMENTS

The SPR and SEI assessment methods are both widely used, and both uncover useful information about software process strengths and weaknesses. Several organizations, such as AT&T and Hewlett Packard, have used both methods concurrently.

Both the SPR assessments and the SEI assessments begin with a kick-off meeting; training of the local staff in the questionnaires; interviews of selected projects; aggregation and analysis of the results; a report of strengths and weaknesses and suggested improvements.

Differences of the SPR and SEI Question Sets

With a total of 400 questions, SPR covers a broader range of topics than the SEI assessment method. In particular, strategic topics such as organizational structures, management cohesiveness, compensation policies, and hiring practices are covered by SPR. At the tactical or project level, SPR includes questions on office space and ergonomics, and on both development and user experience levels that are not included in the SEI questions. Of course the SEI assessments also include questions not used by SPR.

An example of a question used by SEI, but not by SPR, can be illustrated by the SEI question which asks if the organization uses a software estimating tool. Since the primary SPR assessment tool, CHECKPOINT®, includes an estimating model, it would be redundant to ask such a question. The usage of the tool itself provides a de facto "Yes" answer to the SEI question.

The SEI questions are generally binary, requiring "Yes" or "No" answers. The SPR questions use a five-point scale. Following are examples of how SPR and SEI address the same topic, which, in this case is the existence of a software quality assurance function.

- **The SEI question on software quality assurance:**
  Does the software quality assurance function (SQA) have a management reporting channel separate from the software development project management? (Yes or No)

- **The SPR question on software quality assurance:**

Quality Assurance Function?

1) Formal QA group with adequate resources
2) Formal QA group, but understaffed (<1 to 30 ratio)
3) QA role is assigned to development personnel
4) QA role is performed informally
5) No QA function exists for the project

As may easily be seen, both the SPR and SEI question are driving toward the same goal, but use quite different structural methods.

In spite of the differences in focus and question format and structure, both the SPR or SEI assessment methods can diagnose many common problems. A number of organizations use both assessment methods, and look for convergence between the two. This is just as reasonable an approach as using two separate medical diagnostic procedures to validate significant findings.

SPR Effectiveness Levels and SEI Maturity Levels

From the patterns of key answers to various subsets of the SEI questions, projects and enterprises are assigned a capability maturity level. Indeed, this aspect of the SEI assessment process is one of the most publicized aspects of the entire SEI approach.

The SEI capability maturity level is an absolute scale, which does not have a mid-point or "average" in its maturity schema. Of the enterprises assessed by SEI to date, the numeric average is only about 1.5 which implies a fairly low level of sophistication.

The five SEI maturity levels are:

- **Level 1—"Initial" Processes**
  (Unpredictable and poorly controlled)

- **Level 2—"Repeatable" Processes**
  (Can do follow-on projects without making the same mistakes)

- **Level 3—"Defined" Processes**
  (Uses a well-defined and effective methodology)

- **Level 4–"Managed" Processes**
  (Methods are not only effective, but are measured!)

- **Level 5—"Optimizing" Processes**
  (Leading-edge, with full reusability, modern methods, etc.)

The SPR effectiveness level scale runs in the opposite direction from the SEI maturity level scale, and 1 means excellent while 5 means poor. Following is the SPR scale:

- **1 Excellent**
  (Superior to 90% of U.S. enterprises in this factor)

- **2 Good**
  (Superior to 65% of U.S. enterprises in this factor)

- **3 Average**
  (In the middle third of U.S. enterprises in this factor)

- **4 Below Average**
  (Lags 65% of U.S. averages in this factor)

- **5 Poor**
  (Lags 90% of U.S. averages in this factor)

The SPR method expresses results to two decimal places. Thus scores of 2.65 or 3.25 are perfectly acceptable using the SPR approach. The SEI maturity level concept was originally based on integer values, but is moving toward a decimal interpretation.

It is sometimes asked why the SPR and SEI scoring methods move in opposite directions. The most probable answer is that the two methods were published more or less at the same time, and neither the SEI nor SPR assessment developers were aware of the other's work until publication occurred.

The SEI and SPR approaches both have pros and cons. The SEI approach has been criticized as being rigid, inflexible, and biased toward large enterprises and mainframe software. The SPR approach has been criticized since the SPR mid-point, which is intended to represent U.S. norms, does not always accomplish this goal. Moreover, norms change from year to year, so the SPR questionnaire must be modified annually.

In spite of the differences in the form and structure of the SPR and SEI questions, it is possible to carry out very rough correlations between the SPR and SEI results. Indeed, the CHECKPOINT® and CHECKMARK tool produces an overall *SPR Effectiveness Level* that is more or less equivalent to the SEI maturity level, although the numbering systems run in opposite directions. Here are the rough equivalencies between the SPR and SEI levels:

SPR Effectiveness Level	SEI Maturity Level
1.00 to 1.99 Excellent	5) Optimizing
2.00 to 2.49 Good	4) Managed
2.50 to 3.49 Average	3) Defined
3.50 to 3.99 Marginal	2) Repeatable
4.00 to 5.00 Poor	1) Initial

The above correlations are crude and imperfect, but show that at least both groups are concerned with similar issues. In particular, the SPR performance levels include staff experience factors which are not included in the SEI assessment questions. For projects and companies where staff and managerial experience is high, the standard SPR performance level will give more positive results than the SEI assessment method. Also, for smaller organizations which lack the funding and infrastructure which the higher SEI maturity levels assume, the SPR approach will be more equitable.

Both the SEI and SPR methods are evolving, and must continue to stay current with the state of the art. New concepts such as client-server applications, object-oriented analysis and design, rapid application development (RAD), Quality Function Deployment (QFD), and Total Quality Management (TQM) did not exist 10 or 15 years ago. Both the SEI and SPR assessment techniques must be updated at least once a year, and sometimes twice a year, to keep abreast of evolving technologies.

CHAPTER

2

The Most Common Software Risks

Software assessments and software risk management have started to become formal sub-disciplines of software engineering within the last five years. The journal literature on these topics is increasing rapidly. In the domain of risk management, books such as Dr. Barry Boehm's *Software Risk Management* (Boehm, 89), Dr. Robert Charette's *Software Engineering Risk Analysis and Management* (Charette, 89) and the same author's *Application Strategies for Risk Analysis* (Charette, 90) are adding rigor to risk management approaches.

Software project audits and assessments have been used for years to identify risks and enough empirical data has been collected to identify the common patterns of risk that are associated with various kinds and sizes of software projects. For example, both the SPR assessment method and the well-known Software Engineering Institute (SEI) assessment technique have noted significant variances in risk patterns as maturity levels change (Humphrey, 89).

The author, his colleagues at Software Productivity Research (SPR), and many of their clients are engaged almost daily in carrying out formal assessments of software development and maintenance technologies in the United States and abroad (Miller and Tucker, 1992). A natural byproduct of formal assessments using either the SEI or SPR methods, or other methods such as Hewlett Packard's or SDC's, is the identification of the risk factors that affect each project undergoing assessment.

As a result of assessing projects in several hundred enterprises, over one hundred risk factors have been observed. Few projects have more than 15 risk factors at any time, but many projects have half a dozen simultaneously.

This book details 60 of the most common risks, and makes references to other risks where detailed analysis is not appropriate or possible. For example, a very common risk factor that is difficult to quantify is that of litigation. In the software industry, the risks of litigation are high as are the associated expenses. Indeed, litigation has put more than a few companies out of business. However, the risk of litigation is not easy to categorize. The solutions to legal problems are usually outside the authority of most software managers and legal advice would be necessary to say anything definitive. In the course of various SPR assessments, the following kinds of litigation have been observed:

- Law suits for wrongful termination, brought by employees.
- Law suits for copyright violation, brought by publishers whose work was infringed.
- Law suits for nonperformance of contractual obligations.
- Law suits to recover fees asserted to be wrongly withheld by clients.
- Law suits for violation of employment agreements.
- Law suits for trade secret misappropriation.
- Law suits for violation of fiduciary duty against officers of corporations.
- Law suits for consequential damages due to alleged errors in software.
- Law suits between clients and contractors based on disputed ownership of work.

One of the most intriguing observations on risk patterns is that the elements of significant risk are not the same across all software domains. For convenience in analyzing risk, consider the patterns of six generic software classes:

1. Management information systems (MIS) projects such as accounting systems, claims handling systems, and the like.

2. Systems software projects such as operating systems, telecommunication systems, or other software applications which control physical devices.

3. Commercially marketed software projects, such as spreadsheets, word processors, or CAD packages that are leased or sold to end users.

4. Military software projects, which can include all those constrained to follow U.S. military standards such as DoD-STD-2167A.

5. Contract or outsourced software projects in the civilian domain, where the bulk of the software is produced by contract personnel, as opposed to employees of the client organization.

6. End-user software projects, where the software was developed by the intended user rather than by a professional programming staff.

There are of course other types of software, such as scientific software. However, the six discussed here are the ones where SPR has performed enough assessments to have identified the major risk elements.

Each of these classes has a characteristic risk pattern. Some elements of risk are common across all domains, but the characteristic patterns of each class are surprisingly diverse.

The following section contains short discussions of the five most frequently encountered risk factors in each of the six software classes.

Management Information System (MIS) Risks

Management information systems are normally created for specific classes of users such as insurance claims handlers, accountants or order entry personnel. The applications are custom-built to meet their requirements. MIS software projects themselves are normally funded by the user organizations, and are created to improve the speed or work performance of the client organization. These facts in part determine the patterns of observed risks.

Risk Factor	Percent of projects at risk.
Creeping user requirements	80%
Excessive schedule pressure	65%
Low quality	60%
Cost overruns	55%
Inadequate configuration control	50%

By far the most common risk encountered for management information systems is that of creeping user requirements, or changes to requirements which occur after the formal requirements phase. The magnitude of new and unanticipated user requirements is proportional to the size of the project, but averages about 1% per month. Thus for a three-year project, about one third of the total requirements will be added after the formal requirements phase ends. Creeping user requirements are not due to caprice, but rather to the fact that the problems of the business world often change faster than the ability to build software solutions.

The phrase "excessive schedule pressure" is defined as an attempt by user demand or management fiat to force the completion of a software project so far ahead of the technical capabilities of the team that quality, functionality, or the project itself are put at risk. Any attempt to shave more than about 20% off the normal schedule for a software project once it is underway is an invitation to disaster, and especially so when the only approaches used are overtime or adding staff.

The phrase "low quality" is defined as delivered software which either does not work at all, or which fails repeatedly in operation. Projects where users report more than about 0.5 bugs or defects per Function Point per calendar year can be considered to have low quality also. Low quality for MIS projects is endemic, and is normally the result of two common problems often associated with information systems. The first problem is inadequate defect removal such as failing to use inspections and carrying out testing in a casual or unprofessional fashion. The second problem is inadequate defect prevention such as failing to use standard techniques like Joint Application Design (JAD) or Information Engineering (IE), and sometimes failing to produce adequate specifications for the project.

The phrase "cost overruns" is defined as software which exceeded its planned budget by significant amounts, such as 50%. Major information systems sometimes double their planned budgets, and even an "average" MIS project may miss its budget by 15% or more. MIS cost overruns are due to both creeping user requirements and low penetration of formal software estimating methods among MIS managers. Although there are about 50 commercial software estimating tools marketed in the U.S., only about one third of MIS project managers use such tools as of 1993.

The phrase "inadequate configuration control" is defined as lack of rigor in controlling source code, specifications, plans, and documents so that all updates are formally controlled. Failure to use adequate configuration control methods appears endemic to the information systems domain, although there are more than a dozen commercial-grade configuration control tool suites marketed in the United States.

Systems Software Risks

Systems software is normally created to control the operation of physical devices, such as computers, switching systems, fuel injection systems. Systems software is often aimed at thousands of clients, rather than just a few. In order to operate at all, systems software needs very high quality and reliability levels, and most systems houses know this. Therefore quality control is normally more rigorous for systems software projects than for MIS software projects. However, there are still some common quality control problems observed for systems software. The pattern of most common risks for systems software are:

Risk Factor	Percent of projects at risk
Long schedules	70%
Inadequate cost estimating	65%
Excessive paperwork	60%
Error-prone modules	50%
Canceled projects	35%

The phrase "long schedules" has no exact definition, but for practical purposes can be viewed as any systems software project that takes longer than three calendar years. Certainly all projects in excess of five calendar years can be considered to have long schedules. The initial releases of major systems software projects (larger than 5000 Function Points) are normally quite lengthy. Some indeed exceed eight years, although follow-on releases occur at shorter intervals such as 18 to 24 months. In part, long schedules for systems software are due to the fact that the software controls incomplete hardware. Long schedules for systems software are also attributable to the need for rigorous specifications and defect removal.

Long schedules are troublesome for systems software because of the way they interact with hardware development schedules. Normally hardware design starts slightly before software design, so that about 15% to 20% of the allotted schedule time for a mixed hardware/software product is past before software is fully begun. The late start of the software components always puts software on the critical path for final integration, systems testing, and delivery. If integrated hardware/software products do miss critical dates at the end of the development cycle, software tends to receive the blame in more than 75% of the observed cases.

The phrase "inadequate cost estimating" is defined as using manual estimating techniques for predicting the costs, schedules, and deliverables of major software projects (larger than 5000 Function Points in size). There are currently about 50 commercial-grade software estimating tools marketed in the U.S. However, only about 10 of them are aimed at systems software and deal with such projects explicitly.

For what appears to be cultural reasons, the systems software world has not adopted estimating technology as rapidly as other domains. As of 1993, only about 17% of systems software managers use automated estimating tools, which is only about one-half the frequency of the MIS domain and only about one-fourth the frequency of the military domain.

A corollary problem is that the systems software domain has also lagged in adopting functional metrics. It is a well-known problem that "lines of code" metrics are ambiguous and paradoxical for both measurement and estimation purposes (Jones, 1986). For what appears to be cultural reasons, systems software is significantly behind MIS in adopting effective productivity and quality metrics, although there are certainly exceptions.

The phrase "excessive paperwork" has no exact definition, but paperwork can be considered excessive under these conditions: 1) More than 50 discrete document types are produced; 2) the cost of paperwork approaches or exceeds 50% of the total software project expense, and 3) more than 2000 words are created per Function Point. Systems software ranks second behind military software in the magnitude of paperwork production. Unfortunately in both domains, much of the paperwork appears either redundant or overlarge for the work at hand.

A deeper and more subtle derivative problem lurks beneath the surface of excessive volumes of software paperwork: to date there is no published literature on the optimum quantity, volume, structure, or style of the set of paper documents that surround software projects.

The phrase "error-prone modules" means modules within a large system which contain an unusually high proportion of the total error content of the entire system. Error-prone modules were originally discovered in the 1960's in IBM operating systems, when it was noted that 4% of the modules of OS/360 received 38% of all error reports.

Error-prone modules are especially common and severe for systems software, and are frequently encountered in operating systems, switching systems, process control systems, and most other types of systems software (Dunn and Ullman, 1982). Since this phenomenon was discovered almost 30 years ago, some of the leading systems software producers have long-since eliminated this problem. Nonetheless, the problem is still endemic in the systems software domain and especially common within smaller systems software enterprises which lack formal quality assurance methods.

The phrase "canceled projects" is defined as a software project which is terminated prior to delivery to customers. The systems software domain is particularly hard-hit by canceled projects. Computer manufacturers and telecommunication manufacturers may cancel over one-third of their projects prior to completion. Between 1980–1983, ITT canceled three out of four switching system projects. There is no simple answer to why this problem is so common but some observations on canceled projects include the following: 1) Many canceled projects are about a year behind schedule and over budget by more than 50% at the time of cancellation; 2) Many canceled projects cannot meet performance or quality targets.

Commercial Software Risks

Commercially-marketed software runs the gamut from fairly simple games through very sophisticated AI or neural net projects. This includes word processors, spreadsheets, data base projects, language compilers, CASE tools, and a host of other categories.

Commercial software is heavily impacted by competitive pressures and the need to build applications which satisfy users with many different skill levels. Both competitors and clients are known to engage in frequent and expensive litigation. These facts help explain the pattern of observed risks.

Risk Factor	Percent of projects at risk
Inadequate user documentation	70%
Low user satisfaction	55%
Excessive time to market	50%
Harmful competitive actions	45%
Litigation expense	30%

The phrase "inadequate user documentation" is defined as user information which is incomplete, unclear, wrong, or inconvenient. The user information can include on-line help and published material. This is the most widespread problem of the commercial software world. Indeed, the problem is so widespread that it has spawned a large and growing sub-industry of third-party publishers who bring out books and on-line support to augment the normally deficient material produced by the vendors themselves.

Technical writing is such a comparatively scarce skill that those who do it well often produce strings of best-selling books on related topics. Examples of technical writers who deal with software products and concepts of various kinds include Van Wolverton, Ed Yourdon, James Martin, and Jerry Pournelle.

Adequate user manuals are rare in commercial software because: 1) documenting the first release of any new software package is notoriously difficult; 2) some vendors can't afford or don't use competent technical writers and illustrators, and 3) the state of the art of software user documentation is still primitive and evolving.

The phrase "low user satisfaction" means that many software clients are displeased with one or more of several factors: 1) low quality; 2) inadequate functionality; 3) complex or arcane command structures; 5) steep learning curves; 5) tricky or troublesome installation procedures; 6) poor service or customer support, and 7) excessive utilization or monopolization of disk space or other hardware components by the software. As of 1993, some of these problems occur on more than half of commercially-marketed software.

The phrase "excessive time to market" has no exact definition, but can be viewed in both absolute and relative terms. A software product that requires more than three years of development may find that the market has changed significantly. A software product that hits the market more than a month or two after a major competitor's product may find seriously reduced market potential, unless the latter product offers some spectacular functionality that the former product lacked. The recent intense jockeying for release dates positioning between IBM's OS/2 and Microsoft Windows illustrates how important time-to-market issues have become to major software producers.

The phrase "harmful competitive actions" is defined as one or more of the following: 1) negative marketing campaigns; 2) false advertising claims; 3) overt or explicit copyright violations; 4) "look and feel" imitations of successful product concepts or interface conventions; 5) patent or trademark violations; 6) predatory price cutting. Such problems are fairly common in commercial software.

The phrase "litigation expense" is defined as lawsuits, injunctions, or legal actions which require overt actions or responses by legal counsel. The software industry appears to be entering a highly litigious phase. The recent major lawsuits between Microsoft, Apple and Hewlett Packard are prime examples as are the lawsuits between Computer Associates and EDS. Lawsuits between clients and software vendors are becoming common, as are lawsuits between rival vendors. The probability of risk of litigation appears to increase year by year. By the end of the decade it could approach 50% and become a major cost element of the commercial software industry.

Military Software Risks

Software produced in the United States for a uniformed military service or for the Department of Defense must normally adhere to various military standards, such as DoD-STD-2167A. While these standards are fairly rigorous and ensure reasonable consistency from project to project, they also create a number of very expensive problems and create risks in their own right. U.S. military standards are the dominant factor that determine the risks of military software, and explain the patterns of observed risk.

Risk Factor	Percent of projects at risk
Excessive paperwork	90%
Low productivity	85%
Long schedules	75%
Creeping user requirements	70%
Unused or unusable software	45%

Large military projects routinely create up to 100 discrete document types and more than six pages of paper per Function Point, (equivalent to some 400 English words per Ada statement). Military software paperwork in all its manifestations absorbs about 52% of the total cost of military software projects. Coding, on the other hand, is often less than 25% of the total cost. While some of the military paperwork is useful and adds rigor, quite a lot appears to be redundant. Unfortunately, it appears to be much easier to add to military standards than to subtract from them.

The phrase "low productivity" has no exact definition, but a reasonable definition would be that any project which is lower than U.S. averages by more than 50% might be considered to have low productivity. As of 1991, the published U.S. average for all software projects was five Function Points per staff month (Jones, 1991). The published average for military software projects was only three Function Points per staff month, and many large military projects drop below one Function Point per staff month. So long as military paperwork costs exceed military coding costs by a margin of more than 2 to 1, technologies such as Ada and its supporting environment cannot be fully effective, and military software will always rank below civilian software in productivity.

The phrase "long schedules" is a relative term, and is roughly equivalent to the phrase "excessive time to market." For civilian software projects, schedules longer than about three years are troublesome. For military software projects, schedules longer than about five years tend to be troublesome since the real world can change more rapidly than the software can be completed. Really major military software projects, such as those associated with the Strategic Defense Initiative, can exceed 10 years in development.

Creeping user requirements are endemic in the military software domain. Unlike civilian projects, where creeping requirements are often not separately tracked or priced, the military domain tends to keep fairly good records of requirements changes and their associated costs. Indeed, this situation is common enough in military projects so that it is now anticipated, and mechanisms are starting to evolve which assume *continuous* requirements changes throughout the development cycle.

The magnitude of military project requirements changes is similar to civilian projects, and runs about 1% per month. However, since military projects typically have longer schedules, the accumulated totals are greater. Thus on a typical four-to five-year military project, from 50% to more than 60% of the delivered functionality can be in the form of creeping user requirements.

The phrase "unused or unusable software" is defined as software projects which, when delivered, are in fact not used by the intended user community. The risk of unused or unusable software is common to governmental software in general, and to military software in particular. The reason for this phenomenon appears to be partly due to the fact that the length of time it takes to complete large military software projects is long enough for the planned users to have changed jobs, or for the work content of the jobs to have evolved beyond the point where the software has little or no utility. Sometimes the hardware for which the software is being created can become obsolete prior to completion of the software project.

Note: A major and growing problem with military hardware procurement contracts for computers, work stations and the like is the fact that over 50% of the initial selections are now being challenged by competitors. This has stretched out the duration of proposal/contract cycles to more than two years, and the duration is growing rapidly as more and more challenges occur. Should this problem move into the software domain, it may become a major problem before the end of the century.

Contract or Outsourced Software Risks

Between one-fourth and one-third of U.S. software projects involve contractors or subcontractors. As of 1993, just over 5% of U.S. software projects are part of formal outsourcing agreements, but the percentage is increasing rapidly. Contract development and outsourcing are popular in part for reasons of efficiency and cost control, and in part because of load balancing. On the whole, contract and outsourced projects tend to have higher productivity rates than similar projects carried out by personnel employed by the enterprise itself. However, contracting and outsourcing do have some associated risks. The concern here is that of projects which are carried out by a contracting organization, or where the software development is outsourced to a separate company.

Risk Factor	Percentage of projects at risk
High maintenance costs	60%
Friction between contractor and client personnel	50%
Creeping user requirements	45%
Unanticipated acceptance criteria	30%
Legal ownership of software and deliverables	20%

The phrase "high maintenance costs" has no exact definition, but can roughly be defined as projects where the annual maintenance costs for defect repairs and minor updates are notably higher than U.S. norms, and where the amount of existing software which one person can maintain is notably lower than U.S. norms. The current average annual maintenance cost for software (defect repairs and minor enhancements) is about $125 per Function Point (Jones, 1991). The average quantity of existing software which one person can maintain averages about 500 Function Points, and can range up to 1500 Function Points.

Contract projects may exceed $200 per Function Point in annual maintenance costs, and have a maintenance assignment scope of less than 300 Function Points under a very common set of circumstances—software where development is contracted out but maintenance is performed in-house will experience high maintenance costs. The reason is not because the software is intrinsically hard to maintain, but because in-house personnel who must perform the maintenance are usually unfamiliar with it for the first year or so. An obvious solution to this problem would be to include maintenance and/or maintenance training in the contract, but this seldom occurs.

The phrase "friction between contractor and client personnel" implies disagreements, arguments, and sometimes enmity between the client organization and the contracting organization. Such problems are fairly common in all industries, and software is no exception. In extreme cases, this kind of friction can jeopardize contracts and projects.

This friction between clients and contracters often leads to litigation. The author, for example, receives about three requests per year to testify as an expert witness in various software trials dealing with such things as quality and schedules. Although the author routinely rejects these requests because they take too much time, it appears that a new subdiscipline of management consulting which might be called "professional expert witness" could possibly occur before the end of the century.

The risk of creeping user requirements for contract projects is actually slightly lower than the risk for in-house software projects. However, when creeping requirements do occur on contracts they are often more difficult to deal with and more visible. Normally the contractor will expect or demand additional payments for creeping improvements or unplanned requirements. However, the client may assert that the requirement was always implicitly present, and the vendor failed to realize it. Varying opinions about funding for creeping user requirements is a major source of friction between clients and contracting groups.

The phrase "unanticipated acceptance criteria" is defined as new and sometimes stringent criteria levied on a contractor by a client as a condition of product acceptance or payment of funds, outside the scope of the initial contract or agreement. Examples of unanticipated acceptance criteria can include very stringent quality or performance targets for the software, or the need to retroactively specify or document the software.

Unanticipated acceptance criteria can result from a failure to establish criteria early in the contract, or can be due to friction and hard feelings by the client that the work was not satisfactorily performed. In either case, the situation can be damaging to the project and the relationships. In a few extreme situations, unanticipated acceptance criteria can lead to litigation or termination of the contract prior to completion.

The phrase "legal ownership of software and deliverables" refers to a risk factor that is not widespread, but is very serious when it occurs. Agreements between contractors and clients should normally be prepared by attorneys, and should ensure that the ownership of the work products is assigned to the client, if this is the intent of the agreement. Otherwise, and the situation can vary from state to state and case to case, and it may turn out that ownership of the deliverables resides with the contractor and not the client. Several recent court cases have occurred because of this situation.

End-User Software Risks

As computer literacy becomes more widespread, an ever-growing number of end users can program well enough to develop applications for themselves. The phenomenon of end-user development is fairly common among technical knowledge workers such as engineers and architects. As of 1993, computer literacy is so widespread that end-user applications are no longer uncommon among accountants, managers and executives and even attorneys. By the end of the century, computer literacy will be common enough for perhaps 50% of all U.S. knowledge workers to produce software applications should they choose to do so. However, end-user development has a significant pattern of associated risks:

Risk Factor	Percentage of projects at risk
Non-transferable applications	80%
Hidden errors	65%
Unmaintainable software	60%
Redundant applications	50%
Legal ownership of software and deliverables	20%

The phrase "non-transferable applications" refers to end-user software that is so quirky or unique that only the originator knows how to use it. End-user applications may or may not use standard human interface conventions. End-user applications almost never have user documentation or training material. This means that if the author of an end-user application leaves the enterprise or changes jobs, there is a very high probability that his or her successor cannot use the program.

The phrase "hidden errors" is defined as logical or programming errors that are latent within an end-user application without the knowledge of the author or anyone else. Hidden errors are extremely common in end-user applications, due to the lack of formal reviews, inspections, testing, audits, or quality assurance activity. In enterprises where several knowledge workers have produced similar end-user applications, it is astonishing how often the results differ because one or more of the end-user applications contained hidden errors.

37

When the author of an end-user application leaves the enterprise, who exactly will be responsible for maintenance of his or her applications? The phrase "unmaintainable software" refers to end-user applications that are so poorly structured, commented and specified that maintenance becomes essentially impossible after the original author departs or changes jobs.

The phrase "redundant applications" refers to both lateral and chronological redundancy of essentially similar applications. As an example of lateral redundancy, assume that a particular department employs 10 electrical engineers all doing similar work. If each engineer develops his or her own circuit design application, then obviously there are 10 redundant applications. As an example of chronological redundancy, assume that the average assignment in a particular departmental position is 18 months. If each incumbent develops an end-user application, then a new version of the application will be created at 18 month intervals.

As previously noted for contract software, ownership of software and associated deliverables may not automatically vest with the enterprise. The phrase "legal ownership of software and deliverables" refers to risk situations where end-users who developed applications wish to take the application with them when they leave the enterprise. Here too, legal counsel should be sought, and explicit employment agreements should include wording that covers the ownership of end-user developed applications.

PREVENTING AND CONTROLLING COMMON SOFTWARE RISKS

Not every form of software risk is fully controllable. However, for those that are, the most difficult aspects of software risk management appears to be cultural and sociological. Most of the common risks noted here have available technologies that can prevent, control, or minimize the significance of the risk. That fact does not ensure that the technologies will be used, however. Thus software risk management needs effective change agents and an active program of technology transfer. The following sections contain short discussions of known therapies for selected common software risks.

Creeping User Requirements

Although creeping user requirements occur more often than any other risk factor, there are powerful technologies available to improve this situation. The use of prototypes is a proven preventive measure. The use of Joint Application Design (JAD) for requirements creation is also a proven approach in the MIS domain. Creating requirements via Information Engineering (IE) methodologies is a proven approach, although used primarily for MIS projects. The use of functional metrics to measure the growth of user requirements is also a proven and effective control method, and one which works on all classes of software.

A new solution to creeping user requirements has begun in recent years—base the contract on the number of Function Points to be delivered and the anticipated cost per Function Point. For example, a contract might call for the development of a 1000 Function Point application at a cost of $600 per Function Point, or $600,000 total. Thus if 50 new Function Points are added by the user, the costs would rise by $30,000.

Since functional metrics are normally quantified during the requirements phase, some very interesting research is now taking place that attempts to couple and automate requirements gathering and functional metric creation.

Although not yet commercially available, it now appears technically feasible to create requirements automation tools built around tables of common functions and features which will not only add speed and rigor to requirements gathering, but also feed data directly into both Function Point enumerators and cost estimating tools. Data may also be fed directly into various CASE, data modelling, and design tools.

There is at least the possibility of creating reusable requirements, which in turn can augment the creation of reusable plans, reusable estimates, and reusable designs.

Schedule Pressure, Long Schedules, and Excessive Time to Market

Various forms of schedule-related risks are endemic to the software industry. Two classes of technologies must be used to minimize such risks: 1) technologies to improve schedule estimation and planning, and 2) technologies to reduce schedule durations.

As of 1993, there are more than 50 commercial-grade software estimating tools marketed in the U.S. with schedule estimating capabilities and more than 70 project planning tools. There are no reasons, other than cultural or sociological ones, why all software project managers should not have access to such tools.

The sociology of schedule prediction should be noted. If an estimating tool or a manual estimate predicts a delivery date that is significantly longer than client or management expectations, there is a tendency to reject the prediction out of hand.

Schedule reduction technologies are more narrow in focus, and here the selection depends upon the class and size of the application. Some of the schedule-reduction approaches that are known to be effective include: A) creating libraries of reusable designs, reusable code, and other artifacts; B) object-oriented analysis, design, and coding methods; C) CASE tool suites; D) Information Engineering (IE) and Rapid Application Development (RAD) for small or medium MIS projects; E) Structured analysis and design methods for large systems and commercial software projects, and F) Reviews, inspections, and quality control approaches for large systems.

Cost Overruns

Cost overruns and schedule overruns typically go hand in hand. The technologies for prevention and control are similar too, with 3 notable exceptions: 1) technologies which improve the accuracy of cost estimates; 2) technologies which actually reduce software costs; 3) technologies for accurately measuring software costs.

Cost estimation and cost reduction technologies are essentially identical to schedule estimation and schedule reduction. However, measurement of software costs is rapidly improving under the impact of functional metrics such as Function Points and Feature Points. Functional metrics resolve many of the ambiguities and paradoxes of the former "lines of code" metrics, and are rapidly becoming the preferred metrics for large-scale productivity and cost studies of software projects.

The non-profit International Function Point Users Group (IFPUG) already has some 500 enterprises as members, and its membership appears to be growing by more than 40% per year. Of the 50 commercial-grade software estimating tools marketed in the U.S. in 1993, about 30 of them currently support functional metrics. Of the five commercial software measurement tools in the U.S. in 1993, four of them support functional metrics as a standard metric.

An emerging method for dealing with cost overruns and high software costs in general is international outsourcing. The average development cost for software in the United States is about $900 per Function Point as of 1993. Military software runs to more than $2500 per Function Point, but some civilian PC applications are less than $600 per Function Point. There are several countries such as India, Hungary, Poland, and Mexico where the average development costs are less than $200 per Function Point, due to low wage scales and low overheads. There is a growing trend toward international outsourcing.

Low Quality and Error-Prone Modules

For all major software projects and large systems, quality control is on the critical path to schedule reduction and cost control. There are four classes of technologies that have proven to be effective for software quality control: 1) quality estimation and reliability estimation tools; 2) defect prevention methods; 3) defect removal methods, and 4) quality measurement programs.

As of 1993, there are six commercial-grade software quality and reliability estimating tools on the U.S. market, and several more are planned for release before the end of the year. The current penetration of software quality estimation is low: less than 10% of U.S. software managers use such tools in 1993 since this is a fairly new technology. However, the rate of growth for quality estimation tool usage is very steep. All major software projects should have access to quality and reliability estimating tools.

Defect prevention includes all technologies which can reduce the chance of making mistakes or errors, and includes: A) any of the structured analysis and design techniques; B) prototypes; C) high-level and object-oriented languages; D) rigorous usage of structured coding techniques for procedural languages; E) the

40

Quality Function Deployment (QFD) approach; F) the Total Quality Management (TQM) approach; G) Software Quality Assurance (SQA) departments, and H) Cleanroom development methods.

Defect removal includes design reviews, structured walkthroughs, formal code inspections, correctness proofs, and all forms of testing. Formal reviews and inspections have the highest measured defect removal efficiencies of any form of defect removal, and are in fact used by all of the U.S. quality leaders such as AT&T, IBM, Motorola, and Raytheon. Testing works best if carried out by trained specialists in a formal manner.

All of the U.S. leaders in software quality control (i.e. Baldrige Award winners) have established full quality measurement programs. Some companies, such as IBM, have been measuring software quality and user satisfaction for more than 25 years.

One of the newest extensions of functional metrics is in the quality domain. The older "lines of code" metrics were so ambiguous and paradoxical for measuring requirements, design, and documentation error levels that there was essentially no literature on many important quality topics. Function points were used in 1991 to establish U.S. national quality averages for military, systems, and MIS projects (Jones, 1991). As of 1993, functional metrics are also being used to measure and predict the number of test cases and test runs for software projects

SPR was commissioned in 1992 by several Baldrige Award winners to explore aspects of software quality internationally. Part of the study involved contact with companies which had received certification under the ISO 9000–9004 quality standards. Companies producing similar software but which had not received ISO certification were also contacted. It is unfortunate to report that there is no evidence to date which indicates that ISO certification improves quality in any tangible way. However, there is evidence that ISO certification is fairly expensive and time consuming. Of course, the ISO certification process is too new to have developed any long-range studies so future evidence may change this picture.

High Maintenance Costs

The phrase "maintenance" is ambiguous in common usage, where it tends to be used for both enhancements and defect repairs. This discussion centers on the defect repair aspect of maintenance. Enhancements, or adding new functions to existing software, is not necessarily a risk. On the other hand, excessive volumes of defect repair work implies significant front-end deficiencies.

Although the risk of high maintenance or repair costs have been endemic to the software industry, there are many technologies that can now be deployed to lower such risks to safe or at least tolerable levels: 1) structural complexity analyzers; 2) restructuring tools (primarily for COBOL and C); 3) reverse engineering tools; 4) re-engineering tools, and 5) error-prone module analysis and removal.

Those companies which have attacked high maintenance costs have been remarkably successful. IBM achieved a full order of magnitude reduction in annual defect reports against its IMS data base product, for example, by means of error-prone module elimination and other techniques.

Some of the best recent results noted to date are a 50% reduction in overall corporate maintenance costs and a 300% expansion in average maintenance assignment scopes in the course of a five-year period.

Hartford Insurance Corporation provides an interesting case study of successfully reducing software maintenance costs. In an industry where most competitors average more than 50% of their annual budgets going to maintenance and enhancement, the Hartford is now below 19% and dropping.

More than 10 years ago executives at Hartford Insurance realized that maintenance would become a major problem. They adopted a vigorous program of complexity analysis, restructuring, reverse engineering, and reengineering, and have been tracking the results ever since.

Systems and applications with long-range strategic value are refurbished intermittently to keep them well structured, well documented, and easy to modify.

An interesting and cost-effective aspect of the Hartford's strategy is that nothing at all is done to an application unless it is scheduled for enhancement, and then prior to the enhancement it will either be moderately refurbished or fully refurbished, based on its strategic value and the nature of the planned enhancements.

Nowhere is the impact of culture more evident than in the maintenance domain. A new sub-industry appeared circa 1985 of products, services, and companies which can provide geriatric care for aging software and legacy systems. Yet most enterprises that report annual maintenance costs in excess of 50% of their total software budgets have not made any explicit attempt to explore these offerings, and are still using "brute force" maintenance approaches for what appears to be purely sociological reasons.

In addition to gathering data from assessments, it is also useful to do quick surveys at conferences and seminars. When speaking about maintenance at conferences and seminars, the author asks for a show of hands from the audience to represent various percentages of annual costs devoted to maintenance. Then a show of hands is requested for those actively engaged in exploring geriatric services and tools. It is a striking phenomenon that less than 5% of the people who assert that their maintenance costs exceed 50% of their budgets per annum have made any attempt at all to reduce those costs or explore geriatric technologies. On the other hand, about 65% of the people whose annual maintenance costs are less than 25% have active geriatric programs underway.

RISK FACTORS WHICH ARE RESISTANT TO CONTROL

Unfortunately, not all of the most common risk factors are fully controllable. Those which are based on the human psyche or which involve major sociological changes are extremely resistant. Also resistant are risk factors embedded in military standards or the nature of the software itself. Here are short discussions of risk factors which are resistant to improvement.

Excessive Paperwork

As of 1993, excessive paperwork for military projects appears to be mandated by military standards themselves, and hence this problem can be viewed as highly resistant. For civilian systems software, which also tends to have excessive paperwork, there is a fundamental technology gap—no one knows what an optimum set of paper documents (plans, specifications, user documents, etc.) would contain.

From analysing the volume and kind of information created in support of software projects, the author has concluded that displacement of physical paper documents is about to become economically feasible. All talk of "paperless offices" in the past failed to deal with a fundamental issue: the cost per byte of storage on paper was cheaper than for magnetic disk or tape. Further, access from paper documents was easier for executives and others who lacked access to or training in computers.

The convergence of optical storage technologies, object-oriented data base technologies, hyper-text technologies, and low-cost, hand-held optical disk reading devices is now approaching the point where storing and retrieving information via optical media may be both cheaper and more convenient than paper.

Inadequate User Documentation

The percentage of human beings who can write clearly is not very high. Therefore software user documentation is likely to remain marginal, except for software produced by large companies with full technical writing, editing, and illustration departments.

The emergence of multi-media technologies and graphical user interfaces are likely to change the nature and appearance of user documentation in fundamental ways. However, it is premature in 1993 to judge the actual impact of these technologies.

Low User Satisfaction

This problem is not totally resistant, but it is not easy to improve. User satisfaction surveys, human factors experts, and the migration toward Graphical User Interfaces (GUI) can reduce one source of user dissatisfaction. Improving customer support, improving HELP functions, and improving user documentation are also beneficial, but not easy to accomplish. However, software products such as some Windows applications that require 20 megabytes of hard-disk storage space and 8 megabytes of memory to execute are forging new kinds of dissatisfaction.

User satisfaction survey instruments are increasing in sophistication. Further, the quantity of data on features and services which improve or downgrade user satisfaction is becoming more plentiful. The long-range prognosis for this problem is favorable, even if the short-range prognosis is not.

Friction Between Clients and Contractors

This problem appears to be a basic phenomenon of human nature, and it is not clear if anything can alter the probability of its occurrence. Software is not unique in experiencing this problem, and disputes between clients and contractors have been known throughout human history.

Legal Issues and Litigation Expense

Of all of the risk issues discussed here, the probability of encountering legal problems and expensive litigation is the only one that is growing more severe with the passage of time. Unless something unexpected occurs, litigation will be a major factor of the commercial software industry by the end of the century. Unfortunately, the U.S. tends to be the world leader in expensive litigation. The situation is severe enough to jeopardize U.S. leadership and damage a favorable balance of trade for software products.

From conversations with other management consultants during 1992 and 1993, it now appears possible for a technical expert in various aspects of software quality, costs, or schedules to perform almost full-time consulting work as an expert witness should he or she choose to do so.

SUMMARY AND CONCLUSIONS

Formal risk management analysis and formal project assessments are effective and useful approaches that are starting to add rigor to the phrase "software engineering." Not every risk factor is fully controllable, and several risk factors exceed the authority of software managers, such as the risk of excessive paperwork caused by military standards themselves. Nonetheless, risk analysis and assessment methods are quite effective in the identification of significant problems. Once problems are identified and examined, solutions can often be developed.

References

Boehm, Barry W.; *Software Risk Management;* IEEE Computer Society Press; Los Alamitos, CA; 1989; Catalog No. 106; 508 pages.

Charette, Robert N.; *Software Engineering Risk Analysis and Management;* McGraw-Hill, New York, NY; 1989; 325 pages.

Charette, Robert N.; *Application Strategies for Risk Analysis;* McGraw-Hill, New York; 1990; 570 pages.

Humphrey, Watts; *Managing the Software Process;* Addison-Wesley, Winthrop, MA; 1989; 486 pages.

Miller, Sharon E. and Tucker, George T.; *Software Development Process Benchmarking;* IEEE Communications Society; New York, New York; December 1991 (Reprinted from IEEE Global Telecommunications Conference; December 2–5, 1991).

Jones, Capers; *Programming Productivity;* McGraw-Hill Book Company; New York, New York; 1986; pp 7–26.

Dunn, Robert and Ullman, Richard; *Quality Assurance for Computer Software;* McGraw-Hill Book Company; New York, New York; 1982; 351 pages.

Jones, Capers; *Applied Software Measurement;* McGraw-Hill Book Company; New York; 1991; pp 123–183.

3

The Most Serious Software Risks

Software has long been regarded as one of the most risk-prone of all engineering activities. Risks such as schedule slips and cost overruns tend to occur on more than 50% of all large systems. Even more severe risks, such as cancellation of the project prior to completion or serious quality deficiencies are not uncommon.

Many projects tend to lack formal risk management approaches. Risk identification and risk avoidance often depends informally upon the skills and experience levels of software managers. Unfortunately, the magnitude and severities of risks that slip through informal controls leads to the conclusion that management experience, by itself, is not a sufficient safeguard against software risks.

Formal process assessments, risk control audits, and formal software quality assurance organizations are visibly more effective in identifying and minimizing risks than casual, informal means.

Many risk factors are annoying, but do not actually jeopardize the health of an organization or its ability to make progress. Some risk factors, however, are so serious that unless they are handled, projects and enterprises may be in jeopardy.

A topic of considerable importance is the *severity* of risks. Companies must consider which risks are the most serious and have the greatest potential for doing major damage to software projects and software-producing enterprises.

It is an interesting observation that the pattern of serious risks is not identical between military and civilian projects, nor between MIS, systems, commercial, and end-user software. On the whole, military software projects tend to be more formal in their approaches and military standards such as DoD 2167A do add substantial rigor. However, there are still serious problems with military software that are outside the current scope of military standards.

The risk factors included here are the ten which have the greatest potential for doing serious damage. The basis for the assertion of "serious damage" are the observations on productivity, quality, and project outcomes derived from using the SPR assessment method.

Unfortunately, these risks tend to be cumulative in the damage that they can do, just as arsenic accumulates in a human body. A project or enterprise can probably survive one or two of these serious risk factors, but if more than three or four are present at the same time, then the mortality rate reaches alarming levels.

Also included are observations on the different probabilities of having each risk between military and civilian organizations, and between various classes of software.

CLASSES OF SOFTWARE PROJECTS

1. Management information systems (MIS) projects such as accounting systems, claims handling systems, and the like.

2. Systems software projects such as operating systems, telecommunication systems, or other software applications which control physical devices.

3. Commercially marketed software projects, such as spreadsheets, word processors, or CAD packages that are leased or sold to end users.

4. Military software projects, which can include all those constrained to follow U.S. military standards such as DoD-STD-2167A.

5. Contract or outsourced software projects in the civilian domain, where the bulk of the software is produced by contract personnel, as opposed to employees of the client organization.

6. End-user software projects, where the software was developed by the intended user rather than by a professional programming staff.

There are other types of software besides these six, such as scientific software. However, for these six, SPR's assessment method has collected sufficient data to note the problems which follow.

Although the serious risk factors are ranked in nominal order, in real life the most serious problems must be matched to specific projects. Consider the analogy of medical risks. For the United States as a whole, the highest medical risks are those of cancer and heart disease. That does not mean that every single individual is equally at risk to these two conditions.

The following are the 10 most serious risk factors, as derived from SPR assessments:

1. Inaccurate Metrics—It was proven in 1978 that "lines of code" or LOC metrics cannot safely be used to aggregate productivity and quality data when multiple languages are involved. There is a consistent bias with "lines of code" metrics that penalizes high-level languages, and the magnitude of the penalty is directly proportional to the power of the language. In other words, LOC metrics conceal productivity and quality data rather than revealing trends.

The continued use of metrics proven to be ineffective is as unprofessional for the software community as was the refusal of doctors to sterilize their instruments after Lister had demonstrated the hazards of disease transmission.

Usage of inaccurate metrics is the most serious risk of all, since mistakes derived from this problem can slow productivity and quality progress to a standstill. The usage of inaccurate and paradoxical metrics such as "lines of code" has been a major obstacle to software engineering since the industry began.

This problem is so common and so severe that until it can be overcome, it is unlikely that the phrase "software engineering" will be anything other than an oxymoron. A strong case can be made that usage of "lines of code" metrics should be declared to be professional malpractice after 1995.

Functional metrics are now beginning to replace LOC metrics, and are opening up many new fields of exploration and research. Functional metrics are not perfect and have their own problems. However, functional metrics do not violate standard economic and quality assumptions as do LOC metrics.

Economic studies, quality studies, and value studies derived from modern functional metrics are increasing in number and significance. Indeed, as of 1993 the International Function Point Users Group (IFPUG) is the largest software measurement organization in the United States, and is growing rapidly in Europe, Asia, and South America.

There are six serious problems with LOC metrics: 1) Lack of standardization for any single language; 2) Lack of conversion rules for cross-language comparisons among the 400 or so languages in common use; 3) Paradoxical behavior in the presence of high-level languages such as Ada, object-oriented languages, or generators (one of the reasons why usage of the LOC metric should be considered malpractice); 4) Inability to measure non-coding tasks such as plans, specifications and user documents which together comprise more than half of large system expenses (yet another aspect of malpractice); 5) Inability to measure software bugs or defects in requirements, specifications, and non-code deliverables (another form of malpractice); 6) Difficulty in determining source code size during requirements, at the time when this information is needed for estimating purposes.

The ambiguity with LOC and KLOC is caused by the impact of the inelastic costs of certain activities that are always part of software projects. The problem of measuring productivity in the presence of fixed costs has long been understood for manufacturing economics, and appears to have been worked out more than 200 years ago during the industrial revolution. (Studies of manufacturing in the classical world indicate that the impact of fixed costs on manufacturing economics may possibly have been known more than 2000 years ago by Roman industrialists, and even before that in India and China.)

There is a basic law of manufacturing economics—if a manufacturing process includes a high percentage of fixed costs, and the number of units produced goes down, the cost per unit will go up. This same law also applies to software. An illustration can clarify the concept.

Consider a program that was written in basic assembly language and required 10,000 lines of code. The non-coding tasks for requirements, specifications, and user documentation would take about three months of effort, and the code itself would take about seven months to develop and test. The total project would thus require 10 months of effort, and net productivity would be 1000 LOC per person month for this example.

Now consider the same program written in Ada. Only about 2,000 Ada statements would be required as opposed to the previous 10,000 basic assembly statements.

The Ada coding and testing effort would be one month rather than seven months, for a real saving of six months. However, the non-coding tasks for requirements, specifications, and user documentation would still take three months of effort and hence tend to act as fixed costs.

Thus the total project in Ada would require only four months of total effort, for a clear improvement of 60% in terms of real economic productivity (i.e. goods or services produced per unit of labor or expense).

However, when productivity of the total project is measured with LOC, the Ada version of the same project averages only 500 LOC per month for an apparent *reduction* in productivity of 50% versus basic assembly language. This is counter to the improvement in real economic productivity, and constitutes a notable paradox for the software industry.

Since both versions of this sample application perform exactly the same functions, the Function Point total of the assembler and Ada versions would obviously be the same: assume 35 Function Points.

Using the Function Point metric, the assembler version has a productivity rate of only 3.5 Function Points per month, while the Ada version has a rate of 8.75 Function Points per month. Function Points match the increase in real economic productivity, while the LOC metric conceals the power of Ada and other high-level languages.

The usage of LOC metrics ranks as the most serious problem of all for these reasons: A) It is professionally embarrassing for an industry to try and use a productivity and quality normalization metric that goes backwards; B) No effective scientific or engineering research can occur without the ability to measure the results, and the LOC metric has essentially blinded many software researchers.

MIS projects are least likely to use inaccurate metrics. The usage of Function Points in the MIS domain is now approaching 50%. Although not free from this risk by any means, MIS now ranks first in avoiding this problem.

Contract software groups are the second most likely to resist inaccurate metrics now that companies like ISSC in the United States, TATA in India, and DMR in Canada have started to use Function Points for contract software and as the basis for outsourcing agreements. Many major contract and outsourcing groups are now moving toward functional metrics.

Third would be systems software. Many systems software groups tend to look on Function Points with disdain, because of the MIS origin of this metric. However, variations and extensions to Function Points, such as SPR's Feature Point metric and Boeing's 3-D Function Points are starting to attract attention within the systems, embedded, and real-time domains.

Through the start of 1993, military projects are fourth, and are much more likely than civilian projects to utilize inaccurate LOC metrics. This is partially because SEI has lagged in endorsing Function Points, and indeed is lagging in many measurement topics. However, other military software research centers such as the Air Force Institute of Technology and the Naval Post-Graduate School are exploring functional metrics. Some excellent military measurement studies are being produced with functional metrics, such as those of the Surface Weapons Systems group in Dahlgren, Virginia.

Fifth, and highly susceptible to inaccurate metrics, are commercial software houses. Somewhat surprisingly, even the most successful software houses unfortunately tend not to measure productivity or quality using state-of-the-art methods. Some don't measure at all. One gets the impression that the managers and staff within some of these organizations live in their own world, and don't really know or care about what the rest of the industry is doing. As an example of this observation, managers and technical employees from companies such as Microsoft, Borland, and Lotus tend to be significantly underrepresented at conferences and seminars dealing with software quality, software metrics, software measurement, and software management.

In sixth place, would be end-user software. Essentially there is no measurement of end-user software, so accurate or inaccurate metrics are a moot point.

2. **Inadequate Measurement**—This is the second most serious problem. Tracking and cost collection systems for software projects tend to "leak" and omit major portions of software expense. Unpaid overtime, managerial effort, administrative effort, user effort, and many specialist groups such as quality assurance and technical writing are often omitted from project data. In some cases, there is no project tracking at all and hence the leakage is 100%. For enterprises that do attempt software cost tracking, SPR has noted an average leakage that ranges from 35% to 50%.

Leakage from cost tracking systems is serious because it prevents historical data from being used to make accurate predictions of future project costs. The whole technology of calibrating estimating models against historical data is thrown out of kilter, since the historical data is often less reliable than the outputs of the estimating tools.

Leakage from cost tracking systems also impacted several studies of cost estimating accuracy, which seem to have contained a fatal flaw: the authors assumed, without validation, that the historical data used for comparison to the estimating models was itself correct. Therefore, any differences between historical data and cost estimates were assumed to be errors in the estimates.

When the authors of these studies were contacted as to how they knew that the historical data was complete and accurate, the response was that the accuracy was merely assumed.

When some of these studies are revisited with historical data that was itself validated, not only were the differences between the estimates and the historical data closer, but it sometimes happened that the original historical data had a higher margin of error than the estimating tools!

Most cost tracking systems were not created specifically for software project control, and hence are far from optimal. For many projects, the measurement tools themselves are capable of handling factors such as unpaid overtime, slack time between assignments, and managerial effort but local policies tend to bar the recording of such information.

A major leak from cost tracking systems is the work performed by users themselves. For large civilian MIS applications, direct user work on tasks such as requirements, participating in reviews, writing portions of the user documentation, and acceptance testing can sum to almost 20% of the total effort. Yet this effort is almost never recorded, since user time is not part of most projects' cost accounting structure. For military software, user effort is even larger, and may exceed 25% of the total. Here too, the effort is seldom tracked or applied to the overall costs of the project. These quantities are too large to ignore.

Although military projects lag in the use of metrics, they are often superior to civilian projects in controlling resource leakages and rank in first place. But even among military projects, leakage such as early requirements, unpaid overtime, and client performance of technical tasks can exceed 25%. That is, as much as 25% of the effort applied to software projects can be in the form of activities and tasks which are not tracked using the project cost accounting system.

Second in controlling resource leakages are contract software projects. It is surprising that such projects would not rank first, given the importance of accurate time recording to contract work. However, accurate time recording is usually only associated with time and materials contracts. For many fixed price contracts, sizable quantities of unpaid overtime are worked that are not tracked at all.

Third in controlling resource leakages are MIS applications in large corporations, where costs are routinely collected because the software function operates as either a cost center or a profit center. Smaller enterprises are often quite careless in cost tracking, as are enterprises where software is treated as an overhead item. However, tracking user costs is a major gap in most companies' historical data.

Fourth are system software producers. Large companies such as AT&T and IBM which produce systems software may have adequate cost tracking systems in place. Smaller companies often do not. Cost tracking is especially lax for bundled hardware/software products where the software is given away with the hardware.

Fifth in controlling resource leakages are the commercial software houses. The software engineers in such companies (including SPR, incidentally) tend to work around the clock and are seldom required to keep accurate time records.

Sixth are end-user software developers, who seldom record their time spent on building applications at all.

3. **Excessive Schedule Pressure**—Irrational schedules and excessive schedule pressure have occurred on more than 65% of all large projects assessed to date. Excessive schedule pressure is a key contributor to poor quality, canceled projects, low morale, fatigue, burn-out, and high attrition rates among software personnel. Some of the other serious problems were chronic and caused trouble over long time

spans. This problem is acute. It is also a killer that can destroy a project, a contract, staff morale, and even a company.

Two critical root problems have been observed leading to excessive schedule pressure: 1) The original schedule was derived by decree, demand, or some other arbitrary method; 2) The requirements for the project continued to change after the end of the nominal requirements phase.

Ranking first in schedule pressure avoidance are end-user software projects. Often this kind of software is written in spare time, and is not subjected to any kind of schedule constraints at all.

Second in schedule pressure avoidance are large systems software projects such as switching systems. The reason, apparently, is because enough historical data exists for this domain so that schedules are fairly well understood by both clients and managers. That is not to say that schedule pressure is absent, but that *irrational* schedule pressure is somewhat reduced.

The other kinds of software (MIS, commercial, contract, and military) are tied for third place. No significant difference has been noted between military and civilian domains in the area of excessive schedule pressure: both are equally susceptible. Also susceptible are commercial software houses and contract software houses.

Since schedule pressure is more intense on large projects than on small ones, projects larger than 1000 Function Points of any class and type are the most likely to experience this problem. Above 5000 Function Points in size, the incidence approaches 100%.

Note however, the usage of schedule estimating tools (i.e. tools such as ASSET-R, CHECKPOINT®, COCOMO, PRICE-S, REVIC, SPQR/20, SLIM etc.) is somewhat more common in military and defense systems than it is among civilian projects.

4. **Management Malpractice**—This topic is seldom discussed in risk management literature, but ranks as one of the most critical problems of the software industry. Unfortunately, software managers are seldom adequately trained for their jobs, and many lack even rudimentary skills in normal managerial tasks. Management malpractice is both more common and more severe than technical staff malpractice.

The root cause of management malpractice can be traced back to inadequate curricula at the undergraduate, graduate, and professional levels. Most software managers do not receive adequate training in the six basic tasks of software project management: sizing, estimating, planning, tracking, measurement, and assessment. End-user software is obviously first in avoiding this problem, since the work is usually self-managed.

Second in avoiding the problems of management malpractice are the large system software producers such as AT&T and IBM. These organizations typically have in-house management training that is quite sophisticated and overcomes the poor education which managers receive via normal university curricula.

The large systems houses also have excellent infrastructures for identifying malpractice and minimizing its consequences: formal appraisals, opinions surveys, and other techniques for judging performance are quite common.

Third, although the facts are less certain here, would probably be the military domain. The military services also have on-the-job training and go to some pains to ensure that at least some relevant information is given to those who need it. Programs such as the Air Force BOLD STROKE seminars where senior officers are brought up to speed, and the existence of the Air Force Institute of Technology and the Naval Post Graduate School indicate fairly successful attempts to keep military officers more or less up to speed. There are exceptions, such as the high use of LOC metrics by the military, however.

Unfortunately, the above does not hold true for defense contractors. Often they have no training, or very little training, available for either managers or technical staff due to the nature of the contracts under which military work is performed.

Fourth are the managers in the contract houses. These organizations depend upon capable managers for significant portions of their revenue, and although they are not ample in on-the-job training, they are fairly good in selection of qualified managers and weeding out those that are not qualified.

Below this level, results are ambiguous and tend to blur. MIS software producers and commercial software houses all seem to operate under random patterns in regard to the problem of management malpractice.

The only general observation that seems to correlate with avoiding malpractice is that profitable enterprises with available cash tend to do a better job in avoiding this problem than enterprises that have marginal funds for discretionary purposes.

This topic has almost no citations in the software literature, and is not addressed by SEI assessments at all. Clearly this is an area that needs extensive study.

5. **Inaccurate Cost Estimating**—As of 1993 there are more than 50 commercial software estimating tools and more than 70 project planning tools marketed in the United States. In spite of the availability of powerful tools, less than 25% of U.S. software managers use estimating tools, and less than 50% use project planning tools. Since there are no accurate manual methods for planning and estimating large software projects, this factor explains many of the cost overruns and schedule overruns which occur.

Military and defense software producers rank first in avoiding this problem (although no industry is very good in an absolute sense), and are somewhat ahead of their civilian counterparts in the usage of estimating tools. Military software is also ahead in the usage of estimating and cost analysis specialists. In one particular aspect, which is using multiple estimating tools and looking for convergence, U.S. military software producers are perhaps the world leaders.

As mentioned, there are currently some 50 commercial software estimating tools marketed in the United States, and the number grows monthly. Some of these tools are aimed purely at civilian projects, while others are aimed at military and defense projects, and others are general-purpose and can support all classes of software. Among the tools widely used for military software project estimation are (in alphabetic order): ASSET-R, CHECKPOINT®, COCOMO, GECOMO, PRICE-S, REVIC, SEER, SOFTCOST, SLIM, and SPQR/20.

Usage of automated software estimating tools is about twice as frequent for military software projects as for civilian. Usage of multiple tools concurrently (i.e. simultaneous usage of COCOMO, SLIM, CHECKPOINT®, etc.) is about an order of magnitude more common for military software than for civilian.

Second in avoiding inaccurate cost estimates are the MIS producers. The software estimating tools which serve the MIS market are generally quite a different set from the military estimators. Tools such as the Bridge, BYL, ESTIMACS, and SPQR/20 are widely encountered in the MIS domain. Some tools, such as CHECK-POINT®, can be tuned to any domain by means of explicit class and type settings.

Also present in the MIS domain are estimating tools that are closely coupled to CASE tools: AGS FirstCase, Andersen Foundation, CGI PACBASE, Texas Instruments IEF, and Unisys LINC are examples of CASE tools with integral if somewhat rudimentary estimating capabilities.

Third are the contract and outsourcing houses. Now that Function Points are starting to be used for contract and outsourcing agreements, the contract software houses are moving rapidly into software estimation with tools that support Function Points. The contract and outsourcing folks still lag in estimating automation, but their rate of progress is very fast.

Somewhat alarming to U.S. software producers is the fact that several offshore software outsourcing groups in India (and elsewhere) are starting to use cost per Function Point as a marketing tool.

The 1993 average cost to build a Function Point in the United States is around $600 for civilian projects and $2500 (and up) for military projects. In India, the average costs to build a Function Point appear to be around $125. Even with substantial profits built in, outsource projects to India are typically contracted for less than $300 per Function Point.

Commercial off the shelf software packages for personal computers can be purchased for less than $0.20 per Function Point, which shows why there has been such an explosion in personal computers and the software which runs on them.

Fourth are the systems software houses. Tools that estimate effectively for systems software such as operating systems and telecommunication systems are not as common as either MIS or military estimators. CHECKPOINT®, SLIM, ASSET-R, are perhaps most widely encountered in this domain.,

Fifth are the commercial software houses. The general failure to use automated estimating tools in the commercial domain appears to be cultural and sociological. Although a number of commercial software houses are very large now, a low-end hacker mentality is still so pervasive that many managers in the commercial domain actually scorn estimating tools, and prefer to do their estimates manually in spite of the problems this technique can lead to.

Comparatively few estimators can handle some of the aspects of commercial software. CHECKPOINT®, for example, includes estimating functions for customer support, field service, warranty repairs, marketing materials, and course development. These topics are major cost drivers in the commercial domain but may not occur at all for several other classes of software.

Sixth is end-user software. Although several estimating tools can actually estimate end-user software, to date, no end-user has ever bought an estimating tool and few even use one simply for their own personal software.

6. **Silver Bullet Syndrome**—The naive belief that a single factor, such as moving to CASE, trying out Total Quality Management, or moving to the Object-Oriented (OO) paradigm will create large productivity and quality gains has been noted in more than 65% of all projects assessed. The silver bullet syndrome is a key factor in slow technology transfer, since it tends to serialize improvements which should be implemented in parallel. Enterprises that succumb to the silver bullet syndrome tend to never improve at all, and indeed often go backwards.

First in avoiding the problems of the silver bullet syndrome are the larger systems software producers, such as AT&T, Motorola and IBM. These organizations have built complex systems for many years, and they know it takes more than a single tool or a minor technology change to generate large improvements. In the large-system domain, multi-faceted approaches which encompass tools, methods, social factors, and the environment in parallel are the preferred way of making process improvements.

Second are the contract and outsourcing shops. These organizations' entire revenue comes from successful software, and they usually will not risk their business by taking silver bullet claims at face value.

Third in avoiding this problem are the commercial software houses. Here too, painful experience has taught them that multiple approaches are best. However, the OO paradigm is exploding through this domain, and in spite of the merits of the OO approach, some of the vendors are making silver-bullet claims without adequate justification. The GUI and client/server tool vendors, in particular, are claiming marvelous virtues and not quantifying where their assertions were proven.

Fourth is military software. Left to their own devices, military software producers would probably rank higher. Unfortunately, they operate under the auspices of the DoD, and this organization has a tendency to succumb to silver bullet thinking and simplistic solutions from time to time. In fairness, the DoD also recognizes the need for multi-faceted approaches and has invested quite a bit into multi-disciplinary research at the Software Engineering Institute (SEI).

Fifth are the end-user software developers. They would probably rank lower, except that there are not too many silver bullet ads aimed squarely at the end-user market.

Sixth is the MIS community. Unfortunately, the MIS domain is deluged in silver bullet ads from every fad and technology that surfaces: fourth-generation languages, CASE, RAD, and many other tools and methods are advertising "10 to 1" or "20 to 1" or even "1000 to 1" improvements in productivity if you only buy their wares. Most of these claims are spurious and lack all empirical data.

7. **Creeping User Requirements**—New and unanticipated user requirements can now be directly measured with functional metrics such as Function Points and Feature Points, since those metrics deal with the external factors which users care about (i.e. inputs, outputs, inquiries, logical files, and interfaces).

The rate of growth of creeping user requirements is about 1% per month. Thus for a three-year project, about a third of delivered functionality will have been added after the formal requirements phase. This is one of the hidden risk factors which was suspected, but not directly observed in the past.

The differences between military and civilian domains in this problem area are interesting. Both civilian and military projects are roughly equal in the rate at which requirements change. However, since military projects normally have better cost tracking systems, creeping user requirements are more often tracked and priced for military software projects than for civilian. On the other hand, since the schedules for military software projects are somewhat longer than for civilian projects of the same size, the total quantity of creeping requirements is larger in the military domain than in the civilian.

First in avoiding creeping user requirements are end-user software applications. When users develop their own software, the requirements are purely up to them to implement. Also, end user applications are usually fairly quick in development: a month would be a long schedule. Since the rate of creeping requirements is proportional to the schedule, a one-month schedule might, at worst, trigger a 1% increment in functions.

Second are the MIS developers. Although creeping user requirements is a chronic problem for MIS projects, a suite of powerful technologies are available that can minimize this problem for typical MIS applications. Joint Application Design (JAD) and prototyping, for example, can reduce the severity and volume of unplanned user requirements. Quality Function Deployment (QFD) is also effective.

Third are contract software houses and the outsourcing shops. These groups have a brutal and straight-forward approach to reducing unplanned requirements: they charge for them.

Fourth are commercial software houses. These shops are at a disadvantage, because new requirements tend to come in from the companies' own executives or from their own sales and marketing groups, rather than from actual customers. Also, with commercial software such as spreadsheets or word processors, there are thousands of users. Therefore approaches such as JAD or QFD, which assume a small number of users, are difficult to implement.

Fifth are military and defense contractors. If the contracts are on a time and materials basis, the contractors eagerly welcome new requirements. If the contracts are on a fixed price basis, the enthusiasm for new requirements is greatly diminished.

However, some outstanding military research is starting to occur on requirements problems. The U.S. Navy's NAVAIR group's experiments on high-speed prototyping directly from requirements using advanced automation is leading to requirements stability and closure in a remarkable fashion.

Academic research is also being applied to military requirements problems. George Mason University is beginning a program of linguistic analysis of military software requirements, with a view to identifying high-frequency, common requirements and also potentially troublesome requirements. This research may also lead to the ability to do automatic sizing and estimating directly from requirements, as well as creating reusable requirements sets.

Systems software is sixth. They seldom use approaches such as JAD, because they don't have the right mix of users. Their development schedules are long, so normal changes in business and technology can surface requirements that were not envisioned when the projects began.

8. **Low Quality**—The current U.S. average for software quality is a defect potential of about 5 defects per Function Point, coupled with a cumulative removal efficiency of less than 85%. That means that a typical software project will be deployed with a total of some 0.75 defects per Function Point still latent within it. Low quality is a key contributor to low levels of user satisfaction, to low productivity, and to loss of market shares.

The defect potential is the sum of the defects or bugs found in requirements, specifications, source code, user documents, and "bad fixes" or secondary mistakes made while repairing a primary error.

Embedded military software is visibly more complex than many civilian projects, and tends to have higher defect potential in the range of 6 to 7 defects per Function Point. However, U.S. military projects rank among the best in the world in terms of defect removal efficiency. Critical U.S. weapons systems may exceed 99% in cumulative defect removal efficiency, while less critical systems may still exceed 95% in cumulative defect removal efficiency.

There are several industries which rank first in avoiding problems of low software quality: Defense (military software); computer manufacturers (systems software and some commercial software); telecommunications manufacturers (systems software), medical instruments, and on-board flight control and navigational software.

U.S. military software projects typically rank among the best projects assessed in terms of test planning, test methods, number of defect removal operations carried out, defect recording, and use of formal quality methods.

The U.S. industries which consistently produce high-quality software can successfully compete against Japan, Europe, or any other country.

U.S. military software projects exceed civilian information systems by 20% to 25% in cumulative defect removal efficiency, or the total percentage of errors eliminated prior to deployment of the systems. Civilian computer manufacturers such as IBM, Motorola, and Hewlett-Packard and civilian telecommunications manufacturers such as AT&T are equal to military software producers in quality control, however.

Second are the commercial software houses, although they address quality in a peculiar way. The commercial software houses are often lax on defect prevention and pre-test defect removal methods. However, they may use as many as 10,000 customers during Beta Test. Since the number of bugs that is found during Beta testing correlates strongly with the number of users, any time a product is tested simultaneously by more than 1000 people the results are likely to be good.

Third are the contract and outsource software houses. These organizations can be fairly good if the contract includes quality. If the contract does not include quality, they can be careless and perfunctory in quality control.

Fourth are the MIS producers. Unfortunately, most MIS shops depend almost exclusively upon testing by their general software population. Techniques such as formal inspections, testing specialists, test case libraries, formal defect tracking, and the other paraphernalia long deployed by the top-ranked groups are seldom encountered in the MIS arena. This is not as it should be.

Fifth are the end-user software developers. Poor quality control on end-user software explains why only the author would ever want to use it. End-user software does very poorly as legacy applications after the originator has changed jobs or departed.

9. **Low Productivity**—The current U.S. average for military software projects is about 3 Function Points per staff month, for systems software the rate is about 4 Function Points per staff month, and for information systems the average is about 8 Function Points per staff month. The overall U.S. average (taken from Capers Jones' *Applied Software Measurement*) (7) is about 5 Function Points per staff month.

The risk of low productivity is particularly severe for military projects, since it is not possible to follow military specifications such as 2167A and achieve high productivity levels. The four most expensive aspects of software development are, in rank order: 1) paperwork, 2) defect removal, 3) meeting and communications, and 4) coding.

U.S. military software projects consistently rank first in paperwork costs, and are often first in defect removal costs, due to the costs of independent verification and validation, independent testing, and other defect removal activities which seldom occur for civilian projects. Military meeting and communication costs are also more expensive than civilian norms, although civilian projects which are geographically dispersed (such as large operating systems or switching systems) tend to have the greatest communication expenses. Coding costs for military projects are roughly equivalent to and sometimes lower than civilian norms.

Low productivity is a serious problem because it is so often associated with canceled projects. An average canceled software project in the U.S. is about one year late and 100% over budget at the time of cancellation. The average productivity rate for canceled projects is less than 2 Function Points per month at the time of cancellation.

First in avoiding low productivity are end-user applications, where even the average can exceed 25 Function Points per staff month, and the peaks often go above 100.

Second are the commercial software producers, or at least they were in second place before Windows entered the market. Low-end DOS based PC software was averaging 15 to 20 Function Points per staff month in the pre-Windows era. The difficulty of the early Windows applications dropped the rate down to 6 to 10 Function Points per staff month. New tools and more experience are bringing the rates slowly back up, however. (Since Apple does not measure productivity itself, there is almost no data on Macintosh or Apple software.)

Third are the contract and outsourcing software shops. These organizations tend to average 10 to 12 Function Points per staff month, which is somewhat higher than U.S. norms.

Fourth are the MIS shops, where the average is around 8 Function Points per staff month. There are a few peak projects in the MIS domain that have run up to 140 or so Function Points per staff month, but these are outliers.

The disparity between outsourcing and contract software and internal MIS productivity is pushing quite a few companies toward the outsource market, incidentally.

The factors which explain the differential are these: A) Clients are more stable with requirements changes with contractors than with their own people; B) To get a contract, the contractor is fairly far along the learning curve; C) Having often done similar projects, contractors tend to have reusable designs and code available; D) Contractors often work more hours than they bill—especially for fixed-price contracts.

Fifth are the systems software producers, with an average of about 4 Function Points per staff month. The systems world has to do a lot more work for the same sized application than does the MIS domain, and often the hardware itself is unfinished or unstable for systems software. Paperwork costs (plans, specifications, documents, etc.) are also high in the systems software domain.

Sixth are military software projects. The culprit here is paperwork: 400 English words per Ada statement is the current norm, with paperwork costs being three times larger than for MIS projects and twice as large as systems software. Military projects average only around 3 Function Points per month, and seldom exceed 10.

10. **Canceled Projects**—The cancellation rate for software projects is directly proportional to the overall size of the system, and is particularly acute above 10,000 Function Points or 1,000,000 source statements. For large systems in excess of 10,000 Function Points, such as operating systems, telecommunication systems, major defense systems, and the like, the cancellation rate approaches 50%. Ominously, an "average" canceled project is about a year late and approaching or exceeding twice its planned budget at the time of cancellation.

Military and civilian projects of the same size are roughly equivalent in the frequency with which they may be canceled. However, the average size of military software projects is much larger than for civilian software projects, and the number of large systems in excess of 10,000 Function Points is about double in the military domain. This means that the absolute probability of canceled projects is greater for military software than for civilian.

First in avoiding canceled projects are the commercial software producers, although some cancellations occur in this domain. When project cancellations do occur, it is often because the company itself has gone bankrupt.

Second in avoiding cancellations, surprisingly, are end-user applications. Often users tackle jobs that are too big or too difficult, and give up somewhere along the way.

Third for avoiding cancellations are MIS projects. They rank so high primarily because the size range of MIS projects is comparatively small. When MIS producers tackle really large systems of 10,000 Function Points and up, their cancellation rates exceed most other domains.

Fourth in avoiding cancellations are military projects. The size range of military projects can be so large that cancellations are a risk to be dealt with. However, military software projects may sometimes continue on long after a civilian project would have been canceled, due to the absence of profit and loss analysis.

Fifth are contract software projects. Canceled contracts are endemic to the industry. The most common reasons cited for cancellation are: 1) Severe schedule slips; 2) Severe cost overruns; 3) Excessive creeping requirements; 4) Unacceptable quality levels.

Sixth are systems software projects. Some systems software producers begin competing projects and select the stronger as a way of strengthening their R&D's competitiveness. Although cost and schedule overruns are common here too, canceled systems software (especially real-time software) may have other kinds of problems such as inadequate performance.

The ten risks cited here are only the tip of the iceberg. The encouraging aspect of software risk management is that new methods such as process assessments and the use of functional metrics are proving to be remarkably effective in identifying risks that were long hidden. A combination of vigorous process assessments, accurate measures and metrics, and multi-thread process improvement programs can minimize or eliminate many risk factors, and begin to make the phrase "software engineering" take on serious meaning.

Risk management is becoming a formal sub-discipline of software engineering. Readers may wish to pursue the literature for additional information. Following are suggested readings on risk management.

Suggested Readings

Boehm, Barry W.; *Software Risk Management;* IEEE Computer Society Press; Los Alamitos, CA; 1989; Catalog No. 106; 508 pages.

Brooks, Fred P. Jr.; *The Mythical Man-Month;* Addison-Wesley; Reading, MA; 1975 (revised 1982); 195 pages.

Charette, Robert N.; *Software Engineering Risk Analysis and Management;* McGraw-Hill; New York, NY; 1989; 325 pages.

Charette, Robert N.; *Application Strategies for Risk Analysis;* McGraw-Hill; New York, NY; 1990; 570 pages.

DeMarco, Tom; *Controlling Software Projects;*

DeMarco, Tom and Lister, Timothy; *Peopleware;* Dorset House; New York, NY; 1987; 188 pages.

Humphrey, Watts; *Managing the Software Process;* Addison-Wesley; Winthrop, MA; 1989; 486 pages.

Jones, Capers; *"Risky Business; The Most Common Software Risks";* American Programmer Magazine (special issue on risk management); August 1992.

Jones, Capers; *"Process Assessments and Software Risks;"* STSC Crosstalk; November 1992.

Jones, Capers; *Critical Problems in Software Measurement;* Information Systems Management Group monograph series; 1993; 70 pages.

Jones, Capers; *Software Productivity and Quality—The Worldwide Perspective;* Information Systems Management Group monograph series; 1993; 150 pages.

Jones, Capers; *Modelling the Costs of Military Software;* Software Productivity Research, Inc.; January 1993; 12 pages.

Weinberg, Gerald M.; *Quality Software Management—Volume 1 Systems Thinking;* Dorset House; New York, NY; 1992; 318 pages.

Weinbereg, Gerald M.; *Quality Software Management—Volume 2 First Order Measurement;* Dorset House; New York, NY; 1993; 346 pages.

Yourdon, Edward; *Decline and Fall of the American Programmer;* Yourdon Press; Prentice Hall; Englewood Cliffs, NJ; 1992; 352 pages.

ALPHABETIC LISTING OF 60 RISK FACTORS

This book follows the format of a medical text entitled *Control of Communicable Diseases in Man*. The primary contents of that book was an alphabetic listing of 64 communicable diseases, starting with actinomyosis and ending with yellow fever. For each disease, methods of prevention and control were discussed.

This book is similar in its structure, and what follows are discussions of 60 software risk factors arranged in alphabetic order, starting with "Ambiguous Improvement Targets" and concluding with "Slow Technology Transfer." Here too, for each risk factor methods of prevention and control are discussed.

Since software is not as advanced a technology as medical practice, this book includes some additional information which was not present in the medical book. For example, this book includes discussions of whether the cited risk factors are: a) taught at the university level; b) are discussed in software journals; c) are discussed in software books; d) have tools available; e) have consulting assistance available.

This book and the medical book used as a model share a common phenomenon: neither can be completely up to date. New diseases occur with surprising frequency, and hence medical texts must be constantly updated. For example, neither AIDS nor Lyme disease are discussed in medical texts printed in the 1970's, but both have grown to become major health problems.

In a similar fashion, new software risk factors will also occur in response to new domains and new kinds of software. As of 1993. it is unknown what the future will bring forth, but for both software and medicine it is likely that new risks will occur at least as fast as cures are found for risks that already exist.

CHAPTER

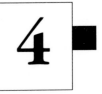

Ambiguous Productivity or Quality Improvement Goals

1. **Definition**—A) Goals or targets for improving software productivity or quality that are abstract or so ambiguous that there is no way of accurately interpreting them and hence no way of achieving them; B) All goals or targets which are based on multiples of an unknown starting value, such as "improve productivity by 10 to 1"; C) All goals or targets which are based on percentage values against unknown origins, such as "improve schedules by 50%".

2. **Severity**—The average severity of ambiguous improvement targets is about a 3 on the following five-point scale:

   Severity 1: No improvement goals or targets of any kind exist

   Severity 2: Goals exist that are very ambiguous and probably unachievable

   Severity 3: Goals exist that are so ambiguous that multiple interpretations occur

   Severity 4: Mixture of ambiguous and tangible goals exist

   Severity 5: Goals are tangible, but probably unachievable

3. **Frequency**—Ambiguous improvement goals or targets have been endemic to the software industry since it began, due to the widespread lack of a firm quantitative base of knowledge about software productivity and quality levels.

   Unfortunately, some of the more common goals encountered even within leading companies tend to be abstract and ambiguous in that they lack a starting point. The most commonly encountered goals include:

   ♦ Improve productivity by 10 to 1 within five years.

   ♦ Improve quality by 10 to 1 within five years.

4. **Occurrence**—This problem tends to occur in companies that have awakened to the importance of software, and are struggling to make improvements. Although the problem is widespread, it is comparatively benign and indeed is a sign that software is starting to be viewed as a serious corporate issue by senior executives.

5. **Susceptibility and resistance**—Software tool and CASE vendors are extremely susceptible to this problem, as well as the associated problem of *False Productivity Claims*. Among software users and developers, this problem is surprisingly more common among leading software producers than it is among trailing or lagging software producers: the laggards have either given up on software, or don't believe improvements are possible. The problem is much more common among enterprises where the senior executives themselves lack software backgrounds. Military, systems, commercial, and MIS software producers appear roughly equivalent in susceptibility to this problem.

6. **Root causes**—The basic root cause of this problem is a simple lack of good, quantitative data about software productivity and quality levels. In turn, this root cause can be traced back to the fact that accurate quantitative data cannot be expressed using historical metrics such as "lines of source code" or "cost per defect." Therefore the problem of ambiguous goals was endemic to the software industry prior to the development of functional metrics in the late 1970's.

7. **Associated problems**—Ambiguous improvement targets correlate strongly with the problem of *False Productivity Claims* by software tool and CASE vendors. This problem is also strongly associated with the *Silver Bullet Syndrome*. It has less direct correlations with *Canceled Projects, Cost Overruns,* and *Excessive Time to Market*.

   Ambiguous improvement targets themselves are often caused by *Inaccurate Metrics, Inadequate Measurement, Inadequate Software Management Curricula,* and *Inadequate Standards*.

8. **Cost impact**—The problem of ambiguous improvement targets is comparatively benign in terms of its cost impact. Somewhat surprisingly, enterprises that have ambiguous improvement targets are often in the upper 50% of their industries in terms of both quality and productivity when measurements are taken. The reason for this is apparently because the senior executives view software as a critical topic, and have therefore provided funds and motivation for improvement, even if the targets themselves are ambiguous when expressed.

9. **Methods of prevention**—The establishment of formal software measurement programs and the adoption of functional metrics are both effective preventive measures for eliminating ambiguous targets.

   There is a real art to setting goals or targets. The goals should be much better than today's norms, but they should actually be achievable. (To leave software for a moment, it might be reasonable to set a target for a track star to "run a mile in less than 3 minutes and 45 seconds." However, to set a target to "run a mile in less than 30 seconds" would be ridiculous.) Also, the goals should be set for managers and executives, who are authorized to spend money and make changes happen. It is of little value to set goals for individual contributors, since they have only limited abilities to acquire improved methods, tools or education on their own.

10. **Methods of control**—The most effective method of control is to rephrase the improvement targets from ambiguous to concrete form. The following are a number of possible targets derived from the actual performance levels of Baldrige Award winners and organizations in the upper 10% of United States industries in terms of both productivity and quality levels. Any enterprise that can achieve these targets can be justifiably proud of its accomplishments.

Software Quality and User-Satisfaction Goals

- Achieve defect potentials of less than 1 defect per Function Point
  (Sum of defects in requirements, design, code, documents, and bad fixes)

- Achieve an average cumulative defect removal efficiency higher than 95%
  (All defects found during development compared to first year's usage)

- Achieve less than 0.025 user-reported bugs per Function Point per year on the average (Measured against valid, unique defect reports)

- Achieve 90% "excellent" ratings from user-satisfaction surveys
  (Measured on topics of functionality, quality, and customer support)

- Allow zero error-prone modules in released software
  (Modules which receive disproportionate quantities of defect reports, such as more than 0.08 defects per Function Point per year)

- Strive to improve software quality levels by > 40% per year
  (Baseline is current year's volume of customer reported defects)

Development Cycle and Time to Market Goals

- Less than 6-month development cycles for software < 250 Function Points in size

- Less than 12-month development cycles for software < 1000 Function Points in size

- Less than 24 month development cycles for software < 5000 Function Points in size

- Less than 36 month development cycles for software < 10,000 Function Points in size

- Strive to reduce cycle times by > 15% per year (Baseline is current year's average cycle time for each class and size of software)

Productivity Goals for New Development Projects

- Average > 25 Function Points per staff month on projects up to 250 Function Points (Including all activities: requirements, design, code, test, documents, management)

- Average > 15 Function Points per staff month from 250 to 1000 Function Points (Including all activities: requirements, design, code, test, documents, management)

- Average > 10 Function Points per staff month on projects above 1000 Function Points (Including all activities: requirements, design, code, test, documents, management)

- Average > 6 Function Points per staff month on projects above 5,000 Function Points (Including all activities: requirements, design, code, test, documents, management)

- Average > 5 Function Points per staff month in gross annual productivity (Total Function Points delivered divided by total software employees x 12)

- Strive to improve new development productivity levels by > 25% per year (Baseline is current year's average productivity rate.)

Productivity Goals for Enhancement Projects

- Average > 20 Function Points per staff month on minor enhancements (Enhancements ranging from 1 to 50 Function Points in size)

- Average > 15 Function Points per staff month on medium enhancements (Enhancements ranging from 50 to up to 250 Function Points in size)

- Average > 10 Function Points per staff month on large enhancements (Enhancements larger than 250 Function Points in size)

- Average > 6 Function Points per staff month on major releases (Enhancements larger than 1,000 Function Points in size)

- Use complexity analysis tools on 100% of aging software. (Software in production for more than three years)

- Use restructuring tools on 100% of aging COBOL, C, or other languages where such tools are supported

- Strive to improve enhancement productivity levels by > 25% per year (Baseline is current year's average rate for enhancement productivity)

Productivity Goals for Migration and Conversion Projects

- Average > 50 Function Points per staff month for migration to a new platform

- Average > 100 Function Points per staff month for conversion to a new data base

- Average > 100 Function Points per staff month for conversion to a new language

Productivity Goals for Maintenance Projects (Defect Repairs/Minor Updates)

◆ Average > 1500 Function Points in maintenance assignment scope (Total portfolio size divided by number of people working on maintenance)

◆ Strive to improve the maintenance assignment scope by > 25% per year (Baseline is current year's average value)

◆ Provide essentially zero wait time for customers reporting a bug or defect (On-line defect recording is necessary to achieve this target)

◆ Average < 24 hours in repairing severity 1 (high severity) defects

◆ Average < 5 days in repairing severity 2 defects

◆ Average < 15 days in repairing severity 3 defects

◆ Average < 30 minutes in providing temporary "work around" solutions for defects (On-line defect recording is necessary to achieve this target)

◆ Average < 1 minute from customer dial-in to service representative contacts

◆ Achieve a bad fix rate of < 2.5% (Secondary defects inserted as a byproduct of repairing previous defects)

Quantified Goals for Sociological and Morale Factors

◆ Provide at least 10 days of annual training for technical staff members

◆ Provide at least 15 days of training for software managers

◆ Provide at least 5 days of training for software and corporate executives

◆ Provide at least 90 square feet of quiet office space for software staff members

◆ Achieve 90% "good" or "excellent" responses on annual morale and opinion surveys

Quantified Goals for Reusability Technologies

◆ Develop an architecture of full reusability that can in theory if not in fact encompass 100% of an enterprise's software projects

◆ Achieve levels of > 70% reuse for software project requirements

◆ Achieve levels of > 50% reuse for project estimates (Templates)

◆ Achieve levels of > 50% reuse for project plans

◆ Achieve levels of > 50% reuse for design of applications (Blueprints)

◆ Achieve levels of > 95% of reuse in human interface conventions from application to application

◆ Achieve levels of > 75% reuse for source code in every application

◆ Achieve levels of > 75% reuse for test cases and test scripts

◆ Achieve levels of > 85% reuse for data and information

♦ Achieve levels of > 60% reuse for user information (both paper manuals and on-line information)

Quantified Goals for Project Management Technologies

♦ Use automated defect tracking tools on 100% of software projects

♦ Use automated cost estimating tools on 100% of software projects > 50 Function Points

♦ Use automated planning tools on 100% of software projects > 50 Function Points

♦ Use quality estimating tools on 100% of software projects

♦ Measure 100% of completed projects > 50 Function Points

11. **Product support**—Some commercial software estimating tools include built-in knowledge bases and comparison modes which allow projects to be compared against U.S. averages for similar projects, or against better than average projects if selected.

Starting in 1993, a new kind of add-on product called "templates" that are associated with software estimating tools may enter the market. Templates are based on the analysis of historical projects, and include both the quantified results (schedules, resources, costs, etc.) and "soft" factors (methods, experience, tools, etc) that affected the outcome of software products.

Several estimating tool companies (Applied Business Technology (ABT), Quantitative Software Methods (QSM), and Software Productivity Research (SPR), are now capable of producing templates. One of the first sets of templates available from SPR will include settings that match the best-in-class data presented here.

Other templates from multiple vendors can match the SEI capability levels and illustrate the differences between projects developed at SEI Levels 1, 2, 3, 4, and 5.

Within a year or two, commercial templates should also be available for dealing with ISO 9000–9004 standards, Baldrige Awards, and other advanced topics.

Templates are also being planned for vertical markets. Examples of such templates would include typical software projects found within insurance companies, banks, public utilities and State and municipal governments.

12. **Consulting support**—Now that functional metrics and Function Points have become the most widely utilized metrics, a number of consulting groups have begun to express baseline data in this form. Examples of consulting groups who deal with both quantified baselines and tangible improvements in productivity and quality include (in alphabetical order) Computer Power, DMR Group, Keane Associates, Quantitative Software Management, Real Decisions, and Software Productivity Research. The Software Engineering Institute (SEI) may also begin to deal with quantified goals or targets. There are also many others.

13. **Education support**—As far as can be determined, there are essentially no university level courses or graduate courses that deal with quantified goals or targets. Commercial education courses such as those offered by Digital Consulting, QSM, SPR, etc. are more readily available than academic courses.

   Most of the courses certified by IFPUG (The International Function Point Users Group) will include some quantified case studies, and a few may also include a section on setting numeric targets using Function Points. Some in-house courses in companies such as AT&T or IBM also deal with quantified targets.

14. **Publication support**—There are many books on software productivity and quality, but comparatively few which deal with tangible improvements and the rates at which those improvements might occur. *Applied Software Measurement* (McGraw-Hill, 1991) contains approximate U.S. averages for quality and productivity expressed in Function Points, and hence is a good starting point for dealing with improvements. *Software Productivity and Quality—The Worldwide Perspective* (IS Management Group, 1993) includes preliminary international comparisons for software productivity, quality, and other tangible factors. Gordon Schulmeyer's *Zero Defect Software* (McGraw-Hill, 1990) deals with tangible goals, although ones that are not easy to achieve. Dr. Larry Putnam's *Measures for Excellence* (Prentice-Hall, 1992) also contains quantified data. Robert Grady and Deborah Caswell's *Software Metrics: Establishing a Company-Wide Program* (Prentice-Hall, 1986) and Grady's more recent *Practical Software Metrics for Project Management and Process Improvement* (Prentice-Hall, 1992) also contain quantified data. Among the first books to deal quantitatively with software is Dr. Barry Boehm's monumental *Software Engineering Economics* (Prentice-Hall, 1981). A recent publication which contains samples of software data from Europe is that of Dr. Karl Moller and Daniel Paulish of Siemens, *Software Metrics—A Practitioner's Guide to Improved Product Development* (IEEE Press, 1993, also published by Chapman and Hall, 1992).

15. **Periodical support**—Many journals are starting to run articles with quantitative data. In recent months, journals such as American Programmer, CASE Outlook, CASE Trends, and even the IEEE Transactions on Software Engineering have included articles with quantified data. For quality data, the fairly new journal by Chapman and Hall, Software Quality Journal, is filling a useful niche. The well-known IEEE Transactions on Engineering Management has quantified data from time to time. House journals such as the IBM Systems Journal or SPR's Knowledge Base also include quantified data from time to time. The IFPUG journal, Metrics Views, is also useful. The Swiss-published ISO 9000 journal includes occasional articles on quality in the ISO domain. The major business journals such as Harvard Business Review, The Economist, and Fortune magazine contain intermittent articles with some quantified data, but not on a regular basis.

16. **Standards support**—The major standards organizations have lagged seriously in the topic of quantified goals or targets. In particular, ANSI, DoD, and ISO stan-

dards are far behind the state of the art or ignore the topic entirely. For example, the well-known ISO 9000–9004 quality standards have no quantification at all for quality. The IEEE Quality standards deal in quantified results, although unfortunately normalization via KLOC is often a result.

To make the situation worse, several important standards tend to *lower* software productivity by demanding extraordinarily large volumes of documentation and paperwork. Projects using DoD 2167A and the new ISO 9000–9004 standards tend to create more words and more text than any other software projects yet observed. It is not clear if the value added by adherence to these standards offsets the increase in the costs they incur.

17. **Professional associations**—The non-profit International Function Point Users Group (IFPUG) is the organization that is currently leading in quantification of software goals and targets. The well-known Software Engineering Institute (SEI) is starting a measurement program, but as of early 1993 is still behind the state of the art in terms of both metrics themselves and quantification methods. Other associations such as the ACM and IEEE, deal with quantified data when they can, and have special-interest sub-groups. The various regional quality assurance groups and the CASE user groups also deal with quantified data from time to time.

18. **Effectiveness of known therapies**—The use of functional metrics for target setting appears to be the most effective approach yet developed for software. It is visibly superior to the older "LOC metrics" for all forms of economic and quality targeting.

19. **Costs of known therapies**—The costs of setting tangible, quantitative goals (as opposed to abstract, ambiguous goals) are approximately zero if the task is assigned to someone with a useful store of historical data. If no data is available and research and study are required before setting goals, then at least two weeks of reference checking will be needed.

20. **Long-range prognosis**—The prognosis is highly optimistic. Now that usage of functional metrics has become widespread throughout the software industry (the growth rate of IFPUG membership has been 46% per year) it is possible to set tangible targets or goals and measure the rate of progress toward those goals. Functional metrics are not the only aspect of targeting, of course, but they have definitely added a rigor that was long missing from the software industry.

CHAPTER 5

Artificial Maturity Levels

1. **Definition**—A) Abstract models or paradigms of software processes, methods, or life-cycles B) Categorization schemes applied to software organizations or projects that divide them into discrete segments based on artificial criteria such as "generation," "maturity" or "levels"; C) Arbitrary categorization schemes that are used to determine vendor performance, contract eligibility, or to restrain trade.

2. **Severity**—Historically, the average severity of artificial paradigms and maturity levels has been about a 3 on the following five-point scale, but the U.S. Department of Defense may elevate the severity level up to 2.0 for military software projects:

   Severity 1: The scheme is false or invalid, and created to restrain trade unfairly

   Severity 2: The scheme is biased, and may be used to restrain trade unfairly

   Severity 3: The scheme is severely biased, but is not used to restrain trade

   Severity 4: The scheme is moderately biased, incomplete, or irrelevant

   Severity 5: The scheme is incomplete

3. **Frequency**—For unknown and perhaps sociological reasons, artificial paradigms and categorization schemes have been a cyclical occurrence throughout the history of software and tend to occur with a period that runs from five to ten years. Examples of artificial categorization schemes within the software discipline include *generations* (i.e. 1st generation languages, 2nd generation languages, etc. which originated in the 1960's; McPherson and Nolan's *seven stages of data processing growth* which originated in the 1970's; *upper CASE* and *lower CASE* which originated in the 1980's; Crosby's *quality maturity levels* which originated in the 1970's and ran into the 1980's; and Humphrey's derivative of the Crosby concept, the SEI *maturity level* concept, which has become popular in the 1990's.

4. **Occurrence**—When the origins are known, it is interesting that artificial level schemes that affect software tend to originate from three primary sources: 1) Universities; 2) the trade press; 3) very large corporations such as ITT or IBM. Once a scheme originates, it can then spread rapidly throughout the industry.

5. **Susceptibility and resistance**—Artificial categorization schemes are endemic to the human condition and have been known throughout history. Their general purpose is to simplify complex phenomena so that concepts can be easily envisioned and discussed. At this level, categorization schemes are often benign. When artificial categorization schemes are used for actual business or government operations, they tend to become malignant. Witness the hideously malignant effects of artificially categorizing humans into *aryan* and *non-aryan* categories during World War II.

The patterns of susceptibility and resistance to artificial categorization schemes are not well known. A majority of organizations, managers, and professionals appear susceptible. That is to say, they tend to accept the tenets of the categorization scheme without serious evaluation. This situation is ordinarily benign, but it becomes malignant when the scheme is simultaneously unjustified and used for purposes that restrain trade. For example, a DoD or ISO requirement that a software vendor must be at or above SEI maturity level 3 in order to receive a contract would tend to disenfranchise small vendors with less than 30 employees and become a notable setback for U.S. software.

6. **Root causes**—Throughout human history there has been a tendency to simplify complex phenomena by creating artificial categories. In the Middle Ages, an artificial concept called *the great chain of being* organized life forms into a hierarchy of plants, animals, humans, and angels.

In his well-known book, *The Prince,* Niccolo Machiavelli created a famous three-level taxonomy: 1) Those who can understand problems by themselves; 2) those who can understand problems once they have been explained to them; 3) those who can never understand problems at all. (An unknown wag created an amusing recursive binary taxonomy: "People can be divided into two groups: those who divide people into groups and those who don't.")

Taxonomies that are carefully worked out, extensible, and based on scientific observations are a major part of scientific progress. For example, the way biologists deal with *phylum, genera, class, species,* and *subspecies* has passed the test of time and has become a powerful organizing principle. On a more mundane level, the Dewey decimal system used to organize books in libraries is also a valid taxonomy.

The problem lies with taxonomies or paradigms that are rigid, artificial, arbitrary, invalid, and not capable of extension or modification.

The primary root cause of artificial taxonomies and paradigms for software is the basic lack of good quantitative information. In the absence of firm knowledge of the factors which truly influence software projects, the industry has long been prey to various cults and "silver bullet" syndromes.

7. **Associated problems**—If the artificial taxonomy is merely used as a convenient way of dealing with complex information, then no serious problems tend to occur. If the artificial taxonomy is used to constrain business, however, then it is a manifestation of the *Silver Bullet Syndrome* and will almost certainly be associated with the problem of *Litigation Expenses*. If the artificial taxonomy or level scheme should find its way into civilian or military standards, then it will obviously be

associated with the problem of *Inadequate Standards*. For enterprises damaged or prevented from doing business by the artificial taxonomy, the problems of *Layoffs and Cutbacks* may occur.

Artificial maturity levels themselves are often caused by *Inadequate Assessments, Inadequate Software Management Curricula,* and *Inadequate Research and Reference Facilities.*

8. **Cost impact**—The costs of artificial taxonomies or levels only occur in situations where the scheme is used to govern contracts or business relations, In such cases, the costs can be divided into direct and indirect components. The direct costs include both the costs of additional staff required to adhere to the scheme and the cost of additional work required by the scheme (i.e. additional reports, forms, etc.). The indirect costs can include lost business opportunities and possible litigation expenses.

To illustrate the difference between benign and potentially malignant artificial taxonomies, consider two versions of a similar taxonomy: Crosby's 1979 *quality maturity level* and Humphrey's 1987 *software process maturity level* which is the basis for the Software Engineering Institute's (SEI) maturity levels.

	Crosby Quality Maturity Levels	Humphrey Process Maturity Levels
Level 1	Uncertainty	Initial
Level 2	Awakening	Repeatable
Level 3	Enlightenment	Defined
Level 4	Wisdom	Managed
Level 5	Certainty	Optimizing

Note: As a matter of minor historical interest, the Crosby maturity level concept is very similar to the sequence of the path of enlightenment which several Mahayana Buddhist sects have described for more than 2,500 years. It is not known if this resemblance is deliberate or coincidental.

An interesting metaphor for the search for enlightenment used by Tantric Buddhists is that of searching for a lost bull. For example, the steps on the path to enlightenment include 1) The initial search; 2) Discovering the bull's footprints, 3) Perceiving the bull; 4) Catching the bull; 5) Taming the bull, and so forth.

Both the Crosby and Humphrey stage concepts seem to replicate these Eastern teachings very closely, although perhaps coincidentally rather than by design.

As originally stated and intended, both of the Crosby and Humphrey maturity level schemas were created primarily to facilitate discussion of the general characteristics of enterprises. As tools for simplifying complex subjects, both are benign. Of the two, the earlier Crosby maturity level is more intuitive and easier to grasp, since Humphrey's was creating new and sometimes arcane definitions for common words such as "repeatable" and "defined" while Crosby was using words whose definitions were already well known.

However, when the U.S. Department of Defense began to consider moving in the direction of preferential business arrangements with enterprises in the Defined, Managed, and Optimizing levels, that is threatening to convert a benign taxonomy into a possibly malignant one.

If the Humphrey/SEI maturity level scheme should become a feature of military software procurements, the results would probably be unfortunate. The Humphrey's SEI maturity scheme is based on an additive series of departments and activities that tend to become progressively more expensive as the levels increase.

The costs of achieving maturity levels 4 and 5 appear to be so high that: A) It is unlikely that small or start-up companies can achieve those levels; B) The overhead costs would be so high that companies at SEI levels 4 and 5 may not be able to win any contracts other than those where high SEI levels are mandated.

Another artificial but widely utilized taxonomy is that developed by Allan Albrecht when defining the Function Point metric. Function Points divide the external characteristics of a software project into five "atomic" components:

Inputs
Outputs
Inquiries
Logical files
Interfaces

Yet another widely utilized taxonomy are the 5- to 8-level Phase Structures long used to illustrate software lifecycles. For example:

Phase 1: Requirements
Phase 2: Analysis
Phase 3: Preliminary Design
Phase 4: Detail Design
Phase 5: Coding
Phase 6: Testing

All of these artificial taxonomies (i.e. Crosby's, Humphrey's, Albrecht's, etc.) simplify some rather complex phenomena, and make discussions more convenient. At this level, all are benign.

Because none of these artificial taxonomies are a *perfect* match to the real-world situations which they discuss, there is always some uncertainty about how to map various concepts into the artificial taxonomy. For example, what it truly means to be at SEI Level 5 is uncertain in 1993, as are questions dealing with the costs versus the value of the SEI maturity scheme.

This kind of uncertainty in mapping the complexities of the real world into the constraints of the artificial taxonomy tends to create "priesthoods" of consulting specialists who assist in dealing with arcane topics.

As of 1993, consulting specialists dealing with Baldrige Award criteria, Business Process Reengineering, IFPUG Function Point counting, Information Engineering, ISO certification, and SEI capability levels can be found in most large management consulting firms, among specialized consultants, and as internal consultants within large corporations.

Historically, these specialists do not always agree. When disagreements are unresolvable, the various "priesthoods" tend to split up and create rival sects. An example of this split can be seen today in the differences between U.S. Function Point counting as certified by IFPUG, and British Function Point counting using the Mark II Function Point metric.

9. **Methods of prevention**—From reviewing the history of psychology, medicine, chemistry, physics, and other sciences, it appears that the slow accumulation of knowledge over long time spans (i.e. 75 years or more) is the most effective prevention. Since the software industry more or less started in 1943, another 25 years of accumulated knowledge may be necessary to prevent this class of problem.

10. **Methods of control**—If an artificial taxonomy or level scheme is used in restraint of trade, there are very few methods of control. The known methods of control include: A) Requesting and receiving a waiver; B) Successful litigation which would void and eliminate the burdensome requirement. Both methods are uncertain, and method B is both uncertain and extremely costly.

11. **Product support**—There are no known products that deal with eliminating artificial taxonomies. There are hundreds of products that support various paradigms, however.

12. **Consulting support**—There is no direct consulting support that deals with the topic of artificial taxonomies and maturity level schemas. However, there are many consulting groups who compete with the Software Engineering Institute (SEI) and who offer consulting in their own specialties. There are also consulting groups which deal with each of the major cults or artificial taxonomies of the industry. Terry Bollinger and Clem McGowan of The Software Productivity Consortium (SPC) have published a very thoughtful analysis of the logical underpinnings of the SEI maturity level concept, and the hazards of attempting to fit real enterprises into an artificial taxonomy from very sparse data.

13. **Education support**—As far as can be determined, there are no standard software engineering or management school courses which deal with artificial taxonomies and artificial maturity levels in a scholarly or scientific way. Such courses are available under philosophy and psycho-linguistic departments, but these departments have only remote intersections with standard software engineering and business curricula. Unfortunately, there are many courses in both software engineering and business schools which teach artificial taxonomies and questionable paradigms without serious consideration or evaluation of their fundamental premises.

14. **Publication support**—There are no known software-related books that deal with artificial taxonomies and artificial maturity levels. Unfortunately, many books which discuss such topics accept the artificial taxonomies at face value. There are interesting books that are relevant to artificial categorization schemes, however: Charles Mackay's *Extraordinary Popular Delusions and the Madness of Crowds* (Harmony Books, 1980) is relevant and quite entertaining. Thomas Kuhn's often-cited *The Structure of Scientific Revolutions* (University of Chicago, 1962) is another relevant volume, as is I. Bernard Cohen's *Revolution in Science* (Harvard University Press, 1985). Dr. Leon Festinger's theory of cognitive dissonance tends to explain why artificial taxonomies are difficult to abandon. Refer to Jack W. Brehm and Arthur R. Cohen's *Explorations in Cognitive Dissonance* (John Wiley & Sons, 1962).

Although it is not widely known, a report on the SEI assessment method and maturity schema commissioned by DARPA in 1992 and carried out by the Institute of Defense Analysis (IDA) would probably be of some interest since it evaluated other assessment approaches too. A summary version was cleared for external publication in October of 1992, and may be available from the Institute of Defense Analysis. The summary report is IDA Document D-1202, "Policy Assessment for the Software Process Maturity Model."

15. **Periodical support**—There are no standard software journals or periodicals which deal with artificial taxonomies and maturity levels per se. From time to time specific articles on this topic may be published.

16. **Standards support**—There are no known standards published by ANSI, DoD, IEE, IEEE, or ISO that deal with the hazards of artificial taxonomies. There is an unfortunate tendency, however, for standards themselves to include artificial taxonomies.

17. **Professional associations**—There are no known software professional groups that deal with artificial taxonomies. There are many associations, on the other hand, which endorse and support specific paradigms.

18. **Effectiveness of known therapies**—Eliminating or minimizing artificial taxonomies can normally be accomplished only by: A) replacing them with a more accurate model; B) replacing them with yet another artificial taxonomy. Method A is preferable, but obviously difficult to accomplish. Method B is more common, but unsatisfactory. On the whole, there are few effective therapies for the problem of artificial taxonomies. The best therapy is the long-term accumulation of knowledge.

19. **Costs of known therapies**—There is no known empirical data available on the costs of eliminating artificial taxonomies.

20. **Long-range prognosis**—Artificial taxonomies and maturity level schemes appear to be a normal part of the human condition, and there is no reason to doubt that the future will resemble the past in this respect. The most favorable long-range prognosis for software is that the steady accumulation of knowledge derived from accurate measurements will gradually improve the software paradigms and may

enable future taxonomies to be based on facts rather than unsupported opinions, which has so often been the case.

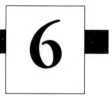
Canceled Projects

1. **Definition**—Software projects that are terminated prior to delivery to their intended customers.

2. **Severity**—The average severity of canceled projects is about a 2.5 on the following scale:

   Severity 1: Project canceled during late testing phase

   Severity 2: Project canceled during late coding or early testing phase

   Severity 3: Project canceled during late design or early coding phase

   Severity 4: Project canceled during early to mid design phase

   Severity 5: Project canceled during late requirements or early design phase

3. **Frequency**—Canceled software projects correlate with the size of the project. For projects larger than 10,000 Function Points, the probability of cancellation is greater than 65%. For projects larger than 5,000 Function Points, the probability of cancellation is around 50%. For projects between 1,000 and 5,000 Function Points, the probability of cancellation is around 25%. Below 1,000 Function Points, cancellation rates drop rapidly with decreasing size.

4. **Occurrence**—Canceled projects are very common for military software and for systems software such as telecommunication projects. MIS projects are not as likely to be canceled, but the reason is because MIS projects are usually smaller in size than systems or military projects. Large MIS projects have the highest severity levels when they are finally canceled, since MIS producers usually let them run on far too long.

5. **Susceptibility and resistance**—It is revealing that the "average" canceled project in the U.S. is about a year behind schedule and almost double its anticipated budget at the time of cancellation. This indicates that projects which are out of control are the most susceptible to cancellation. Small projects are quite resistant to cancellation. Large projects that use careful, automated planning and estimating methods are fairly resistant to cancellation.

6. **Root causes**—The root causes for canceled projects include: 1) The project was poorly planned, incompetently estimated and tracked; 2) Development spanned so

many years that the business or technical situation for which the project was intended changed; 3) Two or more similar projects were started, and only the technical winner was allowed to survive; 4) Extrinsic factors such as the sale of the business negated the need for the project; 5) The project could not achieve technical goals, such as critical performance or throughput targets; 6) The project was so poorly developed that it was discovered during testing that it would probably not work well enough to be released; 7) Creeping requirements changes and unreasonable client demands de-stabilized the project to such a degree that it could not ever be finished.

7. **Associated problems**—Canceled projects are almost always associated with *Friction with Users*, and *Friction with Senior Management*. Unless an extrinsic business factor such as sale of the company caused the cancellation, then there is a strong association with *Low Employee Morale*, and *Low Managerial Morale*, and *High Staff Attrition*. Canceled projects are strongly associated with *Lost Business Opportunities* and *Low Market Shares*.

Canceled projects themselves are often caused by the problems of *Inadequate Planning, Inadequate Cost Estimating, Missed Schedules, Long Schedules, Excessive Time to Market, Cost Overruns, Inexperienced Management, Management Malpractice, Inexperienced Clients, Creeping User Requirements, Inadequate Development Processes, Low Productivity* and *Low Quality*.

8. **Cost impact**—The cost impact of canceled projects is alarming and potentially serious for the entire U.S. software industry. Since canceled projects are very common for large systems, and since they typically occur very late in the development cycle, the quantity of wasted effort devoted to canceled projects in the U.S. is a serious drain on the national software economy. Roughly 15% of the total U.S. software effort in any one year may be dissipated on canceled projects. For 1993, the approximate dimensions of canceled projects in the U.S. are these: 12,000,000 Function Points worth of canceled projects, with a total dollar wastage of $14.3 billion, and a loss of productive staff time of over 285,000 person-years of total software effort. Alarmingly, the frequency of canceled projects in Japan appears to be only about half that of the U.S. The U.S. wastage on canceled projects is larger than the total software effort of most countries.

9. **Methods of prevention**—The most effective prevention is careful planning and careful estimating. As of early 1993 there are some 70 commercial planning tools and 50 commercial estimating tools marketed in the United States, and a significant number of proprietary tools which companies have built for their own usage. In spite of the availability of such tools, their penetration is not yet 100%. About 75% of U.S. software managers use automated planning tools, and about 20% to 25% use automated estimating tools. Failure to use automated planning and estimating tools on large systems of more than 5,000 Function Points should be considered to be management malpractice.

For large mission-critical projects, it would be appropriate to use more than one software estimating tool and look for convergence or divergence in the outputs. Indeed, this is common practice among leading software producers.

10. **Methods of control**—If a large system of more than 5,000 Function Points begins with inadequate requirements, and inadequate planning and estimating, there are no effective methods that can bring it under control.

Note that planning and estimating can *only* be accurate for projects with stable requirements that are competently developed and use structured methodologies. There are no commercial or proprietary estimating tools that can accurately predict the follies of incompetent management or personnel, or the demands of unreasonable clients, and the chaos which they may create. For chaotic and unstructured projects, or those with irrational client demands, massive amounts of unpaid overtime, truncation or deferrals of planned functions, and long schedule slips are the only effective controls and none of them are desirable situations.

11. **Product support**—With some 70 project planning tools and 50 software estimating tools commercially available in the United States, all software project managers should have access to both technologies. Failure to use automated estimating and planning tools for large systems is management malpractice. Note that some estimating tools are optimized for military software, some for MIS projects, some for systems software, and some can handle all classes and types. It is important to select the tool or tools that match enterprise needs.

While estimating tools and manual estimating may sometimes generate equivalent results, the advantages of estimating tools are these: 1) They capture the assumptions of the project at the time of the estimate, and can easily be updated if the assumptions change; 2) They don't omit or forget activities, which are common failings with manual estimates; 3) Their knowledge base is often derived from thousands of projects, and few human managers observe more than 30 or 40 projects in their entire careers.

12. **Consulting support**—The most effective form of consulting for a project suspected of being in serious trouble is an objective project assessment or a project audit. A number of consulting organizations offer assessment and auditing services.

13. **Education support**—The subject of canceled projects is not taught by the majority of software engineering or management schools. This is a serious gap in standard academic curricula. Some seminars, conferences, and commercial courses on project management, project estimating, and project planning will discuss canceled projects from time to time.

14. **Publications support**—Fred Brooks' *The Mythical Man-Month* (Addison Wesley, 1982) should be required reading for all managers. Tom DeMarco's classic *Controlling Software Projects* (Yourdon Press, 1982) is filled with practical advice for heading off the problems which might trigger cancellation. Richard Thayer's *Software Engineering Project Management* (IEEE Press, 1988) is a useful overview. Peter

DeGrace and Leslie Stahl's *Wicked Problems, Righteous Solutions* (Yourdon Press, 1992) is also relevant. Robert Block's *The Politics of Projects* (Yourdon Press, 1993) takes a look at one of the major trouble spots of software management. Another look at a major problem which triggers cancellation is provided by John Boddie's *Crunch Mode: Building Effective Systems on a Tight Schedule* (Yourdon Press, 1992). Two books by Capers Jones, Chairman of SPR, deal with canceled projects and risks. *Programming Productivity* (McGraw-Hill, 1986) deals with the factors influencing long schedules and causing cancellation. *Applied Software Measurement* (McGraw-Hill, 1991) covers the topic of measuring risks, and also includes current U.S. averages for canceled projects for military, systems, and MIS software projects. Dr. Robert Charette's two books, *Software Engineering Risk Analysis and Management* (McGraw-Hill, 1989) and *Application Strategies for Risk Analysis* (McGraw-Hill, 1990) touch upon this subject. Dr. Barry Boehm's *Software Risk Management* (IEEE Press, 1989) also contains much of value.

15. **Periodical support**—In spite of the seriousness of this problem, normal software journals and periodicals seldom discuss canceled projects at all. Only in the case of spectacular failures is there likely to be coverage, and in such cases ordinary business magazines such as Business Week, Time, and Fortune are more likely to include coverage. The journal Risk Management provides reviews of major problems, and covers many industries besides software. Some of the specialized journals, such as Crosstalk which is published by the Air Force Software Technology Support Center, deal with the risks of projects within their domain of specialization, such as military software. The well-known IEEE Transactions on Engineering Management often contains useful articles.

16. **Standards support**—The topic of canceled projects is not covered by any known standard published by ANSI, DOD, IEE, IEEE, or ISO. This is a serious lack of coverage in international standards.

17. **Professional associations**—None of the major professional groups such as the IEEE, ISPA, IFPUG, and the like deal explicitly with canceled projects. Some have special-interest groups on risk management, however.

18. **Effectiveness of known therapies**—Schedule and risk estimation are now easy to perform and surprisingly accurate. Several of the commercial estimating tools estimate the risks and schedules for requirements, design, coding, documentation, and many other activities and tasks. They can also estimate the costs and productivity levels of defect removal activities such as reviews, inspections, and tests. Schedule prediction accuracies to within 10% are now common, and 5% precision is not impossible. Some tools also include "what if" modeling capabilities to explore the impact of improved schedule control methods. However, as a class, such tools have not been fully successful as early warning indicators. The reason is that when such tools indicate serious problems and a strong chance of failure, there is a psychological tendency to disbelieve the warnings.

The best results from leading companies in risk and cancellation reduction are impressive: Canceled project rates of less than 1%; projects that miss schedules reduced to less than 1%. Also, average schedule reductions of about 10% per year have been achieved for four to five consecutive years for development for durations of projects of certain sizes, such as 1,000 Function Points. Military and systems software schedule controls still have higher risks than MIS projects, and are often 30% to 50% longer in their schedules than similar MIS projects. Commercial software, such as spreadsheets, data bases and word processors, also have higher risks and longer schedules than MIS projects.

19. **Costs of known therapies**—Expert-system estimation tools with risk analysis and activity-level and task-level schedule prediction capabilities are in the $5,000 to $20,000 range. (Macro estimating tools are often of lower cost, but also of lower utility than task-level estimating tools, especially for risk control purposes.) Expert-system estimation tools normally return their value in less than six months when used early in the life cycle for projects larger than 1,000 Function Points, or when amortized across ten or more smaller projects.

   Project planning tools range from less than $200 to more than $5000 per set. Planning tools are an effective adjunct to estimating tools, but the two should be used together for optimal results. Project planning tools normally return their value in less than three months when used on projects larger than 1,000 Function Points, or when amortized across ten or more smaller projects.

   An objective project audit or project assessment by an external consultant or consulting group will vary with the size of the project: from a minimum of about $1000 up to $50,000 might be anticipated, with the higher costs associated with major systems in excess of 10,000 Function Points in size.

   Risk of cancellation avoidance techniques vary too widely in cost for convenient generalization, except that careful planning and estimating, structured methods, and formal reuse at the design and coding levels always benefit. Capital investment of more than $25,000 per staff member is often observed in enterprises in the upper quartile of successful project completion rates. Military, systems, and MIS projects typically use different techniques, as do small programs and large systems. Schedule control methods differ for new projects, enhancements, and maintenance projects also. However, since high quality levels tend to correlate with minimum risk levels, quality improvement methods are on the critical path to risk reduction and schedule control, and are usually cost-justified in less than 12 months.

20. **Long-range prognosis**—Canceled projects are likely to remain common for large systems throughout the remainder of the century and perhaps into the next. While the technology exists in 1993 to reduce this problem significantly, the cultural, sociological, and educational support is clearly deficient. A favorable indicator is that the sales of software estimating and planning tools are increasing by more than 30% per year, as are the power and capabilities of such tools.

CHAPTER 7

Corporate Politics

1. **Definition**—Internal disputes, feuds, or power struggles within an organization that are harmful or disruptive enough to jeopardize the work products of the organization or the organization's ability to survive intact.

2. **Severity**—The average severity level of corporate politics is about a 3 on the following five-point scale:

   Severity 1: Corporate politics are severe enough to jeopardize enterprise survival

   Severity 2: Corporate politics are severe enough to jeopardize major units

   Severity 3: Corporate politics are widespread, and there are no effective controls

   Severity 4: Corporate politics are localized, and there are no effective controls

   Severity 5: Corporate politics exist, but control mechanisms dampen the harm

3. **Frequency**—Corporate politics are endemic to the human condition, and have been present in all civilian, governmental, religious, and military organizations throughout human history. Corporate politics are present in essentially 100% of all enterprises with more than 20 employees. Failure to control the harmful effects of corporate politics occur in about 50% of all enterprises larger than 20 employees.

4. **Occurrence**—Corporate politics affect all large organizations regardless of the nature of the work performed. Civilian, military, governmental, and even religious organizations appear equivalent in having this problem.

5. **Susceptibility and resistance**—Since most organizations experience corporate politics, the subject of interest is how this problem can be mitigated. Enterprises where the senior management fosters and participates in corporate politics are most susceptible. Enterprises where the senior management is aware of the problem and moves to control its harmful manifestations are moderately resistant, although not immune, to corporate politics. Organizations where promotions are based on ambiguous or uncertain criteria are very likely to have harmful corporate politics. Organizations with serious management training and career counseling services are somewhat resistant to corporate politics.

6. **Root causes**—The root causes of corporate politics appear to be fundamental to human psychology and sociology. As far as can be determined, all organized

83

groups larger than a single nuclear family tend to differentiate themselves into factions who compete for status, power, or other intangible benefits.

7. **Associated problems**—Divisive corporate politics have been identified as contributing to *Canceled Projects, Cost Overruns, High Management Attrition, High Staff Attrition, Low Management Morale, Low Staff Morale, Lost Business Opportunities,* and *Missed Schedules.*

Corporate politics themselves are often caused by *Management Malpractice* although it would be more accurate to state that a problem not included in this handbook, "Executive Malpractice" or violation of fiduciary duty is the primary cause, with management malpractice being secondary.

8. **Cost impact**—The cost impact of corporate politics is seldom measured directly. However, from assessments and consulting studies which deal with canceled projects, divisive corporate politics were associated with more than one-third of all terminated projects larger than 5000 Function Points.

No human organizations are 100% efficient, in that all employees and managers devote all of their time and energy to performing useful work. When the time spent on corporate politics and other harmful activities is considered (i.e. canceled projects, useless meetings, fixing bugs that should not have occurred, etc.) a case can be made that many companies are less than 35% efficient. In situations where corporate politics or divisive in-fighting are rampant, it is possible that the efficiency drops down below 25%. However, this is not a proven or well-supported hypothesis and is based only on observations made during consulting engagements in enterprises where corporate politics are uncontrolled.

9. **Methods of prevention**—A chief executive or senior management team that is aware of how harmful politics can be is a good preventative. Social experiments carried out in summer camps and prep schools with students indicate that if conflicting groups can work toward a common goal that political divisiveness will be minimized.

10. **Methods of control**—The control mechanisms for corporate politics include the following: A) Establishing clear and unambiguous goals (i.e. fairness, honesty, and respect for the individual) as part of corporate culture; B) Using an objective merit appraisal system for both management and staff; C) For large enterprises, allowing or facilitating transfers to different cities for managers who may be capable, but who have become embroiled in disputes or politics; D) Instituting annual opinion surveys throughout an enterprise, with questions aimed at identifying harmful corporate politics; E) Instituting "Open Door" programs through which employees or managers who feel mistreated can appeal to higher management for adjudication, with a guarantee that no reprisals will be forthcoming.

From time to time, charismatic leaders with strong personalities can so dominate an organization that corporate politics temporarily abate. However, upon the departure or death of such a leader, politics will normally erupt with extreme vigor. The literature dealing with "succession disputes" is plentiful and unequivocal.

One widely used but seldom discussed technique is for the winning side in a political dispute to terminate or force the resignation of the losing side. However, this is only a short-term solution since the winning side will often fragment itself into new political segments, and disputes will begin again.

11. **Product support**—As far as can be determined, there are no commercial products of any kind that deal with corporate politics. It would be possible to include corporate politics in an "artificial life" management game using principles found in commercial games such as Sim Life, Sim City, and Sim Ant.

12. **Consulting support**—The topic of corporate politics is a sensitive and delicate topic, which most larger consulting organizations tend to avoid. Individual consultants who are sensitive to this topic may include it in their analyses. Most standard project audits or project assessments do not deal with corporate politics. There are consulting groups that specialize in personnel-related topics, and such groups deal with corporate politics also.

13. **Education support**—The topic of corporate politics is seldom discussed in either business schools or software engineering schools. However, a topic as common as this often receives intermittent and informal discussion in academic contexts. However, Dr. Albert Lederer of Oakland University in Rochester, Michigan, is one of the U.S. leaders in the exploration of how corporate politics affects estimating accuracy and MIS performance.

14. **Publications support**—The software literature is slowly recognizing the importance of politics, but had comparatively little to say about this topic for years. Robert Bloch's *The Politics of Projects* (Yourdon Press, 1983) is a useful volume. Tom DeMarco's classic *Peopleware* (Dorset House, 1987) has started a whole new school of human-oriented software and management research. Fred Brook's classic *The Mythical Man-month* (Addison Wesley, 1982) is highly relevant. Dr. Gerald Weinberg's *Becoming a Technical Leader* (Dorset House, 1986) is a good source of guidance on heading off political problems. Robert Glass's *Software Conflict* deals with a number of interesting political topics. Barbara Bouldin's *Agents for Change* (Yourdon Press, 1989) talks about using political concepts for beneficial rather than harmful purposes. Rob Thomsett's new *Third Wave Project Management* (Yourdon Press, 1993) also looks at politics and tries to move them in beneficial directions.

The general business literature is filled with interesting and candid discussion of politics and in-fighting among the executives of major corporations. Representative titles include Antony Jay's *Management and Machiavelli: An Inquiry into Corporate Politics* (Bantam Books, 1967). For titles on specific company politics, see Thomas J. Watson's *Father, Son, and Company* (Bantam Books, 1990) which deals with IBM's founding and growth. Rand Araskog's *The ITT Wars* (Henry Holt and Company, 1989) discusses the corporate politics of ITT under Harold Geneen and successive chairmen. Richard Miller's *CITICORP: The Story of a Bank in Crisis* (McGraw-Hill, 1993) also covers politics. A fascinating look at both inter-company and intra-company politics can be found in David Halberstam's *The Reckoning*

(Avon Books, 1987) which deals with the automotive industry, and how the U.S. lost market shares. Rodney Clark's *The Japanese Company* (Yale University Press, 1979) points out that the U.S. is not alone on dealing with corporate politics.

Some of the more recent titles relevant to software include James Wallace and Jim Erikson's *Hard Drive* (Harper Business, 1992) which discusses Bill Gates and Microsoft. Also relevant is Robert X. Cringley's *Accidental Empires* (Harper Business, 1992) which discusses politics among the Silicon Valley enterprises. Covering the opposite coast is Susan Rosegrant and David Lampe's *Route 128* (Basic Books, 1992) which discusses the high-technology companies in the Boston area.

Interestingly, the topic of military history is surprisingly open and candid in discussing the impact of this phenomenon on military affairs. An astonishing number of campaigns and battles were lost, in part, because generals on the same side hated one another and refused to cooperate. Major General J.F.C. Fuller's three volume *A Military History of the Western World* (Minerva Press, 1954) is an excellent overview of the impact of divisive politics on military affairs.

General science is also filled with cases where politics, intrigue, and other manifestations interfered with scientific advances: any standard biography of Thomas Edison or Nikolai Tesla will illustrate the amount of time these brilliant minds devoted to politics. Indeed, the fight between adherents of alternating and direct current in the closing years of the 19th century was one of the bitterest political fights in all of scientific history. The same involvement in political disputes are true of Isaac Newton, Lee De Forest, and Henry Ford, and many other prominent scientists.

15. **Periodical support**—The general computing and software periodicals deal with corporate politics only intermittently, when some noteworthy example that is visible to the outside world manifests itself. Recent examples include the overthrow of Steve Jobs at Apple Computers, Ken Olson's management shake-up at Digital Equipment, the firing of Rod Canion at Compaq, Bill Gates' reorganization of Microsoft, and John Akers' reorganization of IBM. However, periodicals tend to treat these situations as unique events, rather than being the normal operational mode of human organizations. Computer Personnel in July of 1991 contained a fascinating article by Dr. Albert Lederer and Dr. Jayesh Prasad on the impact of political pressure on software estimation. The same authors, and several colleagues, also published an intriguing study of cost estimating practices in the June 1990 issue of MIS Quarterly. Management journals such as CIO, Harvard Business Review, and the IEEE Transactions on Engineering Management may touch upon politics from time to time.

16. **Standards support**—There are apparently no current standards published by ANSI, the DoD, IEE, IEEE, or ISO that deal with corporate politics. It is unlikely that there will ever be a standard that deals with this topic.

17. **Professional associations**—None of the professional organizations such as ADAPSO (now ITAA), ACM, ASM, IEEE, seem to deal specifically with corporate politics.

18. **Effectiveness of known therapies**—Since corporate politics are endemic in human organizations, it can be concluded that none of the therapies are fully effective. Large corporations or large military and government organizations that use transfers to minimize personality and power conflicts can be moderately effective. Enterprises of any size where goals are clear, unambiguous, and all factions strive to achieve them can minimize but not eliminate corporate politics. Enterprises with particularly strong and charismatic leaders can experience a temporary cessation of corporate politics.

19. **Costs of known therapies**—As of 1993 there are no known cost studies which deal with the minimization of corporate politics. The costs must be considered unknown.

20. **Long-range prognosis**—Corporate politics have always been a problem for human organizations, and there is no reason to expect that the future will be any better than the past.

CHAPTER 8

Cost Overruns

1. **Definition**—Complete projects or significant deliverables whose actual costs exceed planned, budgeted, or estimated costs.

2. **Severity**—The average severity of cost overruns is about 2.5, and the severity rises to about 1.5 for projects larger than 5000 Function Points in size:

   Severity 1: Overrun causes project cancellation

   Severity 2: Overrun exceeds estimated cost by more than 100%

   Severity 3: Overrun exceeds estimated cost by more than 50%

   Severity 4: Overrun exceeds estimated cost by more than 25%

   Severity 5: Overrun between 5% and 25%

3. **Frequency**—Cost overruns are endemic to software, and to date have occurred on more than 50% of all software projects larger than 2,500 Function Points. The probability of high-severity cost overruns rises steeply with the size of the project.

4. **Occurrence**—Cost overruns tend to balloon in seriousness and probability near the end of a project's development cycle. Cost overruns are uncommon early at requirements and design but grow steadily in frequency during coding, testing, user documentation, and integration. Cost overruns during testing are normally the most common and also the most serious since there is no way to recover.

5. **Susceptibility and resistance**—Large systems of more than 5000 Function Points that are new in concept and have inexperienced management and staff are the most susceptible to cost overruns. Applications and systems of any size with ambiguous requirements and no ability to control creeping requirements are also highly susceptible. Large systems that attempt manual cost estimating without use of proprietary or commercial planning and estimating tools are highly susceptible to cost overruns: the probability exceeds 90% in these cases. Small, well-understood applications with experienced management supported by automated cost estimating tools are most resistant: the probability here is only about 5%.

6. **Root causes**—Four major root causes exist for the problem of cost overruns:
   1) The costs were not achievable as initially estimated but the project started anyway;

2) The scope of the deliverable or project expanded after the costs were set;

3) The cost estimating methodologies were inadequate;

4) The enterprise failed to collect useful historical cost data.

7. **Associated problems**—Cost overruns are a significant contributor to the problem of *Friction with Users* and the problem of *Friction with Senior Management*. Cost overruns are also associated factors for the problems of *Canceled Projects, Excessive Time to Market, Long Schedules,* and for *Missed Schedules*. Cost overruns also contribute to the problems of *High Staff Attrition* and *Low Staff Morale*. Cost overruns are a contributing factor to *Low Quality*.

Cost overruns themselves are often caused by the problems of *Inexperienced Management, Management Malpractice, Inexperienced Staff, Creeping Requirements, Inadequate Estimating, Inadequate Planning, Inadequate Measurements,* and *Excessive Schedule Pressure*.

8. **Cost impact**—The costs of overruns grow in direct proportion to the magnitude of the miss and the size of the project. For small projects of 100 Function Points or less, cost overruns seldom exceed $2,500. For projects of 1000 Function Points, cost overruns average about $100,000. For projects of 10,000 Function Points, cost overruns of about $3 million to more than $10 million can occur. For massive military projects in excess of 20,000 Function Points, cost overruns can exceed $50 million. For contract software and for commercially marketed software, there may be additional cost penalties for non-performance. Such additional costs require knowledge of the specific situation.

9. **Methods of prevention**—There are four major preventive techniques for eliminating or minimizing the impact of cost overruns: A) Use of commercial-grade software project estimating tools; B) Use of commercial-grade project planning tools; C) Using functional metrics to quantify the changes in the growth of project requirements; D) Full software measurement programs that include activity-level measurements.

10. **Methods of control**—Controlling cost overruns grows progressively harder as the project proceeds. The standard control techniques in frequency of normal occurrence are: A) Voluntary unpaid overtime; B) Reducing project functions or delaying selected functions to a later release; C) Canceling the project completely.

11. **Product support**—The use of commercial-grade software estimating tools and project planning tools are effective against cost overruns. With some 50 software estimating tools and 70 to 75 planning tools marketed in the U.S., such tools should be used on all significant software projects. Failure to do so on large projects can be viewed as management malpractice. Accurate project cost tracking is also desirable. There are many accounting and cost tracking systems commercially available, and even more in-house systems. However, most of them have serious flaws and are not fully effective for software because they do not support full work breakdown structures, and often have no capabilities for recording slack

time, unpaid overtime, user time, and other significant software cost elements. Sometimes more than 50% of the accrued costs for software projects are absent from standard cost tracking systems. Data from cost tracking systems should be validated by interviews with project managers and team members before it is accepted as accurate. Failure to do so is management malpractice.

Starting roughly in 1993, a new kind of supplemental product should reach the software cost estimating marketplace. This is the sale of cost estimating "templates" derived from specific projects or classes of projects. Several vendors Applied Business Technology (ABT), Quantitative Software Methods (QSM) and Software Productivity Research (SPR) are already exploring templates. Template sets can include both horizontal and vertical markets. For example, templates reflecting SEI maturity levels should soon be available. Also, templates of software applications within specific industries such as banking or insurance should also soon be commercially available.

12. **Consulting support**—For projects that are suspected of being in trouble, a form of consulting termed a project assessment or a project audit are often helpful. Many software consulting groups can perform audits and assessments. The assessment service should also identify cost-related issues, including the root causes of overruns. A number of management consulting companies, and many estimating tool vendors, can provide support for specific projects if commissioned to do so.

13. **Education support**—Many academic curricula do not cover cost overruns, although some are starting to do so. Case Western University, for example, is exploring the impact of creeping requirements on cost estimating errors. Carnegie Mellon, DePaul, George Mason University, MIT, the University of Seattle, and several other universities have estimating topics and some even have estimating research laboratories. (Check catalogs for local availability.) Several commercial courses deal with this topic explicitly, including courses by Quantitative Software Management, the Atlantic Systems Guild, Software Productivity Research. Since so much cost and productivity data uses functional metrics, knowledge of Function Point Analysis is highly desirable. There are few academic courses on this topic, but almost one hundred commercial courses available. A course by Allan Albrecht (the inventor of Function Points) was the first such course certified by IFPUG.

14. **Publication support**—In chronological order: Dr. Barry Boehm's monumental *Software Engineering Economics* (Prentice Hall, 1981) is dated but useful. Tom DeMarco's book *Controlling Software Projects* (Dorset House, 1982) contains valuable insights. Capers Jones' book *Programming Productivity* (McGraw-Hill, 1986) deals with the factors that influence costs. His book *Applied Software Measurement* (McGraw-Hill, 1991) contains current U.S. averages for resources in person-months, which can easily be converted into cost data. For example, the current U.S. average productivity rate is about five Function Points per person-month, so the average cost per Function Point would be $1,000 using a standard burdened salary rate of $5,000 per month. Dr. Larry Putnam's book *Measures for Excellence*

(Prentice Hall, 1991) summarizes Dr. Putnam's many years of metrics experiences. Frank Wellman's *Software Costing* (Prentice Hall, 1992) is also relevant. A new 1993 monograph by Capers Jones, *Critical Problems in Software Measurement* (IS Management Group, 1993) deals with capturing enough "soft" data to discover if cancellation may perhaps occur.

15. **Periodical support**—In spite of the seriousness of this problem, normal software journals and periodicals seldom discuss moderate cost overruns at all. Only in the event of spectacular overruns is there likely to be coverage. This is often provided by general business magazines such as Business Week, Time, and Fortune. The magazine Computer Personnel (July, 1991) contained an article by Dr. Albert Lederer and Dr. Jayesh Prasad on the impact of political pressure on software estimation. The same authors and several colleagues also published an intriguing study of the sociology of cost estimating practices in the June 1990 issue of MIS Quarterly.

16. **Standards support**—Unfortunately, some of the basic standards dealing with software costs and productivity cannot be recommended for serious usage on commercial-grade software. The IEEE Standard for Software Productivity Metrics (P1045) should be read, but is too incomplete for serious business purposes. The SEI standard for Software Project Effort and Schedule Measurement is also somewhat deficient even though it is quite recent and it cannot be recommended.

17. **Professional associations**—The non-profit International Society of Parametric Analysis (ISPA) and the non-profit International Function Point Users Group (IFPUG) have the widest membership and are most active in cost-related studies. The Society of Cost Estimating And Analysis (SCEA) is also relevant. SCEA primarily supports the government, and is not limited to software.

18. **Effectiveness of known therapies**—Cost estimation is now a standard feature of some 50 commercial-grade software estimation tools in the United States. Standard project planning tools, of which there are about 70 to 75 on the U.S. market, also support costs, and most include Gantt charting, PERT charting, staff-loading, and critical path analysis as well. However, project planning tools are usually not expert cost control systems, and give the best results with the most experienced managers. Failure to use estimating and planning tools on large projects should be considered management malpractice.

The impact of commercial cost estimating "templates" may change the cost estimating market place in significant ways. However, templating is still too new in 1993 to judge the overall impact. It can be hypothesized that accurate templates derived from careful measurement of similar projects should enhance the accuracy and credibility of the estimating tool business.

Cost overrun recovery is more troublesome. Unpaid overtime can assist recovery by about 15% to 20% if the overrun potential is seen in time. For cost overruns, during testing, overtime cannot usually exert more than a 5% to 10% recovery impact. For cost overruns of greater magnitude, deferred functions or cancellation will normally occur. It is obvious from the paucity of cost control mechanisms that prevention is the best solution.

19. **Costs of known therapies**—Expert-system cost estimation tools are typically in the $5,000 to $20,000 range. They will normally return their value immediately (i.e. in less than six months after purchase) when used on projects larger than 500 Function Points, or when amortized across ten or more smaller projects. There are also public domain or low-end cost estimating tools available that center around Dr. Barry Boehm's well-known COCOMO model. Note that these are not full life-cycle estimating tools, and normally do not include sizing logic or any algorithms for dealing with paperwork costs. The low-end tools may or may not return their value. Since paperwork costs are greater than coding costs for many large systems, and for all U.S. military software, estimating tools that cannot predict the costs of plans, requirements, specifications, and user documentation should be avoided.

Project planning tools are typically lower in price than estimating tools, and run from less than $100 up to perhaps $5,000. In the hands of experienced managers, planning tools return their value almost immediately. In the hands of novice managers, the return period may be longer than the first project for which the tool is used, unless substantial training is also available.

Project audits or assessments will vary with the size of the project. From a low of about $10,000 for a sample of small projects up to as much as $50,000 for massive projects in excess of 10,000 Function Points have been observed.

Cost control techniques vary too widely in costs and effectiveness for generalization. The methods that are used on large systems may not be the same as those on small projects, and there are also variances between military, systems, and MIS applications. Interestingly, there are also international variations, since unpaid overtime is uncommon in parts of Europe and also in Canada. The use of careful planning and automated estimating tools, coupled with well-structured development methods typically give the best results.

For cost estimating tools to work with acceptable accuracy (i.e. better than 10% precision) the project itself must be under control. There are no effective techniques for estimating the chaotic and random patterns of costs that occur when inexperienced managers cross paths with creeping or unreasonable user requirements and careless development methods.

20. **Long-range prognosis**—While the problem of cost overruns is serious in 1993, the rate of growth of the usage of software cost estimating tools leads to the conclusion that this problem should be under control before the end of the century. By 1997, more than 50% of all software project managers should be equipped with commercial-grade estimating tools.

CHAPTER 9

Creeping User Requirements

1. **Definition**—A) New requirements or significant modifications to existing requirements that are made after the basic set of requirements have been agreed to by both clients and developers; B) Widespread failure to anticipate changing requirements and hence make no plans for how to deal with them.

2. **Severity**—The average severity of creeping requirements is about a 3.5 on the following scale:

   Severity 1: New or changed requirements exceed 50% of original requirements

   Severity 2: New or changed requirements exceed 40% of original requirements

   Severity 3: New or changed requirements exceed 30% of original requirements

   Severity 4: New or changed requirements exceed 20% of original requirements

   Severity 5: New or changed requirements exceed 10% of original requirements

3. **Frequency**—Creeping requirements are endemic to the software industry, and seem to occur on more than 70% of all applications over 1000 Function Points. The severity of requirements creep is directly proportional to the size of the application. The average creep for a sample of 60 projects was 35%. The largest observed creep in unanticipated requirements is an astonishing 200%. Expressed chronologically, creeping requirements changes average about 1% per month, so for a three-year project, about one-third of the delivered requirements would have been added after the requirements were initially defined. This rate of requirements change seems higher than for electrical engineering, mechanical engineering, civil engineering or most other forms of engineering.

   The basic problem of the software industry is not with creeping requirements per se, which have been common occurrences for 50 years. The problem is with inadequate methods, tools, and approaches for dealing with creeping requirements in a way that minimizes damage to the structure of the software, schedule slippage, and the other associated problems which manifest themselves.

4. **Occurrence**—All classes of software experience creeping requirements to some degree. Military software is more likely to experience major requirements creep than most other classes of software, since military software schedules are so long. Other large software projects, such as operating systems and switching systems, are also highly sensitive to creeping requirements. However, the problem is widespread and occurs for any and all software applications where the users themselves are uncertain of their true needs. Creeping requirements are unfortunate for time and materials contract software and catastrophic for fixed price contracts.

5. **Susceptibility and resistance**—Applications that are novel or where the users are uncertain as to their true needs are most susceptible to creeping requirements. Applications that have been done many times, such as compilers or PBX switches, are most resistant to creeping requirements. Prototyping and Joint Application Design (JAD) makes projects unusually resistant to creeping requirements.

   Requirements changes usually deal with changes in the external aspects of a software project, such as adding a new input or output. Since the external aspects of software are dealt with by functional metrics, it has been noted that the usage of functional metrics provides a very accurate way of measuring the rate of requirements creep and their magnitude.

6. **Root causes**—The root causes of creeping requirements include the following: 1) Each time new users commission a new project there will be some uncertainty in resolving true needs; 2) For large projects that take several years, normal business or even statutory changes may occur that must be part of the application; 3) The use of effective preventive technologies such as prototypes or JAD sessions may not occur due to corporate culture or the nature of the application itself; 4) The fundamental technologies for exploring and modeling requirements are fairly primitive; 5) Software measurement technology prior to 1979 had no effective way of measuring creeping requirements.

7. **Associated problems**—Creeping requirements are associated with the problems of *Friction with Users* and sometimes with *Friction with Senior Management*. Creeping requirements are often causative factors to the problems of *Missed Schedules, Excessive Time to Market,* and to *Cost Overruns.* Creeping requirements are a contributor to the problem of *Excessive Schedule Pressure* and *Low Staff Morale.*

   Creeping requirements themselves are often caused by the problems of *Inexperienced Users, Inexperienced Management, Inadequate Methodologies,* and *Inadequate Cost Estimating. Inadequate Measurement* is also a contributing factor for creeping requirements.

8. **Cost impact**—The cost impact of creeping requirements can be quantified with very high precision by means of Function Point metrics. Assume that the average cost to build a project is $1000 per Function Point (which is the approximate U.S. average), and the project starts with requirements that total to 1000 Function Points. Obviously the project will have an initial cost estimate of $1 million. Now assume that new requirements are added that total to 25%, or some 250 new Func-

tion Points. The project will now cost $1.25 million since the creeping requirements portion cost $250,000. In real life the situation is somewhat more complex, since the costs of creeping requirements may be higher than the costs of the original functionality if the requirements occur too late in the development cycle.

9. **Methods of prevention**—In the long run, an accurate measurement program based on functional metrics is the most effective prevention for creeping improvements. Software estimating tools that use Function Points or Feature Points are also beneficial. Since creeping improvements have been observed for many years, some estimating tools can actually predict the probable growth in unplanned requirements. Note that the advantage functional metrics offer vis a vis lines of code is two-fold: Function Points are aimed specifically at what users care about, and they are first calculated during the requirements phase.

Many organizations are exploring the implications of creeping requirements, and some significant new breakthroughs might be anticipated. In both England and the United States, research is underway on fully automated requirements collection and analysis tools. These tools can not only capture requirements and requirements changes, but can also be closely coupled to Function Point sizing tools, software estimating tools, software planning tools, and upper CASE design tools. In early 1993 this work is still experimental, but commercial manifestations may occur before the end of the year and almost certainly by 1994.

The U.S. Navy's NAVAIR group has been conducting interesting experiments in fully automated high-speed prototyping as a way of minimizing creeping requirements. By building a replica of, for example, an aircraft control panel directly from requirements, they are able to speed up the requirements analysis process by as much as 12 to 1, and achieve notable reductions in requirements creep. It is also possible to extract data from the requirements tool and feed it directly into Function Point sizing tools.

The University of Virginia is also exploring requirements creep, and methods of controlling them. Interesting research is also underway by George Mason University in performing a linguistic analysis of historical requirements, and using the results to construct a vocabulary of common requirements. This research may also lead to reusable requirements, and direct coupling of requirements to sizing and estimating tools. Case Western University is also exploring creeping user requirements, and at least one doctoral thesis is being prepared on this topic as this book is written.

As of 1993, the requirements domain is experiencing a notable burst of research which seems to be moving in very positive directions.

10. **Methods of control**—Several technologies are effective in controlling creeping requirements. The use of prototypes is highly beneficial in minimizing this problem, and empirical results are quite favorable. Creeping requirements are usually less than 10% for projects that use this technology. The Joint Application Design (JAD) technology is also effective, and it too can reduce creeping requirements to below 10%. The simultaneous usage of JADs and prototypes together appears to

be synergistic, and can drop creeping requirements below 5%. For very large systems of over 5000 Function Points, establishing a formal change control board would be effective.

Quality Function Deployment (QFD) is also adding rigor to the requirements gathering process, with special emphasis on quality requirements.

Several other technologies appear of potential value in reducing creeping requirements, but to date have not published quantitative data in support. Information Engineering (IE) methodologies and object-oriented analysis and design are two that may be of potential value. Control becomes more difficult as the overall size of the application grows. For projects above 10,000 Function Points, development cycles are often four or five years. Over that time span, creeping requirements may be uncontrollable, although they can certainly be reduced.

11. **Product support**—Creeping requirements are best identified by the use of functional metrics and the commercial or proprietary estimating tools which support such metrics. Of the 50 or so commercial software estimating tools marketed in the United States, about 20 of them support functional metrics and hence are capable of dealing with creeping requirements. Failure to use such tools on systems larger than 5000 Function Points can be considered to be management malpractice.

A new class of requirements-gathering tool which is closely coupled to Function Point enumerators, estimating tools, and design tools may soon be available, although the concepts are still largely experimental as this book goes to press.

Examples of some of the kinds of tools used in requirements gathering, updating, and control include: ACT/1 by Certified Software Specialists; APS by Intersolv; Artessa/3000 by Quality Consultants; A.S.A. by Verilog; AD/VANCE data modeller by On-Line Software; ADW/ADS by KnowledgeWare; BACHMAN/ Analyst; CASE Dictionary by Oracle; CORVision by Cortex; EPOS by Software Products and Services; Excelerator by Intersolv; FirstCASE by AGS Management Systems; GeneXus by ARTech; GEODE by Verilog; Mini-ASYST by Sterling Software; NATURAL Architect by Software AG; PRIDE by M. Bryce Associates; ProtoScreens by Bailey & Bailey; Silverrun by Computer Systems Advisers; Statemate by iLogix; STRADIS by McDonnell Douglas; and Teamwork by CADRE.

12. **Consulting support**—A large number of consulting organizations offer Joint Application Design (JAD) or prototyping consulting services and training. Several consulting companies can facilitate JAD sessions and assist in getting the approach operational. Other consulting companies can assist in monitoring the growth of a project using Function Points, and can assist in estimating incremental costs. Information Engineering (IE) and Object-Oriented Analysis are both available from many commercial educational facilities and some academic institutions.

13. **Education support**—Several university software engineering and management schools are now studying the problem of creeping requirements. Case Western University, George Mason University, and Rochester University in Michigan come

to mind. Check local catalogs or with local faculty to explore other university offerings in this topic.

Several commercial courses, including "Applied Software Measurement" (Software Productivity Research and DCI) and "Managing Software Projects" (Atlantic Systems Guild and TTI) deal explicitly with creeping requirements. A course on Function Point Analysis, although hard to find, is a useful prerequisite for controlling creeping requirements.

14. Publication support—Donald Gause and Gerald Weinberg's *Exploring Requirements: Quality Before Design* (Dorset House, 1992) is an excellent overview with important insights. Alan Davis *Software Requirements* (IEEE Press, 1993) is a new book with a very broad range of topics and many useful concepts, including a discussion of intangible requirements.

Richard Thayer and Merlin Dorfman's *System and Software Requirements Engineering* (IEEE Press, 1990) is a massive overview with more than 700 pages and 44 articles. A companion volume by the same authors, *Standards, Guidelines, and Examples on Systems and Software Requirements Engineering* (IEEE Press, 1990) is also relevant.

Judy August's *Joint Application Design* (Yourdon Press, 1991) is a useful overview of one of the popular methods for reaching requirements closure. Stephen McMenamin and John Palmer's *Essential Systems Analysis* is a good bridge between requirements and subsequent analysis and design stages. Ken Orr's *Structured Requirements Definition* (Ken Orr & Associates, 1981) is a good overview of the data analytic approach to gathering requirements. Also recommended as a companion volume covering the same domain is Jean Dominique Warnier's *Logical Construction of Systems* (Van Nostrand Reinhold, 1981). Any of James Martin's books in the series on information engineering (Prentice Hall) provide a useful overview to this mainstream technology. The book *Applied Software Measurement* by Capers Jones (McGraw-Hill, 1991) contains current U.S. averages for creeping requirements, by the size of the overall application.

15. Periodical support—In spite of the widespread nature of this problem, normal software journals and periodicals seldom discuss creeping requirements. Only in the case of spectacular overruns or failures caused by this problem is there likely to be coverage. In such cases, general business magazines such as Business Week, Time, and Fortune are more likely to include coverage. More recently, specialized journals have started dealing with this topic, such as Metrics Views published by IFPUG, and Cross Talk published by the Air Force Software Technology Support Center. North Holland's Information and Decision Technologies has some relevant articles from time to time, such as James Palmer and Yiqing Liang's "Indexing and Clustering of Software Requirements Specification" in 1992.

16. Standards support—The topic of creeping user requirements is not covered by any known standard published by ANSI, DoD, IEE, IEEE, or ISO. However, DoD standards do specify formal techniques for requesting changes to requirements and designs.

17. **Professional associations**—There are a number of associations of software professionals connected to specific industries that deal with cost overruns, although not necessarily with creeping requirements. LOMA for the insurance industry is an example. The non-profit International Function Point Users Group (IFPUG) is also a useful association, since Function Points are the method of choice for measuring creeping requirements. Both ISPA (International Society of Parametric Analysis) and SCEA (Society of Cost Estimating and Analysis) are starting to deal with this topic.

18. **Effectiveness of known therapies**—The effectiveness of known therapies is excellent for small to medium applications, but sags for large systems of more than 10,000 Function Points in total size. JAD sessions, prototypes, or both together can reduce creeping requirements down to under 10%, where the problem is more a nuisance than a serious threat. Information Engineering (IE) and Object-Oriented Analysis appear to be useful in controlling creeping requirements, but have not yet published any definitive supporting data.

   The effectiveness of the new class of requirements tools which are closely coupled to Function Point enumerators, cost estimating tools, and CASE tools has not yet been worked out, but can be hypothesized to have significant value.

   Some of the other new techniques, such as automatic prototyping from requirements, using tools such as Document Director and Statemate, are too new for full economic analysis, but are returning very promising early results.

19. **Costs of known therapies**—Learning to count Function Points is fairly inexpensive, and the cost of a one-day or two-day workshop is usually less than $1,000 per student. Joining IFPUG, the International Function Point Users Group, is also inexpensive since it is a non-profit organization. Estimating tools that support Function Point counting range in price from below $1,000 up to $40,000. Function Point metrics and tools that support them normally return their value in less than 12 months when used for projects of 1,000 Function Points or larger, or when amortized across several smaller projects.

   JAD training is available from several sources, and normally costs less than $1,000 per student. It will usually return its value on the first project for which it is used. Prototyping tools vary in costs from less than $500 to more than $30,000 based on the richness of the feature set. In general, disposable prototypes done with very powerful languages and tools give the best results. A method called "time box" prototyping is also very effective in reducing creeping requirements.

   Since requirements problems are endemic and critical, large software-producing organizations should mount sustained research efforts on this topic. Full time research by up to half a dozen individuals within companies the size of an AT&T would not be excessive.

20. **Long-range prognosis**—As the industry matures, more and more projects will be entering their second, third, or Nth generation. The magnitude of creeping user requirements should gradually decline, but this problem can be expected to remain severe for the remainder of the 20th century.

While creeping requirements will no doubt remain common (and may even be desirable) it is the response to creeping requirements that has lagged historically. A burst of significant research and many prototypes of new kinds of requirements gathering tools may improve our ability to include creeping requirements without doing catastrophic damage to system structures, schedules, costs, and quality. The best-case scenario indicates the creeping requirements may be under control well before the end of the century. On the whole, the prognosis now looks remarkably good.

CHAPTER 10

Crowded Office Conditions

1. **Definition**—Office space for software professionals that provides less than 80 square feet per staff member of relatively private and noise-free working space.

2. **Severity**—The average severity of crowded office conditions for software staffs in the U.S. is about a 3 on the following scale:

   Severity 1: Less than 40 square feet of private work space per staff member

   Severity 2: Less than 50 square feet of private work space per staff member

   Severity 3: Less than 60 square feet of private work space per staff member

   Severity 4: Less than 70 square feet of private work space per staff member

   Severity 5: Less than 80 square feet of private work space per staff member

3. **Frequency**—Crowded office conditions have been endemic to the software industry since the 1970's, when computer usage and software personnel exploded throughout business and government operations.

4. **Occurrence**—Crowded office conditions for software staffs occur throughout the U.S. and indeed throughout the world. From U.S. surveys and consulting engagements by Software Productivity Research, more than 70% of all software organizations have crowded office conditions.

5. **Susceptibility and resistance**—Susceptibility is general and widespread. In an industry that grew as fast as software, few companies could build or acquire office space at the rates required. Resistance to crowded offices today follows a curious distribution. A few very profitable companies are resistant, and a somewhat larger set of companies that are unprofitable and thus are down-sizing and laying off personnel are resistant.

6. **Root causes**—The explosive demand for software and software professionals throughout the 1960's, 1970's, and 1980's is the root cause for crowded office conditions. Throughout those decades, software professionals were increasing by as much as 15% per year in many organizations. Few organizations can increase

available office space by more than 5% to 10% per year, so crowding was inevitable.

Now that some of the same companies that grew explosively are shrinking even faster (i.e. DEC, IBM, Wang, etc.) one might think that office space would become more available. Unfortunately, as companies downsize in personnel, they also close buildings and move into less expensive offices. The net results of downsizing to date have been to make crowded office conditions worse rather than better.

7. **Associated problems**—Crowded office conditions are associated with the problems of *Low Productivity, Low Staff Morale, Missed Schedules, Long Schedules, Cost Overruns,* and *Excessive Time to Market.*

Crowded office conditions are sometimes caused by the problems of *Inexperienced Management,* and *Inadequate Measurement.* A more general problem is the lack of controlled studies and the sparse citations in the literature.

8. **Cost impact**—U.S. organizations with less than about 45 square feet of noisy, crowded office space are at the low end of software productivity rates in the U.S. U.S. organizations averaging more than about 75 square feet of relatively private, noise-free office space are at the high end of software productivity rates in the U.S.

Note that crowded office space does not seem to affect software performance in Japan to the same degree as it does in the U.S. Interviews with software personnel carried out by various researchers such as Gerald McCue, Dean of Architecture at Harvard; Tom DeMarco and Tim Lister for their book *Peopleware;* and the author and his colleagues at SPR indicate strong preferences for adequate office space by software personnel at all levels. When IBM's Santa Teresa lab was occupied, with 100 square foot private offices for all personnel, productivity was about 11% higher than the previous year when the staff had been located in shared cubicles with less than 50 square feet per programmer.

9. **Methods of prevention**—Careful environmental and ergonomic planning are moderately effective as preventions. Several companies, including IBM, ITT, and TRW have constructed experimental "office of the future" layouts, and have had volunteers work in them to judge their effectiveness. Such research is an excellent preventative for crowding, although obviously one only major corporations can afford.

A whole new domain of telecommuting and work-at-home approaches overlaps the topic of inadequate office space. As of 1993, SPR has not been commissioned to gather sufficient data on these topics, so we cannot say anything definitive in this book. The topic of telecommuting is an important one, and the gap in empirical knowledge will hopefully be corrected in the near future.

10. **Methods of control**—Control of crowded office conditions is very difficult due to the costs involved. In major urban environments such as Boston, New York, and San Francisco, office space is extremely expensive to lease, and even more expensive to build. Indeed, one of the reasons why so many companies are either out-

sourcing or moving their headquarters and data centers out of cities has to do with the high costs of adequate office space.

One response to both crowded office conditions and rapid growth of software personnel is to turn the whole software function over to an outsourcing group. If the outsourcing arrangement merely takes over the current personnel and office space, the impact on crowded conditions may not change. If the outsource arrangement moves the software function to some other facility, then space may be affected for either good or ill.

In a 1991 visit to several Japanese software factories, the author noted that conditions were crowded by the standards discussed here (i.e. less than 75 square feet of office space) but productivity did not seem to be adversely affected. From informal observations of software work habits in the United States and Japan, it appears that the conversational noise levels are higher in U.S. offices than in Japan. (In one software factory, the only loud voices noted were visiting Americans.) U.S. software workers appear more likely to interrupt one another with business or social topics than was observed in Japan.

11. **Product support**—As of 1993, comparatively few commercial estimating tools are sensitive to office conditions. The SPR CHECKPOINT® product includes a predicted impact of various office space plateaus on U.S. software productivity. In measurement mode, CHECKPOINT® can also be used to input hard data about office space and noise.

12. **Consulting support**—Comparatively few consulting groups deal with the impact of office space and noise levels on software performance. The Atlantic Systems Guild and Software Productivity Research, Inc. do cover this topic, however. The SPR assessment approach includes an evaluation of software office conditions, although the SEI assessment approach does not.

13. **Education support**—Most schools of commercial architecture deal with ergonomics and the impact of various office layouts. This knowledge is seldom transferred to either business schools or software engineering, however. The well-known course based on the book *Peopleware* (Tom DeMarco and Tim Lister, Dorset House) by the Atlantic Systems Guild on Controlling Software Projects covers the impact of office space and noise levels. The course "Applied Software Measurement" by Software Productivity Research discusses the impact of crowded offices on software productivity.

14. **Publication support**—Susan Braybrooke's *Design for Research: Principles of Laboratory Architecture* (John Wiley & Sons, 1986) discusses the general concepts of productive office environments. See also Pierre Goumain's *High Technology Workplaces: Integrating Technology, Management, and Design for Productive Work Environments* (Van Nostrand Reinhold, 1989). Capers Jones' book *Programming Productivity— Issues for the Eighties* (IEEE Press, 1986) discusses office space, and includes the landmark study by Gerald McCue, Dean of Architecture at Harvard on the design of IBM's Santa Teresa Programming Laboratory. The same author's two

McGraw-Hill books, *Programming Productivity* (1986) and *Applied Software Measurement* (1991) both discuss the impact of office space on productivity. The best-known recent publication on the impact of office space is *Peopleware* by Tom DeMarco and Tim Lister (Dorset House, 1987). This book has started a whole new school of human-oriented research that is beginning to pervade the software management community, with beneficial results.

15. **Periodical support**—Somewhat surprisingly for such a significant topic, until recently, most software journals have not discussed the impact of office space on software performance at all. This is true of general-purpose periodicals such as Computerworld, Datamation, and Information Week and also special-purpose journals such as CASE Trends, CASE Outlook, IEEE Transactions on Software Engineering, and Software Management News. American Programmer is now starting to run special issues on ergonomics and peopleware related issues, and other major journals should soon follow.

16. **Standards support**—So far as can be determined, there are no known standards by ANSI, DoD, ISO, IEE, IEEE or other standard organizations that deal with optimal or even minimal office arrangements for software professionals. There are of course various health and safety-related standards dealing with access by handicapped personnel, fire alarms and fire exits, smoking facilities, and so forth. These standards are administered by various local, county, state, and federal agencies. However, they are concerned with safety and not with productivity or optimizing human performance.

17. **Professional associations**—None of the major software associations to date have dealt explicitly with crowded office conditions for software professionals.

18. **Effectiveness of known therapies**—Moving staff into bigger quarters is effective, but not at all easy to carry out. The most sophisticated companies have a number of interesting criteria about the physical locations and amenities of their software development facilities. These criteria cover not only office space and noise levels, but also geographic proximity to major universities, airports, and related corporate facilities. Unfortunately, the sagging economic conditions and the downsizing of the computer industry in terms of personnel have more or less stopped ergonomic improvements from occurring, at least for the time being.

19. **Costs of known therapies**—The costs of adequate office space are fairly high: roughly $35 per square foot in several major U.S. urban areas. Indeed, many companies tend to expand from urban areas to rural or suburban areas precisely because the square foot costs decline rapidly outside of urban limits. The productivity gains from adequate office space are not fully known, and the IBM data indicating about 11% improvement is one of the few published benchmarks. The DeMarco and Lister study definitely associated adequate office space with both improved performance and improved morale.

20. **Long-range prognosis**—The problem of crowded office conditions is likely to increase in seriousness for the remainder of the century, under the multiple impacts of the sagging economy, office closings, and consolidation of staff in less expensive offices. Even companies where software staffs are growing, such as the pure software houses like Microsoft face increasing real estate costs that might be troublesome. There is an outside chance that productivity rates may increase rapidly enough to offset this problem, but the probability is only moderate.

There is also a chance that downsizing, layoffs, and shrinkages may continue to occur in the software industry. If so, there will no doubt be an impact on office space availability since whole facilities may be closed and the remaining staff moved to other locations.

11

Error-Prone Modules

1. **Definition**—Modules or components within software systems that receive a disproportionate number of defect reports, such as more than 0.5 defects per Function Point per year after release to users.

2. **Severity**—The average severity of error-prone modules is about a three on the following scale:

   Severity 1: About 5% of the modules in the system are error prone

   Severity 2: About 4% of the modules in the system are error prone

   Severity 3: About 3% of the modules in the system are error prone

   Severity 4: About 2% of the modules in the system are error prone

   Severity 5: About 1% of the modules in the system are error prone

3. **Frequency**—Error-prone modules are strongly correlated with the sizes of systems, and become very serious problems for systems over 5000 Function Points. They seldom occur in applications smaller than 500 Function Points.

4. **Occurrence**—Complex systems software such as operating systems are the most likely to experience error-prone modules, although MIS and military software are not immune to this problem. Specific kinds of systems where error-prone modules have been observed in the past include central office switching systems such as AT&T's ESS5 and ITT's System 12; large operating systems such as MVS and UNIX; large commercial software products such as IBM's IMS. Among the newer application types, client/server applications both tend to have error-prone modules, and it is rather difficult to immunize against them.

5. **Susceptibility and resistance**—Large, complex systems developed without use of structured methods and formal inspections are most susceptible. Small, simple applications seldom have error-prone modules. Near-immunity can result from the use of structured techniques and formal design and code inspections. A formal quality measurement system can immunize companies and projects against error-prone modules. Various kinds of geriatric services for aging software, such as restructuring and re-engineering can also eliminate error-prone modules.

6. **Root causes**—The root causes of error-prone modules have been studied for more than 30 years by companies such as IBM and AT&T, and are now well understood. The root causes include: 1) Failure to measure defect quantities and removal efficiency; 2) Failure to use structured methods; 3) Failure to use formal design and code inspections; 4) Casual changes or updates to master copies of software by developers; 5) Excessive schedule pressure; 6) High complexity levels, which may or may not be necessary; 7) Carelessness or inexperience by management; 8) Carelessness or inexperience by technical staff members.

7. **Associated problems**—Error-prone modules are associated with the problems of *High Maintenance Costs, Missed Schedules, Long Schedules, Cost Overruns, Low User Satisfaction, Low Market Shares, Low Productivity,* and *Low Quality.*

    Error-prone modules themselves are often caused by the problems of *Inexperienced Management, Management Malpractice, Inexperienced Staff, Technical Staff Malpractice, Excessive Schedule Pressure, Inadequate Measurement,* and *Inadequate Quality Estimating.*

8. **Cost impact**—The cost impact of error-prone modules is enormous. Error-prone modules are the most expensive artifacts in all of software, and may cost up to 500% more than a normal module. (Pay once to develop the module originally, pay again to maintain it until it can no longer be updated, pay a third time to redevelop the module on an emergency basis, pay a fourth time to maintain the new version, and pay a fifth time to finally get it right.) Normal modules typically cost from $500 to $1000 per Function Point to develop, and about $125 per year or less to maintain. Error-prone modules will run from $2000 to more than $4000 per Function Point to develop, and maintenance costs can exceed $300 per Function Point per year. To pay several times for a defective product is not a landmark of good business management and explains why software managers often appear less than competent to senior executive management.

9. **Methods of prevention**—For new software systems, error-prone modules are completely preventable, and the success rate of companies such as IBM and AT&T is at or very near 100%. The best prevention is to use carefully structured methods, formal inspections, and formal quality measurement. Formal integration and configuration control, and the prohibition of casual updates by developers after unit tests must also be enforced. Quality estimation tools can predict the probability of having error-prone modules in any given application. Complexity analysis tools which calculate cyclomatic and essential complexity can also be useful in identifying potential error-prone modules. Some complexity analysis tools include specific risk of error-prone modules.

10. **Methods of control**—For existing software, error-prone modules should be isolated and eliminated as quickly as possible. Incoming defect reports from users should be analyzed for "spikes" or modules that receive more than their share of bugs. These candidate modules should then be formally inspected to see if they are true error-prone modules. (About 3% of the modules in any large application

are likely to be error-prone modules.) If they are error-prone modules, then they should be redeveloped, using modern and careful techniques. Restructuring and re-engineering of aging software will help to isolate potential error-prone modules, and in some cases may eliminate them. However, human carelessness is a root cause of this problem. The new concept of Total Quality Management (TQM) or Total Quality Control (TQC) may be effective against error-prone modules, but empirical results have not yet been published. Quality Function Deployment (QFD) is also helpful in deterring error-prone modules, and here the empirical evidence, although still sparse, is favorable. In the future, the ISO 9000–9004 standards may affect the incidence of error-prone modules, but as of 1993 there is no empirical evidence that they do currently. (Indeed, the ISO standards do not mention error-prone modules at all.) As of 1993, there is insufficient data to ascertain the impact of the SEI maturity level concept on error-prone modules, but in theory error-prone modules should be essentially non-existent above Level 2. Indeed, the discovery of error-prone modules in SEI Level 3 or 4 organizations would present a major challenge to the validity of the SEI maturity model itself.

11. **Product support**—A number of commercial tools can analyze the structure and complexity of source codes and highlight areas of unusual complexity. Such areas may not be error-prone, but the probability of error-proneness does rise with increasing complexity. The most widely used forms of complexity analysis center around the concepts of *cyclomatic complexity* and *essential complexity*. These concepts were originally developed by Tom McCabe of McCabe Associates. His company has several products which calculate both forms of complexity. Other companies such as Viasoft and Peat Marwick have adopted the same or similar concepts, however.

A number of commercial estimating tools can predict the likelihood of error-proneness, as derived from the nature of the development process itself. For example, large software projects of more than 1000 Function Points which do not use formal reviews or inspections have a very high probability of containing error-prone modules. Indeed, failure to use inspections on systems larger than 5000 Function Points is an instance of both managerial and technical malpractice.

12. **Consulting support**—Several quality-oriented consulting groups deal with the topic of error-prone modules and their elimination. These groups include Bender & Associates, Computer Power, Ernst & Young, the Quality Assurance Institute, Peat Marwick, Software Productivity Research, and Software Quality Tools.

13. **Education support**—The topic of error-prone modules is seldom covered in the standard curricula of business schools, computer science, or software engineering schools. However, a number of commercial education courses do deal with this topic. Courses offered by Digital Consulting, the Technology Transfer Institute, the Quality Assurance Institute, Computer Power Group, and other management consulting firms discuss error-prone modules. The in-house education programs of many quality-oriented companies such as AT&T, Hewlett Packard, IBM and

Motorola, deal very thoroughly with error-prone modules. Courses on formal design and code inspections are also useful, since inspections have very high levels of efficiency in error-prone module removal.

14. **Publication support**—Two books by the author deal with software quality measurement and estimation and include discussions of error-prone modules: *Programming Productivity* (McGraw-Hill, 1986) deals with the measurement and estimation of quality and discusses error-prone modules. *Applied Software Measurement* (McGraw-Hill, 1991) deals with the topic of establishing quality measurement programs, and also includes current U.S. averages for software quality for military, systems, and MIS software projects which can serve as a benchmark for validating quality estimates. It also explains how to isolate and measure error-proneness.

Two books by Robert Dunn, formerly of ITT, also cover error-prone modules: *Quality Assurance for Computer Software* (McGraw-Hill, 1982) and *Software Defect Removal* (McGraw-Hill, 1984) discuss the frequency of error-prone modules and suggest strategies for their elimination.

Error-prone modules are often associated with higher than average levels of complexity. Horst Zuse's *Software Complexity Methods and Measures* (Walter de Gruyter, 1991) is a massive compendium of 605 pages that covers all aspects of complexity analysis.

Since formal reviews and inspections are the most effective method yet discovered for the elimination of error-prone modules, this topic should be surveyed carefully. Among the titles are: Daniel Freedman and Gerald Weinberg's classic *Handbook of Walkthroughs, Inspections, and Technical Reviews* (Little, Brown and Company, 1982 and Dorset House, 1993). See also Ed Yourdon's *Structured Walkthroughs* (Yourdon Press, 1989).

Other relevant books include Gordon Schulmeyer's *Zero Defect Software* (McGraw-Hill, 1990); Keith A. Jones' *Automated Software Quality Measurement* (Van Nostrand Reinhold, 1993); and Gordon Schulmeyer and James McManus' *Total Quality Management for Software* (Van Nostrand Reinhold, 1992).

What is a surprising gap in the literature is the widespread failure of books on software reliability to touch upon the topic of error-prone modules. Authors of several reliability models were queried as to why they assumed homogeneous distributions of defects, when in fact all empirical evidence indicates a clumping effect. The answers were essentially variants of the assertion that theory and fact sometimes diverge. In any case, an interesting survey of reliability concepts, as well as an actual reliability model, can be found in John D. Musa, Anthony Iannino, and Kazuhira Okumoto's *Software Reliability* (McGraw-Hill, 1987).

15. **Periodical support**—Although error-prone modules were first studied in the 1960's, and have been identified as occurring in essentially all large systems of more than 5000 Function Points in size, this topic is seldom discussed in either standard software journals or even in special purpose journals such as Software Quality Times or the Journal of the American Testing Association.

16. **Standards support**—So far as can be determined in 1992, none of the major quality standards published by ANSI, DoD, IEE, IEEE, or ISO even discuss the existence of error-prone modules. This is a serious omission in quality standards coverage, since the phenomenon of error-prone modules had been observed as early as 1965. The omission is particularly troublesome for the ISO 9000–9004 standards. One would expect such a pervasive standard to at least caution about error-prone modules.

17. **Professional associations**—While many of the software professional associations may have an interest in error-prone modules, none to date has shown signs of directly attacking this serious problem. The most likely organizations to be interested in error-prone modules should be the Society for Software Quality, Society for Information Systems Quality, ISO, SEI, ITAA, and some of the regional software quality groups such as the Atlanta group or the Bay area group in California. However, these organizations seldom broach the topic, probably because serious quality data is in very short supply.

18. **Effectiveness of known therapies**—Error-prone modules appear to be a completely treatable condition, and the effectiveness of the available therapies is at or very near 100%. The only barrier to the total elimination of error-prone modules is inexperience or malpractice of software managers, coupled with excessive schedule pressures and unwise shortcuts.

19. **Costs of known therapies**—The costs of adopting structured methods, formal reviews and inspections, quality measurement, and careful configuration control techniques are fairly low in pure dollar terms. Training costs should amount to about $2000 per manager and staff member. Tools and equipment, such as configuration control tools or restructuring tools, are too variable for convenient generalization, but are not extremely expensive. Error-prone module removal returns value more quickly than almost any other process change: positive value would be returned in less than six months.

20. **Long-range prognosis**—The technologies for preventing and removing error-prone modules were developed in the early 1970's and have been successfully deployed by many leading organizations. The widespread lack of knowledge of error-prone modules, and the widespread lack of software quality measurement systems, indicate that this problem will probably fester and decline only gradually throughout the rest of the century. This is unfortunate, since error-prone modules are a fully treatable condition.

CHAPTER 12

Excessive Paperwork

1. **Definition**—A) Software projects that produce notably more paperwork than is normal for their class and type; B) Software projects that create a total of more than about 50 distinct documents, with page counts of over six pages or 3,000 words per Function Point.

2. **Severity**—The average severity of excessive software paperwork in the U.S. is about a 3 on the following five-point scale:

   Severity 1: More than 6 pages and 3,000 words produced per Function Point

   Severity 2: More than 5 pages and 2,500 words produced per Function Point

   Severity 3: More than 4 pages and 2,000 words produced per Function Point

   Severity 4: More than 3 pages and 1,500 words produced per Function Point

   Severity 5: More than 2 pages and 1,000 words produced per Function Point

3. **Frequency**—Excessive paperwork is rare and almost non-existent for civilian projects under 500 Function Points. (Excessive paperwork is the standard condition for all sizes of military software projects, however.) For large systems of more than 5000 Function Points, excessive paperwork occurs with more than 50% of all such systems.

4. **Occurrence**—Military specifications such as DoD 2167A make excessive paperwork mandatory for U.S. defense projects. The ISO 9000–9004 series of standards may also lead to excessive paperwork. Systems software such as operating systems and telecommunication systems are also prone to excessive paperwork. Commercial software such as Lotus, WordPerfect, and various Microsoft projects are also prone to excessive paperwork. MIS projects, on the other hand, may go in the opposite direction and create a shortage of paperwork. Projects that deal with multiple languages, such as Canadian projects that use both French and English, are highly likely to create excessive paperwork.

5. **Susceptibility and resistance**—All military software in the U.S. is susceptible, and the occurrence of excessive paperwork is very close to 100%. Systems software is also highly susceptible, although companies such as IBM that are aware of the problem sometimes take corrective actions. MIS projects are the least suscepti-

ble, although here too, large MIS projects are rather susceptible. Projects that use Systems Development Methodologies (SDM's) dating from the 1970's and 1980's tend to produce excessive paperwork. The Information Engineering (IE) method also tends to produce excessive paperwork.

6. **Root causes**—The root causes of excessive paperwork include the following: 1) A commendable desire to ensure that nothing important is omitted from plans and specifications; 2) The large number of words required to express software concepts in natural languages such as English, French, German, etc.; 3) The failure of software engineering to develop effective techniques for expressing software architecture and design without depending heavily on natural language; 4) Lack of understanding, due to lack of widespread measurement, of how expensive paperwork truly is for software projects; 5) The use of "boiler plate" or text that is included because it is required by standards such as 2167A, even though it may be irrelevant; 6) For countries such as Canada, the need to produce specifications and documentation in more than one language; 7) Overcompensating for the many software projects that are underspecified and underplanned.

7. **Associated problems**—Excessive paperwork is associated with the problems of *Low Productivity, Long Schedules, Missed Schedules, Excessive Time to Market,* and *Cost Overruns.* It may also contribute to the problem of *Low Staff Morale.*

    Excessive paperwork itself is often attributed to the problems of *Inadequate Deliverable Sizing, Inexperienced Management, Inexperienced Staff, Inadequate Methodologies, Inadequate Measurement,* and *Inadequate Cost Estimating.* (Note that one of the glaring deficiencies of the LOC and KLOC metrics is that they produce paradoxical results when used for paperwork studies.)

8. **Cost impact**—The term "paperwork" includes the sum of planning documents, requirements, specifications, defect-removal documents, user documentation, and training materials. More than 50 discrete document types are associated with large civilian software projects. Sometimes more than 100 document types are associated with large military software projects. (At their peak, military projects can create twice as many documents as similar civilian projects, and each document can be twice as large.) The cost impact of excessive paperwork is among the largest in the entire domain of software. For large U.S. military software projects, about 52% of the total costs goes to paperwork and about 400 English words are written for every Ada statement. Military projects spend about twice as much on paperwork as they do on coding. Large civilian systems software, such as operating systems and switching systems, run about 35% of total costs for paperwork which is often greater than the cost of coding. Even for MIS projects, paperwork costs can exceed 25% of total costs. Note that about one-third of the pages in software specifications and user documentation may contain graphics or an illustration.

9. **Methods of prevention**—Measurement of the quantity, cost, and usefulness of paperwork produced is an effective prevention. IBM carried out controlled studies on the contents and usefulness of various software documents, and found that to

be an effective preventive activity. The size and costs of maintenance documentation, for example, were reduced at the same time that usability was improved. Using a software cost estimating tool that can predict paperwork volumes and costs is also a good preventive method.

At several Bold Stroke sessions, the topic of excessive military paperwork was brought up to some ranking officers and civilian Department of Defense personnel. There is some interest in reducing the volume of military paperwork, but this will not be an easy task.

It has been hypothesized that the high volume of military paperwork, which visibly slows down development, may improve either software quality or maintenance productivity. The quality hypothesis appears to be untrue, since several other kinds of software are equal to military software in quality and achieve their results with 50% or less of the volume of military paperwork (i.e. computer manufacturers, telecommunication manufacturers, and medical instrument manufacturers achieve quality levels as good as those found in military software, but with less than half of the total page counts of paperwork).

There is insufficient data as of 1993 to ascertain whether the maintenance hypothesis is true. This topic deserves more research.

New multi-media technologies, hypertext, and other advanced methods of communicating technical information can be expected to change the nature of software documentation in profound ways. As of 1993, it is premature to know how soon these changes will occur, and how beneficial they may be.

10. **Methods of control**—For military projects that are constrained to follow military standards such as 2167A, there is no easy way to avoid excessive paperwork. A long-range strategy of revising 2167A may be effective in the distant future. For civilian projects, a review of software specification and documentation practices every two years is an effective control. Some companies such as IBM also establish size and content targets for major specification and documentation types, after having discovered that inexperienced personnel tend to create larger documents than necessary. Reusable specifications and reusable documentation can be very effective, although this technology is still quite new. Note that if you must produce large quantities of paperwork, then formal and automated configuration control becomes a logical necessity.

11. **Product support**—Predicting paperwork volumes and types should be a standard estimating function, but as of 1993 only a few software estimators can do this. When selecting an estimating tool, it is useful to demand that it have powerful paperwork estimation capabilities. Project planning tools can assist in the schedules and production steps for software paperwork, but have no impact on size or contents.

As might be expected, since military specifications are a root cause of excessive paperwork, the military environment has several special-purpose documentation production and control tools that assist in the production of the voluminous paperwork associated with standards such as 2167A. Examples of such tools include DocEXPRESS from Advanced Technologies Applications (ATA), the 2167A Tool Set from Advanced Systems Technology, and the Automatic Documentation Generator from Software Systems Design. These tools are available as stand-alone support tools, or in some instances as functional units of CASE tools. The ATA document tools, for example, are available under CADRE Teamwork.

Military software constitutes only about 22% of the U.S. total of software projects. Areas in the civilian sector, such as information systems, systems software (operating systems and switching systems), scientific applications, process control, spreadsheets, and word processors, documentation templates are unavailable as of 1993. Templates are also unavailable for the European ISO 9000 through 9004 standards, which cause the creation of a document set that rivals U.S. military standards in volume and quantity of plans and documents.

Several companies such as Interleaf in Boston and Frame Technology in San Jose have built special applications for producing technical documentation for engineering projects. These typically integrate text and graphics, and also support indexing, cross references, updating, and other revision services.

Several CASE vendors, in addition to CADRE, have announced plans for extended paperwork production capabilities, but other than support for military specifications, little is commercially available as of 1993 except basic text, drawing, and storage capabilities. The concept of general-purpose "templates" or standard outlines for common documentation and plan types is not yet a part of the majority of CASE tool suites.

Major civilian software projects are surrounded by more than 50 discrete document types, when development plans, test plans, marketing plans, documentation plans, education plans, budgets, cost estimates, reference manuals, and tutorial materials are aggregated. For military software, the total quantity can also exceed 50 document types, and each document may be twice as large as its civilian counterpart.

There is a strong and urgent need for outlines, content guidelines, and human-factors analysis of the appropriate mixture of text, graphic, and tabular material that will combine optimum usability with optimum completeness.

While standard word processors, project management tools, and drawing programs are obviously used for software paperwork, there is a need for much more robust capabilities which also include full configuration control and backwards traceability.

While many software text documents use word processors, very few make use of grammar checkers or complexity analysis tools. Usage of such tools should become standard, since extracting meaning from convoluted text is one of the more difficult human endeavors associated with software.

The topic of paperwork volumes, and the mix of text, graphic, and tabular materials is also a factor in planning for software repositories. Preliminary analysis of this topic leads to some potentially alarming conclusions. Given the volume of information created today in support of software projects, a full repository of *all* software information for a major organization such as AT&T, IBM, or the Department of Defense may require truly enormous storage volumes.

It can be hypothesized that magnetic storage might be inadequate, and that a relational data base may not be a suitable host for the mixture of text, graphics, and non-standard information that is needed in a full repository. From preliminary analysis, it appears that optical storage and object-oriented data bases may be needed for a full repository, coupled with very advanced configuration control facilities, cross-referencing hypertext facilities, and other state-of-the-art features.

12. **Consulting support**—A number of consulting organizations offer support in producing various kinds of plans and specifications, normally specializing in either military or civilian protocols (but not both). Examples of such consulting groups include Mapping, Inc.; Comtech, and the Document Design Center. The Document Design Center, incidentally, is an example of an independent testing laboratory for usability. Comparatively few consulting groups take the position that paperwork is a major cost element which must be under full management and technical control. The SPR assessment deals explicitly with paperwork volumes and control techniques.

13. **Education support**—Most software engineering and business schools deal with paperwork, if at all, in a rudimentary fashion. Several commercial courses such as "Applied Software Measurement" by Digital Consulting and Software Productivity Research deal explicitly with measuring paperwork volumes and costs. Other commercial education vehicles dealing with documentation include courses taught by Comtech, Mapping, Inc., and the AT&T Information Applications Architecture Center.

Internal education within major corporations such as AT&T and IBM are often better than university education for dealing with this topic. AT&T, for example, has a whole curriculum and video courses available on software documentation.

14. **Publication support**—James Martin's and Carma McClure's excellent book, *Diagramming Techniques for Analysts and Programmers* (Prentice-Hall, 1985), is a useful overview of technical specification approaches, but does not cover planning or support paperwork. Two books by Capers Jones, Chairman of SPR, deal with the volumes of software paperwork. *Programming Productivity* (McGraw-Hill, 1986) deals with the quantity of paperwork for various software projects. *Applied Software Measurement* (McGraw-Hill, 1991) deal with the topic of measuring software paperwork, and also includes current U.S. averages for software paperwork for military, systems, and MIS software projects.

Since DoD and government mandates tend to be a fountain of excessive paperwork requirements, it is appropriate to cite William Roetzheim's *Developing Software To Government Standards* (Prentice Hall, 1991). This is a somewhat depressing tour through a host of government standards, which though well intentioned, collectively cause the creation of more paperwork than any other source in human history.

There are quite a number of books on documentation creation, but these seldom include information on the costs and volume of software paperwork. A few examples include Simpson and Casey's *Developing Effective User Documentation* (McGraw-Hill, 1992); and Baeker's *Human Factors and Typography for More Readable Programs* (Addison Wesley, 1992).

For a preview of what may be forthcoming when multimedia approaches and optical storage become substitutes for paper, Gregory Nielson, Bruce Shriver, and Lawrence Rosenblum's *Scientific Visualization* (IEEE Press, 1990) is an excellent overview.

15. **Periodical support**—The general-purpose software journals such as Datamation, Software Magazine, Information Week, and Computerworld seldom discuss this topic. There are many specialized periodicals for publishing, but they are primarily concerned with production of documents and not the folly of having so much extraneous information produced. The ACM special interest group (SIGDOC) publishes a journal entitled Asterisk. One periodical, Business Documents, deals explicitly with forms and paperwork creation for the business world and fills a useful niche. The military journals, who should at least discuss the topic occasionally since DoD standards are a root cause of the problem, are remarkably silent on this topic.

16. **Standards support**—Unfortunately, international standards are a root cause of excessive paperwork. Both DoD 2167A and ISO 9000–9004 tend to cause excessive volumes of "boilerplate" or text that is required but not utilized.

17. **Professional associations**—None of the major professional associations have addressed the problem of excessive paperwork for software projects. Most appear unaware that there is such a problem. Associations such as the Society for Technical Communication and the Society for Documentation Professionals in the Boston area are interested in the problem of excessive paperwork, but are primarily concerned with other issues. The ACM has a special-interest group on software documentation, and publishes an associated journal. SEI may explore software paperwork in the future, since that is a major cost driver for military software. As of 1993, however, excessive documentation costs are not a factor in the well-known SEI process assessment method.

18. **Effectiveness of known therapies**—For civilian projects, a careful analysis of paperwork requirements coupled with size and content guidelines can reduce overall paperwork expenses by more than 25% and improve clarity and usability at the same time. For military projects, it is difficult to make any near-term improvement. Intermittent attempts by the U.S. Federal Government to reduce paperwork, ironically, tend to create more paper than they save.

Object-oriented analysis and design methods may, in the future, have a beneficial impact on software paperwork via reusability. However, this is only speculation and there is no empirical evidence as yet.

19. **Costs of known therapies**—Estimating tools that can predict paperwork volumes and costs are in the $5,000 to $20,000 range. Although their paperwork capabilities

are useful, such tools would normally not be cost justified on the basis of paper-work estimation alone. The costs of actually reducing paperwork are not excessive: perhaps two or three months of staff time to study the situation and create paperwork reduction guidelines: perhaps $20,000 in burdened labor costs. Such a study would normally return its value on a single project of more than 5,000 Function Points in size, or when amortized across several smaller projects. A study of paperwork reduction could also be carried out by external consultants, usually with shorter time schedules but higher costs.

On-line documentation produced by word-processors and by some CASE tools can reduce the cost of document preparation, but has no impact on the contents and volume of documentation. (Some CASE tools even go in the opposite direction, and cause the creation of more documentation.)

The costs of a full software repository with associated configuration control is currently unknown, but likely to be extremely costly. If every software project in a large company such as IBM or AT&T fully utilized a repository for every document, and included both text, graphics, images, and other representations, the volume of storage would be so large as to tax the capacity of current data base products.

Software paperwork and documentation may be affected in profound ways by the advent of graphical user interfaces, multi-media applications, and integrated audio capabilities. It is premature to judge the effect of these technologies, but potentially at least they can substantially replace ordinary paper documents.

In the early 1980's, ITT built an experimental CASE work station that envisioned all information to be available on-line, without any paper documentation except at the option of the user. It was quickly noted that windows on the primary display were not suitable, since the windows tended to overlay and conceal the work at hand.

The experimental ITT work station featured a battery-powered secondary documentation display unit that was about the size of a hard-cover book (the new Sony Data Diskman is similar in concept, but slightly smaller than the ITT prototype).

With integral search features and a mix of high-resolution graphics and text, this experimental unit compared favorably with paper documents in terms of ease of use, learning speed to master software applications, ergonomics, and portability.

The use of optical storage was also environmentally beneficial, since paperwork associated with software utilizes a tremendous quantity of pulp and wood products. Further, with optical storage as the preferred medium, even storage costs were appreciably below those of paper. This is perhaps a preview of how documentation might be dealt with by the end of the century.

20. **Long-range prognosis**—Unfortunately, the short-range prognosis for this problem shows every sign of getting worse rather than better. Both the new ISO standards and the drafts of the new military standards are calling for *more* paperwork rather than less. While optical storage, hypertext, and multi-media will affect and benefit this problem, it is uncertain exactly how soon the impacts will occur.

Excessive paperwork will probably remain at serious levels for large systems, and for all military software projects, for the remainder of the century. There is a fair chance that optical devices, multi-media, and other advanced technologies can move more quickly, but their success depends upon market acceptance of some rather innovative new ideas.

13

Excessive Schedule Pressure

1. **Definition**—A) Coercive demands by software clients to deliver software applications in a shorter time period than is technically achievable; B) Coercive demands by software executives or project managers to deliver code, specifications, or documentation in a shorter time period than is technically possible.

2. **Severity**—The average severity of excessive schedule pressure is about a 3 on the following five-point scale:

   Severity 1: Schedule pressure causes project cancellation and staff termination

   Severity 2: Schedule pressure causes project cancellation and low morale

   Severity 3: Schedule pressure causes low quality, low morale, excessive overtime, and schedule delays

   Severity 4: Schedule pressure causes low quality, low morale, and overtime

   Severity 5: Schedule pressure causes low quality and overtime

3. **Frequency**—Excessive schedule pressure is the most common of all serious software engineering problems. It has been observed in about 75% of all MIS software projects larger than 1000 Function Points in size. For projects larger than 5000 Function Points in size, the frequency approaches 90% and is roughly equal among MIS, contract, commercial, systems, and military software projects.

4. **Occurrence**—Excessive schedule pressure is endemic to the software industry, and will probably remain so as long as software remains a labor-intensive occupation based on skilled human effort. Information systems software, military software, and systems software are all similarly prone to excessive schedule pressure.

5. **Susceptibility and resistance**—Small software projects of less than 100 Function Points in size are normally immune from excessive schedule pressure. Software projects where schedules are set cooperatively among clients, managers, and technical staffs are comparatively resistant. Software projects where schedules are derived using both automated estimating and planning tools are comparatively

resistant. Software projects where functional metrics are used to measure creeping user requirements are also relatively resistant.

Software projects where schedules are set by arbitrary or irrational methods are most susceptible. Projects where schedules are set before requirements are defined are highly susceptible. Projects where creeping user requirements are not or cannot be controlled are highly susceptible. Projects larger than 1000 Function Points in size which use only manual estimating techniques are highly susceptible. Projects where project managers lack estimating tools, planning tools, or both, are susceptible. Both susceptibility and severity rise with increasing project sizes.

6. **Root causes**—The root causes for excessive schedule pressure can be divided into two sets: 1) Factors associated with the way initial schedules are determined; 2) Factors associated with the long schedules that are endemic to large software projects.

The primary causes for excessive schedule pressure resulting from faulty derivation include irrational schedules set by arbitrary means long before the technical content of the project is known. Another root cause is the attempt to develop schedules for large and complex software projects manually, without using estimating or planning tools. For projects larger than 5000 Function Points, manual planning and estimating can be considered malpractice. Another root cause deals with the whole proposal and contracting cycle: unless optimistic schedules are included, there is a strong probability that a contractor will not be awarded the job. Yet another root cause is the paucity of accurate historical data on the observed schedules of completed projects. As of 1993, accurate historical data is kept on less than 10% of U.S. software projects, within less than 5% of U.S. software-producing enterprises. Following are the average schedules from requirements to delivery, and the average gaps between actual and anticipated delivery dates:

Project Size (Function Points)	Anticipated Schedule	Actual Schedule	Difference
10	1 month	1 month	0
100	6 months	6 months	0
1000	12 months	18 months	6 months
10000	36 months	60 months	24 months

It is obvious that excessive schedule pressure correlates strongly to the overall size of the software being constructed, since the difference between anticipation and actuality grows with overall size.

A totally unexpected root cause for excessive schedule pressure is that some managers and technical staff members like working under pressure. Tight schedules and high-pressure situations augment the psyche and make the work seem important.

Under the second topic, or lengthy schedules for software projects, this is a natural byproduct of the way software is currently developed. Software in 1993 is primarily a skilled craft, where the artifacts are constructed by hand. In addition, creeping user requirements are endemic to the software industry. All products constructed manually in conjunction with creeping requirements are slow to be completed.

7. **Associated problems**—Excessive schedule pressure is a significant contributor to the problems of *Low Staff Morale* and *High Staff Turnover*. Schedule pressure is also observed on a majority of *Canceled Projects* and those with *Cost Overruns*. Excessive schedule pressure is a main contributor to the problem of *Low Quality*.

    Excessive schedule pressure is often caused by *Creeping User Requirements, Inadequate Estimating, Inadequate Measurement, Inadequate Planning,* and *Management Malpractice*.

8. **Cost impact**—The direct costs of excessive schedule pressure are difficult to measure, since one of the byproducts of schedule pressure is a massive amount of unpaid overtime, sometimes exceeding 30 hours per week! An indirect cost of excessive schedule pressure is that of low quality. The number of bugs reported in the first year of customer usage on projects where excessive schedule pressure was present can be up to four times higher than normal. This phenomenon can raise the first year defect repair costs to over $200 per Function Point, as opposed to less than $50 per Function Point for more carefully developed software.

9. **Methods of prevention**—There are five major preventive techniques for avoiding excessive schedule pressure: 1) Use of commercial-grade software project estimating tools (of which there are about 50 on the U.S. market); 2) Use of commercial grade project planning tools (of which there are about 70 on the U.S. market); 3) Using functional metrics to quantify and control growth in user requirements; 4) Accurate historical data collection and measurement of project schedules, so that future projects can be more rationally scheduled; 5) Utilization of reusable materials which minimize the labor content of software applications. A total of 9 kinds of reusability are possible: architectures, code, data, design, documentation, estimates, human interfaces, plans, and test materials.

10. **Methods of control**—Unfortunately, by the time excessive schedule pressure becomes visible it is usually too late to control it, because the project is already in serious trouble. The only control mechanism that seems to work is reducing the functions of the software, or delaying some functions to a future release. Adding staff members is occasionally effective, but often bringing the new staff up to speed sets the project schedule back rather than accelerating it.

11. **Product support**—Many software estimating tools such as ASSET-R, the Bridge, CHECKPOINT®, COCOMO, ESTIMACS, PCOC, REVIC, SEER, SLIM, SOFTCOST, and SPQR/20 have scheduling capabilities. Essentially all general-purpose project planning tools such as Artemis, the Harvard Project Manager, Project Manager's Workbench, Microsoft Project, Superproject, and Timeline, can deal with schedule-related topics. Failure to use such tools on software projects larger than 5000 Function Points should be considered an instance of management malpractice.

12. **Consulting support**—When schedules are suspect on major software projects, either a project audit or a project assessment can identify causes and recommend therapies. That is not quite the same as identifying excessive schedule pressure. For example, the well-known SEI assessment method deals with secondary manifestations such as the usage of estimating tools. Management consultants who deal with morale and personnel implications are most likely to observe and comment on excessive schedule pressure.

13. **Education support**—Many academic institutions do not deal with excessive schedule pressure as a formal topic in either software engineering or business courses. Commercial courses on project management, planning, and estimation may cover this topic from time to time. Examples of such courses are those offered by the Atlantic Systems Guild, Digital Consulting, Computer Power, Quantitative Software Management (QSM), and Software Productivity Research (SPR).

14. **Publication support**—John Boddie's *Crunch Mode: Building Effective Systems on a Tight Schedule* (Yourdon Press, 1992) is a good treatment on surviving excessive schedule pressure. Robert Charette's *Software Engineering Risk Analysis and Management* (McGraw-Hill, 1989) and *Application Strategies for Risk Analysis* (McGraw Hill, 1990) are useful. Dr. Barry Boehm's *Software Risk Management* (IEEE Press, 1989) is useful. Fred Brooks' *The Mythical Man-Month* (Addison Wesley, 1982) should be required reading. DeMarco and Lister's well-known book *Peopleware* (Dorset House, 1987) deals with some of the sociological implications of excessive schedule pressure. The author, Capers Jones' book *Applied Software Measurement* (McGraw-Hill, 1991) contains U.S. averages for software project schedules, anticipated project schedules, and the gap between the two. It also discusses schedule pressure. The author, Capers Jones' monograph *Critical Problems in Software Measurement* (IS Management Group, 1993) discusses the problems of measuring schedules where activities are overlapped and partially concurrent. Dr. Roger Pressman's book *Software Engineering: A Practitioner's Approach* (McGraw-Hill, 1982) has some interesting remarks on scheduling myths. Dr. Larry Putnam's *Measures for Excellence* (Yourdon Press, 1992) also has useful advice and information. Tarek Abdel Hamid and S.E. Madnick's *Software Project Management* (Prentice Hall, 1992) has much to recommend it.

15. **Periodical support**—There are no software magazines or journals that deal explicitly with schedule pressures. Most of the general software journals have intermittent articles about specific projects where the schedules were unusually long or short.

16. **Standards support**—There are no known standards by ANSI, DoD, IEE, IEEE, or ISO that establish normal delivery schedules for software projects of known sizes, or define excessive schedule pressure.

17. **Professional associations**—Most professional associations do not deal with excessive schedule pressure. In Europe and Canada where programmers often

belong to unions, union policy may affect excessive schedule pressure. Several associations deal with schedule measurement and prediction: The International Society of Parametric Analysts (ISPA) and the International Function Point Users Group (IFPUG) both cover software schedules in almost every meeting and conference. SCEA, or the Society of Software Estimating and Cost Analysis may deal with schedule pressure from time to time. The well-known SEI software risk conferences may have papers or presentations on the risk of schedule pressures.

18. **Effectiveness of known therapies**—Schedule estimation is now a standard feature of essentially all commercial-grade software estimating tools and also of general-purpose project planning tools. However, when these tools yield estimates that are notably longer than client, executive, or contractual expectations, they will often be disregarded. Nonetheless, failure to use such tools on projects over 5000 Function Points can be viewed as an instance of management malpractice.

19. **Costs of known therapies**—Expert-system cost estimating tools for software projects start at less than $1000 and run to more than $40,000. Tools with wide U.S. distribution include The Bridge, COCOMO and its clones, ESTIMACS, CHECK-POINT®, PRICE-S, SLIM, SPQR/20, and REVIC (a COCOMO extension). The COCOMO clones are normally the lowest in cost, since COCOMO itself is in the public domain. The other tools are in the $5,000 to $20,000 range. Some estimating tools are embedded in specific CASE tools, such as the IEF or the CGI PACBASE tool suite. Such tools are often bundled, and are not priced separately.

General-purpose project planning tools run from under $200 up to about $10,000 for mainframe-based tools. Examples of such tools include Artemis, Harvard Project Manager, Microsoft Project, the Project Managers' Workbench, Superproject, and Time Line.

20. **Long-range prognosis**—Excessive schedule pressure is not an easy problem to eliminate, and will likely stay prevalent for the rest of the twentieth century. While the technologies of software estimation and planning are sophisticated enough to bring the problem under control, marketing pressure to include optimistic schedule dates in proposals and contracts is rampant. Also, there is still the psychological factor that some people enjoy schedule pressure. There are also problems of malpractice and poor corporate cultures that affect the incidence of excessive schedule pressure.

CHAPTER 14

Excessive Time To Market

1. **Definition**—A) Any new software product that reaches clients significantly after competitive products that perform similar functions; B) Any software product requiring four or more years from requirements until delivery.

2. **Severity**—The average severity of excessive time to market is about a 3.0 on the following scale:

   Severity 1: The product is more than 12 months later than major competitors

   Severity 2: The product is more than 6 months later than major competitors

   Severity 3: The product is more than 3 months later than major competitors

   Severity 4: The product was planned to beat competitors to market, but did not

   Severity 5: The product and its competitors reached market simultaneously

3. **Frequency**—Under definition (A), above, excessive time to market is always a serious concern for systems and commercial software developers. Under definition (B), above, excessive time to market is endemic to carelessly developed systems of over 5,000 Function Points, and can occur intermittently for any application of more than 2,000 Function Points.

4. **Occurrence**—Excessive time to market is a common condition for commercial software producers, and tends to affect most forms of software products including but not limited to operating systems, telecommunication systems, defense systems, embedded software, and end-user software such as word processors, spreadsheets, data bases, and the like. Since embedded software is used in diverse physical devices including home appliances, automobiles, aircraft, PBX systems, cameras, etc. excessive time to market affects other product classes than software alone.

5. **Susceptibility and resistance**—Products that start development after similar competitive products are susceptible, although "clones" that simply mirror competitive features may often overcome this handicap. Any product that does not use careful and automated planning and estimating is susceptible. Any product that attempts to rush to market by skimping on quality control is susceptible. The most resistant

products are those that use fully automated planning and estimating methods, effective quality control methods, and have the highest percentage of reusable components.

6. **Root causes**—The root causes of excessive time to market include: 1) The widespread failure of software product managers to create competent plans and estimates themselves due to lack of training, skill, and automation; 2) Creeping requirements or changes in the scope of a project during development; 3) The widespread failure of software enterprises to establish formal and fully supported product planning and estimating functions; 4) The surprising phenomenon that automated software planning and estimating tools are used on less than 100% of critical software products; 5) The widespread shortage of academic training in software schedule planning and estimation at universities and business schools; 6) The distressing failure of companies and government agencies to measure software projects, including schedules, so that little historical data has readily been available prior to 1991; 7) Carelessness in quality control, so that the project is discovered to have serious problems late in development, during final testing.

7. **Associated problems**—Excessive time to market is a basic contributor to the problems of *Lost Business Opportunities, Friction with Users* and *Friction with Senior Management.* Excessive time to market is a causative factor to the problem of *False Productivity Claims.* It may sometimes be a factor leading to the problem of *Canceled Projects* and *Layoffs and Cutbacks.*

Excessive time to market itself can be attributed to the problems of *Inadequate Cost Estimating, Incomplete Planning, Inadequate Defect Removal, Low Levels of Reusability,* to *Inexperienced Management, Inexperienced Clients, Creeping User Requirements, Management Malpractice,* to *Excessive Schedule Pressure, Inexperienced Staff, Inadequate Methodologies, Inadequate Tools,* and to *Inadequate Measurements* and *Inaccurate Metrics.*

8. **Cost impact**—The cost impact of excessive time to market has both a direct and indirect component. The direct costs are the losses in revenues from the planned day of delivery until the actual day of delivery. Such losses may be unrecoverable. The indirect costs are those of allowing competitors to establish market shares at the expense of the late product. Also, if a schedule slip is public knowledge (such as the delays experienced by Lotus and Microsoft) then there are also indirect costs associated with loss of industry status and prestige and possible litigation.

9. **Methods of prevention**—The prevention of excessive time to market is largely associated with methods for accurate schedule prediction. As of late 1993, there are some 50 commercial software estimating tools and more than 70 software project planning tools marketed commercially in the U.S. The use of such tools by software project managers should be 100% for all strategic or mission-critical software projects. Failure to use automated planning and estimating methods on projects larger than 5000 Function Points should be considered to be management malpractice. The most sophisticated commercial software producers tend to use at

least three different estimating tools simultaneously, and look for convergence or spread among their schedule estimates. Accurate measurement of the schedules of historical projects is another useful preventive measure, although one that takes several years to reach peak effectiveness.

10. **Methods of control**—The control of excessive time to market is largely associated with methods for schedule reduction. Here, formal reusability programs for both design, source code, and other deliverables comprise the most effective current methods. Also, since defect removal is the most expensive and time-consuming activity of software, formal quality control techniques also benefit schedule reduction. Paperwork cannot be omitted from schedule control programs, since the volume and time required for plans, requirements, specifications, and user documents takes longer than coding.

The most widely advertised schedule control methods today are marketed under the generic name of "Computer Aided Software Engineering" or CASE. The CASE industry has had only a moderate impact on schedules when measured accurately. Many of the claims by CASE vendors for enormous productivity gains (10 to 1 or more) appear to be spurious. The technique termed "Rapid Application Development" or RAD also has claims that seem exaggerated, although the RAD method can be useful for prototyping and even for small to medium projects.

The RAD approach may adopt the following pattern: the initial pilot project which uses the RAD concept is fairly successful. Follow-on usage of RAD for larger or more mission-critical projects are less successful, and critical factors such as quality may not be acceptable. In other words, early success with the RAD approach may push its utilization beyond the envelope where its use is beneficial.

Object-oriented methods are also asserted to be schedule control techniques. The support of object-oriented languages such as Objective-C, Smalltalk, and C++ for reusability via methods and inheritance leads to schedule improvements during coding. (Other languages which support reuse include Ada, Visual Basic, and Turbo C. Here too, tangible schedule reductions during coding are noted.) However, there is insufficient data to validate the claims of object-oriented analysis methods, object-oriented data bases, and the front-end object-oriented concepts.

The best current schedule results are associated with careful and automated planning and estimating methods; experienced technical personnel who are supported by adequate levels of capital investment (> $25,000 per staff member), have quiet and private office environments, use CASE tools matched to well-structured techniques; use high-level languages, object-oriented languages, or generators; use quality control techniques, and make use of formal reusability approaches at both the design and coding levels.

11. **Product support**—Most of the 50 or so commercial software estimating tools marketed in the U.S. have schedule estimating capabilities. A curious problem has been noted when such tools are used: when they estimate schedules that are longer than client or management preconceptions, there is a tendency to disregard the estimate and override its output with arbitrary schedules. Some estimating tools

have a built-in knowledge base of thousands of projects, so any project's schedule can be compared against U.S. norms derived from similar projects in terms of class, type, size, and methods.

12. **Consulting support**—Most management consulting groups and individual management consultants are sensitive to time-to-market issues and can perform project audits or project assessments. A significant number can also assist in schedule estimation and time-to-market predictions.

13. **Education support**—Many business schools deal with time-to-market topics, since it is a standard business problem. Software engineering schools occasionally cover this topic, but not in the depth really needed today. Many commercial courses, such as "Controlling Software Projects" by the Atlantic Systems Guild or "Applied Software Measurement" by Software Productivity Research deals explicitly with measuring schedules at the levels of complete projects and individual tasks and activities. They identify the barriers to schedule reduction, and the need to measure overlap among parallel tasks.

14. **Publication support**—John Boddie's *Crunch Mode: Building Effective Systems on a Tight Schedule* (Yourdon Press, 1992) has much to say. Fred Brooks' *The Mythical Man-Month* (Addison Wesley, 1982) is always valuable. Ed Yourdon's *Managing the System Life Cycle* (Yourdon Press, 1988) is relevant. Rob Thomsett's new *Third Wave Project Management* (Yourdon Press, 1993) seeks to integrate the "peopleware" mode of management with the classic project management disciplines. Also of interest is Mike Walsh's *Productivity Sand Traps and Tar Pits: How To Detect and Avoid Them* (Dorset House, 1992). A small book by the American Management Association, Alec Mackenzie's *The Time Trap* (AMA Press, 1990) is of peripheral interest, but intriguing.

Three books by Capers Jones, Chairman of SPR, deal with software schedules and time to market. *Programming Productivity* (McGraw-Hill, 1986) deals with the factors influencing schedules. *Applied Software Measurement* (McGraw-Hill, 1991) deals with the topic of measuring software schedules, and also includes current U.S. averages for software schedules for military, systems, and MIS software projects. *Critical Problems in Software Measurement* (IS Management Group, 1993) discusses the technical challenges of schedule measurement when activities are overlapped and occur in parallel.

Barry Boehm's monumental *Software Engineering Economics* (Prentice-Hall, 1982) deals with schedules and time-to-market issues. Tom DeMarco's excellent *Controlling Software Projects* (Dorset House, 1987) has also become a standard reference. Larry Putnam's new *Measures for Excellence* (Prentice-Hall, 1992) discusses schedule-related topics and time-to-market also.

15. **Periodical support**—While long schedules and the competitive hazards of being late to market are frequently discussed in both general-purpose and specialized journals, there is a remarkable gap in journalistic coverage: seldom are the exact schedules or the specific times to market included. Basic topics including the aver-

age time required to build standard software packages such as word processor, spreadsheets, PBX switching systems, compilers, or accounting systems, are essentially never covered in the software periodicals. Apparently this kind of coverage is too time-consuming and difficult to carry out. The general business magazines often have articles on time-to-market, such as Fortune's article by Brian Dumaine (February 13, 1989) on "How Managers Can Succeed Through Speed."

16. **Standards support**—International standards occasionally include a requirement that schedules will be stated and measured. No known international standard published by ANSI, DoD, IEE, IEEE, or ISO actually sets time-to-market criteria.

17. **Professional associations**—While many manufacturing industry associations are dealing with time-to-market issues, most of the software professional associations are comparatively helpless because they have no idea what a reasonable time to market should be for any given size and type of software product. The two associations that have the greatest insights into schedule related issues are the International Society of Parametric Analysis (ISPA) and the International Function Point Users Group (IFPUG). The Society of Cost Estimating and Analysis (SCEA) is also concerned with time to market. Most of the major professional groups such as the ACM, AMA, IEEE, ITAA, etc. are interested in this problem, and offer special seminars and courses from time to time.

18. **Effectiveness of known therapies**—Schedule estimation is now easy to perform and surprisingly accurate. Estimating tools such as SPQR/20, CHECKPOINT®, SLIM, ESTIMACS, COCOMO, or REVIC (there are about 50 such tools in 1993) can estimate schedules for requirements, design, coding, documentation, and many other activities and tasks. They can also estimate the costs and productivity levels of defect removal activities such as reviews, inspections, and tests. Schedule prediction accuracies to within 10% are now common, and 5% precision is not impossible. Several tools also include "what if" modeling capabilities to explore the impact of improved schedule control methods, and to assess the impact of reuse, alternate methods, high-level languages, and variations in staffing patterns.

A strong caution is indicated. Many of the studies which compare estimating tools to historical data note a significant one-way deviation: the estimated schedules and costs are much greater than the historical data indicates. There is a natural tendency by the authors of such studies to assume that the estimates are in error. However, it often happens that the errors lie in the historical data itself. Many cost and schedule tracking systems "leak" from 35% to more than 50% of the actual effort and activities.

The best results from leading companies in schedule improvement are impressive: projects that miss schedules can be reduced to less than 1%. Average schedule reductions of about 10% per year have been achieved for four to five consecutive years for development. Military and systems software schedule control still lag, and are often 30% to 50% longer than similar MIS projects. In the case of military software, the enormous volume of paperwork required by military specifications such as 2167A make schedule improvement difficult. In the case of systems software, unstable hardware, severe performance constraints, and severe memory constraints tend to affect schedules negatively.

19. **Costs of known therapies**—Expert-system estimation tools with activity-level and task-level schedule prediction capabilities such as the Bridge, SPQR/20, CHECK-POINT®, and ASSET-R, PRICE-S, SLIM or ESTIMACS are in the $5,000 to $20,000 range. (Low-end macro estimating tools are often of lower cost, but also of lower utility than task-level estimating tools, especially for schedule control purposes.) Expert-system estimation tools normally return their value in less than a year when used early in the life cycle for projects larger than 1,000 Function Points, or when amortized across 10 or more smaller projects. Failure to use such tools on projects larger than 5000 Function Points should be considered an example of management malpractice.

Project planning tools, or "project management" tools as they are often called, range from less than $100 to more than $10,000. Examples include Artemis, the Harvard Project Manager, Microsoft Project, the Project Manager's Workbench, Superproject, and Timeline and XPM. Although such tools can be highly valuable for software project control, it should be noted that they work best with experienced project managers. Novices tend to get bogged down or omit critical tasks, and if activities are left out of the plan, then tools cannot overcome the omission.

Schedule reduction techniques vary too widely in cost for convenient generalization, except that formal reuse at the design and coding levels almost always benefits schedules. Capital investment of more than $25,000 per staff member is often observed in enterprises in the upper quartile of U.S. schedule performance levels. Military, systems, and MIS projects typically use different techniques, as do small programs and large systems. Schedule control methods differ for new projects, enhancements, and maintenance projects also. However, since high quality levels tend to correlate with high minimum time to market periods, quality improvement methods are on the critical path to schedule control and are usually cost justified in less than 12 months.

20. **Long-range prognosis**—This problem is hard to predict. The technologies that can compress software project schedules are slowly getting better. The technologies that can predict software schedules are already well-formed and improving rapidly. However, the culture and sociology of software leads to the tendency to jump blindly into irrational scheduling. For more than half of today's software projects, the schedules were set casually or informally by decree or by executive fiat. Essentially the software schedule problem is one of management and client malpractice, and such problems are hard to cure. Probably excessive time to market for software will remain serious for the remainder of the twentieth century.

CHAPTER 15

False Productivity Claims

1. **Definitions**—A) Any assertion by software tool or service vendors to the effect that the acquisition of their products will improve software productivity, when such assertions are not supported by hard, quantitative data; B) Essentially all assertions by tool or service vendors that include phrases such as "10 to 1 improvement" or "more than 100 Function Points per month" as a direct result of acquiring the tool or service; C) Any assertion by software tool or methodology vendors that indicate productivity improvement rates in excess of 25% per year for projects or companies where more than 10 workers are engaged and where reuse is not feasible.

2. **Severity**—The average severity of false productivity claims is about a 3.0 on the following five point scale:

    Severity 1: Assertion has no supporting evidence of any kind

    Severity 2: Assertion is based on incorrect or invalid measurement

    Severity 3: Assertion is based on subjective, anecdotal findings

    Severity 4: Assertion is based on partial life-cycle data

    Severity 5: Assertion is based on extremely small projects

3. **Frequency**—Under Definitions (A), (B), and (C), above, false productivity claims are associated with about 75% of the commercial advertisements and marketing literature published by U.S. CASE, methodology, language, and software tool vendors, based on SPR surveys of advertisements in commercial software journals between 1990 and 1993.

4. **Occurrence**—The advertisements for CASE tools, Information Engineering (IE) methods, Rapid Application Development (RAD), and 4th Generation Languages are all likely to include false productivity claims. CASE tools have the highest incidence of Severity 1 claims. Information Engineering has the highest incidence of Severity 2 claims. RAD has the highest incidence of Severity 3 claims. Fourth-generation languages have the highest incidence of Severity 4 claims. Object-oriented methods

have the highest incidence of Severity 5 claims. Software estimating companies are also prone to Severity 4 false claims in the related area of estimating accuracy.

As an example of how such claims might come about, the author was contacted in 1992 by a CASE vendor who requested permission to use some data for advertising purposes. The draft ad was to be set up along the lines of "Use this tool and you can achieve these results."

The vendor was informed that their product was not included in the data that they wanted to quote. The vendor was then asked a basic question, "Have you ever done a study or commissioned a study on the actual productivity gains which your tool might give?" The vendor's reply was, "No, that would cost too much."

5. **Susceptibility and resistance**—Both software vendors and clients are highly susceptible to false productivity claims. Indeed, the entire software industry and all users are somewhat susceptible to false productivity claims, given the lack of definitive benchmarks prior to 1991. Enterprises with accurate measurement programs are most resistant to false productivity claims.

6. **Root causes**—The root cause of false productivity claims is not, as one might think, simple dishonesty. Many false claims are made sincerely. The root cause has been the general lack of reliable benchmark data prior to 1991, and the historical difficulties of measuring software productivity accurately.

Thus neither vendors nor clients know current U.S. averages for software productivity, or how a given tool, method, or language will affect projects of various sizes, classes, types, and complexity levels. Neither is the rate at which productivity can be improved widely known (about 15% to 25% per year). However, it must be stated that software advertising and marketing personnel do have a tendency to exaggerate their companies' offerings, and this practice is endemic within the software industry.

However, some claims are essentially nothing more than outrageous fabrications: a recent advertisement by a CASE company implied 1000 to 1 improvements in productivity were possible. This ad had no quantification of either the baseline or the actual results—just an ambiguous quote from a nominal "world famous productivity expert." A letter to the company asking for back-up data in support of these claims has not yet been answered.

7. **Associated problems**—False productivity claims are associated with the problems of *Low Productivity, Friction with Senior Management,* the *Silver Bullet Syndrome,* and *Poor Technology Investments.*

False productivity claims are often caused by the problems of *Inadequate Measurement,* and *Inaccurate Metrics.*

8. **Cost impact**—The cost impact of false productivity claims can be divided into direct and indirect components. The direct costs of false productivity claims to clients are the sums of all dollars spent on tools or methods that are ineffective. The indirect costs of false productivity claims are even more significant: lost opportunities, long schedules, and reduced amounts of discretionary capital to spend on tools

and methods that are effective. Even vendors and those who make false productivity claims are damaged. In the case of vendors, the direct revenues resulting from sales must be balanced against the indirect costs of lost business due to customer dissatisfaction. In some instances, false productivity claims can also lead to litigation expenses if either clients or competitors file suit.

9. **Methods of prevention**—Accurate software measurement is the best long-range preventive method. Commercial software estimation tools are also useful preventive methods that can overcome false productivity claims, although care must be exercised to overcome false accuracy claims by estimating vendors. For software vendors themselves, controlled studies and careful measurement of actual client results are effective preventive approaches. Some companies, such as IBM, also have rigorous screening by Quality Assurance and corporate attorneys of all advertising claims to ensure that false productivity claims are not made. Some vendors have user associations which often serve as an effective preventive method.

10. **Methods of control**—The software industry, unlike many other industries such as the pharmaceutical industry, does not have governmental regulation or prohibition of false productivity claims. There are as yet no effective published ethical guidelines for software advertising claims, and no independent consumer or governmental organizations that can validate or challenge productivity claims.

    As of 1993, software is essentially an unregulated industry with no formal canons of ethical conduct. Some of the software industry associations such as ADAPSO (now ITAA), the IEEE, ACM, and ASM, may have established canons of ethical conduct but none have any particular weight or binding status to date. Specific companies such as IBM, UNISYS, and CADRE have established internal controls to eliminate false productivity claims.

11. **Product support**—Most of the 50 or so commercially marketed software estimating tools have both productivity and cost estimation capabilities. These capabilities can be used to model the impact of tools, methodologies, languages, and even office space. Some tools have a built-in knowledge base and a comparison mode, so any project can be compared against U.S. norms derived from similar projects in terms of class, type, size, and methods.

    A new kind of supplemental tool connected with cost estimating tools may have an impact on false productivity claims. It is now possible to measure projects with enough precision to create very accurate "templates" from historical data.

    Within a few years, commercial templates should be available for many kinds of software projects such as operating systems, financial systems, and embedded systems. With widespread availability of templates derived from historical information, true baselines can be used to actually measure the improvements associated with tools, methods, languages, and process changes.

12. **Consulting support**—Consulting organizations associated with specific CASE tool vendors are likely to be biased and unreliable. Independent consultants who are not associated with specific tools or approaches are most likely to be objective.

Look for those who integrate consulting on high quality, high productivity, lowest cost, and shortest schedules with minimum wastage or susceptibility to false productivity claims. Several consulting groups are starting to create industry baselines, but as of 1993 there is no consistency in what the baselines contain.

Several consulting groups are beginning to specialize in software evaluations to determine the replacement costs of software. When a company is sold, or for tax liability calculations, it is useful to have a standard benchmark for comparative purposes. Consulting groups that are tied to accounting enterprises, such as Deloitte Touche, or Coopers & Lybrand may offer such services. Management consulting groups such as Quantitative Software Management (QSM) or Software Productivity Research (SPR) with substantial collections of empirical data may also offer such specialized consulting services.

13. **Education support**—Unfortunately, both U.S. business schools and software engineering schools are close to useless when dealing with false productivity claims. Several commercial courses, such as "Controlling Software Projects" (Atlantic Systems Guild) or "Applied Software Measurement (ASM)" (Software Productivity Research) deal with the subject of measuring software productivity and costs and avoiding false productivity claims.

A course on Function Point Analysis (preferably one certified by IFPUG) is a good preliminary.

14. **Publication support**—There are no known books that deal explicitly with false productivity claims. Tom Forester and Perry Morrison's *Computer Ethics* (MIT Press, 1990) cover a variety of related topics. Two books by Capers Jones deal with software productivity and measured improvement rates. *Programming Productivity* (McGraw-Hill, 1986) deals with the impact of productivity, software costs, and schedules. *Applied Software Measurement* (McGraw-Hill, 1991) deals with the topic of measuring software productivity, and also includes current U.S. averages for software productivity for military, systems, and MIS software projects with an admittedly high margin of error. Since the author's books use the Function Point metric, Dr. Brian Dreger's *Function Point Analysis* (Prentice Hall, 1989) is a good primer. Frank Wellman's *Software Costing* (Prentice Hall, 1992) is also useful background reading. Dick Brandon and Stanley Segelstein's *Data Processing Contracts* (Van Nostrand Reinhold, 1976) is dated but useful. Good background reading can be found in a book that has nothing to do with software but quite a lot to do with false claims of one kind or another: Charles Mackay's *Extraordinary Popular Delusions and the Madness of Crowds* (Crown Publishers, 1980).

15. **Periodical support**—Coverage of false productivity claims by software journals is unsatisfactory, and the situation cries out for a canon of ethical behavior. As of 1993, there is essentially no validation of either advertisements about productivity improvements or articles dealing with this topic. The software industry would be greatly benefited by a non-profit organization similar to Consumer Reports that assessed the productivity and quality claims of tool and methodology vendors.

16. **Standards support**—As of 1993, software has no effective canons of ethical behavior, no monitoring for malpractice, and no international standards which deal with the subject of false productivity claims.

17. **Professional associations**—As of 1993, none of the major professional associations such as the ACM, ADAPSO (now ITAA), the DPMA, the IEEE and so forth have taken an effective stand on false advertising, or on ethical issues of any type. This is not as it should be if software aims at becoming a true profession.

18. **Effectiveness of known therapies**—Software measurement is a very effective therapy against false advertising claims, but takes several years for the effectiveness to reach full potency. Software estimating tools such as SPQR/20, CHECK-POINT®, COCOMO, REVIC, SLIM, ASSET-R, PRICE-S, ESTIMACS (there are about 50 such tools) can be effective when used to assess false productivity claims. However, care must be exercised in dealing with false accuracy claims by estimating vendors themselves. For products and methods with user associations, contacting experienced users is a very effective preventive method against false productivity claims.

    One major problem must be addressed: As of 1993, any vendor that does not make false productivity claims may be at a competitive disadvantage in markets where similar products are being advertised with false productivity claims. For example, if Vendor A carries out a carefully controlled study and proves that his CASE Tool A can actually improve productivity by 15%, that vendor will be at a disadvantage if Vendor B asserts, without proof, that CASE Tool B can improve productivity by 1000%. This problem makes it difficult for the industry to stamp out false productivity claims piecemeal. Unless all false claims can be stopped simultaneously, accurate and truthful claims will be at a disadvantage.

19. **Costs of known therapies**—Membership in user associations is the least-cost therapy against false productivity claims. Expert-system estimation tools with the ability to predict the productivity impacts of tools, methods, and languages are in the $5,000 to $20,000 range. They normally return their value on a single project when used early in the life cycle as maintenance estimators for projects larger than 1000 Function Points, or when amortized across 10 or more smaller projects. Establishing a productivity measurement program, which is the most effective known therapy, can have costs that approximate 2% of a typical software R&D budget. However, a 2% investment in measurement can prevent wasted expenses for ineffective tools and methods that don't work. Thus the costs of a measurement program can be recovered in perhaps 24 to 36 months by reductions in the money that might be wasted on ineffective productivity improvements.

20. **Long-range prognosis**—This problem is likely to remain severe for the remainder of the 20th century. Unless there is a voluntary adoption of ethical standards, or forced adoption via legislation or litigation for false advertising, the problem is likely to continue unchecked. As of 1993, the forces of the software industry are making the problem worse instead of better. Any tool or methodology vendor is

faced with competitive claims of "10 to 1" or "20 to 1" improvement. If Vendor A behaves ethically and does not advertise false claims, while Vendor B does, there is a strong chance that the sale would go to Vendor B since most clients are incapable of evaluating the truth of any given claim.

CHAPTER 16

Friction Between Clients and Software Contractors

1. **Definition**—A) Enmity or personal antagonism which occurs between clients and software contractors as a result of misunderstandings, unanticipated changes in the scope of the contract, missed or delayed delivery, or some other point of dispute that polarizes the clients and contractors into opposing camps; B) Enmity within an organization between clients of a software development or maintenance group and the managers or personnel within the software group.

2. **Severity**—Friction between software clients and developers is endemic to the industry, and is often acute. The average severity of this problem is about a 3.5 on the following five-point scale:

   Severity 1: Friction leads to contract termination and to litigation

   Severity 2: Friction leads to litigation although contract continues

   Severity 3: Friction leads to contract termination without completion

   Severity 4: Friction leads to contract penalties or serious disputes

   Severity 5: Friction leads to mutual distrust and dislike

3. **Frequency**—Friction between clients and contractors appears to be endemic to the human condition, and is found in many kinds of activities. For example, friction between contractors and home owners is quite common.

   For software contracts, friction occurs with both fixed-price contracts and also time and materials contracts, although the origins differ. For fixed-price contracts, feelings by the contractors that the clients have arbitrarily changed the scope of the contract is the normal seed for friction. The incidence of friction with fixed-price contracts is about 65%. For time and materials contracts, feelings by the client that the contractor is arbitrarily running over estimated costs is the normal seed. The incidence of friction with time and materials contracts is about 50%. In both cases, friction is more likely for large contracts (in excess of $100,000) than for small.

For international contracts where the work is performed in another country, such as India, Singapore, Russia, etc. data is still quite preliminary, since the number of such contracts is comparatively small. Friction to date seems to occur in something over 50% of these international outsource arrangements. International differences in culture and work ethic often exacerbate international business arrangements. (Interestingly, friction on contracts within Japan and between Japanese companies seem to have a lower than average incidence of friction. However, contracts between Japanese companies and U.S. or European companies seem to have a higher than average incidence of friction.)

For internal software, developed within a corporation or government agency for its own purposes, friction is strongly correlated with size: it is much more common for large systems (5000 Function Points and up) and for large enterprises (500 software personnel and up) than for smaller projects and smaller enterprises. It is interesting that friction within a company is sometimes just as severe as friction between companies. In one classic confrontation, the engineering function of an aerospace corporation refused to utilize any services of either the data center or software development group of their own corporation, on the grounds that external clients were receiving preferential treatment and getting better service than employees of the company itself.

For outsource contracts where entire software responsibility is taken over by a contracting organization, data is still preliminary since the number of such contracts is comparatively small. Friction to date seems to be observed in about 40% of such outsource arrangements.

For facilities-management contracts, where data centers and other software functions are operated by contracting organizations, friction is observed in about 40% of such arrangements.

4. **Occurrence**—Friction is much more likely to occur for large contracts than for small. Thus on contracts whose value is larger than $100,000 and for systems whose size is greater than 5000 Function Points, the probability of friction rises steeply. It is also interesting that friction occurs very often when both the client and the contracting organization are fairly large enterprises, with total employment of several hundred each. What makes this surprising is that large enterprises usually have resident attorneys and formal contract management groups. It is possible that for large companies both sides are determined to protect their ends of the arrangement so that friction becomes almost automatic. Smaller organizations often have more flexibility than large.

Friction is also very likely to occur on contracts that have stringent penalty clauses or unusual aspects connected with them than it is on "normal" contracts.

5. **Susceptibility and resistance**—So far as can be determined, the incidence of friction between clients and contractors is more or less equal for military software, systems software, and information systems software.

The kinds of contractual arrangements that seem most resistant to friction are those where the contracting group has done the same kind of software many times, and hence has a firm grasp on schedules, costs, and other critical dimensions. Examples of the kinds of contracts that tend to be more resistant to friction than most are specialized software houses, such as those who build compilers under contract, those who build telecommunications software under contract, and so forth.

Contracts where the work is performed on the customer's premises, rather than remotely at the contracting location, tend to be somewhat more resistant than normal. Indeed, the incidence of friction in this situation drops below 30%.

The kinds of contractual arrangements that seem most susceptible to friction are those where both the clients and the contractors are jumping into new and uncertain kinds of applications where neither side has much prior experience.

Many large corporations have contract administration departments and full-time legal staffs that prepare and review contracts. The incidence of friction between clients and contractors appears to be higher than average for such enterprises. There appears to be a tendency for contract administration groups to perhaps be overzealous, and thereby exaggerate any tendency towards friction.

6. **Root causes**—Friction between clients and contractors is endemic and occurs for software, hardware, construction, and all other contracts where the contracting party builds a product to meet the needs of clients.

For software contracts, there seem to be two discrete sets of root causes: those triggered by the contractor, and those triggered by the client. Both can lead to bad feelings or even to litigation.

The root causes triggered by contractors include: 1) Promising delivery dates that are impossible; 2) Bidding artificially low costs with the expectation of modifying the contract if it is received; 3) Bidding on projects where the contractor has no skills or capabilities; 4) Developing products which have low quality; 5) Missing commitments; 6) Providing inaccurate or inadequate status reports.

The root causes triggered by clients include: 1) Demanding impossible delivery dates; 2) Adding new requirements after the contract is issued, but demanding that the contract price and schedule remain unchanged; 3) Omitting quality or acceptance criteria from the contract itself; 4) Insufficient or ineffective monitoring of the contract's progress.

It has often been noted that the United States is a highly litigious country, and possesses the largest number of attorneys of any country in all human history. This phenomenon is relevant, but the origins and impact go beyond the scope of this book. It should be noted that the cost of litigation is a major component of U.S. business expense.

Other countries, such as Japan, have far fewer attornies and far less frequent litigation.

7. **Associated problems**—Friction between contractors and clients is often associated with the problems of *Litigation Expenses,* and *Low User Satisfaction.* There are

also secondary correlations, such as those of *Low Management Morale,* and *High Management Attrition Rates.* There is also an association with *Low Staff Morale* and *High Staff Attrition Rates* although these problems are more indirect.

Friction itself is often caused by *Creeping User Requirements* on the client side, and by *False Productivity Claims* or *Missed Schedules,* or *Cost Overruns* on the contracting side. Both sides may be affected by the *Silver Bullet Syndrome* or by *Management Malpractice*

8. **Cost impact**—The costs of friction between clients and contractors is very difficult to quantify along general lines. If the friction reaches the point of actual litigation, then it becomes the most expensive single problem in modern business. If the friction leads to refusal to pay for the product, or to pay for some agreed to phase of development, then the contractor has clearly accrued costs and lost revenue. If the friction leads to the contractor adding unplanned creeping functions to meet the demands of the client, then the project will probably run at a loss. This too is expensive. The magnitude of costs associated with friction between clients and contractors are among the top cost items of doing business. There are also secondary and derivative costs, of which the most visible would be associated with high attrition rates, and the direct costs of replacing departing software managers and personnel who left because of contractual disputes with clients.

9. **Methods of prevention**—There are several methods which can minimize the probability of friction between clients and contractors, if thoughtfully applied. A good legal staff or use of corporate counsel trained in the domain of software is both an obvious and an excellent beginning. The Joint Application Design (JAD) methodology, whereby clients and development personnel work together on requirements, has proven to be quite effective. The related topic of Quality Function Deployment (QFD) whereby clients and development personnel work jointly on the quality aspects of the product has also proven to be effective. Prototyping aspects of software applications can be effective, but this method may backfire if clients expect the final product to be built as rapidly as the prototype. The use of Function Points is remarkably effective in minimizing creeping requirements, since this metric can be used to show the exact costs of unplanned additions. Also, commercial cost estimating tools which can quickly create time to complete and cost to complete estimates are highly effective when used during contract negotiations, since they clarify and crystallize product development schedules and costs. When friction is caused by lack of crisp, quantitative data on software progress there are solutions readily at hand. As of 1993 there are some 50 commercial software cost estimating tools, about 70 project planning tools, and 5 software measurement tools commercially available. Almost all of these are far superior to manual methods.

10. **Methods of control**—Once friction between clients and contractors gets started, it is not easy to set the situation right. Indeed, if the estimates for the project were prepared manually, and if Function Points were not used to deal with creeping

requirements, the problems tend to quickly become acute and to resist most known therapies. Prevention is much more effective than anything else for dealing with client/contractor friction.

11. **Product support**—As a class, the 50 or so commercial software estimating tools for software, and the 70 or so project management tools which can illustrate schedules, resources, and costs constitute the most effective product sets for minimizing friction between clients and contractors.

Examples of some of the more common software management tools include (in alphabetic order): ACCENT VUE, ADW, AGS FullCASE, Andersen FOUNDATION, APECS 8000, Artemis, Asset-R, the Bridge, BYL, CA-Advisor, CA-Estimacs, CA-Planmacs, CA-Superproject, CA-Tellaplan, CHECKPOINT®, COCOMO, CoCo-Pro, COSTAR, GECOMO, Harvard Project Manager, ISTAR, MARS, Microman II, MIL/SOFTQUAL, Microsoft Project, MI-Project, MISTER, MULTITRACK, N5500, NES, PADS, PLANNER, PMS-II, POWER, Prestige, PRIDE, PROJECT/2, ProjectBASE, ProjectGUIDE, Project Managers Workbench (PMW), PS4, QQA, RA-Metrics, Size Planner, SIZE Plus, SLIM, SOFTCOST, SOFTQUAL, SPQR/20, SPECTRUM, SPMT, STARpro, Sys/PLAN, Time Line, TRAK, UniPress, VAX Software Project Manager, and XPM.

12. **Consulting support**—Many individual management consultants and most software management consulting companies will take note of friction as part of standard consulting studies or software process assessments. That does not imply that the problems can be solved, however. The SPR and SEI assessment techniques include sections on friction between clients and contractors for example. Here too, the problem may not be solvable even when it is diagnosed. Although not consultants in the normal sense, most attorneys who specialize in contracts and business law can provide adequate warnings of contractual terms that are likely to cause friction.

13. **Education support**—Software engineering curricula and most business courses do not always deal explicitly with the subject of friction between clients and contractors, although short courses on business law may include case studies that result from friction. Obviously law schools deal heavily with this topic. Commercial courses such as those offered by Digital Consulting Inc (DCI) or Technology Transfer Institute (TTI) seldom touch on this topic either. There are a few universities which are exceptions, such as Oakland University in Rochester, Michigan, whose chairman (Dr. Albert Lederer) has done significant research on politics and friction.

14. **Publication support**—There are few books which deal explicitly with friction between clients and contractors. There are many which touch upon this subject peripherally. An excellent primer is Brandon and Segelstein's *Data Processing Contracts* (Van Nostrand Reinhold, 1976). John Marciniak's *Software Acquisition Management* (Wiley, 1990) is often cited. Tobey Marzouk's *Protecting Your Proprietary Rights in Computer and High-Technology Industries* (IEEE Press, 1991) touches upon some of the issues. There are a number of books on doing business with the

government which may cover specialized aspects of potential friction. A good overview is William Roetzheim's *Developing Software to Government Standards* (Prentice Hall, 1991). The DoD has published several volumes itself: DODD 5000.1 *Major System Acquisition* and DODD 5000.2 *Defense Acquisition Program Procedures*. Also worthy of note are the Small Business Innovation Research (SBIR) programs, under which both military services and civilian agencies set aside funding for small companies and innovation research programs.

15. **Periodical support**—As of 1993, none of the software periodicals devote significant space to friction, unless there happens to be major litigation involved such as the lawsuit between EDS and Computer Associates. There may be intermittent articles in software journals from time to time. This is true of both house journals and commercial journals. Examples of house journals include Knowledge Base which is published quarterly by Software Productivity Research, or the Rubin monthly newsletter. Intermittent articles on client/contractor friction may appear in the commercial software journals such as American Programmer, Software Magazine, and Datamation. From time to time other journals have articles of interest, too. For example, Computer Personnel in July of 1991 contained a fascinating article by Dr. Albert Lederer and Dr. Jayesh Prasad on the impact of political pressure on software estimation. The same authors, and several colleagues, also published an intriguing study of cost estimating practices in the June 1990 issue of MIS Quarterly. The journal Risk Management deals with friction from time to time. Many legal and law periodicals discuss such topics, but these journals seldom circulate among the software community.

16. **Standards support**—There are no known standards for dealing with friction between clients and contractors. This is true of ANSI, DoD, IEE, IEEE, ISO, and other standards bodies.

17. **Professional associations**—The topic of friction between clients and contractors is dealt with only peripherally by software and management professional associations. The American Management Association (AMA) discusses the topic from time to time, as do ADAPSO (now ITAA), SMIS, the IEEE, and many others. Obviously bar and legal associations are concerned with this problem.

18. **Effectiveness of known therapies**—The effectiveness of preventative therapies is remarkably high. The effectiveness of curative therapies once the problem gets out of hand is remarkably low. A combination of the preventive approaches of good corporate counsel, Joint Application Design (JAD), Quality Function Deployment (QFD), and the use of both estimating and project management tools can immunize successfully against the problem of friction between clients and contractors.

19. **Costs of known therapies**—Attorney's fees vary too widely to be generalized, but are seldom inexpensive. However, they are always cost-effective if they head off problems that can jeopardize a contract. Neither JAD nor QFD are particularly expensive, since both are methodological approaches which require only basic

training before they can be utilized. Plan on spending from $200 to $800 per student day (depending upon the instructors selected) for training. JAD training is normally two days, and QFD training is normally three days. These technologies will normally return their value in six months or less.

There are three classes of project management tools which relate to friction between clients and contractors: sizing, estimating, and planning.

Sizing tools range in cost from less than $1000 to about $20,000. These tools prevent friction by clearly indicating the quantities of various deliverables which must be produced. Sizing tools are useful for both clients and contractors, although they are primarily used by contractors. Sizing tools with full sizing logic for all deliverables (specifications, source code, test cases) are the most valuable. They normally return their value almost at once (less than 3 months) when used on projects larger than 1000 Function Points in size.

Planning tools range in cost from less than $100 to more than $10,000. They are most valuable for the most experienced managers, and indeed may cause trouble for novices. These tools tend to grow in value in direct proportion to the size of the project being planned. Indeed, for projects larger than 5000 Function Points, not using such tools should be considered to be malpractice. They normally return their value almost at once (less than 3 months) when used on projects larger than 1000 Function Points in size.

Estimating tools range in cost from less than $1000 to more than $25,000. These tools are extremely valuable in preventing friction between clients and contractors. Estimating tools which support Function Points or Feature Points are most effective for minimizing client/contractor disputes since these metrics quantify topics of immediate interest to clients. They also benefit novice managers and clients as well as experienced managers and clients. Their value tends to rise in direct proportion to the size of the project being estimated. Estimating tools normally return their value in less than 12 months for projects exceeding 1000 Function Points. Failure to use such tools on projects larger than 5000 Function Points should be considered to be malpractice, since manual estimating methods have proven to be grossly inadequate for large systems.

20. **Long-range prognosis**—Since friction between clients and contractors has been present throughout human history, it is unlikely that this problem will ever go away. However, for software projects, the set of preventive technologies is now good enough to give a basis for mild optimism. The combination of JAD sessions, QFD, and automated sizing, estimating, and planning tools can minimize the chronic sources of friction: creeping user requirements by the clients, and impossible commitments by the contractors.

CHAPTER 17

Friction Between Software Management And Senior Executives

1. **Definition**—A) Dissatisfaction by senior executives (i.e. corporate officers, CEO's, group executives, corporate vice presidents, etc.) with the performance of the software function supporting their operations; B) Dissatisfaction by senior executives with performance of software executives and personnel in terms of slipped project schedules, cost overruns, or low quality.

2. **Severity**—Friction between the software function and senior executives of corporations and government agencies tends to average about a three on the following five-point scale:

   Severity 1: Friction is severe enough to jeopardize enterprise operations
   Severity 2: Friction is severe enough to jeopardize morale and human relations
   Severity 3: Friction is widespread, frequent, and occasionally severe
   Severity 4: Friction is primarily associated with specific projects and is not general
   Severity 5: Friction is intermittent and due to specific instances

3. **Frequency**—Friction between various software functional groups (i.e. information systems teams; systems software teams) and senior executives has been fairly common and occurs in perhaps 30% to 50% of large enterprises which develop major software applications and systems software projects.

4. **Occurrence**—Friction between senior executives and software executives tends to center around four chronic software problem areas: 1) Long schedules or missed schedules by the software group; 2) Cost overruns or escalating costs; 3) Low quality and low user satisfaction; 4) Nebulous and unquantified status reports or a general lack of solid measurement data dealing with software productivity and quality.

   All four problem areas are endemic to software, and particularly so within enterprises that develop large systems exceeding 5,000 Function Points.

5. **Susceptibility and resistance**—Small companies and software companies such as Borland and Microsoft where the senior executives have software backgrounds are comparatively resistant. Large companies and government agencies where senior executives have minimal hands-on knowledge of software are most susceptible.

6. **Root causes**—There are two different root causes for the problem of friction between senior executives and the software function: 1) Large software projects do take longer, cost more, and miss more schedules than most other kinds of engineered product; 2) Software managers have been handicapped for many years by the flawed and paradoxical "lines of source code metric" which prevented serious study of software economic issues, and made even basic status reports on progress troublesome.

7. **Associated problems**—Friction between senior executives and the software function is often associated with the problems of *Low Management Morale,* and *High Management Attrition Rates.* There is also an association with *Low Staff Morale* and *High Staff Attrition Rates* although these problems are more indirect.

   Friction itself is often caused by *Cost Overruns, Long Schedules, Excessive Time to Market, Low User Satisfaction,* and sometimes by the *Silver Bullet Syndrome, False Productivity Claims,* or *Management Malpractice.*

8. **Cost impact**—The costs of friction between senior executives and the software function is very difficult to quantify. The most visible cost element would be associated with high attrition rates, and the direct costs of replacing departing software managers and personnel.

9. **Methods of prevention**—When friction is caused by cost overruns, long or slipped schedules, and poor quality or low user satisfaction, the available therapies are diverse, and must be tailored to the specific needs of the situation. Improvements in methods, tools, and reusability can be effective, but need several years before significant results begin to be visible (beware of the Silver Bullet syndrome). When friction is caused by lack of crisp, quantitative data on software progress there are solutions readily at hand. As of 1993 there are some 50 commercial software cost estimating tools, about 70 project planning tools, and 5 software measurement tools commercially available. Almost all of these are far superior to manual methods.

10. **Methods of control**—Once friction between senior executives and the software function gets started, it is not easy to set the situation right. Some of the approaches to control introduce radical change, such as out-sourcing the software function and or down-sizing mainframe applications. (The efficacy of out-sourcing and down-sizing is not yet fully known as of 1993.)

    A control technique used by Harold Geneen, the Chairman of ITT, was to establish a "Vice President of Programming" who was charged with both accurate reporting of the status of all software groups, and improving the performance of software groups, throughout the corporation. In turn, the Vice President of Programming created positions entitled "Director of Programming" at the major operating companies within the ITT conglomerate, who were charged with both accurate reporting of software status and with assisting in the improvement of software technologies within the operating units.

It is of interest that at one time Geneen was displeased with both software and computers because every major project cited software as a key reason for delay and cost overruns. As a shrewd businessman, he recognized that simply firing software managers and executives would not solve the problem, so he initiated a national search for a top software executive who could bring the software monster under executive control.

An emerging approach for dealing with internal friction is to resort to external outsourcing, whereby responsibility for the entire software function is transferred to another company. In many outsource arrangements, some or all of the software personnel are transferred to the outsource company. The efficacy, pros and cons of outsourcing have not yet been fully explored as of 1993.

11. **Product support**—There seem to be no products that have a direct impact on the problem of friction between senior executives and the software function.

12. **Consulting support**—Many individual management consultants and most software management consulting companies will take note of friction as part of standard consulting studies. That does not imply that the problem can be solved, however. The SPR assessment technique includes a section on friction. Here too, the problem may not be solvable even when it is diagnosed.

13. **Education support**—Software engineering curricula and most business courses do not deal explicitly with the subject of friction between senior executives and the software function. Commercial courses seldom do either.

14. **Publication support**—There are few books that address the subject of friction between senior executives and the software function as explicit topics. Fred Brooks' classic, *The Mythical Man-Month* (Addison Wesley, 1982) is always a useful background book. Robert Bloch's *The Politics of Projects* (Yourdon Press, 1992) is relevant. See also Peter DeGrace and Leslie Stahl's *Wicked Problems, Righteous Solutions* (Yourdon Press, 1992). Several books deal with the sociology of software, however. Dr. Gerald Weinberg's classic *Psychology of Computer Programming* (Prentice-Hall, 1971) is a good source. The more recent classic by Tom DeMarco and Tim Lister, *Peopleware* (Dorset House, 1987) is also useful. Dean Meyer and Mary Boone attack some of the issues underlying friction in *The Information Edge* (Gage Publishing Company, 1987). Harold Geneen and Alvin Moscow's *Managing* (Avon Books, 1984) is a good overview from a CEO who once hated software, and then went on to fund one of the most powerful software research laboratories in the U.S. in an effort to bring it under control. A monograph by Capers Jones, *A 10 Year Perspective of Software Engineering Within ITT* (SPR, 1988) summarizes the functions and accomplishments of the ITT Programming Technology Center. Shuji Hayashi's *Culture and Management in Japan* (University of Tokyo Press, 1988) dis-

cusses some of the approaches which head off friction in Japanese organizations. For deep background, Miriam Beard's *A History of Business* (University of Michigan Press, 1982) is a fascinating overview of business and business friction in the ancient world and the middle ages.

15. **Periodical support**—Friction between senior executives and the software function is normally covered only when the topic is considered newsworthy. The well-known disputes between Ross Perot of Electronic Data Systems and the Chairman and board of directors of General Motors is the most spectacular incident of friction in recent years.

16. **Standards support**—There are no known standards published by ANSI, DoD, IEE, IEEE, ISO, or any other standards group that even mentions friction between senior executives and the software function.

17. **Professional associations**—The topic of friction does not appear to be covered by any of the software professional groups, nor by the American Management Association (AMA). No doubt many individuals within such groups are aware of the problem, but it has not been treated as a public issue.

18. **Effectiveness of known therapies**—There are no direct therapies that can solve the problem of friction between senior executives and the software function. There are therapies that can compress software schedules and reduce costs, which are frequent causes of friction, and they work moderately well. There are also therapies that can increase the rigor of software estimation, measurement, and status tracking (which are also frequent causes of friction) and they work extremely well.

19. **Costs of known therapies**—Since there are no direct therapies that apply specifically to friction, the cost impact cannot be quantified. Refer to the chapters dealing with cost overruns, long schedules, and inaccurate cost estimation for discussions of the therapy costs for contributing problems.

20. **Long-range prognosis**—There is about a 50/50 chance that the problem of friction will either get much better or much worse by the end of the century. The optimistic scenario is based on the remarkable recent improvements in software estimation and measurement that have occurred since 1985, and the significant improvements in software methods and tools that are continuously occurring. The pessimistic scenario is based on sluggish U.S. economy and its impact on technology acquisition and technology transfer. Organizations that can't afford training in improved methods, or the costs of deploying new tools and methods, are not in a position to solve any serious problems.

18

High Maintenance Costs

1. **Definition**—A) Any software production library where the costs and resources devoted to enhancing existing software and fixing bugs are greater than the costs and resources devoted to new applications; B) Any existing software project or legacy system where the effort devoted to annual defect repairs and minor updates is greater than 1% of the original development resources; C) The maintenance costs of any existing software project with the attributes of having high defect levels, poor structural integrity, poor or missing specifications, no regression test suite available, and one or more error-prone modules.

2. **Severity**—The average severity of high maintenance costs under definition (A), above, can be ranked on the following scale. The current U.S. average is about 3:

   Severity 1:   Maintenance budget is equal to or exceeds 65% of total budget

   Severity 2:   Maintenance budget is equal to or exceeds 55% of total budget

   Severity 3:   Maintenance budget is equal to or exceeds 45% of total budget

   Severity 4:   Maintenance budget is equal to or exceeds 35% of total budget

   Severity 5:   Maintenance budget is equal to or exceeds 25% of total budget

3. **Frequency**—Under definition (A), above, more than 60% of Fortune 500 U.S. enterprises have high maintenance costs, as do Federal and State governments and the military services. Under definitions (B) and (C) about 70% of the systems larger than 5000 Function Points have high maintenance costs. For applications of 500 Function Points or smaller, the frequency drops to about 15%.

4. **Occurrence**—High maintenance costs are strongly associated with large enterprises which maintain portfolios of over 250,000 Function Points, including a significant number of large systems in excess of 5,000 Function Points. Thus a number of major U.S. industries are prone to high maintenance costs: banking, insurance, government operations, defense and manufacturing.

   In the fullness of time, maintenance will become the primary work of the software industry as more and more enterprises achieve levels of automation commensurate with their business goals. Some enterprises are already at that level in 1993, so their entire workload is related to updating, enhancing, and fixing problems in existing legacy applications.

5. **Susceptibility and resistance**—In general, susceptibility to high maintenance costs rises with the size of the enterprise, the average size of its production library and the average size of the systems within it. Well-structured software that used careful processes during development are fairly resistant. Formal reviews and inspections are noteworthy for raising the resistance of software maintenance costs and problems. Formal configuration control, integration, and regression test libraries also augment resistance.

Consider the analogy of maintaining a fleet of utility vehicles. When the vehicles are new (say less than 10,000 miles) maintenance will normally consist of oil changes, tuneups, and replacement of spark plugs. But if the fleet is used for many years, so that the average mileage begins to approach 100,000 miles, the costs of maintenance will normally escalate severely. Toward the end of a vehicle's life cycle, new transmissions, valve replacement, brake replacement, and many other costly repairs tend to occur more and more frequently.

Software does not decay under usage as do mechanical devices, but the entropy of software does rise under the long-term impact of many small changes. If the specifications and written descriptions are not updated, if the basic structure of an application is modified, and if structural changes are not reflected in fresh comments, then little by little updating a system will become more expensive and more error-prone over time.

Note that the word "maintenance" as commonly used is highly ambiguous, and has several discrete components with quite different economic outlooks. The term maintenance tends to include *enhancements* (adding new functions), *defect repairs* (fixing errors or bugs), *mandatory changes* (modifications due to law or policy), *conversions* (moving an application to a different platform), *restructuring* (usually performed to reduce complexity), *reverse engineering* (extracting hidden, latent information from existing software), and *reengineering* (moving an application to a new platform and a new technology simultaneously).

6. **Root causes**—The major root causes for high maintenance costs are: 1) The fact that software decays under the impact of many small changes; 2) Inadequate defect prevention; 3) Inadequate use of reviews and inspections; 4) Insufficient or careless testing; 5) Inadequate rigor for configuration control and integration; 6) Lack of quality measurements; 7) Lack of understanding by senior and project management that development quality is an effective preventive step; 8) Excessive schedule pressure during initial development leading to unwise attempts to short-cut quality control techniques, which yields a bitter harvest during maintenance; 9) Rapid decay of the utility of paper specifications for an application, which are seldom updated as system modifications occur.

From both assessments and surveys carried out at conferences, there appears to be a strong cultural component associated with high maintenance costs. A large majority of the enterprises which report high maintenance costs appear to have made no deliberate effort to explore geriatric tools and services, and indeed some managers within these enterprises are surprised at how many tools are available.

On the other hand, enterprises which report low or shrinking maintenance costs tend to be quite active in the exploration of geriatric tools and services.

From long-range studies of applications, some interesting trends have been observed. The rate at which the entropy or complexity of a software application increases appears to correlate quite strongly with the level at initial deployment. For example, an application where the average cyclomatic complexity at deployment is near one can maintain its structure more or less intact through several years of enhancements and updates.

On the other hand, applications which are deployed with high levels of cyclomatic and essential complexity (say an average cyclomatic complexity of 20) tend to increase their entropy quite rapidly. Within a few years, the structure may have degraded so severely that testing becomes very difficult, and "bad fixes" or secondary defects injected as a byproduct of modification can increase sharply.

The increasing problems of maintaining poorly structured applications over long time periods may explain a seeming paradox in empirical studies: well structured applications tend to accumulate higher enhancement costs than poorly structured applications. What seems to be occurring is that the poorly structured applications are frozen except for mandatory changes, since the probability of bad fixes is so great.

7. **Associated problems**—High maintenance costs are key contributors to the problems of *Low User Satisfaction* and *Friction with Users*. High maintenance costs are causative factors in the problems of *Friction with Senior Management, Low Staff Morale*. High maintenance costs are often associated with *Low Productivity, Low Quality, Error-Prone Modules,* and *Long Schedules* since this problem shares some of the same root causes.

High maintenance costs are often caused by the problems of *Inexperienced Management, Inexperienced Staff, Inadequate Estimating, Inadequate Planning, Inadequate Defect Removal, Inadequate Configuration Control, Inadequate Measurements,* and *Excessive Schedule Pressure*.

8. **Cost impact**—The costs of maintenance can be calculated separately for enterprises and for the projects within the enterprise. At the enterprise level, the ratio of the amount spent on maintenance to the total budget is a good indicator (see the "Severity Level" ratings, above). Another powerful indicator is the "maintenance assignment scope." This metric is calculated by dividing the total quantity of Function Points in the production library by the number of people required to handle routine updates and defect repairs. The current U.S. average for maintenance assignment scopes is about 500 Function Points, which implies that annual maintenance in the U.S. costs about $120 per Function Point. Once corporate maintenance costs are established for any given year, it is important to look for year-to-year trends.

At the level of specific projects, software estimating technology is now sophisticated enough to estimate for up to 20 years the maintenance costs of enhancements, defect repairs (by severity level), duplicate defects, invalid defects such as user errors, field service for commercial software, maintenance programming and management, and customer support.

9. **Methods of prevention**—Maintenance costs and quality control share common preventive methods to a large degree: formal quality plans; the use of JAD sessions for MIS projects; prototyping; structured analysis and design techniques; reusable designs and code from certified sources; software quality assurance (SQA) teams; total quality management (TQM) methods; quality function deployment (QFD) methods; clean-room development methods; quality measurement programs; reviews and inspections; and the use of defect estimation and measurement tools. Measurement of defect origins, volumes, and removal efficiencies is the best long-term preventive method.

   The defect removal methods of formal design reviews and code inspections are also excellent preventive steps for high maintenance costs, and indeed have the highest measured defect removal efficiencies of any technique: they can be more than 60% efficient. Most forms of testing are less than 30% efficient. However, formal testing by trained specialists is a good preventive step. Test coverage analyzers, complexity analyzers, test case generators, and formal test libraries are also useful.

10. **Methods of control**—Formal configuration control tools, integration tools, and regression test library support tools are the classic control methods for the high costs of aging software. However, in 1985 a new sub-industry was formed of companies that were providing explicit geriatric care for aging software. Restructuring of aging COBOL was the first such technology to surface, and that has now become a standard technique among the more sophisticated COBOL users. Automated complexity analysis also is useful in reducing maintenance costs, and here many languages are supported besides COBOL: C, PL/I, FORTRAN, Ada, and so forth.

    In 1989, two new technologies were added to the set of geriatric methods: reverse engineering and re-engineering. Reverse engineering is useful in extracting latent design information from aging applications whose specifications have long since disappeared or fallen into decay. Re-engineering provides automated support for migrating the functions of aging software into new and robust versions, often changing platforms and moving to relational data base technology at the same time.

    CASE vendors originally tended to ignore maintenance, but that situation is changing. Bachman, CADRE, Intersolv, KnowledgeWare, Texas Instruments, and many others are now starting to offer geriatric support.

11. **Product support**—An entire spectrum of products that can assist in maintenance are now commercially available. Tools that analyze complexity and indicate maintainability problems have been available since the mid 1980's, and are growing in number. McCabe's Analysis of Complexity Tool (ACT) and Battlemap are exam-

ples. KnowledgeWare's Inspector tool and Peat Marwick's Pathvu are also complexity analyzers, as is PM/SS by ADPAC. This technology is so common that some bulletin boards have public-domain tools (including one developed in Russia) that can be down-loaded.

Tools that can restructure software have also been available since 1985: Recoder, Structured Retrofit, and operate against COBOL and are widely deployed. Many tools are also available that can convert COBOL to COBOL II. Support for other languages, such as C, PL/I, FORTRAN, etc. are much scarcer, due to the huge COBOL base versus all other languages.

Re-engineering and reverse engineering are newer technologies, and have been commercially available only since 1989. The Bachman tool set for COBOL applications and the CADRE tool set for C applications come readily to mind. These technologies are expanding rapidly, in terms of both vendors entering the market and clients. The results from re-engineering and reverse engineering are still preliminary, but favorable.

Estimating maintenance (defect repairs) and enhancements (new features) requires special calibration, since the methodologies are distinct and both productivity and quality rates diverge from new applications. Estimating tools which support maintenance and enhancements include SPQR/20 and CHECKPOINT®. SPQR/20 can predict maintenance and enhancement costs for up to five years. CHECKPOINT® can predict maintenance and enhancements for up to 20 years, and deals specifically with the rate at which software structures decay over time. The impact of geriatric methods such as restructuring can also be estimated.

Estimating tools for commercial software producers are fairly scarce. However, some tools such as CHECKPOINT® can predict customer service, field service, programming, and management expenses for commercial and contract software. Commercial software vendors have also produced their own proprietary tools for this purpose. Some estimating tools for software also estimate defects by severity level, valid and invalid defect reports, and duplicate defect reports for high-volume commercial software with many users.

Examples of commercially available maintenance tools include Aide-De-Camp from Software Maintenance and Development Systems; CCC/Manager from Softool Corporation; Customer Support Manager from Repository Technologies; ENDEAVOR from Legent; POLYTRON from Intersolv; Software Management System from Intasoft; Source Management Utility from COSMIC; SOLOMAN from Information Systems Consultants; SURE from the Software Clearing House; and the VAX DEC/MMS from Digital Equipment.

12. **Consulting support**—A number of consulting organizations either specialize in or have major practices in the domain of maintenance support. One of the best ways of exploring what is available is to join the non-profit Software Maintenance Association (now renamed as the Software Management Association). Many of the re-engineering and reverse engineering companies have captive consulting groups,

as do the major CASE vendors. Although such consulting groups are wedded to particular tools, they are often helpful and knowledgeable.

13. **Education support**—Academic institutions such as computer science departments have had little to offer in terms of maintenance or enhancement training. The maintenance research center at the University of Durham in England is a notable exception. Also an exception is the work of Paul Oman and colleagues at the University of Idaho. The non-profit Software Maintenance Association (renamed to Software Management Association) offers major conferences, and some seminars on maintenance-related topics. Courses in Design Reviews and Code Inspections deal explicitly with software maintenance. SPR's course on Applied Software Measurement (ASM) deals explicitly with the subject of measuring software maintenance, as well as the quality topics of defect origins, defect volumes, and defect removal efficiency.

14. **Publication support**—Maintenance books are now increasing in number and quality. Ten years ago, Girish Parikh and Nicholas Zvegintzov produced an interesting compilation of maintenance literature entitled: *Tutorial on Software Maintenance* (IEEE Computer Society Press, 1983). Dan Couger and Mel Colter wrote a pioneering maintenance book called *Maintenance Programming: Improved Productivity Through Motivation* (Prentice Hall, 1985). Girish Parikh's *Handbook of Software Maintenance* (John Wiley & Sons, 1986) was also among the first to deal with maintenance. James Martin and Carma McClure's *Software Maintenance: The Problem and its Solution* (Prentice-Hall, 1988) is a good introduction to this important topic. Lowell Jay Arthur's *Software Evolution—The Software Maintenance Challenge* (John Wiley & Sons, 1988) is a useful analysis. David Higgins' *Data Structured Software Maintenance* (Dorset House, 1992) is an interesting recent application of Warnier-Orr principles to the maintenance arena. Roger Fournier's *Practical Guide to Structured System Development and Maintenance* (Yourdon Press, 1991) takes a holistic approach to both development and maintenance. Robert Arnold's *Software Reengineering* (IEEE Press, 1992) tackles a recent technology by means of selected articles. A useful companion volume is that of David Longstreet, *Software Maintenance and Computers* (IEEE Press, 1990). Yet another recent addition to the maintenance literature is Landsbaum and Glass' *Measuring and Motivating Maintenance Programmers,* (Prentice Hall, 1992).

A catalog by Applied Computer Research, *Guide to Software Productivity Aids,* includes almost all maintenance tools marketed in the United States. The catalog is updated twice a year. The University of Idaho has published an excellent bibliography on software maintenance: Jack Hagemeister, Bruce Lowthar, Paul Oman, Xiaokang Yu, and Weiguo Zhu's *An Annotated Bibliography on Software Maintenance;* University of Idaho, 1991 (Report #91–06 BB).

Three books by the author, Capers Jones, also deal with software maintenance. *Programming Productivity* (McGraw-Hill, 1986) deals with the impact of maintenance on life-cycle costs. *Applied Software Measurement* (McGraw-Hill, 1991) deals with the topic of measuring software maintenance, and also includes current

U.S. averages for user-reported software defect levels, life expectancy of software projects in the field, and annual enhancement volumes. A book new in 1993, *Software Productivity and Quality—The World Wide Perspective* (IS Management Group, 1993), deals with the software maintenance levels of major European and Pacific-Rim countries and includes international comparisons.

15. **Periodical support**—Three journals support the maintenance arena: *Software Maintenance News* (renamed *Software Management News* in early 1992) is published in the U.S. and *Software Maintenance: Practice and Research* is published in the United Kingdom. Most software-related journals have intermittent articles on maintenance-related topics. The *Journal of Software Maintenance* should also be cited. In addition, the house journals and newsletters of companies with maintenance-related tools such as McCabe Associates, Bachman, Viasoft, CADRE, and SPR may have articles on maintenance from time to time. The defense journal, CrossTalk, discusses this topic too.

16. **Standards support**—There are no current standards published by ANSI, DoD, IEE, IEEE, or ISO that cover maintenance and enhancement explicitly. Many standards touch upon some aspect, such as the standards dealing with configuration management, quality, testing, and so forth.

17. **Professional associations**—Until 1992, the Software Maintenance Association was the most visible U.S. professional group covering this area. As of 1992, that group changed its name to the Software Management Association, and has broadened its focus. It will still cover maintenance topics, however. Many other professional associations focus on maintenance from time to time, or have special interest subgroups. For example, the IEEE's annual software maintenance conferences are well attended, and quite useful.

18. **Effectiveness of known therapies**—The effectiveness of geriatric services and products is remarkably high. Companies that vigorously attack their maintenance problems can and do make major improvements. A full-spectrum approach including complexity analysis, restructuring, re-engineering, and reverse engineering can lower overall maintenance effort by several hundred percent. However, the costs of these technologies is not trivial, and their impact will build up over several years.

Maintenance estimation is now fairly easy to perform and acceptably accurate. Some tools can estimate annual maintenance and enhancement for five and 20 years, respectively. They can also estimate the impact of defect removal efficiencies of standard forms of review, inspection, and test on maintenance costs. Maintenance prediction accuracies to within 15% are now possible for the first three years of production, and within 25% for the first five years. No one can achieve accurate maintenance estimation beyond five years, and the long-range estimates of up to 20 years are produced because of U.S. government requirements for very long-range maintenance estimates for military software. The accuracy is questionable.

The best results from leading companies and military services in maintenance cost reduction are impressive: a 75% reduction in total annual maintenance costs have been achieved in less than four years. This level of performance implies a maintenance assignment scope of more than 1500 Function Points per staff member and an annual maintenance cost of less than $40 per Function Point. Complexity analysis, restructuring, re-engineering, and reverse engineering are the technologies associated with the best results in reducing maintenance costs. Note that high defect removal efficiencies and the elimination of error-prone modules are also associated with reduced maintenance costs.

Hartford Insurance has been exploring maintenance costs for more than 10 years, and has published some impressive results which include a tripling of their maintenance assignment scope, and an annual budget for maintenance below 19% and dropping. Since insurance companies are similar in software methods and operations, Hartford has produced some interesting comparative statistics on their results vis à vis the rest of the industry. Most insurance companies suffered an *increase* in annual maintenance costs over the same years that Hartford was achieving an annual *decrease*.

It is interesting that Hartford's decreasing maintenance expenses were not caused by a decrease in the volume or amount of changes. Rather, the decreases were attributable to their program of restructuring and remodularizing legacy systems prior to carrying out extensive updates. If the legacy system had long-range strategic value, then it was given a full geriatric treatment program of both manual analysis and automated restructuring. If the legacy system was targeted for replacement in the near future, but interim updates were needed, then they used a fully automated restructuring process. If no updates were anticipated, and the legacy system had acceptable reliability, then no action was taken at all.

Independently of the Hartford work, separate experiments in performing the same update on poorly structured (cyclomatic complexity > 20) and well structured software (cyclomatic complexity < 5) were performed by Language Technology of Salem, Massachusetts. The conclusion was that updating a well-structured existing application took 40% less effort than making the same change to a poorly structured application.

In the 1970's, the author interviewed 26 programmers within IBM, of whom half were fixing bugs in existing software and half were adding new functions. Their subjective opinions were that working on well-structured, well-commented source code allowed any given change to be made in about half the time as working on poorly-structured existing software. Test runs, for example, were reduced by about 3 to 1. However, this was not a controlled study but merely the opinions of programmers whose work consisted of modifications to existing applications which they had not created.

19. **Costs of known therapies**—Complexity analysis tools are the least expensive, and range from free (public domain tools) up to several thousand dollars. They

normally return their value in the first year, assuming a normal mixture of chaotic and unstructured applications.

Restructuring tools for COBOL are in the $15,000 to $40,000 class. Reverse engineering and re-engineering tools are similar, but full corporate licenses may exceed $100,000. Such tools normally return their value in the first year if a COBOL portfolio exceeds 100,000 Function Points.

Re-engineering and reverse engineering tools are in the price range from about $1000 to more than $10,000 per copy. However, as more and more companies enter this business segment, prices can be expected to decline over the next few years.

Expert-system estimation tools with maintenance and quality prediction capabilities such as SPQR/20 and CHECKPOINT® are in the $5,000 to $20,000 range. They normally return their value on a single project when used early in the life cycle as maintenance estimators for projects larger than 1000 Function Points, or when amortized across 10 or more smaller projects. However, since projects of 1000 Function Points and larger are normally multi-year development efforts, the return value due to maintenance cost reduction may not occur for 24 to 36 months.

Maintenance improvement techniques vary too widely in cost for convenient generalization. Military, systems, and MIS projects typically use different techniques, as do small programs and large systems. Also, maintenance methods vary significantly with language: COBOL is far and away the language with the most effective geriatric services available. The C language is a distant second. Several other widely-used languages such as PL/I, PASCAL, and Basic have very little available in terms of geriatric support, so the return is hard to calculate.

20. **Long-range prognosis**—The technologies for improving maintenance and enhancement are rapidly improving, so this problem may be brought under control by the end of the twentieth century. However, cultural and sociological resistance might dilute or reduce the effectiveness of the emerging technology base.

Maintenance, more than almost any other problem, is plagued by inactivity and passive management. At conferences and seminars as well as during assessments, attendees are queried as to the magnitude of their maintenance costs. They are also queried as to steps taken to explore or reduce those costs. Most of the managers citing maintenance costs in excess of 50% of their annual budgets have taken no action at all to reduce their costs. On the other hand, almost all managers who cite less than 25% of their budgets apply to maintenance have created active and energetic maintenance technology research groups.

A special case consists of enterprises where no new software is required and existing applications are viewed as sufficient. In this situation, enhancement and maintenance work may constitute 100% of the programming effort. But here too, geriatric services applied to legacy software can make the work easier and faster and reduce annual expenses.

CHAPTER 19

Inaccurate Cost Estimating

1. **Definition**—A) Automated estimating methods that vary by more than 30% when calibrated against fully measured control projects; B) Automated partial estimating methods that omit, ignore, or fail to include more than 30% of the activities and tasks associated with software projects (such as documentation or management) unless specifically limited to selected activities; C) All forms of manual estimating over 1000 Function Points.

2. **Severity**—The average severity of resource and cost estimating accuracy problems under definitions (A) and (B) above is about a 3 on the following scale:

Severity 1:   Estimates miss control projects by more than 50%

Severity 2:   Estimates miss control projects by more than 40%

Severity 3:   Estimates miss control projects by more than 30%

Severity 4:   Estimates miss control projects by more than 20%

Severity 5:   Estimates miss control projects by more than 10%

Note that the consequences of cost and resource estimating errors are usually more serious when the estimates are low and understate resources, rather than when estimates are high and predict more resources than truly needed. The fail-safe mode of estimating technology is to be conservative rather than optimistic.

Note that a very common problem occurs when using software estimating tools initially. Comparisons between historical data and trial estimates for completed projects show large discrepancies of 50% to 100% or more, with the estimate generating larger costs and longer schedules than history indicates. The natural assumption is to consider that the estimate is wrong. Surprisingly, it often happens that the error resides in the historical data. Most of what passes for historical data in the software industry is incomplete, and omits from 30% to more than 70% of the real work that was performed. This problem is common enough and severe enough to have accumulated ranges of the most probable missing data, such as unpaid overtime, management effort, documentation effort, and the like. This problem is severe enough to have invalidated a number of studies of cost-estimating accuracy.

3. **Frequency**—Under definitions (A) and (B), over 50% of U.S. software projects larger than 1000 Function Points are inaccurately estimated. Under definition (C), more than 90% of projects larger than 1000 Function Points are inaccurately estimated, since there are no consistently accurate manual methods for large software projects. (About 10% of manual estimates will be acceptably accurate due to chance or random factors).

4. **Occurrence**—Estimating errors are endemic to the software industry, and are severe for both large and small software projects. However, the serious consequences of estimating errors rise in direct proportion to the size of the project. For projects of more than 1000 Function Points, estimating errors are very common for information systems, and somewhat less common for systems and military software projects. Above 5000 Function Points, failure to use automated estimating tools should be considered as an example of professional malpractice. (Such tools do not forget activities and deliverables, which is a common fault for manual estimates.) As a general rule, U.S. military projects have the lowest incidence of estimating errors, although the large sizes of military projects make estimating errors a serious problem.

Cost and resource estimating errors can be divided into major subcategories: "errors in sizing," "errors in task selection," "errors in assignment scope analysis," and "errors in production rate assumptions," "omission of creeping requirements," and "special or unique situations."

Sizing errors are those of miscalculating deliverable sizes such as the quantity of source code or number of screens. Predicting source code size (almost 400 languages are now supported as of 1993), predicting documentation quantities and sizes, and test case prediction are standard functions of modern software estimating tools, although missing from those developed prior to about 1985. (Historical note: SPQR/20 was the first commercial software estimating tool which included sizing logic for source code, documentation volumes, and test cases. This tool pioneered the usage of Function Points as the uniform basis for sizing all software deliverables: documents, source code, and test cases.)

Task selection errors are those of omitting tasks from an estimate, such as user documentation. Expert task selection from a repertory of several hundred tasks, with the estimating tool automatically adjusting its selection to match military, civilian, and project class or type characteristics, is now a standard function on modern software estimating tools. User override of task selection is also a standard function. Several modern software cost estimating tools support the creation of "templates" which utilize historical projects or custom templates created by the user as the basis for task selection.

Assignment scope errors are those of miscalculating the quantity of work which can be handled by the staff, so that they become overloaded. Assignment scope prediction in terms of both natural metrics (pages of specifications, source codes, number of test cases) and synthetic metrics (Function Points, Feature

Points) is now a standard function on modern software cost estimating tools. Templates defined by users or created from historical data can also be used.

Production rate errors are those of excessive optimism, such as assuming coding rates in excess of 3,000 statements per month. Production rate prediction using both natural metrics such as source code and synthetic metrics such as Function Points is now a standard function on modern software cost estimating tools. Templates defined by users or created from historical data can also be used.

Omission of creeping requirements refers to the very common phenomenon of failing to adjust an estimate for the growth rate in unplanned requirements after the conclusions of the formal requirements phase. The phenomenon of creeping requirements is so common that predicting the amount of requirements creep, and adjusting the estimate accordingly, have become standard functions of modern cost estimating tools.

The phrase "special or unique situations" refers to uncommon factors which can affect a specific project, but which do not occur with enough regularity to fit into standard estimating algorithms or common templates. A few examples of special situations which can affect project costs will clarify the point: A) Closure of an office or evacuation of staff due to weather conditions or natural disasters; B) Voluntary termination or work stoppage of more than 50% of project team members; C) Physical relocation of a project team from one city to another during the project development cycle; D) Injunctions or legal actions which freeze project specifications or source code at a particular point; E) Travel costs for trips among geographically dispersed projects; F) Moving, living, and real-estate fees for hiring new employees.

5. **Susceptibility and resistance**—Susceptibility is widespread, but more serious among enterprises that build large software systems than among those that build a majority of small one-person software projects. Susceptibility is high for projects adopting new technologies, languages, or using new methods for the first time. Susceptibility is also high when dealing with inexperienced users and with contract software.

Resistance is high for enterprises that measure software projects accurately. Resistance is high for enterprises that have "software estimator" as a job title. Commercial software producers, computer manufacturers, and contract software developers are fairly resistant. U.S. military services and U.S. defense contractors are fairly resistant except for situations where the inaccurate "lines of code" metric distorts results.

Susceptibility is surprisingly high among commercial software producers: witness the public embarrassment of Lotus and Microsoft when announced delivery dates were slipped.

6. **Root causes**—The root causes of inaccurate estimates include: 1) Failure by project managers to use effective estimating tools (example of malpractice); 2) Failure to measure completed projects or accumulate a historical data base; 3) Failure to use standard and granular charts of accounts for resource data collection; 4)

Failure by many estimating tool vendors to use standard and granular charts of accounts in estimating; 5) The tendency of estimating tool vendors to leave out significant activities and factors such as unpaid overtime, user effort and costs, requirements, documentation and paperwork, and managerial effort and cost; 6) Basing resource estimates on inaccurate metrics such as "lines of code"; 7) A mistaken belief among project managers that manual methods can produce accurate estimates; 8) Failure to include in the estimate the impact of project sizes, programming languages, technologies, skills, and other influential factors; 9) Growth in a project's scope and requirements after an estimate is made; 10) Failure of business schools and university software engineering curricula to include relevant courses or even to have estimating tools available for student and faculty usage; 11) Politics or social distortion of estimating results.

There is a major cultural barrier to accurate estimation which must be highlighted as a notable root cause. If an early estimate predicts higher costs, longer schedules, or lower quality than client or management expectations, there is a strong tendency to challenge the validity of the estimate. What often occurs in this situation is that the project manager is directed to recast the estimate so that it falls within preset and arbitrary boundary conditions. Then, when the project later exceeds those arbitrary bounds, the project manager is blamed for "missing the estimate."

7. **Associated problems**—Inaccurate resource and cost estimates are associated with *Cost Overruns, Long Schedules, Missed Schedules, Excessive Time to Market, Lost Business, Friction with Senior Management, Friction with Users, Inaccurate Quality Estimates, Inaccurate Reliability Estimates, Low Quality,* and *Canceled Projects.*

Inaccurate cost estimates can often be attributed to one or more of the problems of *Corporate Politics, Creeping Requirements, Inadequate Measurement, Inadequate Software Management Curricula, Inadequate Software Engineering Curricula, Inexperienced Management, Lag Time in Technology Adoption, Inaccurate Metrics, Poor Support Structures,* and *Poor Technology Transfer.*

8. **Cost impact**—The direct costs of inaccurate cost and resource estimates depend upon whether the initial estimate was low or high. If the initial estimate were low, for example, the estimate was $60,000 and the project cost $100,000, then the direct costs of the estimating error would be $40,000. Estimating low is the most hazardous kind of error.

If the initial estimate were high, for example an estimate of $125,000 for a project that costs $100,000 then the direct costs of the estimating error may be zero unless personnel or equipment were acquired as a result of the error in the estimate. The normal "fail safe" mode of commercial software estimating tools is to strive to be either accurate or slightly high. (However, if the high estimate caused the project to be terminated or created lost business, then the indirect costs would be severe.)

The indirect costs of inaccurate estimates are often severe, and are one of the commonest reasons for canceled projects. It is very significant that more than 50% of the software projects that are canceled are more than one year late, and are approaching twice their anticipated costs, when the cancellation occurs. Lost business opportunities, such as failure to get a contract, are another aspect of the indirect costs of inaccurate estimation.

9. **Methods of prevention**—Clearly, the most effective prevention for all forms of inaccurate estimating is accurate measurement. Indeed, accurate measurement of many different kinds and sizes of software projects will gradually build up a total immunity to significant software estimating errors. The use of functional metrics is an excellent preventive for sizing errors, since these metrics allow very early sizing of source code in all known languages, number of screens, pages of specifications, pages of documentation, and even numbers of test cases. The use of commercial micro-estimating tools that operate at the level of activities and tasks is a good preventive for task-selection errors. (Failure to use automated estimating tools on projects larger than 5000 Function Points is an example of management malpractice.)

10. **Methods of control**—As of 1993, some 50 commercial software estimating tools are being marketed in the United States. (For the calendar years of 1991 and 1992, at least one new estimating tool entered the U.S. market each month). In addition, a number of enterprises have built proprietary software estimating tools that are tailored to their particular software needs. While not all of the estimating tools are acceptably accurate, most of them are far superior to manual estimating methods. Micro-estimating tools that work at the level of activities and tasks are more effective than macro-estimating tools that work only at the levels of projects and phases.

11. **Product support**—Commercial software estimating tools have been marketed in the U.S. since the year 1973. Some of the better-known tools include ASSET-R, the BRIDGE, BYL, CHECKPOINT®, COCOMO, ESTIMACS, GECOMO, PRICE-S, REVIC, SLIM, SPQR/20, and SOFTCOST.

Software estimating tools tend to be focused on particular industries and kinds of software, although some can handle multiple software project types. In the MIS domain, tools such as The BRIDGE, BYL, ESTIMACS are aimed primarily at MIS projects. Tools such as SPQR/20 and CHECKPOINT® have an MIS mode, but can be set for other types of software as well. MIS applications also have available special estimators that are tightly coupled to CASE design tools: Texas Instruments IEF, CGI PACBASE, and AGS FirstCase are examples of tightly coupled estimating tools.

Estimating tools encountered in the military software domain include COCOMO and its many clones such as GECOMO. Also encountered are REVIC (which stands for "revised COCOMO"), FAST, PRICE-S, ASSET-R, SLIM, SPQR/20, CHECKPOINT®, the JS estimating series, and SoftCost. Surprisingly, there are few if any close-coupled estimating tools that extract information from design and specifications in the military domain. This is probably due to the fact that military projects tend to utilize the obsolete LOC metric, rather than functional metrics. (Functional metrics facilitate the extraction of estimating parameters from specifications.)

In the systems, real-time, and embedded domains tools such as CHECKPOINT® and SLIM predominate, although COCOMO, ASSET-R, and several others are also encountered. Here too, there is shortage of closely-coupled estimating tools which extract information directly from specifications. Here too, clinging to the obsolete LOC metric probably explains this technology gap.

The more powerful estimating tools will estimate both the resources and schedules of standard software development phases, maintenance and enhancements. They also estimate quality. Ideally, MIS, systems, and military projects should be supported at will, as should estimating for various languages and combinations of multiple languages.

Some of the more powerful recent estimators have extremely powerful estimating capabilities for quality and reliability, and also include measurement capabilities. Quality predictions for defect volumes, defect severities, and defect removal efficiency for various reviews, inspections, and tests have been available since 1985, and new releases of estimating tools are beginning to add support for Total Quality Management (TQM), Quality Function Deployment (QFD), Baldrige Award criteria, and ISO 9000–9004 support.

Maintenance and enhancement estimating are also supported by modern estimating tools, and some can predict the impact of restructuring, re-engineering, or reverse engineering legacy systems.

As an example of other recent capabilities offered during the 1990's, there are now "variable focus" estimators which switch levels and display data for complete projects, eight standard phases, 25 standard activities, and 140 standard tasks.

To continue with modern capabilities, it is now possible to have multiple-project aggregation and averaging capabilities for exploring entire portfolios. Portions of portfolios can be aggregated together to create templates derived from similar projects.

Modern estimators also support reusability estimating, and the knowledge-base can even predict the probable quantities of reusable artifacts. Object-oriented approaches are also included within the capabilities of estimating tools offered since about 1990.

Estimating support for all known languages also occurs. A few of the most complete estimating tools can deal with multiple languages as part of the same project. (Note: as many as 12 languages have been observed on a single system. About one third of software projects use at least two languages, such as COBOL and SQL or C++ and Assembly.)

For convenience in performing a "what if" analysis, some modern estimating tools include a side-by-side comparison mode, so two projects, or two scenarios for the same project, can be seen on the screen at once.

Estimating vendors are also starting to produce commercial "templates" for both vertical and horizontal markets. Examples of templates include sample projects at SEI maturity levels 1, 2, 3, 4, or 5. Other examples include projects set up in adherence with various standards such as DoD 2167A or the ISO 9000–9004 series.

Modern estimating tools tend to use functional metrics as their primary internal measure, but several offer automatic metrics conversion capabilities among multiple metrics (i.e. LOC, KLOC, Function Points, Feature Points, etc.).

For international projects, currency conversion is a standard feature as are European date numeric formats. At least one software estimating vendor is planning to release an international version that will adjust document sizing and estimating equations for specifications and paperwork costs based on national language (i.e. German, Japanese, French, etc.) and paper size (i.e. U.S. 8.5 by 11, European A4 size, etc.)

12. **Consulting offerings**—Most estimating tool vendors also offer consulting support. For example, Quantitative Software Management (QSM) is the vendor of the SLIM estimator, and offers both public and private estimating consulting and seminars. The same is true of Software Productivity Research, the vendor of CHECK-POINT® and SPQR/20. Rubin Associates also offers consulting seminars in support of the ESTIMACS tool marketed by Computer Associates. Many different vendors offer training in COCOMO, since it is in the public domain. Consultants are often used to identify the factors (i.e. the tools, methods, languages, and environmental factors), that impact estimates, selecting normalizing metrics, and assisting in baselines that will assist in building historical data bases that can be used to validate estimates. A good focal point for estimating knowledge are the non-profit ISPA and SCEA organizations. ISPA is the International Society of Parametric Analysis, and SCEA is the Society for Cost Estimating and Analysis. IFPUG, the International Function Point Users Group, also has an estimating and tools subgroup.

13. **Education offerings**—As of 1993, software estimating is such a rapidly expanding discipline that new courses are springing up almost monthly. However, commercial software estimating tools are only about 20 years old and many of the inventors and originators of such tools are still active as instructors and teachers. To cite but a few estimating pioneers who also have courses or who teach estimating: Dr. Barry Boehm, Frank Freiman, Randall Jensen, Capers Jones, Dr. Larry Putnam, and Dr. Howard Rubin have all developed estimating tools, and all lecture on software estimation methods. Dr. Albert Lederer of Oakland University in Rochester, Michigan, is one of the academic leaders in software estimating. Dr. Richard Fairly is one of the better-known U.S. estimating specialists, and has a course which utilizes three separate estimating tools. Dr. Victor Basili of the University of Maryland is also well known in the estimating domain. Dr. Albert Lederer of Rochester University is known in the sizing and estimating domain.

14. **Publication support**—Dr. Barry Boehm's dated but classic *Software Engineering Economics* (Prentice-Hall, 1981) describes the COCOMO estimating methods in depth. COCOMO is the only public-domain estimating method, and has spawned perhaps 20 software tools. Tom DeMarco's classic *Controlling Software Projects* (Dorset House, 1982) discusses the well-known "Bang" or DeMarco functional metric, and also estimation methods based on it. Frank Wellman's *Software Costing* (Prentice Hall, 1992) is relevant. Bernard Londiex's *Cost Estimation for Software Development* (Addison Wesley, 1987) is relevant, but discusses only a few of the many software estimating tools available.

Three books by the author, Capers Jones, deal with software measurement and estimation. *Programming Productivity* (McGraw-Hill, 1986) deals with the measurement and estimation of productivity, software costs, and schedules, and "soft" factors. *Applied Software Measurement* (McGraw-Hill, 1991) covers the topic of establishing measurement programs, and also includes current U.S. averages for software productivity for military, systems, and MIS software projects which can serve as a benchmark for validating estimates. This book also contains a full discussion of the new Feature Point metric. *Critical Problems in Software Measurement* (IS Group, 1993) discusses a multi-tier taxonomy for organizing large data bases which contain thousands of measured or estimated projects. It is quite a technical challenge to ensure apples to apples comparisons when dealing with thousands of heterogeneous projects.

Dr. Larry Putnam's book *Measures for Excellence* (Prentice-Hall, 1991) discusses estimating technology as well as measurement. Charles Symons' *Mark II Function Points* (Addison-Wesley, 1991) describes estimating using the British Mark II method.

A few books attempt to cover multiple estimating models and include comparisons. One of the most useful is a large monograph by Captain Kevin Burk, Dean Barrow, and Todd Steadman of the U.S. Air Force's Software Technology Support Center: *Project Management Tools Report,* March 1992. Bernard Londiex's *Cost Estimation for Software Development* (Addison Wesley, 1987) discusses three of the older models: COCOMO, SLIM, and PRICE-S. Lois Zells' *Managing Software Projects* (QED Information Sciences, 1990) covers more than a dozen planning tools, and a few estimating tools are thrown in. Thomas Gulledge, William Hutzler, and Joan Lovelace's *Cost Estimating and Analysis* (Springer Verlag, 1992) covers software estimation in context with other product estimation methods. A very useful catalog which includes most of the estimating tools marketed in the United States is published semi-annually by Applied Computer Research of Scottsdale, Arizona: *Guide to Software Productivity Aids.* This catalog also includes CASE tools and many other kinds of software tools.

Many books include chapters on estimation, or provide background information on models and metrics. Examples of books which cover estimation among other topics include: S.D. Conte, H.E. Dunsmore, and V.Y. Shen's *Software Engineering Metrics and Models* (Benjamin/Cummings, 1986); K.H. Moller and D.J. Paulish's *Software Metrics* (IEEE Press, 1993); Robert Grady and Deborah Caswell's *Software Metrics: Establishing a Company-Wide Program* (Prentice Hall, 1986); Robert Grady's *Practical Software Metrics for Project Management and Process Improvement* (Prentice Hall, 1992); and Horst Zuse's *Software Complexity—Measures and Methods* (Walter de Gruyter, 1991).

15. **Periodical support**—The only journal that deals explicitly and regularly with estimating is the ISPA Journal (International Society of Parametric Analyses). ISPA is a non-profit organization which encompasses all forms of parametric estimation, not just software. The journal Metrics Views of the International Function Point User's

Group (IFPUG) contains articles on estimating in almost every issue, but is not devoted specifically to estimation. The journal American Programmer published by Ed Yourdon occasionally has a special issue devoted to measurement and estimation. The journal IEEE Transactions on Software Engineering has been promising a special edition on metrics for more than a year, with perpetually delayed publication dates. The Society of Cost Estimating and Analysis (SCEA) also has a newsletter which covers software estimating, among other kinds of estimating. The ordinary software journals such as IEEE Transactions on Software or Communications of the ACM feature articles and even special issues on this topic from time to time.

16. **Standards support**—There are no current standards published by ANSI, DoD, IEE, IEEE, or ISO that cover software estimation in the sense that they specify contents of an estimate, accuracy levels, or significant parameters to be included.

17. **Professional associations**—The Society of Cost Estimating and Analysis (SCEA) is a fairly new group, and growing rapidly. The International Function Points Users Group (IFPUG) has been growing at a rate of almost 50% per year, and is now one of the larger professional associations. The International Society of Parametric Analysis (ISPA) is the major non-profit professional group, and has many chapters and meetings in Europe as well as in the United States that cover software estimating, among other topics. Specific interest groups within other associations such as the ASM, ACM, and IEEE may deal with estimation. Local CASE and Quality Assurance groups may also deal with specialized aspects of estimation. The Software Process Improvement (SPIN) network of regional groups also discusses estimating from time to time.

Most of the commercial estimating tools have non-profit user groups associated with them. To name but a few, COCOMO, CHECKPOINT®, ESTIMACS, PRICE-S, and SLIM are examples of tools with user groups.

18. **Effectiveness of known therapies**—Estimation is now easy to perform at the project level, and surprisingly accurate when compared against accurate historical data. (Watch out for the problem of comparing estimates against incomplete or partial history.) Commercial estimating tools can estimate requirement, design, coding, documentation, and many other activities and tasks with acceptable precision. Some tools, such as CHECKPOINT® and SLIM, can also estimate the costs and productivity levels of defect removal activities such as reviews, inspections, and tests. Productivity estimation accuracies to within 15% are now common, and 5% precision is not impossible (note that estimation is often more accurate than historical data recording). Estimating tools that integrate quality and productivity estimates have the best overall accuracy, since defect removal is such a large portion of total software costs. Estimating tools that predict specification and documentation costs are also more accurate overall, since paperwork can sometimes consume more than 50% of all total software project costs. Some software cost estimating tools also support international estimation, with built-in currency conversion and European numeric and date formats available.

The best results from the leading companies who use commercial estimating technologies are quite favorable: elimination of canceled projects, minimization or elimination of cost and schedule overruns, improvement in staff morale, and reduced friction with users and executive management are the normal results.

Note, however, that when estimating tools give bad news, such as predicting long schedules or high costs, there is a tendency to challenge the validity of the estimate or replace it with a more optimistic scenario.

Military and systems software estimation tools are widely used, but some-what out of date in terms of technical sophistication, due to a strong emotional attachment to unacceptable "lines of code" metrics as the basis for the estimates. However, the military services and major defense contractors are almost unique in several respects when it comes to estimation: A) They have recognized positions such as "cost estimator" and "cost analyst"; B) They use multiple estimating tools and look for convergence or divergence. Both of these practices augment accuracy and are steps in the right direction.

For cost estimating tools to work with acceptable accuracy (i.e. better than 10% precision) the project itself must be under control. There are no effective techniques for estimating the chaotic and random patterns of costs that occur when inexperienced managers cross paths with creeping requirements and careless development methods.

Note that before a software cost estimating tool can successfully estimate the impact of new technologies, languages, or other factors, several completed projects that used the technologies must be measured. This introduces a lag time of at least a year between the introduction of a new approach, and the ability of estimating tools to deal with the new factor. For example, as of 1993 developing multi-media applications is outside the scope of most commercial software estimating tools.

Note also that every commercial estimating tool has a hidden implicit assumption that a project will be managed and developed with at least moderate competence. In situations where this assumption is not true, and for situations where user demands are unstable and grow continuously and randomly, none of the estimating tools can be successful. There are no estimating techniques that can predict the follies and random results of incompetent management, technical staff, or clients.

19. **Costs of known therapies**—Ordinary project planning tools by themselves are not adequate for estimation purposes, since they have no way to assess the impact of "soft" factor influences such as methods, tools, languages, skill levels and the like. Expert-system, full software estimating tools with soft-factor analysis, activity-level and task-level estimation, integrated quality and document estimation, (such as SPQR/20, SLIM, and CHECKPOINT®) are in the $5,000 to $20,000 range. (Partial estimating tools and macro-estimating tools such as the public-domain COCOMO method and its derivatives cost less, but are also less useful than full life-cycle estimation tools.) Software estimation tools normally return their value in less than 12

months when used early in the development (i.e. requirements phase) of projects over 500 Function Points, or when amortized over 10 or more smaller projects.

Companies that measure quality and productivity are obviously in a position of measuring the costs of measurement itself. A full quality measurement program that includes both user-satisfaction and defect measurements tends to absorb about 2% of the annual costs of a software organization. A full productivity measurement program that includes "soft" data collection and both monthly reports on on-going projects, and annual reports of completed projects, is also at about the 2% level. Thus a full software measurement program will add about 4% to the overall cost of software. These expenses will be recovered via shorter schedules, higher quality, and other benefits in about 18 to 20 months.

20. **Long-range prognosis**—Use of commercial grade estimating tools is increasing in the U.S. by about 30% annually. New vendors and new tools are becoming available at a rate of about one per month. Under these conditions, accurate estimates should become the norm by the end of the 20th century, and possibly as early as 1997. However, empirical observations indicate a major cultural problem that may not be solved so rapidly: when estimating tools predict failure, long schedules, and poor quality software managers tend to disbelieve the estimate and ignore the warnings. By the time the estimate is proven correct, it is too late for effective recovery. Here too, social and cultural problems are intertwined with technical problems.

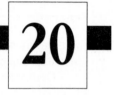

CHAPTER 20

Inaccurate Metrics

1. **Definition**—A) Common software metrics that violate standard economic assumptions; B) Common software metrics that behave in paradoxical, counter-intuitive, or unpredictable ways; C) "lines of source code" and "KLOC" metrics when used as general-purpose software quality or productivity metrics; D) "Cost per defect" when used as an indicator of quality costs; E) "Software Science" metrics when used as general productivity or quality indicators; F) Ratios and percentages when used as general productivity indicators.

2. **Severity**—The average severity level of inaccurate metrics is embarrassingly high, and averages about 1.5 on the following scale:

   Severity 1: Inaccurate metrics are used for key technical and business decisions

   Severity 2: Inaccurate metrics are used as general productivity and quality indicators

   Severity 3: Inaccurate metrics are used as primary metrics, but not exclusively

   Severity 4: Inaccurate metrics and rational metrics are used concurrently

   Severity 5: Inaccurate metrics are used as supplemental metrics to rational metrics

3. **Frequency**—Inaccurate metrics of types (A) through (D), above, are used by about 75% of U.S. software producing enterprises. Inaccurate metrics of types (E) and (F) are used by about 15% of U.S. software producing enterprises.

4. **Occurrence**—Inaccurate metrics are common in the U.S., Europe, the Pacific Rim, and South America. Military and systems software producers are more likely to use inaccurate metrics than are MIS producers. Universities and academic institutions are both a source and vector for the transmission of inaccurate metrics, as are journals and book publishers. Even software standards organizations such as ISO, ANSI, and the IEEE are prone to using inaccurate metrics such as "lines of source code." The Software Engineering Institute (SEI) core metrics program is also a vector for transmission of inaccurate metrics, since it includes "lines of code" with no cautions or warnings that this metric is unreliable.

5. **Susceptibility and resistance**—Susceptibility to inaccurate metrics is general and widespread among academics, practitioners, managers, and software authors. Resistance to inaccurate metrics occurs whenever inaccurate metrics are examined

carefully using standard economic and logical analytic techniques. Users of functional metrics are somewhat more resistant to inaccurate metrics than other classes.

6. **Root causes**—The root causes of inaccurate metrics include the following: 1) The widespread tendency to use concepts without examining their validity; 2) The common tendency to use concepts as long as colleagues also use the same concepts; 3) The implicit but incorrect assumption that if a metric is used in published articles it must be valid; 4) The lack of any rational alternatives to inaccurate software metrics prior to 1979; 5) The unfortunate tendency of civilian and military standards to include certain inaccurate metrics such as "lines of code"; 6) The dismal failure of U.S. universities, business schools, and software engineering curricula to include any courses at all in metrics analysis; 7) Resistance to change and slow technology transfer.

The mathematical problems with "lines of code" metrics are so damaging to economic understanding of software that an illustration is desirable.

Assume that we are concerned with two versions of a military application which provide *exactly* the same functions to end users. The quantity of Function Points is therefore the same for both the Ada and Assembly language versions: assume 15 Function Points for both versions.

The code volumes, on the other hand, are quite different. The Assembly Language version required 5000 statements, while the version in the more powerful Ada language required only 1,000 statements, or only 20% of the Assembly-Language code.

Assume that the burdened salary rate in both the Ada and Assembly versions of the project was $10,000 per staff month. Here are the two versions shown side-by side:

Activity	Assembly Language Version (5000 Source Lines) (15 Function Points)		Ada Language Version (1000 Source Lines) (15 Function Points)	
	Months	**$**	**Months**	**$**
Requirements	1.0	$10,000	1.0	$10,000
Design	2.0	$20,000	1.0	$10,000
Coding	3.0	$30,000	0.75	$7,500
Testing	2.0	$20,000	0.75	$7,500
Documentation	1.0	$10,000	1.0	$10,000
Management	1.0	$10,000	0.5	$5,000
Totals	10.0	$100,000	5.0	$50,000

In standard economic terms (i.e. goods or services produced per given amount of labor or expense) the Ada version is clearly twice as productive as the

Assembly language version, since delivering the same application costs half as much and took half as much effort.

However, are these economic advantages of Ada visible when productivity is measured with "source lines per month" or "cost per source line?" Indeed they are not. The productivity of the Assembly Language version of the project is 500 LOC per month. The productivity of the Ada version is only 200 LOC per month.

There are similar reversals when costs are normalized: the Cost per LOC for the Assembly Language version is $20.00 while the Cost per LOC for the Ada version has soared to $50.00.

(There are also similar reversals when quality data is normalized. Data expressed in "Defects per KLOC" form also tends to penalize high-level languages.)

Plainly something is wrong here. The more expensive version (Assembly Language) looks more than twice as productive as the Ada version when measured using "lines of code" metrics. Yet the Ada version cost only half as much. What is wrong?

The fundamental problem is that there are fixed costs tied up in activities such as requirements, design, and documentation that are the same in both versions. Thus when LOC is selected as a manufacturing unit, and there is a switch from a low-level language to a high-level language, then the number of units that must be manufactured is clearly reduced, but the fixed costs are not reduced.

Since both the Assembly Language and Ada versions produce the same functions, observe how closely productivity can be when measured with Function Points. The Ada version nets out at 3.0 Function Points per month, which is double that of the Assembly Language version which nets out at only 1.5 person-months per staff month.

When Function Points are selected as the manufacturing units, as opposed to LOC, the paperwork costs are included in the unit of measure itself and no longer act as external fixed costs.

The cost per Function Point also favors Ada too: The Ada cost per Function Point is $3,333 while the Assembly version is $6,666. As can be seen, Function Points actually correlate with standard manufacturing economics and productivity assumptions, while LOC metrics move paradoxically in the wrong direction.

This illustration shows how inaccurate metrics are the root cause to a host of other software problems. Without being able to measure or understand improvements in software economics, and LOC metrics prevent that from occurring, many derivative and supplemental problems occur. A strong case can be made for declaring "lines of code" metrics to be professional malpractice starting in 1995. It is professionally embarrassing for the software industry to continue using a normalization metric that works backwards for both productivity and quality.

7. **Associated problems**—Inaccurate metrics are key contributors to the problems of *Poor Technology Investments, False Productivity Claims, Inadequate Cost Estimating,* and *Inadequate Measurements.* Inaccurate metrics are also causative factors in the problems of *Missed Schedules, Long Schedules,* and *Low Productivity,*

and even to *Canceled Projects*. Inaccurate metrics are also contributing factors to the problems of *Friction with Executives, Friction with Users,* and *Friction with Contractors,* and *Low Management Morale.*

Specific inaccurate metrics are associated with specific problems. The two most harmful inaccurate metrics are "lines of source code" and "cost per defect" since they are by far the most widely used. Both "lines of source code" and "KLOC" metrics are associated with *Poor Technology Investments, False Productivity Claims, Low Productivity, Inadequate Cost Estimating,* and *Inadequate Measurements.*

The "cost per defect" is associated with *Poor Technology Investments, Low Quality,* and *Inadequate Defect Removal.*

Inaccurate metrics are often caused by the problems of *Academic Malpractice, Management Malpractice, Inadequate Management Curricula,* and *Inadequate Standards.*

8. **Cost impact**—The direct costs of inaccurate metrics can be quantified in specific cases, but are difficult to generalize. An example of a direct cost associated with inaccurate metrics would be investing in an estimating tool that only supported "lines of source code" metrics and hence would generate irrational estimates when used with object-oriented languages or program generators.

The indirect costs of inaccurate metrics are enormous. Indeed, it is fair to say that the use of inaccurate metrics has been the main bottleneck in making "software engineering" a true engineering discipline. One example of the indirect costs of inaccurate metrics is the failure of "lines of source code" metrics to demonstrate the economic productivity gains associated with object-oriented languages, program generators, and graphic icons. All of these methods improve economic productivity, but are not directly measurable with "lines of source code" metrics.

Another example of the indirect costs of inaccurate metrics is the fact that software paperwork (requirements, design, specifications, and user documentation) often costs more than twice as much to produce as the source code for a large system, but paperwork costs are essentially invisible with "lines of source code" metrics. Therefore enterprises that use "lines of source code" are seldom able to carry out serious research into front-end economic problems and effective technologies.

The dual problems of inaccurate metrics and inadequate measurement are root causes for many of the cost overruns, canceled projects, and inefficiencies of the software industry.

9. **Methods of prevention**—The examination of a candidate metric using standard economic methods and generally acceptable accounting practice is an effective preventive step for incorrect metrics. Analogies with metrics used by other disciplines are also effective. For example, from the standpoint of normal accounting it is obvious that "lines of source code" ignores the costs of non-coding activities such as requirements, design, and documentation. With high-level languages, the non-coding activities absorb the bulk of the effort and paperwork costs tend to

behave as though they were fixed costs. Thus, the metric "lines of source code per staff month" will get lower as the level of language gets higher.

Consider the analogy of studying compensation of software managers internationally. It is obvious that dollars, yen, lire, pounds, francs, and deutschmarks cannot simply be added together and averaged. Doing so would obviously violate the laws of standard economics and create irrational results. It is equally obvious that for large-scale productivity studies spanning multiple languages, it is not possible to add and average the results of projects in assembly, Ada, C, C++, Fortran, Chill, Smalltalk, and other languages.

The metric "cost per defect" also ignores factors such as preparation of test cases and training of maintenance staff which are essentially fixed costs. Thus as quality improves, the "cost per defect" metric will get larger and larger. In the case of zero-defect software, there will still be costs associated with preparing and running test cases and training maintenance personnel, so with zero-defect software the "cost per defect" will be infinity!

10. **Methods of control**—Surprisingly, the most effective control for inaccurate metrics is to use them on a large sample of diverse projects, such as 50 or more. It is difficult to perceive the inaccuracies of metrics when they are used on only a single project, but as more and more projects are analyzed, the problems and paradox become clearly visible.

(Note: the original discovery of the LOC paradox occurred in 1973. It was made after about 25 projects in various languages had been compared. Prior to that study, the author had never bothered to question the validity of LOC metrics, and had tacitly assumed that LOC was a perfectly reasonable sizing unit. The first solution to overcoming the paradox, also developed in 1973, was to use "equivalent assembly language statements" for productivity and quality comparisons. The paradox was published in the IBM Systems Journal in 1978. Albrecht's more elegant solution of Function Points was published in 1979.)

Since one of the primary reasons for continuing to use inaccurate metrics is sociological, it may be appropriate to consider a sociological remedy. That remedy, which is admittedly controversial, is to declare the use of "lines of code" metrics for productivity and quality studies to be regarded as professional malpractice starting in 1995. The two-year lead time should be sufficient to allow challenges to the thesis that LOC metrics are a serious enough problem to deserve being viewed as malpractice.

11. **Product support**—Software measurement and estimation tools that support Function Points and, Feature Points are the best defense against misuse of "lines of code" metrics. Commercial measurement tools that support functional metrics include CHECKPOINT®, FP Expert, MARS, and RA Metrics. Commercial estimation tools that support functional metrics include Before You Leap, the Bridge, and GECOMO. The CHECKPOINT® tool also has powerful conversion capabilities and can switch data between IFPUG function points, SPR function points, SPR feature

points, and LOC metrics at will. Direct conversion from LOC metrics to functional metrics is termed "backfiring." Backfiring is now possible for over 350 languages.

12. **Consulting support**—More than a hundred consultants and consulting companies now support functional metrics, and the rate of increase in such support is larger than 30% annually. Some of the consulting groups supporting functional metrics include, in alphabetical order, Computer Power, DMR Group, Huffschmidt Associates, Nolan, Norton & Company, QAI, Real Decisions, and Software Productivity Research (SPR). The SPR metrics methods also deal with activity and task level metrics from requirements forward. The non-profit International Function Point Users Group (IFPUG) now has more than 300 member organizations throughout the world, and is an excellent source of consulting and training assistance.

13. **Education support**—Academic support for functional metrics has lagged the commercial world, but Dr. Chris Kemerer at MIT's Sloan School has become well-known internationally for his research on Function Points. Many universities in the U.S. and abroad are starting to add courses in functional metrics, and to carry out research using functional metrics. A few recent examples include George Mason University, the Air Force Institute of Technology, the Naval Post Graduate School, and the University of Rochester in Michigan. The International Function Point Users Group (IFPUG) has a certification service to ensure that function point courses are current and accurate. Historical note: The course on Function Point Analysis developed by Allan Albrecht (the inventor of Function Points) was the first course certified by IFPUG.

14. **Publication support**—The first college text book on functional metrics is *Function Point Analysis* by Dr. Brian Dreger (Prentice Hall, 1989). It was published exactly 10 years after Function Points were publicly announced in October of 1979.

Four books by the author, Capers Jones, deal with software metrics and measurement. *Programming Productivity* (McGraw-Hill, 1986) deals with the metrics and measurement of productivity, software costs, and schedules, and "soft" factors. *Applied Software Measurement* (McGraw-Hill, 1991) deals with the topic of inaccurate metrics, and uses case studies to demonstrate common problems. *Critical Problems in Software Measurement* (IS Management Group, 1993) discusses the nature of synthetic versus natural metrics, and analyzes the problems of "LOC" metrics. *Software Productivity and Quality—The World Wide Perspective* (IS Management Group, 1993) deals with the software metrics and measurements methods and includes comparative data from major European and Pacific Rim countries as well as North and South America.

Dr. Larry Putnam's book, *Measures for Excellence* (Prentice-Hall, 1991) discusses both measurement, estimating, and statistical analysis of results. A book by Charles Symons, *Mark II Function Points,* (Addison Wesley, 1991) discusses the Mark II function point variant, which is used primarily in the United Kingdom.

Tarik Abdel-Hamid and S. Madnick's *Software Project Dynamics—An Integrated Approach* (Prentice Hall, 1991) discusses an emerging form of dynamic modelling for software that has been made popular by its usage in the "management war games" seminars offered by Tom DeMarco and Ed Yourdon.

Cautions are necessary in regard to several well-known books that deal with metrics. Dr. Barry Boehm's *Software Engineering Economics* (Prentice Hall, 1981) and Robert Grady's and Deborah Caswell's *Software Metrics* (Prentice Hall, 1987) both use LOC metrics without cautioning readers of the situations and circumstances under which LOC metrics will generate paradoxical and incorrect results. The same is also true of Grady's new *Practical Software Metrics for Project Management and Process Improvement* (Prentice Hall, 1992). Therefore, readers should be cautious in using quantitative information from these books, (as indeed they should from most books on software, including this one). The books have many excellent features and are well regarded throughout the industry. But LOC is too hazardous a metric to use without warnings or cautions about its deficiencies.

Many books include background information on numerous models and metrics. Examples of such books include: S.D. Conte, H.E. Dunsmore, and V.Y. Shen's *Software Engineering Metrics and Models* (Benjamin/Cummings, 1986); K.H. Moller and D.J. Paulish's *Software Metrics* (IEEE Press, 1993); and Horst Zuse's *Software Complexity—Measures and Methods* (Walter de Gruyter, 1991).

15. **Periodical support**—Most of the general software and software management magazines are starting to include articles and discussions on the use of functional metrics: CIO, Datamation, Information Week, ComputerWorld, and the like. The journal of the International Function Point Users Group (IFPUG), Metric Views, is dedicated to coverage of functional metrics. The journal of the International Society of Parametric Analysis (ISPA) does not deal with software metrics exclusively, but often runs articles on this topic. American Programmer will do a special issue on metrics and measurement in 1993. Other journals, such as the IEEE Transactions on Software Engineering also cover the metrics field from time to time, and may even have special issues. A military journal, STSC Crosstalk, is starting to become one of the most diverse software journals, and often has articles on software metrics and measurement. Software is now a major industry, and mainstream publications are running articles about software with increasing frequency. To cite a few, Fortune, The Economist, Newsweek, and Business Week have all had articles on software metrics and related topics in 1992 and 1993.

16. **Standards support**—The canonical standard for counting Function Points in the U.S. is the *IFPUG Counting Practices Manual* which is updated by the IFPUG Counting Practices committee. The IEEE Standard on Software Productivity Measurement (IEEE 99n) discusses Function Points, and refers to the IFPUG counting practices manual. There are no standards for Feature Points or Mark II Function Points, although books are available which describe these methods in detail. Both SEI and SPR have published quasi-standards dealing with counting LOC. (Neither organization is an official standards body.) The SPR and SEI standards are not iden-

tical, however. The IEEE and the Software Engineering Institute are collaborating on a draft standard for software measurement, which is slated for external review in the Spring of 1993. Major changes will probably be necessary before final voting and acceptance—a process that can take a year or more.

17. **Professional associations**—The non-profit International Function Point Users Group (IFPUG) is the most effective current association for dealing with measurement and metrics issues. Membership in IFPUG has been increasing by almost 50% annually, and as of 1993, IFPUG is probably the largest software measurement association in the world. There are also IFPUG chapters or affiliated groups in England, Australia, New Zealand, France, the Netherlands, Brazil, and many other countries. Associations and groups still mired in "lines of code" metrics should be avoided or at least viewed cautiously, by reason of visible malpractice. Another well-known organization dealing with metrics is ISPA, or the International Society of Parametric Analysis. The Society of Cost Estimating and Analysis (SCEA) also deals with metrics from time to time. The older non-profit associations such as the ACM, IEEE, ITAA, and the like, may have metrics special interest groups.

18. **Effectiveness of known therapies**—Metrics research is now fairly easy to perform at the project, activity, and task levels. Tools such as CHECKPOINT® and GECOMO can convert raw data back and forth among a variety of metrics at will, and thus illustrate how metrics vary in response to factors such as fixed costs and improved quality with very high precision. Metrics conversion accuracies to within 1% are now common, and 0.1% precision is not impossible.

The best results from the leading companies who use accurate metrics are favorable: improvements in operating effectiveness, reduction of expenses, and quantified productivity improvement rates of about 15% per year have been achieved for four to five consecutive years for development productivity and more than 40% annually for software quality. In certain situations, maintenance productivity has improved as much as 25% to 30% per year. Metrics are not necessarily causative factors for such improvements, but do assist in making rates of progress visible.

19. **Costs of known therapies**—Note that neither resource tracking systems nor ordinary project planning tools are adequate for metrics research purposes, since neither class typically supports common software metrics at all. A full software metric and measurement tool with metrics conversion capabilities such as CHECKPOINT® or the BRIDGE and MARS or RA METRICS would be in the $20,000 range. (Partial metric and measurement tools such as function point collectors are often of lower cost, but also of lower utility.) Full metric and measurement tools with integrated estimating capabilities tools normally return their value in about 12 to 18 months when used for a typical set of projects in medium to large enterprises that handle 20 or more software projects per year.

20. **Long-range prognosis**—The technical problems of measuring software accurately have been solved. The cultural and sociological resistance to accurate measure-

ment is a harder problem. The United States as a country is very slow to adopt leading metrics: for example, only the U.S. and Burma still use miles and have not fully adopted metric highway signs. Given cultural resistance, it is likely that poor measurements will remain widespread throughout the remainder of the 20th century. Since companies that do measure software well have a good chance of stealing market shares from those that do not measure software, the very long range prognosis for solving the problem is good.

The Department of Defense is moving more slowly than the civilian sector in metrics research, and the Software Engineering Institute (SEI) is also somewhat behind the current state of the art on metrics topics. However, individual research efforts within the Army, Navy, Air Force, and Marines are sometimes quite good.

An encouraging sign of progress is the push by the U.S. Air Force to create a national software database. However, the proposal is so recent (September of 1993) that the effects cannot be judged as this book is printed.

21

Inaccurate Quality Estimating

1. **Definition**—Failure to predict the defect origins, defect potentials, defect severities, defect removal efficiencies, and delivered defect levels of software projects.
2. **Severity**—The average severity of quality estimating is distressingly high, and in the U.S. the average approaches 1 on the following scale:

Severity 1:   Neither formal nor informal defect estimates of any kind

Severity 2:   Informal delivered defect estimates

Severity 3:   Formal delivered defect estimates

Severity 4:   Informal defect removal and delivered defect estimates

Severity 5:   No defect potentials, but formal removal and delivery estimates

3. **Frequency**—The total number of U.S. companies and government agencies with accurate defect estimating capabilities in 1993 is less than 600, so the problem of inaccurate quality estimating currently affects about 97% of all U.S. enterprises.

4. **Occurrence**—Quality estimating errors are endemic throughout the software industry, and are severe for all sizes and classes of enterprises and projects.

5. **Susceptibility and resistance**—Susceptibility is widespread, and includes MIS, systems, and military software producers. MIS is more susceptible than systems and military software, although all classes are susceptible to a high degree. Resistance is normally found only in the leading 1% to 3% of the most sophisticated U.S. enterprises. Computer manufacturers, telecommunication manufacturers, U.S. military services, defense contractors, and commercial software producers are the most resistant U.S. industries. Organizations with formal quality assurance departments are somewhat more resistant than organizations without such groups, but not very much. As a class, Baldrige Award winners are the most resistant and a majority of such enterprises tend to use both defect prediction and defect measurement methods.

6. **Root causes**—The root causes of inaccurate quality estimation include: 1) The widespread U.S. cultural tendency to ignore quality; 2) The short-range concentra-

tion of U.S. management and the tendency to ignore long-range problems and solutions; 3) The U.S. failure to measure software quality; 4) Failure of business schools and university software engineering curricula to include relevant courses; 5) Failure of standards organizations such as ANSI, IEEE, and ISO to establish adequate standards for quality estimation; 6) The shortage of commercial software quality estimating tools in the U.S. prior to 1985; 7) The widespread shortage of trained quality assurance personnel in the U.S.; 8) Underfunding of U.S. quality assurance organizations.

A fairly significant root cause which has been noted during both assessments and also surveys carried out at quality association meetings is the fact that many software quality assurance groups are understaffed, underfunded, and undercapitalized. Software QA groups where the staffing levels are less than 3% of the general software population often reflect lip-service to quality. These minimal groups seldom have the discretionary funding available to either build or buy quality estimation tools.

7. **Associated problems**—Inaccurate quality estimates are associated with *Cost Overruns, Long Schedules, Missed Schedules, Excessive Time to Market, Lost Business, Loss of Market Share, Friction with Senior Management, Friction with Users, High Maintenance Costs, Low User Satisfaction, Inaccurate Cost and Resource Estimating, Inaccurate Reliability Estimating, Low Quality,* and *Canceled Projects.*

Inaccurate quality estimates can often be attributed to one or more of the problems of *Unanticipated Requirements, Inadequate Measurement, Inadequate Software Management Curricula, Inadequate Software Engineering Curricula, Inadequate Standards, Inexperienced Management, Lag Time in Technology Adoption, Inaccurate Metrics, Poor Support Structures,* and *Poor Technology Transfer.*

8. **Cost impact**—The direct costs of inaccurate quality estimation are difficult to enumerate, but can be calculated along the following lines: For example, a U.S. software project of 1000 Function Points will have a defect potential of 5,000 total defects. If only normal testing stages are used, then about 70% of the defects will be removed prior to release. This leaves about 1,500 defects still present when the software is delivered to its customers. The direct costs of inaccurate defect estimating can be derived from the costs of repairing the 1,500 delivered defects.

The indirect costs of inaccurate quality estimation are enormous, and potentially threaten the current U.S. dominance in global software markets. At a somewhat lower level, every producer of commercial products which use software is at risk, since high quality is the factor that has the greatest single impact on market shares. Also, defect potentials and the direct costs of defect removal constitute major factors in reducing the time to market of software-intensive products.

9. **Methods of prevention**—The most effective prevention for inaccurate quality estimating is accurate measurement. Indeed, accurate quality measurement of many projects from requirements onward throughout the life cycle will gradually build up a total immunity to significant quality estimating errors. The use of func-

tional metrics is an excellent preventive for quality errors, since these metrics allow very early prediction of requirement and design errors, which often outnumber coding errors. Also, functional metrics provide a new and powerful technique for predicting the number of test cases that will be required (i.e. raise the Function Point total to the 1.20 power for civilian software, and the 1.25 power for military software to predict the rough volume of test cases needed). The use of commercial micro-estimating tools that operate at the level of specific defect-removal activities and predict defect origins and severities is a good preventive for quality estimation errors.

10. **Methods of control**—Historical note: SPQR/20, marketed since 1985, appears to be the first commercial tool marketed in the United States that included defect potential, removal efficiency, and quality estimation capabilities as standard functions. As far as can be determined, the first such tool of any kind to create quality estimates including defect potentials and removal efficiency was IBM's Interactive Productivity and Quality (IPQ) estimator which was designed by the author and developed in APL by Dr. Charles Turk of IBM's San Jose Programming Laboratory in 1973.

   As of 1993, several other commercial software estimating tools besides the SPR products are being marketed in the United States that include at least partial quality estimation. The best include defect potential prediction for requirements, design, code, documentation, and bad fix defect categories; as well as defect severity level prediction. The best also include removal efficiency prediction for all standard types of review, inspection, and test activity. Modern tools also allow custom "templates" that are tailored to their particular software needs. Not all of the quality estimating tools are acceptably accurate, but most of them are far superior to manual methods.

11. **Product support**—Quality estimation tools were first marketed in 1985 in the United States. The vendors which market such tools include Computer Power, Quantitative Software Management (QSM), Software Quality Tools, and Software Productivity Research. However, new tools are frequently planned and announced. By the end of 1993 or early 1994, perhaps eight to 10 quality estimation tools may be in the U.S. market. This market, however, has been characterized by under capitalization and at least two start-up quality estimation companies went out of business before their products reached commercial availability.

12. **Consulting support**—A number of consulting organizations have specialized practices in software quality. These include Bender & Associates, Computer Power, Ernst and Young, Howard Rubin Associates, the Quality Assurance Institute (QAI), the Software Engineering Institute (SEI), Software Research Associates, Software Productivity Research, and Software Quality Engineering. All support quality-related estimation and measurement.

13. **Education support**—Unfortunately, commercial education in software quality seems more complete than that of the academic institutions. Several well-known

public courses on quality estimation include those of the estimating pioneers who have developed quality estimation tools. To name but three, Dr. Larry Putnam of QSM, Dr. Howard Rubin, and Capers Jones of SPR all offer quality prediction courses in 1993. Look for a course that deals with the subject of estimating software quality, and includes current U.S. ranges for defect potentials and removal efficiency. Look also for coverage of the culture and sociology of quality control. Since quality measurement is the underlying technology of quality estimation, the two topics are closely intertwined.

The technology of software quality control is being transformed, and new topics are appearing often. Since about 1990, the topics of Total Quality Management (TQM) and Quality Function Deployment (QFD) have become increasingly common. Other fairly new quality topics include "Clean Room" development, the Japanese Kaizen methods, and Motorola's well-known six-sigma quality goals (i.e. reducing defects to one part per million, or raising defect removal efficiency to 99.9999%). So many changes are occurring so rapidly that it is difficult to assess the impact of the newer technologies either by themselves, or in concert with older technologies.

14. **Publication support**—Many books deal with software quality control and quality improvement methods. However, only a few books deal with software quality estimation. Three by the author, Capers Jones, follow. *Programming Productivity* (McGraw-Hill, 1986) deals with both the measurement and estimation of quality. *Applied Software Measurement* (McGraw-Hill, 1991) deals with the topic of establishing quality measurement programs, and also includes current U.S. averages for software quality for military, systems, and MIS software projects which can serve as a benchmark for validating quality estimates. *Critical Problems in Software Measurement* (IS Management Group, 1993) discusses the need to measure defect potentials and defect removal efficiency.

Several books on reliability analysis include discussions of defect estimation, or at least defect estimation after release of the software. An example is *Software Reliability: Measurement, Prediction, Application* by Musa, Iannino, and Okumoto (McGraw-Hill, 1987). Unfortunately the literature on software reliability is sometimes at cross-purposes with the literature on software quality.

S.D. Conte, H.E. Dunsmore, and V.Y. Shen's *Software Engineering Metrics and Models* (Benjamin/Cummings, 1986) attempts to cover the whole universe of software metrics, and discusses quality estimation in several places.

15. **Periodical support**—The only journal that deals with software quality estimation, and then only on occasion, is the ISPA journal (ISPA is the non-profit International Society of Parametric Analysis). From time to time other journals such as the IFPUG's Metric Views will have specific articles on software quality estimation. SPR's house journal, Knowledge Base, has intermittent special issues on defect prediction and measurement.

Curiously, the software testing journals seldom cover this important topic. The newsletter of SCEA, the non-profit Software Cost Estimating and Analysis organization, also covers defect estimation from time to time. The Journal of Risk Management may include articles occasionally. The standard software engineering journals such as IEEE Transactions on Software and Communications of the ACM have intermittent articles on quality-related topics. A journal that should deal with quality metrics and quality prediction, but seldom does, is the Swiss-published ISO 9000 journal.

16. **Standards support**—It is embarrassing to the industry that neither the IEEE quality standard nor the ISO 9000–9004 quality standard series even discusses quality estimation in terms of defect potential prediction or defect removal efficiency estimation. Both standards lag the state of the art by several years, which is not uncommon for standards, unfortunately. Military standards also tend to have a gap in the topic of software defect predictions, and this topic is not included in the current version of DoD 2167A as of 1993.

17. **Professional associations**—Interestingly, it is the non-profit International Function Point Users Group (IFPUG) that seems most active in software quality estimating, rather than the quality associations themselves. The non-profit International Society of Parametric Analysis (ISPA) also deals with software quality estimating. The ISO organization is perhaps interested in the topic, but seems not to publish much about it. The Software Engineering Institute (SEI) is also beginning to move into quality topics, but is not yet particularly advanced. The industrial quality groups such as the Juran Institute and Phil Crosby Associates don't often deal with software quality as a separate topic.

    While there are many useful software quality associations, such as the Society for Information Systems Quality (SISQ), and many regional quality groups in cities such as Atlanta and San Francisco, the topics of defect prediction are not widely discussed in their journals and meetings.

18. **Effectiveness of known therapies**—Quality estimation is now easy to perform and surprisingly accurate. Modern Software Quality estimation tools can estimate requirements, design, coding, documentation, and "bad fix" defect origins. They can also estimate the costs and resources for defect removal activities such as reviews, inspections, and tests. Defect potential estimates to within 15% are now common, and 5% precision is not impossible. Defect removal efficiency has a higher margin of error, but 15% to 20% accuracy is now common. Estimating tools that integrate quality with productivity estimates have the best overall accuracy, since defect removal is such a large portion of total software costs. While this precision is not as high as might be desired, it is certainly better than having no quality estimates at all.

    The best results from the leading companies who use commercial quality estimating technologies are quite favorable: elimination of canceled projects, reduction of potential defect levels, elevation of removal efficiencies above 95%, minimization or elimination of cost and schedule overruns, improvement in staff morale, and reduced friction with users and executive management are the best results.

Military and systems software quality estimation tools are widely used, but somewhat out of date in terms of technical sophistication, due to a strong emotional attachment to unacceptable "lines of code" and "cost per defect" metrics as the basis for the estimates.

19. **Costs of known therapies**—Expert-system quality estimating tools such as SPQR/20 and CHECKPOINT® are in the $5,000 to $20,000 range. Other tools from other vendors such as QSM, Computer Power, etc. are in a similar price range. Software quality estimation tools normally return their value in less than 12 months when used early in the development (i.e. requirements phase) of projects larger than 500 Function Points, or when amortized over 10 or more smaller projects.

20. **Long-range prognosis**—The technologies for estimating software quality exist today and can be acquired fairly easily. The sociological and cultural resistance to estimating or measuring software quality is a harder problem. Because of that cultural resistance, poor quality estimation and measurement are likely to remain serious problems for the rest of the twentieth century.

Inaccurate Sizing of Software Deliverables

1. **Definition**—A) Failure to estimate the size of major software development components such as specifications, source code, user documents, test cases, or output screens; B) Errors in estimating the size of major software components, where the errors exceed 25% of the actual size; C) Essentially all attempts to size software components using "lines of code" metrics when the language of the product being sized is different from the language from which the sizing algorithms were developed.

2. **Severity**—The severity of sizing errors for software under definitions (A), (B), and (C) above is extremely high in the U.S. and abroad, and seems to be about a 1.5 on the following scale:

   Severity 1: No formal attempt to size any software components

   Severity 2: Formal sizing attempts for source code, but not for specifications

   Severity 3: Formal sizing algorithms are derived from "lines of code" metrics

   Severity 4: Informal sizing using only experience-based approaches

   Severity 5: Informal sizing using functional metrics, without complexity adjustment

3. **Frequency**—Sizing, or predicting the volumes of source code and other software deliverables and work products, was long considered to be one of the most difficult tasks of software engineering. Prior to the advent of functional metrics in 1979, the frequency of sizing problems exceeded 95% of all software projects. The unexpected power of functional metrics since 1979 to perform both source code sizing and also sizing of other deliverables is rapidly reducing the frequency of sizing problems by perhaps 10% to 15% per year.

4. **Occurrence**—Prior to 1979, sizing problems were endemic throughout the software industry and occurred with equal severity among information systems, systems software, commercial software, and military software projects. The advent of functional metrics has changed the pattern of sizing problems. The incidence of sizing problems for projects using functional metrics is now comparatively low. This means that military software and systems software, which have lagged in

adopting functional metrics, now experience the bulk of the remaining software sizing problems.

5. **Susceptibility and resistance**—Susceptibility is high among all projects and enterprises that fail to measure historical data. Susceptibility is also high among projects and enterprises that still attempt to use "lines of source code" as their metric of choice.

Resistance to sizing problems is very high among enterprises using functional metrics, including standard IFPUG Function Points, SPR Function Points, SPR Feature Points, and the British Mark II Function Points. Functional metrics have remarkable powers for sizing both source code in all known languages, and also specifications, test cases, and other software work products and deliverables. Note that size algorithms must be adjusted to match the specific functional metric employed. In particular, the British Mark II Function Points are not fully compatible with U.S. functional metrics.

6. **Root causes**—The primary root causes for software sizing include: 1) sizing is a very difficult intellectual problem; 2) the widespread lack of historical data of the sizes of software deliverables gave sizing researchers little to work with; 3) historical attempts to normalize size by means of the "lines of source code" metric invalidated all efforts to develop general sizing algorithms for requirements, specifications, user documentation, and other deliverables whose size was de-coupled from the volume of source code in the application.

7. **Associated problems**—Inaccurate size data is a key contributor to the problems of *Canceled Projects, Cost Overruns, Long Schedules, Missed Schedules, Excessive Time to Market, Friction with Users, Inaccurate Cost Estimates, Inaccurate Quality Estimates, Low Productivity,* and *Low Quality.*

Inaccurate sizing itself can often be attributed to one or more of the problems of *Creeping User Requirements, Inaccurate Metrics, Inadequate Measurement, Inadequate Software Engineering Curricula, Inexperienced Management,* and *Slow Technology Transfer.*

8. **Cost impact**—The direct costs of inaccurate sizing are normally unidirectional, and are serious primarily when the deliverable is substantially larger than its anticipated size. For example, if the estimated quantity of C code for a given application is 10,000 source statements, and the application actually requires 20,000 C statements, it is obvious that additional costs must be accrued. In this example, the costs for coding the application would be perhaps 75% higher than expected. (Doubtless unpaid overtime would be applied when the magnitude of the sizing error became visible, so the empirical cost difference would be slightly less than what might be anticipated.)

The actual cost of sizing errors depends upon what deliverable was mis-sized, and on the magnitude of the error itself. The commonest sizing errors are those associated with pages of specifications, volumes of source code, number of screens in an application, and pages of user documentation

9. **Methods of prevention**—The most effective prevention for sizing errors is accurate measurement of the sizes of all deliverables, the resources required to produce the deliverables, and the "soft" factors which influenced the deliverables.

The use of functional metrics has had a remarkable impact on software sizing technology, and such metrics are highly recommended as preventive measures for sizing problems. Recall that functional metrics are synthetic metrics rather than natural metrics. Synthetic metrics can be applied to a wide class of problems, and hence sizing algorithms using functional metrics are in rapid development for requirements, specifications, source code, pages of user documentation, and test cases.

Sizing technology using functional metrics is still a new field of research, and many of the results are still preliminary. Nonetheless the results are quite encouraging. Here are a few examples:

The size of *software requirements* appears to run from 0.25 to 0.75 pages per Function Point, assuming civilian projects, normal U.S. paper, single-spaced text, and 10 point type.

The size of *software functional specifications* appears to run from 0.5 to 1.5 pages per Function Point, assuming civilian projects, normal U.S. paper, single-spaced text, and 10 point type.

The quantity of *source code* per Function Point is now known, at least approximately, for almost 400 programming languages. For example, Ada averages 71 statements per Function Point, COBOL averages 105 statements per Function Point, C averages 128 statements per Function Point.

The number of *test cases* per Function Point can be approximated by raising the Function Point total of a civilian application to the 1.2 power and expressing the results as an integer. Thus for an application of 100 Function Points, about 250 test cases are indicated. For an application of 1000 Function Points, about 3,980 test cases are indicated. For a major system of 10,000 Function Points, about 63,000 test cases are indicated.

The size of general-purpose *users' guides* for software applications appears to run from 0.3 to 1.2 pages per Function Point, assuming civilian projects, normal U.S. paper, single-spaced text, graphics or illustrations on 30% of the pages, and 10-point type.

The technology of sizing with functional metrics still has a substantial margin of error, but the initial results are extremely encouraging. The first major publication on sizing with functional metrics appeared in only 1986 (*Programming Productivity*, McGraw-Hill). After less than 10 years of research, it is now possible to use functional metrics to size more than 50 paper documents, the volume of source code in almost 400 languages, and the number of test cases for ten different kinds of software testing.

10. **Methods of control**—The most effective control is to include full sizing logic in either proprietary or custom estimating tools. Although there are some 50 commercial software estimating tools marketed in the United States, not all of them support

sizing with functional metrics, and some do not support sizing at all. The first commercial software estimating tool to utilize sizing from functional metrics was SPQR/20 in 1985. The current commercial software estimating tool with the most complete sizing logic including sizing for specifications, source code, user documents, and test cases is the CHECKPOINT® tool, which was first marketed in 1989.

Many commercial software estimating tools will shortly be adding both Function Point support and sizing features, so the available tools should increase significantly over the next few years. Tools such as ASSET-R, the Bridge, BYL, GECOMO, PRICE-S, and many others are beginning to support sizing from functional metrics or from some modified form of functional metric as standard features.

11. **Product support**—The commercial software estimating and measurement products with the most complete sizing capabilities as of 1993 can now predict the sizes of more than 50 paper documents, source code size in all languages, source code size when multiple languages are used, test cases for all standard test steps, and the number of screens for interactive applications.

Commercial software estimating tools with at least partial source code sizing support include ASSET-R, the Bridge, BYL, GECOMO, SPQR/20, and SLIM.

Several CASE tools such as Texas Instruments' IEF, UNISYS LINC, AGS FIRST-CASE, Andersen's METHOD/1, and CGI PACBASE are starting to include integral sizing and estimating capabilities.

12. **Consulting support**—The estimating tool vendors whose products include sizing algorithms normally offer consulting support as well. For example, both Quantitative Software Management (QSM), the developer of SLIM, and Software Productivity Research (SPR), the developer of SPQR/20 and CHECKPOINT®, offer consulting services for sizing-related issues. Consultants who are familiar with functional metrics and with Function Points in particular are often useful for size-related issues. SEI is also exploring sizing methods.

13. **Education support**—Universities and academic institutions, by and large, have not offered explicit courses on software sizing. However, there are intermittent exceptions. Check local schools for availability of sizing courses. Several commercial courses deal with this topic, including courses offered by the companies formed by sizing pioneers such as Quantitative Software Management (QSM) or Software Productivity Research (SPR). Generalized courses on the rules of counting with Function Points are a normal prerequisite for using such metrics to size software deliverables. There are many excellent courses in counting with Function Points, although it is desirable to select courses endorsed by IFPUG. As of 1993, about 20 courses have now been IFPUG-certified.

14. **Publication support**—Brian Dreger's *Function Point Analysis* (Prentice Hall, 1989) is a useful primer which assumes no prior knowledge of functional metrics. The first book to cover source code sizing from Function Points as an explicit topic was the author's *Programming Productivity* (McGraw-Hill, 1986). The first

book to deal with paperwork and test case sizing from Function Points as an explicit topic was the author's *Applied Software Measurement* (McGraw-Hill, 1991).

Charles Symons' *Software Sizing and Estimating* (Wiley Interscience, 1991), covers sizing from the basis of the British Mark II Function Point metric, which differs substantially from the American IFPUG Function Point.

Anyone interesting in sizing from Function Points should join IFPUG (a non-profit association) and thereby receive the various IFPUG Counting Practices manuals, which are the de facto standards for dealing with this metric.

15. **Periodical support**—The journal Metrics Views of the International Function Point Users Group (IFPUG) is the periodical with the most frequent coverage on software sizing. The journal of the International Society of Parametric Analysis (ISPA) also includes software sizing articles from time to time.

Many software management and engineering journals will have articles on sizing from time to time: American Programmer, Communications of the ACM, CIO, Datamation, IEEE Software, IEEE Transactions on Software Engineering, and so forth.

16. **Standards support**—There are no current standards published by ANSI, DoD, IEE, IEEE, or ISO that cover software sizing for major deliverables in a generic way. There may occasionally be specific sections that require sizing of test cases and source code.

17. **Professional associations**—The non-profit International Function Point Users Group (IFPUG) is the most active association for size-related topics. The non-profit International Society of Parametric Analysis (ISPA) is also relevant for sizing topics. The Society of Cost Estimating and Analysis (SCEA) also deals with sizing topics.

18. **Effectiveness of known therapies**—Sizing with functional metrics is too new a technology to assert that it will be totally successful, but the preliminary results are highly encouraging. Source code sizing from functional metrics is now routinely accurate to about plus or minus 25%, and often even better. (Note that Creeping User Requirements must be dealt with also.) Sizing of paper documents has a higher margin of error, but accuracies of plus or minus 30% are now common, and often results are even better. Sizing of test cases is still too new to state accuracy ranges since many projects lack historical data on the number of test cases created or used. However, from the comparatively few projects where test-case data exists, accuracies of plus or minus 30% have been noted.

As of 1993, sizing technology from functional metrics has not yet been applied to multi-media applications, hypertext, or graphics and visual representation methods. However, active research is occurring in these new technical domains.

19. **Costs of known therapies**—The costs of learning to count Function Points, which is the basis of modern sizing technology, is comparatively low. Standard two-day or three-day Function Point courses range from about $200 to $1000.

Commercial estimating tools which support software sizing via functional metrics range from less than $1000 up to $20,000. At the higher-priced end, tools may offer very complete sizing logic for paper documents, source code, and test cases.

20. **Long-range prognosis**—The use of functional metrics for sizing purposes has created an explosion of new data and new techniques. Commercial software estimating tool vendors are already starting to include new sizing algorithms, and the usage of commercial software estimating tools is increasing by perhaps 30% per year. If the current rate of basic research and applied practices continues, software sizing should become an effective standard of engineering within five years. Even academic curricula, which normally lag the state of the art by about 10 years, should include sizing materials and courses by the end of the century.

CHAPTER · 23

Inadequate Assessments

1. **Definition**—A) Software process assessments that omit known and important factors which have a significant impact on quality, productivity, or staff performance; B) Software process assessments which lack the ability to perform valid comparisons between similar projects, organizations, or enterprises in terms of software performance levels; C) Software process assessments which lack follow-on process improvement activities to correct discovered problems.

2. **Severity**—As of 1993, most U.S. software-producing enterprises have not used any form of software process assessment, so the average severity of inadequate assessments is fairly high, and ranks as about 1.5 on the following five-point scale. For enterprises which use only SEI assessments, the severity is about a 3:

   Severity 1: No process assessments or improvement programs are utilized

   Severity 2: Inadequate assessments are used, with no improvement plans afterward

   Severity 3: Inadequate assessments are used, with inadequate improvements

   Severity 4: Adequate assessments are used, with no improvements afterward

   Severity 5: Adequate assessments are used, with inadequate improvements afterward

3. **Frequency**—As of 1993, perhaps 70% of all software-producing enterprises have not used any form of serious process assessment and follow-on improvement program, based on informal surveys at conferences and seminars. Of the 30% who have used software process assessments, about half tend to use marginal assessment methods such as the SEI approach, without also exploring the many important factors which are not covered by SEI assessments. This severely limits their ability to implement improvement plans. The other half (i.e. about 15% of U.S. software producing enterprises) use either non-SEI assessments, or multiple assessment methods such as SEI, SDC, SPR, Hewlett-Packard, or a proprietary method concurrently, and look for convergence. About half of this group (i.e. about 7.5% of software-producing enterprises) then implement effective software improvement programs. A very small number (less than 1%) of U.S. software-producing organizations are sophisticated

enough in their software processes and methods that they do not require significant process improvements as a byproduct of their assessments.

4. **Occurrence**—In principle, a software process assessment is similar to a medical examination, and is basically a form of structured analysis applied to software development itself, using standard checklists and questionnaires to ascertain if all important and relevant functions are performed. The more mature assessment methods also explore how well the relevant functions are performed, against the background of U.S. or industry standard practices.

Failure to perform any software assessment at all is common for small enterprises with less than about 50 total software staff members, other than DoD contractors. Failure to perform any software process assessments is also fairly common among MIS producers. Military software producers often use only the marginal SEI assessment process. This is becoming common among systems software producers as well.

5. **Susceptibility and resistance**—Military and defense software producers are highly susceptible to using only the marginal SEI assessment process, since SEI is funded by DARPA and the U.S. Department of Defense is strongly biased in favor of SEI assessments. (Many DoD executives and military personnel do not even know that other and more widely used assessment methods exist.)

Resistance to inadequate assessments is high among enterprises that have analyzed the structure and deficiencies of the SEI approach. Resistance is also high among industries and enterprises which have developed their own forms of software assessment. Resistance is also high among enterprises which use multiple assessment approaches, including alternate methods which compensate for the gaps and deficiencies of the current SEI assessment model.

6. **Root causes**—The technology of formal process assessments is somewhat analogous to an annual medical examination. Annual medical examinations use standard tests and diagnostic techniques (X-rays, blood pressure, glucose levels, etc.) to seek out and identify possible conditions that need treatment before they become severe. Formal software process assessments also use standard examination techniques to seek out possible conditions that may need correction. Unlike standard medical examinations, which have been evolving for several hundred years, the technology of formal software process assessments is comparatively young. The best-known assessment techniques in the U.S. (the SEI and SPR approaches) have been in use only since about 1985. However, both of these approaches were developed within different divisions of IBM in the 1970's and 1980's. Informal assessments and audits have been used since the 1950's for software, and derive from the pioneering work on operations research which took place during World War II.

The root cause of the lack of process assessments is the youth of the fundamental technologies. When technologies are quite new, they have not yet been incorporated into software management or software engineering curricula so many professionals lack knowledge of available options. The root causes of selecting and using only the SEI assessment methodology is because of pressure by the U.S. DoD in the military domain (SEI assessments are starting to be required by the U.S. DoD). Usage of the SEI assessment method in the civilian domain is due to the popularity of Watts Humphrey's well-known book *Managing the Software Process* (Addison-Wesley, 1989).

7. **Associated problems**—Failure to perform any kind of software process assessment can be either benign or malignant, depending upon whether the enterprise has major problems with software development, maintenance, staff morale, or user-satisfaction. If there are major problems, then failure to utilize formal assessments can be considered a manifestation of management malpractice.

The SEI assessment process is much better than nothing, but is currently deficient for several reasons. (Note that SEI has plans to improve their assessments in the future.) The following deficiencies of the SEI assessment process should be considered: 1) The SEI assessments are incomplete and ignore factors such as staff morale, high or low compensation plans, organizational structures, recruiting methods, office space and noise levels, and many other elements of software risk; 2) SEI assessments fail to capture quantitative data on productivity, quality, schedules, or other tangible matters; 3) SEI assessments are essentially manual, and hence more expensive than need be; 4) The SEI assessments have been biased in favor of large enterprises, and biased against small enterprises which lack the minimum complement of staff members necessary to climb above SEI maturity level 2 (Note: this problem may have been eliminated by the time this book is published); 5) SEI has asserted without any empirical proof that productivity and quality rates correlate strongly with maturity levels; 6) The SEI maturity level concept is a manifestation of an artificial maturity level and is not necessarily correct in its assumptions; 7) The binary question structure used by SEI is inadequate, and creates patterns of forced answers; 8) The SEI maturity level concept lacks a mid-point or average, and is not really useful for large-scale statistical studies since too many data points clump at level 1; 9) The SEI concept is geared to large mainframe producers, and tends to ignore some of the factors that are associated with object-oriented development, client-server development, multi-media development, and the like; 10) The SEI approach is not being modernized as rapidly as software technologies are changing, and does not cover recent topics such as Quality Function Deployment (QFD) and object-oriented analysis and design; 11) Now that SEI maturity levels are important for government contracting, contractors are beginning to learn the method and intimidate their managers to provide only positive patterns of answers; 12) SEI personnel have reported privately that some companies whose assessments turned up problems have used intimidation on managers who provided "negative" information; 13) The SEI approach is rather ambiguous, and there is no guarantee that assessments by two different groups of licensees would return the same results.

It must be concluded that an SEI assessment, if used by itself, is associated with the *Silver Bullet Syndrome,* and sometimes results in *Low Staff Morale.*

Marginal assessments such as the current SEI approach are often caused by *Inexperienced Management, Slow Technology Transfer,* and perhaps *Management Malpractice.*

8. **Cost impact**—The cost impact of inadequate assessments can be divided into direct and indirect components. The direct costs of inadequate assessments are the total costs for the assessment itself; i.e. staff salaries while they participate, and any fees paid to consultant groups for performing the assessment. In round numbers, this ranges from about $25,000 for assessing a small enterprise through perhaps $250,000 for large-scale corporate assessments of a multi-national enterprise.

The indirect costs of inadequate assessments are potentially much greater than the direct costs. (Consider the analogy of an inadequate medical examination for a patient with a serious condition which was not detected!) Quantifying the indirect costs is easy for specific cases, but difficult to generalize.

9. **Methods of prevention**—The most effective prevention approach for inadequate assessments is to use multiple approaches concurrently, such as SEI in conjunction with the SPR method, the SDC method, the Hewlett-Packard method, or the Pressman method. It is also possible to analyze assessment methods, and select the most relevant. (Since the author of this book is the developer of the SPR method, there is an obvious potential for conflict of interest.) Following are some general principles for evaluating the maturity level of software process assessments themselves:

Assessment Maturity Level 1—Rudimentary

The method uses incomplete and biased factor analysis questions (less than 150 total questions). The questions are structured in binary form, and tend to create artificial patterns of forced answers. Management provides the bulk of information and technical staff members are queried as a secondary consideration. The method lacks all quantitative data collection for resources, schedules, costs, or quality. There is no intrinsic ability to carry out multiple regression analysis from the collected data. Question sets are static, and do not change in response to new technologies. There is no automation of the question sets, and no convenient way to create a useful data base for multiple projects, enterprises, or industries. Follow-on process improvement programs are either not present, or likely to be ineffective due to the gaps in the assessment process itself.

Assessment Maturity Level 2—Developing

The assessment method is fairly complete in factor analysis (more than 250 questions). The questions are structured in binary form and tend to create artificial patterns of forced answers. Both management and technical staff members are interviewed. The assessment process still lacks all quantitative data collection for resources, schedules, costs, or quality. The questions are updated at least annually to stay current with new technologies and approaches, such as Quality Function

Deployment (QFD), Total Quality Management (TQM), and the like. There is no automation of the question sets, and no convenient way to create a useful data base for multiple projects, enterprises, or industries. Follow-on improvement programs are likely to be ineffective, due to lack of quantitative data on expense patterns and causative factors.

Assessment Maturity Level 3—Meaningful

The assessment method is fairly complete in factor analysis (more than 250 questions). The questions are structured in multiple-choice form, and do not create significant artificial patterns of forced answers. Both management and technical staff members are interviewed. The assessment process lacks quantitative data collection for resources, schedules, costs, or quality. The question sets are updated at least annually to stay current with new technologies and approaches. There is automation for the question sets, and it is possible to create a useful data base for multiple projects, enterprises, or industries. Follow-on improvement programs are the norm, but are sometimes ineffective due to lack of quantitative data. Follow-on improvement programs are common, but not always fully effective due to the gaps in the quantitative data available, or to the usage of inadequate metrics such as "lines of source code."

Assessment Maturity Level 4—Effective

The assessment method is very complete in its coverage (more than 350 questions) and includes strategic information such as total portfolio size as well as tactical information derived from specific projects. Senior executives, software managers, technical staff members, and software users or clients are interviewed. The assessment method captures basic project-level data for resources, schedules, costs, and quality. The questions and assessment instruments are frequently updated to stay current with evolving technologies such as the object-oriented paradigm and Quality Function Deployment (QFD). Automation exists to support the assessment process, and it is comparatively easy to create a powerful data base for multiple projects, enterprises, and industries. Quantitative data can be normalized to all standard metrics, such as IFPUG Function Points, SPR Feature Points, Mark II Function Points, and even the inadequate "lines of code" metric if desired. Follow-on improvement programs are tightly focused on key problems, and tend to be cost effective.

Assessment Maturity Level 5—Advanced

The assessment method covers all known factors which influence the outcomes of software projects (perhaps 500 questions). It includes strategic information on topics such as total portfolio size as well as tactical information on specific projects. It also explores the value and usage patterns of software within the enterprise being assessed. Senior executives, software managers, technical staff members, and software users or clients are interviewed. Very precise quantitative data is collected down to the levels of activities, tasks, and sub-tasks. Very complete user-satisfaction data is collected. Very complete value and software usage patterns are collected. Quantitative data can be normalized using all standard metrics, such as IFPUG Function Points, SPR Feature Points, Mark II Function Points, DeMarco Function Points, and even the inadequate "lines of code" metric if desired. Quality data is collected for all projects and for the enterprise. The question sets are updated frequently to stay current with evolving technologies. The questionnaires themselves are validated, and include built-in safeguards against bias and forced answer patterns. Advanced automation exists which not only creates a useful data base of information, but includes expert-system capabilities for generating improvement plans and quantifying their costs and value.

10. **Methods of control**—It is much easier to prevent inadequate assessments than it is to control them once underway. If an enterprise does commission or perform inadequate assessments, then the most effective (but expensive) control technique is to do another assessment using a better methodology. Note that following the analogy of annual medical examinations, software assessments should have periodic check ups. Empirical studies within enterprises such as AT&T, Hewlett-Packard, and SPR clients indicate that an annual assessment cycle may be optimal.

11. **Product support**—Assessments are normally performed by consultants or by assessment specialists. Tools such as SPR's CHECKPOINT® product, QSM's SLIM product, or Computer Power's MARS product are often used to support data collection. Standard statistical tools such as SAS are also used in support.

12. **Consulting support**—Many consulting companies can perform assessments. Very few can perform adequate ones. Consider the assessment maturity levels shown above when selecting an assessment consulting group. Note that the Software Engineering Institute (SEI) licenses consulting groups to use their method officially. However, many other companies are using flavors or variants of the SEI approach since the basic concepts are in the public domain.

13. **Education support**—Most universities have had no courses that deal with either adequate or inadequate assessments as part of the standard software engineering or management school curricula. Due to the popularity of the SEI assessment approach, there are now some university courses and many commercial courses available. Check local catalogs for current information. Commercial courses dealing with assessments are offered by groups such as Digital Consulting Inc. (DCI), the Technology Transfer Institute (TTI), and other commercial software education companies. Most of the companies that perform assessments also have courses or seminars available: Computer Power, SDC, SEI Hewlett-Packard, Pressman Associations, QSM, and SPR all have courses in their assessment approaches.

14. **Publication support**—Watts Humphrey's well-known book *Managing the Software Process* (Addison-Wesley, 1989) is the basis of the SEI assessment approach, and is one of the best-selling books of the industry.

The author, Capers Jones, describes the SPR assessment process in two books published by McGraw-Hill, *Programming Productivity* (1986) and *Applied Software Measurement* (1991). Obviously this book, *Assessment and Control of Software Risks* (Prentice Hall, 1993), describes many of the findings of SPR's assessments. The monographs *Software Productivity and Quality—The Worldwide Perspective* (IS Management Group, 1993) and *Critical Problems in Software Measurement* (IS Management Group, 1993) describe results from SPR assessments, and some of the problems of collecting assessment data internationally.

Roger Pressman's book *Software Engineering—A Practitioners' Approach* (McGraw-Hill, 1986) describes his approach. Dr. Bill Curtis' book *Human Factors in Software Engineering* (IEEE Press, 1984) is not about assessments, but illustrates many important topics that should be explored as part of assessments. Since Dr. Curtis headed the SEI assessment group, this book is perhaps a preview of new SEI approaches.

An entire suite of publications by SEI discuss their approach, with the 1991 *Capability Maturity Model for Software* by Paulk, Curtis, Chrisis, et al., being a good overview.

Phil Crosby's book *Quality is Free* (Mentor Books, 1979) is interesting because it is the background of Watts Humphrey's maturity-level concept.

A short description of how AT&T performs software assessments using the SEI and SPR methods concurrently was published as a monograph by the IEEE Press: *Software Development Process Benchmarking,* IEEE Communications Society, CH2980–1/91/0000–0153, December 1991. Clem McGowan, Shari Pfleeger, and Terry Bollinger, formerly of Contel's Software Engineering Laboratories, have published several thoughtful critiques of the SEI assessment approach.

A report on various assessment methods has only recently become available in summary form. That is the 1992 analysis of several assessment methods (SEI, SDC, SPR, etc.) commissioned by DARPA and carried out by the Institute of Defense Analysis (IDA). The summary is available in limited quantity. The document is Beth Springsteen's *Policy Assessment for the Software Process Maturity Model,* IDA Document D–1202 dated August of 1992, but not declassified until October.

(A letter to the author from Dr. Barry Boehm, dated September 22, 1992, stated that the full report would not be released due to the government sensitivity of the materials. That is to say, the report pointed out some gaps in the SEI approach.)

It would be unfortunate to mandate the SEI approach or require, for example, SEI maturity level 3 as a precondition for doing business with the military. Such a mandate would seem to be an unwarranted restraint of trade, and perhaps challenged in court. Of the approximately 32,000 U.S. software producers in 1993, only about 50 (or less) are at SEI level 3. A government mandate that disenfranchises 99.9% of U.S. companies in the absence of any strong empirical evidence that level 3 is truly more effective than level 2 would be most unwise.

Further, one of the military services has recently noted that software delivered by contractors who are at SEI level 3 is not necessarily of outstanding quality.

The companies most seriously at risk would be the many small companies that cannot afford the infrastructure and overhead required to climb above SEI level 2. Such groups would be placed at a serious disadvantage in competing with large enterprises. Essentially, all enterprises with less than about 50 employees would lose out. Even large enterprises such as WANG and DEC, which have been losing money of late, would be at a disadvantage.

Neither SEI, DARPA, military personnel, nor the DoD seem to realize that several off-shore software producers in India and elsewhere are already at or approaching SEI level 3, and yet have cost structures that amount to perhaps one-fifth of U.S. norms. A government mandate to contract only with SEI level 3 or higher enterprises might force substantial volumes of software business away from the United States and toward overseas producers.

Neither SEI, DARPA, many military personnel, nor the DoD seem to realize that a number of alternate assessment approaches and capability models exist in the United States and abroad. Several of them include the collection of quantitative data as well as assessment data. At least one is automated, while the SEI approach is manual. It is uncertain why so much public money is being spent creating SEI's assessment approach, when commercial off the shelf (COTS) methods exist which appear to equal and perhaps surpass the SEI approach.

Four interesting aspects of this situation deserve comment: A) The policy of favoring the SEI approach is perhaps being made without an adequate review or study of alternate and perhaps superior methods; B) Studies of alternate methods, such as the IDA research have been arbitrarily classified and not released promptly even though funded with public money; C) These important policy decisions are being made without any convincing empirical data which demonstrates a tangible superiority for SEI level 3 vis a vis level 2; D) The SEI assessment method is being deployed without prior validation or empirical evidence. It would be hazardous to deploy a weapons system on an aircraft with so little prior testing.

It is interesting that such a critical policy should originate in a fashion that spends public money without adequate review, controls, or consideration of viable alternatives.

A final point is that the costs of achieving SEI levels 4 and 5 are high enough so that it is uncertain that American enterprises at those levels could win competitive bids in the civilian sector. (On the other hand, companies in India, Hungary, Mexico, etc. where labor costs are low may well be able to win bids on costs as well as maturity level.) So far as can be determined from conversations with DoD and SEI personnel, no research has yet been carried out into the costs of achieving the higher SEI maturity levels.

While SEI has asserted that productivity rises with maturity level, that currently appears to be untrue or at least unsupported by empirical data. However, there is a serious shortage of long-range empirical studies on this topic, and future data may change the situation.

It is also asserted that high SEI maturity levels benefit quality. Here, too, the data is ambiguous. Some early data does show a correlation with quality, but there are exceptions too. Being at SEI level 3 does not seem to guarantee high quality. There are many unanswered questions about the actual results accruing from the various SEI maturity levels. Here too, more research and more empirical data are needed.

Note that there are five classes of software that are essentially equal in achieving high quality levels, and all five typically use careful software development processes: 1) medical instrumentation software; 2) central office switching systems software; 3) military weapons systems software; 4) operating system software; 5) on-board software for aircraft flight control and navigation. It is interesting that the costs of U.S. military software are significantly greater than any of the others, even though quality levels are essentially equal.

15. **Periodical support**—Because software assessments are becoming a significant subindustry, the standard software journals publish something about this topic almost every month. Check out American Programmer, the IEEE Transactions on Software Engineering, CASE Outlook, and other journals for frequent articles and occasional special issues. Terry Bollinger and Clem McGowan's now classic "A Critical Look at Software Capability Evaluations" in the July 1991 issue of IEEE Software is worth reviewing by those who regard the SEI approach as fully perfected.

16. **Standards support**—The DoD is considering the possibility of making SEI assessments a military standard, which appears to be premature. The International Standards Institute (ISO) is also exploring assessments, and will hopefully not simply recommend the current and marginal SEI approach. Other standards organizations such as ANSI, IEEE, IEE, and the National Bureau of Standards have not yet made any overt move towards standardizing assessments. This is probably the best policy, given the volatility of the assessment methods themselves.

17. **Professional associations**—Most of the major professional associations such as the ACM, IEEE, IEE, and Software Publishers Association are now aware of process assessments. From time to time meetings, seminars, newsletter articles, and the like deal with this topic.

18. **Effectiveness of known therapies**—For large corporations and large software projects, almost any assessment method is better than none and even the SEI approach generates useful information. However, small enterprises with less than about 50 software professionals should be very cautious about using the SEI assessment method, since it is severely biased in favor of large corporations. The most effective approaches are those practiced by industry leaders such as AT&T, Hewlett-Packard, and Motorola. These approaches involve the concurrent use of multiple assessments. Multiple assessment methodologies tend to complement one another, and when they converge on specific problems the results are highly convincing.

19. **Costs of known therapies**—The costs will vary with the size of the enterprise, the assessment method(s) used, and whether the assessment is self-administered or uses outside consultants. Costs range from less than $25,000 for small enterprises to

more than $250,000 a year for major multi-national corporations who annually assess all of their software groups. For example the SPR assessment approach, which has the largest volume of published cost data available, takes from two to four hours per project to collect the data (ten to 24 staff hours since up to six people are interviewed concurrently for each project). Data reduction, analysis, and results preparation normally takes from a week to 15 days and from 80 to 360 hours.

20. **Long-range prognosis**—The prognosis is somewhat favorable. The Software Engineering Institute (SEI) was taken by surprise by the success of Watts Humphrey's book, and by the interest in their assessment approach. Thus, a technique that was still under development was suddenly being treated as though it were fully perfected. SEI is working to modernize and update their assessment process. (Unfortunately, the DoD may force the current method on defense contractors, ready or not.) The other major assessment methods, such as SDC's, SPR's, Hewlett-Packard's and Pressman's, are also evolving. It would be highly desirable for the various assessment techniques to share common data, or at least to have their scales and evaluation results be commensurate. By the end of the century, the most optimistic scenario would be that software process assessments will become as accurate and effective as full annual medical examinations.

CHAPTER 24

Inadequate Compensation Plans

1. **Definition**—A) Compensation plans for software professionals and support personnel which are poor enough to lower morale or raise voluntary attrition; B) Compensation plans for software professionals and support personnel which top out well below managerial compensation plans; C) Compensation plans significantly below competitive and industry norms; D) Compensation plans significantly below regional averages.

2. **Severity**—The average severity of inadequate compensation plans for software staffs is about a three on the following five-point scale:

   Severity 1: Staff compensation > 30% below competitive or management norms

   Severity 2: Staff compensation 25%–30% below competitive or management norms

   Severity 3: Staff compensation 20%–25% below competitive or management norms

   Severity 4: Staff compensation 15%–20% below competitive or management norms

   Severity 5: Staff compensation 10%–15% below competitive or management norms

3. **Frequency**—Inadequate compensation plans are endemic among governmental organizations at local, state, and national levels where the frequency exceeds 95%. For academic institutions and universities, inadequate compensation also appears endemic, and can reach 75%. (Universities often allow faculty members to receive consulting, speaking, and publishing fees which offsets somewhat modest compensation plans.) For major service and manufacturing business enterprises with more than 100 software professionals, the frequency of inadequate compensation plans is perhaps 45%. For smaller organizations, inadequate compensation plans exceed 70% because small enterprises are often undercapitalized and lack adequate funds. In many small business and start-up situations, some form of equity is used as a partial substitute for salary and benefit compensation.

4. **Occurrence**—For small businesses, academic institutions, and government agencies inadequate compensation plans are the norm due primarily to limited available funds. For large companies, the occurrence of adequate or inadequate

compensation plans does not have a clearly defined pattern. On the whole, profitable industries and profitable companies tend to have better compensation plans than less profitable industries and companies, but there are some notable exceptions. So far as can be determined, corporate culture is the major factor involved.

5. **Susceptibility and resistance**—Enterprises where the founders, for various reasons, wished to develop long-term employment tenures and attract topnotch professional personnel have been the most resistant to inadequate compensation. Enterprises where long-term employment is not a goal, or where topnotch professionals are not actively recruited, tend to often be marginal in compensation. There are exceptions to both situations, however.

6. **Root causes**—The root causes of inadequate compensation can be divided into "financial" and "cultural" categories. The financial root cause includes enterprises which are undercapitalized or which lack funding for adequate compensation plans. The cultural root cause includes enterprises with adequate capitalization and funding, but where compensation plans are inadequate due to policies set by the owners, shareholders, or senior executives. One reason for low compensation levels for software personnel may be the comparatively low status of software in the eyes of senior executives.

7. **Associated problems**—The impact of good or bad compensation plans appears to be the following: good compensation plans do not directly improve morale or performance, but do make it easier to recruit capable personnel. Bad compensation plans have the very harmful impact of raising the voluntary attrition rate among the most capable employees. The most common compensation-related problem for software is the situation where technical staff compensation is significantly below managerial compensation. This means that senior technical staff at the top of their compensation levels have two choices, neither of which are beneficial to the enterprise: A) Enter management; B) Leave the company.

Inadequate compensation plans are directly associated with *high staff attrition rates* and *low staff morale*. There are indirect associations with *low productivity, low quality, long schedules,* and *excessive time to market.*

Inadequate compensation plans themselves may be caused by *inadequate capital investment, low status of software engineering personnel,* or even by *management malpractice.*

8. **Cost impact**—The cost impact of inadequate compensation plans has only recently been amenable to study, and the results are far from accurate. When the metric "gross enterprise productivity" is used, enterprises with marginal to inadequate compensation plans usually rank well below enterprises with good to adequate compensation plans. The metric of "gross enterprise productivity" is calculated by dividing the sum of the Function Points (new and changed) which the enterprise delivered to users in a year by the total quantity of staff months expended. The total quantity of staff months is calculated by multiplying the entire software staff (managers, programmers, software engineers, and administrative personnel) by 12.

Thus an enterprise with a total staff of 100 would obviously expend 1,200 months of effort in a year (more or less). If the enterprise delivered 2,400 new and changed Function Points in a year, the gross enterprise productivity would average 2 Function Points per month (more or less).

As of 1991, the gross enterprise productivity average for the U.S. appeared to be about 1.55 Function Points per month (Capers Jones, *Applied Software Measurement*, McGraw-Hill, 1991). The compensation plans of the enterprises that averaged more than 2 Function Points per staff month were often (but not always) superior to the enterprises that averaged less than 1 Function Point per staff month. However, many other factors were also present.

Within two industries—banking and insurance—gross software productivity levels seem to correlate with average compensation level. This may be an accidental phenomenon, and not a causative relationship.

Most comparisons between government and civilian productivity rates for software (and most other kinds of work) clearly favors the civilian sector, as do compensation levels. It has been recognized for some years that government positions usually do not pay enough to attract many researchers or knowledge workers in the top 10% of their fields. Of course, there are some civil servants who are highly capable and are willing to sacrifice higher compensation levels for the public good.

9. **Methods of prevention**—Quite a number of approaches are available for preventing compensation plan imbalances. Many professional associations such as the ACM, AMA, AEA, ADAPSO (now ITAA), the IEEE, and regional groups such as the New England Software Council publish annual surveys of compensation levels by job title, city, geographic region and the like. There are also special industry-wide compensation groups which provide "blind" comparisons of compensation practices to subscribers within an industry. An annual review of compensation levels for all employees is a good general practice. A deliberate policy of establishing a dual compensation plan, with technical salaries on a parity with management salaries up to about the level of a third or fourth line manager is also a good preventive. Carrying out annual opinion surveys is also a good preventive.

10. **Methods of control**—Correcting inadequate compensation plans is more difficult than preventing them. It is normally necessary to cost-justify such changes in considerable detail, and quantify the benefits that might occur in considerable detail. Also, to be fair, compensation plans must cover all employees of the enterprise, and not just the software professionals. Several New England companies have modernized and improved their compensation plans and introduced dual-salary plans within the past five years. The observed time spans to accomplish such changes ranges from about 12 months to over 24 months.

A method of control used fairly widely in Canada and Europe, although rare in the U.S., South America, and the Pacific Rim are craft unions for software personnel. For organizations where software personnel are unionized, union contracts tend to keep compensation levels somewhat above normal.

11. **Product support**—There appear to be no commercial products that assess the impact of good or bad compensation plans on enterprise performance.

12. **Consulting support**—Many management and personnel consulting groups deal with personnel and compensation-related issues: Andersen Consulting, A.D. Little, Dean Meyer Associates, DMR Group, Ernst & Young, the Index Group, and Peat Marwick are examples. Some, indeed, can even provide data on industry or regional compensation averages. The SPR assessment approach investigates compensation plans as part of its normal mode of operation when exploring strategic factors.

13. **Education support**—Most business schools have courses on compensation planning. There are also commercial courses available from both profit-making and non-profit groups such as the ACM, AMA, the Massachussets Software Council, etc. Note that there is a tendency to run into potential antitrust or conspiracy problems if universities, companies, or public utilities share or coordinate their compensation data.

14. **Publication support**—There are a number of personnel-related books that discuss compensation in general ways. There are also a number of books which deal with the topic of how good or bad compensation plans affect the morale and performance of employees, in general ways. Only a few books deal with the topic of software staff and management compensation as specific topics. Dr. Gerald Weinberg's classic *The Psychology of Computer Programming* (Prentice Hall, 1971) is very good on the motivational aspects of compensation. The more recent classic, Tom DeMarco and Tim Lister's *Peopleware* (Dorset House, 1987) deals with the measured impacts of salary levels on performance. Also useful are the annual surveys of compensation levels for various programming and software jobs published by organizations such as the American Management Association, the Bureau of Labor Statistics, the Massachusetts Software Council, and other professional groups.

Labor economics is a topic rich in books and citations, although only a small subset deal specifically with software. The Department of Labor's annual *Occupational Outlook for American Industry* is useful. Lloyd Reynolds, Stanley Masters, and Collette Moser's *Readings in Labor Economics and Labor Relations* (Prentice Hall, 1982), gives a useful broad coverage of many interrelated topics. Belton Fleisher and Thomas Kneisner's *Labor Economics: Theory, Evidence, and Policy* (Prentice Hall, 1980) is also relevant. An intriguing book that has useful information, although not specifically on compensation plans, is Robert Levering, Milton Moskowitz, and Michael Katz' *The 100 Best Companies to Work For in America* (New American Library, 1992).

Small companies and start-up companies are often undercapitalized, and may substitute equity for compensation. Several books discuss such topics: William Hancick's *The Small Business Legal Advisor* (McGraw-Hill, 1982) and Marc Lane's *Legal Handbook for Small Businesses* (Amacom, 1977) are examples of this genre.

15. **Periodical support**—A number of software magazines feature intermittent or annual articles on software compensation levels. Datamation and Software magazines, for example, have annual compensation articles.

16. **Standards support**—So far as can be determined, there are no known standards by ANSI, DoD, IEE, IEEE, ISO, or other standards organizations that deal with compensation levels. In organizations where software personnel are members of unions, there may be union salary standards. These will vary by specific case.

17. **Professional associations**—Several professional associations report on or survey compensation levels of various software-related jobs. The ACM, AMA, IEEE, Software Publishers Association, and the New England Software Council are examples. There are also vertical groups within specific industries, such as LOMA for the insurance industry, where topics such as this are considered.

18. **Effectiveness of known therapies**—For compensation problems based on inadequate capitalization or inadequate available funds, there is little that can be done. For compensation problems based on lack of a merit system or corporate culture, the problems are not insoluble, but are not easy to rectify. The most effective therapies seem to be enterprises where senior executives seek to attract top-caliber personnel and are very interested in morale and employee satisfaction. A topic of great interest, but little empirical data, is the exploration of the exact impact of compensation on performance. For example, what are the average productivity and quality levels produced by software personnel with annual compensation levels of $50,000, $75,000, $100,000 and $125,000? As of 1993, this kind of information essentially does not exist, although software measurement technology is now capable of performing such studies.

19. **Costs of known therapies**—The costs of good compensation plans are fairly easy to quantify. If the average fully-burdened compensation package for software personnel averages $65,000 per year in 1993, then any upward adjustment can be calculated and compared to current levels.

20. **Long-range prognosis**—The probability is high that compensation plans for software personnel will stay relatively flat, or indeed may decline, throughout the remainder of the century. So long as the U.S. economy is sluggish, there may not be an explosion of new companies and job opportunities, and many large software employers (such as DEC, WANG, Data General, Prime, etc.) have experienced shrinking or even negative profits. Further, the status of software is rather low in the eyes of many senior executives. Also, off-shore competition from countries such as India on the basis of costs may have a negative impact on U.S. compensation levels. Finally, outsourcing arrangements also are growing in popularity and tend to keep compensation levels fairly flat. Given the current economic and job situation, the prospect of tangible improvements in compensation levels against the background of cost-of-living expenses is not favorable. As usual, really capable experts (say the upper 10%) are more or less immune since they can move quickly from position to position.

25

Inadequate Configuration Control and Project Repositories

1. **Definition**—Lack of formal and automated capabilities for dealing with the synchronization, cross-referencing, integration, and updating of software planning documents, contracts and business materials, specifications, graphic materials and images, user information, source code, defect repairs, and test cases.

2. **Severity** —The average severity of inadequate configuration control is about a three on the following five-point scale:

   Severity 1: Neither manual nor automated configuration control of any kind

   Severity 2: Formal manual configuration control, but no automation available

   Severity 3: Automated source code control; manual document and test case control

   Severity 4: Source code and document control automation using uncoordinated tools

   Severity 5: Source code and document control using inappropriate tools

3. **Frequency**—The technology of configuration control has been evolving since the 1960s. IBM, for example, built a proprietary configuration control system in 1967 that integrated source code control, document control, and defect tracking. The concept of a project encyclopedia (dynamic cross-referencing among materials) was added in the 1970's, and the concept of a full project repository for synchronizing all software deliverables (text, graphics, images, source code, and test cases) was added in the 1980's. Nonetheless, lack of such capabilities is still endemic to the software industry. As of 1993, about 30% of U.S. software producers have no configuration control automation of any kind; about 30% have some form of source code automation, but lack automation for documentation, test cases, and defect tracking. About 30% have automation for source code, documentation, and test libraries but the configuration control tools are separate for each domain, and there is no integration or cross-referencing between the tools. About 10% are moving toward full integration of all configuration control tasks.

4. **Occurrence**—In general, large computer companies such as IBM and DEC, large telecommunication companies such as AT&T, and large defense contractors such as Raytheon typically have the most powerful and effective configuration control capabilities. Indeed, both IBM with its AD/Cycle repository concept and DEC with its CMS and MMS under the Cohesion repository concept are attempting to expand the envelope of traditional configuration control. In general, systems software producers and military software producers do a better job of configuration control than MIS software producers. Also, large companies tend to do a better job of configuration control than small companies.

5. **Susceptibility and resistance**—Inadequate configuration control is a problem that tends to creep up on companies unexpectedly. For small stand-alone programs operating on a single platform under a single operating system, configuration control is scarcely a problem. However, if an application is ported to different operating systems (i.e. DOS, Windows, UNIX, and VMS) then configuration control becomes more important. For commercial software producers such as Lotus, Borland, Microsoft, etc. with hundreds of applications, each of which has multiple releases, and which operate across multiple platforms and multiple operating systems, configuration control is a critical aspect of company business.

    The most susceptible organizations to inadequate configuration control are small commercial software houses, whose products are being ported across multiple hosts. Almost equally susceptible are MIS producers who build applications that are slightly customized for various states, countries, or operating units. The most resistant organizations are the larger and more sophisticated defense contractors, since military specifications mandate rigorous configuration control. Certain industries, such as computer manufacturing and central office telecommunications manufacturing are rather resistant too, with a few exceptions in each industry.

6. **Root causes**—The primary root cause of inadequate configuration control is that it is a very complex problem which not everyone understands, and which even fewer people can solve. If the problem is dealt with piecemeal, such as keeping track of code updates, paperwork updates, defect repair updates, and test library updates using separate tools and approaches, the difficulty is reduced, but the chance of missing important relationships goes up.

    A second root cause is that once the need for adequate configuration control is typically realized within a company, a lot of the damage has already been done. For example, a software company with 10 products in the field, all of which have multiple releases and operate under various operating systems, has a lot of material that would have to be brought under configuration management. The effort of making the initial migration to configuration control is so great that some companies can't find the resources, since their staffs are already operating at full capacity.

    A final root cause is the way companies track resources and measure costs: configuration control is a multiple-phase activity that often involves quite a few people, but only intermittently. Cost and resource tracking systems are usually set up to record costs within a single phase, or activities where essentially full-time resources are identified. The costs of configuration control tend to escape notice, since the expense pattern is not one which most tracking systems were set up to handle.

7. **Associated problems**—Inadequate configuration control is a key contributor to the problems of *high maintenance costs, low quality,* and *low productivity.* It is a very significant contributor to the problems of *excessive time to market, long schedules, missed schedules,* and *cost overruns.* Inadequate configuration control is an indirect contributor to *low morale* and *low user satisfaction.* Inadequate configuration control is also a barrier to eliminating the problems of *low levels of reusable code* and *low levels of reusable design.*

Inadequate configuration control is caused by *inadequate capital investment, inadequate management curricula, inadequate software engineering curricula,* and *inadequate standards.*

8. **Cost impact**—The costs of inadequate configuration control have both a direct and an indirect component. The direct costs are those of the increased manual effort required to keep track of updates to plans, specifications, source code, documents, test libraries, and other deliverables. The indirect costs are those associated with correcting the mistakes and errors attributable to inadequate configuration control.

Both the direct and indirect costs vary strongly with the size, complexity, and volumes of software deliverables. For projects smaller than 1000 Function Points in size, the difference between adequate and inadequate configuration control is only a few percentage points. For large systems of 10,000 Function Points and higher, adequate configuration control is a critical path item leading to successful completion, and the cost differentials between adequate and inadequate support is alarmingly high. Also, for products that operate under multiple environments and operating systems, configuration control is a basic requirement.

For a system of a nominal 10,000 Function Point aggregate size (equivalent to about 1,250,000 C statements) the following are approximate amounts of effort in staff work-months that might be devoted to configuration control with and without adequate automation support. The effort shown is for the mechanical tasks of updating, cross-referencing, and synchronizing material. Obviously the effort devoted to initial creation of the deliverables would be much larger.

Configuration Item	Without Automation (Staff months)	With Automation (Staff months)	Difference
Plans, estimates, budgets	15	3	–17
Requirements, specifications	30	6	–24
Graphics, illustrations	15	3	–12
Source code	50	10	–40
Test cases	35	5	–30
Defect reports, repairs	65	15	–40
Totals	210	42	168

As may be seen, full automation of configuration control is an essential aspect of large system development.

9. **Methods of prevention**—One of the most effective preventive steps for inadequate configuration control is to carry out a complete analysis of all of the kinds of materials which are produced for software projects, how they interconnect, and how frequently they are updated. Studies such as this were carried out in the 1960's within IBM, and in the 1970's and 1980's by other major organizations such as ITT and the corporations which were owned by ITT. Each company and government agency would be advised to perform their own surveys, but some of the findings are of common interest.

Configuration control should start early—ideally, during requirements. Late starts, such as after design and partial configuration control, are not sufficient.

Counting development plans, test plans, proposals, requirements, specifications, user documents, educational materials, and other paper documents reveals that large software projects may create more than 100 discrete document types, which contain in aggregate more than 400 words for every source code statement. Using modern metrics, the maximum quantity of paperwork observed is more than six pages per Function Point, which would total to about 3000 words per Function Point. The volume of information is large enough so that optical storage appears to be a logical necessity for full repositories within large corporations and government agencies. Magnetic storage may not be sufficient.

Any given software function is likely to be discussed in from six to 10 discrete documents, as well as being encapsulated in source code, and having specific test cases created for it. Cross-referencing of all citations for a given function requires a hyper-text-like linkage.

Projects which operate across multiple operating systems (i.e. UNIX, MS-DOS, Windows, MVS, etc.) require much more care in configuration control than monolithic products which operate under a single operating system. The effort for configuration control goes up by about 25% for each platform or operating system supported.

Software projects for the U.S. Department of Defense or the U.S. military services are required to support backwards traceability from source code to original requirements. While backwards traceability is not required for civilian projects, it is a useful although difficult concept. Backwards traceability appears to add about 30% to the effort required for configuration control.

Projects which are marketed internationally, or which require translations into various national languages (such as English, Japanese, and German) are very taxing for configuration control. The additive configuration control effort may exceed 100% for each language supported.

About one third of all pages in specifications and user documents contain graphics, illustrations, or special characters (i.e. mathematical symbols, formulae, etc.). It is obvious that a relational data base which assumes all information to be either alphabetical or numerical is not a good choice for a full repository manager.

An object-oriented data base would appear to be a more suitable host for full configuration control of all deliverables. This is especially true for modern software products with a high graphic and image content.

User requirements tend to grow at a rate of about 1% per month, using the size in words of the original approved requirement as the starting point. Specifications and design documents tend to change at a rate of about 3% to 5% per month, using the initial functional specifications as the starting point. Source code tends to change at a rate of more than 10% per month, using the volume of code or the first clean compile as the starting point. It is obvious that manual configuration control is not capable of keeping up with the volume of changes required. It is less obvious, but true nonetheless, that separate configuration control tools for text, graphics, source code, test cases, defect reports, and other deliverables are inefficient and inadequate.

U.S. software projects routinely create from two to more than six test cases per Function Point. Since test cases have residual value for regression testing after the initial release, test libraries, test cases, and test scripts should also be under configuration control and should be part of software project repositories.

The current U.S. average for software projects is to find about five defects per Function Point over the development cycle of software projects. Defects are found in requirements, plans, designs, specifications, code, user documents, and even in test cases. Many defects affect multiple deliverables. For large systems, the total defect quantities can exceed 100,000. Plainly, a full configuration control system must be capable of tracking and synchronizing defects and the repairs made in response to defects. Also, defect repairs themselves are a source of fresh defects: almost 10% of all bugs can be traced to attempts to fix previous bugs.

Although changes to software deliverables occur spontaneously on a daily basis and should be under configuration control, it is not a good strategy to release modified versions of software to users at random intervals. The optimal release interval for software packages which include new functions and accumulated defect repairs appears to be about every six months for personal computer applications, and about every 18 months for main-frame applications.

When new releases of software products occur with major new functions included, it is preferable from the vantage point of user convenience to send out complete new user manuals, rather than sending out changed and added pages which must be incorporated into manuals by the users themselves. It is more expensive, of course, to republish full manuals.

After the initial first release of a software product, all major deliverables continue to evolve over time. The normal growth in functionality is 5% to 10% per year, for as long as a product is successful in its market place.

The entropy or complexity of software products tends to increase over time. The actual rate of increase correlates strongly with the initial starting point: highly complex and poorly structured applications tend to decay quickly. This means that configuration control costs also tend to increase over time.

10. **Methods of control**—Once the costs and problems of configuration control become apparent to software-producing organizations, there are three normal control responses: 1) Lease or purchase configuration control tools from external vendors; 2) Build proprietary configuration control tools; or 3) Purchase or lease a configuration control tool from an external source and customize it to local requirements. Method one is the most cost effective for small to medium organizations with software staffs from less than 10 up to perhaps 1000. For very large organizations with thousands of software professionals, methods two and three may be advantageous in matching unique corporate requirements, although the costs and timing are much greater than method one.

11. **Product support**—There are dozens of change managers, integration tools, and repository tools on the current U.S. market, and new tools are occurring almost daily. Some of the major players include IBM with its evolving repository concept, and DEC with its Code Management System (CMS) and Module Management System (MMS) repository concept. Major CASE vendors are also starting to offer configuration control capabilities, and some of them are even moving toward full repository support. A few of the other players in the configuration control and repository market place include Atherton Technologies, Bachman, CADRE, CaseWare, Computer Associates (CA), DEC, IMACS, IBM, Intersolv, Knowledgeware, LEGENT, OPCODE, Oregon Software, RMR, Pansophic, Softool, Texas Instruments, SMDS, and UNISYS.

    One caution is indicated: source code management is important, but it is not by itself sufficient for total configuration management. Look for tools which integrate control of text, graphics, source code, test cases, and defect reports. In the near future, look for full multi-media configuration control. Examples of commercial configuration control tools include: Aide-de-Camp, AMPLIFY CONTROL, CA-LIBRARIAN, CCC/DM, CCC/Manager, CCC/Resolve-IT, Change Man, CONDOR, CMF, ENDEAVOR, FLEE, Historian Plus, IMPACT, ISTAR, LCS/CMF, OCS/LIBRARIAN, PANVALET, PolyLibrarian, Polytron, SCONS, Software Backplane, SOLOMAN, SMU, SOURCEBANK, SURE, TIME, VAX DEC/CMS, VAX DEC/MMS, and VMLIB.

12. **Consulting support**—The major vendors of configuration control tools often have consulting staffs as part of a package arrangement. Curiously, except for configuration control tool vendors, the topic of consulting about configuration control is under-represented in the civilian domain. Because of the stringent configuration control requirements in the military world, consultants which support the DoD community are often well-versed in this topic. Among the newer areas in consulting is that of the theory (but not the practice) of repositories. A number of well-known international consultants such as James Martin and Carma McClure have added repository consulting to their repertory.

13. **Education support**—Software engineering curricula in many universities tend to skimp on configuration control. Some, indeed, have no courses on this topic at all. The impact of major vendors such as IBM and DEC have sensitized universities to the importance of this topic, and so courses that touch on repositories are finally

starting to be developed. On the whole, better and more current training is available from private sources such as major configuration control vendors.

14. Publication support—Configuration control is seriously under-represented among software engineering and software management titles. Fletcher Buckley's *Implementing Configuration Management: Hardware, Software, and Firmware* (IEEE Press, 1992) is a welcome recent addition.

Indeed, a survey of several standard software engineering textbooks found that the topic was not even discussed. Considering the importance of the topic, this is a curious situation. Software configuration control vendors such as IBM and DEC often publish white papers, monographs, and sometimes even books. An example of a relevant book is that of ex-IBM employees Ronald Radice and Richard Phillips, *Software Engineering: An Industrial Approach* (Prentice Hall, 1988).

Given the absence of general software engineering references, some of these are quite useful. For example, *Requirements for a Modern Configuration Management System* (CaseWare, January 1992) and *Software Configuration Management Redefined* (CaseWare, March 1992) are both thoughtful explorations of the functionality required to support large heterogeneous software applications.

The IEEE Press publishes the annual conference proceedings on Systems Integration (1992 marked only the second year for this conference) and the papers are often useful.

15. Periodical support—Unfortunately, basic configuration control and integration methods are complicated and not particularly glamorous, and hence seldom attract journalistic attention. On the other hand, the theory of repositories as put forth by IBM has generated a burst of articles which tend to outpace the technology itself. What is needed is a better balance between how configuration management is carried out today, and how it might occur when repositories are fully operational. The situation is slowly improving. Intermittent articles in American Programmer, Software Magazine, and IEEE Software are beginning to appear.

16. Standards support—Although the U.S. Department of Defense standards are often cumbersome, they tend to be fairly thorough. DoD standards for configuration control are probably the most exhaustive. Other standards groups with relevant materials include ISO and the IEEE. The IEEE "Guide to Software Configuration Management" (IEEE Catalog No. SH11973, 1987), and the IEEE standard on "Software Configuration Management Plans" (IEEE Catalog No. SH13714, 1990) should both be useful.

17. Professional associations—Although major corporations may actually use job titles such as "configuration control specialist," "integration specialist," or "repository specialist" there appears to be no software association devoted to this topic. More generalized associations such as the IEEE, ACM, GUIDE, SHARE, DECUS, and others may have special-interest groups devoted to this topic. User associations for configuration control tools also exist. For example, Softool has a rather large international user group, as do other vendors. On-line support from vendors or special-interest groups is available from various services such as CompuServe, Delphi, Prodigy and Genie.

18. **Effectiveness of known therapies**—Discussing the effectiveness of configuration control tools brings to mind a statement once made by Samuel Johnson when he observed a dog walking on its hind legs: "It isn't done well, but it is surprising that it can be done at all." Configuration control is a *very* difficult problem and tools which can fully support all major deliverables (text, graphics, source code, test cases, and defects) are only just starting to appear. Multi-media configuration control is actually beyond the current state of the art. Even basic source code control is not a trivial problem, and when the need to synchronize changes to multiple documents, versions, and other materials occurs the problems mount up rapidly.

19. **Costs of known therapies**—Simple source code control tools can be purchased for less than $100, or even acquired as free-ware or share-ware from bulletin boards. Full configuration control or repository tools which can handle documents, source code and defects, can approach $100,000 in costs, plus annual maintenance fees of up to 15%. The value of configuration control correlates strongly to the size and complexity of the application. For large systems, multi-platform systems, and other systems where synchronization is both difficult and frequently required, configuration control tools tend to justify their value in less than 12 months.

20. **Long-range prognosis**—The fundamental technologies for full configuration control exist in 1993, and include object-oriented data bases, optical storage, hypertext links, and other forms of dynamic links across heterogeneous information. It will probably be near the end of the century before a full repository manager exists that contains all desirable functionality. However, the prognosis is guardedly favorable: some very bright minds supported by large sums of money are exploring configuration control and repository capabilities. This combination has a good chance of succeeding.

Inadequate Curricula (Software Engineering)

1. **Definition**—A) Academic curricula for software engineering and computer science at the university level which do not equip the graduates to design or develop commercial-grade software upon entering the software work force; B) Specific omissions in undergraduate software education in the topics of reviews, inspections, software quality control, large-system development methods, configuration control, maintenance and enhancement of aging software, military software criteria, software metrics, complexity analysis, and software documentation methods.

2. **Severity**—The average severity of inadequate software engineering and computer science curricula among U.S. universities and business schools is about a three on the following five point scale:

   Severity 1:   Graduates require more than three years of remedial on-the-job training

   Severity 2:   Graduates require more than two years of remedial on-the-job training

   Severity 3:   Graduates require more than a year of remedial on-the-job training

   Severity 4:   Graduates require remedial training in quality control methods

   Severity 5:   Graduates require remedial training in large-system or military methods

3. **Frequency**—Inadequate software engineering curricula are a widespread problem for U.S. universities and colleges, and the frequency seems to exceed 85% based on reviews of university catalogs. Similar problems occur overseas. The former head of ITT in the United Kingdom once observed that graduate software engineers in the U.K. required three years of on-the-job training before they could be entrusted with commercial-grade software development.

4. **Occurrence**—Modern, practical university curricula are a fairly recent phenomenon. The first deliberate attempt in the U.S. to form a curriculum that was directly related to the job market only occurred after the Civil War, when Robert E. Lee became president of Washington University (Now Washington and Lee) and introduced practical subjects to help in easing former confederate soldiers into civilian

life. With this as background, universities that recognize the need for graduates to enter the job market tend to have the most practical curricula.

5. **Susceptibility and resistance**—For reasons that are outside the scope of this report, state universities and urban universities with close links to the business and manufacturing community seem to be most resistant to inadequate software engineering curricula. Some fairly prestigious universities appear to have curricula that do not equip graduates for commercial-grade software engineering. On the whole, software engineers seem not as well prepared to commence work as engineers in other fields.

6. **Root causes**—The root causes of inadequate software engineering and computer science curricula can be traced to the fundamental weakness of software engineering as a discipline: inadequate measurement and inaccurate metrics. The long dominance of the flawed "lines of source code" metrics made serious research into effective and practical software engineering technologies extraordinarily difficult. The results were some 40 years of software research with unreproduceable results and questionable conclusions. Only since the advent of functional metrics in 1979 has this situation improved.

7. **Associated problems**—Inadequate software engineering curricula is a contributor to the problems of *canceled projects, long schedules, low productivity, low quality, missed schedules,* and of course *technical staff malpractice.*

   The problem of inadequate software engineering curricula itself can be traced to the problems of *inadequate measurement, inaccurate metrics,* and *slow technology transfer.*

8. **Cost impact**—The direct costs of inadequate software engineering curricula include the costs which companies and government agencies must bear before new entry-level personnel just out of college can begin to work effectively on software projects. An example of such direct costs is that of Electronic Data Systems (EDS) which requires an intensive 10-week training program for new software engineers. Assuming normal salary rates, travel and incidental expenses, and educational material costs, EDS would appear to spend about $25,000 per software engineer to put them through this period of remedial training. Other companies may utilize on-the-job training, or courses staggered over a year or two. The final costs are probably similar to EDS', but would be spread out over longer time spans.

   The indirect costs of inadequate software engineering curricula include all of the rework, repairs, and corrective actions which may occur to correct the damage done by poorly trained software engineering staffs. Here exact quantification is difficult, and will vary from case to case.

9. **Methods of prevention**—Universities and software engineering schools modernize their curricula as often as they think necessary, which is unfortunately not often enough. Establishing ties between universities and companies which pro-

duce software is moderately helpful. Academic participation in major professional groups such as the ACM, IEEE, and IFPUG is also beneficial.

A modern software engineering curriculum at the university level should include both standard offerings and courses similar to the following:

Software Design Reviews and Code Inspections

Design reviews and code inspections have the highest measured efficiencies of any forms of defect removal yet discovered, and are often more than twice as effective in removing defects than standard testing approaches. All undergraduate software engineers and computer scientists should receive a thorough grounding in these methods and should actually participate in reviews and inspections of their own work and their colleagues'.

Software Configuration Management, Library Control, and Integration Methods

One of the major factors of commercial-grade and military software development is the need for rigorous control of updates to specifications, source code, and other deliverables. A corollary need is that of integrating the work of many developers in either discrete builds or via a continuous integration mode. Software engineering undergraduates should become familiar with these technologies.

Principles of Measurement and Metrics

All graduate software engineers and computer scientists should understand the basic tools of measurement and metrics. The hazards of LOC and "cost per defect" should be clearly addressed. Approaches such as functional metrics should become standard topics. (As this book was being prepared, the author was approached after giving a speech in San Jose, California by a member of the audience. This was the query which the attendee made: "I'm a graduate student in computer science at Stanford, and I've never heard of Function Points. Can you tell me what they are?")

Design of Experiments

Nowhere is the difference between software engineers and graduates of the "hard" sciences more visible than in the literature they produce. Software engineering has become accustomed to anecdotes rather than experiments, and this is quite unfortunate. Commercial education institutes, such as Motorola University, are starting to teach this important topic. Hopefully the concept will spread.

Principles of Complexity Analysis and Reduction

Complex code with "spaghetti bowl" structure has been recognized as harmful since Professor Edger Dijkstra's famous 1968 letter, "Go To Statements Considered Harmful." While the basic structuring theorems for procedural code are often taught at the undergraduate level, many related topics are not taught at all. For example, there are well-known techniques for measuring and reducing the complexity of textual documents such as specifications, but these approaches are not always taught to undergraduate or even graduate software engineers and computer scientists. In addition, there are a variety of commercial source code complexity analysis and restructuring tools which software engineers will encounter upon graduation. It is reasonable that they should learn such topics at the university level.

Maintenance and Enhancement of Aging Software

As of 1993, more than half of the professional programmers and software engineers in the United States are actually employed on maintenance and enhancements of aging software. Surprisingly, university courses on these topics are seldom offered. (One notable exception is the maintenance research center at the University of Durham in England.) Undergraduates should learn the basic facts of software entropy, and the specialized tools and methods needed to keep aging software operational, including complexity analysis, restructuring, reverse engineering, and re-engineering.

Principles of User Documentation and Interactive Screen Design

All software engineers should receive basic training in the planning and development of documents for end users, and in the usage of standard conventions for screen design. In addition, standard conventions for using pointing devices such as track-balls, mice, and pens should be introduced at the undergraduate level.

Principles of Commercial and Military Software Development

Modern commercial software that is marketed internationally must conform to ISO standards 9000 through 9004. U.S. military software must conform to a variety of military specifications, such as DoD STD–2167A. Even though these topics may be dreadfully boring, undergraduates should at least be exposed to the facts of life of working on commercial and military software projects.

Principles of Reusable Software Design and Reusable Software Modules

This course would cover the technical aspects of constructing software from reusable designs and reusable modules. It would also cover the technical aspects of constructing reusable designs and reusable modules; i.e. specific design approaches, certification methods, interconnection protocols, and library and configuration control of reusable artifacts.

Principles of Standard Software Applications

Now that the software industry is 50 years of age, there is a growing body of empirical data about the best methods for building certain applications where many thousands of such applications have actually been constructed. This course would be an overview of the state-of-the-art of those software types where the basic principles of design and construction are now known based on hundreds of instances: examples of such software applications include accounting systems, banking systems, CASE tool suites, compilers, data base products, network control systems, operating systems, payroll systems, PBX switching systems, public switching systems, spreadsheets and word processors.

Global Software Engineering

Software is a highly international occupation. Both software engineers and managers should know and understand the principles of building and marketing software for global markets. They should also know the basic facts of international competition, and the demographics of software professionals in the major cities and countries of the world. This course would cover in summary form international standards; what must be done to allow software to operate in multiple countries (i.e. variances in date formats, paper sizes, numeric delimiters, etc.). As of 1993, the U.S., Europe, and the Pacific Rim are all competing for software markets. Countries such as India are also entering the global software arena. The course would also cover the varying methods of software management and engineering that are associated with particular geographic localities. For example, the Merise methodology is a standard approach in France. Formal specification approaches are more common in England than in the United States. The Japanese methods of Kaizen and Quality Function Deployment (QFD) are having an impact. The Canadian approach of Joint Application Design (JAD) is now spreading world wide. The U.S. invention of Function Points has forged the largest international association of metric users in the world.

10. **Methods of control**—The most effective control method for inadequate software engineering curricula is to supplement gaps in academic training with either commercial courses, in-house courses, or on-the-job training after employment. These three methods are used by more than 90% of U.S. companies which employ 100 software engineers or more. The need for this kind of supplemental training is so pervasive that it has been asserted (by Lyman Hamilton, former Chairman of ITT) that the U.S. Fortune 500 companies employ more software instructors than all U.S. universities put together. Indeed, the in-house software engineering curricula of several major corporations such as AT&T and IBM are superior to almost any university curriculum in both quantity and quality of course offerings. There is also a large and profitable sub-industry of companies which provide commercial software engineering education.

11. **Product support**—So far as can be determined, there are no commercial products available in 1993 that can assist in software engineering curriculum planning. Software Productivity Research (SPR) has built an experimental prototype that uses assessment data to generate software curricula for both managers and technical staff, based on the patterns of weakness which the assessment uncovers.

Some years ago, ITT developed an experimental curriculum planner for retraining electrical and mechanical engineers who wished to change disciplines and become software engineers. An engineer could enter both academic and commercial courses already taken, and the kind of software engineering position which was the target occupation. The tool would then generate a full curriculum of both university-level courses, ITT internal courses, and suggested commercial or vendor-supplied courses.

12. **Consulting support**—In the United States there is a major sub-industry of companies and individual instructors that provide supplemental software engineering training. Examples of such companies include Andersen Consulting, American Management Systems, Computer Power, DEC, Digital Consulting, Inc. (DCI), Hewlett-Packard, IBM, UNISYS, and many more. The Software Engineering Institute (SEI) commissioned the development of a software engineering curriculum, but the results seem somewhat incomplete.

13. **Education support**—Some of the universities which have attempted to bring their curricula into synchronization with industry needs include Boston University's Wang Education Center, the University of Bridgeport (prior to being acquired by the Reunification Church), Carnegie-Mellon University, the University of Colorado in Boulder, George Mason University, Oakland University in Michigan, the University of Virginia, Seattle University, and Washington University in St. Louis. Dr. Everald Mills of Seattle University also worked with the Software Engineering Institute (SEI) on a joint curriculum program.

14. **Publication support**—Several books attempt to provide overviews of the kind of information which software engineers need to be effective in the commercial world. Examples of these books include Roger Pressman's well-known *Software Engineering—A Practitioner's Approach* (McGraw-Hill, 1982) which has become a "best seller." Richard Fairley's *Software Engineering Concepts* (McGraw-Hill, 1985) also covers many topics needed by commercial software engineers. There are of course hundreds of books dealing with specific software engineering topics.

15. **Periodical support**—Probably the most explicit source of academic curriculum information is the bi-monthly "Computer Science Syllabus" from Sunnyvale, California. This journal features the computer science curricula of several universities and colleges in every issue, and also contains interesting articles dealing with academic topics. Various IEEE periodicals such as IEEE Transactions on Software Engineering and IEEE Spectrum have articles on software engineering curricula from time to time.

16. **Standards support**—Both the IEEE and the Software Engineering Institute (SEI) have draft curricula for software engineering and computer science. Neither curriculum includes all of the courses cited in section nine.

17. **Professional associations**—The IEEE Computer Society and the ACM are perhaps the two associations with the broadest membership of software engineers. Many regional and local associations also exist, such as the Boston Computer Society and regional software quality associations. All such groups offer courses and

workshops from time to time, which are quite useful for professional software engineers.

18. **Effectiveness of known therapies**—The effectiveness of in-house and commercial training to supplement academic training varies with the size of the organization, available funds, and corporate culture. The best U.S. companies, such as AT&T, DEC, EDS, Hewlett-Packard, IBM, Motorola and UNISYS are very effective. Such companies typically provide entry-level training of at least several weeks' duration, and then supplemental annual training of ten to 20 days per software engineer.

19. **Costs of known therapies**—From analyzing the entry-level training of organizations such as AT&T, EDS, and IBM, it appears that about $15,000 to $25,000 in training costs may be required before a graduate software engineer can be entrusted with commercial-grade software projects in a major company.

20. **Long-range prognosis**—Academic curricula for all engineering disciplines normally lag the state-of-the-art by at least five years. (It takes about three years of research and field trials to validate a new approach, and then about two years to create text books and training materials.) Software engineering and computer science, unfortunately, tended to lag the state-of-the-art by more than ten years. As an example, formal inspections were proven to be the most efficient defect removal method in the early 1970's, but courses on this topic are still rare in software engineering curricula. However, that is past history. Since 1979 functional metrics have been rapidly replacing the flawed "lines of source code" metrics, and this phenomenon is leading to remarkable progress in understanding software quality, productivity, and economic topics. The first college text book on this topic was not produced until 1989, almost ten years to the day after Function Points were put into the public domain. Although the projection may be optimistic, it appears technically possible for software engineering curricula to achieve parity with other engineering curricula by the end of the century.

CHAPTER 27

Inadequate Curricula (Software Management)

1. **Definition**—A) Academic curricula within business schools or universities that do not equip candidate software managers with sufficient knowledge to perform their jobs with reasonable competence; B) Specific omissions in software management training including some or all of the topics of software sizing, planning, estimating, tracking, measurement, organization planning, assessments, quality control, risk analysis, value analysis, and competitive analysis; C) Management courses and curricula which lag the current state of the art by many years; D) Management courses on software projects that are built around the flawed and paradoxical "lines of source code" metric.

2. **Severity**—The average severity of inadequate management curricula among U.S. universities and business schools is about a three on the following five point scale:

   Severity 1: Curricula is incomplete, and lags state of art by more than ten years
   Severity 2: Curricula is incomplete, and lags state of art by more than seven years
   Severity 3: Curricula is incomplete, and lags state of art by more than five years
   Severity 4: Curricula is incomplete, and lags state of art by more than three years
   Severity 5: Curricula is incomplete, but current in topics that are covered

3. **Frequency**—Inadequate curricula for educating software managers is endemic to software, and the frequency exceeds 90% in 1993 based on reviews of business school and university catalogs.

4. **Occurrence**—Given the nature of university course development and the way curricula are planned, it is not surprising that there is a lag of several years between the emergence of "best current practices" and their appearance in university or business school curricula. It normally takes at least three years of field trials and empirical results to develop and validate a "best current practice." After that, it would take another two or three years to write text books and develop educational materials. Therefore one would expect about a five-year lag between the state of the art and the appearance of a topic in standard university and business curricula.

Software management education has been handicapped far beyond most other engineering and management disciplines by the 40-year dominance of "lines of source code" metrics, which essentially negated serious economic studies and the development of adequate management courses and curricula. Only since 1979 with the publication of the Function Point metric has it been possible to develop rational and effective software management courses and curricula.

Unfortunately, the first college text book on Function Points, Dreger's *Function Point Analysis* (Prentice Hall, 1989), did not appear until ten years after Function Points had been in use, and more than three years after the International Function Point Users Group (IFPUG) had been formed. Indeed, IFPUG had over one hundred member companies before functional metrics appeared in any university courses at all. As of 1993, modern software management curricula based on functional metrics still remain to be seen.

5. **Susceptibility and resistance**—Universities and business schools that have established close ties to industry, and particularly to leaders such as AT&T, IBM, Hewlett-Packard, and Motorola, are the most resistant and tend to have the most dynamic and modern curricula. Universities and business schools that are more or less detached from daily contact with actual software producing companies are the most susceptible. Defense contractors seldom have adequate training, due to the fact that the costs are considered to be overhead. The military services themselves, however, are sometimes better than average in providing management training. For example, the Naval Post-Graduate school in Monterey, and the Bold Stroke program at the Air Force University at Maxwell Air Force Base in Alabama are attempting to provide state-of-the-art education for senior officers and some DoD civilian personnel.

6. **Root causes**—The root causes for inadequate management curricula are partly grounded in the sluggishness with which any academic curricula changes, and partly grounded in the deficiencies of historical management practices. There are strong feedback loops between the effective state-of-the-art in the commercial world and what universities teach. In the case of software, the state-of-the-art of management practice had been fairly primitive prior to the advent of functional metrics in 1979. Since that time, however, the usage of functional metrics and the new managerial concepts derived from those metrics have been exploding through the commercial software world. Unfortunately, universities and business schools have been slow to respond: as of 1993 the numbers of software managers trained in functional metrics and derivative approaches by private instructors and management consultants exceeds the number of students trained in university and business school courses by perhaps 1000 to 1!

7. **Associated problems**—Inadequate software management curricula is a contributor to many classic software problems. Inadequately trained managers are noted with distressing frequency on *canceled projects,* and projects that experience *cost overruns* and *missed schedules*. Inadequate management training is also commonly

associated with the problems of *low productivity, low quality,* and of course *management malpractice.* Inadequate software management curricula is a frequent contributor to the problems of *friction with users* and *friction with senior management.*

The problem of inadequate software management curricula itself is primarily caused by the long time required to modernize university curricula in the presence of major paradigm shifts. More pragmatically, a number of state of the art software management topics such as project management using Function Points do not even have standard text books as of 1993.

8. **Cost impact**—The cost impacts of inadequate management curricula are difficult to quantify and enumerate. The direct costs would include all software projects which overran their budgets or experienced other problems due to poorly trained managers. The indirect costs include the inability of companies and government agencies to tackle really large systems, because the probability of a successful outcome is too low. In neither case is it reasonable to assign explicit dollar values.

9. **Methods of prevention**—Universities and business schools modernize their curricula as often as they think necessary, which is unfortunately not often enough. Establishing ties between universities and software management communities is moderately helpful. Academic participation in technical associations such as the non-profit International Function Point Users Group (IFPUG) would also be beneficial. On the whole, prevention is difficult and uncertain. In theory, association with the Software Engineering Institute (SEI) should be beneficial, but a caution is indicated here: some parts of the SEI curricula and research, such as measurement and metrics, lag the state-of-the-art by several years.

A modern software management curriculum at the university or business-school level should include the following courses:

Principles of Software Sizing, Planning, and Estimating

This would be a course built around the emerging state-of-the-art of using functional metrics to predict the sizes of all software deliverables and work products. This is coupled with how this information would be used in conjunction with software planning and estimating tools. Since there are about 50 software cost estimating tools and 70 project planning tools on the U.S. commercial market, management curricula should deal broadly with their capabilities and uses.

Principles of Software Metrics, Measurement, and Assessment

This would be a course on standard software metrics, and on the collection of both "hard" and "soft" data associated with software projects. The course would review the pros and cons of all software metrics (i.e. LOC, Function Points, Feature Points, Cost per Defect, complexity metrics, etc.). It would also cover the principles of hard data and soft data. The hard data consists of the effort, resources, and schedules of producing major deliverables. The soft data consists of the analysis of the effectiveness of the methods, tools, languages, and environment which affect the outcome of software projects. The course would not be limited to only the SEI assessment, but would also include the SDC and SPR assessment methods, the Hewlett-Packard and AT&T assessment methods, standard project audits, and some of the specialized Independent Verification and Validation approaches used on military software. The course would give full attention to modern functional metrics, and would point out the serious paradoxes associated with "lines of code" metrics.

Principles of Software Quality Control

This would be a course built around the twin concepts of "defect prevention" and "defect removal." The technologies of defect prevention include all those which minimize complexity and reduce the tendency of humans to make mistakes. (A few examples of notable defect prevention approaches include prototypes, Joint Application Design (JAD), Quality Function Deployment (QFD), Total Quality Management (TQM), and "Clean Room" development.) The technologies of defect removal are those for seeking and eliminating errors in all deliverables. (Examples of defect removal include all forms of review, inspection, test, and correctness proofs.) The course would use recent findings on the use of functional metrics to predict defect volumes and numbers of test cases. It would also cover the measured defect removal efficiencies of common reviews, inspections, and test activities.

Principles of Software Risk and Value Analysis

This would be a course built around the contrasting topics of risk analysis and value analysis. For risk analysis, the course would discuss the most common software risks, and the most effective preventive and control methods. For value analysis, the course would utilize the new and emerging concept of using functional metrics to enumerate the software used by enterprises, divisions within enterprises, and specific classes of knowledge worker. For example, software project managers in 1993 tend to have available about 15,000 Function Points of processing power in the form of estimating tools, planning tools, spreadsheets, and the like. Major corporations tend to own from 250,000 to more than 1,000,000 Function Points in their full portfolios, and there is growing evidence of some correlation between portfolio size and corporate performance.

Principles of Software Reusability Management

This would be a course on the management of reusable data, reusable documents, reusable code, reusable designs (blueprints), and reusable plans and estimates (templates). This course would deal with the economics of reuse, the need for centralized control of reusable resource libraries, and the roles of management in establishing such libraries. One managerial role is modifying software productivity measures so that "delivery productivity" rather than "development productivity" is stressed. Another managerial role is dealing with the social and public-relations aspects of large-scale reuse. The course would also deal with the commercial aspects of purchasing or leasing reusable artifacts.

Principles of Software Package Evaluation and Acquisition

From 20% to 40% of the software applications operating within large companies was acquired from vendors. For small companies that lack in-house programming staffs, the total may approach 100%. This course would cover the basics of "make or buy analysis," evaluating packages, sources of evaluation data such as user groups and comparative reviews, and the basic aspects of package contracts and agreements. The course would also cover the hazards of package modification after acquisition, which may degrade the economic advantages of packages below acceptable levels.

Principles of Software Organization Planning

This course would cover major topics such as the pros and cons of matrix management, optimal placement of software organizations within corporate structures, and the organization structures typically associated with small staffs (less than 10 software professionals), medium staffs (from 50 to several hundred professionals), and large staffs (hundreds or thousands of software professionals). The course would discuss the productivity and quality levels associated with organization size and structure, and the numbers and kinds of specialists needed as organizations grow larger.

Principles of Corporate Politics

The only real difference between a large corporation and the Court of the Borgias is that poison is seldom used to eliminate rivals. Every major organization has an authority structure, which is based on its normal organization chart. However, every major organization also has a power structure, which may not resemble the organization chart at all. That power structure, also known as corporate politics, would be the basis of this course. In some large companies, such as IBM, smoothing out political disputes is one of the commonest reasons why executives transfer from place to place. At a more mundane level, politics has been revealed to be a key component of important business decisions and affects the accuracy of software cost estimates. It also slows down the spread of measurement systems, since there is a "reflective layer" of senior managers who fear that rivals might rank above them if quality or productivity is truly revealed, so they would prefer not to know.

Global Software Engineering

Software is a highly international occupation. Both software engineers and managers should know and understand the principles of building and marketing software for global markets. They should also know the basic facts of international competition, and the demographics of software professionals in the major cities and countries of the world. This course would cover in summary form international standards; what must be done to allow software to operate in multiple countries (i.e. variances in date formats, paper sizes, numeric delimiters, etc.). As of 1993, the

U.S., Europe, and the Pacific Rim are all competing for software markets, and countries such as India are also entering the global software arena. The course would also cover the varying methods of software management and engineering that are associated with particular geographic localities. For example, the Merise methodology is a standard approach in France. Formal specification approaches are more common in England than in the United States. The Japanese methods of Kaizen and Quality Function Deployment (QFD) are having an impact. The Canadian approach of Joint Application Design (JAD) is now spreading world wide. The U.S. invention of Function Points has forged the largest international association of metric users in the world.

Software Geriatrics and Legacy Systems

This would be a course that concentrated on the suite of technologies available for stretching out the useful lives of aging software systems. The topics included would be complexity analysis, automated and manual restructuring, reverse engineering, re-engineering, and documentation recovery.

Case Studies of Software Failure and Success

This course would be an in-depth analysis of the opposite ends of the software managerial spectrum: A) The factors associated with notable failures and canceled projects; B) The factors associated with notable successes such as Baldrige awards, zero-defect levels, and significant schedule and cost underruns. The course would be built around real case studies.

Managing Standard Software Applications

Now that the software industry is approaching 50 years of age, there is a growing body of empirical data on the costs, schedules, and optimal methods for building standard applications that have been constructed thousands of times. This course would be an overview of the state-of-the-art of those software types where the basic principles of management are now known from many trial and error projects. Examples of standard applications built hundreds of times include accounting systems, banking systems, CASE tool suites, compilers, data base products, network control systems, operating systems, payroll systems, PBX switching systems, public switching systems, spreadsheets, and word processor. In each of these cases, the average costs, schedules, and resources for at least 50 projects can now be collected and analyzed.

Standards and Software

Since 1992, when the ISO 9000–9004 standards became mandatory throughout Europe, standards issues have become an important topic for software managers. Surprisingly, it is almost impossible to find a course that covers all of the international and national standards groups, and the industry groups as well. This course would discuss who can issue standards, which standards are important, and how to gain access to them. Topics such as ANSI standards, DoD standards, IEEE standards, ISO standards, sector standards, major corporate standards from companies such as AT&T, Motorola, IBM, would all be covered.

10. **Methods of control**—Lyman Hamilton, the former Chairman of the ITT Corporation, once observed in a speech that the number of software instructors employed by the Fortune 500 companies in the U.S. exceeded the total number of academic instructors by a significant margin. Indeed, the management training provided by major corporations such as AT&T and IBM is generally superior to that of most universities and business schools, in both quantity and quality. Corporate training is often better funded, the physical facilities are superior, and corporations often have funding available to bring in major world-class experts as guest lecturers. The best current solution to inadequate academic and business school curricula is to provide adequate management training via commercial or in-house education. It is interesting and significant that while courses such as the ones shown above do not occur in most U.S. universities or business schools, they are offered as internal courses within major corporations and by private management education and consulting organizations.

11. **Product support**—There are no commercial products available in 1993 that can assist in software management curriculum planning. Software Productivity Research (SPR) has built an experimental prototype that uses assessment data to generate software curricula for both managers and technical staff, based on the patterns of weakness which an assessment discovers. The prototype can be made available to universities and non-profit educational groups for research purposes.

12. **Consulting support**—In the United States there is a major sub-industry of management consulting companies and education providers whose curricula fill in the major educational gaps of universities and business schools. Examples of such private education include Andersen Consulting, Computer Power, Digital Consulting, Inc. (DCI), DMR Group, Extended Intelligence, James Martin Associates, the Quality Assurance Institute (QAI), Quantitative Software Management (QSM), and Software Productivity Research (SPR), and the Technology Transfer Institute (TTI). The number of managers trained by these private and commercial education sources appears to be greater than the sum of all U.S. universities and business schools.

13. **Education support**—Some of the universities and business schools that are actively engaged in modernizing their management curricula and building new courses based on economically valid functional metrics include the Air Force University, the Air Force Institute of Technology (AFIT), George Mason University, Kansas Newman College, MIT's Sloan School, New York University, Oakland University in Rochester, Michigan, New York University, University of California (several campuses), Seattle University, the University of Virginia, Washington University in St. Louis, The University of North Texas and Wichita State University.

Some of the best training for both managers and software engineers are the in-house curricula offered by major enterprises. The curricula at AT&T, Hewlett-Packard, IBM, and Motorola, for example, are superior to most universities and are far more modern. This is not an uncommon phenomenon: many of the guest instructors within major corporations are pioneers and industry leaders. For example, within enterprises such as the above, it is possible to hear lectures from colleagues who have been part of winning a Baldrige Award or even the Nobel Prize.

The U.S. Air Force's Bold Stroke program is an interesting and effective approach to bringing senior officers up to speed on software-related topics. This program has been run several times a year at the Air Force University located at Maxwell Air Force Base. Officers of the rank of Lt. Colonel and above are eligible, as are senior civilian managers from the Department of Defense.

14. **Publication support**—The best place to begin is a large public or university library which stocks catalogs of U.S. business schools and universities. A general overview of university and corporate relations is Thomas Langfitt et al.'s *Partners in the Research Enterprise: University-Corporate Relations in Science and Technology* (University of Pennsylvania Press, 1983).

There are hundreds of books on software management topics, but essentially none that describe a complete management curriculum and discuss all of the knowledge a software manager should have before commencing practice. Dr. Everald Mills of Seattle University has attempted a monograph on a software management curriculum commissioned by the Software Engineering Institute (SEI), but it failed to include modern functional metrics and hence is not fully up to date.

15. **Periodical support**—There are dozens of software periodicals, but none which deal specifically with the topics of software management curricula. From time to time the IEEE Transactions on Software Engineering will run special articles on this topic. Ed Yourdon's American Programmer also discusses managerial training from time to time. The bi-monthly Computer Science Syllabus deals mainly with undergraduate curricula, but has articles from time to time on managerial topics. The well-known IEEE Transactions on Engineering Management frequently contains interesting and relevant articles. Communications of the ACM also includes managerial-level articles rather frequently.

16. **Standards support**—The IEEE standard on software engineering curricula is updated from time to time, but still lacks modern managerial topics derived from functional metrics. The proposed SEI curricula is also woefully deficient, and indeed lags the state of the art substantially.

17. **Professional associations**—Most of the professional software associations are interested in training and curriculum planning. Examples include the ACM, ASM, the IEEE, IFPUG, the Software Management Association (SMA), and even local associations such as the regional CASE User Groups and the Boston Computer Society. These groups tend to offer specific courses and seminars on topics of interest, but typically do not provide a full curriculum.

18. **Effectiveness of known therapies**—A judicious mixture of academic training, commercial courses and seminars, conferences, and in-house training appears to

be relatively effective in bringing software managers up to speed. The university portion would include older and well-known concepts such as basic grounding in economics and the span of control concept. The commercial courses and seminars would include the newer and more advanced topics, such as integrating functional metrics into a corporation measurement program or performing software assessments. Conferences are normally used to seek out topics of potential interest, such as the impact of CASE on software, or how Total Quality Management (TQM) might be utilized. The in-house training would cover specific topics of interest to particular companies or divisions, such as budgeting and tracking systems.

19. **Costs of known therapies**—Academic costs are normally based on some form of unit rate such as cost per credit hour, or occasionally on a fixed-fee basis. Commercial software management courses are often based on a fee per student day, and rates vary between $100 and about $1000 per student day. Commercial courses tend to average from one to three days in length and hence are tightly focused on specific topics such as "Function Point Counting." Conferences normally charge a one-time fee to attend, with rates that range from nothing up to several hundred dollars. In-house training varies widely, and may either be given for nothing if the education group operates as a cost center, or have fees assigned if the education group operates as a profit center.

A software manager in a major corporation that wants to stay current in the state of the art would probably have from 10 to 15 days of training per year, with annual costs of perhaps $10,000 for the courses themselves, and another $5,000 for travel and incidental expenses. The observed ranges in the industry in 1993 are from a low of zero annual education costs to a maximum of more than $25,000 per manager.

20. **Long-range prognosis**—University curricula tend to lag the state of the art by about five to 10 years in all scientific and engineering topics, and software is no exception. This is not necessarily a bad situation: it is merely the way academic curricula tend to evolve. In-house management training within major corporations is usually far more current and relevant than academic curricula. Also, the emergence of a growing and profitable commercial software education business, and the availability of a synergistic mix of academic, commercial, and in-house training for software managers yields a favorable long-range prognosis.

CHAPTER 28

Inadequate Measurement

1. **Definition**—Failure to record the basic and special factors that influence software projects coupled with either inaccurate or missing quantitative data on size, staffing, schedules, resources, costs, and quality coupled with the usage of paradoxical or unsound metrics.

2. **Severity**—The observed U.S. severity levels for inadequate measurements average about a two on the following scale:

   Severity 1: Neither influential factors nor quantitative data are recorded

   Severity 2: Some resource data recorded, but neither influences nor deliverables

   Severity 3: Partial influential factor recording and partial resource data

   Severity 4: Substantial influential factor recording but partial resource data

   Severity 5: Substantial influential factor and resource data, but paradoxical metrics

3. **Frequency**—Inadequate measurement is endemic to the software industry, and is present in more than 90% of all U.S. companies, government agencies, and military services. Inadequate measurement is an international problem, and includes Europe, Asia, and South America as well as North America. Even basic cost and resource tracking in the U.S. tends to omit unpaid overtime, managerial costs, and is often in error by 30% to 70%.

4. **Occurrence**—Inadequate resource measurements or no measurements at all are the normal mode for both artistic activities and for pure research in topics such as mathematics and physics. Inadequate resource and cost measurements are also common in other professions such as medical practice and law, although medicine is quite sophisticated in diagnostic metrics. Until the number of software practitioners began to exceed 5% of the total staff of several industries, the work connected with software was treated as an unmeasurable, artistic activity rather than as a standard business or engineering function.

5. **Susceptibility and resistance**—Susceptibility is wide-spread and is virtually universal among small enterprises with fewer than 50 software practitioners. As the

226

size of the enterprise grows, measurement programs become more common. The computer and telecommunication industries also are more resistant than most. However, resistance follows a surprising pattern, and so far as can be determined, is associated with strong financial performance and strong executive management. The most successful companies within an industry are the ones most likely to have measurement programs, and the most successful industries are also the ones most likely to have measurement baselines. It is not the case that measurement causes success, but rather that successful executive performance and successful enterprise performance are both based on facts. Therefore a pattern of using quantified data is part of the overall pattern of successful enterprise management. It is an interesting observation that as a class, Baldrige Award winners have among the best software measurement programs of any group yet surveyed.

Organizations which follow the SEI capability model literally are highly susceptible, since SEI places measurement in Maturity Level 4. This is clearly a mistake, since measurement belongs at all levels including Maturity Level 1. (Note that SEI itself is trying to correct the misunderstanding. The SEI model merely suggests that full measurement programs are most often encountered at Level 4; it does not bar measurements at the lower levels.) An SEI assessment is itself a form of measurement, and both SPR and SEI recommend doing assessments at Level 1 as the basis for climbing the sequence. Also, standard cost accounting is a form of measurement. It is obvious that SEI does not suggest that profit and loss reporting, tax payments, cash flow, and other financial measures be delayed until the enterprise achieves Level 4 status. This of course would lead to the financial ruin of the organization, and perhaps to the arrest of the corporate officers.

6. **Root causes**—The root causes of inadequate measurement include: 1) Lack of serious metrics research in the early periods of software development, so that economically valid metrics were unavailable prior to 1979; 2) The lack of valid metrics prior to 1979, causing the software industry to develop a dogma that "software is unmeasurable," which became a feature of the software culture; 3) An inclination in the U.S. to ignore preventive methods (which measurement is) and an inclination in the U.S. to ignore problems that do not have large and immediate direct costs; 4) A vested interest on the part of software executives, managers, and staff to oppose measurements, on the grounds that if measurement revealed their performance to rank below enterprise or national averages that would be disadvantageous; 5) A vested interest on the part of CASE and tool vendors to discredit measurements, since accurate measurements would reveal the spuriousness of their improvement claims; 6) Failure of the software engineering schools and business schools to include adequate metrics training; 7) Failure of the software standards organizations such as the IEEE, ANSI, and ISO to establish a valid basis for software measurements, such as standard occupation codes, standard deliverable metrics and definitions, standard influence factor recording methods, and a standard chart of accounts for software cost and resource accumulation at the activity and task levels.

7. **Associated problems**—Inadequate measurement is itself a root cause for many of the most severe problems of the software industry, including *low productivity, false productivity claims, low quality, long schedules, missed schedules, excessive time to market, inadequate estimating, friction with senior management, friction with users, low user satisfaction, canceled projects, inadequate methodologies, inadequate tools, poor organization structures, inadequate specialization, inadequate capital investment,* and *inadequate office environments.*

Inadequate measurements can often be attributed to one or more of the following: *inadequate software management curricula, inadequate software engineering curricula, inexperienced management, lag time in technology adoption, inaccurate metrics, poor organization structures, poor technology transfer,* and *poor corporate culture.*

8. **Cost impact**—The direct costs of inadequate measurement are normally considered to be zero. Note that there is a "Catch 22" associated with the direct costs of measurement: only companies that measure know what it costs and what its value is, so that those which do not measure have no quantified data for comparison. Productivity measurements use about 2% of software management and staff resources. Quality measurements also use about 2%, so a full Applied Software Measurement program can total to about 4% of software management and staff time.

It is significant that companies that have established full Applied Software Measurement programs often have improved quality by more than 60% and productivity by more than 30% within three years, using their initial measurement baseline for comparison. Those companies that do not measure may achieve equal improvements, or they may go backwards by the same amount, but without measurement there is obviously no way for the company or anyone else to verify either progress or regression. Note also that Baldrige Award winners, as a class, typically have state-of-the-art measurement programs in place.

The indirect costs of inadequate measurement are enormous, and are a significant percentage of the sum total of costs of the associated problems identified in section 7. Companies and software producing organizations, like any other system, tend to have a characteristic efficiency at which they work.

The software industry on the whole seems to be about 35% efficient, in that almost two thirds of the total resources are spent on things that have no positive benefit to the enterprise (based on a study carried out within ITT).

The 65% wastage is the effort spent on harmful or non-productive activities: buying productivity tools that do not work, delayed projects, unnecessary projects, reworking carelessly developed projects, canceled projects, bug and defect repairs for problems that might have been prevented or removed early, and the like. Thus, for a large Fortune 500 enterprise with an annual software budget of $500 million, about $325.5 million will essentially be dissipated because of the "friction" associated with current software problems. For both mechanical systems such as engines, and for social systems such as software production, measurement is a key factor in raising efficiency.

Note that wastage of 65% or so is not uncommon among human affairs. Somewhat more extensive studies of military operations suggest that large human organizations seldom put more than 30% of their resources into direct accomplishment of tasks.

9. **Methods of prevention**—The most effective preventive methods of inadequate measurements are cultural. Those enterprises where the corporate culture is oriented toward excellence and "management by fact" have the best situation for prevention of this problem. Enterprises where corporate politics are harmful and divisive, or where schedules are the only real goal, are the least likely to prevent this problem. It is surprisingly beneficial to have a CEO who has been frustrated with software in the past, and who demands improved software performance in the future.

10. **Methods of control**—Fortunately, inadequate measurements are a fully controllable condition. The normal sequence of control is: A) A measurement manager or a measurement focal point is established; B) The current measurement literature, seminar offerings, and consulting services are reviewed; C) The set of monthly and annual quality and productivity reports is defined; D) A chart of accounts is developed for software resource data collection; E) The defect origins, severities, and removal steps are defined for quality measurement; F) The "soft" influential factors that will be collected are determined; G) Normalizing metrics such as Function Points or Feature Points are selected and taught ("lines of code" are not economically valid and are unsuited for quality measurements as well); H) The input questionnaires for "soft" factor and resource data are developed or acquired from a commercial source; I) The measurement work plan is presented to both management and staff so there will be buy-in to the concepts; J) One or two projects are measured as pilot studies; K) The initial pilot studies are reviewed and possible improvements made; L) The full measurement program is implemented.

Moving from step A to step L is normally about a 12 to 18 month undertaking, although a few energetic companies have managed to establish a full measurement program in about six months.

11. **Product support**—A full software measurement system should record resource and cost data, deliverable size data, milestone data, "soft factor" data, and normalized data using functional metrics. In 1993, only four commercial tools approach these capabilities: CHECKPOINT® by SPR, MARS by Computer Power, RA Metrics by Howard Rubin Associates, and PADS by QSM. While there are dozens of resource tracking systems marketed, unless they support functional metrics, deliverable sizes and soft factors, they are not sufficient for serious managerial analysis. A full software measurement tool should include productivity, quality, and "soft" factor measurement capabilities concurrently. For example, measurement at the project level should be "variable focus" and encompass the levels of complete projects, standard phase structures, standard development activities, tasks and subtasks. In addition, the tool should handle multiple-project aggregation and averaging capabilities, for exploring measurements of entire portfolios.

12. **Consulting support**—Only a small number of consulting organizations specialize in accurate software measurements: Computer Power, Howard Rubin Associates, Quantitative Software Management, Real Decisions and Software Productivity Research are the best known. The Software Engineering Institute at Carnegie Mellon University has started a software measurement initiative. In Europe, the Pyramid Project and the Esprit Group are examining software metrics. There is also a Function Point Users Group in Amsterdam. Consulting groups can also assist companies by helping them select the combination of "soft" factors (i.e. the impact of tools, methods, and environmental factors), normalizing metrics, charts of accounts, and sample baselines that will assist in creating useful software measurement programs. A large number of individual management consultants have started practices in software measurement and metrics, and the number is growing rapidly. There is essentially no shortage of consulting support on this topic.

A full measurement and assessment consulting service should include topics that influence the outcomes of software projects, such as tools, methods, languages, corporate politics, organization structures, and physical office space. The measurement service should include conversion capabilities among various normalizing metrics such as Function Points, Feature Points, and even the obsolete "lines of code" and "cost per defect" metrics upon demand (with suitable caveats and cautions).

13. **Education support**—For many years, serious measurement and metrics courses could not be found in either software engineering schools or business schools. Since about 1990, the situation has improved. Now a growing number of universities are starting to include measurement-related topics. A few of these are the Air Force Institute of Technology, Carnegie Mellon University, George Mason University, the University of Maryland, MIT, and Washington University in St. Louis. There is a growing number of commercial measurement courses available, including those which deal explicitly with the subject of measuring software productivity, quality, "soft" factors, and also with the culture and sociology of measurement. An IFPUG-certified course on Function Point Analysis is a good prerequisite to a full software measurement program. Counting Function Points is about as difficult as learning to play chess or checkers. The basic rules are simple, but practice is needed to become proficient. A formal course is a definite advantage. The error rate of novice and untrained Function Point counters is fairly high. The error rate of LOC counting is also high in the absence of training and standard concepts.

14. **Publication support**—Alan Perlis, Fred Sayward, and Mary Shaw's *Software Metrics* (MIT Press, 1983) covers some interesting topics, including design of experiments and data collection and validation. S.D. Conte, H.E. Dunsmore, and V.Y. Shen's *Software Engineering Metrics and Models* (Benjamin/Cummings, 1986) discusses measurement as well as metrics. Brian Dreger's *Function Point Analysis* (Prentice Hall, 1989) is a good primer which deals with an important sub-element of software measurement.

Four books by Capers Jones, Chairman of SPR, deal with software measurement. *Programming Productivity* (McGraw-Hill, 1986) deals with the measurement of productivity, software costs and schedules, and "soft" factors. *Applied Software Measurement* (McGraw-Hill, 1991) covers the establishment of measurement programs, and also includes current U.S. averages for software productivity for military, systems, and MIS software projects. *Critical Problems in Software Measurement* (IS Management Group, 1993) discusses measuring a host of software topics, including occupation groups, schedules of concurrent activities, international projects, and many others. *Software Productivity and Quality—The World Wide Perspective* (IS Management Group, 1993) includes international comparisons, and discusses nine discrete levels at which measurements can be taken, ranging from gross national averages to the level of individual named employees.

Dr. Larry Putnam's book, *Measures for Excellence* (Prentice Hall, 1991) covers measurements and metrics. The well-known book by Bob Grady and Deborah Caswell, *Software Metrics: Establishing a Company-Wide Program* (Prentice Hall, 1987) discusses Hewlett-Packard's corporate measurement system. A more recent book by Robert Grady, *Practical Software Metrics for Project Management and Process Improvement* (Prentice Hall, 1992) continues the Hewlett-Packard story. David Card and Robert Glass's *Measuring Software Design Quality* (Prentice Hall, 1990) covers a number of topics that are seldom discussed, such as measuring optimal module sizes.

A book by Dr. Karl Moller and Dr. Anton Paulish, *Measurement of Software* (IEEE Press, 1982) discusses software measurement from the perspective of the European view. Also giving an overseas flavor from the United Kingdom is Charles Symons' *Software Sizing and Estimating MK II Function Point Analysis* (John Wiley & Sons, 1991). Also from Europe are a number of specialized books on measurement by Horst Zuse, of which *Software Complexity Measures and Methods* (Walter de Gruyter, 1991) is among the most complete treatments of this topic.

15. **Periodical support**—As of 1993, there are no journals fully dedicated to software measurement and metrics except IFPUG's Journal *Metrics Views*. Most of the general software magazines have occasional articles on this topic. A few, such as American Programmer, the IEEE Transactions on Software Engineering, or Communications of the ACM will have intermittent special issues devoted to measurement. On the whole, the coverage has been embarrassingly low. However, the situation seems to be improving. The journal of the International Society of Parametric Analysis (ISPA) includes measurement articles from time to time.

16. **Standards support**—There are no current standards by ANSI, DIN, DoD, IEE, IEEE, or ISO that deal with the full collection of "soft" factors that influence software projects. This is a major gap in international standards. The IFPUG counting practices manual is the canonical reference and equivalent to a standard for counting Function Points. The IEEE standard on software productivity measurement and the IEEE standard on software quality measurement both exist, but neither is very thorough and they give too much unwarranted and uncritical credence to the

obsolete "LOC" metric. There are several DoD standards on software tracking, but most attempt to normalize to the obsolete "lines of code" metric and hence are worthless for serious economic or quality purposes. In conjunction, the DARPA-funded Software Engineering Institute (SEI) is developing a draft standard on source code counting, and also a draft standard on software measurement in conjunction with the IEEE. The draft standard has not been finalized or approved as this book is written. The SEI core metrics include LOC as a standard, without any caution or warning about its paradoxical nature. This is a serious omission.

17. **Professional associations**—The non-profit International Function Point Users Group (IFPUG) is the most active measurement association in the industry, and the only one that is doing state-of-the-art analysis. Since its annual growth rate is about 50%, IFPUG has become the largest measurement association in the United States. The Software Engineering Institute (SEI) is also a non-profit, and has an expanding program of software measurements. The International Society of Parametric Analysis (ISPA) is also concerned with measurement topics, since measurements provide the basis for parametric estimation. The Society of Cost Estimating and Analysis (SCEA) has a similar interest in measurement. Many local societies and organizations are also concerned with measurement: regional or urban CASE users groups, regional software quality groups, SPIN groups, and the like.

18. **Effectiveness of known therapies**—Measurement is now fairly easy to perform at the project level, and surprisingly accurate. Measurement tools can measure requirement, design, coding, documentation, and many other activities and tasks with very high precision. It can also measure the costs and productivity levels of defect removal activities such as reviews, inspections, and tests. Productivity measurement accuracies to within 5% are now common, and 1% precision is not impossible as are quality and defect measurements. Some of these tools also include international measurement capabilities, with multiple currencies, and "what if" modeling capabilities to explore the impact of alternate technologies.

   The best results from the leading companies who use measurement technologies are favorable: improvement in staff morale, coupled with quantified annual improvement rates of about 15% have been achieved for four to five consecutive years for development productivity, and more than 40% per year for software quality. (In certain situations, maintenance productivity has improved as much as 25% to 30% per year.) Military and systems software often lag in measurement technology compared to information systems, due to a strong emotional attachment to unacceptable "lines of code" metrics.

19. **Costs of known therapies**—Note that neither resource tracking systems nor ordinary project planning tools are adequate for measurement purposes, since neither class can be used to explore "soft" factor influences such as methods, tools, languages, skill levels and the like. (Also, resource tracking systems typically "leak" and tend to omit from 30% to 70% of the actual effort applied to software projects.) A full software measurement tool with soft-factor analysis, activity-level and

task-level measures, and integrated quality measures is about $20,000. (Partial measurement tools such as Function Point collectors are often of lower cost, but also of lower utility than full measurement tools.) Full measurement tools normally return their value in about 18 to 36 months when used for a typical set of projects in a medium to large enterprise that handles 20 or more software projects per year.

20. **Long-range prognosis**—The technologies of measuring both "hard" and "soft" factors are now well formed and improving rapidly. Cultural and sociological resistance to measurement is a harder problem. Due to that resistance, poor or inadequate measurement is likely to remain a problem for the rest of the 20th century. However, since companies that measure software well can take market shares from companies that do not, the very long-range prognosis is favorable due to natural selection.

Inadequate Package Acquisition Methods

1. **Definition**—A) For individual departments or units, acquiring software packages without adequate evaluation of how the package matches unit needs; B) For large multi-site enterprises, having various sites or units acquire copies of packages without arranging any kind of volume discount; C) Acquiring packages with similar functions that are mutually incompatible, without realizing that this situation is occurring (i.e. acquiring several incompatible data base tools, word processors, etc.); D) Acquiring packages which are so incompatible with existing software that either the new package or old software requires extensive modifications in order to interconnect; E) For software vendors, acquiring marketing rights to products which are incompatible with stated market targets and goals; F) Failure to arrange for training in acquired packages, if that is necessary to commence usage.

2. **Severity**—The average severity of inadequate package acquisition methods and policies is about a three on the following five point scale:

    Severity 1: Wastage on redundant or inappropriate packages exceeds 60%

    Severity 2: Wastage on redundant or inappropriate packages exceeds 50%

    Severity 3: Wastage on redundant or inappropriate packages exceeds 40%

    Severity 4: Wastage on redundant or inappropriate packages exceeds 30%

    Severity 5: Wastage on redundant or inappropriate packages exceeds 20%

3. **Frequency**—Given the importance of software packages to modern industry and government operations, it is quite astonishing how careless some enterprises are in the way they acquire packages. For example, a major manufacturing enterprise with more than 25 locations in the United States does not attempt to arrange any kind of corporate discount for volume purchases or leases of software. Each of the 25 locations negotiates its own contracts with vendors, leading to both enormous duplication of effort and artificially high prices. Similar situations occur with local and state governments. The same problem has been observed at the national level, such as in Canada where government agencies often make purchases or contracts indepen-

dently of other groups. (The U.S. Federal Government tends to acquire software via General Services Administration or GSA lists of approved vendors and prices.)

The Department of Defense and the United States military services have started an expanded program of trying to use commercial-off-the-shelf (COTS) software packages whenever possible. This is a laudable goal, but unfortunately it is in direct opposition to another DoD policy of mandating the Ada programming language. Since few COTS packages are written in Ada, the military services are faced with an unfortunate binary choice. Only one of the two directives can be followed.

SPR assessments indicate that about 30% of acquired packages do not meet enough user needs to be effective (about 10% are never even used after acquisition); about 20% of acquired packages duplicate similar packages which an enterprise may already own; about 25% of packages suffer from lack of usage once acquired, since training was not planned but was actually necessary; about 15% of acquired packages are seriously incompatible with existing applications, and hence trigger some form of modification work to fit the package into the intended environment.

There is an opposite side to the package acquisition coin. Not only do companies and government agencies waste money on packages they don't use, don't need, or which don't work, these same organizations often fail to acquire packages which would solve long-standing problems. For example, many of the companies which complain loudly about high maintenance costs have never acquired or even explored tools such as complexity analyzers, restructuring tools, reverse engineering tools, or re-engineering tools.

For perhaps cultural reasons, both sides of the package acquisition problem tend to occur within the same enterprises. That is, organizations that are the most careless in package acquisition and waste the most money on ineffective packages also tend to have the biggest gaps in their tool and technology suites.

4. **Occurrence**—Failure to have adequate policies and methods in place for package acquisition seems to be most related to corporate culture. There are no clear trends by industry. For example, within the telecommunications industry, several companies have formal package evaluation and screening methods, while several competitors simply acquire packages based on local option. Surprisingly, even wholesale/retail chains, whose primary business is buying and selling commodities, are not always rigorous when it comes to buying software packages for their own use. In theory, large companies should be more careful in package acquisition than small enterprises. However, the majority still do not exercise proper care in software selection.

In general, acquisition rigor correlates somewhat to the costs of the package being acquired. Thus packages in excess of $10,000 tend to be acquired more thoughtfully than packages in the $500 range, for example. However, even here there are exceptions. Several companies have acquired project estimating tools in the $20,000 range which were not even calibrated for the kinds of software the enterprise was building. As an even more embarrassing example, a major computer vendor attempting to penetrate the MIS market-place, actually entered into agreements to market two separate estimating tools that were not calibrated for MIS projects, and could only perform adequately for systems and military applications.

5. **Susceptibility and resistance**—Susceptibility and resistance tend to be random. They may be based on cultural factors or even on the habits of specific executives. Enterprises where the controller or CFO tends to be careful in acquisitions may sometimes have better policies than similar enterprises where the culture is more laissez faire.

Among the most resistant organizations are the U.S. Federal Government agencies who acquire software from the General Services Administration (GSA) schedule. While the GSA schedule does not guarantee that software will meet an agency's needs, at least the price is firm and the conditions are clear.

Small enterprises who depend entirely on purchased or leased packages are often quite susceptible. Sometimes these enterprises do not even have any resident technologists who can evaluate vendor claims, which places them at the mercy of unsupported marketing and sales assertions. This is always hazardous.

What is surprising about susceptibility is how several major companies, who are technical leaders in many respects, are remarkably uncautious in their package acquisition policies. One would think that every Fortune 500 enterprise would have full-scale package evaluation teams and departments, since almost any company in the Fortune 500 class has more than $1 billion in acquired software packages. The incidence of careful package acquisition methods and policies among the Fortune 500 set seems to be less than 50%.

6. **Root causes**—The root causes of inadequate package acquisition methods and practices can be traced back to the fact that software is a fairly new industry, whose entire history is barely 50 years of age. This, in turn, leads to a scarcity of training. There appear to be no U.S. university courses in software engineering schools or even business schools which deal explicitly with software package acquisition. There are also few on-the-job or in-house training courses available. Essentially package acquisition is unknown in terms of software curricula and literature.

A second and derivative root cause is that there are no effective civilian standards for package acquisition. There are a number of local exceptions within specific companies, where corporate policies and practices are fairly thorough when it comes to package acquisition.

Package acquisition is perhaps one of the rare domains where governments are more effective than civilian organizations. However, an alarming trend has started to occur with at least U.S. military procurements. Something like 50% or more of hardware procurements are now being challenged by rival vendors who were not selected. This is stretching out the procurement window from months to years. Should such a situation arise for software, the results would be equally time consuming.

7. **Associated problems**—Inadequate package acquisition methods and policies can be correlated with *cost overruns, long schedules, missed schedules,* and also with *high maintenance costs* and *low levels of user satisfaction.*

Inadequate package acquisition is often associated with *inadequate management curricula, inadequate software engineering curricula, inadequate standards,* and sometimes with *management malpractice.*

8. **Cost impact**—The cost impact of inadequate package acquisition policies can be viewed from two directions: 1) The costs of acquiring packages that are ineffective, redundant, or don't work; 2) The costs of *not acquiring* packages that would benefit enterprise operations in positive and tangible ways.

As a rule of thumb, enterprises which have casual or random package acquisition strategies tend to waste about 50% of all money spent on tools, by acquiring tools which don't meet local needs, which don't work, or which duplicate similar tools.

Even enterprises with formal package acquisition methods can waste a little bit (anyone can be fooled once or twice) but the magnitude of waste usually drops below 10%.

It is easiest to see the costs of inadequate package acquisition when dealing with specific examples. The following example is based on a very common situation in software cost estimating. Company ABC has 100 managers and 1000 personnel in the software engineering function. Due to repeated problems with inaccurate estimating, the VP of software engineering decides to acquire an estimating tool. Not being aware of the number and diversity of such tools (about 50 are being marketed as of 1993) he or she acquires ten copies of one of the older kinds of estimating tools without any serious investigation of local needs and modern estimating capabilities. The cost of the ten copies might be $100,000. The tool which was acquired requires the staff to be trained, so 20 of the managers are trained by the vendor in a one-day session, which costs $2500 in direct costs, plus $5,500 for the burdened labor costs of the 20 managers. Unfortunately, the selected tool was not calibrated for the kind of software which the enterprise builds, requires a guess at "lines of source code," and hence tends to generate inaccurate estimates. Within three months, the tool has become shelfware and is no longer utilized. The inaccurate estimating problem still remains.

9. **Methods of prevention**—The most effective prevention is to recognize that tool acquisition is a major business function that needs to be dealt with in a professional manner.

It is most appropriate for a mid-sized company to appoint a tools committee of perhaps three managers and three technical staff members. The first task of the tools committee would be to make their existence known, and solicit recommendations from managers and technical staff members about tool needs.

Tool recommendations would include a discussion of the problem area where the tool was expected to make improvements and the capabilities which tools must have to solve the problems.

The tools committee would be empowered to acquire all of the relevant catalogs of available software engineering and software management tools, and would also collect vendor literature. In addition, the tools committee would find contact points within the user groups of any interesting tools, where such groups exist.

The tools committee would use literature references and contacts with tool users to narrow down the search (in the estimating domain, a first pass might narrow the possibilities down from about 50 to perhaps five). Vendors from the short list would be invited to demonstrate their tool capabilities to both the tools committee and to potential users, ideally on problems taken from within the company.

Note that some vendors provide 30-day to 90-day trial periods, although fees are usually levied. These trials normally provide adequate time to be sure that the tools actually meet enterprise needs. The only caution is that if the tools necessitate training, the vendor and company must provide it.

The company and the winning vendors (there may be more than one) would then negotiate volume purchase arrangements, training, maintenance, and any other ancillary agreements.

Those tools which had been successfully evaluated would become part of a permanent library of tool information which could be circulated within the company.

A six-person committee such as the one discussed here which meets perhaps six days a month normally costs around $10,000 per month. For a small company which uses a three-person committee, the monthly rate would be around $5,000.

A new method for exploring and evaluating packages is on the horizon, although the results are still very preliminary. Function Point metrics are beginning to be used for both contractual purposes, and also starting to show up in package evaluations.

Here are some examples: Typical word processors and speadsheets operating on personal computers range from 500 to 1500 Function Points in size. The acquisition costs per copy range from a low of about $0.10 to a high of about $0.75 per Function Point. It is now possible to explore both functional capabilities and effective costs, utilizing Function Points as one aspect of the research.

This method of analysis is new, but leads to some interesting fields of research. For example, personal computer software is often available for less than $1.00 per Function Point. Software operating under UNIX, however, tends to be in the range of $10.00 per Function Point. Some mainframe packages exceed $100.00 per Function Point.

10. **Methods of control**—For the problem of inadequate tool evaluation and purchasing, prevention is the solution. There are few if any control methods available once tools have been acquired and are in use. Some vendors provide 30-day, 60-day, or 90-day return policies, although there may be some kind of associated restocking charge if the package is returned.

11. **Product support**—There is a major gap in the software industry in the domain of package acquisitions. For example, most CASE vendors assume that all software

will be custom-built, and have no intrinsic capabilities for trying out packages or, in some instances, even importing or exporting information.

Tool vendors themselves provide three layers of product support: 1) Self-running demonstrations of tool capabilities; 2) Working versions of tools with some functions cut out or disabled; 3) The complete tool itself operating under some kind of 30-day to 90-day temporary license.

12. **Consulting support**—The larger tool vendors have captive consulting groups who obviously are biased in favor of their company's tools. There are a few consulting and publication companies, such as Auerbach and the Gartner Group, which evaluate and review tools. There are also journals such as CASE Trends and CASE Outlook which review tools from time to time, and even publish tool catalogs. However, for serious in-depth tool evaluations, the smaller independent consulting groups or individual consultants who know particular tool classes predominate.

13. **Education support**—There are few sources of education available from either universities or private companies that deal explicitly with tool evaluations or tool or package acquisition. Several universities, such as the University of North Carolina or Washington University in St. Louis have set up demonstration labs where various commercial tools and packages can be tried out. On the whole, package acquisition is not well served by either university or private educational curricula.

14. **Publication support**—Here too, there is a major shortage of information. John Marciniak and Don Reifer's *Software Acquisition Management* (John Wiley & Sons, 1990) is a recent title. Dick Brandon and Sydney Segelstein's classic *Data Processing Contracts* (Van Nostrand Reinhold, 1976) is also a useful book. William Roetzheim's *Developing Software to Government Standards* (Prentice Hall, 1991) is a very useful book for companies who want to do business with the government.

There are a number of useful tool catalogs. For example, the semi-annual *Guide to Software Productivity Aids* (ACR Press) edited by Phil Howard is a useful compendium. Also useful is a similar volume edited by Gene Forte and produced by CASE Outlook. Eliot Weinman of CASE Trends also produces such a catalog. Auerbach and DEC produce catalogs too. Many large computer companies and software vendors produce catalogs of all software which operates on their platforms or using their operating systems.

15. **Periodical support**—For personal computers, clones, and Apple users there are usually excellent reviews of software products in every issue of many journals, such as PC Magazine, Macworld, PC Sources, PC Computing, PC Week and Computer Language. From time to time, there are special reviews of collected suites of packages, such as reviews of 20 spreadsheets, 15 word processors or a dozen CAD tools. For companies doing software business in Europe, the Swiss-published ISO 9000 newsletter contains articles of interest.

Several companies, such as Auerbach, have reviewed hardware and software products for many years, and offer commercial subscriptions to their reviews. The

Gartner Group comes to mind as one of the specialists in reviewing software management tools.

The general software engineering literature is more lacking on software reviews than the specialized journals. However, CASE Trends or CASE Outlook will occasionally review products.

What would be desirable would be a non-profit association and journal similar to Consumer Reports, only specializing in software packages.

16. **Standards support** —There are no known non-government U.S. civilian standards dealing with software acquisition, other than local policies and standards within specific companies. The General Services Administration (GSA) has rather strict standards for government software package acquisition, however. There are also DoD standards. Starting in 1992, software products (and other products too) marketed in Europe have been required to be certified under various ISO standards from 9000 through 9004. It is therefore quite important for all companies exporting software to have copies of these standards.

17. **Professional associations**—Many package vendors and quite a few tools and packages have non-profit user associations connected to them. These associations are an excellent source of real-life information on the pros and cons of the tools themselves, and the vendor support of tools as well. A few examples (there are more than a thousand in all) include the Artemis user group, the CADRE Teamworker user group, the CHECKPOINT® user group, the CGI PACBASE user group, the DEC DECUS user group, IBM's GUIDE, SHARE, and COMMON user groups, the IEF user group and the Oracle user group.

There are also many non-profit associations which encompass entire classes of tools. For example, the International Function Point Users Group (IFPUG) deals with all tools which support functional metrics. The International Society of Parametric Analysis (ISPA) deals with all tools for parametric modeling. The Society of Cost Estimating and Analysis (SCEA) deals with all kinds of estimating tools, and so forth.

There are also many regional groups which discuss tools: CASE user groups, local quality assurance groups, the Boston Computer Society, etc.

There are also bulletin boards and user associations which communicate via CompuServe, Internet, Prodigy, or some other on-line service. (Note: the author seldom fails to receive at least a dozen first-hand responses about how well or poorly various packages operate when a query is placed via CompuServe or Internet. These on-line services have become a major component of modern marketing research for software tools, and for other products as well.)

There would appear to be a good opportunity to create a "Consumer's Union" type of non-profit organization which would carefully evaluate and review various software packages, without bias. Such an organization would be very beneficial for the industry as a whole.

18. **Effectiveness of known therapies**—Once an enterprise becomes aware of wastage and inefficiency in package acquisition methods, the available therapies are quite effective. Seeking information from users of various packages is the most effective of all known therapies. Trying out packages under local conditions is the second most effective therapy.

19. **Costs of known therapies**—Establishing a permanent or semi-permanent committee for dealing with package acquisition is the most costly of the therapies. Such groups will typically run from a low of $5,000 per month within small enterprises to more than $100,000 per month for a Fortune 500 class enterprise. Since these groups can pay for themselves by eliminating a single tool purchase mistake, they will usually return their value within six months.

    Other aspects of package acquisition rigor, such as buying catalogs, subscribing to relevant journals, and joining non-profit user associations are so inexpensive that the costs are almost negligible: less than $1,000 per year.

20. **Long-range prognosis**—The prognosis is guardedly optimistic. The technologies and non-profit organizations which can assist in package acquisition are very good already. The basic weakness seems to be in corporate culture, plus a lack of firm quantitative data on the costs and wastage associated with inappropriate or unusable package acquisitions. Cultural problems are harder to solve than technical problems, but they are not impossible. By the end of the century, most medium and large enterprises should have fairly rigorous package acquisition methods in place.

Inadequate Research and Reference Facilities

1. **Definition**—A) Lack of convenient enterprise library support for exploration of software engineering and management topics; B) Lack of on-line reference facilities or lack of access to on-line research data bases; C) Lack of convenient access to university or public reference libraries with software engineering and software management sections containing both journals and more than 500 volumes of relevant books.

2. **Severity**—The average severity of lack of research and reference facilities is about a three on the following five-point scale:

   Severity 1: No enterprise, public, or on-line library support at all
   Severity 2: No enterprise or public library support; but on-line support
   Severity 3: No enterprise library, but public and on-line support available
   Severity 4: Minimal enterprise and public libraries, but on-line support
   Severity 5: Minimal enterprise library, adequate public and on-line support

3. **Frequency**—With any technical discipline, one of the problems facing practitioners is staying current with new and emerging information. Software engineering, computer science, and software management produce new information in ever-increasing volumes. As of 1993, a library of useful books on software engineering and management would contain more than 2000 titles of current works, and add about 100 to 200 titles annually. In addition, about 50 software-related journals and magazines exist that have articles of residual value. There are also a number of on-line data bases and useful reference sources. Access to this information is valuable to professional competence and growth. As of 1993, less than 20% of U.S. software-producing organizations seem to have adequate local facilities for keeping professional and management staffs up to date.

4. Occurrence—Reference facilities and library support correlate strongly with the size of the enterprise. Large enterprises such as AT&T, DEC, IBM and Hewlett-Packard usually have good to excellent library and research facilities. Companies with less than 1000 employees have marginal or no on-site research facilities. Companies with less than 100 total employees seldom have any on-site research capabilities at all, other than access to various on-line data bases.

5. Susceptibility and resistance—As already stated, small enterprises tend to be more susceptible than large enterprises. However, high-technology enterprises in the computer, software, bioengineering, and telecommunications business sectors tend to be fairly resistant at all size levels due to the need for research facilities connected to the business itself. Civilian government organizations tend to be more susceptible than companies when software populations are of equal size. Military organizations, on the other hand, are approximately equal to companies in resistance. Banks, insurance companies, and MIS software producers tend to be more susceptible than systems software producers with the same population size.

6. Root causes—The root causes of inadequate reference facilities can be divided into three sets: financial, cultural, and technological. Small and undercapitalized enterprises tend to regard research and reference facilities as an expensive luxury, and therefore seldom have them, since both on-site libraries and heavy usage of on-line reference services tend to be expensive.

Software is still a comparatively new discipline, and it often escapes notice that there is a large and growing literature of useful topics. Medium to large companies that are profitable and lack reference libraries normally omit them for cultural reasons. Indeed, from time to time assessments turn up enterprises where things like libraries or reference facilities are regarded as useless time wasters which might take away from available work hours.

The technological root cause is that software lacks some of the reference facilities of older disciplines such as medicine. There is no software equivalent of the *Index Medicus* nor the ready availability of abstracting services and even audio cassettes of current topics. Optical storage and multi-media support are about to revolutionize reference services, incidentally.

7. Associated problems—Lack of adequate reference and research facilities are often associated with *management malpractice* and *technical staff malpractice*. There are also associations with *slow technology transfer, low status of software professionals*, and with *low morale*.

Lack of reference and research facilities itself is caused by the problems of *inadequate capital investment* and *poor corporate culture*.

8. Cost impact—There is very little information on the costs associated with lack of adequate reference and research facilities. In both telecommunications software and systems software, a surprising correlation was noted in the 1980's: software quality and productivity levels correlated with the number of volumes in the on-site research library. Locations such as AT&T in Naperville or IBM in San Jose with

243

more than 20,000 volumes in their reference libraries tended to outperform locations with smaller libraries. However, it is probable that the correlations were coincidental and due to deeper factors. Obviously locations with large libraries had adequate discretionary capital available, and had many other tools and productivity factors available at the same time.

9. **Methods of prevention**—As of 1993, reference and research capabilities are being deeply transformed by the technologies of optical storage, on-line data bases with search and retrieval capabilities, hyper-text, new data compression algorithms, and multi-media representation. Enormous volumes of information are starting to appear on optical disks, complete with search and cross-reference capabilities. While these technologies are not yet mature, they are evolving so rapidly that anyone can now have powerful and personal research facilities both at home and at work. Indeed, as portable optical readers show up on the consumer market, it is now technically possible to carry the equivalent of a small library in an attache case.

On-line reference services such as Lockheed Dialog, the data bases of Mead Data Central, and the specialized data bases provided by commercial services such as CompuServe, Internet and Ziffnet, are also quite useful.

10. **Methods of control**—The most effective control is to establish an on-site library of the relevant books, magazines, and multi-media information needed by software managers and professional staffs. This is a recommended approach for organizations with more than about a dozen software professionals.

11. **Product support**—As of 1993, the technologies of multi-media information storage and retrieval are in rapid evolution and new products are appearing monthly. Products that can perform key-word searching and facilitate hyper-text links are on the critical path to ease of reference.

12. **Consulting support**—Reference and research facilities are seldom dealt with by management consulting groups, or by individual consultants either. Professional librarians are the most likely source of useful consulting assistance. Also useful is access to good book stores. For example, the author is fortunate to have both a B. Dalton general book store and a Softpro technical book store within walking distance. It is actually easier to stay current on relevant topics by scanning the recent acquisitions within a book store than by visiting a library. Indeed, an interesting form of research is to enumerate the titles on various topical areas in a technical book store such as Softpro. It is obvious that the OO paradigm and client-server computing are on an upswing, since the titles dealing with those topics increase weekly.

13. **Education support**—There seem to be no courses in software engineering or business schools that deal explicitly with research and reference facilities. There are obviously many courses on library science, but these are seldom mixed with a software curriculum. Private education and seminars seldom discuss this topic

either, except in the limited context of bibliographic references for specific topics. Universities and academic institutions tend to have good to excellent libraries and research facilities.

There is an interesting correlation among large companies such as those in the Fortune 500. The number of patents, inventions, and research publications correlates fairly closely with the volume of their research libraries. Indeed, until the hard economic times of the 1990's damaged companies such as DEC, IBM, PRIME, and Data General, it might have been claimed that profits and revenues had a similar correlation.

14. **Publication support**—There is no single book or bibliography that covers all of the relevant software engineering and management literature. Specific publishers such as Prentice Hall, Addison Wesley, Dorset House, and McGraw-Hill publish their own catalogs, of course. Major technical book stores and university book stores also publish catalogs.

A group called "Single Source" which is a division of Software Quality Engineering in Jacksonville, Florida, has attempted to create a unified catalog of software engineering, computer science, and software management books from all relevant publishers. Some technical and computer-science oriented book stores also publish consolidated catalogs. For example, in Burlington, Massachusetts, there is an annual catalog of software engineering, computer science, and management books published by the Softpro book store. These consolidated catalogs are quite useful to researchers, since they encompass multiple publishers and list books by topic.

What might be an interesting contribution to the literature would be a book that reviewed other software books. A book containing about 100 full-length reviews or perhaps 250 short reviews of the major software titles would be an interesting project. Such a book would need updating on an annual basis to stay current. Eventually such a project might grow to a set of related books, such as reviews of software project management, reviews of maintenance and enhancement, and reviews of quality assurance publications.

15. **Periodical support**—Specialized library periodicals deal with research and reference facilities, but they are comparatively scarce among the software engineering community. The standard software and management journals seldom touch on this topic. The ACM Computing Reviews attempts, with moderate success, to stay current with new books. There are often book reviews in the normal software journals such as American Programmer, CASE Outlook, CASE Trends, The Software Practitioner, Software Magazine, and System Development.

16. **Standards support**—So far as can be determined, none of the major standards organizations have addressed the topic of research and reference capabilities. There are emerging standards on data interchanges and multi-media formats that will facilitate future reference capabilities.

17. **Professional associations**—Most of the professional associations are interested in reference and research facilities, but none do more than publish occasional bibliographies.

18. **Effectiveness of known therapies**—In 1993, it is premature to judge the effectiveness of the new research and reference capabilities such as multi-media representations and hypertext. Conventional research and reference methods, i.e. books, periodicals, and libraries have been effective for several thousand years. On-line reference material is also effective. Particularly useful for research purposes are key-word searches for topics such as "Function Points" or "Software Productivity" which are applied to current periodicals and books stored on-line.

19. **Costs of known therapies**—An "average" technical book in 1993 costs around $35 and an "average" journal subscription for one year is about the same amount. Therefore a library of 5000 volumes and 100 journals would cost more than $200,000 plus the costs of shelves, space, and at least part-time library support. Multi-media and optical costs are too unstable to be definitive, but the average street cost for a typical CD disk of useful information is less than $100. Optical readers or multi-media drives and software are less than $1000.

    One of the most cost-effective ways of performing some kinds of research is membership on Internet, CompuServe, Genie, Prodigy, or some other on-line service. Such services not only have other members who can answer queries, but offer gateways into major data bases such as Lockheed's Dialog, or the Mead Data Central resources.

20. **Long-range prognosis**—The emergence of optical storage, multi-media representations, data compression techniques, hyper text, and on-line data bases are of enormous potential significance. The printing press made reading a common skill, and opened up new facilities for learning and transferring information. Optical storage supported by sophisticated search and retrieval algorithms can augment these basic capabilities by allowing researchers to pursue related topics through literally hundreds or even thousands of reference sources. It is not impossible that by the end of the century, every knowledge worker can be equipped with a personal library that is equivalent, for his or her specialty, to a university library today.

Inadequate Software Policies and Standards

1. **Definition**—A) Standards or policy statements that enforce the usage of harmful or obsolete technologies; B) Standards or policies that cause excessive work for no increase in value or usefulness of the projects which adhere to them; C) Major problem areas where there are no standards, or where current standards and policies are out of date in describing appropriate preventive or control mechanisms.

2. **Severity**—The observed severity levels for inadequate standards is fairly high, and averages about a 2.5 on the following scale:

   Severity 1: The standard requires usage of methods known to be harmful

   Severity 2: The standard requires usage of methods known to be obsolete

   Severity 3: The standard requires usage of methods known to be irrelevant

   Severity 4: The standard excludes or fails to cover important topics

   Severity 5: The standard causes excessive work without compensating value

3. **Frequency**—Unfortunately, more than 50% of the standards and policies that deal explicitly with software are inadequate under the definitions cited above. It appears that every standards-creating organization for software tends to create inadequate standards. This statement appears true of ANSI, DoD, IEE, IEEE, and ISO. The statement also appears true of quasi-standards organizations such as IFPUG and SEI, which do have authority to issue formal standards but which are in de facto control of specific technologies.

4. **Occurrence**—Inadequate policies and standards appear endemic to the software industry. The fundamental reason seems to be that as of 1993, software has not really evolved into a true engineering discipline. In particular, software lacks an adequate volume of empirical data derived from accurate measurements. Therefore many software standards reflect the subjective opinions of the standards committee members, rather than true engineering knowledge.

   One of the more uncertain aspects of the standards situation for software is to enumerate exactly how many standards exist for software, and which organizations are empowered to create and modify such standards. Following is a rough attempt to identify the major standards-producing organizations which may impact software:

International Software Standards

1) CCITT
2) IAEA
3) IEC
4) ISO

National Software Standards

1) AFNOR	6) CSA
2) ANSI	7) DIN
3) AS	8) JIS
3) BSI	9) SDA
4) CEN	10) Spain
5) CEN	

Professional Association Standards

1) ASME	6) IEEE
2) ASQC	7) IFPUG
3) ASTM	8) ITAA
4) Baldrige criteria	9) SAE
5) IEE	10) SEI

Sector Standards

1) AIAA	8) EEA	15) MOD
2) ANS	9) EIA	16) NASA
3) ARINC	10) EPRI	17) NBS
4) DIA	11) ESA	18) NIST
5) DOD	12) FAA	19) NSCAC
6) DPC	13) GPA	20) RTCA
7) ECMA	14) MIL	21) UK DOH

Corporate/Group Standards

1) Formal corporate standards
2) Formal group or divisional standards
3) Informal standards/guidelines
4) Formal policies
5) Informal policies/practices

In round numbers, there are perhaps as many as 50 different organizations who can establish either actual standards or de facto standards which may sometimes be enforced.

No individual software project is likely to find itself subjected to 50 different standards groups, but many software projects might find themselves being pulled in different directions if, for example, they must concurrently adhere to CCITT standards, IEEE standards, ISO standards, and DoD standards. The maximum number of standards which a given project might be constrained to follow concurrently is in excess of 30.

It is a reasonable question to ask if adherence to formal standards is a beneficial or harmful activity. Surprisingly, this important topic has very little in the way of empirical data on either side of the question.

5. **Susceptibility and resistance**—Standards created for topics where there are no proven engineering practices are most susceptible. For software engineering, lack of proven engineering practices is a distressingly common condition. Most resistant are standards created for topics where empirical data are derived from accurate measurement. As of 1993, both empirical data and accurate measurement are uncommon for software, although there are signs of progress. Specific standards-creating organizations seem to have patterns of common error conditions:

ANSI/IEEE standards for software tend to run about three to five years behind the state of the art (which is the average length of time required to produce an IEEE standard) and tend to be very spotty and incomplete in their coverage. For example, the 1991 edition of the IEEE Standard Glossary of Software Engineering Terms (IEEE 729–1983) omits all references to the terminology of functional metrics, even though they have been in use since 1979. The IEEE Standard on Measures for Reliable Software (IEEE 982.1–1988) omits all references to the measure of defect removal efficiency, even though this topic has been in use since the 1960's. It also specifies "LOC" for quality normalization, in spite of proof that this metric is paradoxical for quality purposes. The IEEE standard on software productivity measures (IEEE Computer Society P1045/D3.1 8/28/90) omits references to the interaction of the paradoxical LOC metric with fixed costs. The positive aspects of the ANSI/IEEE standards is that they are updated fairly often, and include a proviso that if they are not endorsed at five-year intervals, they should be considered obsolete.

Department of Defense (DoD) standards tend to run about five to seven years behind the state of the art, and create enormous quantities of paperwork, some of which appears useless or irrelevant. The best feature of DoD standards is that they tend to enforce rigor in initial specifications, change management, quality assurance, and configuration control. The worst feature of DoD standards such as DoD 2167A, 2168, 1521 B, etc. is that the paperwork requirements are so voluminous that the standards create about 400 English words for every Ada statement. A careful pruning of document types and contents might preserve the essential rigor of DoD standards, and simultaneously improve their usefulness.

International Function Point Users Group (IFPUG) is not a formally constituted standards organization endorsed by a professional committee such as the IEEE or by national governments. IFPUG is, however, the primary coordinating body for Function Point usage, and the IFPUG Counting Practices Committee has become the de facto standards organization for the counting rules associated with U.S. Function Points (but not British Mark II Function Points). The IFPUG Counting Practices are updated fairly often and attempt to stay current. However, they include a few anomalies and debatable points. For example, there is strong disagreement with the counting of menu items. At a deeper level, the IFPUG practice of counting deleted Function Points as though they were part of a delivered system appears to violate standard economic practices. It would be more appropriate to keep separate accounts for deletion size and effort.

International Standards Institute (ISO)—The ISO standards of most importance to software are the ISO 9000 through 9004 series which deal with quality plans, levels, and measurement. Although these standards are fairly new and became operational in 1992, the contents of the ISO standards appear to be seven to ten years out of date. The basic definitions of "quality" are curiously obsolete and include topics such as "portability" which has no place in a quality standard at all. Major quality topics such as defect potential enumeration, defect removal efficiency measurement, warranty repairs and duplicate defects, are not covered at all. Another flaw with the ISO quality series is that they approach DoD standards in requiring enormous quantities of supporting paperwork, some of which appears to be unnecessary or redundant. U.S. companies marketing in Europe will be required to conform to ISO standards, so in spite of their problems they are important and should be carefully analyzed. The redeeming feature of ISO is that it provides a basis for European cooperation which may develop into something useful.

(From contacting organizations which have been certified to ISO standards, and similar organizations which have not been certified, there is no empirical evidence to date which suggests that the ISO 9000–9004 quality series improves quality in any tangible way. There is empirical evidence that ISO certification adds to project costs, however.)

Software Engineering Institute (SEI) is not a formally constituted standards organization, but due to SEI being a non-profit organization with funding from DARPA, it is becoming a quasi-standards organization for several topics. SEI is most prominent for its five-stage maturity level scheme, and for having developed a widely used assessment technique. The SEI core metrics draft standard, which may be accepted by the Department of Defense, is woefully inadequate and continues to recommend the obsolete LOC metric without any caution as to the paradoxical results which might occur.

Other SEI work that overlaps the standards domain can be seen in the SEI measurement initiatives. The SEI maturity model was made famous by Watts Humphrey in his well known book *Managing the Software Process* (Addison-Wesley, 1987) now augmented by a host of supplemental SEI guides. Humphrey, of course, picked up the maturity concept from an older book, Crosby's famous *Quality is Free* (McGraw-Hill, 1979).

The draft SEI measurement standards, produced in conjunction with the IEEE, are unfortunately several years behind the state of the art, and would not be acceptable for civilian or commercial software usage in their present form. They lack adequate granularity of data collection, use normalization metrics such as LOC that are known to be harmful, and in general are too far removed from current best practices in measurement to be effective. However, the SEI standards are still at the draft level and may yet be updated and modernized before final publication occurs.

6. **Root causes**—The root cause of inadequate standards is that software engineering is not as advanced a technology as other forms of engineering. (The 50th anniversary of software is 1993, since the contract for the ENIAC computer was signed in June of 1943.) In particular, software engineering lacks a valid data base of empirical results derived from accurate measurements.

   Standards committees are staffed by volunteers who work hard and attempt to do a good job. The inadequacies are certainly not deliberate. The fundamental problem is basically lack of valid data on which a standards committee can build reasonable standards.

7. **Associated problems**—Inadequate standards are associated with *low productivity, low quality, low user satisfaction,* and *inadequate methodologies.*

   Inadequate standards are caused by *inadequate measurement, inadequate metrics, inadequate software engineering curricula,* and *slow technology transfer.*

8. **Cost impact**—The cost impact due to inadequate standards must be dealt with on a standard-by-standard basis. Some of the costs can be quantified readily. For example, the paperwork costs associated with DoD 2167A are about three times larger than would be experienced for civilian projects of the same size and complexity levels.

   There are also indirect costs associated with inadequate standards. For example, companies who used ISO 9000–9004 series and still produced low-quality software might reasonably attribute some of their problems to the basic inadequacy of the standards themselves.

9. **Methods of prevention**—Accurate measurement of software projects and the factors which influenced them (methods, tools and languages) is the best long-term preventive for inadequate standards. As the knowledge base of software engineering improves, so will the adequacy of standards.

10. **Methods of control**—Most standards organizations have a procedure for challenging a given standard, granting a waiver for not using it, or some other mechanism for correcting major standards deficiencies. For political and sociological reasons, it is not always easy to use these methods but at least they exist in theory. Another control method is to simply ignore an inadequate standard and do some-

thing better. This strategy can be used with civilian standards such as the IEEE, but it is not an option with DoD or ISO 9000–9004 standards.

11. **Product support**—There are too many standards to discuss this topic completely. For DoD standards, there are documentation production tools that come pre-configured with required section titles and content guides. For standards such as those dealing with comments and code structure, there are a variety of tools that can scan source code and report on standards adherence. For quality standards, there are tools that can facilitate test coverage analysis, test plan development, and defect reporting and measurement. There are also tools that can predict defect potentials and defect removal efficiencies, and also measure these same factors. On the whole, tool coverage for standards is spotty and inconsistent. Some standards are well covered, while others have essentially zero coverage.

12. **Consulting support**—Many consulting groups and individual consultants specialize in various standards. There is no current shortage, for example, of consultants well versed in DoD 2167 A. Due to the significance of ISO 9000–9004, many consulting groups are gearing up to handle this domain.

13. **Education support**—Academic training in standards is spotty, and tends to be on the skimpy side. Obviously specialized educational facilities such as the Air Force Institute of Technology (AFIT) and the Naval Post-Graduate School are exceptions when it comes to military standards. Commercial and private courses are available on DoD and ISO standards.

14. **Publication support**—The U.S. Government Printing Office (GPO) and the National Technology Information Service (NTIS) deal with U.S. governmental and military standards. The IEEE publishes a semi-annual standards collection, *IEEE Software Engineering Standards Collection* (IEEE Press, New York). The ISO standards, *ISO 9000, 9001, 9002, 9003, 9004* are published commercially by Global Engineering Documents, New York, New York. The *IFPUG Counting Practices Manual* is published by IFPUG, Westerly, Ohio. The SEI quasi-standards are published by the Software Engineering Institute, Carnegie-Mellon University, Pittsburgh, PA. William Roetzheim's 1991 book *Developing Software to Government Standards* (Prentice Hall) is a very good survey of the major standards and how to follow them. Also relevant is Susan MacManus' *Doing Business with the Government* (Paragon House, 1992). Standards are also available from various retail establishments, such as Global Engineering Documents in Washington, D.C., which sells ISO standards, military standards, and various other standards.

15. **Periodical support**—The general software journals do not discuss standards as a normal practice, but may run specific articles. The IEEE, the Air Force, and a number of specialized journals such as the IFPUG newsletter deal with standards and changes to standards from time to time. The IEEE publishes an interesting quarterly journal entitled *The IEEE Standards Bearer* that discusses the status of various standards and the committees who are involved with them. The Swiss-published

ISO 9000 News is also of interest. For military and defense personnel, the well-known STSC Crosstalk journal published from Ogden Air Force Base in Utah frequently includes articles on DoD and military policies and standards.

16. **Standards support**—Curiously, there are no known standards that deal with validating and verifying the accuracy, usefulness, and completeness of standards themselves. This appears to be a major omission. Another major omission would be a "sunset" clause that automatically terminated standards after a period of three to five years unless the standards were revised or recertified.

   It would be technically possible to build an expert system, with perhaps some fuzzy logic, that could select the relevant standards that must be followed for any particular software project. At least one software cost estimating company is exploring the market value of such a standards planning function as an add-on feature. The costs of implementation may be greater than the market value.

17. **Professional associations**—Many professional engineering societies such as the IEE in England, and the IEEE world-wide, create and distribute standards. Obviously the major standards groups, such as ANSI, ISO, and JUSE create standards and approve those created by others. Other organizations such as the Software Engineering Institute (SEI) and the International Function Point Users Group (IFPUG) create de facto standards which may be adopted as formal standards by the ISO or some other standards group.

18. **Effectiveness of known therapies**—The most effective therapy for improving on the usefulness and value of standards is to derive them from empirical, measured data. Standards based solely on subjective opinions, even the opinions of experts, are less likely to be effective. It is also recommended that standards include a "sunset" clause, which limits their applicability to a three-year or five-year time period. If the standards are not modified or recertified before the expiration date, then they might be considered null and void. As the situation stands now, it is much easier to create new standards than it is to eliminate obsolete and even harmful standards.

19. **Costs of known therapies**—A software standards selection group in major companies or government agencies that actually considers the adequacy of standards would require the effort of from three to 10 senior personnel, and would probably work for about two weeks each year. A sort of "Consumer Reports" that reviewed and commented on standards would be useful too, but no journal has yet stepped up to this task.

20. **Long-range prognosis**—The software engineering standards have been improving from decade to decade. Given the current rate of progress, it can be hypothesized that adequate standards may occur early in the first decade of the 21st century, and perhaps as early as 1999. The short-term prognosis is not as optimistic: the U.S. Department of Defense and the International Standards Organization are both actively at work on some very regrettable standards.

CHAPTER 32

Inadequate Software Project Risk Analysis

1. **Definition**—A) Failure to consider or properly evaluate the risk potentials of significant software projects prior to commencement; B) Failure to consider or properly evaluate the risk potentials of significant software projects based on changes after development begins; C) Failure to consider risks associated with tools, methods, and approaches prior to acquisition and deployment.

2. **Severity**—The average severity of inadequate risk analysis is about a three on the following five-point scale:

   Severity 1: No risk analysis is performed at all on significant projects

   Severity 2: Perfunctory or trivial risk analysis is performed on significant projects

   Severity 3: Preliminary risk analysis is performed, but none in response to changed conditions after the initial risk assessment

   Severity 4: Risk analyses are performed that cover too small a percentage of major software risks to be effective

   Severity 5: Risk analyses are performed, but hazardous conclusions are rejected or denied due to political pressures

3. **Frequency**—In the past, before 1990, failure to perform adequate risk assessments of software projects had been observed for 80% of all major (> 1000 Function Point) projects observed. Since that time, risk analysis has started to become more common under the combined impact of new books, journal articles, and new emphasis on risk management by groups such as the Software Engineering Institute (SEI). Inadequate risk analysis appears to be decreasing, and a 1993 estimate is that inadequate risk analysis is now down to perhaps 65%, and dropping by about 10% to 15% per year. However, these findings have a high margin of error.

4. **Occurrence**—Risk (and value) assessment rigor varies widely from enterprise to enterprise. As a class, military software projects tend to be somewhat more rigorous in risk assessments than civilian software projects. On the other hand, civilian projects are much better at value assessment.

Internal MIS applications are seldom thorough in risk analysis, and indeed often ignore risks until far too late to take effective corrective actions. Although internal MIS projects often go through the motions of value analysis, it cannot be said that they do this particularly well. Indeed, the value of many MIS applications hovers around zero or a negative value.

5. **Susceptibility and resistance**—Since the problems of inadequate risk analysis grow with the size of the application being constructed, the most serious manifestation of the problems are found in very large enterprises such as the Fortune 500 class, or within large government and military organizations which build large software systems.

   The most resistant organizations (although resistance is not perfect) are those which require both formal risk and value analysis steps as a precondition for funding software projects. Companies which have such requirements include AT&T, IBM, ITT, and Motorola for example.

   The most susceptible organizations are those which tend to ignore risk analysis entirely, and where value analysis is based on artificial or spurious criteria.

6. **Root causes**—The root causes of inadequate risk analysis are not the same as the root causes of inadequate value analysis, so it is appropriate to consider each one separately.

   The root causes of inadequate risk analysis include the following: 1) Risk analysis is not taught under most software engineering or software management curricula; 2) Risk analysis is not taught under many on-the-job or enterprise training curricula; 3) The corporate culture of the enterprise tends to ignore risk-related conditions, or even to penalize managers or staff members who point out risks.

   Another root cause is that serious emphasis on risk analysis is a fairly recent phenomenon. The bulk of the literature on software has been produced since about 1989, and the first annual SEI risk conference was held in 1990.

7. **Associated problems**—Inadequate risk analysis is associated with *canceled projects, cost overruns, excessive time to market, missed schedules, friction with senior executives,* and *low levels of user satisfaction.*

   Inadequate risk analysis is often associated with *inadequate management curricula, inadequate software engineering curricula, inadequate standards, inadequate cost estimating,* and sometimes with *management malpractice.*

8. **Cost impact**—The cost impact of inadequate risk analysis should be considered separately for each of the major categories of risk.

   All of the costs of projects which have low or negligible value can reasonably be considered to be wastage. Sometimes, however, value changes after a project is already funded and underway. This is a special situation, which needs to be considered. An example of a project where the value changed after commencement was a benefit-tracking system being created for a company. When the project was being planned, the company was profitable and the employee benefits were rather good. After two years of serious financial losses, many of the benefits were being cut back or eliminated so the value of the benefit tracking system was reduced to nearly zero.

The cost impact of inadequate risk analysis varies with the nature of the risk, but includes a significant percentage of the costs of canceled projects, and projects with major cost and schedule overruns.

9. **Methods of prevention**—Risk analysis is becoming a recognized subdiscipline of software engineering management. The most effective preventive step for this problem is to bring all managers up to speed in the topics of software risk management, software cost estimating, software measurements, software assessments, and other relevant disciplines.

Most of the formal process assessments that operate on specific projects (as opposed to dealing only with managers) are capable of carrying out rather sophisticated risk analysis. However, value analysis is often outside the scope of process assessment.

Another preventive step, often reasonably successful, is to introduce a formal risk and value analysis step into local or company standards and policies for software projects.

Strong caution is warranted. Some software projects should be done for business and competitive reasons even if they don't make money or improve your operations. Consider the following syllogism: A) If a competitor builds such a project, and you do not, what harm will befall your organization in terms of prestige or market share? B) If you build such a project, and your competitors do not, what benefit will accrue to your organization in terms of prestige and market share?

Another useful preventive measure is to use a checklist of common risk categories, as a mnemonic aid to ensure that significant categories of risk are not accidentally omitted from consideration. As an example, the risks included in the table of contents of this book provide a useful initial checklist of common risk topics.

10. **Methods of control**—Unfortunately, it is quite difficult to control the problems of low value or high risk once a project is well underway and is in full development. Indeed, in spite of many pleas of "early warning" systems there are major cultural problems which prevent the early warnings from being taken seriously. A cost, schedule, or quality estimate which predicts serious problems may well be dismissed or challenged even when the results are highly likely to occur.

On the whole, risk prevention is the best approach. However, risk containment is not impossible. There are "top gun" project managers and management consultants who specialize in putting risky projects back on track, and they succeed often enough to stay in business. Risk minimization can sometimes be accomplished if a project is included in an SPR or SEI assessment. Indeed, the objectivity of the assessment process tends to add credibility to risk findings. However, the people and the same factors which created the risks in the first place are still present.

11. **Product support**—Software cost estimating tools and software project planning tools can both be useful in minimizing risks and maximizing value of software

projects. Some of these tools have explicit risk and value analysis functions. As of 1993, there are about 50 commercial software cost estimating tools and about 70 project management tools being marketed in the U.S.

12. **Consulting support**—Risk and value analysis consulting are normal aspects of many management consulting groups, such as Andersen, A.D. Little, Deloitte Touche, DMR, Ernst & Young, Keane Associates, and many others. The Software Engineering Institute (SEI) also deals with risk management, and indeed sponsors major annual conferences on software risk management. Many individual consultants also cover these topics. Finally, many tool vendors have captive consulting groups which can deal with risk and value analysis in the context of specific tools.

13. **Education support**—Prior to about 1990, risk and value analysis tended to be covered in perfunctorily, if at all, by normal software engineering and management school curricula at the university levels. However, this situation is slowly changing and since about 1990 more and more courses on risk management have appeared.

14. **Publication support**—The literature on software risk analysis is much more extensive than the literature on value analysis. Dr. Robert Charette's *Software Engineering Risk and Management* (McGraw-Hill, 1989) and the same author's *Application Strategies for Risk Analysis* (McGraw-Hill, 1990) are good examples of the risk management genre. Dr. Barry Boehm's *Software Risk Management* (IEEE Press, 1989) is also a good introduction to the risk side of the picture. The Software Engineering Institute (SEI) conference proceedings on risk management are good surveys of the state of the art, and have the advantage of being updated annually.

Tom DeMarco's classic *Controlling Software Projects* (Yourdon Press, 1982) and Fred Brooks' equally classic *The Mythical Man-Month* (Addison Wesley, 1982) were pioneers in covering software risk topics. Robert Block's less widely cited *The Politics of Projects* (Prentice Hall, 1983) covers a rarely discussed aspect of risk. John Boddie's *Crunch Mode: Building Effective Systems on a Tight Schedule* (Yourdon Press, 1987) also covers a major risk topic. A compendium of many different authors' articles can be found in Alan Brill's *Techniques of EDP Project Management: A Book of Readings* (Prentice Hall, 1984).

Controlling or calculating the probability of various kinds of risks is a standard sub-domain of operations research and mathematical modelling. A useful overview of general risk calculation approaches can be found in Robert Behn and James Vaupel's *Quick Analysis for Busy Decision Makers* (Basic Books, 1982).

15. **Periodical support**—The journal Risk Management is the most explicit in dealing with risk-related topics. The IEEE Transactions on Engineering Management will discuss risks from time to time. Both risk and value analysis have intermittent topical coverage in the software engineering journals. American Programmer, for example, ran a special risk management issue. For military and defense applications, the STSC Crosstalk journal and the STARS journal have articles on risk management. CASE Trends and CASE Outlook sometimes have articles on software risk

analysis. The major business journals (Forbes, Fortune, the Economist, Business Week, Wall Street Journal, Harvard Business Review, etc.) are starting to deal with software more often, and with the risks of software projects too.

16. **Standards support**—There are no known national or international standards which deal with software risk analysis as a general topic in 1993. There are many aspects of standards which deal with specific kinds of risk, however. Both DoD 2167A and the ISO 9000–9004 standards, for example, deal with topics which can affect risk in lesser or greater degree. Several IEEE standards also discuss risk-related topics.

17. **Professional associations**—Both risk and value analysis are discussed informally within many associations, but so far as can be determined there are no associations that are fully dedicated to these topics. The Software Engineering Institute (SEI) has been holding interesting annual conferences on risk management, and has become a well-known research organization on this emerging topic. The International Society of Parametric Analysis (ISPA) covers risk prediction fairly often.

18. **Effectiveness of known therapies**—The therapies for risk analysis are much more advanced than those for value analysis. Risk analysis using modern estimating and planning tools is now extremely effective. Cultural resistance and sociological problems remain, however. The value analysis therapies lag far behind, and except for the subdomains of value in the forms of revenue prediction and operating cost reductions, the effectiveness of therapies is marginal.

19. **Costs of known therapies**—Software project planning tools start at about $100 and run to more than $10,000. Software project estimating tools start at about $300 and run up to more than $25,000. Both of these tool classes are relevant for risk analysis, and somewhat relevant to value analysis.

A software process assessment, which includes risk analysis as a normal function, can run from less than $25,000 to more than $250,000 for a large, multisite, multi-national assessment. Such assessments tend to find corporate or enterprise-wide risks (i.e. inadequate compensation plans, sluggish technology transfer) as well as risks associated with specific projects.

20. **Long-range prognosis**—The prognosis for improvements in software risk analysis is very good. Risk analysis is already a recognized sub-domain of software engineering management, and the books and literature on this topic are growing steadily. By the end of the twentieth century, the most optimistic scenario is that risk analysis will be a standard part of software engineering and management curricula, and fully supported by advanced tools and methods.

CHAPTER 33

Inadequate Value Analysis

1. **Definition**—A) Failure to consider or properly enumerate the value potentials of significant software projects prior to commencement; B) Failure to consider or properly enumerate the value potentials of significant software projects during development; C) Failure to measure or enumerate the value of significant software projects after deployment; E) Failure by the software engineering management community to have developed a standard value analysis method and supporting tools.

2. **Severity**—The average severity of inadequate value analysis is about a two on the following five-point scale:

   Severity 1:   No value analysis is performed at all prior to development, during development, or after deployment

   Severity 2:   Initial value analysis is based on incorrect or unsupported assumptions; no subsequent value analysis is performed to validate initial results

   Severity 3:   Perfunctory value analysis based on current industry fads

   Severity 4:   Perfunctory value analysis based on minimal, uncontrolled empirical data

   Severity 5:   Value analysis based on studies or projects too different to be applicable

3. **Frequency**—Failure to perform adequate value assessment of software projects has been recorded for 60% of all projects observed during SPR assessments. However, this constitutes a significant problem only for larger projects in excess of about 1,000 Function Points in size. Failure to perform adequate value assessment for large software projects occurs in about 35% of such cases.

4. **Occurrence**—Both risk and value assessment rigor varies widely from enterprise to enterprise. As a class, military software projects tend to be somewhat more rigorous in risk assessment than civilian software projects. On the other hand, civilian projects are often much better in value analysis than military software projects.

   Commercially-marketed software (i.e. software such as spreadsheets, CAD packages, operating systems that are leased to other companies) usually have the best and most accurate value analysis, since they generate tangible revenues that can be quantified easily. However, these same projects do not excel in risk analysis, particularly in the risk of schedule slippages and cost overruns.

Internal MIS applications often go through the motions of value analysis, but the results are frequently spurious or built on false assumptions. Indeed, many enterprises have a set of artificial and arbitrary criteria for funding software projects. Examples of these arbitrary criteria may include requirements that funded applications must lower operating costs, or must return value in 24 months. Some of these criteria are reasonable, but some are irrational. As an example, the CFO of a company that was in serious financial distress decided not to fund any software projects that did not reduce operating costs. Thus a proposed software project which would have augmented the company's revenues did not initially receive funding until the CFO amended the directive.

Value analysis of software projects is sometimes biased by the usage of new and unproven software tools and methods. Sometimes the value analysis is even based on vendor productivity claims, which in general are exaggerated and untrustworthy. These assumptions can throw off value assumptions by notable amounts.

An emerging and potentially important domain of value analysis is that of calculating the value of software for tax purposes, or to quantify the value of software as assets when companies are bought and sold. The U.S. Internal Revenue Service, many accounting companies, many management consulting groups, and many large corporations are exploring and debating software evaluations. Although this topic is still unsettled, the usage of Function Points appears to be very well suited to dealing with the value of software for both taxation and asset evaluation purposes.

5. **Susceptibility and resistance**—Since the problems of inadequate value analysis grow with the size of the application being constructed, the most serious manifestation of the problems are found in very large enterprises or within large government and military organizations.

The most resistant organizations (although resistance is not perfect) are those which require both formal risk and value analysis steps as a precondition for funding software projects. Companies which have such requirements include AT&T, IBM, and ITT for example.

Overall the most resistant organizations are those which have full software measurement programs and hence accurate historical data on which to base initial value judgments. The most susceptible organizations are those which have no measurement programs at all, and hence must depend upon unsupported assumptions for ascertaining value.

6. **Root causes**—The root causes of inadequate value analysis for projects are not the same as the root causes for inadequate value analysis of tools and technologies, so it is appropriate to consider each one separately.

The root cause of inadequate value analysis for software projects is that a number of aspects of software value are outside the scope of standard financial planning, and have not yet been adequately absorbed into management science. Only three forms of value analysis are normally dealt with in standard financial planning: 1) Direct revenues for leased or marketed software packages; 2) Indirect revenues for software which tends to augment sales of related hardware devices or other software packages; 3) Operating cost reductions for software projects which might displace human or mechanical effort.

Software projects which are difficult to analyze in terms of value include: 1) Projects which bolster enterprise prestige; 2) Projects which affect human life or safety; 3) Projects which affect employee morale; 4) Projects which affect national defense; 5) Projects which affect competitive positioning; 6) Projects which are required by state, local, or federal law or regulation; 7) Projects which might open up new but unproven business opportunities.

The root cause of inadequate value analysis prior to investment in software tools, methods, and technologies can be traced to a lack of both accurate metrics and adequate measurement of productivity and quality. Now that these twin problems are coming under control, much more sophisticated value analysis should be available in the future.

However, some corollary root causes of inadequate value analysis include the following: 1) Value analysis is not taught in most software engineering or software management curricula; 2) Value analysis is not taught in many on-the-job or enterprise training curricula; 3) There is a shortage of tools and standard approaches for dealing with value analysis.

7. **Associated problems**—Inadequate value analysis is associated with *canceled projects, false productivity claims, friction with senior executives, low levels of user satisfaction,* and the *silver bullet syndrome.*

Inadequate value analysis is often associated with *inadequate management curricula, inadequate measurement, inaccurate metrics, inadequate software engineering curricula, inadequate standards, inadequate cost estimating,* and sometimes with *management malpractice.*

8. **Cost impact**—The cost impact of inadequate value analysis for projects, tools and methods should be considered separately.

All of the costs of projects which have low or negligible value can reasonably be considered to be wastage. Sometimes, however, value changes after a project is already funded and underway. This is a special situation, which needs to be considered. An example of a project where the value changed after commencement was a benefit-tracking system being created for a company. When the project was being planned, the company was profitable and the employee benefits were rather good. After two years of serious financial losses, many of the benefits were being cut back or eliminated, so the value of the benefit-tracking system was reduced to nearly zero.

The cost impact of low-value tools and methods shows up in many significant ways. Companies which invest heavily in tools with low value tend to lag their competitors in important business factors such as time to market. Also, the software managers and executives who are responsible for the poor investments may find their advancement or even their careers in jeopardy.

An emerging topic of both academic and commercial research is that now called "the productivity paradox." Most large companies have been investing in computers and software for many years, with the expectation that their overall performance would improve. The productivity paradox is based on the observation that the returned value of the entire computing and software complex may be only about $0.80 for every $1.00 invested.

As of 1993, fierce debate is raging around the topic of the productivity paradox, with some researchers saying the observations are based on invalid data and false assumptions, and others saying the observations may be true.

Another recent topic which is now sweeping through the industry is "business process realignment." The fundamental concept is that business operations and the software which supports those operations have drifted apart, and existing software may now be a barrier to modernization of procedures and operations.

Here too, fierce debate is raging, and a new set of courses and management consulting practices are building up.

9. **Methods of prevention**—Value analysis is becoming a recognized sub-discipline of software engineering management. The most effective preventive step for this problem is to bring all managers up to speed in the topics of software value analysis, software cost estimating, software measurements, software assessments, and other relevant disciplines.

Another preventive step, often reasonably successful, is to introduce a formal value analysis step into local or company standards and policies for software projects, and for acquisitions of tools, methods, and technologies.

However, poor value analysis is a more difficult topic to prevent, due to the fact that the non-financial aspects of software value (i.e. enterprise prestige, employee morale, etc.) are outside the domain of management science as of 1993.

Simplistic financial cost and value analysis are no longer sufficient. Today's systems offer strategic advantages, and the value of strategic factors is notoriously difficult to quantify.

A strong advisory is indicated: some software projects should be done for business and competitive reasons even if they don't make money or improve operations. Consider the following syllogism: A) If a competitor builds such a project, and you do not, what harm will befall your organization in terms of prestige or market share? B) If you build such a project, and your competitors do not, what benefit will accrue to your organization in terms of prestige and market share?

Also, some tools and methods may be used for cultural reasons even if the proof of value is sparse. Without some exploratory usage of tools or methods before value is established, there would be no way of determining value. Brand new methods and brand new tools being used for the very first time obviously have no historical data available. However, if such tools appear potentially useful, then experimental deployment is often valuable in its own right.

10. **Methods of control**—For specific projects, it is quite difficult to control the problems of low value and high risk once a project is well underway. Prevention is the best approach. Value augmentation is extremely difficult once software development begins. Risk minimization can sometimes be accomplished, but not very often. Usually the same factors which triggered the risks in the first place are still present. The same value factors are present too.

11. **Product support**—Software cost estimating tools and software project planning tools can both be useful in minimizing risks and maximizing value of software projects. They can also be used to model the potential value of tools, methods, and technologies. Some of these tools have explicit risk and value analysis functions. As of 1993, there are about 50 commercial software cost estimating tools and about 70 project management tools being marketed in the U.S.

    Although used more often by accounting and financial managers than software managers, there are a host of tools which can calculate various kinds of value such as accounting rates of return, internal rates of return, and others.

12. **Consulting support**—Value analysis consulting is not a standard aspect of many management consulting groups. Therefore it is necessary to seek out specialists in this emerging topic. Software estimating tool and project planning tool vendors may have consulting groups that can demonstrate potential value of various concepts by simulating their effect using estimating or planning tools. As management consultants, both DMR Group and Andersen Consulting have been experimenting with different kinds of value analysis approaches. Other management consultants such as Deany Myer Associates, Ernst & Young, Peat Marwick, Rubin Associates, QSM and SPR also explore these topics from time to time.

    Note that the topics of "the productivity paradox" and "business process realignment" are sweeping through the industry as of 1993, and many new consulting practices are being formed around these topics. It is premature to judge the results of either.

    Also sweeping through the industry is the need to evaluate software for taxation and asset management purposes when companies are bought and sold. Here too, new consulting specialties and tools are starting to appear.

    A specialized form of consulting which touches upon the value of companies is that associated with venture capital and mergers and acquisitions. Many consultants can help start-up companies with business plans and other aspects that are peripherally related to corporate value. When companies are put up for sale, similar specialists are also available.

13. **Education support**—Software value analysis in a general sense is becoming a fairly hot topic within both software engineering and management school curricula at the university levels. However, value analysis of particular software tools, methods, and technologies does not seem to be part of any business school or software engineering curriculum as of 1993. This situation may change in the future.

14. Publication support—The literature on software value analysis of specific projects is anecdotal and unsatisfactory. From time to time, books will feature "scare" discussions on some notable failure or canceled project. Few positive results are featured. So far as can be determined, the value side of specific software projects is not represented by any significant books at this time.

However, Paul Strassman's *The Business Value of Computers* (Information Economics Press, 1990) is widely cited for information on the value of the computers and software within an enterprise. Also Weil's *Do Computers Pay Off* (ICIT Press, 1990) covers this topic. A book edited by Thierry Noyelle of the United Nations also discusses relevant value data: *Skills, Wages, and Productivity in the Service Sector* (Westview Press, 1990).

Dean Meyer and Mary Boone tackle the problem of the value of the entire software and computing complex by means of interviews and case studies of many different managers and companies. The resulting book, *The Information Edge* (Gage Publishing Company, 1987), contains many intriguing insights drawn from practical day to day observations.

Milt Bryce and Tim Bryce, developers of the PRIDE methodology, have approached the value analysis of information in their book *The IRM Revolution: Blueprint for the 21st Century* (Milt Bryce Associates, 1988). The book is more philosophical than quantitative, but the value of information is an important sub-element of value analysis.

William Perry's *Data Processing Budgets* (Prentice Hall, 1985) is more down to earth, and deals with calculating various kinds of value as a step toward creating pragmatic budgets for software organizations. Frank Williams' *Software Costing* (Prentice Hall, 1992) is relevant.

Although not specifically on the topics of software value, Michael Porter's *Competitive Strategy: Techniques for Analyzing Industries and Competitors* (The Free Press, 1980) covers value in a global context. Peter Drucker's *Managing for the Future* (Truman Talley Books, 1992) is also of interest. Tom Peters' *Thriving on Chaos* (Harper Row, 1987) also takes an eclectic look at value. Richard Foster's *Innovation: The Attackers Advantage* (McKinsey & Company, 1986) discusses the value of innovative products and services. Kenichi Ohmae's *The Mind of the Strategist—The Art of Japanese Business* (McGraw-Hill, 1982) considers value analysis and strategic planning from a Japanese business perspective. John Guaspari's *The Customer Connection* (Amacom, 1988) considers value (and quality) from a customer's point of view.

There are a host of books which deal with various aspects of financial value, such as net present value, accounting rate of return, profitability, and return on investment. Robert Vichas' *Handbook of Financial Mathematics, Formulas, and Tables* (Prentice Hall, 1979) is an enormous tome of 870 pages which contains more than 50 types of value calculation methods. The book does not discuss software at all, but it covers a very large number of standard value methods.

Value analysis overlaps game theory, if winning is considered to be valuable. Morton Davis' *Game Theory—A Nontechnical Introduction* (Basic Books, 1970) is a simple introduction to the mathematics of winning and losing.

See also the section of this handbook dealing with return on investment in various software tools and technologies.

15. **Periodical support**—Value analysis has intermittent topical coverage in the software engineering journals. Unfortunately, what passes for value analysis is often some kind of an article announcing the discovery of a new "silver bullet" that can solve major problems of quality, productivity, or schedule control. On the whole, there is no effective literature dealing with value analysis of specific tools, methods, and technologies. From time to time, journals such as The Economist, Forbes, Fortune, or the Harvard Business Review will feature in-depth articles on the value (usually expressed in terms of revenue) of major software products such as Lotus or Windows. Internal projects are featured less often.

   Fred Brooks' widely quoted article entitled "No Silver Bullet" was published in IEEE Computer, Volume 20, Number 4, 1987 and remains of current interest.

   The author, Capers Jones, published preliminary research on the use of Function Points for value analysis in CASE Trends, January 1993: "Software Value Analysis—A New Approach." The thesis is that the quantity of Function Points in management tools and CASE can determine, at least in part, the power or value of the tool suite.

   One interesting offshoot of value analysis that is becoming notable are articles dealing with what is called "the productivity paradox." Huge amounts of money have been invested in computers and software with the expectation that service and productivity would improve. Current data, however, suggests that the return on investment on the entire computing establishment within major corporations may be only $0.80 for every $1.00 invested. In particular, clerical and office productivity has not jumped ahead as might be expected, and the reasons why are now being explored.

   Some of the studies on this topic are those of Erik Brynjolfsson of MIT's Sloan School (in Communications of the ACM); Richard T. Due; the Canadian economist who publishes with Auerbach (Due's "The Productivity Paradox" in the winter 1993 issue of Information Systems Management discusses this topic quite succinctly); Michael Hammer, who published in the Harvard Business Review; and many other authors.

16. **Standards support**—There are no known national or international standards which deal with software value. (There are many aspects of standards which deal with various kinds of risk, however. Both DoD 2167A and the ISO 9000–9004 standards, for example, deal with topics which can affect risk in lesser or greater degree. Several IEEE standards also discuss risk-related topics.)

17. **Professional associations**—Both risk and value analysis are discussed informally within many associations, but no groups appear to be fully dedicated to these top-

ics, especially not to value. An interesting exception is that the United Nations has had an active research program in the value of various kinds of technologies for the emerging countries. Since software requires little in the way of machinery, does not pollute, and has a high value per shipped ton, the software business is an attractive goal for countries such as India, Poland, Hungary, or Mexico which couple low labor costs with good technical schools.

18. **Effectiveness of known therapies**—The therapies for risk analysis are much more advanced than those for value analysis. Risk analysis using modern estimating and planning tools is now extremely effective. Cultural resistance and sociological problems remain, however. The value analysis therapies lag far behind, and except for the subdomains of value in the forms of revenue prediction and operating cost reductions, the effectiveness of therapies is marginal.

19. **Costs of known therapies**—Software project planning tools start at about $100 and run to more than $10,000. Software project estimating tools start at about $300 and run up to more than $25,000. Both of these tool classes are relevant for risk analysis, and somewhat relevant to value analysis.

    For value analysis of commercial software, most major corporations—enterprises such as Borland, IBM, and Microsoft—have fairly sophisticated models for predicting revenues of software products. In general, these are proprietary models which are not commercially available. Some are even regarded as trade secrets.

    Note that software process assessments, which are one of the key technologies of software risk management, are not as useful when it comes to value analysis. Neither the SEI nor the SPR assessments actually quantify the value of projects, although both query as to whether a value analysis was performed.

20. **Long-range prognosis**—The long-range prognosis for improvements in software value analysis is moderately good, although inconsistent. The value of the entire computing and software complex is now receiving lots of attention, so the prognosis here is favorable. The value of specific software projects is also getting attention, although major problems exist for quantifying the strategic and competitive value of software projects. The value of individual tools, methods, and approaches can now be studied, but lags in terms of published research. Even here, some progress should occur between now and the end of the century. Hopefully, progress in this topic will reduce the incidence of false claims and misleading advertisements which are so much a part of the software industry.

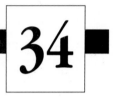

Inadequate Tools and Methods (Project Management)

1. **Definition**—Inadequate automation and methodological approaches applied to the six generic activities of software project managers: 1) Sizing source code and other deliverables; 2) Estimating schedules, resources, costs, defect levels and removal efficiency; 3) Planning the critical paths and key milestones of software projects; 4) Tracking actual milestones, costs, and resources; 5) Measuring both "hard" factors (deliverable sizes, resources expended, schedules) and "soft" factors (experience, methods, tools, etc.) of software projects; 6) Performing post-mortem assessments to evaluate the processes, tools, languages, requirements creep, organization structures, and other influential factors which influenced the outcomes of projects.

   Note: Software project managers perform many more activities than the six cited here, which constitute the primary activities of project management, however. There are many activities associated with managing departments (budgeting, capital equipment, space planning, travel authorization, etc.). There are also many activities associated with personnel management (hiring, appraising, promoting, transferring, etc.).

2. **Severity**—The average severity level of inadequate project management tools and methods is high: about a 2.5 on the following five-point scale:

   Severity 1: No automated management tools of any kind

   Severity 2: Automated resource tracking or project accounting tools only

   Severity 3: Project planning and resource tracking tools are both available

   Severity 4: Planning, estimating, and resource tracking tools are available

   Severity 5: Automation is lacking only for measurement and assessment

3. **Frequency**—The frequency of inadequate project management automation is surprisingly varied across the normal activities which project managers perform.

Based on SPR assessments, the overall performance of U.S. software project managers (and also European, Canadian, Australian, and Japanese managers) is not very good.

Management Activity	Average Performance by Project Managers	Percent of Projects Lacking Automation
Sizing software deliverables	Poor	85%
Estimating project resources	Poor	75%
Planning project schedules	Fair	35%
Tracking expenses and costs	Poor	65%
Measuring software projects	Very Poor	95%
Post-mortem assessments	Poor to Good	90%

4. **Occurrence**—Both sociological and technical factors explain the occurrence of inadequate use of project management tools. As of 1993 there are about 70 commercial project planning tools marketed in the United States, and about 50 commercial software estimating tools.

Commercial project planning tools have been marketed in the United States since the early 1960's, and indeed were one of the first business applications ever computerized. For large projects with thousands of activities and tasks, only automated planning tools can handle the critical path calculations with reasonable efficiency. Manual methods are so hazardous and unsatisfactory for large projects that failure to use some form of planning automation for software projects larger than 5000 Function Points should be considered an example of professional malpractice.

Commercial project estimating tools have been marketed in the United States since 1973. The intrinsic accuracy of many of these tools is no higher than unaided manual estimates. However, automated estimating tools do not "forget" major activities and deliverables. Also, when project requirements or assumptions change, automation allows fresh estimates to be prepared in moments. Companies and government agencies with the best overall results of cost and schedule control tend to utilize multiple estimating tools concurrently.

The intrinsic accuracy of software cost estimating tools has been difficult to evaluate due to a serious flaw in the methodological procedures used. Accuracy has normally been calculated by comparing estimated results against historical data from completed projects. Any deviation is then assumed to be due to errors on the part of the estimating tool. Such errors are normally in one direction only: estimated results for costs, schedules, and resources are greater than what historical data indicated.

However, most studies of estimating accuracy did not validate or check the accuracy of the historical data itself. When the contents of the historical data itself is explored, it is often found that factors such as unpaid overtime, managerial effort, specialist effort, and many other kinds of work were not captured by the tracking system used to record the historical data. Sometimes errors in the historical data are significantly larger than errors from the estimating tools.

Project sizing, or predicting the quantity of source code, number of pages of specifications, number of test cases, etc., is a fairly new technology. The first U.S. commercial estimating tool to feature sizing logic for predicting source code, pages, and test cases (SPQR/20) has only been available since 1985. Modern tools now include complete sizing logic: close to 400 languages, mixed languages, test cases, and more than 50 document types. Older software estimating tools, such as COCOMO or its clones required manual size input by users. Sizing is starting to become a standard feature of software estimating tools, but more than 50% of such tools still lack this feature. Most modern sizing logic is derived by calculating the quantity of various deliverables produced for a given quantity of Function Points.

Project tracking and cost accounting tools have been in use since the early 1960's. Very few are optimal for software projects, however. Use of inadequate project tracking tools is often outside the scope of a project manager's authority. If the corporation or government agency mandates the use of a project accounting or tracking tool that is not set up to handle software projects well (and most are not) then few software managers can change the situation.

The most common problem with inadequate tracking is resource leakage or failure to record all effort that was actually applied. Resource leakage averages from 35% to 50% in the U.S. for civilian projects. A few outliers have actually omitted as much as 75% of the actual effort, since tracking was only utilized for coding and unit testing. Some of the commoner omissions from tracking systems include unpaid overtime, managerial expenses, user effort when performing technical tasks, and the work of specialists who support multiple projects (i.e. quality assurance, technical writers, etc.).

Software project measurement tools which can capture methods, languages, and other "soft" factors as well as hard data are new on the U.S. market: the first such tools have only been available since 1989. It normally takes from 10 to 20 years before a new technology becomes commonplace, and so knowledge of this technology is not yet pervasive, although it is expanding rapidly.

Manual assessments or project audits have existed since the 1950's for software and long before that for non-software projects. However, automation of assessment factors is comparatively recent. Major software projects should normally conclude with a formal post-mortem assessment to explore all of the factors that went right, and all of the factors which went wrong. This information can then be used to head off future difficulties in similar projects.

Several standard assessment approaches such as those used by SEI, SPR, Pressman, and Hewlett-Packard can be used for such purposes. As of 1993, the SPR approach is supported by automated data collection tools, and plans exist to add SEI automation capability. Indeed, it is now possible to create templates that show representative projects at SEI maturity levels 1 through 5. While manual recording of post mortem and assessment data is useful, automation is highly desirable. When assessment and post mortem information is automated, results from many projects or a whole portfolio of hundreds of projects can be analyzed to look for patterns of strength and weakness.

5. **Susceptibility and resistance**—The patterns of susceptibility and resistance are diverse, and some appear to be even contradictory.

Small companies with less than 100 software engineers and 10 software managers are the most susceptible, and often lack any kind of software management automation, due in part to being undercapitalized, and in part to the fairly high costs for software estimating tools. However, the need for such automation is also lowest for small organizations. Several lower-cost software estimating tools should reach the commercial market during 1993 and 1994.

Military software organizations are *least* susceptible to inadequate tracking and to inadequate project planning, but are highly susceptible to inadequate sizing, estimating, and assessment automation. (This is due to the DoD failure to move away from obsolete "lines of code" metrics and into the modern world of functional metrics; plus the DoD espousal of the limited and manual SEI assessment approach.)

Systems software managers tend to be advanced in usage of project planning tools and project tracking, but lag somewhat in software sizing, estimating, measurement, and assessment automation.

MIS software producers tend to be advanced in terms of sizing, estimating, and planning, but lag in assessment, measurement, and tracking.

Commercial software producers tend to be advanced in project planning, but backward in sizing, estimating, tracking, measurement, and assessment automation.

6. **Root causes**—The root causes of inadequate automation of standard software project management activities include business, technical, and cultural components.

The *business component* has to do with the history of the software management tool market. Although the six functions discussed here (sizing, planning, estimating, tracking, measurement, and assessment) are logically coupled and synergistic, the companies which produce such tools have all been different and have been aiming at different markets. For example, until several recent acquisitions occurred, different companies produced software estimating tools and software planning tools.

Unfortunately, the project planning tool market, which predates estimating tools by about a decade, utilized the word "project management" for basic tools whose only functions were producing PERT charts, Gantt charts, and critical path analysis. Companies which produced such tools often knew little or nothing about the specific requirements of software project management. Such tools also lack capabilities for dealing with quality, with influential factors, and with a host of other management-related topics and considerations. The usage of the phrase "project management" for such incomplete tools is poorly chosen.

Only recently has it become obvious that all software project management functions needed to be carried out using a common tool strategy, or at least sharing data and information. This is leading to a wave of mergers and acquisitions in the software management tool arena, with software estimating, sizing, measurement, and planning tool groups forming strategic alliances or acquiring one another. Examples of mergers include the acquisition of the MACS corporation and the ESTIMACS tool by Computer Associates, and the coupling of the BRIDGE estimating tool with the Project Managers Workbench (PMW).

The *technical component* of inadequate management automation can be traced to the technology history of the software industry. For example, the most common sizing approach in current usage (predicting source code and other deliverable sizes from Function Points) was only developed in 1985.

Informal post-mortems and informal assessments or audits have been used for many years, but the two most widely utilized methods today (SPR's and SEI's) did not occur until 1985 and 1987, respectively.

Inadequate measurement and metrics are contributing root causes to inadequate management automation in many serious software projects. The widespread lack of accurate historical data about software projects has made any kind of software management tool automation unusually difficult.

Project tracking tools were often custom developed for accounting and financial clients. Seldom are project accounting systems really optimal for software projects, and most are useless for serious project controls. Generic project tracking systems have existed since the early 1960's, and manual cost tracking and project accounting systems for hundreds of years. However, tracking systems aimed specifically at software projects only started to become available in the late 1980's. Since it normally takes from 10 to more than 20 years for new technologies to achieve widespread deployment, the need for full integration of all software management functions was only recognized less than 10 years ago and still is not fully operational in 1993.

The *cultural component* for inadequate management tool automation can be traced to the normal human reaction to change. When confronted with new tools and methods, the natural reaction of many project managers is to ask, "Who else is using these tools?" Less than 15% of the normal management population is willing to jump into a new technology without some form of social endorsement. When tools are truly new (such as sizing and measurement tools, which are less than 10 years old) it can be five or six years before a critical mass of pioneering users have accumulated enough success stories for widespread deployment to occur.

Another aspect of resistance to management tool automation is fear of displacement by the managers themselves. Software projects are quite complex, and software managers tend to enjoy the perception of being keepers of arcane knowledge, such as the ability to estimate schedules and resources. When software estimating tools are used, there is a fear that some of the perceived mystery of software project management will be taken away. Indeed, this is exactly what occurs, but the results tend to benefit the enterprise as a whole. A more appropriate response by project managers would be to become the experts in how such tools operate, rather than merely avoiding them.

7. **Associated problems**—Inadequate use of automation for project management functions is strongly associated with *canceled projects, cost overruns, missed schedules, excessive time to market, long schedules, excessive schedule pressure, friction with clients,* and *friction with senior management.* There are also less direct correlations with *low quality* and *low staff morale.*

Inadequate use of automation for project management can be caused by *inadequate capital investment, inadequate management curricula, slow technology transfer, inaccurate metrics, inadequate measurement,* and sometimes by *management malpractice.*

8. **Cost impact**—The costs of inadequate project management are related to some specific deficits:

Inadequate sizing automation typically results in under-estimating the amount of source code and the volumes of other deliverables which must be produced. (Over-estimating seldom occurs for social and political reasons.) The error range observed when manual sizing occurs averages about 35% to 50% for source code size, and 40% to 60% for plans, specifications, and user documents. The costs of inadequate sizing will vary with the magnitude of the sizing errors. Manual estimates by experienced managers have been observed to do a creditable job in sizing the quantity of source code that must be produced. However, manual size estimates have not been effective in guessing at creeping requirements. Therefore projects have tended to grow far beyond the initial expectation.

Modern sizing logic based on functional metrics is now able to deal with difficult factors such as creeping user requirements. Automated sizing is now possible for more than 50 kinds of specifications and paper documents, source code in almost 400 languages, test cases, and even sizing of the number of on-line screens. Software sizing is now a standard function of several commercial software estimating tools, and the costs range from less than $1000 for rudimentary source code sizing to more than $20,000 for full sizing of all deliverables.

Inadequate estimating automation typically results in under-estimating the staffing, resources, costs, and schedules required to build software projects. However, over-estimates may occur too, for business or political reasons. Normally people who have to build the software tend to want some padding. People who have to pay for the software want all padding removed, and may insist on both costs and schedules so far below U.S. norms that the projects are technically impossible.

Starting in 1995, it is proposed that manual estimation of projects larger than 5000 Function Points in size should be considered to be professional malpractice. The average observed error of manual estimates for software projects is to under-estimate schedules by about 35% and costs by about 50%. Manual estimating has been associated with more than half of all canceled software projects. Since the cancellation rate of large systems approaches 35%, it can be hypothesized that manual estimation is a factor in more than 17% of all canceled projects. This is one of the reasons why manual estimation should be considered malpractice.

Usage of estimating tools which do not support functional metrics should be avoided, since such tools are intrinsically error-prone and have too high a margin of error.

The costs of inadequate estimation are related to the cost overruns and canceled projects which the inadequate estimates tend to trigger. With some 50 software estimating tools on the U.S. market, there is no shortage in the basic technology of automated software estimation. The costs of commercial software estimating tools start at less than $1000 for rudimentary tools such as COCOMO or its clones, and go beyond $20,000 for the high-end tools which integrate sizing, quality estimates, maintenance estimates, and other advanced functions.

Inadequate planning automation typically results in schedule delays or project inefficiencies since the critical path items are out of sequence. Starting in 1995, it is proposed that manual planning of software projects larger than 5000 Function Points in size should be considered to be professional malpractice.

The average observed error of manual plans for software projects is that the schedules run about 35% to 50% longer than anticipated. (With more than 70 project planning tools on the U.S. market, and prices that start below $100 for simple planning tools, only cultural resistance explains why such tools are not universally employed.)

Inadequate tracking automation results in historical data that is essentially useless for either cost control or for estimating future projects. The most common problem with tracking systems is leakage of project resources, such as unpaid overtime by exempt professionals, management costs, user costs when they perform technical work, and so forth. About 35% to 50% of the true effort devoted to software projects is omitted from U.S. tracking systems.

The costs of inadequate tracking automation show up in several different ways: 1) reduced profits or actual loss if the tracking data is used for billing or contract purposes; 2) inability to use historical data for estimating purposes. Starting in 1995, it is proposed that usage of tracking systems which omit significant resources such as unpaid overtime should be considered to be professional malpractice. Unfortunately, software project managers seldom have authority to select tracking systems: normally this authority vests in controllers or financial executives, who are seldom knowledgeable about software needs and requirements. The costs of mainframe tracking systems often exceed $100,000 although client-server tools and personal computer tools can lower the costs to less than $1000.

Inadequate measurement automation normally results in a total lack of knowledge about the factors which influence software projects. Inadequate measurement tends to make managers fall prey to the "silver bullet syndrome" or the naive belief that a single tool or methodology will make dramatic improvements in productivity or quality.

Full measurement automation collects not only the "hard" data dealing with project resources and deliverables, but also the "soft" factors on the methods, languages, tools, and other items which determined the outcome of the project.

Measurement automation is new on the U.S. market, and the first full software measurement tools only became available in 1989. Therefore failure to use such tools is not unexpected. As of 1993, several competitive tools are also available, and therefore measurement tool usage should expand rapidly.

The costs of inadequate measurement automation center around the reduced ability of companies that do not measure to make rapid or tangible improvements in their software processes. Software measurement tools in 1993 are in the $10,000 to $25,000 range.

Inadequate assessment automation normally results in data which cannot easily be analyzed statistically, averaged across multiple projects, or compared against other enterprises and industries. The Software Engineering Institute (SEI) has not produced any automated support for their widely used assessment method. However, it is possible to add an SEI mode to the automated tools used during SPR assessments, and to create templates that reflect SEI maturity levels one through five. Such templates allow comparison of the results of any given project against similar projects developed under the protocols of any of the five SEI maturity levels.

The direct costs of inadequate assessment automation is approximately two staff weeks on every project assessed, which is the time required to manually process the assessment results. By contrast, automated assessment approaches can produce an assessment report for a specific project essentially in real time at the end of the assessment interviews. They can also aggregate any number of projects and produce statistical results on a daily basis as new projects are assessed.

Automated assessment tools are in the $20,000 range. Note: general-purpose statistical tools, data bases, and even spreadsheets could be used to automate the SEI questions. The cost of such automation including labor and the tool used would probably amount to about $15,000 to $25,000.

9. **Methods of prevention**—The most effective approach for preventing inadequate management tool usage is quite new. The new approach is to perform surveys of the kinds of tools needed by software project managers and the frequency with which such tools are utilized. From this kind of analysis, it is then possible to evaluate the consequences of:

A) Not having tool capabilities at all
B) Having low-end tools or partial automation
C) Having high-end tools or full automation
D) Having full integration of all project management tool functions

The Function Points metric is now starting to be applied to studies of tool capabilities, and also to studies of tool usage. The results are still preliminary, but encouraging. It is possible that a whole new form of software value analysis may result.

The following table gives preliminary results of tool usage as of the middle of 1993:

**Tools Used by Software Project Managers
(Size Range in Function Points)**

Tool Categories	Lagging	Average	Leading
Project Planning		1250	2500
Project Measurement			2000
Project Assessment			2000
Project Estimating			2000
Spreadsheet	750	1250	2000
Graphics/Presentations		1250	2000
Word Processing	500	1000	2000
Data Base	500	1000	1500
Project Resource Tracking		750	1500
Project Sizing			1000
Electronic Mail	300	500	750
Appointments/Calendar	100	300	750
Phone/Address File	100	150	500
Totals	2250	7450	20800

From interviews with software project managers during assessments and at seminars, a number of interesting findings can be discussed about the usage patterns of project management tools. About 85% of managers use at least some software daily. Software project managers average about two hours per day actually using software. The three smallest applications—electronic mail, appointment/calendar files, and phone/address files—are used most often and usage here is essentially daily.

About 75% of software project managers have project planning tools (i.e. tools such as Artemis, Timeline, the Project Managers Workbench, etc.) and usage tends to occur several times a week throughout a project's development cycle.

Five separate kinds of sizing tools are starting to be used: A) Estimating tools such as CHECKPOINT® that size all deliverables including source code, documents, screens, and test cases as integral functions; B) Estimating tools such as SLIM with source code sizing logic; C) Separate sizing modules offered as add-ons for older estimating tools such as COCOMO and its clones; D) Sizing capabilities as part of front-end CASE tools. CASE vendors are starting to develop automatic Function Point enumerators that are closely coupled to front-end CASE design tools. Texas Instruments and UNISYS already have such tools, and most other CASE vendors (Bachman, CADRE, KnowledgeWare, Intersolv, etc.) have either announced such capabilities or are known to be exploring the prospects of this kind of integration; E) Direct conversion from source code size to functional metrics is termed "backfiring." This technology is already supported by several project estimators such as SPQR/20 and CHECKPOINT®. Tools for scanning source code in various languages and generating Function Points are already available as share-ware from bulletin boards and from commercial software companies such as Viasoft.

About 25% of software project managers have project estimating tools (i.e. CHECKPOINT®, COCOMO, SPQR/20, SLIM, etc.) Usage for such tools tends to be intermittent. When projects are first being discussed and initial estimates are needed, usage is intense: sometimes as many as 20 to 25 trial estimates will be prepared in a single day. Once an initial estimate is agreed to, several weeks or even a month may go by before the estimating tool is used again. Normally changes in the scope of the project (i.e. creeping user requirements) or the move from one phase to another triggers the need for fresh estimates. Occasionally a fresh estimate will be triggered when the magnitude of actual expenses differs from planned expenses by more than about 10%.

Within several industries (i.e. defense, computer manufacturing, telecommunications manufacturing) it is a common practice to have "estimating specialist" and "cost analyst" as formal job titles, and to have software estimating departments as formal organizations. These two practices appear to have a significant impact in terms of reducing estimating errors.

Although the data on the usage of software management tools is still sparse and preliminary, some interesting observations are already starting to occur. For example, software projects where the project managers have more than 10,000 Function Points of management tools available tend to have better schedule and cost control than similar projects where less than 5,000 Function Points of management tools are available.

10. **Methods of control**—The most difficult aspects of inadequate project management tool support are cultural and sociological. Those are the problems of convincing project managers that such tools are intrinsically superior to manual methods, and that usage of such tools will not detract from their mystique. It is interesting that the U.S. organizations which have the best software quality, productivity, and schedule control typically use multiple tools and methods for the three management tasks where prediction and subjective information are most common—sizing, estimating, and assessment. Using multiple tools and looking for convergence or divergence is an effective approach, and similar to approaches used in medical diagnosis where multiple tests are used to ensure an accurate diagnosis of uncertain conditions. For example, sometimes estimates will be produced using three separate estimating tools such as CHECKPOINT®, COCOMO, and SLIM. Multiple assessment approaches such as SEI and SPR are used concurrently. Sizing will be performed both from functional metrics and by analogy with similar projects. Usage of such tools is evolving too rapidly to know what kind of usage pattern will finally result.

11. **Product support**—As of 1993, there are some 70 project planning tools and about 50 commercial software estimating tools on the U.S. market. There are also integrated planning, estimating, and sizing tools in several CASE tool suites, such as those offered by AGS Management Systems, CGI, Texas Instruments, and UNISYS.

New tools in both classes have appeared at approximately monthly intervals for the last 18 months, so the market is too dynamic for a full listing.

Examples of some of the more common software management tools include: ACCENT VUE, ADW, AGS FullCASE, Andersen FOUNDATION, APECS 8000, Artemis, Asset-R, the Bridge, BYL, CA-Advisor, CA-Estimacs, CA-Planmacs, CA-Superproject, CA-Tellaplan, CHECKPOINT®, COCOMO, CoCoPro, COSTAR, ESTI-MACS, Estimator, Estiplan, GECOMO, Harvard Project Manager, ISTAR, MARS, Microman II, MIL/SOFTQUAL, Microsoft Project, MI-Project, MISTER, MULTI-TRACK, N5500, NES, PADS, PCOC, PLANNER, PMS-II, POWER, Prestige, PRIDE, PROJECT/2, ProjectBASE, ProjectGUIDE, Project Managers Workbench (PMW), PS4, QQA, RA-Metrics, REVIC, SEER, Size Planner, SIZE Plus, SLIM, SOFTCOST, SOFTQUAL, SPQR/20, SPECTRUM, SPMT, STARpro, Sys/PLAN, Time Line, TRAK, UniPress, VAX Software Project Manager, and XPM.

12. **Consulting support**—Consulting support is offered by both product vendors such as Quantitative Software Methods (QSM), Reifer Associates, Rubin Associates, and Software Productivity Research (SPR), and ABT) and by general management consulting groups such as DMR, Nolan & Norton, or Roger Pressman Associates. Specific consultants may have a bias toward certain tools. A strong caution would be to avoid tools and consulting which only support "lines of source code" since this metric has been proven to be paradoxical for dealing with paperwork, object-oriented methods, high-level languages, and a number of modern topics.

13. **Education support**—Universities and business schools are slowly modernizing their curricula for dealing with software project management, but it will be many years before most universities are up to speed. Universities that have close ties with business and industry (such as Seattle University, Washington University in St. Louis, or the University of Colorado) are probably the most advanced. Universities which happen to have project management specialists on their faculties, such as George Mason University, MIT, Oakland University in Rochester, Michigan, the University of Minnesota, and the University of Dayton, are also comparatively modern in specific courses taught by these experts.

14. **Publication support**—The topic of automated software management tools is not very well covered by book publishers as of 1993. Some of the most interesting books tend to dwell on manual methods rather than automation. Barry Boehm's *Software Engineering Economics* (Prentice Hall, 1981) contained the fundamental algorithms for the COCOMO model and hence was quite influential in the growth of the software estimating business. As of 1993, there may be as many as 20 COCOMO clones available.

Tom DeMarco's *Controlling Software Projects* (Yourdon Press, 1982), Thomas Rullo's *Advances in Computer Programming Management* (Heyden Press, 1980), and Richard H. Thayer's *Software Engineering Project Management* (IEEE Press, 1988) are all interesting, but stress manual methods, as do Phil Metzger's *Managing a Programming Project* (Prentice Hall, 1977 but revised), T. Gilb and S. Finzi's

Principles of Software Engineering Management (Addison Wesley, 1992); Watts Humphrey's *Managing the Software Process* (Addison Wesley, 1987); and Marciniak, Fry, and Zempolich's *Software Project Management* (John Wiley, 1991). All of these, and others too, are interesting, but deal with manual rather than automated software project management methods.

Specific tool vendors also write books which tend to emphasize how their tools work, but are seldom generalized. Nonetheless, such books are often useful and should not be discounted. Examples of this genre include Larry Putnam's *Measures for Excellence* (Prentice Hall, 1992), and this author Capers Jones' *Applied Software Measurement* (McGraw-Hill, 1991). Both books tend to emphasize the proprietary tools of the authors, but both contain useful data from industry sources.

Capers Jones' publication *Applied Software Measurement* includes an appendix that illustrates the usage of automated sizing, estimating, measurement, and assessment tools although that is not the main purpose of the book. The book also includes a history of functional metrics, and the only detailed discussion of the Feature Point metric.

One of the more useful compendiums of automated software management tool information was produced by Captain Kevin Berk, Dean Barrow, and Todd Steadman of the U.S. Air Force's Software Technology Support Center at Ogden Air Force Base in Utah (March of 1992). This is a very large catalog of perhaps 150 planning, estimating, and measurement tools. Although this is a good first step toward a complete catalog, even this 200-page effort appears to omit at least 20 of the more recent tools. The rate at which new software management tools appear (approximately monthly) make it essentially impossible to stay current via normal books and catalogs.

An explicit but not totally successful attempt to deal with project management automation is Lois Zell's *Managing Software Projects—Selecting and Using PC-Based Project Management Systems* (QED Press, 1991). Unfortunately this book tends to blur together planning and estimating tools, ignores soft-factor measurement, is skimpy on tracking, does not mention resource leakage at all, and was published before assessment automation was well known. Perhaps a revised edition in the future can rectify these faults. The book also omits about 70% of the available tools.

Another book attempts to discuss software cost estimation but does not succeed very well: Bernard Londeix's *Cost Estimation for Software Development* (Addison-Wesley, 1987). This book is somewhat embarrassing, since it only discussed two out of the 50 or so commercial estimating tools available. The two, COCOMO and SLIM, are fairly dated in their estimating approach and do not support modern functional metrics. The author, from the United Kingdom, appears to be unaware of how large and dynamic the estimating tool market is in the United States and does not discuss those tools.

Dr. Richard Fairley has produced an interesting video tape on software project management, which includes actual demonstrations of a number of such tools at work. Dr. Fairley's course on software estimating is interesting in that three separate estimating tools are used and their functions compared. Three out of 50 or so is not a great percentage, but it is still useful to witness the various assumptions and operating modes at play on the same project.

For those interested in acquiring commercial software project management tools, a useful resource is the *Guide to Software Productivity Aids* published by Applied Computer Research, Inc. (ACR) of Scottsdale, Arizona. This is a catalog of various tools, including management tools, which are marketed in the United States. The catalog contains a short section describing each tool (provided by the vendor), the price, vendor's address and phone number, and other useful information. Cross-reference sections and appendices show tools by platform, by type, etc. Similar catalogs are produced by CASE Trends and CASE Outlook.

Since so many modern software cost estimating tools utilize Function Points as the basis for both sizing and estimating, a background knowledge of this topic is highly recommended. Dr. Brian Dreger's *Function Point Analysis* (Prentice Hall, 1992) is a college primer that assumes no prior knowledge. Charles Symons' *Software Sizing and Estimating Mk II Function Point Analysis* (John Wiley & Sons, 1991) illustrates the British Mark II Function Point method. Anyone interested in Function Points should consider joining the non-profit International Function Point Users Group (IFPUG), since membership includes copies of the current IFPUG counting practices guidelines, which are the de facto standard for the Function Point metric.

15. **Periodical support**—As of 1993, the only periodicals that devote significant space to software project management tools are the house journals of the tool vendors, such as Knowledge Base which is published quarterly by Software Productivity Research, or the Rubin monthly news letter. Intermittent articles appear in the commercial software journals such as American Programmer, Metrics Views, Software Magazine, and Datamation. From time to time other journals have articles of interest too. For example, Computer Personnel in July of 1991 contained a fascinating article by Dr. Albert Lederer and Dr. Jayesh Prasad on the impact of political pressure on software estimation. The same authors, and several colleagues, also published an intriguing study of cost estimating practices in the June 1990 issue of MIS Quarterly. The Journal of the International Society of Parametric Analysis (ISPA) and the newsletter of the Society of Cost Estimating and Analysis (SCEA) both discuss project management tools and estimating tools in almost every issue. The defense software journal, Crosstalk, produced by the Software Technology Support Center at Ogden Air Force Base has intermittent articles about management tools, sometimes in the context of I-CASE.

16. **Standards support**—As of 1993 there are no standards by ANSI, DoD, IEE, IEEE or ISO that mandate any specific combination or suite of software project management tools. There is an IEEE standard on project management plans, however.

17. **Professional associations**—Several interesting associations deal with software project management tools, among others. SCEA (Society of Cost Estimating and Analysis) is a non-profit association which centers on military software estimation and cost analysis (and on military hardware too). ISPA (the International Society of Parametric Analysis) is a world-wide non-profit association of companies and individuals which build and use parametric models. For example, ISPA members include Barry Boehm, Larry Putnam, Don Reifer, the author of this book Capers Jones, and many other software estimating tool builders. IFPUG (the International Function Point Users Group) has a tools sub-section, and the interest of this group centers around tools which support functional metrics.

    A number of specific tools have their own non-profit user associations. For example, there are national Artemis user groups, COCOMO user groups, SLIM user groups, CHECKPOINT® user groups, and a number of others.

    Many larger companies such as Microsoft have electronic bulletin boards or special interest groups about their management tools using services such as CompuServe and Prodigy. From time to time, conferences and special events on management tools will be hosted via such electronic means. Smaller companies such as SPR will have bulletin boards too from time to time.

    The older and more traditional professional associations, such as the IEEE and the ACM, are interested in project management and have management sub-groups. However, the most active research in management tools and approaches seems to center in the newer groups such as ISPA, SCEA, and IFPUG.

18. **Effectiveness of known therapies**—The effectiveness of software project management tools is improving fairly rapidly. Sizing methods derived from functional metrics can now be used to size essentially all software deliverables, and the accuracy is improving from study to study. Planning tools have long been effective in the hands of experienced managers, but are still only marginally effective for novices and amateurs. Estimating tools add rigor and precision to software cost modeling, but such tools should be carefully calibrated and validated before accepting their output without question. Tracking tools continue to leak resources and are often ineffective, but the main reason for leaking in 1993 is cultural rather than technical. Measurement tools, a new technology since 1989, are rapidly proving their value and effectiveness. Assessment tools, also new since 1989, are rapidly spreading and creating large volumes of useful information that was seldom available in the past.

19. **Costs of known therapies**—*Sizing tools* range in cost from less than $1000 to more than $20,000. Such tools are available under DOS, Windows, UNIX, and some mainframe systems. These tools are useful for both new managers and experienced managers, and for all classes of software (military, civilian, real-time, MIS, etc.) Sizing tools with full sizing logic for all deliverables (specifications, source code, test cases) are the most valuable. They normally return their value almost at once (less than 3 months) when used on projects over 1000 Function Points.

Planning tools range from less than $100 to more than $10,000. Here, too, most operating systems and many hardware platforms have such tools available. As of 1993, personal computer versions under DOS or Windows tend to outsell other kinds of planning tools, with UNIX being in second place. Planning or project management tools are most valuable for the most experienced managers. These tools tend to grow in value in direct proportion to the size of the project being planned. Indeed, for projects larger than 5000 Function Points, not using such tools should be considered to be malpractice. They normally return their value almost at once (less than 3 months) when used on projects larger than 1000 Function Points in size.

Estimating tools range in cost from less than $1000 to more than $25,000. Tools are available under DOS, Windows, UNIX, and for some mainframe systems. These tools are valuable for both novice managers and for experienced managers. The value tends to rise in direct proportion to the size of the project being estimated. They normally return their value in less than 12 months for projects larger than 1000 Function Points. Failure to use such tools on projects exceeding 5000 Function Points should be considered to be malpractice, since manual estimating methods have proven to be grossly inadequate for large systems.

Tracking tools range in price from less than $1000 to more than $100,000. Tracking tools which are intrinsically inaccurate (i.e. have no provision for recording slack time, unpaid overtime, etc.) have *negative value* and indeed constitute a major problem for the software industry. Accurate tracking tools, although very scarce, will typically return their value in less than 12 months for projects over 1000 Function Points.

Measurement tools range in price from $10,000 to $20,000. These tools will typically return their value in less than 18 months when used on projects larger than 1000 Function Points. They can return their value in less than 12 months when used on 10 or more small projects. The absolute value of measurement tends to rise with both the size of software projects and the number of projects measured. A strong case can be made that failure to measure projects over 1000 Function Points should be considered to be malpractice.

Assessment tools range in price from about $2,500 to $20,000. These tools are normally intended to be used across many projects, where they can be extremely helpful in identifying patterns of strength and weakness. Assessment tools will normally return their value in less than 12 months, if used on a portfolio of at least 10 projects.

As of 1993, acquiring a full suite of project management tools which provide support for the six generic functions performed by project managers is expensive, and requires dealing with different vendors. Exchanging data or interfacing various tools is not trivial.

However, a visible trend of the management tool arena since about 1989 has been consolidation, as various independent tool vendors merge, acquire one another, and form strategic alliances. As of 1993, only partial integration of all project management tools exists, and the overall cost for equipping a project manager with a full suite of tools supporting all six functions (sizing, planning, estimating, tracking, measurement, and assessment) is about $30,000 to $40,000. Site licenses, shared tools, and volume discounts can lower the effective per-seat cost to less than $10,000. Annual maintenance fees would amount to another 10% to 15%. Prices can be expected to decline over the next few years, due to increasing competition. Also it can be expected that the pattern of mergers, acquisitions, and strategic alliances will begin to offer integrated management tool suites at lower prices than today's separate and unconnected tool combinations.

20. **Long-range prognosis**—By the end of the century, software project managers in leading corporations and government agencies should have access to powerful, integrated management tool suites which are closely coupled to CASE tools. Services such as automatic creation of functional metrics from design, backfiring from source code, conversion among metrics, and automatic cost to complete estimates should become common. On the whole, the long-range prognosis for software project management tools is quite favorable. A very interesting form of research is the direct coupling of requirements methods to Function Point sizing tools, and also to CASE design tools. The prospects of being able to automatically create full size and cost estimates directly from requirements are improving rapidly.

Inadequate Tools and Methods (Quality Assurance)

1. **Definition**—Inadequate automation and methodological approaches applied to the 10 generic activities performed by software quality assurance (SQA) departments: 1) Predicting defect potentials; 2) Predicting defect removal efficiencies; 3) Predicting quality levels of deployed software; 4) Predicting reliability levels of deployed software; 5) Measuring defect volumes, severity levels, origins, and causes; 6) Measuring and calibrating defect removal efficiency levels; 7) Assisting development teams in the selection of optimal defect prevention approaches; 8) Assisting development teams in the selection of optimal defect removal activities; 9) Performing actual tests in addition to validating those performed by development and testing organizations; 10) Performing research and technology transfer in state-of-the-art software quality control methods.

2. **Severity**—The average severity of inadequate software quality assurance tools and methods in the United States is alarmingly high: about a 1.5 on the following five-point scale. This problem is severe enough to jeopardize the health of the U.S. software industry, and may actually jeopardize the survival of individual companies.

Severity 1: No SQA function exists, and no SQA tools or methods are used

Severity 2: SQA function exists, but cannot measure or predict defect levels

Severity 3: SQA function performs manual defect measurement and prediction

Severity 4: SQA function has automated measurement, but manual prediction

Severity 5: SQA function has only partial automation of key functions

Note: In early 1993, the author was invited to speak at two separate software quality assurance associations, one in the South and one on the West Coast. The number of certified quality assurance personnel was about 60 in each event, and about 50 companies and some state, municipal, and federal government groups were present at each meeting. The attendees were asked to raise their hands if they used automated quality estimating tools, and no hands went up in either event. It is interesting that usage of quality estimating tools is common among winners of Baldrige Awards and enterprises in about the upper 10% of quality results, but extremely rare elsewhere.

3. **Frequency**—Lack of adequate software quality assurance tools and methods appears to be endemic to the U.S. software industry. Based on SPR assessments, the overall performance of U.S. companies in software quality control is generally inadequate, although there are some striking exceptions:

Quality Activity	Average Performance by U.S. Companies	Percent of Sites Lacking Automation
Predicting defect potentials	Very Poor	97%
Predicting defect removal	Very Poor	97%
Predicting delivered defects	Very Poor	95%
Calibrating removal efficiency	Very Poor	97%
Predicting reliability	Poor	85%
Measuring defect levels	Poor	85%
Assisting in defect prevention	Poor to Fair	95%
Assisting in defect removal	Fair	65%
Quality R&D	Poor	75%
Performing testing	Fair to Good	25%

4. **Occurrence**—The problem of inadequate software quality assurance automation is so common and widespread that it is better to start by discussing those industry segments which tend to have effective control of software quality.

As of 1993 there are only five U.S. industries that stand out as having consistently superior software quality control methods and automation: 1) Large mainframe computer manufacturers such as IBM, Hewlett Packard, Tandem, or UNISYS; 2) Telecommunications manufacturers such as AT&T, Motorola, and GTE; 3) Defense companies such as Raytheon and TRW; 4) Medical systems producers such as GE, Siemens, and Hewlett Packard; 5) Aircraft producers such as Boeing and McDonnell Douglas or the companies which produce the on-board flight control and navigational software. It is not coincidental that U.S. companies within these five industries are able to compete successfully in international markets, where quality control is a major factor.

Many of the other 250 or so U.S. industries and government sectors at federal, state, and local levels are seriously deficient in software quality control approaches and automation, although there are exceptions within most industries. For example, banks, insurance companies, wholesale and retail marketers, and manufacturing companies (i.e. automobiles, airlines, machine tools, etc.) are seldom adequately equipped for software quality control. Civilian government agencies at city, state, and federal levels are seldom adequately equipped for software quality control. Somewhat surprisingly, commercial software developers are often poorly equipped for software quality control.

Most small companies with less than 100 software professionals are seldom equipped for adequate software quality control.

Most universities and academic institutions are neither equipped for adequate software quality control in their own applications, nor do they teach quality control very well as academic subjects.

Most publishers of software engineering books and journals (including publishers of books on software quality) are ill-equipped for effective software quality control. When visiting or assessing large publishing houses, one forms the impression that the software managers seldom read the books which the company produces.

Software has become one of the most pervasive technologies of the 20th century. Within the past 30 years, software has spread from a small number of comparatively specialized applications to become a critical factor in almost all engineered products. Software has also become a major factor in consumer goods, and in company operations, military operations, and government operations. Thirty years ago, poor software quality was often annoying, but today poor software quality can literally shut down a phone system, a defense system, and even a company. Any reasonable prognosis makes software even more critical in the future, and hence software quality will become more critical as well.

Somewhat surprisingly, software quality is also on the critical path for reducing software development schedules and improving the time-to-market of commercial products with a high software content. The reason that quality is so important for schedule and cost reduction is because, historically, the most expensive and time-consuming aspects of software development have been the time and costs of finding and fixing software bugs or defects. Thus when software defects are either prevented or removed early, schedules and costs benefit significantly.

Progress in all forms of engineering is heavily dependent upon accurate measurement and precise metrics. Software achieved notoriety as being the worst measured engineering discipline of the 20th century. The main barrier to software quality control in the 1950's, 1960's, and 1970's was a simple lack of good quantitative data about software quality levels, reliability, defect removal efficiency and other basic quality data.

This lack of data was not because software managers and professionals did not care about quality, but because there were no effective metrics prior to 1979 that could actually be used to measure software quality.

Historically, software quality was measured crudely in terms of "defects found per 1000 source code statements" (normally abbreviated to KLOC, where K stands for 1000 and LOC stands for lines of code). Unfortunately, the KLOC metric contains a built-in paradox which causes it to give erroneous results when used with newer and more powerful programming languages, such as Ada, object-oriented languages, or program generators. The results derived from KLOC studies were so poor that several leading companies stopped trying to measure software, and lagging companies never started.

The main problem with the KLOC metric is that this metric conceals, rather than reveals, important quality data. For example, suppose a company has been measuring quality in terms of "Defects per KLOC" which has been a common practice in the past. A project coded in FORTRAN might require 10,000 lines of code, and might contain 200 bugs, for a total of 20 defects per KLOC. Now suppose the same project could be created using a more powerful language such as C++, which required only 2,000 lines of code and contained only 40 bugs. Here too, there are 20 defects per KLOC, but the total number of bugs is actually reduced by 80%.

In the FORTRAN and C++ examples, both versions provided the same functions to end users, and so both contain the same number of Function Points. Assume both versions contain 100 Function Points. When the new metric "Defects per Function Point" is used, the FORTRAN version contained 2.00 defects per Function Point, but the C++ version contained only 0.40 defects per Function Point. With the Function Point metric, the substantial quality gains associated with more powerful high-level languages can now be made clearly visible.

One of the advantages of the Function Point metric is that it can be used to predict and measure all sources of software errors, and not just coding errors. Based on a study of more than 4000 software projects published in Capers Jones' book *Applied Software Measurement* (McGraw-Hill, 1991), the average number of software errors is about five per Function Point. These defects are not found only in code, but originate in all of the major software deliverables, in the following quantities:

Defect Origins	Defects per Function Point
Requirements	1.00
Design	1.25
Coding	1.75
Document	0.60
Bad fixes	0.40
Total	5.00

These numbers represent the total numbers of defects that are found and measured from early software requirements through the remainder of the life cycle of the software. The defects are discovered via requirement reviews, design reviews, code inspections, all forms of testing, and user-reported problem reports.

Complementing the Function Point metric are measurements of defect removal efficiency. The U.S. average for defect removal efficiency, unfortunately, is currently only about 85% although top-ranked projects in leading companies such as Motorola, Raytheon, IBM, and Hewlett Packard achieve defect removal efficiency levels well in excess of 99%.

Requirements errors, design problems, and "bad fixes" tend to be the most difficult to eliminate. Thus, on the day when software is actually put into production, the average quantity of latent errors or defects still present tends to be about 0.75 per Function Point, with the following distribution:

Defect Origins	Defect Potentials	Removal Efficiency	Delivered Defects
Requirements	1.00	77%	0.23
Design	1.25	85%	0.19
Coding	1.75	95%	0.09
Document	0.60	80%	0.12
Bad fixes	0.40	70%	0.12
Total	5.00	85%	0.75

Note that at the time of delivery, defects originating in requirements and design tend to far outnumber coding defects. Data such as this can be used to improve the upstream defect prevention and defect removal processes of software development.

The best companies are using state-of-the-art methods to lower their defect potentials, and coupling that with state-of-the-art methods for removing defects with high efficiency. The results can be quite impressive: Defect potentials of less than 2.0 defects per Function Point coupled with removal efficiencies in excess of 99%.

5. **Susceptibility and resistance**—The pattern of susceptibility and resistance to inadequate quality control automation is not fully known, but some preliminary observations are possible.

Systems software (i.e. software that controls physical devices such as computers, aircraft navigational instruments, medical devices, or telephone switching systems) may not work at all, and certainly will not work well, without careful quality control. Therefore systems software producers are normally better equipped for quality control purposes than MIS producers and are among the most resistant groups. Systems software also tends to be the source of much of the relevant literature on defect prevention, defect removal, and reliability modeling. Examples of systems software producers with capable SQA functions include AT&T, Hewlett-Packard, IBM, and Motorola.

Military software (i.e. software that conforms to DoD standards such as 2167A) are required to have quality assurance approvals, and hence tend to be well equipped with software quality tools. U.S. military software producers are quite resistant to inadequate quality automation. However, military software quality control is often flawed by dependence on the obsolete "lines of source code" metric for normalization purposes. Examples of military software producers with capable SQA functions include Raytheon and TRW.

Large commercial software producers (i.e. Microsoft, Borland, Lotus, Word Perfect, Dun & Bradstreet, Computer Associates, etc.) with hundreds of software personnel have learned the hard way that low-quality products do not sell well, and hence have moved into the domain of software quality automation. Some but not all tend to lag behind computer manufacturers, however, and are only moderately resistant to inadequate quality automation. The large software houses tend to approach quality in a unique fashion. Some releases of major products may utilize 10,000 or so external Beta testers. Since defect removal efficiency correlates closely to number of product users, any product tested by more than 1000 people concurrently is likely to achieve good to excellent levels of removal efficiency. Plainly, this approach is not possible for low-volume or custom software.

Medium commercial software producers (i.e. companies with 25 to perhaps 100 software personnel) are at serious risk due to lack of software quality automation. Companies of this size are often in head-to-head competition with huge companies such as Microsoft or Computer Associates. Yet mid-size companies are often undercapitalized or subject to cash flow limitations so that they cannot acquire adequate SQA tooling. Further, it is difficult to have only top-notch software engineers when companies begin to have 50 or so total software employees. This is a hazardous combination, and mid-size commercial software producers are in a position of serious risk. They compete against major computer and software vendors with full SQA teams and automation, and yet the mid-size companies are seldom adequately staffed or equipped.

Small commercial software producers (i.e. companies with less than 25 software professionals) tend to be highly susceptible to inadequate quality control. This is due in part to undercapitalization and marginal cash reserves. However, small companies seldom build or market software products larger than 2000 Function Points, so small companies with fairly talented software engineers can sometimes produce high-quality products even without formal SQA methods and tools.

Information systems producers (i.e. banks, insurance companies, wholesale and retail chains, health care providers, etc.) tend to be highly susceptible to inadequate quality control. This situation appears to be largely the result of sociological and cultural factors: These organizations typically did not have any quality assurance groups at all prior to the advent of computerization and hence were not aware of how important the topic of software quality would be. One by one, in the wake of various disasters, litigation, outsourcing, and outraged customers, MIS producers are gradually moving toward improved quality control.

Active versus passive quality assurance: Software quality assurance tends to operate in two diverse modes, which can be defined by the phrases "active" and "passive." U.S. quality leaders such as AT&T, IBM, Motorola, Raytheon, and Hewlett-Packard typically use the active form of quality assurance.

An active quality assurance team normally requires about 5% of the staff and resource levels of the groups they support. In other words, 1 employee out of every 20 employees in the software function will be in quality assurance. The role of an active QA group is, as the name implies, quite energetic. Some of the tasks performed by the active QA organizations typically include: A) Building custom QA tools; B) Estimating and modeling quality levels for projects under development; C) Measuring quality levels during and after development; D) Teaching and participating in formal inspection methods; E) Teaching and participating in Total Quality Management (TQM) programs; F) Teaching and participating in Quality Function Deployment (QFD) methods; G) Specialized testing of critical components and systems; H) Research and instruction in critical quality topics such as ISO 9000–9004 standards.

Passive quality assurance teams range in size from less than 3% of the staff (i.e. 1 QA person is supporting more than 35 developers) to less than 1%. At the 1% level, however, QA is really only a token organization and has no ability to influence quality. The role of a passive QA team is primarily observational, and typically includes these functions: A) Observing reviews and inspections; B) Observing the results of software test activities; C) Ensuring that corporate or external quality standards are adhered to.

6. **Root causes**—The root causes of inadequate software quality automation include financial, technical, and cultural components.

The financial component of inadequate software quality automation is the fact that many software quality assurance groups are understaffed and underfunded. An SQA organization that constitutes less than 3% of the overall software population cannot do an effective job. A healthier ratio would be in the vicinity of 5%.

Unfortunately, many U.S. companies establish small SQA groups where the ratio of QA personnel to the project personnel they support is less than 2%. These small groups seldom have adequate funding for building or buying effective QA tools.

The technical component of inadequate software quality automation is because defect prediction is a fairly new technology. The first commercial software tool which could predict software defect potentials (SPQR/20) was only marketed starting in 1985. The first (and as of 1993, the only) tool which could predict the specific defect removal efficiencies of various kinds of reviews, inspections, and tests (CHECKPOINT®) was only marketed starting in 1989.

Tools for measuring software quality and defect removal are also new to the commercial market: none were available before the mid 1980's, although proprietary quality measurement tools were in use in companies such as AT&T and IBM as far back as the middle 1960's.

The cultural component is the distressing fact that quality, and software quality in particular, is not high on the priority lists of many U.S. product managers and senior corporate executives.

Actually, achieving high levels of software quality is on the critical path for minimizing product schedules and for maximizing market shares. Quality is on the critical path for schedule reduction because finding and fixing bugs is one of the most expensive and time-consuming activities in the entire history of the software industry. Quality is on the critical path for maximizing market shares because the customer perception of quality is the dominant market factor for all high-technology products.

A deeper cultural problem can be seen lurking behind the surface problem of poor quality. U.S. software managers and executives have not done a very good job of measuring quality, schedules, costs, or market factors or they would already have known about the strong correlations between quality, time to market, and market shares.

7. **Associated problems**—Inadequate use of automation for software quality assurance (SQA) functions is strongly associated with *canceled projects, cost overruns, missed schedules, excessive time to market, long schedules, excessive schedule pressure, friction with clients, low user satisfaction, low market shares,* and *friction with senior management.* There are also less direct correlations with *low staff morale* and *high attrition rates.*

Inadequate use of automation for software quality assurance can itself be caused by *inadequate capital investment, inadequate management curricula, inadequate software engineering curricula, slow technology transfer, inaccurate metrics, inadequate measurement,* and sometimes by *management malpractice.*

8. **Cost impact**—The costs of inadequate software quality automation are both acute and chronic, and have a sinister impact on corporate performance, as follows:

Loss of market share. Customer perception of poor quality is the shortest and most certain way to lose market share for all high-technology products, including software. Quality levels and market shares can be quantified for specific products, but general rules are difficult.

Cost and schedule overruns. Products with poor quality invariably hang up during integration and test, when the deficiencies finally become visible. Poor quality control is the top-ranked reason for both cost and schedule overruns. (Creeping user requirements rank number 2; irrational cost and schedule estimates rank number 3. Note that two of the top three reasons could be alleviated by adequate predictive and measurement tools.) The magnitude of the potential disaster can be quantified explicitly for specific projects, and indeed this is one of the primary functions of software quality automation.

Canceled projects. The average canceled software project in the U.S. is about a year late and twice its anticipated budget at the moment of cancellation. Almost half of all canceled projects are in a protracted integration and test cycle at the point of cancellation, and the specific reason for cancellation is that the quality levels are too low for acceptable delivery. The probability of cancellation rises with the size of the project, and for systems larger than 5000 Function Points the probability of cancellation can exceed 30%.

High maintenance costs. Delivering software products with poor quality invariably creates a huge and unnecessary bulge of customer support and maintenance costs for the first three years after deployment (assuming the product and the vendor survive that long). The maintenance assignment scope for software products with poor quality seldom exceeds 300 Function Points. By contrast, the maintenance assignment scope for high-quality software products often exceeds 1000 Function Points. There is about a 300% differential in maintenance costs between low-quality and high-quality software products.

9. **Methods of prevention**—The most effective approach to preventing inadequate SQA tool usage is quite new. The approach is to perform surveys of the kinds of tools needed by software project managers, and the frequency with which such tools are utilized. The following table gives an overview of SQA tool suites as of 1993.

This table shows the tool suites utilized by active quality assurance teams in major corporations in the computer, defense, and telecommunications sectors. These sectors typically have the highest U.S. quality levels and the most widespread utilization of active quality assurance teams:

Tools Used by Software Quality Assurance
(Size Range in Function Points)

Tool Categories	Minimum	Median	Maximum
Statistical Analysis Tools			3000
Quality Estimation Models			2500
Spreadsheet	750	1250	2000
Graphics/Presentations	750	1250	2000
Word Processing	500	1000	2000
Configuration Control	500	1250	2000
Test Case Generators			1750
Data Base	500	1000	1500
Defect Tracking/Analysis	500	750	1000
Reliability Estimation Models		500	1000
Symbolic Debuggers	250	500	750
Electronic Mail	300	500	700
Appointment Calendar	100	300	750
Phone/Address File	100	150	500
Complexity Analyzers			350
Test Path Coverage Analyzers		200	350
Test Execution Monitors		200	350
Totals	4250	8850	22250

The study of performance levels correlated to available functionality is still in its infancy, so the margins of error are very high. However, for SQA tasks, the available evidence indicates a sharp demarcation in overall effectiveness: SQA teams that lack quality estimation tools, statistical analysis tools, and defect tracking tools appear to be much less effective than teams which are adequately supplied. Although the sample size is quite limited and probably biased, there appears to be about a 15% to 30% differential in annual customer-reported defect rates between teams that have adequate SQA tool suites and those which do not.

While all of the SQA tools are useful, U.S. industry quality leaders such as Baldrige Award winners tend to have available a nucleus of six specific SQA tools that smaller companies may not even know about. This nucleus consists of the following: 1) Statistical analysis tools; 2) Quality and defect estimation models; 3) Reliability estimation models; 4) Defect tracking tools (used from requirements forward); 5) Complexity analysis tools; 6) Test-path coverage analysis tools.

10. **Methods of control**—The most difficult aspects of controlling inadequate SQA tool suites are financial and cultural. A full SQA tool suite can cost in excess of $50,000 as of 1993, and many small enterprises who lack discretionary capital or who are strapped for cash flow cannot afford a full tool complement.

Further, many SQA organizations are themselves understaffed and underfunded even for ordinary manual activities. This is due to the unfortunate tendency by U.S. enterprises to establish minimal SQA groups, and then believe that "they support software quality."

The cultural difficulty of controlling inadequate SQA tooling is the fact that powerful SQA tools are fairly new on the U.S. market. It takes about 14 years for civilian inventions to move into widespread deployment, and about 17 years for military inventions. Since the first U.S. defect estimation model was only introduced in 1985, SQA tools are still in the mode of establishing credibility. It can be hypothesized that full SQA automation will not become common until about 1996 or 1997, if such tools follow a typical rate of penetration.

11. **Product support**—Commercial off the shelf software (COTS) is now available for most SQA functions. Unfortunately, the SQA tool market is dominated by small, independent companies so fully integrated SQA tool suites do not exist as of 1993 on the commercial market place. Examples of various SQA tools that are commercially available include (in alphabetic order): ACT, AdaQuest, Battlemap, CHECK-POINT®, DEC/Test Map, Design Test Tool, Impact, Inspector, MIL/SOFTQUAL, PADS, Pathvu, ProTEAM, Q/Auditor, QualityTEAM, QQA, RA-Metrics, RevuGen, SPQR/20, S-TCAT, SLEUTH, SLIM, SMARTS, SPMT, SOFTQUAL, Software Test-Works, SQAMANAGER, TCAT, TestGen, TestPro, TIE(Q), T-Scope, Verify, VIA/SmartTest, and XRunner.

12. **Consulting support**—Consulting support in the SQA arena is offered by both tool vendors and generalized management consulting organizations that specialize in more strategic concepts such as Total Quality Management (TQM). Some of the consulting groups with well known software quality practices include Andersen Consulting, Bender & Associates, Computer Power Group, Ernst & Young, Phil Crosby Associates, Juran Institute, Quality Assurance Institute, QSM, Software Productivity Research, and Software Quality Tools.

13. **Education support**—Most U.S. software engineering and business schools are barely adequate in teaching SQA concepts at all. Those that have full SQA tool

suites are virtually nonexistent. Military universities, such as the Air Force Institute of Technology and the Naval Post-Graduate School are interested in software quality automation, but tend to be underfunded and hence lack full SQA tool suites.

Aspects of quality, such as testing, may be taught effectively by universities but the overall topic is not often well served. Some possible exceptions include the University of Virginia, which is doing very innovative research in software quality attributes. Washington University in St. Louis is also doing interesting work on testing methods.

Quite a number of private, commercial courses are available and some of these feature the usage of software quality estimating tools, reliability models, and the like. Courses offered by companies such as Computer Power, Digital Consulting, Inc., QAI, QSM, SPR, etc., are often more current than university courses and more complete in their coverage of automation. The down side of private education, of course, is that courses offered by tool vendors are likely to be heavily biased in favor of the vendor's proprietary approach.

14. Publication support—Books that deal with software quality automation are scarce in 1993. This is a major gap in the software engineering literature. One of the few is Keith A. Jones' *Automated Software Quality Measurement* (Van Nostrand Reinhold, 1993). Of the books that deal with partial aspects of software quality automation, testing is the best covered. For example, Dr. Daniel Mosley's *The Handbook of MIS Application Testing* (Prentice Hall, 1993) includes some citations to tools and automation. Even here, automation is treated as a minor and subordinate topic, rather than as a primary focus of concern. Vendor manuals from companies which market software quality tools, such as quality estimating tools and test coverage analyzers are often useful, but quite narrow in their focus.

Even though automation is not stressed, the quality literature per se is growing rapidly and contains some excellent references. Gordon Schulmeyer's *Zero Defect Software* (McGraw-Hill, 1990) and Gordon Schulmeyer and James McManus' *Total Quality Management for Software* (Van Nostrand Reinhold, 1992) are both fairly broad in coverage. A few older citations include Robert Dunn's *Quality Assurance for Computer Software* (McGraw-Hill, 1982) and the same author's *Software Defect Removal* (McGraw-Hill, 1984). It is a minor historical note that Dunn was one of the many software researchers at ITT's famous Programming Technology Center during its years of operation.

Dr. Gerald Weinberg's many books are always interesting. His two recent books *Quality Software Management Volume 1 Systems Thinking* (Dorset House, 1991) and *Quality Software Management Volume 2 First-Order Measurement* (Dorset House, 1993) have much to recommend them. Jerry Weinberg also has a historical connection to the ITT Programming Technology Center, since he not only served as a consultant there but in his youth he and Jim Frame, the former ITT Vice President of Programming, shared an office at IBM.

The literature on testing and testing automation was sparse for many years, but is now improving. Daniel Mosley's new *The Handbook of MIS Application Soft-*

ware Testing (Yourdon Press, 1993) contains an extensive bibliography and includes discussions of test automation.

Ulma Gupta's *Validating and Verifying Knowledge-Based Systems* (IEEE Press, 1991) examines the tools and techniques for dealing with the quality of complex expert systems. Also relevant is Martin Stitt's *Debugging* (Wiley Interscience, 1993).

A very useful catalog which includes quality estimation tools, test tools, CASE tools, and many other tool types is published semi-annually by Applied Computer Research of Scottsdale, Arizona: *Guide to Software Productivity Aids*. This is one of the most complete single-volume catalogs of automation for various aspects of management, quality control and testing.

15. **Periodical support**—Here too, there is a major gap in the software engineering literature. From time to time, individual articles on software quality automation will occur in the general software magazines such as American Programmer, IEEE Transactions on Software Engineering, Communications of the ACM, or Quality Times. There appear to be no current journals which deal explicitly and repeatedly with software quality automation. The journal of the International Society of Parametric Analysis (ISPA) will run occasional articles on software quality estimation. The newsletter of the Society of Cost Estimating and Analysis (SCEA) may also be relevant. Many regional software quality groups, such as the Bay Area group in San Francisco and the Atlanta quality group have local newsletters that may contain articles on quality automation. For military software, STSC Crosstalk, produced at Ogden Air Force Base, deals with many aspects of software automation. The Swiss-published ISO 9000 journal may discuss quality automation from time to time.

16. **Standards support**—While there are many standards, such as DoD 2167A, ISO 9000–9004, and various IEEE standards that deal with software quality in a generic manner, there are no known standards as of 1993 that deal with software quality automation.

17. **Professional associations**—There are a number of national and regional software quality non-profit associations. National groups include the Society for Software Quality (SSQ) and the Society for Information Systems Quality (SISQ). Regional groups include those in the San Francisco Bay Area, Atlanta, and New York. There are also special interest quality groups within larger organizations such as the IEEE, ACM, IFPUG, and ASM. The non-profit International Society of Parametric Analysis (ISPA) has a number of member companies and individuals who build quality and reliability models, and SQA automation is often discussed within this forum. The Software Cost Estimating and Analysis (SCEA) non-profit association also has an interest in quality automation, although this topic is subordinate to cost estimating. The well-known Software Engineering Institute (SEI) has not yet done much research in the domain of software quality automation.

Although they are not non-profit organizations, the Quality Assurance Institute (QAI), Quantitative Software Management (QSM) Software Quality Tools, and Software Productivity Research (SPR) have user associations and conferences where quality automation is a frequent topic.

The International Standards Organization (ISO) is now famous for the fact that ISO quality standards 9000 through 9004 are now mandated, and ISO certification is necessary to market many kinds of software packages in Europe. It is a very interesting occurrence that a quality standard was one of the first examples of the power of a unified Europe. It is unfortunate that the ISO standards themselves are not very good, and to date have not demonstrated any empirical evidence that they improve quality in any tangible way. Essentially ignoring quality prediction, defect removal efficiency, and quality tools are among the many deficiencies of the current ISO standards. Of course, there is less than two years of data as this book is being prepared, and the ISO situation may improve in the future.

Various on-line services such as CompuServe, Internet, Prodigy, and Genie may have special-interest groups which deal with software quality automation.

18. **Effectiveness of known therapies**—The effectiveness of software quality automation is high enough so that companies with full SQA tool suites have a good chance of dominating their industries and putting weak competitors out of business. It is an interesting fact that a majority of Baldrige Award winners tend to use both predictive and measurement tools for software quality. Predictive software quality estimating models and software quality measurement tools head the list of effective SQA tools. Essentially all enterprises with reputations of producing software of excellent quality tend to use quality and reliability estimators, and have quality measurement capabilities as well.

19. **Costs of known therapies**—*Software quality estimation models* are in the price range of $5,000 to $20,000. Such tools are expert systems, and the high cost tends to reflect the value of the embedded knowledge and the proprietary reasoning algorithms. They normally return their value in less than 12 months for companies that produce commercial software or large systems.

Software reliability models are less expensive than software quality estimation tools, and range from less than $500 to about $5000. The reason for the cost differential is that reliability models are normally based on statistics, rather than expert-system reasoning rules. The return on investment in reliability tools is not fully understood, but there is some evidence which suggests that value and size tend to correlate, as do the number of users. Thus reliability modeling of software projects larger than 1000 Function Points in size, or where more than 10 users are intended, seems most valuable.

Software quality measurement tools are less expensive than estimating tools, since they do not contain embedded knowledge. The costs of COTS defect tracking tools range from less than $1000 to over $5000. However, large computer and telecommunication manufacturers such as AT&T and IBM may have custom software quality measurement tools where the costs exceed $1 million. These high-end tools can track defects from the first day of requirements through the rest of the life cycle. They can also produce a variety of powerful quality reports, such as defect trends over time, defects by laboratory or development site, kinds of defect reported by various client categories, and defect reports by state, city, and country. Quality measurement tools will normally return their value in between 24 months and 36 months (it takes that long to accumulate the first set of life-cycle quality data points).

Software complexity analyzers range from close to being free (some are available as share-ware from bulletin boards) to a high of more than $10,000. Most tools operate with specific programming languages, or with families of selected programming languages. There is yet another set of complexity analyzers that work with natural language text, such as specifications, and can produce reports on grammatical or syntactic complexity. Curiously, the text and programming complexity analyzers are developed and marketed by separate companies, use quite different approaches, and do not import or export data between one another. The value or return on investment of complexity analyzers is not fully understood as of 1993.

Software test coverage analyzers range in cost from about $500 for personal computer tools, up to $15,000 or more for main-frame tools. The value of test coverage analyzers is not fully understood as of 1993, but preliminary studies indicate that the value of such tools is proportional to the size of the software being tested. It may take as many as 5 or more small programs of less than 500 Function Points to generate positive value. However, a single system of 5000 Function Points or larger will generate positive value. The time span for positive value seems to be in the range of 18 to 36 months.

The costs of constructing a reasonably complete SQA tool suite from COTS components in 1993 can range from a low of about $15,000 to a high of more than $100,000. Since such tools are normally acquired for a Quality Assurance Department, rather than for individual SQA personnel, the effective cost per seat will range from less than $3,000 up to about $20,000. Such a tool suite would probably have a return on investment of 6 to 18 months of usage.

20. **Long-range prognosis**—The future of software quality automation is guardedly optimistic. The individual SQA tool capabilities are already fairly good, but suffer from being developed by small, independent, and competitive companies. This has tended to make the tools incompatible, and has fragmented the SQA market into many small sub-markets. It is fairly obvious that the first large company that acquires or builds a fully integrated SQA tool suite for the commercial market is going to be a near monopoly, and will probably do very well indeed. Given the number of large companies that are now awake to the importance of quality, it is probable that by the end of the century fully integrated SQA tool suites will be commercially available.

Inadequate Tools and Methods (Software Engineering)

1. **Definition**—Inadequate automation and methodological approaches applied to the 12 generic activities which software engineers should be able to perform well: 1) User requirements analysis; 2) Reusable component analysis; 3) Functional design and specification; 4) Logical design and specification; 5) Data design and specification; 6) System segmentation and sequencing; 7) Reusable component acquisition; 8) New component development; 9) Defect removal operations against all defect classes; 10) Integration and configuration control of all deliverables; 11) Restructuring of aging software; 12) Reverse engineering and re-engineering of aging software.

2. **Severity**—The average severity of inadequate software engineering tools and methods is fairly high: about a 3.0 on the following five-point scale:

   Severity 1: Automation for only one activity (usually compilers or assemblers)

   Severity 2: Automation for two activities (usually compilers plus debuggers)

   Severity 3: Automation for three or four activities out of 12

   Severity 4: Automation for five or six activities out of 12

   Severity 5: Automation for seven or eight activities out of 12

3. **Frequency**—The frequency of inadequate software engineering automation varies widely across the 12 generic activities. Following are U.S. observations based on SPR assessments:

Software Engineering Activity	Average Performance by Software Engineers	Percent of Projects Lacking Automation
Requirements analysis	Poor to fair	95%
Reusability analysis	Very poor	99%
Functional design	Poor to fair	75%
Logical design	Poor to fair	75%
Data design	Poor to fair	75%
System segmentation	Poor	99%
Reusable components	Very poor	99%
New code development	Poor to excellent	00%
Defect removal	Poor to good	50%
Configuration/integration	Poor to good	30%
Restructuring	Poor to excellent	65%
Reverse and re-engineering	Poor to good	75%

4. **Occurrence**—The widespread lack of effective software engineering automation has impacted systems software, military software, commercial software, and MIS software, although not equally.

The military software domain is mounting a very energetic push toward integrated CASE or I-CASE tool suites. This is one of the few areas where the Department of Defense and the military services may be somewhat ahead of their civilian counterparts.

The systems and military domains tend to lag in the areas of requirements and data design, and also in the areas of restructuring, reverse engineering, and re-engineering. However, they are ahead in defect removal and configuration control.

The MIS domain is severely behind in defect removal and configuration control, but ahead in requirements acquisition, restructuring, and both re-engineering and reverse engineering.

The commercial software domain (i.e. companies such as Microsoft, Borland, Lotus, etc.) are ahead in new code development, configuration control, and integration, but tend to have surprising gaps in areas such as defect removal, restructuring, and both re-engineering and reverse engineering.

Small enterprises with less than 50 software technical staff members are often undercapitalized, and hence lag in software automation. Many companies which are in economic distress or which have chronic cash flow problems also lag in effective software automation.

There are technical, economic, and sociological reasons behind these variations in software engineering automation.

The technical reason for lack of effective engineering automation is that tools which support all 10 of the generic software engineering activities have only recently started to become available. The Computer-Aided Software Engineering (CASE) sub-industry only started in about 1985, and the CASE vendors themselves have not yet been able to fully automate every major software engineering activity. Even in 1993, there are many severe gaps in CASE automation, such as inadequate support for reusable components; inadequate support for defect removal operations; and inadequate support for configuration control and integration. The technical situation is improving fairly rapidly, but some of the underlying technical problems are quite severe and full automation is not easily accomplished.

The economic reason for lack of effective engineering automation is that integrated CASE tool suites are expensive to build, and also expensive to acquire. In the early 1980's the ITT corporation explored the full suite of CASE tools needed to support a large multi-national corporation. A total of about 110 tools were identified, and the cost of building those tools was estimated at about $85 million. Further, assuming that construction started in 1980, the full suite of 110 tools would probably not have been fully operational prior to 1990, even with the early tools being used to bootstrap the subsequent tools. Should ITT have decided to market the CASE tool suite it was considering building, the probable market price to clients would have been in the range of $25,000 to $50,000 per seat.

In 1993, integrated CASE tool suites range in price from less than $5,000 per seat to about $50,000 per seat. Gaps and omissions occur at all cost levels, but the gaps tend to be more severe at the low end than at the high. Failure to support defect removal and quality control, failure to support reusable deliverables, failure to include adequate configuration control and integration capabilities, and failure to support restructuring, reverse engineering, and re-engineering are the most prevalent gaps.

The sociological reasons for lack of effective engineering automation are multiple, and include: 1) The normal difficulty of adopting new technologies and changing paradigms; 2) Exaggerated claims and false advertising by many CASE vendors, which slows down market acceptance of CASE tool suites; 3) The "silver bullet syndrome" or the naive expectation by managers and executives that tool purchases, by themselves, will have a major impact on software productivity, schedules, or quality. To be effective, even optimal tool suites require training, capable managers and staffs, good organization structures, and comfortable, noise-free office environments. Acquiring CASE tools for staffs that are already overworked and are crowded into noisy office conditions will not create immediate improvements, and indeed will initially slow things down.

5. **Susceptibility and resistance**—The patterns of susceptibility and resistance include both economic and cultural components.

The economic component of inadequate software engineering tool usage centers around the high expense levels to rectify the problem. As a general rule, small software development groups (less than 50 total employees) tend to be chronically under-funded and often have severe cash flow problems.

It should be noted that the entire software industry has a history of being undercapitalized and under-funded for the work at hand. It is not uncommon for enterprises to support electrical, telecommunication, or mechanical engineers with more than $150,000 worth of tools and software per seat. Software engineers, on the other hand, have long been supported by less than $10,000 worth of tools and software per seat. Not only that, but software engineers are often crowded together in less than adequate office space, to a greater degree than most other forms of engineering. Part of the reason for excessive crowding of software engineers is that there are so many of us, due to the lack of effective automation and tools.

Enterprises and organizations which tend to be marginal in financial strength such as start-ups and small software houses invariably under-equip their software staffs. This is also true of enterprises which are in economic trouble due to the current recession or due to competitive pressures.

The cultural component of inadequate software engineering tool usage centers around the natural human resistance to changing technologies. Further, for software, the impact of false advertising and fraudulent claims by software tool vendors has increased resistance to CASE tool usage. Software personnel and managers tend to react negatively to advertising claims of "10 to 1" (or higher!) productivity improvement since they will be held responsible for achieving those targets if the tools are acquired. A rational and common defensive posture in the face of exaggerated claims is to dismiss the tools out of hand as being inadequate and spurious. Thus exaggerated claims have tended to slow down and reduce the usage of tools which are effective.

The cultural factors associated with inadequate software engineering tool usage tend to vary in ways which are not fully explainable. It frequently occurs from assessments of similar companies, all of which are profitable and have adequate funding available, that some will be at state-of-the-art levels in terms of tooling, while others will be years behind. What seems to be the key cultural factor is the vision the enterprise has of itself as being a leader or a laggard.

6. **Root causes**—Inadequate software engineering automation occurs because the software and CASE industries are still young enough so that trial-and-error methods have not yet fully revealed the complete sets of tools which software engineers truly need to be effective.

A derivative root cause has been the chronic lack of adequate measurement of software projects, which long prevented proper understanding of major software expense elements. For example, the fact that paperwork, defect removal, and meetings and communication all cost more than coding for large software systems is still not common knowledge. Enterprises and managers who believe that coding is the dominant cost element have a high probability of acquiring tools which will not be sufficient to make tangible improvements.

However, the CASE and software industries are making fairly rapid progress in filling in the gaps and providing enhanced tool capabilities. Considering 1985 as the starting point of the CASE industry, progress in software tool functionality almost seems to be following a Fibonacci series. A slow beginning, but a rapid acceleration in tool functionality in recent years.

7. **Associated problems**—Inadequate use of automation for software engineering functions is strongly associated with *canceled projects, cost overruns, missed schedules, excessive time to market, long schedules, excessive schedule pressure, friction with clients,* and *friction with senior management.* There are also less direct correlations with *low quality* and *low staff morale.*

Inadequate use of automation for software engineering can be caused by *inadequate capital investment, inadequate management curricula, inadequate software engineering curricula, slow technology transfer, inaccurate metrics, inadequate measurement,* and sometimes by *management malpractice.*

8. **Cost impact**—The costs of inadequate software engineering tools vary from tool function to tool function. Following are some of the commonly observed phenomena:

Inadequate requirements tools and methods result in a high level of creeping requirements, in missed requirements, and in low levels of customer satisfaction. These problems can add 10% to 30% to the direct costs of building software systems in the first release. Missed or omitted requirements may constitute more than 50% of the second release as well. New research on requirements methods is leading to the potential of creating fully automated, reusable requirements that can feed data directly into both project sizing and estimating tools, and also into lower-level design tools. Even direct coupling of requirements to application generators or prototyping tools is now on the technical horizon.

Inadequate reusability analysis tools and methods result in excessive volumes of custom work and the associated manual effort to build components which should be reused. These problems can add 25% to 75% to the direct costs of constructing software systems.

Inadequate functional design tools and methods can result in designs that are intrinsically inadequate from the users' view, and also in designs that are expensive to modify or update. These problems can add 10% to 30% to the direct costs of building software systems.

Inadequate logical design tools and methods can result in designs that are irrationally structured, are difficult to maintain, and which exhibit low reliability and high defect levels, as well as poor operational performance. These problems can add 15% to 40% to the cost of initial development of software, and well over 100% to the cost of long-term maintenance.

Inadequate data design tools and methods can result in arcane data structures which fail to fulfill user needs, in polluted data, and in very sluggish performance for queries, updates, and other data management functions. These problems can add from 5% to 15% to the cost of initial development of software, and more than 50% to the cost of long-term maintenance.

Inadequate system segmentation tools and methods are problems whose impact varies with the size of the application. For small programs, the impact can be close to zero. For large systems, however, inadequate segmentation into discrete builds and failure to develop rational components, programs, and modules can

301

add 20% to 40% to the cost of initial development, and can add well over 100% to the costs of long-term maintenance.

Inadequate tools and methods for accessing reusable components is a chronic problem for the software industry. A nominal target for software would be to achieve about 85% reuse for specifications and source code. Anything less than that adds cost in direct ratio. Thus, for a project which might have achieved 85% reuse but in fact achieved only 15% reuse, the cost impact is 70%.

Inadequate tools for new code development can result in long schedules, excessive defect rates, excessive rework, and sometimes severe performance problems. Such problems can add from 10% to 50% to the costs of any new code required for a given application.

Inadequate tools for defect removal can result in poor quality, obviously, but also in long schedules and low levels of user satisfaction. Inadequate defect removal is a chronic problem for the software industry, and typically adds from 15% to 50% to the costs of software. The magnitude of the costs rise with the size of the application.

Inadequate tools for configuration control and integration have the greatest impact on large systems and on military projects. For small stand-alone programs, the cost impact is close to zero. For large systems, inadequate configuration control and integration can add 10% to 30% to the cost of initial development, and more than 50% to the cost of long-range maintenance.

Inadequate tools for restructuring software adds cost to both initial development and to long-term maintenance. Knowledge and ability to create well-structured applications is not common among software engineers, and automated restructuring tools can be applied during new development, as well as during maintenance. Inadequate restructuring tools tend to add from 5% to 15% to new development, and from 15% to 40% to long-term maintenance.

Inadequate tools for reverse engineering and re-engineering tend to have the greatest impact when aging software is being modernized or replaced. Lack of adequate reverse engineering and re-engineering tools can add more than 100% to the cost of modernizing or replacing aging applications.

The cumulative impact of lack of effective tooling for software engineering can be of major proportions. For a large system of 10,000 Function Points that uses no tools or automation except basic compilers and source code debuggers, productivity will seldom exceed a rate of 1 Function Point per staff month.

If the same system is developed with full automation from requirements forward, and with reasonable volumes of reusable components (more than 50%), the productivity rate can approach and sometimes exceed 10 or even 15 Function Points per month.

If the application is developed with an "average" tool suite of partially automated design tools, compilers and source code debuggers, 10% or so reusable code, and some form of automated configuration control, productivity would typically be in the range of three to five Function Points per staff month.

9. **Methods of prevention**—The most effective approach for preventing inadequate software engineering tools is quite new, having only had published citations since 1991. This new approach is to perform surveys, using functional metrics such as Function Points or Feature Points, of the kinds of tools used by software engineers. Studies of usage patterns are complementary to the primary study of the functionality of both stand-alone tool suites, CASE tool suites, and Integrated or I-CASE tool suites.

The following table gives preliminary results as of the middle of 1993 in terms of the size ranges of various software engineering tools, ranked in descending order by maximum size:

Software Tools Utilized by Software Engineers
(Size Range in Function Points)

Tool Categories	Minimum	Median	Maximum
Code Editors	750	1250	3500
Design Tools		1500	3000
Reverse Engineering Tools			3000
Program Generators			3000
Compilers	750	1500	2500
Assemblers	750	1250	2000
Word Processing	500	1000	2000
Restructuring Tools			2000
Configuration Control	500	1250	2000
Test Case Generators			1750
Symbolic Debuggers	250	500	750
Electronic Mail	300	500	700
Appointment Calendar	100	300	750
Phone/Address File	100	150	500
Complexity Analyzers			350
Test Path Coverage Analyzers		200	350
Defect Tracking			300
Test Execution Monitors		200	350
Totals	4000	9600	28800

The effective total of software tools for well-equipped software engineers is actually about two to three times larger than the table indicates, due to the fact that often multiple versions of specific tools will be utilized. For example, a software engineer may use C++, PASCAL, and Ada compilers; several different editors; and several different testing tools. The total volume of software tools for software engineers may exceed 50,000 Function Points.

Programmers and software engineers, as might be expected, utilize computers and software more intensively than software project managers. Even so, usage

303

during the normal business day only averages four or five hours. Meetings, status reports, discussions, and other business functions occupy the rest of the normal business day.

However, software engineering is not a normal 9 to 5 kind of occupation. Many software engineers average another one to three hours of computer and software usage in the evenings, and many will average four to six hours of computer and software usage on weekends. Thus the total quantity of hands-on software usage by a professional programmer will sometimes exceed 40 hours a week when overtime is factored in.

The most widely used software development tools are code editors coupled with either compilers, assemblers, or generators. Usage of such tools occurs in essentially 100% of software development projects.

For software developed in large enterprises, electronic mail tends to be among the most widely used kind of software, often on a daily basis.

The usage pattern of many software engineering tools tends to be intermittent, and is based on the size, phase, and needs of specific projects. For example, the usage of design tools averages less than 50% overall. However, usage of design tools correlates closely with the size of the application: for applications smaller than 500 Function Points less than 30% of projects use such tools, but for systems larger than 5,000 Function Points, usage climbs to more than 60%.

The method of using Function Points to explore software engineering and CASE tool suites is still too new to determine if the method will make a permanent contribution, or only become a transient experiment. The preliminary results are quite intriguing, however, and the method deserves additional experimentation and utilization.

No long-range studies have yet been published on the growth of software tool capabilities by era. However, programmers working 30 years ago in the IBM 1401 era seldom had more than about 500 Function Points of tools available: basic assemblers, sorts, and a few other rudimentary tools were all that were available.

By the 1970's, design tools and some testing tools were available, and compilers were beginning to offer some integral debugging support. A well equipped IBM System 370 programmer might have as many as 5000 Function Points of processing power available.

By the mid 1980's, restructuring tools, complexity analyzers, and the early forms of CASE tool suites were starting to appear. UNIX tool suites were also increasing in power and sophistication. A well equipped programmer on a VAX under UNIX, or on an IBM mainframe under MVS might have more than 10,000 Function Points of processing power available.

As already noted, software engineers in the 1990 era tend to have up to 50,000 Function Points available when using the newer CASE and I-CASE tool suites.

Projecting forward to the end of the century, it might be hypothesized that a well-equipped software engineer may top 100,000 Function Points of processing power. Some of the tools soon to be added to a standard software engineering tool suite include reusability support tools, network analysis tools, multi-media development and debugging tools, client-server development tools, viral protection tools, and on-line defect tracking and analysis tools.

10. **Methods of control**—The most difficult aspects of inadequate software engineering tool usage are technological, financial, and sociological.

The technological problem of inadequate software engineering tool utilization is that there are still many gaps and missing functions, even in CASE and I-CASE tool suites which advertise "full life cycle" support. No CASE tool vendor today truly provides all of the support needed for software engineering of large and complex systems in geographically dispersed organizations.

Some of the most obvious gaps in today's CASE and I-CASE tool suites include: 1) Lack of support for defect removal, defect tracking, and for quality control; 2) Lack of support for viral protection and security in general; 3) Lack of support for configuration control and integration; 4) Lack of support for reusable designs, test libraries, and source code; 5) Lack of support for restructuring, reverse engineering, or re-engineering existing software; 6) Lack of support for geographically and organizationally dispersed development teams.

The financial problem of inadequate software engineering tool utilization is the comparatively high cost involved. Even today's more powerful CASE and I-CASE tool suites in the 15,000 Function Point and higher domain can exceed $25,000 per seat. When supplemental and stand-alone tools are added to the equation, the costs can rise to more than $50,000 per seat. (This is still cheaper than a full CAD tool suite for an electrical engineer, but there are many more software engineers than electrical engineers in today's world.) Unfortunately, the low-end CASE tool suites at less than $5,000 per seat are often somewhat low in functionality: many of them contain less than 5,000 Function Points of capability.

The sociological problem of inadequate software engineering tool utilization is the age-old story of the natural human resistance to change. An interesting experiment was performed by Hewlett Packard in the years 1989 to 1991 in which several CASE tools were given to internal development labs, on the condition that their experiences would be recorded and used to help in technology transfer. Although several of the groups using CASE tool suites recorded favorable results, none of the groups that did not receive the tools for free were motivated to buy the tools and use them. Even after three years of moderately good results, the number of non-CASE development projects was almost unchanged. The conclusion of the study was that successful tool usage, by itself, is not a sufficient reason for rapid technology transfer.

11. **Product support**—As of 1993, well over 1200 stand-alone software engineering tools and more than 50 CASE and I-CASE tool suites are being marketed in the United States. New stand-alone tools are entering the market about once a week. New CASE tools are entering the market more slowly, but three to four new tool suites a year have been appearing since 1990. The functionality of existing CASE tool suites marketed by major vendors is increasing by perhaps 5% to 10% each

year. This is an encouraging sign, and implies that full life-cycle and cross-life cycle support may become an actuality by the end of the century.

Examples of some of the more common software engineering tools and CASE tool suites include ABLE, ACT/1, Ada Software Toolset, ADS, AIMS, ALL, APPGEN, APS, APTools, ARIS, ARTESSA/3000, AS/SET, Automator, BACHMAN/ Analyst, BACHMAN/Re-Engineering, BIBLOS, BLACKSMITH, CASEworks, CASE-PM, CHARM, CISLE-C, COGEN, COHESION, CONDOR, CorVision, Cradle, Design Aid, DESTINY, Deft, DEVELOPER, DOME, EasyPath, EasySAA, EPOS, Excelerator, EXPRESS, firstCASE, FOUNDATION, GAMMA, GENER/OL, GEODE, GeneXus, GURU, I-CASE, IDEAL, IEF, IEW, Informix-4GL, INFRONT, IPF, ISPF, KEE, LINC II, MAESTRO II, MAGEC, MAGNA 8, MANAGER, MANTIS, MAPPER, Micro Focus Workbench, Millennium, MITROL, MODEL, NATURAL, NETRON/CAP, NOMAD, NOVA, Object Plus, OMNI, PACBASE, PACE, PASSPORT, POSE, Power Builder, PowerCASE, PowerHouse, PRISM, PREDICT CASE, PRODOC, ProKit Workbench, ProMod, PSL/PSA, QUEO, RAMIS, Reliance, Sculptor, SEE, SIMPLE, SMARTsystem, SNAP, Software Backplane, Software Through Pictures, STAR, superCASE, Synon/2E, System Developer II, System 1032, SYSTEMS ENGINEER, TAOS, Team-Work, TELON, TIGRE, TODAY, Transform, UFO, UNIX System V, and Visible Analyst Workbench.

The software engineering tools market has both horizontal and vertical groupings. The horizontal groupings tend to follow typical software life cycles, and include requirements tools, specification and design tools, data dictionary tools, coding tools, debugging tools, maintenance and restructuring tools, and so forth. Many CASE vendors adhere to this traditional grouping, and indeed IBM's AD/CYCLE concept, DEC's COHESION concept, and many others provide instances of horizontal integration of major tool functions.

The vertical groupings tend to have three main components: 1) Tools for information system developers; 2) Tools for real time and systems software developers; 3) Tools for military software developers.

A number of specialized tool suites have been developed under one or another aspect of this triad. For example, tool suites that center around COBOL are almost exclusively used by the MIS community, but constitute by far the largest number of vendors. Examples of MIS tool and CASE vendors include Bachman, CGI, COGNOS, IBM, Intersolv, and Visible Systems.

Tool suites centering around C, Objective-C, or C++ are most widely used by the systems and real-time software community. Example of tool and CASE tool vendors for systems software include CADRE, DEC, Hewlett Packard, Sabre, and Stepstone.

Tool suites centering around Ada are most widely used by the military software community. Examples of tool and CASE tool vendors for military software include AETECH, CADRE, Carman Group, Iconix, and McCabe & Associates.

Several new and specialized groupings have started to appear, although it is premature to state whether these groupings will coalesce into new markets, or will gradually be subsumed under the existing horizontal and vertical groups.

The Information Engineering (IE) paradigm is being cited as a distinct form of software engineering aimed at MIS applications. As of 1993, perhaps 10% to 15% of U.S. MIS projects utilize the IE paradigm. Examples of vendors within the IE domain include KnowledgeWare, Texas Instruments, and James Martin Associates. The IE domain has an extended horizontal activity list, which commences with enterprise data modeling prior to any actual project development.

The Object-Oriented (O-O) paradigm is currently on an upsurge, and seems to be growing at a compound rate of more than 15% per year. Currently less than 10% of U.S. software projects use the O-O paradigm, but the number of enterprises who are considering using it or evaluating it is about 25%. Examples of vendors within the O-O domain are Borland, Easel, Microsoft, and ObjectVision. The O-O paradigm has developed its own argot, which includes both special terms and redefinitions of older terms. The O-O paradigm started with a few O-O languages such as SmallTalk, C++, Eiffel, and Objective-C. It now includes O-O analysis, design, and data base components.

The Client-Server paradigm is also on an upsurge. Currently less than 5% of existing applications actually use the client-server paradigm, but the percentage of enterprises who are considering using it or evaluating it is about 30%. As of 1993, separate tool vendors tend to support the client side and the server side, although simultaneous support for both sides exists too. Examples of vendors within the Client-Server domain include many of the more significant data-base vendors such as Oracle, Ingres, and Computer Associates and also vendors such as Easel.

The Expert-System paradigm is expanding slowly, and is now starting to incorporate the older artificial intelligence concept and decision support concept, and the more recent neural-net concept. Expert systems constitute less than 1% of U.S. software projects as of 1993, but the concepts are extremely powerful and far-reaching. Examples of vendors in this domain include AICorp, DEC, and Hewlett-Packard. The expert-system domain has an extended life cycle, including knowledge acquisition. It also includes some new occupation groups, such as knowledge engineers.

The Multi-Media paradigm appears to be poised for an explosion of new applications, new tools, and probably new vendors as well. Multi-media applications deal with sounds, animation, video and photographic images, and a number of other rather complex topics. As of 1993, multi-media appears to be reaching a critical mass of hardware components and software support. Less than one-tenth of 1% of U.S. software projects are multi-media applications in 1993, but by the end of the century the percentage could approach 5%. This may be a fast-growth business. Examples of vendors in the multi-media domain include Microsoft and Borland.

The Pen-Based paradigm is starting to scale up in 1993, as new hardware products and software tools appear. Pen-based applications deal with hand printed or hand written information, and therefore require special approaches including fuzzy logic and pattern recognition. Examples of vendors in the pen-based paradigm include Microsoft and Poquet.

The Virtual Reality paradigm is not yet advanced enough to know if it will be a commercial success. Virtual reality software includes full holographic displays, tactile feedback, and conceivably even odor or taste manipulation. It is premature to talk about vendors for an experimental technology, but due to the military and civilian implications of this technology, quite a lot of money is now going into virtual reality research.

12. **Consulting support**—The software tool and CASE domain is supported by more consultants than almost any technology in human history. As of 1993, there are probably more than 1000 consulting organizations and perhaps 15,000 individual CASE consultants in the U.S. alone. Essentially all CASE and tool vendors have associated "captive" consulting groups which support their proprietary methods and tools. In addition, many industry luminaries such as Dr. Richard Fairley, Dr. Carma McClure, Dr. James Martin, Dr. Roger Pressman, Ed Yourdon, and Tom DeMarco, also consult and speak on CASE and tool-related topics.

13. **Education support**—There is a significant gap between academia and the private sector in education and training in software tools and CASE products, with academia lagging far behind. There are so many possible tools, and the costs are so high, that most universities cannot afford the time or expense of dealing with more than the basics, and often the available tools in universities are older ones as well. A few universities, such as Washington University in St. Louis, Carnegie-Mellon in Pittsburgh, and MIT have extensive tool suites available and up-to-date curricula. However, private educational groups such as Digital Consulting (DCI) and Extended Intelligence, rather than academia, tend to deal with the cutting-edge of software engineering tool and CASE tool issues.

Supplementing the somewhat sparse academic offerings on CASE are a host of private and semi-public courses, conferences, and seminars. To name but a few, the Digital Consulting, Inc. CASE conferences and seminars attract thousands of attendees and hundreds of CASE vendors each year, in both the United States and Europe. The annual IEEE Software Engineering symposia also attract thousands of participants, and have associated seminars as well as the symposia themselves. There are also regional CASE user groups, such as the ones in the New York area, the New Jersey area, the Raleigh area, the Atlanta area, the San Francisco Bay area, and many other regions.

14. **Publication support**—The literature on software tools, CASE, and ancillary topics is enormous and growing rapidly. Over 1000 books are already in print on these topics, and new ones are appearing at a rate that exceeds 10 volumes per month or 120 volumes per year. It is not possible to cite more than the tip of the iceberg in this domain.

Among the best-sellers in this domain for the past few years are Dr. Roger Pressman's *Software Engineering: A Practitioner's Approach* (McGraw-Hill, 1987), Dr. Carma McClure's *CASE is Software Automation* (Prentice Hall, 1989), and Dr. Richard Fairley's *Software Engineering Concepts* (McGraw-Hill, 1985). The IEEE

Press is perhaps the largest publisher of software engineering materials by volume. The annual proceedings of the IEEE Software Engineering Conferences are always interesting, for example.

Paul Tinnirello has edited a massive compendium entitled *Systems Management Development and Support* (Auerbach, 1992) that integrates the views of perhaps 60 authors on tools and approaches for software development and maintenance.

Since so many tools are available, and so many new ones appear monthly, it is useful to acquire one or more catalogs which attempt to stay current. Auerbach, Gartner Group, and Datapro are all widely-cited publishers of software tool evaluations and tool catalogs. Other sources of tool reviews and catalogs are the major CASE journals such as CASE Trends and CASE Outlook (both of which publish annual catalogs). The British OVUM group also publishes tool reviews and intermittent tool catalogs, with special emphasis on CASE and client-server approaches. A very useful book for anyone considering the lease or purchase of CASE tools or other software tools is a rather massive catalog edited by Phil Howard of ACR, *Guide to Software Productivity Aids.* This catalog is published twice a year, and contains summary data on most of the software tools marketed in the United States.

David Marca and Geoffrey Bock's *Groupware: Software for Computer-Supported Cooperative Work* (IEEE Press, 1992) discusses an emerging topic of considerable importance. Dorine Andrews and Naomi Leventhal's *Fusion: Integrating IE, CASE, and JAD* (Yourdon Press, 1993) discusses tool integration in the specialized context of information engineering. Barbara Bouldin's *Agents of Change* (Yourdon Press, 1989) deals with the social changes necessary to handle new tool suites.

Luca-Dan Serbanati's new book *Integrating Tools for Software Development* (Yourdon Press, 1993) takes a holistic approach to the need to integrate large suites of very diverse tools. Also new is D. Schefstrom and G. Van den Brock's *Tool Integration* (John Wiley, 1993).

Once again, new tools and new books on tools are occurring almost daily and it is not possible to do more than recommend that catalogs, book stores, and libraries be scanned often for the latest materials.

15. **Periodical support**—The CASE and software tool domain is supported by more journals and magazines than any other: about 50 different journals as of the middle of 1993. In the CASE domain, the major periodicals are CASE Outlook, CASE Strategies, and CASE Trends. Ed Yourdon's American Programmer magazine is also a good source of information. Various IEEE journals, such as IEEE Spectrum, IEEE Software, and IEEE Transactions on Software Engineering are excellent sources of information. At a somewhat lower level, but quite interesting, are magazines such as Computer Language, PC Magazine, Dr. Dobbs Journal, Windows Magazine, the UNIX Journal, and many more. Many such journals are available on-line via services such as CompuServe or Prodigy. House magazines by computer manufactur-

ers and software vendors are also interesting: the IBM Systems Journal, the Microsoft Systems Journal, the Bell Labs journal, and many others.

16. **Standards support**—There are far too many tools, and they are evolving much too rapidly, for standards to be either complete or even desirable as of 1993. What is useful, although rare, are catalogs of tools which have passed successful benchmarks and have demonstrated their effectiveness. Many large corporations have tool evaluation groups which carry out the benchmarks, and then add successful tools to the corporate catalog of accepted vendors. These are not formal standards, but they are useful.

17. **Professional associations**—Essentially all of the non-profit software professional associations have tool subgroups. Any one of these organizations are concerned with tools: ACM, ADAPSO, ITAA, Software Publishers Association, IEEE, IFPUG. Most large software tool vendors and essentially all computer manufacturers have user groups. Some of the user groups, such as COMMON, GUIDE, and SHARE which are comprised of IBM customers, have many thousands of members. Other examples of non-profit user groups include Borland's, CADRE's, the IEF user group, and the UNISYS user group.

18. **Effectiveness of known therapies**—With hundreds of vendors and thousands of tools, there is no simple answer to this question. Design and specification tools, for example, are quite effective for large systems in excess of 5000 Function Points, but often of marginal utility for small applications of under 100 Function Points. Coding and debugging tools appear to be the most consistently effective, but here there are too many choices to make general statements. Software engineers with less than 10,000 Function Points of support tools are often less productive and have longer schedules than software engineers with more than 25,000 Function Points of support tools. However, this form of analysis is so new that it is premature to make definitive judgments.

19. **Costs of known therapies**—The cost range of software engineering tools is from less than $1.00 per Function Point to more than $20.00 per Function Point. Personal computer and Macintosh developers have the largest selection of low-cost tools (less than $1.00 per Function Point). UNIX developers have quite a few tools available, but the cost of UNIX tools is often in the range of $10.00 per Function Point, so equipping a software engineer is much more expensive than for the PC domain. Mainframe software developers and military software developers must often use more expensive tools (more than $100.00 per Function Point).

It may be seen that a well-equipped software engineer with a tool suite in excess of 25,000 Function Points could accrue one-time costs that range from $25,000 to more than $200,000 (i.e. acquisition costs that range from less than $0.25 per Function Point to more than $25.00 per Function Point.) However, site licenses and volume purchase arrangements can lower the per-seat cost. Annual maintenance and enhancement fees would normally amount to some 10% to 15% of the one-time expenses. The true economics of software engineering tools are not fully understood at this time, but rapid progress is being made in this domain now that functional metrics are being applied to these economic topics.

Another dimension to the economics of tools is the cost of training. Current data indicates that from $0.50 to about $1.00 in training costs must be spent for every dollar spent on tools themselves. A rough rule of thumb is to allow one day of training for every 2000 Function Points of tool capability. Therefore, an abrupt migration to a full I-CASE tool suite containing 25,000 Function Points might require 12 to 13 days of training and hands-on experience to get fully up to speed.

The pay-back period and return on investment in software engineering tools are uncertain as of 1993. In general, software engineers have been undercapitalized and under-equipped for many years. It is suspected from preliminary data that tool suites in excess of 25,000 Function Points will return their value in 18 to 36 months. This same data tends to indicate lower productivity for the first 12 months, due to the need to factor in training and learning-curve escalation.

20. **Long-range prognosis**—The long-range prognosis for software engineering tools is very good. By the end of the century, well-equipped software engineers should have more than 100,000 Function Points of support tools, and most of the current gaps will have been closed. When Function Point analysis is used retrospectively on tool capabilities in the past, the rate of progress for software engineering tools is actually rather rapid. Between 1962 and 1993, the quantity of software engineering tools for a well-equipped programmer went from perhaps 500 Function Points to about 50,000 Function Points: a two-order of magnitude increase in 30 years.

Inadequate Tools and Methods (Technical Documentation)

1. **Definition**—Inadequate automation and methodological approaches applied to the 10 generic activities which software technical writers should be able to perform well: 1) Structuring software documents and document sets for optimal clarity and reader convenience; 2) Freely intermixing text, graphics, images, and tabular materials as the subject matter demands; 3) Cross referencing and cross linking topics within and between documents; 4) Full configuration control of changes and updates; 5) Reference acquisition and fact checking; 6) Index preparation and maintenance; 7) Glossary preparation and maintenance; 8) Validation of all examples and specific instructions; 9) Validation of grammatical usage and reading levels; 10) Validation of spelling accuracy and consistency.

2. **Severity**—The average severity of inadequate technical documentation tools and methods has dropped significantly under the impact of personal computers. As of 1993, the average is about a 3.5 on the following five-point scale:

Severity 1: No automation; typewriters and manual methods only

Severity 2: Basic word-processing automation only

Severity 3: Word processing plus spelling checker only

Severity 4: Word processing and some graphics automation

Severity 5: Word processing, graphics, and limited ancillary tools

3. **Frequency**—The frequency of inadequate software documentation tools varies widely across ten generic activities surrounding software technical writing. Following are U.S. observations based on SPR assessments:

Technical Writing Activity	Average Performance by Software Writers	Percent of Projects Lacking Automation
Document structuring	Poor to Fair	99%
Text, graphics integration	Poor to Excellent	40%
Cross referencing	Poor to Fair	90%
Configuration control	Poor to Good	65%
Reference acquisition	Poor	80%
Index preparation	Poor to Good	50%
Glossary preparation	Poor to Good	65%
Validation of examples	Very Poor	99%
Validation of grammar	Fair to Good	50%
Validation of spelling	Good to Excellent	10%

4. **Occurrence**—The software profession is among the most documentation-intensive industries in all of human history. The total quantity of discrete documents produced for large software projects can exceed 100. The total amount of effort devoted to software paperwork (plans, specifications, user documents) is often greater than the effort devoted to coding, and occasionally exceeds 50% of the total effort applied to software projects.

Some of the more common documents produced in support of software projects include the following:

- Development plans and schedules
- Integration and test plans
- Requirements specifications
- Initial functional specifications
- Final functional specifications
- Software logic specifications
- Data flow specifications
- User's guides
- Reference manuals
- Message manuals
- Programming manuals
- Maintenance manuals
- Training and educational materials

The MIS software community tends to produce the smallest volume of documentation and paperwork in support of software projects, and is also the least sophisticated in terms of documentation technologies.

The military software community tends to produce far and away the greatest volume of paperwork (sometimes more than 400 English words per Ada statement). Documentation automation for military software lags in graphics and usability analysis, but leads in configuration, cross-referencing, and update control.

The systems software community tends to produce enormous volumes of planning documents and specifications, and also fairly large volumes of user documentation and tutorial materials. Systems documentation technology varies from company to company. In general, large corporations do a better job than small companies.

The commercial software community (Microsoft, Borland, Lotus, etc.) are marginally adequate for plans, specifications, and internal documents. They do a slightly better job on user documentation and external tutorial material, but their performance is still much less than desired. Indeed, a robust and growing sub-industry exists of free-lance writers and publishers who supplement the often tedious and poorly structured documents which the software vendors themselves create.

5. **Susceptibility and resistance**—The patterns of susceptibility and resistance to inadequate documentation automation are not fully understood. There is a global shortage of really good technical writers, although not of journeyman technical writers. This means that only companies which recognize the value of excellent documentation, and go out of their way to attract and support capable writing staffs, are likely to achieve consistently good documentation results.

However, there are rapid improvements in the tools and technology for creating technical documentation. The decade from 1980 to 1990 witnessed a burst of new text, graphic, and editing support tools which essentially revolutionized the way technical documents can be produced.

6. **Root causes**—The primary cause of inadequate technical documentation is the widespread inability of human beings to write well, to enjoy writing, or to have any particular innate skill in conveying complicated technical topics by text, graphics, or any other medium.

Approximately, less than 10% of the U.S. population finds any enjoyment in writing, and less than 1% can do it well. Similar percentages no doubt apply to communication via graphics and visual symbols. Given the huge volume of written and graphic material which is produced in support of software projects, there is an obvious imbalance: much of the technical software documentation must perforce be created by people who do not enjoy such work, and who are not very good at it.

7. **Associated problems**—Inadequate document automation is strongly associated with *missed schedules, excessive time to market, long schedules,* and *low user satisfaction.*

Inadequate documentation itself may be caused by *inadequate capital investment,* by *slow technology transfer* and by a chronic problem which is outside the scope of this book: inadequate curricula for training technical communicators.

8. **Cost impact**—The costs of inadequate documentation tools and methods have two major components: 1) Costs that affect document production; 2) Costs that affect document users, and slow down learning or operational performance.

Inadequate document structuring has only a nominal impact on document production costs, but is a major source of user dissatisfaction and user costs. Individual documents or document sets which are poorly organized slow down learning and make day to day usage difficult. Poor document structure can add 10% to 15% to the length of a typical terminal session when using software.

Inadequate text and graphic integration affects both document production costs, and also document utilization efficiency. Manual integration of text, graphics, halftones, tables, etc. can add 25% to more than 70% to the cost of document production, based on the number of elements to be included. A survey by the author of software journal articles noted about 35% graphics content in the articles considered "clearest and most understandable" by readers.

Inadequate cross referencing within a document, and between documents, has only a nominal impact on document production costs, but is a major source of user dissatisfaction and user costs. Poor cross referencing can add up to 5% to the length of a typical terminal session when using software.

Inadequate configuration control of changes to software documentation in response to new product features, corrections, or any other reason can add from 5% up to 10% to the cost of document production during a revision cycle.

Inadequate reference acquisition is a major source of expense for journalists and technical book authors, and a significant source of expense for authors of reference and tutorial materials as well. This factor can add perhaps 10% to the effort and costs of technical book authoring. In addition, poor utilization of references and fact checking can degrade the technical accuracy of publications to unacceptable levels.

Inadequate indexing is one of the most common complaints cited by software users. Poor indexing automation has only about a 1% impact on technical book production costs, but can slow down usage and add to reader expenses by as much as 5%. Poor indexing is particularly troublesome during the start-up period when users are just exploring software capabilities: here the impact on usage can add up to 10% to an average terminal session.

Inadequate glossaries are an endemic problem for software. The rate at which new software terms are being created is still quite large. Several hundred new terms are created on an annual basis. Many common software terms have only ambiguous meanings as of 1993: for example "CASE" or "4th generation" or "full life cycle." Inadequate glossaries add only nominal costs to document development and to document usage, but are frequently annoying.

Inadequate validation of examples is an acute and chronic problem for software technical publications. Nothing is more frustrating to a software user than to follow an example step by step, and find that the example itself contains an error. Failure by software authors to validate every example should be considered to be professional malpractice. The direct cost of validating all examples can add perhaps 5% to the cost of document production. However, incorrect examples can add 5% to 10% to any terminal session where such examples are encountered. This is a major cause of reader and user dissatisfaction with software documentation.

Inadequate grammar checking is a problem for novice or amateur technical writers. Actual mistakes in grammar are scarce, but convoluted syntax and excessive textual complexity are very common. Automation applied to grammar and syntax checking is now quite sophisticated. Using such tools has only a nominal impact on document production (possibly even reducing costs by making editing easier). Convoluted text can add 2% to 5% to the time required to read and learn a technical document, however.

Inadequate spelling checking has become almost non-existent in 1993, due to the fact that on-line dictionaries are available for almost every word processing program on the market. However, personal names, brand names, and many technical terms are not included in standard dictionaries. Spelling problems have only a nominal impact on document production and usage, with one exception: errors in key words or specific parameters can be frustrating to users.

The cumulative impact of these problems can add up to significant totals. A well equipped technical author with a full suite of automated tools available (word processing, graphics support, on-line reference sources, etc.) can produce a technical document better than at any time in human history. Indeed, the advance in technical document production in the three decades from the 1960's through the 1990's is perhaps as profound as the development of the printing press and the development of the typewriter.

On the other hand, there is no empirical evidence that users or readers have achieved substantial gains in reading or learning rates as a result of these same technologies.

Much research remains to be done in the domain of optimizing reading, learning, and knowledge acquisition costs. For example, as of 1993 there is no hard evidence that on-line information is more effective than hard-copy information.

An entirely new set of multi-media capabilities is starting to emerge. Technical authors in the future will utilize animation, sound, full-color graphics, hypertext links among document sections, on-line linkage to executing software to create "live" examples, and many other capabilities that a few years ago might have seemed impossible. Unfortunately, as of 1993, neither the costs nor the value of these new methods are fully understood. It can be anticipated that the production of user documentation will be affected in profound ways, and that the nature of documentation production by the end of the twentieth century may be quite different from past history.

9. **Methods of prevention**—The most effective approach for preventing inadequate technical documentation automation is quite new, having only had published citations since 1991. This new approach is to perform surveys, using functional metrics such as Function Points or Feature Points, of the kinds of tools utilized by software technical authors.

The following table gives preliminary results as of the middle of 1993 in terms of the size ranges of various authoring tools, ranked in descending order by maximum size.

**Software Tools Utilized by Technical Writers and Editors
(Size Range in Function Points)**

Tool Categories	Minimum	Median	Maximum
Desktop Publishing		2000	3000
Word Processing	500	1000	2000
Graphics/Presentations			2000
Spreadsheet			2000
Data Base		1000	1500
Grammar Checkers		750	1000
Dictionary/Thesaurus	300	500	750
Electronic Mail	300	500	750
Appointments/Calendar		300	750
Phone/Address File	100	150	500
Totals	1200	6200	14250

Not all functions are used at every session with a computer, of course. Typical usage patterns for software writers and technical editors would involve three to four hours per day of computer usage, during which time around 3,500 Function Points might be utilized. This is roughly equivalent to a rate that ranges from 900 to 1200 Function Points per hour.

Data from a study carried out by the author in the 1970's on the usage of electronic typewriters versus word-processing systems was retroactively examined, with interesting but arguable results: writers using electronic typewriters can seldom perform work equivalent to more than about 50 to 100 Function Points per hour. It can be crudely hypothesized that a well-equipped technical writer in 1993 is nine to 24 times more productive than a writer from the typewriter era, for the actual tasks of text and graphics production.

Obviously research, interviews, reference checking, fact checking, copy reading, and many other manual and knowledge-based activities are outside the domain of this analysis. Even so, it is interesting to have a quantified approach for exploring software usage patterns by various knowledge-based workers such as technical authors.

10. **Methods of control**—The primary difficulties of improving software documentation automation are cultural and financial.

The cultural problem of inadequate document automation is that many executives do not recognize how important good documentation methods can be, in terms of both productivity and user satisfaction.

The financial problem is a derivative of the cultural problem, and manifests itself in the fact that many technical documentation departments are under-staffed, under-capitalized, and under-equipped for the work at hand. This phenomenon should not occur, since documentation tools are actually rather inexpensive compared to software engineering tools, management tools, and other kinds of tool suites such as CASE, CAD, and so forth.

Excellent software documentation tools are available on personal computers as commercial off the shelf (COTS) packages for costs of less than $0.10 per Function Point. This means that even the most powerful documentation tool suite would total to less than $7,500 per seat.

11. **Product support**—As of 1993, more than 50 vendors and 500 products are available in the general area of technical documentation support tools. New products are coming out at monthly intervals, and new vendors are arriving several times a year. This is a dynamic and fast growing market.

Examples of some of the more common software documentation tools include: 2167A Tool Set, ABSTRACT, Adobe Illustrator, Applause II, Arts & Letters, Automatic Documentation System (ADS), Aldus Persuasion, Ami Pro, AutoDoc, Correct Grammar, Corel Draw, DOCGEN, DOCPAK, Document Publishing System (DOC), DOCU/MANAGER, Documentation Aid, FrameMaker, Grammatik, Microsoft Word, NAPER-DOC, Pathfinder, PolyDoc, Power Point, Rightwriter, ROBOT/3000, VAX Document, VIA/SmartDoc, Word Perfect, and Word Star.

The market for document support software has long been fragmented into six discrete segments which should logically be integrated. The four major fragments have been: 1) Word processing and ancillary tools (dictionaries, thesaurus, grammar checkers, etc.); 2) Art, free-form graphics and ancillary tools; 3) Tables, spreadsheets, business graphics and ancillary tools; 4) Desktop publishing and ancillary tools; 5) Configuration control and multi-document cross-reference and update support; 6) On-line reference sources such as Lockheed Dialog, Ziffnet, and the like.

12. **Consulting support**—Consulting in the technical documentation arena has been a niche practice dominated by individual consultants or small specialist consulting groups. The large consulting organizations (Andersen, Ernst & Young, A.D. Little, etc.) usually have no practices in the technical documentation domain. Some of the documentation tool vendors (such as Microsoft and Word Perfect) have captive consulting groups which concentrate on the vendors' tools, but are often useful within that context. Some of the documentation consulting groups include Mapping, Inc., Comtech Services, and the Document Design Center.

13. **Education support**—Technical communication for software is an awkward gap in most university curricula. Software engineering schools, by and large, have comparatively few courses available at all on software documentation. Journalism schools and departments may offer courses in technical writing, but seldom are these aimed at software. Perhaps the best source of training in this area are the inhouse courses run by computer companies and software producers such as AT&T, IBM, DEC and Microsoft.

14. **Publication support**—Software documentation, surprisingly, is severely underrepresented in the software engineering literature. There are many books which

are narrow in focus and deal with specific forms of documentation, such as the set of documents required by the DoD 2167A standard, or those to be produced when using Object-Oriented (OO) Analysis or Information Engineering (IE). There are few books which cover the entire gamut of plans, specifications, user documents, on-line HELP, and other broad topics. Robert Glass' *Software Communication Skills* (Prentice-Hall, 1988) is rather broad in coverage. Dr. James Martin and Dr. Carma McClure's *Diagramming Techniques for Analysts and Programmers* (Prentice Hall, 1985) is specialized, but does a rather good job within its niche. Lawrence Peters' *Software Design: Methods and Techniques* (Yourdon Press, 1981) is also specialized, but at least recognizes the need to explore multiple alternatives. Haramundanis's *Art of Technical Documentation* (Digital Press, 1992) is a good overview of computer and software user documentation methods. Darrow et al.'s *Digital Stylebook* (Digital Press) is an example of a useful genre; standardized styles for capitalization, nomenclature and usage, among other things.

The IEEE Press often publishes useful books that are compendiums of many different authors' articles. Freeman and Wasserman's *Software Design Techniques* (IEEE Press, 1983) and Neilsen, Shriver, and Rosenblum's *Visualization in Scientific Computing* (IEEE Press, 1990) are examples. Two books by the author, Capers Jones, attempt to quantify the number and sizes of various kinds of software documents, and the costs of their production: *Programming Productivity* (McGraw-Hill, 1986) and *Applied Software Measurement* (McGraw-Hill, 1991).

Caroline Chappell and Ronnie McBryde's *Open Document Architecture* (OVUM, 1991) discusses fairly recent trends in document interchange methods.

Susan Schultz, Jennifer Darrow, Frank Kavanaugh, and Marjorie Morse of DEC have published two relevant books: *The Digital Style Guide* (Digital Press, 1993) and *The Digital Technical Documentation Handbook* (Digital Press, 1993). Scott Jones et al. from DEC have also published *Developing International User Information* (Digital Press, 1992) which discusses software documents in a global context.

It should be noted that optical storage, multi-media applications, virtual reality, animation, hypertext, fractal-based storage of graphic images, and many other emerging technologies may change software documentation in profound ways. As of 1993, it is premature to judge the rate and depth of the evolution of documentation methods.

15. **Periodical support**—The major software engineering journals occasionally run articles on software documentation, but not very often. These journals do review new releases of word processors, graphics packages, and other ancillary tools in almost every issue. A fairly large and growing set of specialist journals support the software documentation community in various flavors. Examples include Desktop Communication, Desktop Publishing, and New Media. Several vendors have their own house journals that are often useful and interesting. For example, Word Perfect has a house journal that is occasionally even sold at news stands.

16. **Standards support**—There seem to be no standards that encompass all of the 100 or so kinds of documents which might surround and support software products. There are a number of standards that deal with specialized forms of documentation, however. The DoD 2167A standard, for example, defines the 20 or so documents that must be produced for U.S. military software. The ISO 9000–9004 standards define the set of documents required for ISO certification. There are also quasi-standards, such as the materials dealing with what must be submitted for Baldrige awards. Since the fundamental technology of software documentation is evolving rapidly, it would be premature in 1993 to establish rigid standards.

17. **Professional associations**—The ACM has a special interest group on software documentation, SIGDOC. At the national level, the Society of Technical Communication is useful. There are also a number of regional non-profit associations which support documentation and technical writing personnel. The Society of Documentation Professionals (SDP) in the Boston area is a typical example. There are also user groups for some of the more widely utilized documentation tools, such as Word Perfect, Microsoft Word, and the like. Some of the large non-profit associations such as the IEEE have special-interest sub-groups which deal with document-related issues.

18. **Effectiveness of known therapies**—With scores of vendors and hundreds of tools, there is no simple answer to this question. Design and specification tools, for example, are quite effective for large systems over 5000 Function Points, but of marginal utility for small applications under 100 Function Points. Word processors and graphics tools are consistently effective, but here there are too many choices to make general statements. Grammar checkers have substantial value for novice or amateur writers, but have a negligible impact on experienced professional technical communicators. Technical authors with less than 5,000 Function Points of support tools are often less productive and have longer schedules than software authors with more than 10,000 Function Points of support tools. However, this form of analysis is so new that it is premature to make definitive judgments.

19. **Costs of known therapies**—The cost range of software technical documentation tools is from less than $0.10 per Function Point to more than $25.00 per Function Point. Personal computer and Macintosh developers have the largest selection of low-cost tools (less than $0.10 per Function Point). UNIX personnel have a large tool selection available, but UNIX tools may exceed $1.00 per Function Point and some exceed $10.00 per Function Point. Mainframe software technical authors must often use more expensive tools (more than $15.00 per Function Point) because of the normal pricing differential for mainframe applications. A well-equipped software technical author with a tool suite in excess of 15,000 Function Points could accrue one-time costs that range from $3,750 to more than $15,000 (i.e. acquisition costs that range from $0.10 per Function Point to $15.00 per Function Point.) However, site licenses and volume purchase arrangements can lower the per-seat cost. Annual maintenance and enhancement fees would normally

amount to some 10% to 15% of the one-time expenses. The true economics of software documentation tools are not fully understood as of 1993, but rapid progress is being made now that functional metrics are being applied to documentation topics.

The pay-back period and return on investment in software documentation tools are uncertain as of 1993 but appear to be only a matter of a few months. In general, software documentation specialists have been under-capitalized and under-equipped for many years. It is suspected from preliminary data that documentation tool suites in excess of 10,000 Function Points will return their value in 6 to 12 months.

20. **Long-range prognosis**—The long-range prognosis for software documentation tools is very good. By the end of the century, well-equipped software documentation specialists and authors may have more than 50,000 Function Points of support tools available. Whole new vistas of tools for dealing with animation, full-color graphics, hypertext links, and new visualization methods are on the horizon. When Function Point analysis is used retrospectively on documentation tool capabilities in the past, the rate of progress for software documentation tools indicates one of the most rapid technical progressions in human history. Between 1962 and 1993, the quantity of software documentation tools for a well-equipped technical author went from essentially zero to perhaps 15,000 Function Points. Few other kinds of knowledge work have had such a dramatic increase in automation capabilities.

CHAPTER 38

Lack of Reusable Architecture

1. **Definition**—A) The unconscious mind-set of the software community which has focused on the development of unique, custom artifacts rather than reusable components; B) The lack of a social and cultural infrastructure for supporting the usage of reusable artifacts within corporations and government groups; C) The lack of standard approaches for requirements, design, and code creation which assume that usage of reusable artifacts are normal parts of the software process.

2. **Severity**—The most appropriate way to consider the severity of the lack of reusable architecture is to evaluate the percentage of reusable artifacts within applications compared to the potential for reuse based on the number of common, widely known functions and standard deliverables produced with the application. The average severity appears to be about a two on the following five-point scale:

Severity 1: Application contains < 05% reused material; potential is > 95%

Severity 2: Application contains < 10% reused material; potential is > 90%

Severity 3: Application contains < 15% reused material; potential is > 85%

Severity 4: Application contains < 20% reused material; potential is > 75%

Severity 5: Application contains < 25% reused material; potential is > 65%

3. **Frequency**—The frequency of lack of a reusable architecture or framework tends to vary with specific deliverables that are part of software projects. Following are the results of observations by Software Productivity Research on the percent of a sample of 300 companies exploring each of the 10 subdomains of software reusability.

As may be seen, reuse of various software artifacts such as data and code is fairly common within the software industry, but this kind of reusability tends to be spontaneous and unplanned. Formal exploration of the discipline of reuse, and the creation of a full architectural framework to support reuse among all components is much more rare.

Reusable Material	Percent of Enterprises Investigating	Percent of Projects Utilizing
Reusable architecture	1%	1%
Reusable data	25%	50%
Reusable designs	3%	5%
Reusable code	20%	50%
Reusable estimates	5%	20%
Reusable human interfaces	10%	50%
Reusable plans	5%	10%
Reusable requirements	2%	10%
Reusable user documents	2%	10%
Reusable test cases	10%	20%

4. **Occurrence**—Within the client set of Software Productivity Research, there are very wide ranges of interest in and usage of reusable materials. In general large enterprises with more than 1000 software professionals, and producers of systems and military software are much more likely to be exploring software reuse than small information systems providers. Essentially 100% of SPR's clients who employ more than 5000 software professionals have formal, on-going reusability research programs underway. By contrast, for SPR clients with less than 500 software employees, formal research programs on reusability are found in less than 10% of the enterprises. There are also national differences in reusability research, with this topic being a major subject in both Japan and the United States.

5. **Susceptibility and resistance**—Reusability is a cultural topic as well as a technical topic. Therefore susceptibility to lack of reuse is greatest among enterprises which have the view that "what we do is so unique that reuse is impossible." Another and surprising aspect of susceptibility and resistance is that companies with good measurement programs are much more likely to have research programs in reuse than companies which lack measurements.

The most resistant enterprises of all are those which have had a reuse program underway for at least five years, and have already established a library of certified reusable components that include requirements, design, plans, estimates, test cases, and documents as well as source code.

In the United States, the Department of Defense and the various military services have active programs underway to explore and expand reusability. This appears to be one of the few domains where government and military software research may be in advance of the civilian sector.

Companies that are exploring and moving toward object-oriented development are somewhat more resistant to lack of reusable architecture than companies that have not yet considered the object-oriented paradigm.

Susceptibility and resistance to lack of reusable architecture varies from industry to industry. Public utilities and police agencies, for example, tend to need the same kinds of software all over the country, and hence tend to explore reusability as a way of controlling costs. Further, with large numbers of possible clients, vendors have started to provide various kinds of reusable artifacts.

Industries with the greatest reuse potential are those where even direct competitors use similar software: banks, insurance companies, hospitals, state governments, municipal governments, public utilities, retail and wholesale chains, defense contractors, and computer manufacturers are examples of industries where reusability research is active and energetic, even if not yet totally successful.

Companies that measure software projects well know how much they spend on software, and also how much they spend on the subactivities of software projects such as paperwork and defect removal.

When the economic value of reuse is explored via measurements, it is necessary to make two major changes in the way software is measured: 1) Measurements should switch from what is *developed* and should instead measure what is *delivered;* 2) The usage of "lines of code" should be abandoned, and modern functional metrics should be adopted. This second change is because the bulk of the costs of large systems are not related to the code, but center in paper-intensive activities and defect removal operations where LOC metrics are known to be paradoxical and incorrect. Further, with some modern languages such as object-oriented languages, application generators, and data base languages LOC metrics are quite misleading.

6. **Root causes**—The primary cause for lack of reusability architecture seems to be because software developed along the lines of a craft, rather than along the lines of engineering or manufacturing. The education, training, and mental attitude of software engineers approximates that of a skilled carpenter or cabinet maker rather than that of an electrical or mechanical engineer. Software engineers are taught techniques for designing and building software artifacts *by themselves*. Electrical engineers and mechanical engineers, on the other hand, are taught how to design components that can be *manufactured*.

Continuing briefly with this analogy, consider the number and volume of the catalogs of various kinds of electrical and mechanical equipment which can be purchased off the shelf and then become part of electrical or mechanical devices. Now consider the number and volume of catalogs of reusable materials available to software engineers. As of 1993, there seems to be a variance of several orders of magnitude between the reusable materials commercially available to the software community, and the reusable materials available to electrical or mechanical engineers.

A secondary root cause in the United States is that U.S. anti-trust laws more or less eliminate cross-company reusability research. In Japan, even competing companies are able to perform research in various aspects of software reuse, and that factor appears to be putting Japan ahead of the United States in establishing high-volume reuse.

All human artifacts which are custom built by skilled craftsmen are fairly expensive to produce. Consider these cost differentials: A) Costs of constructing a Formula 1 race car, versus normal assembly-line manufacture; B) Costs of constructing a 12-meter racing yacht versus the costs of a normal class-built boat; C) Costs of designing and constructing custom homes, versus the costs of normal tract homes.

7. **Associated problems**—Lack of reusable architecture and other materials are key components of *low productivity, long schedules, excessive time to market,* and *low quality.* Lack of certified deliverables are also a secondary contributor to the problem of *high maintenance costs.* Lack of reusable architecture is almost universally associated with the related problems of *lack of reusable designs (blueprints), lack of reusable requirements, lack of reusable data, lack of reusable test cases,* and *lack of reusable plans and historical data (templates),* which are endemic to the software industry.

   Lack of reusable architecture itself is often caused by *inadequate software engineering curricula, slow technology transfer, inadequate capital investment,* and occasionally by *technical staff malpractice* or *management malpractice.* Major contributors to lack of reusable architecture are *inaccurate metrics* and *inadequate measurement.* Measuring development with LOC metrics conceals the value of reuse; measurement should be switched to what is delivered, and normalized using functional metrics to see the value of reusability.

8. **Cost impact**—The overall costs of lack of reusable architecture, and all other aspects of reuse, can be quantified and visualized by means of functional metrics.

   As of 1993, the average cost to build one Function Point in the United States is around $900. To simplify the following illustration, it will be rounded up to make an even $1000 per Function Point. Following are the approximate costs of the major sub-elements of this cost with and without full reusability.

   The economics of using reusable material are highly advantageous. However, the costs of constructing reusable material are much higher than ordinary construction of software today. Each deliverable item must be planned and constructed for reuse in advance, and that adds a premium of 50% to 100% to the initial construction cost and schedule requirements.

   The greatest barrier to effective reuse in most organizations is short-sightedness. Reusable artifacts benefit future users, but have a negative impact when they are first created. Many companies and industries lack the vision to fund and create a library of reusable components. They also fail to set aside the time necessary to certify reusable artifacts to ensure that such materials can safely be used across multiple applications.

Cost Per Function Point With and Without Reusability

Activity	Without Reusability	With Full Reusability
Requirements	$100	$25
Design	$200	$10
Development	$200	$20
Defect Removal	$300	$30
Documentation	$100	$25
Management	$100	$15
Subtotal	$1000	$125
Year 1 Maintenance	$150	$15
Year 2 Maintenance	$200	$10
Year 3 Maintenance	$300	$10
Year 4 Maintenance	$350	$10
Year 5 Maintenance	$400	$05
Subtotal	$1500	$50
TOTAL	$2500	$175

9. **Methods of prevention**—Prevention of low levels of reusable architectural thinking at the enterprise level requires the following sequence: A) Senior management should support a formal reusability program encompassing all software artifacts; B) Senior management should fund a formal reusability program (this is the most important point); C) Existing applications should be surveyed for functions and deliverables which occur with high frequency across multiple applications; D) Functions and deliverables with high-frequency of usage should be carefully acquired, certified, and fully documented. CAUTION—do not attempt to extract and reuse modules from aging, unstructured applications. E) Certification is very critical—it is dangerous to reuse uncertified modules or functions. The certification should cover quality, functionality, connection protocols, and lack of viral contamination; F) A formal reusable artifact library for text, graphics, test materials, and code with browsing capabilities should be created; G) A formal public-relations campaign should be mounted, to prepare the enterprise culture for the move toward reuse; H) A formal user list should be created, so that if errors or problems are noted in a reusable module it can be recalled and all users notified; I) The costs or charge back system for accessing the reusable code library should be worked out; J) Corporate software productivity measurement programs should be converted from measuring "development productivity" to measuring "delivery productivity" so that credit is received for utilizing reusable components.

Moving from step A to step J in a large company or government agency is normally an 18- to 36-month sequence, and costs from a few thousand dollars for a small company up to many millions for an organization the size of the U.S. Department of Defense.

10. **Methods of control**—Once a project is developed without reusable components, it is too late. There are no effective after the fact controls.

11. **Product support**—The products that have done the most to promote reusability at the application level are operating systems. Without MS/DOS, UNIX, OS/2, VMS, MVS, and the like, there would probably be no commercial software industry.

  Most major corporations have on-going programs to develop reusable materials. For example, within the United States, there is active research underway in reusability methods at Andersen Consulting, AT&T, IBM, and Microsoft.

  At the level of reusable modules or specific functions, languages and associated products tend to facilitate reuse. There are many products that support reusable code directly or indirectly for specific languages and compilers. Many vendors such as Borland, Microsoft, Stepstone, etc. market class libraries and reusable modules in support of languages such as Ada, Object PASCAL, Visual Basic, C++, Objective C, and the like.

  Quite a lot of government and military software is in the public domain, and hence potentially reusable. Several companies and catalogs of reusable government components are now being produced or gearing up.

  Indirect support for reusability includes library management tools and configuration control tools for keeping track of libraries of certified, reusable modules. Here too there are many choices.

  The tool suites aimed at restructuring, reverse engineering, and re-engineering of aging software turn out to be synergistic with reusability. These tools are very helpful in identifying candidate reusable modules that occur with high frequency in existing applications. A major new market for such tools may occur when they are tuned to identify candidate reusable modules and then re-engineer and certify them.

  Some of the newer concepts that can support reusability include the On-Line Linking and Embedding (OLE) protocol and neural net architectures. Also massively parallel computer architectures are synergistic with reusability, since one of the useful aspects of reusable modules is that they can often execute in parallel.

  Research into reuse is inconsistent from topic to topic. For example, many groups are exploring reusable source code, and quite a few are exploring reusable designs. However, reusable requirements, reusable test cases, reusable plans, and reusable documentation are seldom cited in the literature and SPR's consulting staff reports little actual research into these topics among clients surveyed.

12. **Consulting support**—Most of the vendors of reusable materials and reuse support tools have consulting and education groups also. A number of management consultants and consulting companies also specialize in reusability. For example, Andersen Consulting is both a researcher into reuse and also has consultants who specialize in this topic.

13. **Education support**—One of the many historical gaps in academic training for software engineers and programmers is the absence of courses such as, "Designing, building, and maintaining reusable material." This gap in academia is slowly starting to be overcome. Also commercial education providers, such as software vendors, and companies such as Dr. Carma McClure's Extended Intelligence, offer commercial courses in reuse.

14. **Publication support**—The body of literature on reusability is growing rapidly, and new books are appearing at the rate of two or three per year. A sample of recent titles include Dr. T.J. Biggerstaff and Dr. A.J. Perlis' massive two-volume work, *Software Reusability* (Addison Wesley, 1989); Dr. Will Tracz's, *Software Reuse—Emerging Technology* (IEEE Press, 1988); Dr. Peter Freeman's well-known *Software Reusability* (IEEE Press, 1987), and Dr. Carma McClure's popular *3 R's of Software Engineering: Reusability, Re-engineering, Repository* (Prentice-Hall, 1992).

Since one of the virtues of the object-oriented paradigm is facile reusability, this technology should be included in all reusability research efforts. However, the literature on the object-oriented paradigm is increasing almost exponentially, so it is necessary to make frequent visits to libraries and book stores to stay current. A few representative titles which overlap the architecture domain include Stephen Mellor and Sallyi Shlaer's *Object Lifecycles: Modelling the World in States* (Yourdon Press, 1992). Ed Yourdon and Peter Coad's *Object-Oriented Analysis* (Yourdon Press, 1991) is also of interest. James Martin, the well known guru and popularizer, covers the O-O paradigm too. His *Object-Oriented Analysis and Design* (James Martin Books, 1992) is an example of a fairly clear explication. The ITT Programming Technology Center was a pioneer in O-O methods during the late 1970's and early 1980's (the Objective C language was invented within ITT). Dr. Brad Cox's *Object-Oriented Programming: An Evolutionary Approach* (Addison Wesley, 1987) shows the thinking of yet another ITT graduate.

There are some major gaps in the software literature on reusability, however: A) What actual functions occur with the greatest frequency in software applications and hence should be reused? B) What is the average and maximum amount of reused code in common applications? C) How many modules are required in a full reusable code library? D) How does the performance of reusable modules compare to custom modules for the same functions? E) What is the synergy between reusable modules and massively parallel computing environments? F) What is the prognosis for reusable test cases? G) How can reusable data be linked to reusable code? H) What is happening in the domains of reusable requirements and design? I) What is happening in the domains of reusable plans and estimates?

15. **Periodical support**—Reusability has become so significant that many journals either have special issues devoted to the topic, or frequent articles. Examples of journals where reusability is frequently discussed include Ed Yourdon's American Programmer, Computer Language, the IEEE Transactions on Software Engineering, and Software magazine. House journals of major vendors such as DEC, IBM,

Microsoft, etc. also contain articles on reusability from time to time. Military software journals, such as STSC Crosstalk often have feature articles on reusability.

16. **Standards support**—As of 1993, there are no known general standards published by ANSI, DoD, IEE, IEEE, ISO, or any other standards organization that deals explicitly with all reusable deliverables. However, many specific standards and protocols are in fact aimed at facilitating reusability at either the module or product levels: IBM's SNA architecture is an example.

17. **Professional associations**—Interestingly, an association was formed as long ago as the 1950's to facilitate reusability of similar applications among companies and government agencies performing similar software activities. This association is SHARE, the non-profit association of IBM scientific software users. User groups and associations of other computer manufacturers, such as DECUS for Digital Equipment, also are concerned with reusability. Some of the "open-system" vendor groups in the U.S. and in Japan are also concerned with reusability. So far as can be determined as of 1993, there is no specific professional association devoted to reusability. There are special-interest groups on reusability within many professional associations, however; for example the ACM, the IEEE, and even local groups such as the Boston Computer Society.

18. **Effectiveness of known therapies**—The economic effectiveness of reuse appears to correlate directly with the volume of reused material in applications. Those applications where reusable designs, code, documents, and test material exceeds 50% of the total volume often have net productivity rates in excess of 35 Function Points per month. Since the overall U.S. average productivity rate as of 1991 was about 5 Function Points per month, this is a significant difference. An important but unanswered question as of 1992 is what is the maximum amount of reusability that is theoretically possible in general-purpose applications, and can it approach 100%.

19. **Costs of known therapies**—Spontaneous and private reuse by experienced software personnel costs essentially nothing. Formal large-scale reusability programs that affect an entire corporation can range in cost from a few thousand dollars to many millions of dollars, depending upon the size of the enterprise. While the costs can be quantified for any specific enterprise or work group, it is difficult to develop generic guidelines.

   An interesting but unanswered question as of 1993 would be the commercial price of reusable components if they are commercially marketed. So far as can be determined, the market costs of reusable plans, estimates, test cases, documents, and designs are essentially unexplored. Reusable code modules are starting to appear, and are being offered at prices between 1/100th and 1/5th of normal development costs.

20. **Long-range prognosis**—Reusability is a very important topic and so many companies and government agencies are performing active research that optimism

appears justified. However, research in Japan may be even more intensive than research in the United States. Further, the Japanese business culture more or less lacks the concept of anti-trust, so Japanese research in reuse tends to cross multiple companies far more often than U.S. research. The best-case scenario would be that reusable deliverables will constitute more than 50% of the volume of all new software applications by the end of the century. Another reason for optimism is that software vendors have discovered that there is a lot of money to be made from marketing reusable artifacts such as software cost templates, software design blueprints, reusable code, and reusable test materials. The profit motive is an even stronger reason for optimism than on-going scientific research. The technologies of fully reusable architecture encompassing reusable data, documents, code, reusable designs (blueprints), and reusable plans (templates) are all synergistic and closely intertwined.

Lack of Reusable Code

1. **Definition**—A) Widespread failure by software development organizations to establish and utilize libraries of certified reusable modules for standard functions that occur within many applications; B) Widespread failure by software engineering schools to teach reusability concepts or explore patterns of potential reuse; C) Partial failure by software compiler and language vendors to market or make available reusable modules or standard functions; D) Failure by various standards organizations to establish meaningful standards or protocols to facilitate reuse; E) Widespread failure by professional software engineers to utilize reusable modules when they are available; F) Any common, generic application (i.e. billing system, PBX, compiler, etc.) that contains less than 35% reused code.

2. **Severity**—The most appropriate way to consider the severity of the lack of reusable code is to evaluate the percentage of reused code within applications compared to the potential for reuse based on the number of common, widely known functions within the application. The average severity appears to be about a 3.5 on the following five-point scale:

   Severity 1: Application contains < 05% reused code; potential is > 95%

   Severity 2: Application contains < 10% reused code; potential is > 90%

   Severity 3: Application contains < 15% reused code; potential is > 85%

   Severity 4: Application contains < 20% reused code; potential is > 75%

   Severity 5: Application contains < 25% reused code; potential is > 65%

3. **Frequency**—Lack of reusable code has been one of the major stumbling blocks to improved productivity and quality for more than 20 years. (Software developed more than 20 years ago, on the average, was so poorly structured and had such high defect levels that reuse would have been dangerous and unwise.) Prior to the advent of personal computers in 1981, the lack of reusable code was endemic to the industry and the frequency of the problem exceeded 90%. (That is, 90% of the applications which might have benefited from reusable code did not in fact use any.) Under the combined impact of companies such as Borland and Microsoft

331

marketing reusable functions in Basic and Pascal for personal computer applications, and the emergence of object-oriented languages and Ada, the frequency of this problem has been cut in half as of about 1991. There is a strong probability that the frequency will be cut in half again by the end of the century.

4. **Occurrence**—Historically, lack of reusable code was endemic to the software industry and affected MIS applications, systems software, commercial software, and military software with approximately equal frequency. Within the last 10 years, there have been technology changes which have altered the distribution of this problem. In the MIS world, mainframe COBOL applications still suffer from a fairly widespread lack of reusable code, and still amount to about half of all MIS applications. Other languages and application generators, however, do provide increasing volumes of reusable code. In the systems software and commercial software world, the advent of C, C++, Objective-C and other object-oriented languages which support inheritance and class libraries have increased the available volume of reusable code by perhaps an order of magnitude, compared to about 1980. For military software, reusable Ada modules are also starting to have an impact, and the volume of reusable code for military software has increased by several hundred percent, compared to 1980.

5. **Susceptibility and resistance**—Mainframe applications written in PL/I or Assembler Language are the most susceptible software projects to low volumes of reusable code. COBOL, FORTRAN, ALGOL, CHILL, and other "classic" third-generation languages are also susceptible to the problem of low volumes of reusable code. COBOL is the most resistant of the third-generation languages.

Object-oriented languages such as ACTOR, C++, Objective-C, SMALLTALK, and the like are highly resistant to this problem, and Ada is fairly resistant. Application and program generators are also fairly resistant, and some indeed support reusability explicitly and hence are quite resistant.

6. **Root causes**—The root causes of low levels of reusable code have technical, educational, business, and cultural components. The technical components include: A) the lack of a good generic catalog of standard functions that occur with high frequency in many applications; B) the fact that unstructured, carelessly developed code is intrinsically hazardous to reuse. The educational component is driven by the technical component, and manifests itself in the fact that the number of university-level courses in the U.S. on reusability is only slightly above zero. Therefore most graduate software engineers have had no academic grounding in this topic. The business component is that establishing a reusable code library of certified modules is fairly expensive (from perhaps $100,000 to more than $1 million) and most companies have not allocated any funding for this.

Further, the productivity measurement practices of many companies focus on "development" rather than on "delivery" and hence give no credit for reuse, since the reusable modules were not developed for specific applications. The cultural component is that many programmers are fairly egotistical, and hence believe that they can program a given function better than any reusable module can.

7. **Associated problems**—Lack of certified reusable code modules is a key component of *low productivity, long schedules, excessive time to market,* and *low quality.* Lack of certified reusable code modules is a secondary contributor to the problem of *high maintenance costs.* Lack of reusable code is almost universally associated with the related problems of *lack of reusable designs (blueprints)* and *lack of reusable plans and historical data (templates),* both of which are endemic to the software industry.

Lack of reusable code itself is often caused by *lack of reusable architecture, inadequate software engineering curricula, slow technology transfer, inadequate capital investment,* and occasionally by *technical staff malpractic* or *management malpractice.* A major contributor to lack of reusable code are the factors of *inaccurate metrics* and *inadequate measurement.* (Measuring development with LOC metrics conceals the value of reuse; measurement should be switched to what is delivered, and normalized using functional metrics to see the value of reusability.)

8. **Cost impact**—The economic impact of reusability can be quantified with fairly good precision using standard manufacturing economics and functional metrics. The normal U.S. cost in 1993 for developing an "average" module of 500 source code statements or 5 Function Points is about $2,500. This is equivalent to about $500 per Function Point for the activities of module-level design, coding, and testing.

The cost of developing and certifying a reusable module of 500 source code statements or 5 Function Points is about $5,000. (Reusable code modules should be certified to approximate zero-defect status.) Thus the initial manufacturing cost of a reusable module is about $1000 per Function Point for the activities of module-level design, coding, testing, and certification, which is twice as expensive as building a normal, non-reusable module.

The economy of reusability can be quantified by evaluating the "cost per application usage" figure: if the module is used 10 times, its cost per application drops to $100, which is substantially below the cost of unique development. If the reusable module is utilized 100 to 1000 times, its cost per application rate would be $10.00 and $1.00, respectively.

Expressed on a per Function Point basis, normal development runs from $600 to $1200 per Function Point in 1993. Building a module specifically to be reused, and hence certifying it to near zero-defect status, will cost from $800 to $2000 per Function Point. However, once available, reusable modules may be acquired by future applications for declining costs based on the number of users. Conceivably, with high enough usage volumes, the costs could drop below $1.00 per Function Point.

Commercial personal-computer software provides a fairly clear picture of the value of large-scale reusability. As it happens, spreadsheets such as Lotus, Excel and Quattro, and word processors such as Word Perfect, Microsoft Word, Textor, contain roughly 1000 Function Points. The "street price" of these personal-computer tools is normally in the vicinity of $300. Any customer of such PC software, therefore, is spending about $0.30 per Function Point. Since it normally takes more than 100 source code statements in a procedural language to code one Function Point, some personal computer software packages are being marketed for as little as $0.03 per source code statement.

9. **Methods of prevention**—For new software projects that are still in requirements or design phase, a straight-forward preventive approach for subsequent lack of reusability is to select a language or generator where reusable code is plentiful, such as Ada, Object PASCAL, C++, Objective-C, SMALLTALK, various generators and 4GLs, and the like. Although empirical data is sparse and incomplete, it would appear that a set of about 150 reusable modules or functions are sufficient to create about 85% of the code in any normal application. The other 15% may require custom development work.

 Prevention of low levels of reusable code at the enterprise level requires the following sequence: A) Senior management should support and fund a formal reusability program; B) Existing applications should be surveyed for modules which occur with high frequency across multiple applications; C) Modules or functions with high-frequency of usage should either be purchased from a reliable vendor, or should be carefully developed, certified, and fully documented. (CAUTION—do not attempt to extract and reuse modules from aging, unstructured applications.) D) Certification is very critical—it is dangerous to reuse uncertified modules or functions. The certification should cover quality, functionality, connection protocols, and lack of viral contamination; E) A formal reusable code library with browsing capabilities should be created; F) A formal public-relations campaign should be mounted, to prepare the corporate culture for the move toward reuse; G) A formal user list should be created, so that if errors or problems are noted in a reusable module it can be recalled and all users notified; H) The costs or charge back system for accessing the reusable code library should be worked out; I) Corporate software productivity measurement programs should be converted from measuring "development productivity" to measuring "delivery productivity" so that credit is received for using reusable components.

 Moving from step A to step I in a large company or government agency is normally an 18- to 36-month sequence, and costs from a few thousand dollars for a small company up to many millions for an organization the size of the U.S. Department of Defense.

10. **Methods of control**—Once a project is hard coded without reusable modules, it is too late. There are no effective controls, other than conversion, re-engineering, or redevelopment.

11. **Product support**—The products that have done the most to promote reusability at the application level are operating systems. Without MS/DOS, UNIX, OS/2, VMS, MVS, and the like, there would probably be no commercial software industry.

At the level of reusable modules or specific functions, languages and associated products tend to facilitate reuse. There are many products that support reusable code directly or indirectly for specific languages and compilers. Many vendors such as Borland, Microsoft, and Stepstone, market class libraries and reusable modules in support of languages such as Ada, Object PASCAL, Visual Basic, C++, Objective C, and the like.

It is a curious omission as of 1993 that the CASE and I-CASE vendors are only beginning to provide formal support for reusability, and there are still gaps in the kinds of support needed. The missing elements for reusability support in typical CASE tool suites include: A) Support for certification and quality control of reusable components; B) Support for associating reusable code, designs, documents, and other artifacts into a cohesive whole; C) Support for selecting and incorporating reusable components while developing new applications (this latter problem is starting to be overcome).

Indirect support for reusability includes library management tools and configuration control tools for keeping track of libraries of certified, reusable modules and their usage. Once an enterprise commits to a reusability program, it is necessary to keep "where used" lists of all reused artifacts, so that recall notices can be sent in case of problems. Here too there are many choices, although few that are optimal for supporting libraries of certified reusable components.

The tool suites aimed at restructuring, reverse engineering, and re-engineering of aging software turn out to be synergistic with reusability. These tools are very helpful in identifying candidate reusable modules that occur with high frequency in existing applications. A major new market for such tools may occur when they are tuned to identify candidate reusable modules and then re-engineer and certify them.

Some of the newer concepts that can support reusability include the On-Line Linking and Embedding (OLE) protocol and neural net architectures. Also massively parallel computer architectures are synergistic with reusability, since one of the useful aspects of reusable modules is that they can often execute in parallel.

The current "world record" for reusability probably belongs to either the "install" functions for personal computer software, or to the hundreds of printer drivers that are now more or less standard throughout the industry. The number of applications which use standard reusable install procedures and standard printer drivers almost certainly exceeds 1 million.

A major gap in reusability products is that of tools for the accompanying documentation sets. Six major kinds of documentation should support reusable modules: 1) Connection protocols for linking the module to an application; 2) "Nearest neighbor" information for what other reusable modules are synergistic with the module in question, and may be used in conjunction to build up larger functions; 3) Structural and functional information on exactly what the module does; 4) User information for invoking and controlling the module's functionality; 5) Modification history of the module, showing both defect repairs and functional additions (if any) over time; 6) A customer catalog of authorized users of the module, so all users can receive notice of recalls or necessary updates. Without the ability to notify all users of changes, a standard reusable module would quickly degrade into a host of unique variants.

It should be noted that software viruses are essentially "reusable modules" although particularly dangerous and virulent ones.

One aspect of reuse that is worthy of comment is the fact that there are certain industries where all or most companies use similar software. In these industries, a host of specialized vertical reusability products, services, and companies have emerged. Examples of industries where special reusability services have come into existence include airlines, banking, construction, insurance, general manufacturing, telephone operating companies, and commercial software development. Industries where reusability is not currently as advanced, but may become so in the future, include city governments, state governments, public utilities, oil companies, wholesale and retail chains, hotels and motels, restaurants, agriculture, and food processing.

12. **Consulting support**—Most of the vendors of reusable code and supporting tools have consulting and education groups also. A number of management consultants and consulting companies also specialize in reusability and are building practices around reuse, such as Andersen Consulting, Computer Power, DMR, IBM, and Software Productivity Research.

13. **Education support**—One of the notable gaps in academic training for software engineers and programmers is the absence of courses such as, "Designing, building, and maintaining reusable modules." This gap in academia is filled by commercial education providers, such as software vendors, and by companies such as Dr. Carma McClure's Extended Intelligence.

14. **Publication support**—The body of literature on reusability is growing rapidly, and new books are appearing at the rate of two or three per year. A sample of recent titles include Dr. T.J. Biggerstaff and Dr. A.J. Perlis' massive two-volume work, *Software Reusability* (Addison Wesley, 1989); Dr. Will Tracz's, *Software Reuse—Emerging Technology* (IEEE Press, 1988); Dr. Peter Freeman's well-known *Software Reusability* (IEEE Press, 1987), and Dr. Carma McClure's popular *3 R's of Software Engineering: Reusability, Reenginering, Repository* (Prentice-Hall, 1992).

Since the object-oriented paradigm is quite fruitful in the reusability domain, this topic should be explored carefully. Examples of O-O books which encompass reuse include Peter Coad and Jill Nicola's *Object-Oriented Programming* (Yourdon Press, 1993); and Gerald Peterson's (editor) *Object-Oriented Computing Volume 1: Concepts* (IEEE Press, 1988) and *Volume 2: Implementation* (IEEE Press, 1988).

There are some major gaps in the software literature on reusability, however: A) What actual functions occur with the greatest frequency in software applications and hence should be reused? B) What is the average and maximum amount of reused code in common applications? C) How many modules are required in a full reusable code library? D) How does the performance of reusable modules compare to custom modules for the same functions? E) What is the synergy between reusable modules and massively parallel computing environments? F) What are the average and optimal size ranges for reusable modules in terms of Function Points and source code? G) What industries have made the greatest usage of reusable code, and what are future probabilities?

15. **Periodical support**—Reusability has become so significant that many journals either have special issues devoted to the topic, or frequent articles. Examples of journals where reusability is frequently discussed include Ed Yourdon's American Programmer, Computer Language, the IEEE Transactions on Software Engineering, and Software magazine. House journals of major vendors such as DEC, IBM, Microsoft, etc. also contain articles on reusability from time to time. Military software journals such as STSC Crosstalk feature articles on reuse fairly often, and tend to include fairly high-level policy statements on reuse by senior Department of Defense officials too.

16. **Standards support**—As of 1993, there are no known general standards published by ANSI, DoD, IEE, IEEE, ISO, or any other standards organization that deal explicitly with reusable modules in terms of interconnection protocols. However, many specific standards and protocols are in fact aimed at facilitating reusability at either the module or product levels: IBM's SNA architecture is an example.

17. **Professional associations**—Interestingly, an association was formed as long ago as the 1950's to facilitate reusability of similar applications among companies and government agencies performing similar software activities. This association is SHARE, the non-profit association of IBM scientific software users. User groups and associations of other computer manufacturers, such as DECUS for Digital Equipment, also are concerned with reusability. Some of the "open-system" vendor groups in the U.S. and in Japan are also concerned with reusability. As of 1993, there is no specific professional association devoted to reusability. There are special-interest groups on reusability within many professional associations, however; for example the ACM, the IEEE, and even local groups such as the Boston Computer Society.

18. **Effectiveness of known therapies**—The economic effectiveness of reuse appears to correlate directly with the volume of reused code in applications. Those applications where reused code exceeds 50% of the total volume often have net productivity rates in excess of 20 Function Points per month. Since the overall U.S. average productivity rate as of 1991 was about 5 Function Points per month, this is a significant difference that should be explored further. An important but unanswered question as of 1993 is what is the maximum amount of reusability that is theoretically possible in general-purpose applications, and can it approach 100%.

A study performed some years ago by IBM of accounting systems found that about 85% of the code had nothing to do with accounting per se: the bulk of the code was concerned with doing accounting via a computer, and consisted of code for storing and retrieving information, error checking, formatting screens and reports, and the like. The conclusion was that more than 90% of the code in accounting applications could probably have been reusable, had reusable modules been readily available.

Interviews with professional programmers by the author and his colleagues at Software Productivity Research noted that even without formal corporate reusability support, experienced programmers spontaneously reuse from 15% to about 35% of the code in their significant applications, using their own private or personal reusable code libraries. With object-oriented languages, the quantity of reused code often exceeds 50%.

SPR assessments, and other kinds of studies as well, often find a striking anomaly in the perception of reusability. Professional programmers tend to have a much different perception of the volume of reusable material in software applications than do managers. One gets the impression that reusability is a kind of secret weapon which professional programmers employ when faced with excessive schedule pressures, although this is an observation and not a definite fact.

19. **Costs of known therapies**—Spontaneous and private reuse by experienced programmers costs essentially nothing. Formal large-scale reusability programs that affect an entire corporation can range in costs from a few thousand dollars to many millions of dollars, depending upon the size of the enterprise. While the costs can be quantified for any specific enterprise or work group, it is difficult to develop generic guidelines.

An interesting but unanswered question as of 1993 would be the commercial price of reusable modules when they are commercially marketed. If such modules are value-priced, then they may sell for more than $1000. If, as appears likely, reusable modules are commodity-priced, then they may sell for only a few dollars, or less than $100 at any rate. The return in investment in reusable code seems to exceed $6.00 for every $1.00 spent which is a good return.

20. **Long-range prognosis**—Reusability is such an important topic and so many companies and government agencies are performing active research that optimism appears justified. The best-case scenario would be that reusable code will constitute more than 75% of the volume of all new software applications by the end of the century. Another reason for optimism is that software vendors have discovered that there is a lot of money to be made from marketing reusable modules. The profit motive is an even stronger reason for optimism than on-going scientific research. The technologies of reusable code, reusable designs (blueprints), and reusable estimates and plans (templates) are all synergistic and closely intertwined, as is research into reusable data.

CHAPTER 40

Lack of Reusable Data

1. **Definition**—A) Corporate or general data stored using proprietary formats that make access by multiple applications difficult; B) Corporate or general data with such a high error content that its reuse by other enterprise applications would be hazardous or unwise; C) Data hard-coded within applications and hence invisible to other applications; D) Key items of corporate data whose existence is not noted in any data dictionary, encyclopedia, or repository catalog; E) Key items of corporate data which exist only in paper form, or some other medium not amenable to automatic search, retrieval, or utilization; F) Prior versions of current data records which are archived in off-line storage or stored on media that is not immediately accessible.

2. **Severity**—The most appropriate way to consider the severity of lack of reusable data is to evaluate the actual percentage of reusable data within applications compared to the optimal amount of potentially reusable data within the same application. The average severity is quite high and appears to be about a 2.5 on the following five-point scale:

Severity 1: Application accesses < 10% reusable data; potential is = 100%

Severity 2: Application accesses < 20% reusable data; potential is > 90%

Severity 3: Application accesses < 30% reusable data; potential is > 80%

Severity 4: Application accesses < 40% reusable data; potential is > 70%

Severity 5: Application accesses < 50% reusable data; potential is > 60%

3. **Frequency**—Lack of reusable data has been a major problem since the industry began. Indeed, during the formative years of the computing and software industries from the 1950's through the 1970's, the basic technical problems of lack of reusable data were compounded by deliberate attempts on the part of storage device and data base vendors to make reuse difficult. The business motivation was to lock customers into unique and proprietary data formats, so they would be forced to use a specific vendor's storage devices or data base tools and methods. Since the 1980's and into the 1990's, the problem of proprietary data organizations

has been reduced somewhat, and data conversion utilities are also available. By the 1990's, both hardware vendors and data base vendors had recognized the folly of proprietary data structures, since they tend to drive customers toward competitors with more generic approaches, rather than lock them into place.

Once it became apparent that sharing data across applications and even across multiple vendors' data base products was a good thing, a new problem surfaced: poor data quality. Traditional Software Quality Assurance (SQA) had more or less ignored data quality since the data was supplied by users, who were outside SQA jurisdiction. However, starting in about 1990, a new sub-discipline of SQA, motivated by the concepts of Total Quality Management (TQM), has appeared which seeks to measure and correct poor data quality. This will be a necessary precursor to achieving truly successful heterogeneous data repositories which include multiple forms of data and tools produced by multiple vendors.

4. **Occurrence**—Lack of reusable data is a chronic problem that affects MIS, systems, military, commercial software applications, and even personal software written for private use (such as spreadsheets). The problem is most acute for MIS applications, where the need for reusable data is greatest. Indeed lack of easily reusable data and poor data quality are two of the most serious problems which plague large corporations and government agencies.

Since reusable data is a logical necessity, and yet difficult to implement, the normal result for most MIS applications is to utilize redundant data rather than reusable data. That is, multiple copies of information will be maintained within, or in support of, the various applications which need access to the information. This of course creates horrendous problems of data synchronization, validity checking, and poor data quality.

As of 1993, alphabetic and numeric data are the most widely utilized kinds of information by software applications, and are in principle the most amenable to reuse. This kind of data can be stored under essentially all file organizations: flat files, hierarchical data bases, network data bases, relational data bases, and object-oriented data bases. Alphabetic information is the most reusable data of any type, due to the ubiquitous support of ASCII text files by thousands of different applications. Numeric and alphanumeric information ranks second, but requires more specialized support. The DIF protocol was perhaps the earliest format for interchanging alphanumeric data.

Graphics and image data, whose utilization is growing rapidly, has lagged in reusability due to incompatible storage organizations, competing standards, and a general failure by data base vendors to recognize the need for this kind of data. Although this kind of data can be stored in various fashions, the object-oriented data base concept seems most amenable to the integration of graphics and image data with other forms.

Other kinds of data (i.e. voice, music, sounds, video animation, sensor-based information, analog data, etc.) are only just starting to be utilized by commercial software, and in some cases do not yet even have any standard protocols for storage and transmission.

Applications using heterogeneous data (i.e. a mix of alphanumeric, graphics, sensor-based, etc.) are inevitably going to experience problems with lack of reusable data. This means, among other things, that a true repository for software project data as of 1992 does not actually exist. A true repository for all of the software data used by large corporations must include a rich mixture of alphanumeric information, graphics, and other heterogeneous forms of data. Most hierarchical and relational data base products do not seem to be suitable hosts. Probably an object-oriented data base using optical storage would be the best choice for dealing with really large volumes of heterogeneous data types.

5. **Susceptibility and resistance**—As of 1993, essentially all applications are susceptible to the problem of lack of reusable data in small or large degree. Applications which use only alphanumeric information are slightly more resistant than most, although not as much as they should be.

Data base applications which share a single vendor's products (such as IBM's IMS, IBM's DB2, Borland's Paradox, dBase III, Foxpro, etc.) are comparatively resistant within the single vendor's context. Should an application need data from two or more competing products, problems mount rapidly and severely. The need for data reuse between applications that use rival data base products is acute enough so that conversion utilities are available for importing and exporting data among the better sellers.

A major problem in the data base domain is the lack of chronological reuse of the prior versions of current data. For example, when someone receives a pay raise, the prior salary level may be archived or moved to off-line storage. Thus applications which deal with trends over time are often difficult to implement.

Within the data base product domain, hierarchical data base products appear to be the most susceptible; relational data base products are fairly susceptible, and object-oriented data base products are (in theory if not in fact) the most resistant to lack of reusable data.

Word processing applications using a single vendor's product (such as Microsoft Word, Word Perfect, Ami Pro, etc.) are comparatively resistant within the single vendor's context if they use only text (not graphics or some other kind of data). For perhaps a dozen of the most widely utilized word processing tools, conversion utilities are available for back and forth data conversion. For example, Microsoft Word for Windows II has a built-in conversion tool that can convert text files from various Word Perfect releases.

A number of word-processing tools (i.e. Word Perfect, Microsoft Word, etc.) support the importation and exportation of certain kinds of data, such as spreadsheets, tables, and graphics from other applications.

Spreadsheet and financial applications using a single vendor's product (such as Pacioli, Excel, Lotus, or Quattro Pro) are comparatively resistant within the single vendor's context. For perhaps 20 of the most widely utilized spreadsheets and financial tools, conversion utilities are available for back and forth data conversion.

Within the personal computer domain, several new concepts have arisen in the last few years to augment data reuse: Dynamic Data Exchange (DDE) and Object Linking and Embedding (OLE). These concepts allow a comparatively new kind of data reuse between applications which are actually running, and where the data may be changing dynamically. The concepts are new enough so that their full impact is not yet known, but the direction of the concept is moving in a very beneficial direction.

Graphics and image applications are highly susceptible to the problem of lack of reusable data, in part because of deliberate attempts to limit access to specific vendors' tools and methods (i.e. Corel Draw, PowerPoint, etc.). As a trivial example, there are several commercial golf games on the U.S. market (Accolade, Links, Microsoft Golf, etc.). All of these games have graphics data which describe some of the same golf courses, but the formats are generally incompatible.

CASE tools which support front-end design, project management and coding, often have integral data bases or repositories available. (Examples include the IEF by Texas Instruments, Teamwork by CADRE, and Foundation by Arthur Andersen.) The more robust tools within this class support at least limited reuse of data among the various components of software planning, design, development, and so forth. However, most commercial CASE tools are extremely hostile to rival CASE tools and even to older stand-alone tools. The best one can expect circa 1992 is some generic form of import and export facilitation.

Repository tools in principle should support heterogeneous data types, and should recognize the need to import and export data to and from other applications as a standard function. Unfortunately, what passes for a "repository manager" in 1992 can range from a low of a source-code library to a high that only encompasses alpha numeric information (source code, text) and some kind of data dictionary. A full repository with facilities for graphics, images, voice records, and animation for dynamic simulation of systems, plus standard alphanumeric data is still in the future. Object-oriented data bases using optical storage would seem to be the most appropriate hosts for a full repository, given the heterogeneous mix of data types and the enormous volumes of information that must be dealt with.

Systems software which controls physical devices (operating systems, telecommunication systems and process control) normally uses highly proprietary data storage methods, and hence is highly susceptible to the problem of lack of reusable data. Since many enterprises utilize multiple hardware devices from multiple vendors, it would be useful to share information back and forth between UNIX, DOS, VMS, MVS, and other widely-used systems. This is not easily done other than via ASCII files, which normally require extensive re-conversion by the receiving application.

Hard copy information is the least reusable of all forms of data. Even though computers have existed for 50 years, much of the information used by corporations and government agencies still exists only on paper in hard-copy form. As of

1993, more than 75% of the data and information used by corporations is still on paper. The problems and limitations of hard copy information are severe, but outside the scope of this book.

Several of the long-standing problems of the "paperless office" concept have now been solved. The two major problems were: A) Storage costs using paper were cheaper than magnetic storage; B) There was no portable, hand-held device of the size and weight of a typical book that allowed access to magnetically-recorded data.

Optical storage now has the lowest costs per byte of any storage medium in human history, so the first barrier has been broken. In 1992 and 1993, several hand-held devices have entered the commercial market for gaining access to optical and magnetic media, so the second barrier has also been broken.

6. **Root causes** —The primary cause of lack of reusable data can be traced back to the early days of computers and automation, when both storage and memory were extremely limited. In the 1950's and early 1960's when computers such as the IBM 1401 were the normal machines used for business purposes, available memory was usually less than 8K bytes, and data storage was either on tab cards, paper tape, or low-density magnetic tape. The limitations of storage space, and the rather slow processing speeds then available, led the industry down a path of keeping only the current values of records, of performing only rudimentary data validation, and of not recording very much supplemental information about the data that was being utilized.

Unfortunately, once bad habits get started it is hard to break them. In the 1990's, storage volumes are essentially unlimited and processing speeds are several orders of magnitude faster than 30 years ago. However, the data base community still employs some fundamental concepts left over from the tab card era. When records are updated, the prior values tend to be destroyed or moved to inconvenient locations. Header information for stored data is still sparse, when there is now plenty of capacity to record many useful facts such as how and when the data was created, or which applications can access it. Even rules for determining the validity of the data could be stored with the data, but this factor does not yet occur in commercial data base products.

The root cause for poor data quality is the fact that this problem falls into a troublesome gap. Most bad data originates *after* the software is delivered to its intended users. Indeed, the users of software are often the source of the poor quality data. Software Quality Assurance (SQA) operations, reviews, inspections, testing, and indeed most forms of defect removal and defect prevention are operational *before* the software is delivered. The new concept of Total Quality Management (TQM) is beginning to recognize that quality is a lifetime commitment, and not a phase-dependent activity. However, TQM applied to data is a new topic which began to emerge as of 1992. The fact that TQM addresses data quality is an encouraging sign of progress.

Yet another new concept, Quality Function Deployment (QFD) is also beginning to have an impact on poor data quality and even on data reusability, although this technology is still too new in the United States to judge its impact.

Another root cause for both poor data quality and low data reusability is the fundamental lack of suitable metrics. As of 1993, there are no standard metrics that deal with data volumes, data quality, or any other quantified aspect of data management. It is a well known aphorism that, "You can't manage what you can't measure." The data and information domain lags far behind every other aspect of software in the availability of metrics and measurement techniques. Even fairly basic questions such as "How much data do you have?" or "Is your data quality better or worse than average?" have no answers, since there are no quantitative methods for expressing data volumes and data quality. Theoretically, the Function Point metric might be applied to the domain of data volumes, but as of 1993 there are no published citations to indicate that this has yet occurred, or even if the concept would be successful or a failure for data measurements.

7. **Associated problems**—Lack of reusable data is a key component of the twin problems of *redundant applications* and *redundant data*. These problems, in turn, are contributors to the problems of *low productivity, excessive time to market, long schedules, low user satisfaction,* and *high maintenance costs*. Lack of reusable data is also a contributing problem to *lack of reusable designs* and *lack of reusable code*.

Several problems that are not discussed in this book are also closely coupled to the problem of lack of reusable data: poor data security and poor viral protection. Almost daily news items appear that discuss hackers entering and disrupting financial data bases, military data bases and personnel data bases. In the future, malicious damage to important data is likely to grow worse rather than better. (As this draft was being written, a neighbor came over to print a document and a variant of the Stoned virus was discovered on the floppy disk.)

Another problem not discussed in this book also impinges upon data reuse: the right to privacy, and the illicit use of data on individuals and companies by government agencies, vendors, and even criminal organizations.

8. **Cost impact**—As of 1993, the economics of creating, using, and maintaining various kinds of data is not clearly understood. Lack of reusable data has not yet been subjected to formal economic analysis, so only rough and provisional assertions are possible.

Redundant data has become a normal operating mode for U.S. businesses and government agencies. There are both direct and indirect costs of substantial magnitude. The direct costs are the mechanical costs of creating and maintaining multiple copies of the same information. The indirect costs are those of resolving the conflicts and correcting the errors when these multiple data bases get out of synchronization.

Lack of chronological reuse has made an important class of software applications difficult and expensive since the industry began. This class consists of applications that analyze long-range trends based on a continuous spectrum of changing data over long time spans. For example, what has been the average salary level for first line managers in a given company every year since 1962? To deal with this kind of basic topic, it would normally be necessary to use off-line data or go through an elaborate data recovery mechanism from archived data.

It should be noted that the disposition of prior data when an update occurs appears to be a fundamental gap in data base technology. The relational model and most standard data schemas seem only to be concerned with current values of information. The fact that data exists in four dimensions (time being the fourth) is essentially an unexplored topic as of 1992.

Poor data quality has become a major expense element for U.S. and global business operations. The costs of poor data quality are both direct and indirect. As a minor example of a direct cost of poor data quality, every week for the past five years the author has received at least half a dozen multiple marketing brochures from the same companies addressed to the various permutations of his name (i.e. addressed to Capers Jones, C. Jones, T. C. Jones, T. Capers Jones, etc.). The author's company receives more than $1000 a week of redundant mail from various software vendors, consulting groups, and educational service vendors.

A major example of the indirect costs of poor data quality include the litigation expenses when indignant consumers and companies bring suit to recover damages due to billing errors, misstated credit ratings, and even errors in criminal records.

Poor data quality also is a critical problem in human tragedy. Recently a murder was committed in the Boston area by a parole violator who had been in police custody shortly before the murder was committed, but his records did not indicate the parole violation and so he was released.

9. **Methods of prevention**—Lack of reusable data and poor data quality are problems whose significance has only recently been recognized. This means that most companies already own significant volumes of redundant data with potentially serious errors already present.

One method of prevention is to perform a thoughtful analysis of all of the data and information needs of the enterprise, and include specific activities as part of such a study to explore reusable data and data quality control. Several standard methods exist for carrying out such enterprise-wide studies, including an entire suite of Information Engineering (IE) approaches which can deal with enterprise data models.

A second preventive step is to evaluate and explore various tools and methods in the data base arena, including but not limited to data dictionaries and encyclopedias, data base products, data entry systems, and query systems. The goal of the evaluation is to deal with long-range enterprise needs for data and information, which can result in maximum reuse, minimum redundancy, maximum security, optimum quality, and optimum user access.

A long-range preventive approach which is now spreading across the entire industry is that of Open System Interconnection (OSI) architectures. This is a very broad topic which encompasses interconnection protocols, reuse of data across heterogeneous environments, interface protocols, and many other topics.

10. Methods of control—For most enterprises, since they already have large volumes of redundant data of questionable quality, control will necessarily occur before prevention. Essentially the industry is playing catch-up ball in the domain of data reusability and validity.

Starting in about 1990, a new sub-industry is slowly forming and comprises companies, products, and services which deal with improving the reuse, accuracy, and quality of on-line data and information. Some of the players in this emerging sub-industry are the data base vendors themselves, and some are new companies such as QDB Solutions. Vendors in the re-engineering and reverse engineering domain are also attacking quirky and error-prone data base problems. Also part of the solution are the non-profit groups such as IEEE, CODASYL, ACM, and DPMA, and the various standards organizations. The software journals are also awakening to the significance of lack of data reuse and poor data quality, and articles on this topic are coming out with increasing frequency.

As of 1993, control starts with a retrospective study of the volumes of data which the enterprise already owns, and an in-depth analysis of both its potential for reuse and its error content.

Once such a study has been carried out, the next step is to purge existing data bases of known or suspected errors, and hence pave the way to a migration to a more stable organization in the future. Anticipate quite a lot of work, and plan for several years of continuous effort. Correcting errors in existing data bases is one of the hardest activities in the entire software domain.

11. Product support—There are perhaps 100 vendors and more than 1000 products in the general domain of data bases and ancillary tools. Some of the specific types of tools include (in alphabetic order): CASE, comparators (for checking inconsistencies in redundant data); configuration control, cross-reference analyzers (for determining where data is used); data base management systems, data validity checkers (a new class of product for finding explicit errors in data); data dictionaries (and encyclopedias); library products; query products, repository products, and security and viral protection products. Unfortunately, these products are often created by different vendors, are not particularly compatible, and indeed are sometimes quite hostile to one another.

Examples of typical products that can affect data reuse include ACCESS/204, ADABAS, ADB, ADDERS, ADW, AID/SPF, APS, AS/400 QUERY, BACHMAN/Analyst, BACHMAN/Re-Engineering, BLACKSMITH INTERCHANGE, CADRE Teamwork, CA-Datadictionary, CA-IDMS, CA-LIBRARIAN, COMPARE, COMPAREX, CREATABASE, DATABASIC II, DATAMANAGER, DATA-XPERT, DB2, DB2 CATALOG MANAGER, DB2-EXPERT, DBOL, DELTA, Dictionary 204, DICTIONARYMANAGER, DMS II, ENDEAVOR, Entry Point 90, ER-Designer, EXDIFF, FILECOMP, FALCON, FOCUS, IEF, IEW, IMS, IMSXREF, Information/System, Informix-QuickStep, INGRES, INTACT, KEY/MASTER, LOOKAT, ODE, ONTOS, ORACLE, PARITY, QDB/Analyze, SUPER-C, SUPERSEARCH, SUPRA, Synchrony, Text Comparator, THE INTEGRATOR, and VAX CDD/Plus.

12. **Consulting support**—There is no shortage of consulting support available in the whole spectrum of data-related topics and problems. Many of the data-base vendors have captive consulting groups which, although primarily locked into a specific product line, are often available for low cost. The Information Engineering (IE) community also has captive consulting groups that serve in the areas of enterprise data modeling and corporate information systems. The object-oriented (OO) paradigm is moving rapidly into the data base domain, and this group is starting to deal explicitly with reusable data. Repository consultants are also beginning to occur as a new specialty, employed either by large vendors such as IBM, or by various independent consulting groups. Ordinary management and technical consulting groups such as Andersen Consulting, DMR, and Ernst & Young, also have practices in the data domain too. There is a shortage of consulting support in data quality, however. Only a few specialized groups such as QDB Solutions and Vality deal with this topic.

13. **Education support**—Basic training in data base fundamentals is a required topic for software engineering students. However, more sophisticated training in topics such as optimizing data for reuse, security and viral protection for data, and data quality control is almost nonexistent at the university level. For this kind of advanced information, private education provided by vendors such as the Quality Assurance Institute (QAI), QDB Solutions or education companies such as Digital Consulting (DCI) or the Technology Transfer Institute (TTI) may be more up to date. Related topics include client-server applications, distributed applications, and object-oriented (OO) applications. For these topics, university courses are slowly starting to appear.

14. **Publication support**—The general topics of data bases and information storage is one of the largest sub-fields of software engineering literature, with perhaps 500 books in print and many thousand journal articles. However, when the topic switches to reusable data across heterogeneous data base systems and data quality control, the number of citations is less than ten. A new book, published in October of 1992, is Thomas Redman's *Data Quality* (Bantam Professional Books). Redman works for AT&T, which has long been a pioneer in data quality.

Jeffrey Clark's *OLE/DDE* (Prentice Hall, 1992) discusses two of the newer concepts for data reuse: object linking and embedding and dynamic data exchange. Dr. Carma McClure's *3 R's of Software Engineering (Reusability, Re-engineering, Repository)* is a rare example that touches on data reuse (Prentice-Hall, 1992). James Martin's books on information engineering are relevant, since that technology tends to facilitate data reuse: *Information Engineering, Volume 1, Introduction and Principles; Information Engineering, Volume 2, Strategy and Analysis* (Prentice Hall, 1990).

Another new book, Dr. Dan Mosley's *Handbook of Testing Business Application Software* also touches upon data quality, and peripherally with data reusability. The two-volume series on reusability by Dr. Ted Biggerstaff and Dr. Alan Perlis are also worthy of acquisition: *Software Reusability, Volume 1, Concepts and Models; Software Reusability, Volume II, Applications and Experience* (Springer-Verlag,

1989). (These two books grew out of the ITT research on software reusability in the early 1980's.) Another reuse book is that of Will Tracz; *Software Reuse—Emerging Technology* (IEEE Press, 1988). A useful primer on OO data base (which facilitates reuse) is that of Ez Nahouraii and Fred Petry; *Object-Oriented Data Bases* (IEEE Press, 1991). The IEEE annual *Proceedings of the International Conference on Data Engineering (COMPDEC)* also contains relevant materials. The 8th such conference was held in 1992. In a similar vein, the IEEE annual *Proceedings of the International Conference on Distributed Computing Systems* is also relevant. The 12th such conference was held in 1992.

15. **Periodical support**—Reusability in general is becoming such a major topic that new articles are appearing at monthly or weekly intervals in the major journals. Data reuse and data quality are also heating up, and recent articles have appeared in PC Week, Computerworld, DBMS, and Data Base Programming & Design. Dr. Mark Hansen of QDB Solutions in Cambridge is a frequent contributor on the topic of data quality and the need to purge data bases of harmful errors prior to safely being able to reuse the information. Dr. Hansen is also attempting to broaden the concept of Total Quality Management (TQM) so that it encompasses data quality: a reasonable extension. The IEEE Data Engineering Newsletters, and many data base vendor journals have articles of relevance from time to time.

16. **Standards support**—In the domain of standards, there are no explicit standards for data reuse or for data quality. There are many standards that impinge upon these topics, however. So many standards deal with aspects of reusable data that it is not possible to cite all of them: it is best to acquire one of the comprehensive standards publications, such as the IEEE Software Engineering Standards Collection. ANSI, IEEE, ISO and other standards dealing with POSIX, LANS, Configuration Management, Quality Assurance, and many other topics are relevant. Particularly relevant to data reuse is the new ANSI SQL-92 standard. The ISO 9000–9004 standards also impinge upon the topic of data reuse, and a relatively minor impact on data quality. So far as can be determined, military and DoD standards have a general impact on data quality, but this topic seems to be lagging. CompuServe has an on-line facility called OASIS (On-Line Access to Standards Information Services) that is very helpful. It should be noted that major vendors also have proprietary quasi-standards which they hope will become de facto standards. In the domain of data reuse, for example, IBM has DRDA (distributed relational data base architecture) standard, and does not support the ISO SQLCLI standard. The new PCMIA II standard is also relevant.

Here are a few emerging standards topics which impinge upon data reuse and data quality: A Tool Integration Standard (ATIS); Broadcast Message Server (BMS); CASE Data Interchange Format (CDIF); Common Object Request Broker Architecture (CORBA); Common User Access (CUA); Information Resource Dictionary System (IRDS), and Portable Common Tool Environment (PCTE).

17. **Professional associations**—Most of the standard non-profit associations are interested in data reusability and data quality, and discuss such topics from time to time. Examples of such associations include the ACM, ADAPSO, ITAA, DPMA, IEEE, and others. Software data base and computer manufacturer user groups may also be interested in data reuse: for example IBM's SHARE and GUIDE. The software quality groups have not yet dealt with data quality, but this topic is likely to surface within the next few years. National quality groups such as SSQ, SISQ, and various regional quality groups will probably devote more time to data quality in the future.

18. **Effectiveness of known therapies**—As of 1993, it is premature to judge the effectiveness of known therapies, since many of them have only been available for 18 months or less. Further, the lack of any standard metric for dealing with data volumes, data reuse, and data quality is slowing down research into this area. However, now that poor data quality and low data reusability are becoming recognized as major problems, it can be anticipated that new therapies will occur in increasing numbers.

19. **Costs of known therapies**—As of 1993, it is premature to evaluate the costs of therapies which can facilitate data reuse and improve data quality. The economics of reusable data within a single data base environment was worked out in the 1960's and 1970's. The topic of concern today in the 1990's is reuse across heterogeneous distributed environments where multiple vendors, multiple data bases, and multiple applications are interacting concurrently. Unfortunately, neither the costs of achieving this kind of data reuse, nor the costs of not achieving it, are understood today.

20. **Long-range prognosis**—The starting point for the recognition that reusable data across heterogeneous data bases would be useful was approximately 1990. If this technology follows a normal pattern of technology transfer, it will take about 14 years for the concept to become a standard practice in the civilian world, and about 17 years in the military world. Thus it will probably be well into the first decade of the twenty-first century before the problems noted here are resolved. However, as of 1993 quite a few large corporations, government agencies, and other groups are exploring the issues. The software journals are now alert to the topic, so technology transfer is getting underway. The down side is that a very large volume of non-reusable data with hidden errors exists in 1993, and converting and correcting this data will be a very expensive, time-consuming undertaking. The long-range prognosis is only guardedly favorable: low data reusability and poor data quality are likely to remain chronic problems for the rest of the 20th century unless there are some remarkable breakthroughs.

CHAPTER

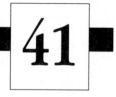

Lack of Reusable Designs (Blueprints)

1. **Definition**—A) Widespread failure by the software industry to have developed generic designs or models of common application types which occur with high frequency (with several exceptions); B) Widespread failure by software engineering schools to teach reusable design concepts (with several exceptions); C) Widespread failure by upper CASE vendors and design methodology vendors to support the concept of reusable designs (with several exceptions); D) Failure by various standards organizations to establish meaningful standards or protocols to support reusable designs; E) Any common, generic application which occurs with high frequency where the entire design is treated as a new and novel artifact. (Examples of common, generic applications include accounting systems, billing systems, compilers, data-base packages, operating systems, payroll systems, PBX switching systems, and many others.)

2. **Severity**—The severity of lack of reusable designs is much greater than the severity of reusable code, and appears to be about a 2.5 on the following five point scale, where the amount of actual reuse is contrasted with the amount of potential reuse:

Severity 1: Design contains < 05% reuse; potential is > 90% reuse

Severity 2: Design contains < 10% reuse; potential is > 80% reuse

Severity 3: Design contains < 20% reuse; potential is > 70% reuse

Severity 4: Design contains < 30% reuse; potential is > 60% reuse

Severity 5: Design contains < 40% reuse; potential is > 50% reuse

    To clarify the severity of the lack of reusable software designs, look at other kinds of multiple-unit construction projects. Consider how expensive it would be to put up a subdivision of 100 tract homes if every home were to be designed uniquely by a different architectural firm. It is obviously more economical to use half a dozen or so standard, generic home designs if the goal is moderately-priced housing. Standard blueprints for home construction have been commercially available for many years. The cost of acquiring such standard blueprints is less than $100, as opposed to architectural fees of more than $10,000 for custom designs. It is this same concept that needs to be applied to software. There is no intrinsic need to custom-design every software application used by modern enterprises.

3. **Frequency**—Lack of reusable designs or blueprints is much more common than lack of reusable code. Many applications are designed and built as unique artifacts by hundreds or even thousands of enterprises, when the applications are more than 90% identical. For example, the payroll systems of every U.S. company contain about 90% common, generic functions. Accounting systems tend to exceed 95% reused functions. Many competitive products (i.e. E-mail, word processors, spreadsheets, switching systems, etc.) contain more than 50% standard, generic functionality.

   Unfortunately, there is currently no easy or economical way to acquire blueprints or reusable designs for most application types. There are a few exceptions, however: generic designs are available for compilers, sorts, operating systems, chess games (and a few other game types), spreadsheets, and viruses. Compiler, sort, and operating system designs are available because software engineering schools tend to use compilers, sorts, and operating systems as training examples. Game designs are available because they occur in several books on game design. Reusable spreadsheet designs are available because the concepts are fairly straightforward and several language products use spreadsheets as examples for tutorial discussion. Virus designs are available because the software industry has developed a pernicious underground of hackers who, like arsonists, gain enjoyment from doing damage.

4. **Occurrence**—Lack of reusable designs is endemic to the software industry in 1993, and occurs for MIS software, systems software, commercially marketed software, and military software. Somewhat surprisingly, games and end-user software tend to make the greatest use of blueprints or reusable designs.

5. **Susceptibility and resistance**—Essentially the entire software industry is susceptible to the lack of reusable designs, with a few exceptions already noted. Resistance as of 1992 is rare and uncommon, although there is reason to believe that this situation may get better within a few years. CASE vendors such as Texas Instruments are starting to recognize that reusable designs are a powerful selling tool for CASE, and indeed may even bring in separate revenue streams. As soon as a company starts making money by selling software blueprints, other companies are sure to follow. (Note that Texas Instruments has started to use the name "templates" rather than "blueprints." This is unfortunate, since the word "template" was already in use to mean reusable plans and estimates, as discussed in the next section.)

6. **Root causes**—The root causes of a lack of reusable designs are multiple and not easy to describe succinctly. The first and most basic root cause is that the software industry has not developed a standard design technique that lends itself to blueprint construction. There are more than 150 specification and design techniques extant as of 1993, including the methods of Yourdon, DeMarco, Gane & Sarson, Warnier-Orr, object-oriented design, Information Engineering (IE), the Jackson

351

design, technique and SADT. None, unfortunately, are fully adequate for blueprint purposes. Object-oriented analysis and design seems to have the best prospects for future blueprinting, however, although far from achieving this goal in 1993.

The second root cause is that there is no software equivalent to the "bill of materials" for manufactured products. That is, software lacks a concise way of describing the reusable modules and functions which will be part of an application. To make an analogy with home construction, a blueprint for a home does not contain a detailed design or specification for the washers, castings, and fittings for every sink in the house. It is sufficient merely to indicate where the sinks will be placed and how the plumbing will be routed. Unfortunately, building software in the absence of reusable modules and standard functions means that essentially every aspect of a generic application is included in every specification every time such a product is built.

The third root cause is derived from the second: the volume of the specification set for software products tends to be enormous. The complete set of blueprints and construction plans for a 1500 square foot tract home requires less than 10% of the quantity of paper that the specifications for a 1500 Function Point software product will require. Only in the case of very large and unusual physical structures (i.e. the Sydney Opera House or a domed athletic stadium) does the blueprint volume approach that of medium and large software applications.

7. **Associated problems**—Lack of reusable designs is a major component of *low productivity, low quality, long schedules, excessive time to market,* and *high maintenance costs.* Lack of reusable designs is universally associated with two other similar problems: *lack of reusable code* and *lack of reusable plans and historical data (templates).*

The lack of reusable designs is itself caused by *inadequate software engineering research, inadequate software engineering curricula, slow technology transfer,* and *inadequate capital investment.*

8. **Cost impact**—The external and internal design phases of software projects in 1992 absorbs from about 10% to almost 50% of the costs of software, and from about 15% to more than 50% of software schedules. The variances are associated with the size, novelty, and complexity of the projects, the experience of the design team, design method used, design tools used, and whether the projects are military or civilian. Expressed in terms of Function Points, the observed productivity range of the design phases of software projects runs from less than two to more than 50 Function Points per staff month.

If the design for a new application were to start from the basis of a reusable design for similar applications instead of starting with a blank screen as happens today, the impact would reduce the costs of design by about 85%, and the schedule required for design by about 90%. This information is derived from instances where reusable designs are available, such as for compilers and sorting programs where the fundamental design issues have long been worked out by trial and error methods.

Unfortunately, empirical data on what it costs to create a reusable design the first time is not as clear. The basic dimensions of creating a reusable design seem to be: A) The designs of at least three similar projects must be carefully reviewed; B) A design representation method must be selected (i.e. Yourdon design, Warnier-Orr design, object-oriented design, etc.); C) The tool platforms for the design must be chosen (i.e. Cadre Teamwork, Knowledgeware, the IEF, etc.); D) The essential common features of the application must be expressed in the chosen design representation; E) The new reusable design must be carefully inspected, and updated if needed; F) The new reusable design must be validated by using it to build at least one new project; G) The new reusable design can now be placed on the commercial market or made available to users.

It is an interesting observation that the technologies associated with reverse engineering and re-engineering of aging software projects are highly relevant to the task of constructing reusable designs or blueprints. Should the re-engineering companies choose to do so, they may well be in an advantageous position to create a significant new market for reusable designs.

Although the empirical data is sparse, it can be hypothesized that the initial creation of a reusable design may be 25% more expensive than and take perhaps 20% more time than ordinary non-reusable design technologies. This means that unless the design will be commercially marketed, or it is known that similar projects will be built in the future, there is no immediate incentive for constructing reusable designs.

This sequence of constructing a reusable software design is more or less identical to the sequence for constructing several other classes of commercial-grade blueprints that are marketed in the U.S. such as: A) kit-built airplanes; B) various classes of small boats; C) vacation homes and tract homes.

A reusable software design or blueprint is somewhat similar to the design of any other complex artifact such as an automobile, sail boat, or motorcycle. It is an abstract model of a generic product. A standard, reusable design needs to include a bill of materials for the functions, algorithms, or objects the product will contain; a data table for the entities and relationships the product will store; the interconnection protocols for how the various components communicate and how the product will connect to other products; usage protocols for information about using the product in general and also specific functions; a discussion of the product's inputs and outputs; and the assembly sequence or the normal steps in constructing the product. Special topics such as installation, local customization, performance criteria, standards to be followed, software dependencies, and hardware dependencies are also to be included. From considering the contents of reusable designs, it appears that their volume would amount to about half a page per Function Point.

9. **Methods of prevention**—The best prevention for the lack of reusable designs appears to be associated with the profit motive. Several CASE vendors have recognized that reusable designs are likely to be marketable commodities. Indeed, the

most optimistic scenario is that the sales of reusable designs may generate more revenues than the sales of upper CASE tools themselves. Major computer companies and software houses which build sets of numerous related software projects (i.e. compilers, data base products, etc.) also have incentives for constructing reusable designs.

Reusable designs that are vertical within specific industries have some very attractive commercial potential. Industries where many different enterprises use similar or identical software applications are the most likely groups to acquire commercial reusable designs. Examples of industries where reusable designs would seem useful and a viable commodity since all enterprises within the industry need essentially identical software include: city governments, state governments, public schools, state universities, junior colleges, public utilities for electricity and water, local and state police and county sheriff departments, banking, insurance, agricultural production, religious institutions and major church groups, telephone operating companies, railroads, bus and transportation companies, airlines, travel agencies, professional athletic teams, hotels and motels, restaurants, retail stores, medical offices, law offices, and dental offices.

Vertical reusable designs within specific industries vary and fluctuate with the industry. Several years ago a number of public utility companies met and decided to consider a reusable design for a generic fleet-management system, since all public utilities own and maintain sizable fleets of vehicles. Reusable designs have also started to occur for various police agencies and for motor vehicle registration systems.

10. Methods of control—Unless reusable designs are available before the commencement of ordinary design, there are no effective controls. Once a design is constructed in the normal way, it is too late to do anything else.

11. Product support—As of 1993, interest in reusable designs and the commercial market for reusable designs are still uncertain. Texas Instruments is perhaps the first CASE vendor to announce support for reusable designs (incorrectly termed "templates" in the TI marketing literature). However, other CASE vendors are known to be exploring these topics as well.

Products which may be useful in analyzing existing software and extracting their generic functions for encapsulation into reusable designs include: A) Complexity analyzers; B) Restructuring tools (especially those using graph theory); C) Re-engineering and reverse engineering tools; D) Data dictionary tools; E) Library control and configuration management tools; F) Upper CASE or front-end CASE tools that support various design methods; G) Object-oriented design methods and tools.

Although not yet commercially available, research on reusable requirements also overlaps the topic of reusable designs. It appears that fully automated table-driven approaches to requirements gathering may assist reusable designs, and have other virtues as well such as direct coupling to sizing and estimating tools.

12. **Consulting support**—Management or technical consulting support for reusable designs is a rare commodity in 1993, and neither major consulting companies nor most individual consultants deal with this topic. Exceptions to this rule may include consultants within specific industries such as banking, insurance, and telephone operating companies who may well be aware of reusable designs for generic applications within the industry. Since Texas Instruments has announced reusable designs as part of the IEF, it is also offering consulting assistance as well. Other CASE and Information Engineering groups no doubt would soon follow. IBM has just created a new object-oriented consulting group.

13. **Education support**—University software engineering curricula do not seem to deal with reusable designs in any significant way. (The fact that many universities share common application types such as compilers as training vehicles is a form of reuse, but only an incidental one.) This is also true of commercial education. The lack of courses on principles of reusable designs, and pragmatic examples of reusable designs, must be considered a major gap in software education.

14. **Publication support**—The body of literature on reusable design is smaller than the literature on reusable code. Many books deal with this topic in passing, however: titles include Dr. T.J. Biggerstaff and Dr. A.J. Perlis' massive two-volume work, *Software Reusability* (Addison Wesley, 1989); Dr. Will Tracz's, *Software Reuse—Emerging Technology* (IEEE Press, 1988); Dr. Peter Freeman's well-known *Software Reusability* (IEEE Press, 1987), and Dr. Carma McClure's popular *3 R's of Software Engineering: Reusability, Reenginering, Repository* (Prentice-Hall, 1992). Dr. Carma McClure's *CASE is Software Automation* (Prentice Hall, 1989) also touches upon design reuse.

Dr. Gerald Weinberg's *Rethinking Systems Analysis and Design* (Dorset House, 1992) is a good primer for those who wish to create potentially reusable designs. Dr. James Martin and Dr. Carma McClure's massive *Diagramming Techniques for Analysts and Programmers* (Prentice Hall, 1985) is also a good primer for those seeking to develop both reusable designs, and also explore the rich variety of design and specification methods. (Author's note: A survey of software design methods carried out at IBM found more than 150 specific techniques. About 40 of them were graphically based, and more than 110 were based on characters and special symbols, or were hybrid methods.)

Both the object-oriented paradigm and the information engineering paradigm are moving in the direction of reusable designs. Therefore keeping current with the literature of these two domains is valuable. However, both domains are on a rapid upsurge in books, articles, and tutorial materials. A few representative titles which impinge upon reusable designs include: Peter Coad and Ed Yourdon's *Object-Oriented Design* (Yourdon Press, 1991); Barry Kurtz, Scott Woodfield, and David Embley's *Object-Oriented Systems Analysis and Specification: A Model Driven Approach* (Yourdon Press, 1991); and James Martin's *Object-Oriented Analysis and Design* (James Martin Books, 1992). Dr. Tom Love's *Object-Lessons* (SIG Books, New York, 1993) discusses design reuse.

Moving to the information engineering paradigm, James Martin's three introductory volumes on this topic are a good comprehensive treatment: *Information Engineering Book 1: Introduction and Principles; Information Engineering Book 2: Planning and Analysis;* and *Information Engineering Book 3: Design and Construction* (all from James Martin Books, 1989).

James Martin is a prolific writer, and his *Application Development Without Programmers* (Prentice Hall, 1982) was a pioneering attempt to encompass various kinds of reuse, among other technologies.

In general, software designs begin by analyzing either the functions that are to be provided or the data which will flow through the application. The data-driven design approaches have been asserted to be more useful for reusable designs than the function-driven approaches. As of 1993, it is not certain if this assertion is really true, but it is interesting. Examples of books which deal with data-driven software designs include Kirk Hansen's *Data Structured Program Design* (Ken Orr & Associates, 1983) and Michael Jackson's *Principles of Program Design* (Academic Press, 1975).

No discussion of software design, reusable or not, would be complete without citing some of the classic books on software design: Glenford Myers *Composite/ Structured Design* (van Nostrand, 1979); Ed Yourdon and Larry Constantine's famous *Structured Design* (Prentice Hall, 1979) and Wayne Stevens' *Using Structured Design* (John Wiley, 1981). Ed Yourdon also has a more recent book on a similar theme: *Modern Structured Analysis* (Yourdon Press, 1989). Tom DeMarco's *Structured Analysis and System Specification* (Yourdon Press, 1979) also deserves a citation among the classics. Interestingly, some of Tom's original ideas of structured English are beginning to resurface in the form of linguistic analysis of requirements and text-based specifications, in order to construct standard vocabularies of significant software terms.

15. **Periodical support**—The general data processing journals run articles or even special issues on reusability from time to time. For example, both Ed Yourdon's American Programmer and the IEEE Transactions on Software Engineering and Communications of the ACM have had special issues on reusability. Some of the vertical, industry-specific journals also deal with reuse for industries such as banking, CASE, and insurance. Reusable design lags other types of reuse, such as reusable code, but interest in this topic is increasing.

16. **Standards support**—There are no known standards as of 1993 published by ANSI, DoD, IEE, IEEE, ISO, or any other standards organization that deals explicitly with reusable designs. This is a significant gap in standards coverage.

17. **Professional associations**—The industry-specific professional associations, such as LOMA for the insurance industry, may have working sessions on reusable designs for common applications from time to time. The general professional associations such as the ACM or the IEEE frequently have sessions dealing with many

aspects of reusability at conferences such as the well-known IEEE Software Engineering Symposia.

18. **Effectiveness of known therapies**—As of 1993, it is premature to really judge the effectiveness of reusable designs for software applications in general. For those few products which have actually utilized reusable designs, such as compilers, the effectiveness seems high.

19. **Costs of known therapies**—As of 1993, it is premature to make general statements about the costs of reusable designs since there is essentially no commercial business in reusable designs currently. As with most other reusable artifacts, the initial design and construction is fairly high. Usage across 10, 100, or 1000 projects would generate substantial economic returns. The economics of reusable designs should be more precise within a few years, and by 1995 a clear economic picture may emerge.

An interesting but unanswered question as of 1993 would be the approximate commercial costs for software blueprints when they are commercially marketed. If blueprints are value-priced, then blueprints might sell for $2,500 to $5,000. If blueprints are commodity priced (like commercial boat and home blueprints are today) then the price would probably be less than $500.

20. **Long-range prognosis**—For reusable code, the long-range prognosis is very favorable. The long-range prognosis for reusable designs is more questionable. There are fairly complex technical issues which must be resolved before reusable designs can truly succeed. For example, what is an optimal design representation for a reusable design, and what will be the volume of reusable designs? The topics are uncertain, but the overall prognosis is moderately optimistic. The need for reusability at all levels is high enough so that no doubt the technical problems can be resolved.

Lack of Reusable Documentation

1. **Definition**—A) User documents and reference materials for common application types which are produced uniquely; B) On-line documents and tutorial materials which are produced uniquely; C) Tutorial and training materials which are produced uniquely.

2. **Severity**—The severity level of lack of reusable documentation is greater than for either reusable designs or reusable code, and appears to be about a one on the following five-point scale, where the amount of actual reuse is contrasted with the amount of potential reuse:

   Severity 1: Documents contain < 01% reuse; potential is > 95% reuse

   Severity 2: Documents contain < 05% reuse; potential is > 90% reuse

   Severity 3: Documents contain < 10% reuse; potential is > 80% reuse

   Severity 4: Documents contain < 20% reuse; potential is > 70% reuse

   Severity 5: Documents contain < 30% reuse; potential is > 60% reuse

3. **Frequency**—Lack of reusable documentation for software packages has been a major problem since the industry began. This is due in part to the historical nature of technical writing, where plagiarism, copyright violations, and even "look and feel" overlaps are normally avoided.

4. **Occurrence**—For civilian projects, lack of reusable documentation is endemic among MIS software producers and systems software producers. The frequency declines slightly for very large software producers (i.e. Microsoft, Borland, Lotus) and for military software producers. Third party book publishers (i.e. Ziff Davis, Sybex, QUE, Prentice Hall, etc.) also have a reduced incidence of this problem.

5. **Susceptibility and resistance**—The kinds of documents most susceptible to lack of reusability are tutorial materials, user manuals, reference manuals, programmer's guides, maintenance manuals, and various on-line tutorial screens and HELP screens. The kinds of documents that are most resistant are test plans, quality

plans, and other relatively generic document types where standards such as ISO 9000–9004 or DoD 2167A determine both the format and some of the contents.

The kinds of document that are most resistant to lack of reusability are maintenance documents produced automatically by some of the commercial restructuring tools. These documents are identical in format if not in content, and facilitate maintenance. In a similar fashion, some of the documents produced semi-automatically by re-engineering tools are also similar in format if not in content.

Another class of highly resistant quasi-documents are the on-screen icons and user instructions for applications which operate under the protocols of the Macintosh, Windows, OS/2, SAA, or Motif. If it were not for the risk of a lawsuit by Apple, there would be a strong possibility that on-screen information would be as reusable as the instrument panels of automobiles. (Imagine the convenience to users of being able to move seamlessly between Macintosh, Windows, and Unix applications without having to relearn fundamental icons and protocols.)

6. **Root causes**—The primary cause for lack of reusable documentation is the feeling that reusing material may be perceived as degrading the writer. Indeed, for many kinds of writing such as fiction and history, reuse is deemed either plagiarism or copyright violation and considered, with some justification, to be quite reprehensible. However, writing about how to utilize software is an industrial occupation and not classic creative writing, and it would be much more cost effective if reusability volumes could be increased.

Two discrete forms of reusability are relevant to software documentation: 1) reusable formats and layouts; 2) reusable text, illustrations, and contents. The former is much more common than the latter. For example, within this book the same format is used for every problem discussion. The contents or problem discussions themselves are not reused to the same degree however. Users of many kinds of software applications need essentially similar information, such as:

A) How to install the application.
B) How to uninstall the application if needed (especially critical for Windows applications).
C) How to adjust the application to fit a particular operating system.
D) How to use physical devices with the application (i.e. printers, plotters, etc.).
E) How to configure the application for optimal results.
F) How to turn the application on and begin usage.
G) How to turn the application off and exit (a topic often omitted).
H) How to use the basic functions of the application, with correct examples.
I) How to use esoteric or seldom utilized functions, with correct examples.
J) How to import and export information to and from other applications.
K) What kinds of problems typically occur, and what to do about them.
L) Where to go to seek help or report problems.
M) How to contact or join user associations (if any exist for the application).

N) How to contact or use on-line support or access relevant bulletin boards.

The latter three points (L, M, and N) are seldom included in vendor-produced material for unknown reasons. For example, Microsoft, Borland, IBM, and Computer Associates all have substantial user groups for many applications, and all have various kinds of on-line support via CompuServe, Prodigy, or various bulletin boards. One would think that such information would be included proudly in these vendors' manuals, but it is not.

The entire topic of creating optimal document sets in support of software (or hardware too for that matter) is under-represented as a serious research topic. There are some basic gaps in the scientific literature that have only recently been fully explored. For example:

1) What mix of text and graphics is most effective for explaining software topics?
2) Are there differences in comprehension between paper and on-line information?
3) How effective are context-sensitive HELP screens?
4) How effective are hypertext links for information retrieval?
5) What are the most and least effective ways of visualizing software structures?
6) Can the object-oriented paradigm be usefully applied to documentation?

Research into the domain of reusable software documentation (or documentation in general) requires synergistic cooperation among domains that have historically been quite disparate: linguistics, cognitive psychology, software engineering, and knowledge engineering. Unfortunately, few individuals are versed in all of these disciplines. Researchers in any one of the disciplines are seldom in a position to carry out broad-based studies involving the others.

Unfortunately, another root problem is that research into reusable software documentation (or documentation in general) has been chronically underfunded and understaffed. Only a few large companies such as IBM, Xerox, General Electric, ITT, and AT&T have carried out formal research programs in this topic.

A final root problem is that when effective approaches surface for various aspects of communicating software usage instructions to end users, they are often regarded as proprietary and defended quite fiercely in the courts. The lengthy lawsuit between Apple, Microsoft, and Hewlett Packard and the fierce defensiveness of Lotus against Borland and other competitors provide examples of the proprietary nature of user interface methods. Ironically, it appears that few of the plaintiffs in these suits actually perform serious research into optimal human communication methods. For the most part their approaches were created by derivation from earlier companies or by accident.

7. **Associated problems**—Lack of reusable documentation is a contributor to the problem of *low user satisfaction, long schedules*, and *high maintenance costs.*

Lack of reusable documentation itself is often caused by the very similar problem of *lack of reusable designs.* In addition, problems not discussed in this book are also relevant. These involve inadequate curricula for technical communication and inadequate research funding into technical communication methods.

8. **Cost impact**—The cost of low levels of reusable documentation can be quantified fairly exactly for specific cases and specific products, but is not easy to generalize.

U.S. military software projects sometimes produce a total of up to 100 discrete documents (or as few as 20) containing an aggregate of about 400 English words per Ada statement. The costs of military paperwork constitute about 52% of the total costs of military software development, so it can be seen that reuse in this domain would be even more beneficial than reusable code.

Civilian MIS projects create about one fourth the volume of paperwork as do military projects, and civilian systems software projects produce about one half the volume. Even though the volumes are smaller, reuse would still be beneficial.

For training manuals and tutorial materials, standard reusable formats are already common among major computer manufacturers, military software producers, and software vendors. However, reusable contents are deemed difficult, and it is improbable for more than about 25% of the contents to be reusable.

For software user manuals and reference documents, increasing the volume of reusable material is fairly difficult, and it is improbable that more than about 30% of the contents can be reusable. However, producing reusable templates of document formats is quite straightforward.

For maintenance manuals, increasing the volume of reusable material is both easier than for user documents, and supported to various degrees by automated tools such as restructuring packages. An achievable goal here would be to exceed 60% reusable material.

For planning documents (test plans, SQA plans, etc.) that follow standards such as ISO 9000–9004 or DoD 2167A, over 80% of the total volume is conceivably reusable.

For on-line usage information under products that support standard protocols (such as Windows, OS/2, the Macintosh, Motif, etc.) reuse in excess of 80% also seems possible.

Among the most reusable of any type of documentation artifact are glossaries and dictionaries. Here reuse from standard sources, such as the IEEE glossary, can exceed 90%.

There are also substantial indirect costs associated with lost user time as they grope and search their way through arcane document structures looking for information which may not even be present. Poor or quirky document structures can be hypothesized to cost software users about 15 minutes a day. Since the U.S. has about 35 million people who use computers and software in 1992, the net loss of productive time can be as high as 5 million hours every working day! For the U.S. as a whole, some 137.5 million working days per year might be considered to be lost time searching for information about how to use a particular software application! That amounts to a loss of almost 7 days per year for every computer user.

9. **Methods of prevention**—There are several possible preventive approaches to the problem of lack of reusable documentation. A fairly inexpensive method used by IBM as early as 1967 was to review the incoming reader comments forms to discover which IBM reference and usage manuals were considered the best by users. Sets of these well-regarded manuals were collected (there were about 20 of them out of a total of several hundred manuals which IBM had published at that point) and supplied to all software publication departments. The purpose was to give software technical writers demonstrably successful patterns to use for the structure of their own manuals.

A somewhat more expensive preventive approach, also pioneered within IBM in the 1960's, was empirical research. In the area of maintenance manuals, several different formats and methods were used to express the maintenance information for one system. Some of the documentation versions used flowcharts, others HIPO diagrams, others had no structural information. Then the product was seeded with a few known bugs, and actual maintenance personnel were asked to find the bugs using the various alternative maintenance manuals. There was a fairly clear winner (a pocket-sized manual containing no flow charts, but clear discussions of what all error messages meant and what kinds of conditions triggered them) and this manual became the template for many others.

The same concept of empirical research has been extended and made more sophisticated by IBM and other companies such as ITT, Xerox, Hewlett Packard, and AT&T, and has developed into actual usability laboratories. In a usability lab, offices and work spaces are fully instrumented for sound and video recording, and various experiments are carried out with users and technical personnel performing normal tasks using different kinds of user documentation, command structures and interface methods. Both the time required to perform standard tasks, and the participants' subjective impressions can be recorded for analysis.

An informal study was carried out by the author in the 1980's on software journal articles considered to be the clearest and easiest to understand. Some of the journals included were Scientific American, IBM Systems Journal, IEEE Transactions on Software Engineering, and Communications of the ACM. The clearest articles had about one-third of their page space devoted to graphics and illustrations. Obviously text alone is not sufficient to illustrate complex and abstract phenomena such as software, so reuse must encompass multiple communication methods.

Reusability of textual materials provides an excellent research platform for studying the fundamental properties of reuse. For example, if the atomic element of textual reuse is considered to be "words" then the volume of reusable material is obviously 100% for any given language such as English, French, or German.

However, if the element of textual reuse is considered to be a coarser unit, such as sentences, paragraphs, pages, or chapters, then the volume of reuse normally drops below 1% within a language, and may be 0% between unlike languages.

It would be an interesting experiment, and a good thesis topic as well, to explore the sets of documents produced for well-defined software product classes (such as spreadsheets or word-processing applications) and determine the potential for maximum reuse within those classes of application.

An extended form of such research would be to explore the sets of documents produced for applications which need to share information (such as word-processors and graphics presentation packages) and also explore the maximum reuse potentials.

In the military, document contents are not reusable but document structures usually follow standard formats as defined by military standards such as DoD 2167A. While this does result in reusable templates for many document types, it also results in very large documents which often contain redundant information. For this approach to be successful, the standards should be reviewed and pruned at least once every two years.

Actually, some of the content of military software documentation is reusable too. Topics such as the list of standards adhered to often occur without change in many different documents. This phenomenon is termed "boiler plate."

A basic but effective reusability approach, and one which is open to companies of almost any size, is to hire experienced technical communicators and technical writers. This results in a spontaneous kind of reusability, since experienced personnel tend to have templates and successful approaches in memory from their prior work.

10. **Methods of control**—The problem of lack of reusable document structures, and lack of reusable contents, is much more amenable to prevention than it is to control. Once a document set has been created, it is too late to introduce standard formats or reusable contents.

11. **Product support**—Reusable documents can be produced using a variety of standard word processing packages. Some of these, such as Microsoft Word for Windows even include reusable templates for common forms of documents such as business letters, FAXes, term papers, and technical articles. There are currently perhaps 30 commercial word processors, such as Ami Pro, Word Perfect, Word Star, Multimate, JustWrite, Zywrite, and the like. In addition, there are also some document production tools aimed explicitly at software technical documentation such as DOC (Document Publishing System) and NAPER-DOC. There are also tools which facilitate reuse by capturing information from one application and allowing it to be moved to another, such as Hi-Jack.

In the military software domain, several vendors produce tools which contain format templates of the 20 or so document types required by DoD 2167 A. For example, the 2167A Tool Set, Auditor, ASSIST/GT, and DOC-GEN.

A number of CASE tools offer documentation support. Since these tools usually include an integral data dictionary or encyclopedia and some form of repository manager, they tend to lend themselves to reusable document construction. Examples of tools in this domain include ARTESSA/3000, BACHMAN/Analyst,

CorVision, CADRE Teamwork, Design Aid II, Document Director, Excelerator, first-CASE, FOUNDATION, GEODE, I-CASE, IEF, IEW, ISPF, MacAnalyst, MAESTRO II, managerVIEW, NATURAL, NAVIGATOR, PowerCASE, ProKit WORKBENCH, PSL/PSA, Software Through Pictures, StateMate, TELON, TRANSFORM, and VAW (Visible Analyst Workbench).

Graphics, illustrations, and screen painters are sometimes integrated with other tools and sometimes available in stand-alone form. Here too, reusability is a goal but one not often encountered. Examples of tools in this domain include Ada-Graphics, The Analyst, BlauBloc, EASEL, IntegrAda, SEE SYSTEM, TIGRE, and WORKSHOP/204.

The most automated and hence most reusable forms of documentation are those derived by examining source code and data base structures. Some of these tools do more than simply document: some can restructure source code or perform other services too. Examples of tools in this domain include ABSTRACT, ADS/IMS and ADS/MVS, AutoFlow (for C, COBOL, FORTRAN, and PASCAL), C-DOC, DATAMANAGER, Docu-Mint, DOCU/MANAGER, DOCU/TEXT, Documentation Aid, DOSSIER PROVE, INDICATOR, PolyDoc, RECODER, RETROFIT, ROBOT/3000, SUPERSTRUCTURE, and VAX DOCUMENT.

12. **Consulting support**—There are quite a number of individual consultants and consulting groups who can perform technical writing, graphics production, and the production of various kinds of software documents. However, when the topic switches to reusable documentation or to fundamental research in optimal documentation methods, the number of consulting practices approaches zero.

13. **Education support**—Technical communication methods for software is seldom offered as a university course. General-purpose technical writing, on the other hand, is quite common. Some of the larger software producers have in-house training in technical writing and technical communication methods which tend to center around their concepts and approaches. Local or regional associations, such as the Society of Documentation Professionals in the Boston area may have courses on technical communication for software. On the whole, technical communication for software is seriously under-represented.

14. **Publication support**—The topic of reusable documentation seems to have few explicit citations in the software engineering literature. An exception is Caroline Chappell and Ronnie McBryde's *Open Document Architecture* (OVUM, 1991). Keith Hales and Judith Jeffcoate's *Document Image Processing* (OVUM, 1990) deals with a more restricted aspect of document reuse.

There are quite a few books on how to write technical documentation for software, however. There are also a number of useful books on the topics of cognitive psychology, and how various kinds of communication methods are perceived by users.

Examples of general guidelines for software documentation, that may be useful as background material leading to reuse, include Katherine Haramundanis' *The*

Art of Technical Documentation (Digital Press, 1992); Susan Schultz et al.'s *The Digital Style Guide* (Digital Press, 1993); Susan Schultz et al.'s *The Digital Technical Documentation Handbook* (Digital Press, 1993). Also relevant for international reuse is Scott Jones et al.'s *Developing International User Information* (Digital Press, 1992).

Software and scientific communication methods in 1993 are in the midst of profound changes caused by the concurrent advent of optical storage, multi-media hardware and software support, hypertext, and advances in scientific visualization approaches. It is premature to judge how all of these technologies will coalesce, but it is now theoretically possible to achieve fundamental improvements in the way complex topics are explained, illustrated, and transmitted from mind to mind.

Some of the titles which are relevant to the topic of reusing software documentation include: Simpson and Casey's *Developing Effective User Documentation: A Human-Factors Approach* (McGraw-Hill); Price and Cummings' *How to Write a Computer Manual: Software Documentation Handbook* (McGraw-Hill); Patterson and Beason's *Writing Effective Software Documentation* (Scott, Foresman & Co.); Brockman's *Writing Better Computer User Documentation* (John Wiley & Sons); Baeker's *Human Factors and Typography for More Readable Programs* (Addison Wesley); and Hein van Steenis' *How to Plan, Develop & Use Information Systems: A Guide to Human Qualities & Productivity* (Dorset House, 1992).

Since static documentation on paper pages and dynamic documentation on screens must be planned and designed concurrently, other relevant titles include: Lauriel's *The Art of Human-Computer Interface Design* (Addison Wesley); Ben Shneiderman's *Designing the User Interface* (Addison Wesley); and Thimbleby's *Human Interface Design* (Addison Wesley).

Effective documentation, and also reusable documentation, must integrate various document types from various document sources. On this topic, Dr. James Martin, the well-known software lecturer and researcher, has provided some useful introductions: *IBM Office Systems Architecture and Implementation* (Prentice Hall, 1990) discusses IBM's SAA (System Application Architecture) for creating composite documents. Also of interest is Dr. Martin's *Hyperdocuments and How to Create Them* (Prentice Hall, 1990).

The emerging topic of multimedia information should be noted also: Bruce Berra's *Multimedia Information Systems* (IEEE Press, 1992) is an example.

For deep background reading on scientific visualization, several new books are relevant: Peter and Mary Keller's *Visual Cues: Practical Data Visualization* (IEEE Press, 1992); and Nielson, Shriver, and Rosenblum's *Visualization in Scientific Computing* (IEEE Press, 1990).

Although not text publications, a number of video tapes discuss relevant topics. For example, the IEEE has an interesting video tape series which includes *Advances in Reusability, Topics in Reuse and Design Recovery,* and *Software Reuse: Past, Present, and Future* and *Visualization in Scientific Computing.*

15. Periodical support—Software documentation tends to be under-represented in the normal software periodicals. A notable exception to this rule are the frequent complaints about inadequate documentation which occur in roughly 50% of all software product reviews. Some aspects of software documentation and desktop publishing are supported by their own periodicals, as are multimedia applications and computer graphics. One of the few periodicals relevant to the topic of software documentation reuse is Business Documents. A notable gap in both book and periodical coverage is the absence of any materials on how Object-Oriented (OO) methods relate to user documents. In theory, OO user documentation would be a logical progression from OO analysis and design. Outside of software, documentation methods and linguistic analysis have a very rich literature. An example of a widely-cited journal is Visible Language, which explores many aspects of human communication.

16. **Standards support**—The IEEE, ISO, and DoD standards tend to provide the backbone of quite a lot of reusable documentation in the domains of plans, specifications, and to a lesser degree, user documentation. The standards tend to err on the side of excessive prolixity, but this problem can conceivably be rectified, although with great difficulty. DoD 2167A is currently the most pervasive in its impact on reusable documents. The new ISO 9000–9004 standards are ramping up quickly in impact, since 1992 is the year when compliance became necessary. The ISO standards create document sets that are as verbose and excessive as the DoD, unfortunately. IEEE Standard 1063–1987 Standard for Software User Documentation is useful, but also tends to create somewhat verbose document sets. As of 1992, none of the standards recognize new technologies such as multi-media, hypertext, or optical storage.

17. **Professional associations**—The major non-profit associations often have special-interest sub-groups that are concerned with documentation and communication: the ACM and IEEE for example. In addition, there are a number of regional or national documentation associations. For example, the Boston area has SDP, or the Society of Documentation Professionals.

18. **Effectiveness of known therapies**—As of 1993, it is premature to judge the effectiveness of known therapies. Documentation reuse has not been the subject of much in the way of formal research nor is there much empirical data available. It is possible, of course, to hypothesize.

For example, this book was written using Microsoft Word for Windows II. That application is approximately 2000 Function Points in size, and the User's Guide is 848 pages in size, for a rough average of 0.4 pages per Function Point. The estimated number of words in the User's Guide is about 170,000 which would yield a total of roughly 85 words per Function Point.

The volume of art (illustrations, graphics) constitutes something over 20% of the total page space, or roughly 180 pages out of 848 devoted to graphics and illustrations. Most of the illustrations are half-page in size or smaller, so the total number of graphics would amount to about 250 illustrations. That is roughly equivalent to 0.125 illustrations per Function Point.

Assuming little or no reuse, a technical writer could create this book in about a year, at a nominal rate of 3.8 pages per day. Assuming a fully burdened salary of $50,000 per year, the book's original creation might be roughly $50,000. (Editing and proof reading would add about another $10,000.) Thus a typical application User's Guide can be produced at a rate of about 167 Function Points per month, and have a cost that is roughly equivalent to $25.00 per Function Point.

Since reusable material must still be selected and merged, there is not a perfect correlation between the volume of reusable material and cost reduction. Roughly, an increase in reuse of 10% should generate a cost (and schedule) reduction of perhaps 7%. Therefore, if the User's Guide contained 50% reusable text and graphics, the cost and schedule might be about 35% lower than normal document creation without reuse. If the User's Guide contained 90% reused text and graphics, the reduction in cost and schedule might be about 63%.

19. **Costs of known therapies**—Reusable documents have not been formally evaluated in economic terms as of 1993, so the costs are not fully quantifiable. Tools which support documentation reuse (i.e. word processors, graphics packages, etc.) start at less than $100 and run up to as much as $5,000.

20. **Long-range prognosis**—Software documentation is going through a period of profound change, which will probably not be complete until the next century. Optical storage, multi-media information, scientific visualization, hypertext, knowledge acquisition and knowledge engineering are beginning to come together in exciting but unpredictable ways. The best case scenario for the end of the century would be to have libraries of reusable multi-media material. The worst case scenario would be to have standard paper documents produced more or less as they are in 1993 with minimal reuse. Adding to the uncertainty of long-range prediction is the specter of expensive litigation for copyright violation or "look and feel" violation for competitors who dare to use approaches similar to other competitors'. The technologies for achieving high-levels of document reuse are advancing quickly, but the business, cultural, and legal climate is not moving as rapidly.

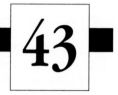

Lack of Reusable Estimates (Templates)

1. **Definition**—A) Lack of an accurate way of defining software projects and their characteristics with enough precision so that historical costs for a particular project can be used as the starting point when estimating similar projects in the future; B) Comparatively low availability of software estimating tools with templating capabilities, or the ability to convert historical data into reusable estimates.

2. **Severity**—The severity level of lack of reusable estimates based on historical data is fairly high, and appears to be about a 1.5 on the following five-point scale, where the amount of actual reuse is contrasted with the amount of potential reuse:

   Severity 1: Estimate contains < 05% reuse; template potential is > 95% reuse

   Severity 2: Estimate contains < 10% reuse; template potential is > 85% reuse

   Severity 3: Estimate contains < 20% reuse; template potential is > 75% reuse

   Severity 4: Estimate contains < 30% reuse; template potential is > 65% reuse

   Severity 5: Estimate contains < 40% reuse; template potential is > 55% reuse

   To clarify the significance of lack of software estimating templates, a software cost estimating template is equivalent to the standard costs used by a number of industries. For example, health insurance companies have standard cost tables for common medical procedures. Most large automobile repair garages have standard shop labor manuals that are used for common repair work.

3. **Frequency**—Lack of reusable cost estimates are endemic to the software industry, and the frequency appears to exceed 90% of all projects. This is not too surprising, since the tools and technologies for creating software estimating templates have only been on the commercial market since about 1985. From suveys of software project managers carried out by Software Productivity Research, the use of commercial grade estimating tools as of early 1993 is between 20% and 25%, although it is growing. Only a few of the 50 or so commercial software estimating tools can convert historical data into reusable estimates, so the usage of templates derived from accurate historical data in 1993 is less than 5%. Indeed, the availability of accurate

historical data is only between 10% and 15%. The availability of any historical data at all for software projects, accurate or not, appears to be less than 50%.

4. **Occurrence**—Lack of effective project cost estimating templates affects information systems, systems software, military software, commercial software, and contract-developed software with equal severity. Only a few major computer companies and large software contracting groups even approach the concept of effective templates.

5. **Susceptibility and resistance**—To start with an even decade, it can be asserted that prior to about 1990, susceptibility to lack of cost templates approached 100% of the software industry. Now that descriptions of template contents have been published, and template construction tools are on the commercial market, it will be interesting to see the rate at which the problem is eliminated.

6. **Root causes**—The fundamental cause for lack of software cost templates is the widespread lack of accurate historical data for completed software projects. Obviously, any effective template or standard-cost table must be derived from accurate measurements of actual software projects.

A secondary but important root cause is the fact that the software cost estimating business has historically been quite distinct from the project management tool business. It is obvious that cost estimating tools such as COCOMO, CHECK-POINT® and SLIM, etc., as well as traditional project management tools such as ARTEMIS, TIMELINE, PRESTIGE, and the others should be either directly coupled or should have convenient interfaces. Starting in about 1991, companies in both the estimating and project management domains have started business discussions leading to cooperative arrangements. Some of these joint arrangements are already commercially available as linked estimating and planning tools.

Following are some of the salient differences between commercial estimating tools and commercial planning or project management tools:

	Software Estimating Tools	Project Management Tools
Uses expert-system technology	Yes	No
Knowledge base of historical data	Yes	No
Sizing logic for code and documents	Yes	No
Function Point and LOC metrics	Yes	No
Influential factor adjustments	Yes	No
Tool and methodology catalogs	Yes	No
Quality and reliability modeling	Sometimes	No
Cost and resource accumulation	Yes	Yes
Gantt chart creation	Sometimes	Yes
PERT chart creation	No	Yes
Critical path modeling	No	Yes

A corollary root cause was the widespread usage of "lines of source code (LOC)" metrics prior to the publication of the Function Point metric in 1979. LOC metrics are worse than useless for software template construction. Indeed, they are extremely harmful.

Another root cause was the lack of a standard recording technique for the factors which influence the outcomes of software projects. It is not sufficient merely to record the schedules, costs and staff for a software project. For templating purposes, it is also necessary to know the languages used, the tools used, the rate at which requirements changed, and many other factors which influence the outcomes of software projects.

One of the most serious root causes has been the lack of a taxonomy for ensuring that two projects are similar enough for their costs to be comparable. It would be folly, for example, to use the costs for a small, civilian project as a template for a large military system. It is surprising that even after 50 years, the software industry still lacks an effective project classification system.

7. **Associated problems**—Lack of software cost templates is a major contributing cause to the problems of *canceled projects, cost overruns, excessive time to market, friction with clients, friction with senior management,* and *long schedules.*

The lack of templates is itself caused by the problems of *inadequate software engineering curricula, inadequate software management curricula, inaccurate metrics, inadequate measurement, lack of reusable plans and historical data, management malpractice,* and *slow technology transfer.*

8. **Cost impact**—The cost impact of lack of reusable software cost estimating templates has both a direct and an indirect component. The direct component is obviously the cost of developing a cost estimate for a product where a template should be available. For software projects with formal cost estimating activities, the direct costs of lack of templates amounts to perhaps a week of effort for every project: roughly $1,500 for every project estimated.

9. **Methods of prevention**—As of 1993, the most effective prevention is to start a full software measurement program that will capture project costs, resources, and influential factors with sufficient accuracy so that the data can be turned into templates for future projects. Within a few years, possibly even in 1993, a new kind of prevention may be commercially available: cost templates purchased from commercial template vendors.

Templates are not universally practical. However, within vertical domains for certain kinds of generic projects, and within certain industries where even direct competitors utilize similar software, cost templates would be extremely useful. Examples of project types where cost templates would be valuable include accounting systems, billing systems, operating systems, process control systems, and public and private switching systems. Examples of industries where even direct competitors utilize similar software include city governments, state governments, police agencies, banking, insurance, travel agencies, steel and metal fabrication, automotive assembly, wholesale and retail chains, and hotels.

Note that in order to use a template successfully, it is important that the projects from which the template is constructed, and the projects for which the template will be used, are very similar. This means that a good taxonomy of software projects is necessary before templating becomes a practical technology.

Following are discussions and examples of the kinds of information which should be recorded about software projects, if the data is going to be used to construct cost templates:

Generalized Format of an Estimating Template

A) Project identification
Project name
Project nature (new, enhancement, etc.)
Project scope (program, system, etc.)
Project class (civilian, military, internal, external, etc.)
Project type (real-time, batch, embedded, etc.)
Project goals (highest quality, shortest schedules, etc.)
Project constraints (caps on staffing, costs, etc.)

B) Estimate identification
Version number of estimate
Estimating personnel
Names
Locations
Contact method
Approval personnel
Names
Locations
Contact method
Estimating tools used
Estimating resources used

C) Client identifications (for specific clients)
Enterprise name
Standard industry classification (SIC)
Enterprise location (country, state or province, address)
Primary contact
Requirements contact
Approval contact

D) Developer identification
Enterprise name
Standard industry classification (SIC)
Enterprise operating units involved
Organization structure of project

E) Project Deliverable Sizing
   Documents to be delivered
      Languages to be used
   Functionality to be delivered
   Source code to be delivered
      Languages to be used
   Test materials to be delivered
   Other deliverables

F) Personnel Required for Project
   Management
   Development software engineering staff
   Maintenance software engineering staff
   Specialists
      Quality assurance
      Technical writing
      Configuration control
      Testing
      Other

G) Accounting Data for Project
   Salary levels for management
   Salary levels for technical staff
   Burden rates
   Overtime premiums
   Accounting year
   Currency exchange assumptions
   Inflation rate assumptions
   Special costs for Project
      Legal fees
      Moving and living
      Travel
      Capital equipment

H) Influential factors
   Developers' SPR effectiveness level
   Developers' SEI capability level
   Requirements changes
   Standards to be followed
   Statutes which affect project
   Methodologies utilized
   Quality control techniques
   Hardware tools utilized
   Software tool used
   Hardware platforms for development

Hardware platforms for operation
Unusual events
    Natural disasters
    Extraordinary attrition
    Other

I) Project Chart of accounts
    Phases to be estimated
    Activities to be estimated
    Tasks to be estimated
    Subtasks to be estimated

J) Critical path and PERT analysis
    Beginning and end of overall project
    Overlap among activities and tasks
    Critical path network among activities, tasks, and subtasks
    Earliest starts and latest endings of critical activities, tasks, and subtasks

K) Project Staffing Plan
    Overall staffing by time period (days, weeks, months)
    Peak staffing—overall project
    Specialist staffing levels

L) Quality and reliability estimate
    Defect potentials (all sources)
    Pre-test defect removal methods and efficiencies
    Testing stages and removal efficiencies
    Delivered defects
    Duplicate, invalid, and abeyant defects

M) Development estimate
    Phase staffing, resources, costs
    Activity staffing, resources, costs
    Task staffing, resources, costs

(Note: The minimum of 25 development activities whose resources, costs, staffing, and schedules comprise a basic template are: 1) Requirements; 2) Prototyping; 3) Architecture; 4) Formal planning; 5) Initial Analysis and Design; 6) Detail Design; 7) Design Reviews; 8) Coding; 9) Reusable Code Acquisition; 10) Purchased Code Acquisition; 11) Code Inspections; 12) Independent Verification and Validation (IV&V); 13) Configuration Management; 14) Integration; 15) User Documentation; 16) Unit Test; 17) Function Test; 18) Integration Test; 19) System Test; 20) Field Test; 21) Acceptance Test; 22) Independent Test; 23) Quality Assurance; 24) Installation and Training; 25) Project Management.)

N) Maintenance estimate
    Number of years of project usage
    Number of customer sites by year

Number of defects by year
Defect reporting methods
Customer support by year
Maintenance programming by year
Maintenance management by year
Field service by year

O) Enhancement estimate
Release intervals
Annual growth in new functions
Annual removal of obsolete functions

P) Normalized data
Development effort, costs, per Function Point, KLOC, etc.
Maintenance effort, costs, per Function Point, KLOC, etc.
Enhancement effort, costs, per Function Point, KLOC, etc.

Note: See also the section on reusable planning, since the capabilities of project planning or project management tools add substantial value to software templates.

As may be seen from the length of even a generalized skeleton of an estimating template, quite a bit of information is needed. For convenience in constructing and using estimating templates, they should obviously be fully automated. Automation brings with it the convenience of pull-down menus and the ability to access substantial volumes of on-line HELP information.

Following are examples of a few of the several hundred factors that can be selected when using an automated template construction tool such as CHECK-POINT®. Note that the ability to record this kind of information, which is so vital for template construction, is usually missing entirely from project management tools. This is why the integration of estimating tools and project management tools is increasing and is valuable.

Project Class

1) Personal program for private use

2) Personal program, to be used by others

3) Academic program, developed in an academic environment

4) Internal program, to be used at a single location

5) Internal program, to be used at multiple locations

6) Internal program, developed by external contractor

7) Internal program, developed by out-source contractor

8) Internal program, with functions accessed via network

9) Internal program (produced by a military service)

10) External program, to be put in the public domain

11) External program, leased to users

12) External program, bundled with hardware

13) External program, unbundled and marketed commercially

14) External program, developed under commercial contract

15) External program, developed under government contract

16) External program, developed under military contract

Project Type

1) Nonprocedural (generators, query, spreadsheet, etc.)

2) Batch applications program

3) Interactive applications program

4) Batch database applications program

5) Interactive database applications program

6) Client/server database applications program

7) Scientific or mathematical program

8) Systems or support program

9) Communications or telecommunications program

10) Process control program

11) Embedded or real-time program

12) Pen-based application

13) Trusted system with high reliability and security levels

14) Graphics, animation, or image processing program

15) Multi-media application

16) Robotics, or mechanical automation program

17) Expert system with substantial knowledge acquisition

18) Artificial intelligence program

19) Neural net application

20) Hybrid application (multiple types)

Standard Development Methods

1) Andersen Method/1

2) Bachman

3) Baldrige Criteria

4) Chen Data Design

5) Clean-Room Methodology

6) DeMarco Structured Analysis

7) DMR

8) Gane & Sarson Structured Analysis

9) Hatley Real-Time Design

10) Hoskyns Structured Analysis

11) IBM AD/Cycle

12) Information Engineering (IE)

13) ISO 9000 series

14) Object-Oriented Analysis

15) LBMS

16) Meiler Page-Jones

17) Merise

18) Pamela

19) Pride

20) SADT/DEF

21) SDM/70

22) Seigler

23) Spectrum

24) Spiral Model

25) SPR Method 2000

26) Stradis

27) Ward/Mellor

28) Waterfall Model

29) Yourdon Structured Design

30) Other _____

31) Mixed _____

Current SPR Effectiveness Level

0) SPR effectiveness level is unknown

1) Level 1—Excellent

2) Level 2—Good

3) Level 3—Average

4) Level 4—Below Average

5) Level 5—Poor

Current SEI Maturity Level

0) SEI maturity level is unknown

1) Level 1—Initial

2) Level 2—Repeatable

3) Level 3—Defined

4) Level 4—Managed

5) Level 5—Optimizing

10. **Methods of control**—Commercial software estimating tools, measurement tools, and commercial software planning tools which each deal with portions of a software template are now starting to be integrated or at least to communicate. This integration is starting to provide the groundwork for an expanding set of template capabilities. Indeed, the more powerful software cost estimating tools such as CHECKPOINT® or SLIM include a built-in template construction capability for software projects being initially estimated, and later measured. The synergistic linkage of a commercial software estimating tool such as CHECKPOINT® with a detailed project planning tool such as PRESTIGE or XPM can produce a powerful template that can be very useful for similar projects. As projects are actually constructed, the same tools allow true templates to be constructed from the accumulation of actual historical information.

11. **Product support**—As of 1993, commercial cost templates for common software types are not yet on the market. However, several vendors are known to be working on templates. (Examples of representative templates would include templates for the various SEI maturity levels, templates of ISO certified projects, and the like.) Tools which can produce such templates are commercially available, and have been on the market for several years. These can collect historical data and influential factors with enough precision to build templates, and have been commercially available for several years. Tools such as CHECKPOINT® from Software Productivity Research (SPR) and SLIM from Quantitative Software Management (QSM) can record historical data and influential factors. When such tools are tightly coupled to related project management tools such as ARTEMIS, PRESTIGE, TIMELINE, MicroSoft Project, the Project Managers Workbench (PMW) and the like, then highly detailed templates can be constructed.

    Note that Texas Instruments (TI) has support for a feature called "templates" as part of their Information Engineering Facility (IEF). However, these are not templates as discussed in this section. An IEF "template" is actually a blueprint or a standard reusable design.

12. **Consulting support**—Software cost template construction is a fairly new discipline, and only a few consulting groups as of 1993 appear to be involved. Quantitative Software Management (QSM) and Software Productivity Research (SPR) have already been identified. Other management consulting groups starting to move

into the template domain include Computer Power and Lucas Management Systems. Surprisingly, the Software Engineering Institute (SEI) has not yet addressed standard cost templates as of 1993. ABT Corporation is now exploring templates.

13. Education support—As of 1993, universities, most business schools, and software engineering schools have no courses on template construction in their curricula. Commercial education dealing with template construction is available from management consulting groups such as Software Productivity Research (SPR) and Quantitative Software Management (QSM).

14. Publication support—As of 1993, the only published book which actually contains an estimating template and explains how to construct one seems to be Capers Jones' *Applied Software Measurement* (McGraw-Hill, 1991).

Many other books cover software estimating, even if they lack discussions of reusable templates. Examples include Dr. Barry Boehm's classic *Software Engineering Economics* (Prentice Hall, 1981) and the more recent book by Charles Symons' *Software Sizing and Estimating Mk II Function Point Analysis* (Wiley Interscience, 1991). S.D. Conte, H.E. Dunsmore, and V.Y. Shen's *Software Engineering Metrics and Models* (Benjamin/Cummings, 1986) also includes material on software estimation methods.

15. Periodical support—As of 1993, none of the major software journals have discussed templates in either special issues or as normal topics. The IFPUG journal Metrics Views and the Journal of the International Society of Parametric Analysis (ISPA) deal with this topic upon occasion. American Programmer runs occasional special issues on reuse, but has not yet dealt with reusable estimates.

16. Standards support—Unfortunately, none of the major standards associations have adequately addressed the needs for template standards. Thus ANSI, DoD, IEE, IEEE, ISO and quasi-standards groups such as IFPUG, ISPA, and SCEA do not have published standards suitable for template construction. The IEEE standard on software productivity measurements may be modified in the future so that it is adequate for templating, but the 1993 version is not sufficient.

17. Professional associations—Most of the software professional associations are interested in templates, but none have addressed the topic explicitly. The International Society of Parametric Analysis (ISPA), and the Software Cost Estimating and Analysis (SCEA) group should be pioneers in templating, but tend to skirt around the central issues. The International Function Point Users Group (IFPUG) is exploring template-related issues. The IEEE, ACM, Software Publishers' Association, and most other professional groups lack formal programs dealing with templates.

18. Effectiveness of known therapies—It is premature in 1993 to make definitive statements about the effectiveness of software cost estimating templates. In non-software domains such as automotive repair, home construction, and medical insurance, the equivalent of templates are standard operating procedure and appear quite beneficial. It can be hypothesized that software cost templates for common, generic software projects will also be quite beneficial.

19. **Costs of known therapies**—Template construction tool sets would normally cost from $10,000 to $40,000. These tools also perform top-down and bottom-up estimation and planning, as well as template construction. The full capabilities of such tools normally return their value in less than 12 months. When only template construction is considered, such tools would return their value after perhaps 36 months, based on the number of similar projects for which the templates are utilized.

An interesting but unanswered question would be the costs of templates when commercially marketed. A template for a typical application such as a compiler, billing system, or PBX would probably be fairly inexpensive: perhaps $200 or less. If templates and blueprints are marketed together as a set, which is likely, then the costs will depend upon whether they are value-priced or commodity-priced. If they are value-priced, then from $3,500 to perhaps $7,500 might be the price for a matched blueprint/template combination for a set of 15 to 20 projects. If they are commodity-priced (as are blueprints and templates for home construction, sailboats, and the like) then the costs may well be under $1,000 and possibly under $250.

20. **Long-range prognosis**—The long-range prognosis for software templates is rather optimistic. If templates turn out to have commercial market potential, which seems likely, then they may explode into the creation of a new sub-industry by the end of the century. Templates and blueprints are technically synergistic, and the long-range prognoses of both technologies are closely coupled.

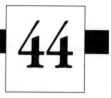

CHAPTER 44

Lack of Reusable Human Interfaces

1. **Definition**—Lack of consistent usage of installation procedures, removal procedures, keyboard commands, function keys, mouse buttons, icons, and HELP information from application to application.

2. **Severity**—The severity level of lack of reusable interfaces from vendor to vendor is fairly high, and appears to be about a two on the following five-point scale. The lack of reusable interfaces by a single vendor is much lower.

   Severity 1: Interface protocols are cumbersome, inconsistent, and non-intuitive
   Severity 2: Interface protocols are cumbersome and inconsistent
   Severity 3: Interface protocols are cumbersome and non-intuitive
   Severity 4: Interface protocols are inconsistent
   Severity 5: Interface protocols are cumbersome

3. **Frequency**—Lack of standard, reusable human interfaces for software packages has been a major problem since the industry began. Originally, this was due to the novelty of computer and software usage and the necessary trial and error period for any novel technology that requires concentrated human effort. More recently, the problem of inconsistent interfaces has been made even worse by "look and feel" litigation involving the nominal owners of some of the more intuitive interfaces, who are seeking to prevent other companies from using similar interfaces.

4. **Occurrence**—For personal computer and mainframe software projects, lack of reusable interfaces were endemic prior to the advent of Windows, X-Windows, Motif, IBM's SAA, and OS/2. For Apple software, inconsistent interfaces were significantly reduced by the interface protocols used for Macintosh applications.

5. **Susceptibility and resistance**—Consider what driving an automobile would be like if the steering wheel could be on the left side, right side, or center of the automobile; or if steering could be performed by paired levers (as in tanks) rather than by a steering wheel. Consider also what would be the result of interchanging the positions of the brake pedal and gas pedal from automobile to automobile. Acci-

dents would be much more common, since drivers would not be able to develop reflex patterns that would allow safe maneuvers when they switched from vehicle to vehicle.

The situation described above is more or less what confronts software users in 1993: the "controls" for performing normal tasks such as getting help or launching an application vary significantly from package to package.

The most susceptible to this problem are software vendors who have been hit by "look and feel" law suits. The most resistant to this problem are software vendors who own best-selling packages or who have established a proprietary claim to interface techniques, such as Apple.

The most resistant to date have probably been Macintosh applications, where the human interfaces are more or less identical across all commercial software packages.

6. **Root causes**—The primary cause for lack of reusable human interfaces was formerly that the state of the art had not advanced far enough to have worked out really good interface protocols. More recently, a second and more malignant root cause has surfaced: litigation involving "look and feel" of software interfaces. (Imagine what typing and word processing would be like if the look and feel of the QWERTY keyboard were subject to proprietary rights.)

Four discrete forms of reusability are relevant to human interfaces with software applications: 1) Usage of keyboard commands; 2) Usage of function keys; 3) Usage of mouse buttons; 4) The appearance of on-screen icons or visual information.

Combinations of these four interface techniques are involved in everything a user might want to do with a software application, including but not limited to:

A) Installing the application.

B) Uninstalling the application if needed (sometimes a very difficult operation).

C) Customizing the application to fit a particular operating system.

D) Using physical devices with the application (i.e. printers, plotters, etc.).

E) Configuring the application for optimal speed or minimum memory.

F) Turning the application on and beginning usage.

G) Turning the application off and exiting (a surprisingly awkward topic).

H) Using the basic functions of the application.

I) Using esoteric or seldom invoked functions.

J) Importing and exporting information to and from other applications.

K) Problem resolution, and what to do about them.

The entire topic of creating optimal human interface protocols for software (or hardware too for that matter) is starting to expand as a serious research topic. There are some basic questions that are still being explored. For example:

1) What mix of HELP text and on-screen graphics is most effective for software?

2) How effective are context-sensitive HELP screens?

3) How effective are hypertext links for information retrieval?

4) What are the most effective ways of finding information?

5) What will be the most effective interfaces for virtual reality applications?

6) What will be the impact of voice and pen-based interfaces?

7) What are the optimal interface approaches for computer users with various physical handicaps?

Research into the domain of reusable software interfaces requires cooperation between areas that have historically been quite disparate: linguistics, cognitive psychology, software engineering, and knowledge engineering. Researchers in any one of the disciplines are seldom in a position to carry out broad-based studies involving the others.

The most serious root problem is that when effective approaches surface for various aspects of dealing with software interfaces, they are often regarded as proprietary and defended quite fiercely in the courts. The lengthy lawsuit between Apple, Microsoft, and Hewlett Packard and the fierce defensiveness of Lotus against Borland and other competitors provide examples of the proprietary nature of user interface methods.

7. **Associated problems**—Lack of reusable human interfaces is a contributor to the problem of *low user satisfaction, slow technology transfer, long learning times, software usage errors*, and *high maintenance costs*.

Lack of reusable interfaces themselves are often caused by the major problem of *litigation potential*. Sometimes the problem is technical, and related to the very similar problem of *lack of reusable designs* and *lack of reusable user documentation*.

8. **Cost impact**—The cost of low levels of reusable human interfaces can be quantified fairly exactly for specific cases and specific products. In general, lack of reusable human interfaces tends to add from one to three days to the time required to learn any given software package. Since a typical computer user in 1993 tends to use from five to 15 separate software applications, and there are more than 20 million computer users in the United States, it is possible to extrapolate the impact of this problem fairly easily. From a low of 100 million working days per year to a high of 900 million working days can be associated with this problem.

There are also substantial costs associated with lost user time as they grope and search their way through arcane paper document structures looking for information which may not even be present. The related problem of poor or quirky document structures can be hypothesized to cost software users about 15 minutes a day. Since the U.S. has about 20 million people who use computers and software in 1993, the net loss of productive time can be as high as 5 million hours every working day! For the U.S. as a whole, some 137.5 million working days per year might be considered to be lost time searching for information about how to use a particular software application! That amounts to a loss of almost 7 days per year for every computer user.

9. **Methods of prevention**—Continuing research into human interface methods is the best preventive method. The concept of empirical research has been extended and made more sophisticated by IBM and other companies such as ITT, Xerox, Hewlett-Packard, and AT&T, and has developed into actual usability laboratories. In a usability lab, offices and work spaces are fully instrumented for sound and video recording, and various experiments are carried out with users and technical personnel performing normal tasks using different kinds of user command structures, interfaces, documentation, and the like. Both the time required to perform standard tasks, and the participants' subjective impressions can be recorded for analysis.

Research within ITT on human interfaces to software packages led to a somewhat surprising conclusion. Standard windowing techniques where explanatory materials, HELP text, and the like appeared in small windows was not optimal. If a user is trying to carry out a complex task, such as circuit design for example, the windows tend to overlay the work in progress. A second display device dedicated to on-line tutorial and HELP information gave better results. The ITT prototype display device was even portable, and could be picked up and handled like a book.

Studies on clarity and learning ease of complex tasks indicate that multimedia information may add a new dimension to the human interface situation. It is now technically possible to have audible messages as well as visual messages. The advent of pen-based computing, and the emerging advent of voice-based command recognition and virtual reality structures will bring a need for very extensive research.

10. **Methods of control**—The problem of lack of reusable human interfaces to software is much more amenable to prevention than it is to control. Once a software package has been created, it is usually too late to introduce new interface formats.

11. **Product support**—The entire domain of interface product support is undergoing transition under the impact of many factors including litigation, new technologies such as multi-media and pen-based computing, and the advent of virtual reality applications.

A number of CASE tools offer interface creation support. Examples of such tools in this domain include ARTESSA/3000, BACHMAN/Analyst, CorVision, CADRE Teamwork, Design Aid II, Excelerator, firstCASE, FOUNDATION, GEODE, I-CASE, IEF, IEW, ISPF, MacAnalyst, MAESTRO II, managerVIEW, NATURAL, NAVIGATOR, PowerCASE, ProKit WORKBENCH, PSL/PSA, Software Through Pictures, TELON, TRANSFORM, and VAW (Visible Analyst Workbench).

Graphics, illustrations, and screen painters also are used for interface creation. Examples of tools in this domain include AdaGraphics, The Analyst, BlauBloc, EASEL, IntegrAda, SEE SYSTEM, TIGRE, and WORKSHOP/204.

12. Consulting support—The topic of consulting on optimal human interfaces is a specialized niche, and successful work in this domain often requires advanced degrees in cognitive psychology, linguistics, or other advanced disciplines. This means that individual consultants are more likely to be found than practices within larger consulting groups. A very specialized form of consulting has become a necessity. There is now a group of attorneys who specialize in the "look and feel" subdiscipline of intellectual property law.

13. Education support—Human interface methods for software is sometimes offered as a university course. The larger software producers such as Microsoft and IBM have in-house courses and in-house interface experts. From time to time, commercial courses are offered, but this is one of the rare subdisciplines of software engineering where academia may be fairly up to date and superior to commercial education groups.

14. Publication support—The topic of standard, reusable human interfaces seems to have few explicit citations in the software engineering literature other than the numerous citations dealing with certain well-known topics such as SAA, Windows, the Macintosh protocols, X Windows, or Motif. There are quite a few books on how to write technical documentation for software, however. There are also a number of useful books on the topics of cognitive psychology, and how various kinds of communication methods are perceived by users.

Jerry Growchow's *SAA: A Manager's Guide to Implementing IBM's Systems Application Architecture* (Yourdon Press, 1991) is an example of one particular concept of reusable interfaces. (James Martin's entire SAA series, available from James Martin books, cover the same topics in a more expansive fashion.) James Larson's *Interactive Software: Tools for Building Interactive User Interfaces* (Yourdon Press, 1988) is more generic in its approach. Geoff Lee's *Object-Oriented GUI Application Development* (Prentice Hall, 1993) is also fairly generic.

Software and scientific communication methods in 1993 are in the midst of profound changes caused by the concurrent advent of multi-media hardware and software support, hypertext, and advances in scientific visualization approaches. It is premature to judge how all of these technologies will coalesce, but it is now theoretically possible to achieve fundamental improvements in the way complex topics are explained, illustrated, and transmitted from mind to mind.

Some of the titles which are relevant to the topic of reusable software interfaces include: Lauriel's *The Art of Human-Computer Interface Design* (Addison Wesley); Ben Shneiderman's *Designing the User Interface* (Addison Wesley); and Thimbleby's *Human Interface Design* (Addison Wesley).

Although addressed more to documentation than to on-line interfaces, other reference works include: Simpson and Casey's *Developing Effective User Documentation: A Human-Factors Approach* (McGraw-Hill); Price and Cummings' *How to Write a Computer Manual: Software Documentation Handbook* (McGraw-Hill); Patterson and Beason's *Writing Effective Software Documentation* (Scott, Foresman & Co.); Brockman's *Writing Better Computer User Documentation* (John Wiley &

384

Sons); Baeker's *Human Factors and Typography for More Readable Programs* (Addison Wesley); and Hein van Steenis' *How to Plan, Develop & Use Information Systems: A Guide to Human Qualities & Productivity* (Dorset House, 1992).

Reuse across national boundaries is also a relevant topic, and here a book by DEC, the *Digital Guide for Developing International Software Corporate User Publications* (Prentice Hall) is of interest.

Effective reusable on-line interfaces and reusable documentation must integrate various information sources. On this topic, Dr. James Martin has provided some useful introductions: *IBM Office Systems Architecture and Implementation* (Prentice Hall, 1990) discusses IBM's SAA (System Application Architecture) for creating composite documents. Also of interest is Dr. Martin's *Hyperdocuments and How to Create Them* (Prentice Hall, 1990).

The emerging topic of multimedia information should be noted also: Bruce Berra's *Multimedia Information Systems* (IEEE Press, 1992) is an example.

For deep background reading on scientific visualization, several new books are relevant: Peter and Mary Keller's *Visual Cues: Practical Data Visualization* (IEEE Press, 1992); and Nielson, Shriver, and Rosenblum's *Visualization in Scientific Computing* (IEEE Press, 1990).

Although not text publications, a number of video tapes discuss relevant topics. For example the IEEE has an interesting video tape series which includes *Advances in Reusability, Topics in Reuse and Design Recovery, Software Reuse: Past, Present, and Future* and *Visualization in Scientific Computing.*

15. **Periodical support**—Software interface methods tend to be under-represented in the normal software periodicals. Special periodicals such as Windows or Apple User tend to cover these topics within their specific domains. Interestingly, software game journals are rather sophisticated in their reviews and discussions of human interfaces.

16. **Standards support**—Unfortunately, the topic of optimal human interfaces is so prone to litigation that it is not really possible to develop standards. If the IEEE, ISO, ANSI or any other standards group inadvertently included a proprietary method in a standard, the probability of a law suit by litigious enterprises such as Apple or Lotus would be quite high.

The IEEE, ISO, and DoD standards tend to provide the backbone of quite a lot of reusable documentation in the domains of plans, specifications, and to a lesser degree, user documentation. The standards tend to err on the side of excessive prolixity, but this problem can conceivably be rectified, although with great difficulty. DoD 2167A is currently the most pervasive in its impact on reusable documents. The new ISO 9000–9004 standards are ramping up quickly in impact, since 1992 is the year when compliance became necessary. The ISO standards create document sets that are as verbose and excessive as the DoD, unfortunately. IEEE Standard 1063–1987 Standard for Software User Documentation is useful, but also tends to create somewhat verbose document sets. As of 1993, none of the standards recognize new technologies such as multi-media, hypertext, virtual reality, pen-based computing, or optical storage.

17. **Professional associations**—The major non-profit associations seldom have special-interest sub-groups that are concerned with interface protocols. Paper documentation and general communication are covered by both the ACM and IEEE. In addition, there are a number of regional or national documentation associations. For example, the Boston area has SDP, or the Society of Documentation Professionals which from time to time has guest speakers on interface methods.

18. **Effectiveness of known therapies**—As of 1993, it is premature to judge the effectiveness of known therapies for dealing with reusable and optimal interfaces. The topic is so litigious that legal issues tend to outweigh technical issues.

19. **Costs of known therapies**—Reusable interfaces using, for example, techniques regarded as proprietary by companies such as Apple or Lotus are generally unavailable without licenses. This means the costs are not readily enumerable.

20. **Long-range prognosis**—Software interface design is entering a period of profound change, which will probably not be complete until the next century. Optical storage, multi-media information, pen-based computing, voice-based computing, scientific visualization, hypertext, knowledge acquisition and knowledge engineering are beginning to come together in exciting but unpredictable ways. The best case scenario for the end of the century would be to have libraries of standard voice commands, pen-based icons, and other new approaches readily available and possibly even taught in grade school. The worst case scenario would be to have litigation bring research to a stand still. The spectre of expensive litigation for copyright violation or "look and feel" violation for competitors who dare to use approaches similar to other competitors' is too serious to ignore. The technologies for achieving high-levels of interface reuse are advancing quickly, but the business, cultural, and legal climates are not moving as rapidly.

CHAPTER 45

Lack of Reusable Project Plans

1. **Definition**—A) Widespread failure by the software industry to measure software projects with enough precision to use the historical data as a basis for project planning; B) Widespread failure by software engineering and business schools to teach project measurement and project planning effectively or at all; C) Widespread failure by vendors of project management tools to develop and market planning templates for common application types; D) Failure by various standards organizations to establish meaningful standards to support software templates; E) Any common, generic application which occurs with high frequency where the entire plan and work-breakdown structure is treated as a new and novel activity. Examples of common, generic applications include accounting systems, billing systems, compilers, data base packages, operating systems, payroll systems, PBX switching systems, and many others.

2. **Severity**—The severity level of lack of reusable plans derived from historical projects is greater than for either reusable designs or reusable code, and appears to be about a 1.5 on the following five-point scale, where the amount of actual reuse is contrasted with the amount of potential reuse:

Severity 1: Plan contains < 05% reuse; template potential is > 95% reuse

Severity 2: Plan contains < 10% reuse; template potential is > 85% reuse

Severity 3: Plan contains < 20% reuse; template potential is > 75% reuse

Severity 4: Plan contains < 30% reuse; template potential is > 65% reuse

Severity 5: Plan contains < 40% reuse; template potential is > 55% reuse

To clarify the significance of lack of software planning templates, a template is equivalent to the bill of materials and routing sheets when manufacturing standard products. A reusable software plan for common application types would contain the standard activities, tasks, and subtasks that will be followed as part of a complete work breakdown structure. The timing and sequence and critical path of the construction process would be derived from many similar projects.

3. **Frequency**—Lack of reusable plans or planning templates are endemic to the software industry, and the frequency appears to exceed 95% of all projects. This is not too surprising, since the tools and technologies for creating software planning templates have only been on the commercial market since about 1989. Prior to that time, there were many planning tools on the market (more than 70 at last count) but they did not cover the full spectrum of information necessary for templating. Successful templating requires three components: A) The work breakdown structures, schedules, staffing, effort, and costs of software projects; B) A way of recording the volume of requirements changes over the development period (about 1% per month); C) The effect of the usage of CASE tools, ordinary tools, methodologies, programming languages, source code quantities, paperwork volumes, and the skill or experience levels associated with the project. Ordinary project planning and management tools have tended to support only A, and have traditionally lacked support for B and C. An effective software project template needs data from all three categories. The integration of traditional project management tools with cost estimating and measurement tools is now leading to the ability to construct templates.

4. **Occurrence**—Lack of effective project planning templates affects information systems, systems software, military software, commercial software, and contract-developed software with equal severity. Only a few major computer companies and large software contracting groups even approach the concept of effective templates.

5. **Susceptibility and resistance**—It can be asserted that before 1990, susceptibility to lack of templates approached 100% of the software industry. Now that descriptions of template contents have been published, and template construction tools are on the commercial market, it will be interesting to see the rate at which resistance builds.

6. **Root causes**—The fundamental cause for lack of software planning templates is the almost universal lack of accurate historical data for completed software projects. Obviously any effective template or standard-cost table must be derived from accurate measurements of actual software projects.

Another root cause is the fact that the project management tool business was historically separate from the cost estimating business. Project management tools such as ARTEMIS, TIMELINE, and PRESTIGE and cost estimating tools such as COCOMO, CHECKPOINT®, and SLIM were developed by separate companies, and did not have close coupling or convenient data interchange mechanisms. That situation is now changing, and the project management and estimating companies are starting to forge strategic alliances or even merge.

A corollary cause was the widespread usage of "lines of source code (LOC)" metrics prior to the publication of the Function Point metric in 1979. LOC metrics are worse than useless for template construction: indeed they are extremely harmful. Yet another root cause was the lack of a standard recording technique for the factors which influence the outcomes of software projects. It is not sufficient merely to record the schedules, costs and staff for a software project. For templating purposes, it is also necessary to know the languages used, the tools used, the rate at which requirements changed, and many other factors which influence the outcomes of software projects.

7. **Associated problems**—Lack of software project templates is a major contributing cause to the problems of *canceled projects, cost overruns, excessive time to market, friction with clients, friction with senior management,* and *long schedules.*

   The lack of templates is itself caused by the problems of *inadequate software engineering curricula, inadequate software management curricula, inaccurate metrics, inadequate measurement, lack of reusable estimates, management malpractice,* and *slow technology transfer.*

8. **Cost impact**—The cost impact of lack of software planning templates has both a direct and an indirect component. The direct component is obviously the cost of developing a plan and cost estimate for a generic product where a template should be available. For software projects with formal planning and estimating, the direct costs of lack of templates amounts to perhaps two months of effort and $10,000 for every such project.

   The indirect cost of lack of planning templates has to do with the errors in customized plans constructed by managers without access to templates. For example, assume that the software for an average PBX switch has a 24 month development schedule, requires a staff of 12 personnel, accumulates 288 months of effort, and costs $1,500,000 to construct. A project manager who naively entered into an agreement to build the software for such a product in 12 months, with a staff of six people, with 72 months of effort, and with expenses of less than $500,000 will become painfully aware that a template would have been useful. The client and senior executives will also become aware that templates are useful as missed schedules and cost overruns begin to mount up toward yet another software catastrophe.

9. **Methods of prevention**—As of 1993, the most effective prevention is to start a full software measurement program that will capture project resources and influential factors with sufficient accuracy so that the data can be turned into templates for future projects. Within a few years, but not in 1993, a new kind of prevention may be commercially available: templates purchased from commercial template vendors.

   Templates are not universally practical. However, within vertical domains for certain kinds of generic projects, and within certain industries where even direct competitors utilize similar software, templates would be extremely useful. Examples of project types where templates would be valuable include accounting systems, billing systems, operating systems, process control systems, and public and private switching systems. Examples of industries where even direct competitors utilize similar software include city governments, state governments, police agencies, banking, insurance, travel agencies, steel and metal fabrication, automotive assembly, wholesale and retail chains, and hotels.

Note that the concept of a template includes a fairly detailed work-breakdown structure. The minimum granularity for an effective software template includes 25 activities. Templates for military software and major systems may include several hundred to more than 1000 activities.

The minimum of 25 activities whose resources, costs, staffing, and schedules comprise a basic template are: 1) Requirements; 2) Prototyping; 3) Architecture; 4) Formal Planning; 5) Initial Analysis and Design; 6) Detail Design; 7) Design Reviews; 8) Coding; 9) Reusable Code Acquisition; 10) Purchased Code Acquisition; 11) Code Inspections; 12) Independent Verification and Validation (IV&V); 13) Configuration Management; 14) Integration; 15) User Documentation; 16) Unit Test; 17) Function Test; 18) Integration Test; 19) System Test; 20) Field Test; 21) Acceptance Test; 22) Independent Test; 23) Quality Assurance; 24) Installation and Training; 25) Project Management.

Recording historical data at coarser levels, such as recording phase-level data (i.e. requirements, design, construction, and testing) is not sufficient for template construction. Imagine how useless an automotive shop manual would be if it only had generic costs for "electrical work," "engine work," and "body work."

Really successful template construction for software projects requires the integration of quite a bit of data from tools which have historically been separate: project tracking tools, project estimating tools, accounting tools, and project management or planning tools.

Full software templates include information about at least 10 specific influential factors associated with software projects: 1) Project class (i.e. military, civilian, etc.), type (i.e. process control, PBX, etc.), and size (Function Points, code, pages, etc.); 2) Requirements volume, methods, and tools; 3) Creeping user requirements after the requirements phase; 4) Design volume, methods, and tools; 5) Programming Language(s); 6) Amounts of reusable code; 7) Configuration control and integration tools; 8) Documentation volumes, methods, and tools; 9) Management methods and tools; 10) Geographic and environmental factors.

Templates also include normalized data for all activities. Function Points and Feature Points are the most accurate normalization metrics, and are preferred, but templates can also include normalized data using essentially any metric, including inaccurate ones such as "LOC" and "cost per defect." If inaccurate metrics such as LOC are used in templates, it is critical to identify the specific language(s) for which the template operates. Templates derived from COBOL, for example, should not be used for projects written in C or C++.

A complete software project template includes a description of the product class the template defines (i.e. compiler, PBX, or whatever); size ranges of the major deliverables and work products (i.e. pages of paperwork, source code volumes, test cases, etc.); the resources, staffing, schedules, and costs for all included activities; PERT and Gantt charts for the construction sequence; and various kinds of supplemental information. Software project templates typically run from about 15 pages to 50 pages in size.

The particular kinds of data which a standard project management or planning tool adds to the template are the elements where such tools are strongest: critical path and PERT analysis.

10. **Methods of control**—Commercial software estimating tools, measurement tools, and commercial software planning tools where each deal with portions of a software template are now starting to be integrated or at least to communicate. This integration is starting to provide the groundwork for an expanding set of template capabilities. Indeed, the more powerful software cost estimating tools such as CHECKPOINT® or SLIM include a built-in template construction capability for software projects being initially estimated, and later measured. The linkage of a commercial software estimating tool such as CHECKPOINT® with a detailed project planning tool such as PRESTIGE can produce a powerful template that can be very useful for similar projects. As projects are actually constructed, the same tools allow true templates to be constructed from the accumulation of actual historical information.

11. **Product support**—As of 1993, commercial planning templates for common software types are not yet on the market. However, tools that can collect historical data and influential factors with enough precision to build templates are commercially available. Tools such as CHECKPOINT® from Software Productivity Research (SPR) and SLIM from Quantitative Software Management (QSM) can record historical data and influential factors. When such tools are tightly coupled to related project management tools such as ARTEMIS, PRESTIGE, TIMELINE, MicroSoft Project, the Project Managers Workbench (PMW) and the like, then highly detailed templates can be constructed.

   Note that Texas Instruments (TI) has support for a feature called "templates" as part of their Information Engineering Facility (IEF). However, these are not templates as discussed in this section. An IEF "template" is actually a blueprint or a standard reusable design.

12. **Consulting support**—Template construction is a fairly new discipline, practiced by only a few consulting groups. Quantitative Software Management (QSM) and Software Productivity Research (SPR) have already been identified. Other management consulting groups starting to move into the template domain include Computer Power and Lucas Management Systems. The ABT Corporation is also addressing templates.

13. **Education support**—It appears that universities, business schools, and software engineering schools have no courses on template construction in their curricula. Commercial education dealing with template construction is available from management consulting groups such as Software Productivity Research (SPR) and Quantitative Software Management (QSM) and tool vendors such as ABT.

14. **Publication support**—As of 1993, the only published book which actually contains a template and explains how to construct one seems to be Capers Jones' *Applied Software Measurement* (McGraw-Hill, 1991).

Lois Zells' *Managing Software Projects* (QED Information Sciences, 1990) is an overview of many PC based software project planning tools. An even larger overview in terms of the number of tools cited is the *Project Management Tools Report* (STSC, March 1992) produced by Captain Kevin Burk, Dean Barrow, and Todd Steadman of the U.S. Air Force Software Technology Support Center (STSC) at Ogden Air Force Base. This report cites at least 150 or so software project managment tools.

A semi-annual catalog which includes many project planning tools, as well as a host of other tool categories, is that of Applied Computer Research of Scottsdale, Arizona: *Guide to Software Productivity Aids*. Other sources, such as the journals CASE Trends and CASE Outlook also produce tool catalogs which contain some planning tool citations.

15. **Periodical support**—As of 1993, none of the major software journals have discussed templates in either special issues or as normal topics. The personal computer and Macintosh journals review planning tools from time to time: Byte, PC Magazine, ComputerWorld, PC Week, PC Resources, etc. The IEEE Transactions on Engineering Management may have planning tool articles from time to time.

16. **Standards support**—Unfortunately, none of the major standards associations have adequately addressed the needs for template standards. Thus ANSI, DoD, IEE, IEEE, ISO and quasi-standards groups such as IFPUG, ISPA, and SCEA do not have published standards suitable for template construction. The IEEE standard on software productivity measurements may be modified in the future so that it is adequate for templating, but the 1993 version is not sufficient.

17. **Professional associations**—Most of the software professional associations are interested in templates, but none have addressed the topic explicitly. The International Society of Parametric Analyses (ISPA), and the Software Cost Estimating Association (SCEA) should be pioneers in templating, but tend to skirt the central issues. The International Function Point Users Group (IFPUG) is exploring template-related issues. The IEEE, ACM, Software Publishers' Association, and most other professional groups lack formal programs dealing with templates.

18. **Effectiveness of known therapies**—It is premature in 1993 to make definitive statements about the effectiveness of software planning templates. In non-software domains such as automotive repair, home construction, and medical insurance the equivalent of templates are standard operating procedure and quite beneficial. It can be hypothesized that software templates for common, generic software projects will also be quite beneficial.

19. **Costs of known therapies**—Template construction tool sets would normally cost in the $10,000 to $40,000 range. These tools also perform top-down and bottom-up estimation and planning, as well as template construction. The full capabilities of such tools normally return their value in less than 12 months. When only template construction is considered, such tools would return their value after perhaps

36 months, based on the number of similar projects for which the templates are utilized.

An interesting but unanswered question would be the costs of templates when commercially marketed. A template for a typical application such as a compiler, billing system, or PBX would probably be fairly inexpensive: perhaps $200 or less. If templates and blueprints are marketed together as a set, which is likely, then the costs will depend upon whether they are value-priced or commodity-priced. If they are value-priced, then from $3,500 to perhaps $7,500 might be the price for a matched blueprint/template combination for a suite of related projects. If they are commodity-priced (as are blueprints and templates for home construction, sailboats, and the like) then the costs may well be under $1,000 and possibly under $250.

20. **Long-range prognosis**—The long-range prognosis for software templates is rather optimistic. If templates turn out to have commercial market potential, which seems likely, then they may explode into the creation of a new sub-industry by the end of the century. Templates and blueprints are technically synergistic, and the long-range prognoses of both technologies are closely coupled.

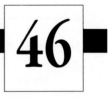

CHAPTER

Lack of Reusable Requirements

1. **Definition**—Failure by the software industry to develop a technique for exploring and capturing user requirements that is simultaneously convenient for the users themselves, and lends itself to comparison and analysis of generic requirements which might be transferred from project to project.

2. **Severity**—An appropriate way to consider the severity of the lack of reusable requirements is to evaluate the percentage of common, generic functional requirements for applications that occur in many similar applications, and hence may be needed in numerous software packages. The average severity is high, and appears to be about a two on the following five-point scale:

   Severity 1: Potential is > 90% reuse of requirements; actual reuse is < 10%

   Severity 2: Potential is > 80% reuse of requirements; actual reuse is < 15%

   Severity 3: Potential is > 70% reuse of requirements; actual reuse is < 20%

   Severity 4: Potential is > 60% reuse of requirements; actual reuse is < 25%

   Severity 5: Potential is > 50% reuse of requirements; actual reuse is < 30%

3. **Frequency**—After some 50 years of software history, many kinds of functions are known to be generic, and occur repeatedly in hundreds of applications. Examples include retrieving and storing data, transmitting data from application to application, input error detection, formatting input and output information, controlling screen colors and display characteristics, and many others.

   What the industry lacks are convenient, reliable methods for capturing this kind of generic user need so that analysis can be performed on the frequency with which common functions occur in many different kinds of software projects.

   Lack of reusable requirements is much more common than lack of reusable code, reusable designs, or any other software deliverable. Many common software applications share numerous requirements with others, and yet are built as unique artifacts when the applications are more than 90% identical. For example, the payroll systems of every U.S. company contain about 90% potentially reusable requirements. Accounting systems tend to exceed 95% potentially reusable requirements.

Many competitive products (i.e. E-mail, word processors, spreadsheets, switching systems, etc.) contain more than 50% standard, generic functional requirements.

Unfortunately, there is currently no easy or economical way to capture reusable requirements for most application types, or even to know of their existence. There are a few exceptions, however: compilers, sorts, operating systems, chess games (and a few other game types), and spreadsheets exist in such large quantities that more or less standard reusable requirements can be said to exist.

Research is underway in both England and the United States (and perhaps elsewhere) on fully automated table-driven requirements gathering approaches that may lead to reusable requirements. These experimental methods may also lead to other advantages as well, such as direct input from requirements to sizing and estimating tools, data modelling tools, and CASE design tools.

Research is also underway to carry out linguistic analyses of requirements and gather data on phrases, nouns, and verbs which occur with high frequency.

4. **Occurrence**—Lack of reusable requirements is endemic to the software industry in 1993, and occurs for MIS software, systems software, commercially marketed software, and military software. Military software is potentially in the best position to do something about this, since the DoD is mounting a well-funded campaign to explore various aspects of reuse.

5. **Susceptibility and resistance**—Essentially the entire software industry is susceptible to the lack of reusable requirements, with a few exceptions already noted. Resistance as of 1993 is rare, although there is reason to believe that this situation may get better within a few years. CASE vendors such as Texas Instruments are starting to recognize that reusable requirements might be a powerful selling tool for CASE, and indeed may even bring in separate revenue streams. As soon as a company starts making money by selling software blueprints or standard requirement sets, other companies are sure to follow.

Enterprises that are already using fairly advanced requirements methods such as Joint Application Design (JAD) and Quality Function Deployment (QFD) are at least potentially more resistant than companies which gather requirements in the old-fashioned adversarial way. Enterprises that use prototyping, modeling, and other approaches for dealing with dynamic requirements are also somewhat more resistant than most.

6. **Root causes**—The fundamental causes of a lack of reusable requirements are not easy to describe succinctly. The first and most basic cause is that the software industry has not yet developed a standard checklist for common requirement parameters. However, early in the 1970's a former IBM researcher (Don Burnstine) attempted to create a set of questions that could be used to generate a reusable requirements checklist for MIS applications. Examples of his basic question set were: 1) Is a client ordering space, skill, or things? 2) Does the supplier bill the customer or is the transaction for cash? 3) Is the item custom built or delivered from stock? 4) Does the supplier keep records by individual customer or not? 5) Is

the price fixed or negotiable? 6) Is the product rented, leased, or sold? 7) Is the service order tracked or not tracked? 8) Is delivery immediate or will it be in the future? From the patterns of answers to questions such as this, a generic set of reusable requirements could be constructed with comparative ease, and much less ambiguity than the customary amorphous descriptions using plain text.

The second basic cause is that there is no software equivalent to the "bill of materials" for manufactured products. That is, software lacks a concise way of describing the higher-level reusable requirements which will be part of an application.

To make an analogy with home construction, a requirement for putting a sink in a home bathroom need not contain a detailed description of what every washer, casting, valve, and fitting is supposed to do. Neither is it necessary for the user to specify water temperature, velocity, drain rates, or other performance-related topics. It is sufficient merely to indicate that a sink is needed, and where the sink will be placed.

The equivalent practice for software, in the absence of both reusable requirements and reusable designs, demand that the users detail every aspect of the performance and structure of the desired software functionality.

The third cause is derived from the second: the volume of the requirement specification set for software products tends to be enormous. The complete set of blueprints and construction plans for a 1500 square foot tract home requires less than 10% of the quantity of paper that the requirements and specifications for a 1500 Function Point software product will require. Civilian requirements usually take about 0.25 pages of text per Function Point; military requirements usually take from 0.5 to 0.75 pages of text per Function Point.

7. **Associated problems**—Lack of reusable requirements is a major component of *creeping user requirements, low productivity, low quality, long schedules, excessive time to market,* and *high maintenance costs.* Lack of reusable requirements is associated with five other similar problems: *lack of reusable architectures, lack of reusable code, lack of reusable designs, lack of reusable data,* and *lack of reusable plans and historical data (templates).*

The lack of reusable requirements is caused by *inadequate software engineering research, inadequate software engineering curricula, slow technology transfer,* and *inadequate capital investment.*

8. **Cost impact**—The initial requirements gathering phase of software projects in 1993 absorbs from about 3% to almost more than 15% of the costs of software, and from about 5% to more than 15% of software schedules. The variances are associated with the size, novelty, and complexity of the projects, the experience of the design team, design method and tools used, and whether the projects are military or civilian. Expressed in terms of Function Points, the observed productivity range of the requirements phase of software projects runs from less than 50 Function Points per staff month to more than 350 Function Points per month.

However, lack of reusable requirements brings hidden costs to software projects in the form of "creeping user requirements." Once the initial requirements are agreed to, they tend to grow at a rate of about 1% per month from that point through the development and even testing phases. Thus for a three year project, perhaps one third of the final requirements will have been added as afterthoughts. The costs associated with creeping user requirements are enormous, and standard sets of reusable requirements could potentially reduce requirements creep to below 5% for projects of any size.

Unfortunately, empirical data is unclear on what it costs to create reusable requirements for the first time. The basic dimensions of creating reusable requirements are these: A) The functional requirements of at least three similar projects must be carefully reviewed; B) A requirements checklist method must be created; C) The essential common features of the application must be expressed using the new method of representation; D) The new reusable requirements must be carefully inspected, and updated if needed; E) The reusable requirements must be validated by using it to build at least one new project; F) The reusable requirements design can now be placed in a catalog for perusal on future or similar projects.

This sequence of constructing reusable software requirements is more or less identical to the sequence used by real-estate companies for cataloging homes. Most multiple-listing real estate services have data on homes organized by geographic locale, cost, number of rooms and lot size. Thus when a client expresses requirements for a new home, it is possible to begin the search by looking at all available homes which meet the client's first set of requirements.

In general, reusable software requirements are somewhat similar to the cataloging practices of other complex artifacts such as automobiles, cameras, stereo equipment, houses, or sail boats.

Reusable requirements should address the functionality of the application (probably using a catalog of standard functions); the performance and security criteria; the inputs and outputs to the application; the kinds of logical data the application will use; and the interfaces to other applications and to the outside world. Requirements for information systems should also address the inquiry capabilities of the application. Requirements for military software projects should be clear and explicit enough to support backwards traceability since that is required for military software.

Reusable requirements should also contain supplemental information about user characteristics and about the usage patterns of the software (i.e. continuous use, intermittent use, etc.); its fault tolerance, permissible failure modes; and criteria for defect repair response times. Further, for long-range planning, reusable requirements should indicate anticipated change rates in terms of new inputs, outputs, algorithms, data elements, and the like. The reusable requirements should also contain information about relevant standards, statutes, or policies which affect them.

It is interesting that the criteria for reusable requirements are fairly close to the elements of the Function Point and Feature Point metrics. This fact leads to the potential of being able to derive functional size metrics automatically from user requirements, and even produce time to complete and cost to complete estimates as an automatic byproduct of the requirements analysis process.

9. **Methods of prevention**—The best prevention for the lack of reusable requirements appears to be associated with the profit motive. Several CASE vendors have recognized that reusable requirements would be valuable additions to their tool suites, and may significantly benefit users as well. Major computer companies and software houses which build sets of numerous related software projects (i.e. compilers, data base products, etc.) also have incentives for constructing reusable generic requirements. The Department of Defense and the U.S. military services are also motivated to create reusable requirements, since they own more software than any other entity on the planet. Indeed, U.S. military software ownership is greater than the total volume of software owned by more than half of the member countries of the United Nations.

Reusable requirements that are vertical within specific industries have some very attractive commercial potential. Industries where many different enterprises use similar or identical software applications are the most likely groups to find reusable requirements of interest. Examples of industries where reusable requirements would seem useful include: city governments, county governments, state governments, public schools, state universities, junior colleges, public utilities for electricity and water, telephone companies, local and state police and county sheriff departments, banking, insurance, agricultural production, religious institutions and major church groups, railroads, bus and transportation companies, airlines, travel agencies, professional athletic teams, hotels and motels, restaurants, retail stores, medical offices, law offices, and dental offices.

Vertical reusable requirements within specific industries vary with the industry. Several years ago, a number of public utility companies met and decided to consider reusable requirements and design for a generic fleet-management system, since all public utilities own and maintain sizable fleets of vehicles. Reusable requirements and designs have also started to occur for various police agencies and for motor vehicle registration systems.

Dr. James Palmer of George Mason University is doing some interesting linguistic analysis of historical requirements, in which they seek to create a taxonomy of common verbs and nouns that frequently occur in requirements. This work may conceivably lead to both reusable requirements, and to the ability to feed requirements directly into associated tools such as Function Point-based sizing tools, cost estimating tools, or CASE design tools.

The U.S. Navy's NAVAIR group is also exploring innovative requirements methods using tools such as Document Director and StateMate. The Navy's interest is in direct and automatic graphic modelling of requirements. The results to date have been impressive, and here too reuse is a distinct possibility. The Navy method also seems amenable to direct coupling between requirements and Function Point sizing and estimating tools.

10. **Methods of control**—Unless reusable requirements are available before the commencement of ordinary requirements analysis, there are no effective controls. Once requirements are constructed in the normal way, it is too late to do anything else.

11. **Product support**—Both interest in reusable requirements and the commercial market for reusable requirements are still uncertain. However, given the critical position of requirements, and the fact that incomplete, creeping user requirements is an endemic problem, it can be predicted that a successful approach to requirements reuse should turn into a highly successful product. If the reusable requirements could also feed directly into Function Point or Feature Point sizing tools, estimating tools, design tools, and even application generators, the success should be even greater.

Ancillary products which may be useful in analyzing existing software and extracting their generic functions for encapsulation into reusable requirements include: A) Complexity analyzers; B) Restructuring tools (especially those using graph theory); C) Re-engineering and reverse engineering tools; D) data dictionary tools; E) Library control and configuration management tools; F) Upper CASE or front-end CASE tools that support various design methods; G) Object-oriented design methods and tools.

A number of vendors currently support aspects of software requirements gathering, and may be moving toward fully reusable requirements. Examples include ACT/1, AdaFlow, ADW/RAD, APS, Bachman Analyst, CA-ADS, Cadre's SHORTCUT, Document Director, DynaShell, IBM's ISPF, PROTO-SDS, PSL/PSA, STATEMATE, System Architect, SPR's JADPoint, VERILOG, and the Visible Analyst Workbench (VAW).

12. **Consulting support**—Direct consulting support for reusable requirements is a rare commodity. Exceptions to this rule may include consultants within specific industries such as banking, insurance, and telephone operating companies who may well be aware of reusable designs for generic applications within the industry. Andersen consulting is working on several different types of reusability, and may offer consulting services on their concepts. Other major companies such as IBM and Microsoft are also working toward establishing new reusability consultancies.

13. **Education support**—It seems that university software engineering curricula do not deal with reusable requirements in any significant way. This is also true of commercial education. The lack of courses on principles of reusable requirements or reusable designs, and lack of practical examples must be considered a major gap in software education.

14. **Publication support**—The body of literature on reusable requirements is even smaller than the literature on reusable designs, data, test cases, and much smaller than the literature on reusable code. Some books deal with this topic in passing, however: titles include Dr. T.J. Biggerstaff and Dr. A.J. Perlis' massive two-volume work, *Software Reusability* (Addison Wesley, 1989); Dr. Will Tracz's, *Software Reuse—Emerging Technology* (IEEE Press, 1988); Dr. Peter Freeman's well-known *Software Reusability* (IEEE Press, 1987); and Dr. Carma McClure's popular *3 R's of Software Engineering: Reusability, Reenginering, Repository* (Prentice-Hall, 1992).

The general literature on software requirements methods is fairly rich, and growing rapidly. Some representative titles that are good background sources include Donald Gause and Gerald Weinberg's *Exploring Requirements: Quality Before Design* (Dorset House, 1993); Alan Davis's *Software Requirements* (Prentice Hall, 1993); and Ken Orr's *Structured Requirements Definition* (Ken Orr & Associates, 1981). See also Dr. Tom Love's *Oject-Lessons* (SIG Books, New York, 1993).

15. **Periodical support**—The general data processing journals run articles or even special issues on reusability from time to time, but seldom discuss reusable requirements. For example, both Ed Yourdon's American Programmer and the IEEE Transactions on Software Engineering have had special issues on reusability. Some of the vertical, industry-specific journals also deal with reuse for industries such as banking, CASE, and insurance.

16. **Standards support**—There are no known standards for reusable requirements as of 1993 published by ANSI, DoD, IEE, IEEE, ISO, or any other standards organization that deals explicitly with reusable designs. This is a significant gap in standards coverage. There are several standards published by the IEEE and DoD that discuss reusable *formats* for software requirements, but this is not the same as reusable *contents*.

17. **Professional associations**—The industry-specific professional associations, such as LOMA for the insurance industry, may have working sessions on reusable requirements and designs for common applications from time to time. The general professional associations such as the ACM or the IEEE frequently have sessions dealing with many aspects of reusability at conferences such as the well-known IEEE Software Engineering Symposia.

18. **Effectiveness of known therapies**—As of 1993, it is premature to really judge the effectiveness of reusable requirements for software applications in general. For those few products which have actually utilized reusable requirements, such as compilers within IBM, the effectiveness seems fairly high.

19. **Costs of known therapies**—As of 1993, it is premature to make general statements about the costs of reusable requirements since there is essentially no current commercial business in this area. As with most other reusable artifacts, the initial design and construction is fairly high. Usage across 10, 100, or 1000 projects would generate substantial economic returns. The economics of reusable designs should be more precise within a few years, and by 1995 a clear economic picture may emerge.

20. **Long-range prognosis**—For reusable code, the long-range prognosis is very favorable. The prognosis for reusable designs, data, test cases, documents, or requirements is somewhat more questionable. There are fairly complex technical issues which must be resolved before reusable requirements can truly succeed. For example, what is an optimal visual representation for a reusable requirement, and what will be the cataloging mechanism for retrieving reusable requirements if they existed? The topics are uncertain, but the overall prognosis is optimistic. The need for reusability at all levels is high enough so that no doubt the technical problems can be resolved by energetic effort.

CHAPTER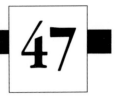

Lack of Reusable Test Plans, Test Cases, and Test Data

1. **Definition**—A) Failure by software-producing organizations to establish regression test protocols or create permanent libraries of test materials which can support multiple releases of evolving applications; B) Widespread failure to utilize general-purpose test plans or templates; C) Widespread commercial unavailability of test cases or test data for common application types.

2. **Severity**—An appropriate way to consider the severity of the lack of reusable test material is to evaluate the percentage of re-used test cases for applications compared to the potential for re-use based on the number of common functions that occur in similar applications, and hence may already have test materials available. The average severity appears to be about a three on the following five-point scale:

   Severity 1: Application uses < 05% reused test material; potential is > 95%

   Severity 2: Application uses < 10% reused test material; potential is > 90%

   Severity 3: Application uses < 15% reused test material; potential is > 85%

   Severity 4: Application uses < 20% reused test material; potential is > 75%

   Severity 5: Application uses < 25% reused test material; potential is > 65%

3. **Frequency**—After about 50 years, many kinds of applications are essentially standard utilities. For example, word processors, compilers, PBX communication systems, spreadsheets and data base products occur in scores and sometimes hundreds of instances. Generic test plans for common application types should be available, but often are not. Further, once useful applications are created, they tend to evolve over periods of many years and go through wave after wave of enhancement and maintenance releases. As of 1992, for example, many of the better-known word processors and spreadsheets and presentation graphics programs are at the release three through seven levels; MSDOS is at release five; Autocad is at release 12; and so forth. Regression test suites to ensure that changes and modifi-

cations have not damaged prior functions unknowingly should be a standard aspect of multi-release software, but often is not.

4. **Occurrence**—Lack of reusable test plans, test cases, and test data for common application types has been endemic to the software industry since it began. Lack of reusable regression test cases and test data for applications which evolve through multiple releases has also been endemic, although not quite as common. The patterns of occurrence of the two problems overlap, but are not identical.

Companies which produce software that evolves over time gradually came to the recognition that reusable testing materials were important to ensure consistency from release to release. Thus companies such as AT&T with its ESS switching system or IBM with various operating systems began to create formal regression test libraries as early as the 1960's. The term "regression test" means a special form of testing to ensure that enhancements to a software package do not destroy or damage functions which were already present in earlier versions.

However, both companies originally had problems implementing the concept of effective regression test libraries. For example, IBM discovered in the late 1960's that they had many different varieties of the same kinds of test case, which added costs to testing but did not add rigor since they tested identical conditions. Indeed, about a third of the entire number of test cases were accidental duplicates. Even worse, some of the test cases often had more errors than the products which they were intended to test! It quickly became evident that reusable test libraries needed pruning of surplus test cases, and more careful control over contents in the future to avoid both redundancy and test cases which themselves had a high error content.

Unfortunately, even in 1993, many companies still have these problems. Their regression test libraries are not under full technical and management control, and hence contain substantial percentages of both redundant and erroneous test cases.

As pure software houses began to occur and prosper they had similar needs to ensure consistency from release to release, platform to platform, and operating system to operating system. There is no cost-effective way to test products which exist in different varieties (i.e. DOS, Windows, OS/2, and UNIX versions of the same application) without reusable regression test libraries. Thus the larger software houses tended to establish formal reusable test libraries of regression test cases by the 1970's.

Unfortunately, some of these libraries are riddled with duplicate test cases and also have many test cases which themselves contain errors. There are also gaps in the functions being tested.

In a similar fashion, software journals which review multiple instances of similar applications (such as PC Magazine's review of various spreadsheets, word processors, CAD applications, etc.) quickly recognized the value of performing common test activities on all of the varieties of similar products. Here too, comparative testing of similar applications began as early as the 1960's.

In the 1990's, a new and important topic has surfaced that has a direct bearing on the need for reusable test cases and test data. When projects are reverse engineered, re-engineered, or down-sized, the test data which supports the earlier version of the product must be converted also. This topic has not yet been fully addressed by the re-engineering and reverse engineering tool vendors.

One would think that trial and error over a period of 40 years or so would have resulted in a substantial literature about reusable testing, and probably the commercial availability of reusable test cases for common application types such as word processors, spreadsheets, PBX switching systems, operating systems, access methods, and the like. However, this market niche appears to be totally unexploited.

As of 1993, one might expect that the object-oriented paradigm would encompass testing, and perhaps lead to a new class of OO test methods and test tools. Unfortunately, the OO literature does not seem to address this topic at all: a surprising gap.

5. **Susceptibility and resistance**—In general very large companies are more resistant than small. Maximum (but not total) resistance is usually found in large computer, telecommunication, or defense companies which have: 1) Formal test departments staffed by trained specialists; 2) Formal Software Quality Assurance (SQA) departments staffed by trained specialists.

The most susceptible companies are MIS software producers, and small to mid-sized software houses who are expanding their products across multiple platforms or operating systems. In both situations, susceptibility can be correlated to using generalists for test library control when specialists are needed.

6. **Root causes**—The root causes of lack of reusable test plans, test cases, and test data appear to be cultural and sociological. Testing in all of its manifestations is under-represented in the software literature, in software engineering curricula, and as a formal software research topic. Construction of reusable test materials is covered even more sparsely.

7. **Associated problems**—Lack of certified, reusable test cases or test data has a strong correlation to *low quality, low user satisfaction, long schedules,* and *missed schedules.*

Lack of certified, reusable test cases itself is often caused by *inadequate tools and methods for software quality assurance, inadequate software engineering curricula,* and *slow technology transfer.*

8. **Cost impact**—The economics of testing is undergoing a remarkable transformation now that functional metrics are being applied to problems of software quality. The older "cost per defect" and "LOC" metrics made economic studies of software testing exercises in frustration and futility.

There is no standard definition for all of the possible kinds of software testing and the sub-activities within testing. For convenience, it is useful to consider test planning, test case construction, test case execution, test coverage analysis, and test library control as the major topics encompassing software testing.

A typical testing expense pattern would be: test case preparation requires 15% of the effort; test case execution requires 20% of the effort; and fixing defects requires 65% of the effort.

Under a TQM approach, overall expenses would be lower, and the expense pattern for testing might be: test case preparation requires 30% of the effort, test case execution requires 30% of the effort; and fixing defects requires only 35% of the effort.

A new method for estimating the number of test cases required for software was developed in 1991, and is starting to produce useful results. A metric termed *Function Points* was invented by A.J. Albrecht of IBM, and placed in the public domain in 1979. This metric is derived from the weighted sums of five parameters: the numbers of inputs, outputs, inquiries, logical files, and interfaces that constitute a software application. The Function Point total of an application can be enumerated during the requirements and design phases.

It is obvious that testing must be carried out for each of the factors utilized by the Function Point metric. Empirical observations indicate that from two to four test cases per Function Point are the normal quantities created by commercial software vendors and computer manufacturers. Thus for an application of 1000 Function Points, from 2000 to 4000 test cases may be required to test the user-defined functionality of the application.

Note: Raising the Function Point total of an application to the 1.2 power gives a useful approximation of the number of test cases that may be required. Thus for a small 10 Function Point application about 15 test cases may be needed. For an application of 100 Function Points, about 250 test cases. For a truly major system of 10,000 Function Points, this method indicates that more than 63,000 test cases may need to be created. Obviously, the need for reuse, technical control, and other forms of careful planning rises in direct proportion to the size of the application that must be tested.

Each test case will require from a few minutes to something over three hours to create initially (and to document what conditions the test case deals with). Thus for large systems, test case creation is a very significant cost element. If test cases are created in a reusable fashion, that tends to add about 10% to 15% to the cost of each test case so created. These additional costs are insignificant if the test cases can be reused for multiple applications. However, the project that is funding their initial creation should receive some form of relief from the delta expenses.

Note that testing can be approached from several directions. Testing which attempts to validate user requirements or the functionality of software, without regard for its inner structure of the application, is termed *black box* testing.

Black-box test case construction for software has long been a largely manual operation that is both labor intensive and unreliable. (Empirical observations of operating system test libraries revealed more errors in the test cases than in the product being tested.) Test case generators have been used experimentally since the 1970's, and are starting to appear as both stand-alone products and as parts of CASE tool suites. However, in order for black box test case generation to work effectively, the specifications or written description of the software must be fairly complete, rigorous, and valid in its own right. It is to no purpose to generate automatic test cases for incorrect specifications.

Testing which attempts to exercise the structure, branching, and control flows of software is termed *white box* or sometimes *glass box* testing. In this domain, a fairly rich variety of tools has come into existence since 1985 that can analyze the structure and complexity of software. For certain languages such as COBOL and C, tools are available that not only analyze complexity but can restructure or simplify it. In addition, there are tools that can either create or aid in the creation of test cases. Quite a number of tools are available that can monitor the execution of test cases, and identify portions of code which have or have not been reached by any given test run.

Although not full test case generators, many supplemental testing tools are available that provide services such as creating matrices of how test cases interact with functions and modules. Also widely used are record and playback tools which capture all events during testing. One of the more widely used testing tool classes is that of test coverage analyzers. Test coverage analyzers dynamically monitor the code that is being executed while test cases are being run, and then report on any code or paths that may have been missed. Test coverage is not the same as removal efficiency: it is possible to execute 100% of the instructions in a software application without finding 100% of the bugs. However, for areas of code that are not executed at all, the removal efficiency may be zero.

Once created, effective test cases will have residual value long after the first release of a software product. Therefore formal test case libraries are highly desirable, to ensure that future changes to software do not cause regression, or damage to existing functionality.

It should be possible to market test cases and test data for various kinds of applications which occur with great frequency. However, this market niche has been essentially unexploited. Indeed, the whole domain of software testing tools and testing support is surprisingly small, given the importance of this topic to the industry.

9. **Methods of prevention**—The first step in a prevention program is to explore whether an enterprise needs reusable test cases and test data. If the enterprise creates software that evolves over multiple releases, the answer is yes. If the enterprise creates software that operates on multiple platforms or under multiple operating systems, the answer is yes. If the enterprise is down-sizing its applications, or reengineering them, the answer is also yes.

For enterprises where reusable test cases would be useful, the next step is to move toward the professionalism of the entire testing function, including any or all of the following: 1) Establishing a formal testing group or department; 2) Establishing a formal software quality assurance (SQA) group or department; 3) Acquiring or building test library support tools; 4) Acquiring or building ancillary tools such as complexity analyzers, test coverage analyzers, test case generators; 5) Exploring the existing test library for instances of redundancy and errors in test cases; 6) Establishing local and formal standards for test case reuse.

10. **Methods of control**—Unfortunately, when the need for control manifests itself, the problems are often far advanced. Every company which supports long-range modifications to its major systems (i.e. enhancements, conversion, down-sizing, etc.) should explore the implications of establishing a formal, reusable test case and test data library.

11. **Product support**—There are quite a few products which support software quality assurance (SQA) and many which support testing. However, products which aim at reusable test cases and reusable test data are in short supply. Tools which have some relevance to reusable test cases or test data include: ACT, AdaQuest, Battlemap, DEC/Test Map, Design Test Tool, Impact, Inspector, MIL/SOFTQUAL, Pathvu, ProTEAM, Q/Auditor, QualityTEAM, QQA, RevuGen, S-TCAT, SLEUTH, SLIM, SMARTS, SPMT, Software TestWorks, SQAMANAGER, TCAT, TestGen, TestPro, TIE(Q), T-Scope, Verify, VIA/SmartTest, and XRunner.

12. **Consulting support**—Consulting support in the testing arena is offered by both tool vendors and generalized management consulting organizations. Some of the consulting groups with well-known software testing and quality practices include Andersen Consulting, Bender & Associates, Computer Power Group, Ernst & Young, Phil Crosby Associates, Juran Institute, Quality Assurance Institute, QSM, Software Productivity Research, and Software Quality Tools.

13. **Education support**—Most U.S. software engineering and business schools are adequate in teaching basic testing concepts but seldom approach reusable test data. Those that have reusable test data themselves are virtually nonexistent. Unfortunately, universities may be interested in topics such as test case reuse or software quality automation, but tend to be seriously underfunded and understaffed.

14. **Publication support**—Books that deal with test case or test data reusability automation are essentially nonexistent in 1993. This is a major gap in the software engineering literature. Of the books that deal with partial aspects of reusability in various manifestations, software testing is the worst covered and has not been a primary focus of concern. Vendor manuals from companies which market software quality tools, such as test coverage analyzers, etc. are often useful, but quite narrow in their focus.

There is a growing set of books which provide useful background information on testing, and some that also deal with test data selection. A few examples of the genre include: Glenford Myers' classic *The Art of Software Testing* (John Wiley & Sons, 1979). A more recent title is Daniel Mosley's *The Handbook of MIS Application Testing* (Yourdon Books, 1993) which has a very useful bibliography attached. Bill Perry's *A Standard for Testing Application Software* (Auerbach, 1992) and the same author's *A Structured Approach to System Testing* (QED Information Sciences, 1988) can be mentioned.

The widely used *Guide to Software Productivity Aids* published semi-annually by Applied Computer Research has a large section on software testing tools, as well as sections on debugging tools, management tools and CASE. Other catalogs are produced by Auerbach, Datapro, CASE Trends, CASE Outlook, and the British OVUM group.

15. **Periodical support**—Here too, there is a major gap in the software engineering literature. Although articles on various aspects of reusability occur fairly often, articles on reusable test cases, test data, and test plans are seldom found. Testing per se has fairly good coverage in the standard software journals such as Communications of the ACM and IEEE Transactions on Software Engineering. Indeed, there are a number of journals which specialize in software testing topics: ITEA Journal of Test and Evaluation; Software Quality World; Testing Techniques Newsletter, and The Journal of the Quality Assurance Institute. House journals of large corporations such as the AT&T Technical Journal, Digital Review, and the IBM Systems Journal cover testing fairly often, and other companies such as Hewlett Packard, Motorola and Microsoft include testing articles in their journals too.

16. **Standards support**—While there are many standards, such as DoD 2167A, ISO 9000, and various IEEE standards that deal with software quality and serve as fairly good sources of reusable test plan skeletons in a generic manner, there are no known standards as of 1993 that deal with software test case or test data reuse.

17. **Professional associations**—Reusable testing is outside the scope of most SQA organizations. However, this topic may be added to their set of issues in the future. There are a number of national and regional software quality non-profit associations that include aspects of testing as topics for discussion. National groups include the Society for Software Quality (SSQ), and the Society for Information Systems Quality (SISQ). Regional groups include those in the San Francisco Bay Area, Atlanta, and New York. There are also special interest quality groups within larger organizations such as the IEEE, ACM, IFPUG, and ASM. The non-profit International Society of Parametric Analysis (ISPA) has a number of member companies and individuals who build quality and reliability models, and SQA automation is often discussed within this forum although not, to date, the impact of reusable test cases and test data. The Software Cost Estimating and Analysis (SCEA) non-profit association also has an interest in quality automation and testing, although this topic is subordinate to cost estimating. The well-known Software Engineering Institute (SEI) has done very little in the domain of software quality automation and essentially nothing in the domain of reusability per se, or of reusable test data. This is a surprising gap considering the SEI charter.

Although they are not non-profit organizations, the Quality Assurance Institute (QAI), Quantitative Software Management (QSM) Software Quality Tools, and

Software Productivity Research (SPR) have user associations and conferences where quality automation, testing, and reusability are frequent topics.

18. **Effectiveness of known therapies**—The economic effectiveness of reusable test cases and test data correlates directly with their quantity or volume. Those applications where reused test materials exceeds 50% of the total volume are visibly lower in test construction costs than groups where every test case is a unique artifact. An important but unanswered question as of 1993 is: What is the maximum amount of test material reusability that is theoretically possible in general-purpose applications, and can it approach 100%?

Interviews with professional programmers by the author and his colleagues at Software Productivity Research noted that even without formal corporate reusability support for test cases and test data, experienced programmers spontaneously reuse from 20% to about 50% of the test cases code in their significant applications, using their own private or personal reusable test libraries. Unfortunately, these private libraries are seldom shared among colleagues and hence are somewhat inefficient for large multi-programmer systems and applications.

19. **Costs of known therapies**—Spontaneous and private re-use of test materials by experienced programmers costs essentially nothing. Formal large-scale reusability of test cases and test data for all of the applications that are evolving within an entire corporation can range in costs from a few thousand dollars to many millions of dollars, depending upon the size of the enterprise. While the costs can be quantified for any specific enterprise or work group, it is difficult to develop generic guidelines.

An interesting but unanswered question as of 1993 would be the commercial price of reusable test cases and test data if and when they are commercially marketed. If such materials are value-priced, then they might sell for more than $500 for low-end products on personal computers and perhaps $5,000 for UNIX based workstations. Since such a market does not currently exist, speculations are not too useful.

20. **Long-range prognosis**—Reusability is such an important topic and so many companies and government agencies are performing active research that mild optimism appears justified even for reusable test cases and test data, which is the least understood of all aspects of reusability. The best-case scenario would be that reusable test cases will constitute more than 50% of the volume of all new software application testing by the end of the century. Note that the technologies of reusable test plans, cases, and data, reusable code, reusable designs (blueprints), and reusable plans (templates) are all synergistic and closely intertwined. Also, it may be that the object-oriented (OO) paradigm will begin to explore reusable test cases and test data. To date, this topic has been outside the scope of OO research.

CHAPTER

Lack of Specialization

1. **Definition**—A) Failure by the software industry to establish a meaningful taxonomy of recognized software engineering specialties; B) Failure of individual enterprises to identify and utilize practitioners trained in relevant specialties; C) The widespread but naive belief that generalists are fully adequate for the construction and maintenance of large and complex systems projects; D) Failure to recognize the need for special skills for software activities where general software engineering and management training are deficient, i.e. architecture, estimating, planning, measurement, quality assurance, testing, human interface design, technical writing, technical illustration, training, configuration control, and maintenance.

2. **Severity**—The average severity of lack of specialization in the United States is rather high, and averages about a two on the following five-point scale:

    Severity 1:   Lack of specialization causes cancellation of a major software project

    Severity 2:   Lack of specialization causes low quality, delays, and cost overruns

    Severity 3:   Lack of specialization causes either low quality, delays or cost overruns

    Severity 4:   Lack of specialization causes delays, overruns, or user dissatisfaction

    Severity 5:   Lack of specialization causes user dissatisfaction

3. **Frequency**—Lack of specialization is endemic to the software industry, and as of 1993 occurs in perhaps 90% of U.S. software-producing enterprises. For software enterprises with less than 50 employees, lack of specialization approaches 99% but the problem is seldom serious for small enterprises. For software-producing enterprises with more than 1000 employees, the frequency is about 75% and is a serious problem when it occurs. Lack of specialization is normally benign for small projects of less than 500 Function Points in size. As the size of the software increases, the need for specialization increases. Failure to use relevant specialties on projects larger than 5000 Function Points in size should be considered an example of management malpractice.

4. **Occurrence**—Lack of specialization is endemic among management information systems (MIS) projects, where the problem is widespread. Systems software, commercial software, and military software are somewhat resistant. Major software-producing enterprises with more than 10,000 software professionals are often highly resistant.

5. **Susceptibility and resistance**—The patterns of resistance and susceptibility are not clearly known. In general, the largest and most sophisticated software-producing companies have recognized the need for and provide specialists in critical activities. Unfortunately, some of these same enterprises tend to utilize the generic title "member of the technical staff" so that identification of specialists or statistical studies involving them are difficult to carry out. Somewhat surprisingly, military software organizations which use formal position descriptions are the most alert to the need for software specialization.

The need for specialization correlates strongly with the overall software population of an enterprise:

Software Employees	Specialists Encountered
Less than 10	None
From 10 to 50	Testing
From 50 to 100	Testing, quality assurance, technical writing
From 100 to 500	Testing, quality assurance, technical writing, maintenance, configuration control, measurement, data base administration
From 500 to 1000	Testing, quality assurance, technical writing, maintenance, configuration control, measurement, data base administration, local area networks
Larger than 1000	Testing, quality assurance, technical writing, maintenance, configuration control, measurement, estimating, data base administration, local area networks, human factors, standards, architecture, process analysis, requirements analysis, data modeling, performance, viral protection, function point analysis, reuse, Total Quality Management (TQM)

Without continuing ad infinitum, a total of more than 100 different software specialties and occupation groups have been observed as of 1993. Eventually software will follow the practice of medicine and law, and establish a standard taxonomy of recognized specialists accompanied by educational prerequisites and performance standards.

Following is a table which illustrates some of the kinds of specialists interviewed in the course of performing SPR software assessments:

Executive and Management Occupations

1) Presidents
2) Vice Presidents
3) Chief Information Officers (CIO)
4) Chief Scientists
5) Directors
6) 3rd Line Management
7) 2nd Line Management
8) 1st Line Management
9) Supervisors
10) Technology Managers
11) Project Managers
12) Career Managers

Primary Technical Occupations

1) Lead Analysts
2) Analysts
3) Programmer Analysts
4) Application Programmers
5) Systems Programmers
6) Software Engineers
7) Data Base Administrators
8) Integration Specialists
9) Configuration Control Specialists
10) Testing Specialists
11) Quality Assurance Specialists
12) Technical Writing Specialists

Specialist Technical Occupations

1) System Architects
2) Reverse Engineering Specialists
3) Reengineering Specialists
4) Restructuring Specialists
5) Information Engineering Specialists
6) Project Library Specialists

7) Repository Specialists

8) Reusability Specialists

9) Package Evaluation Specialists

10) Domain Specialists

11) Hardware Specialists

12) Microcode Specialists

13) Performance Specialists

14) Wide Area Network Specialists

15) LAN Specialists

16) Capacity Planning Specialists

17) Tool Development Specialists

18) Downsizing Specialists

19) CASE Specialists

20) Decision Support Specialists

21) Artificial Intelligence Specialists

22) Object-Oriented Method Specialists

23) Members of the Technical Staff

24) Research Fellows

Maintenance Occupation Specialists

1) Maintenance Programmers

2) Maintenance Customer Support Specialists

3) Maintenance Field Service Support

4) Maintenance Management

5) Maintenance Test Specialists

6) Maintenance Integration Specialists

Customer Support Occupation Specialists

1) Customer Liaison Specialists

2) Customer Support Specialists

3) Information Center Specialists

Education and Communication Occupation Specialists

1) Technical Editors

2) Technical Translators

3) Educational Planners

4) Educational Instructors

5) Communication Specialists

6) Multi-Media Specialists

7) Human Factors Specialists

8) Linguistic Specialists

9) Graphics Specialists

10) Virtual Reality Specialists

Business Occupation Specialists

1) Project Planning Specialists

2) Project Estimating Specialists

3) Project Measurement Specialists

4) Long-Range Planning Specialists

5) Accounting Specialists

6) Financial Audit Specialists

7) Business Planning Specialists

8) Acquisition and Merger Specialists

9) Marketing Specialists

10) Sales Specialists

11) Sales Support Specialists

12) Software Audit Specialists

13) Standards Specialists

14) Methodology Specialists

15) Data Administration Specialists

16) Purchasing Specialists

17) Competitive Evaluation Specialists

18) Outsourcing Specialists

19) Human Resources Specialists

Attorneys and Legal Specialists

1) Attorneys—Intellectual Property

2) Attorneys—Patents

3) Attorneys—International Law

4) Attorneys—Corporate

5) Attorneys—Litigation

6) Paralegal assistants

External Consulting Occupation Groups

1) Strategic Planning Consultants

2) CASE Consultants

3) Methodology Consultants

4) Market Planning Consultants

5) Competitive Evaluation Consultants

6) TQM and Quality Consultants

7) Measurement Consultants

8) Estimating Consultants

9) Function Point Consultants

10) Assessment Consultants

11) Baselining Consultants

12) Domain Consultants

13) Object-Oriented Methodology Consultants

14) Systems Engineering Consultants

15) Acquisition and Merger Consultants

16) Financial Consultants

17) Contract Development Staff

18) Facilities Management Staff

6. **Root causes**—The primary cause for lack of specialization is the comparative youth and immaturity of the software industry. Lack of adequate demographic studies that reveal the number and kinds of software specialists employed by software-producing organizations is another cause. The third reason is the lack of recommended standards or guidelines by professional associations such as the IEEE for the kinds of specialists needed by the industry. The fourth is the failure by universities and academic institutions to recognize the existence of software specialists, and offer appropriate curricula.

Analogies with medical and legal specialization are relevant. When a physician specializes in internal medicine, or an attorney specializes in intellectual property law, that does not mean that they know nothing about other subdisciplines: it simply means that their practices are concentrated in particular domains. Indeed, from time to time both physicians and attorneys may change their specialties, or may be certified in several different specialties concurrently.

For software specialists, working in a particular domain such as quality assurance does not imply inability to do other kinds of work—it simply means that the specialist is concentrating in a recognized subdiscipline. What software lacks today, vis a vis medicine and law, are expanded curricula for the relevant subdisciplines and clear definitions of the roles of various specialists.

7. **Associated problems**—Lack of adequate specialization is very strongly correlated with *low quality.* It is also often associated with *cost overruns, excessive time to market,* and *missed schedules.* Lack of specialization is frequently associated with the problem of *poor organization structures.*

   Lack of specialization is often caused by *inadequate software engineering curricula, inadequate management training,* and occasionally by *management malpractice.*

8. **Cost impact**—The cost impact of inadequate specialization is difficult to quantify. In most human occupations, specialists can outperform generalists by a substantial margin and this appears true for software as well. Anecdotes and specific observations suggest that adequate specialization would probably improve software quality by around 50%, and software productivity by around 15%. These provisional data points are derived from assessments and consulting studies where the quality and productivity levels of enterprises with specialists are compared against the same size organizations which used generalists primarily. However, many other factors exist which could also affect the results. For example, the enterprises with specialists also had better tooling and more sophisticated methodologies deployed, by and large.

9. **Methods of prevention**—The first step in prevention of the problem is the simple recognition that the problem exists and is fairly serious. From that point on, universities and professional associations should be able to establish specialization criteria and training curricula. Software producing organizations that utilize formal job descriptions and which utilize annual demographic surveys are usually able to see the need for specialists long before ordinary enterprises.

   Another method of prevention is to create a *skills inventory* of the kinds of occupation groups employed within an enterprise. This approach has been used for more than 30 years, with varied results. A common problem with skills inventories is that some of the skills that are assumed to be important for a particular position may not be. Conversely, skills that are quite important may not be recognized as such.

10. **Methods of control**—A *project audit* or one of the standard *process assessment* studies carried out using the SEI, SPR, or an equivalent assessment methodology will often diagnose inadequate specialization. Once diagnosed, the problem can be cured by moving away from the generalist concept and towards the specialist concept. Given normal personnel hiring practices and the sluggishness which many enterprises exhibit when making fundamental changes, expect about five years (or more) to fully make the transition from generalists to specialists.

    As companies prosper and grow, there is a normal sequence in which specialists begin to be utilized. When the software population approaches 100, testing and quality assurance specialists tend to occur. When the software population approaches 200, maintenance specialists, data base administrators, and network specialists tend to occur. Obviously these are rough observations, and variations occur often.

11. **Product support**—A few software estimating tools include occupation-group estimates. Some project planning tools such as Artemis, Prestige, Timeline and PMW also allow the entry of occupation groups or specialists, although deliberate user input is required. There are a reasonable number of skills-inventory and personnel-related systems which deal with occupation groups and specialists. Note that one of the major weaknesses of many project tracking and cost accounting systems is that they do not support effort and cost tracking to the level of special occupation groups.

12. **Consulting support**—The subject of skill planning and occupation group planning is not a common specialty, but there are consultants and consulting groups that deal with the topic. For example, the Atlantic Systems Guild, Dean Myer Associates, Nolan, Norton & Company, the Software Engineering Institute (SEI) and Software Productivity Research (SPR) deal with this topic from time to time.

13. **Education support**—The topic of occupation group and skill selection for software projects is seldom covered by either university software engineering curricula, business school curricula, or commercial courses. There are some exceptions, such as the certification program for software quality analysts and for software cost analysts. These certification programs include testing in the basic and advanced topics of the subdisciplines, and are intended to ensure that those receiving certification are in fact knowledgeable.

14. **Publication support**—As of 1993 few books that deal explicitly with software specialization and demographic trends are available. From time to time, chapters or sections within more generalized books will discuss this topic, such as Curtis's *Human Factors in Software Development* (IEEE Press, 1984) or Jones's *Applied Software Measurement* (McGraw-Hill, 1991). Tom DeMarco and Tim Lister's widely-cited *Peopleware* (Dorset House, 1987) is always relevant. Dr. Gerald Weinberg's *Understanding the Professional Programmer* (Dorset House, 1993) tackles the interesting topic of professionalism. The same author's classic *The Psychology of Computer Programming* (Prentice Hall, 1971) is one of the most widely cited and one of the best-selling books ever published on a software topic. Weinberg's *Becoming a Technical Leader* (Dorset House, 1986) is not about specialization, but does deal with the special skills needed to deal with some of the complex topics confronting software professionals. Ed Yourdon's well-known *Decline and Fall of the American Programmer* (Prentice Hall, 1992) takes the dismaying hypothesis that the U.S. software industry may fail before the details of specialization are fully worked out. N. Dean Meyer's *Structural Cybernetics* (N. Dean Meyers, Ridgefield, CT, 1993) is relevant.

Richard Backe's *Employment Guide for Engineers and Scientists* (IEEE Press, 1992) is useful background information. Lawrence Kamm's *Real-World Engineering: A Guide to Achieving Career Success* (IEEE Press, 1992) is useful for deep background information.

Many professional associations produce intermittent surveys of salary ranges for various kinds of software management and technical positions: The AMA, the IEEE, and the Massachusetts Software Council are examples. Check regional groups for local data. Also, regional Quality Assurance groups and regional CASE User groups may have informal networks for various specialists.

The Department of Commerce publishes an annual *Occupational Outlook* for American industries which includes useful information on which industries are growing and shrinking. Some state governments produce more localized equivalents. A few states, such as Alaska, are actively seeking software companies and offering tax advantages and other inducements to relocate. Janet Rule's *The Programmer's Survival Guide* (Yourdon Press, 1989) is not about specialization per se, but is a useful book for software personnel who might have been laid off in one of the many industry down-sizings. Yet another book in this genre (now being sold in Boston area computer book stores) is Christopher Kirkwood's *Your Services are No Longer Required* (Plume Books, 1993) which is aimed at personnel recently laid off.

15. **Periodical support**—Most of the general software engineering periodicals do not deal with specialization or software occupation groups as normal topics. From time to time individual articles may touch upon this subject. Personnel journals may also deal with software specialization, but these journals have low visibility within the software profession. Ed Yourdon's eclectic *American Programmer* is the most likely journal to discuss this topic, since it eventually gets around to most of the major problems of software.

16. **Standards support**—There are currently no ANSI, DIN, DoD, IEE, IEEE, or ISO standards that deal explicitly with software specialization. This is a major gap in standards coverage. Several corporations such as IBM and General Electric have internal position description manuals which define various job titles and responsibilities, but these are not true standards. The military services also have explicit position descriptions for many specialist categories. Here too, these are more akin to policy statements than to true standards. Unfortunately, some companies go in the opposite direction, and lump all technical workers together under generic titles such as "member of the technical staff." This kind of coarse aggregation of multiple skills makes long-range personnel planning remarkably difficult.

17. **Professional associations**—The major professional associations such as the IEEE have formed a number of special interest groups, such as quality assurance and testing. The most widespread organizations for software specialists are those of quality and technical writing, since both subdisciplines have a number of professional associations available. Until recently there was a Software Maintenance

Association, but to survive the recession of 1991 it broadened its scope and name and became the Software Management Association. Other specialized professional associations include technical writing, parametric software cost estimating (ISPA or the International Society of Parametric Analysis), and Function Point measurement (IFPUG, or the International Function Point Users Group). Although the Software Engineering Institute (SEI) is doing research on a number of software-related topics, specialization has not yet been explicitly covered. SEI will probably address this topic in the future, since the higher SEI maturity levels (3, 4, and 5) are built on the precept of increased specialization.

18. **Effectiveness of known therapies**—Enterprises that recognize the need for software specialization and create the organization structures to support it tend to have larger market shares, more satisfied clients, higher productivity, and better quality. From these observations it can be hypothesized that the therapies associated with moving towards specialization are reasonably effective. However, it is possible that the samples are biased or that other factors intervened.

19. **Costs of known therapies**—The direct costs of carrying out annual demographic surveys and establishing enterprise-wide skills inventories constitute the major expense. The exact amount of expense will vary with the size and geographic dispersion of the enterprise. Given the propensity for specialists to outperform generalists, these surveys should return their value in about five years. The timing might be quicker, but once such a survey identifies a gap in specialization, it takes time to either hire from outside or train from inside to fill the gap.

20. **Long-range prognosis**—Every form of science and engineering, as well as medicine and law, went through evolutionary transformation that caused a move from generalists to specialists. The sheer amount of knowledge that builds up in a mature discipline is so great that no human mind can encompass all of it, and so specialization is a natural occurrence. The fact that as of 1993, specialization is starting to accelerate for software is an encouraging sign: it means that we are finally accumulating enough knowledge so that we can begin to consider ourselves a true engineering discipline. The prognosis is favorable for recognizing as many as 100 software engineering specialties by the end of the century.

Long Service Life of Obsolete Systems

1. **Definition**—A) Aging systems whose utility is declining and whose maintenance costs are rising, but which cannot be withdrawn from service for business or financial reasons; B) Prior but still usable releases of applications that remain in service.

2. **Severity**—The average severity of software obsolescence is a complex topic that does not lend itself to a simple five-point scale. As software ages, two phenomena tend to occur simultaneously: 1) The basic structure of the software degrades under the cumulative impact of many small changes. This is an increase in the *entropy* or disorder of the system; 2) The essential functionality of the application tends to become obsolete as technology and business operations evolve. The cumulative effect of these two phenomena is that aging software becomes progressively harder to maintain, and yet the need for functional enhancements and defect repairs steadily increases. The average severity of mainframe software is about a three on the following five-point scale. The average severity of PC software is only about a five, due to more rapid replacements in the PC domain.

   Severity 1:   Age > 15 years, with obsolete functions and very high entropy

   Severity 2:   Age > 10 years, with marginal functions and high entropy

   Severity 3:   Age > 5 years, with marginal functions and increasing entropy

   Severity 4:   Age > 5 years, with adequate functions and increasing entropy

   Severity 5:   Age > 3 years, with adequate functions and increasing entropy

3. **Frequency**—The life expectancy of software tends to rise in proportion to the size of the application. Raising the Function Point total of a program or system to the 0.25 power will provide a crude indication of the probable number of years that the software will be in use before being withdrawn. Thus for an application of 1000 Function Points (about the size of a PC word processor or spreadsheet), the life expectancy would be 5.6 years. For an application of 10,000 Function Points (about the size of a mainframe order-entry or accounting system) the life expectancy would be 10 years. For an application of 50,000 Function Points (about the size of a mainframe operating system or a major defense system) the life

expectancy would be 14.9 years. It should be noted that as of 1992, the optimal economic life of software applications and systems is essentially unknown. Indeed, neither the average nor maximum life expectancies of software have adequate citations in the literature.

4. **Occurrence**—Long service life for aging and obsolete software tends to be concentrated in the domain of medium to large mainframe systems, and hence is most common among large enterprises and government agencies. For enterprises in economic distress and which lack adequate capital and cash reserves, the problem is likely to be both acute and chronic since they cannot afford effective remedies. One way of analyzing the occurrence of this problem is to consider the average age of applications in the five languages where aging and unstable software is most common. The following data is taken from *Knowledge Base* (SPR, Inc. Vol. 1, No. 1, June 1992).

Language	Development Programmers	Maintenance Programmers	Total Programmers	Average Age of Software (Years)
Assembler	9,100	56,900	66,000	> 15
FORTRAN	10,375	39,125	49,500	> 13
PL/I	2,063	6,187	8,250	> 12
COBOL	192,152	385,365	577,500	> 10
C	130,062	76,188	206,250	> 4

As may be seen, these five languages constitute the crux of what has come to be known as "the maintenance problem." That is, applications where the entropy is high and which cannot be withdrawn from service due to business or financial needs.

5. **Susceptibility and resistance**—Aging assembler language applications are the most susceptible to both chronic and acute maintenance distress. Assembler applications are typically the oldest in any corporation's portfolio. Also, assembler language lends itself to the creation of very poorly structured applications, and there is also a shortage of both tools and experienced programmers who can deal with these problems. The geriatric care providers (reverse engineering and re-engineering) have not really done much for assembler, since the problems are tricky and the market only of moderate size.

PL/I suffers primarily from a lack of adequate tools and a shortage of trained programmers. Historically, PL/I is an interesting language. It was developed and sponsored by IBM as a true general-purpose language that could be used for both business, systems, and scientific software. The language turned out to be too baroque, however, and few programmers ever mastered all of its capabilities. When IBM perceived that their strategy was not working (i.e. PL/I would not replace COBOL and FORTRAN) support for PL/I tended to peter out. It is interesting that the Ada language is also being touted as a true general-purpose language, and is also rather baroque.

FORTRAN seems to have the minor advantage that scientific and mathematical applications, where FORTRAN dominated, are somewhat more stable and more resistant to continuing changes once complete. However, the geriatric business (reverse engineering, re-engineering) is more or less passing FORTRAN by except for the availability of complexity analyzers.

Of the major languages where aging software is most common, COBOL is the most resistant. Indeed, an entire new sub-industry has come into being circa 1985 of tools and services for providing geriatric care for aging COBOL: complexity analyzers, restructuring tools, reverse engineering tools, and re-engineering tools are now plentiful.

The C language is still too new to have been used to build up a substantial inventory of aging and obsolete applications in the U.S. as a whole, although AT&T where the language was developed has a substantial inventory. However, C's popularity and widespread current usage indicates that aging and obsolete C applications will become a major problem over the next decade. The C language is difficult and tricky to use, but add-on tools and support are becoming popular. Since major vendors such as DEC, IBM, Microsoft, and Borland are now in the C market, the prospect for geriatric support is pretty good. Many CASE tool vendors are starting to offer both new product capabilities, and geriatric support as well.

Because older legacy systems with high entropy levels are difficult and hazardous to modify, there is a tendency to stay away from modifications other than truly mandatory ones. On the other hand, well-structured applications with low entropy levels can be modified with relative ease and relative safety. This leads to an interesting paradox: the annual costs of enhancements for well-structured applications is often *higher* than for poorly structured applications. The apparent reason is that well-structured applications are modified much more often. On the other hand, the costs of performing any specific enhancement tend to favor the well-structured applications.

A 1991 experiment by Language Technology of Salem, Massachusetts, indicated that the effort for making the same change was 40% less when the change was made to a well-structured base system as when made to the same system in a poorly structured form. A series of 26 interviews by the author with IBM systems programmers in California (13 were fixing bugs; 13 were adding enhancements) reached a similar conclusion: working with well-structured base code was perhaps twice as fast as with poorly structured for any given update.

6. **Root causes**—The primary causes for keeping aging software past its prime are twofold: replacement is too expensive and it takes too long. The average cost of building new software in the U.S. is about $1,000 per Function Point (roughly a range of $600 to $1200 per Function Point). Adding enhancements to existing software can average less than $800 per Function Point for modifying well-structured base systems, but more than $1200 per Function Point for modifying poorly-

structured base systems. The average annual maintenance cost for defect repairs in the U.S. is about $15 per Function Point (roughly a range of $5 to $150 per Function Point). It is slightly cheaper to modify well-structured software than to replace it. Even though it is more expensive to modify poorly structured software, the additions are so much smaller than the base that there are short-term savings. Thus it is easy to see why older systems continue to be used long past their primes. Also, since old systems must be used while replacements are being built, enterprises face a double hit: simultaneously funding new projects while continuing to maintain old versions.

7. **Associated problems**—The long service life of obsolete systems is a key contributor to the problem of *high maintenance costs.* In addition, aging software with high entropy levels are associated with *low productivity, low quality, error prone modules,* and *friction with users.*

Long service life of obsolete software is itself caused by *inadequate planning* and *inadequate maintenance tools and methods.*

8. **Cost impact**—The cost impact of maintaining obsolete systems with high entropy can be predicted with very high precision for specific systems and applications, but is more difficult to generalize. The normal range of maintenance expenses in the U.S. for defect repairs and minor routine modifications is from about $15 per Function Point to $50 per Function Point. The range of maintenance costs for aging and obsolete systems with high entropy is from about $50 per Function Point to $250 per Function Point.

Another useful metric is the "maintenance assignment scope" or the amount of aging software which one person can keep operational in a given year, in terms of defect repairs and minor updates. Current U.S. norms are in the range of 500 Function Points (equivalent to about 50,000 to 75,000 source code statements in languages such as COBOL or C). For poorly structured software, the assignment scope drops, but for well-structured software with few latent defects, the assignment scope can exceed 1,500 Function Points (equivalent to about 150,000 to 200,000 source code statements in procedural languages).

9. **Methods of prevention**—The rate at which entropy increases in software is strongly correlated with the initial structure and quality level when the application is first deployed. The most effective method of prevention, therefore, is to develop high-quality and well-structured software initially. Doing this almost guarantees a long and useful service life. On the other hand, software that is low in quality and poorly structured when first deployed will experience nearly catastrophic increases in entropy and maintenance costs within a three to five year period.

Hartford Insurance has been exploring maintenance and enhancement of aging legacy systems since the early 1980's and is one of the few MIS producers in the United States with ten consecutive years of fairly solid data on maintenance costs. They developed a multi-tier approach to dealing with legacy systems based on the strategic importance of the application. Applications with high strategic value are totally refurbished if necessary, which includes restructuring, remodularizing, redocumentation, and module renaming. A combination of automatic restructuring and geriatric tools, plus manual effort is devoted to the task. Applications with low strategic value are automatically restructured, but little or no manual effort is utilized.

This approach has more than tripled the maintenance assignment scope of the Hartford maintenance personnel, and has led to a continuous annual decline in total maintenance costs. In an industry where many companies spend more than 50% of their budgets on maintenance and enhancement, Hartford is below 19% and dropping.

10. **Methods of control**—For existing software that is already past its prime, where entropy is high and maintenance costs excessive, the methods of control vary strongly by language. COBOL has the greatest quantity of tools and support available. Indeed, a new sub-industry appeared circa 1985 of tools, products, and services which provide geriatric care for aging COBOL applications. The primary components of this sub-industry are complexity analyzers, restructuring tools, reverse engineering tools, and re-engineering tools.

For other languages, control methods are not in such plentiful supply. The second-place language in terms of geriatric support is the C language, where several CASE vendors such as CADRE and DEC provide geriatric services.

Ada is not yet old enough to have built up a library of aging and obsolete applications, but geriatric tools are already being planned for this language.

The languages with minimal geriatric support include Assemblers, APL, BASIC, CHILL, FORTH, FORTRAN, JOVIAL, LISP, and several hundred more.

11. **Product support**—For aging COBOL applications, a growing sub-industry of products exist which are too numerous to list completely. Vendors such as Bachman, CGI, KnowledgeWare, Intersolv, Viasoft, and Visible Systems have continuously expanding capabilities.

For non-COBOL applications, the CASE vendors which specialize in military and systems software are starting to provide geriatric support: CADRE, CORTEX, DEC, Hewlett-Packard, etc.

12. **Consulting support**—Most large management consulting groups have developed practices which deal with geriatric care for aging software: Andersen Consulting, CGI Consulting, Computer Power, DMR Group, Keane Associates, Peat Marwick, and many others. In addition, there are countless smaller consultancies and individual consultants which service this area.

13. **Education support**—Universities and academic institutions, by and large, do not cover geriatric services well, and in many cases, at all. Courses by consulting groups and commercial education services such as Digital Consulting (DCI), the Quality Assurance Institute (QAI), or the Technology Transfer Institute (TTI) are much more plentiful, and tend to be more current than university curricula. The University of Durham in England has a well-known maintenance research center.

14. Publication support—Until about five years ago, books dealing with mainte-nance and aging software were almost non-existent. An informal survey carried out at the McGraw-Hill corporate bookstore in New York in 1986 noted a disparity of titles between development books and maintenance books which exceeded 100 to 1. Recently, however, new books on geriatric care are starting to increase in volume and content maturity. James Martin and Carma McClure's *Software Mainte-nance: The Problem and its Solution* (Prentice Hall, 1989) is a good introduction. The author Capers Jones' *Applied Software Measurement* (McGraw-Hill, 1991) con-tains data on U.S. averages for software life expectancies and annual maintenance costs.

The pioneering maintenance authors Girish Parikh and Nicholas Zvegintzov deserve some credit for dealing with maintenance problems five or ten years before other researchers realized the importance of the topic. Eric Bush is also a well-known pioneer in the maintenance arena. Girish Parikh's *Handbook of Soft-ware Maintenance* (John Wiley & Sons, 1986) was one of the first to hit mainte-nance head-on. Lowell Jay Arthur has also explored maintenance. His *Software Evolution* (John Wiley & Sons, 1988) is widely cited. David Longstreet's *Software Maintenance and Computers* (IEEE Press, 1990) is also relevant.

Lowell Jay Arthur's *Software Evolution—The Software Maintenance Challenge* (John Wiley & Sons, 1988) is a useful analysis. David Higgins' *Data Structured Software Maintenance* (Dorset House, 1992) is an interesting recent application of Warnier-Orr principles to the maintenance arena. Roger Fournier's *Practical Guide to Structured System Development and Maintenance* (Yourdon Press, 1991) takes a holistic approach to both development and maintenance. Robert Arnold's *Software Reengineering* (IEEE Press, 1992) tackles a recent technology by means of selected articles. A useful companion volume is that of David Longstreet, *Software Mainte-nance and Computers* (IEEE Press, 1990). Yet another recent addition to the main-tenance literature is Landsbaum and Glass' *Measuring and Motivating Maintenance Programmers* (Prentice Hall, 1992).

A catalog by Applied Computer Research, *Guide to Software Productivity Aids*, includes almost all maintenance tools marketed in the United States. The cat-alog is updated twice a year. The University of Idaho has published an excellent bibliography of the software maintenance arena: Jack Hagemeister, Bruce Lowthar, Paul Oman, Xiaokang Yu, and Weiguo Zhu's *An Annotated Bibliography on Soft-ware Maintenance;* University of Idaho, 1991 (Report #91–06 BB).

Proceedings of various maintenance conferences are often useful. The IEEE, for example, should be hosting their 9th annual software maintenance conference in 1993.

15. Periodical support—One of the few dedicated journal that deals with mainte-nance and geriatric topics is *Software Maintenance: Practice and Experience.* This journal is published in both the U.K. and the U.S. See also *The Journal of Software Maintenance.* A U.S. journal, *Software Maintenance News,* fell into economic dis-tress during the recession of 1991 and changed its name and scope to *Software*

Management News to attract a broader client base. It still discusses maintenance, however. Most of the standard software journals have frequent articles, but coverage is often slanted toward notable disasters.

16. **Standards support**—There are no known standards published by ANSI, DoD, IEE, IEEE, or ISO that cover service life and aging software.

17. **Professional associations**—Until 1992, the Software Maintenance Association was the most visible U.S. professional group. However, the name was changed to Software Management Association and the focus has broadened. Many other groups, such as the IEEE, DECUS, GUIDE, SHARE, IFPUG, and ADAPSO are interested in these problems and many will have special-interest sub-groups within them.

18. **Effectiveness of known therapies**—For aging software written in either COBOL or C, the current crop of therapies are remarkably effective. For other languages, such as Assemblers or PL/I, there are so few therapies that their effectiveness is quite low.

19. **Costs of known therapies**—For COBOL and C, tools which can analyze complexity and restructure aging software run from a few hundred dollars up to about $50,000. Full re-engineering and reverse engineering is more expensive, and will run from about $150 per Function Point up to perhaps $600 per Function Point. These costs are something less than half as expensive as building brand new applications. For other languages, the costs are not easy to quantify because the services are so sparse.

20. **Long-range prognosis**—The prognosis is favorable. The technologies of complexity analysis, restructuring, reverse engineering, and re-engineering all appear to be reasonably effective, and reasonably cost effective as well. As of 1993 these technologies have focused primarily on COBOL and C because they are the most widely used languages. In time, similar technologies will be aimed at the less popular languages if market demand is sufficient. By the end of the century, a full suite of geriatric tools and services should be available for all major languages that have sufficient numbers of programmers and applications to justify the investment in building geriatric tools.

CHAPTER 50

Low Productivity

1. **Definitions**—A) Software projects that are significantly below U.S. industry averages for their class, type, and size; B) Any project that averages less than five Function Points per person month in net project productivity (the current U.S. average); C) Any project perceived as being of low productivity by its clients or by senior management.

2. **Severity**—The observed severity levels for low productivity under definition (A) tend to average about three on the following scale:

   Severity 1: The project is terminated due to low productivity

   Severity 2: The project is 50% lower in productivity than its class/type/size average

   Severity 3: The project is 25% to 49% lower than its class/type/size average

   Severity 4: The project is 10% to 24% lower than its class/type/size average

   Severity 5: The project is 1% to 9% lower than its class/type/size average

3. **Frequency**—Under definition (A), above, low productivity occurs in from 15% to 25% of U.S. software projects. Under definition (B), above, low productivity occurs in some 49% of U.S. software projects. Under definition (C), above, low productivity is strongly related to project size, and occurs for more than 95% of all software projects larger than 5000 Function Points in size.

4. **Occurrence**—Low productivity is normally associated with all occupations and crafts which require significant amounts of skilled, manual labor, and which lack automated support or manufacturing processes. Software development is among the most prominent of the occupations with low productivity and has the largest number of practitioners. Other such occupations include U.S. medical practice, U.S. legal practice, the construction of delicate mechanical instruments by hand, and the construction of experimental aircraft and weapons' systems. Occupations that are accompanied by low productivity are normally those where manual activities exceed automated effort by more than 10 to 1 in overall performance of the work at hand.

5. **Susceptibility and resistance**—Large and complex systems are more susceptible to low productivity than small and simple programs. However, so long as software

is constructed largely by manual means, all project sizes may be susceptible. Applications with the highest volumes of reusable materials are most resistant. Those projects where more than 75% of the design and 75% of the code are reusable are the most resistant.

6. **Root causes**—The root causes of low productivity include: 1) The high levels of skilled human effort required to design and build software using today's technologies; 2) The limited amount of proven and certified reusable components for software available today; 3) The widespread failure to measure the historical effort and costs of software projects which has led to an almost total lack of quantitative knowledge on the part of software managers; 4) Inadequate levels of capital investment in tools for software practitioners; 5) Inadequate and indeed disruptive office environments for software practitioners; 6) Irrational or at least ill-advised behavior on the part of software clients and managers when attempting to force productivity by ignoring quality; 7) The unfounded and often irresponsible claims of productivity gains by software tool, language, and methodology vendors which sometimes trigger major but ineffective expenses.

7. **Associated problems**—Low productivity is a basic contributor to the problems of *friction with users* and *friction with senior management*. Low productivity is a causative factor to the problem of *false productivity claims*. It may sometimes be a factor leading to the problem of *canceled projects* and *excessive time to market*.

Low productivity itself can be attributed to the problems of *low levels of reusability*, to *inexperienced management*, to *inexperienced staff*, to *inadequate capital investment*, to *inadequate office environments*, to *inadequate methodologies*, to *inadequate tools*, and to *inadequate measurements, inaccurate metrics* and to *short-range improvement planning*.

8. **Cost impact**—The direct costs of low productivity under definition (A), above, may easily be calculated. If an average U.S. MIS project of 320 Function Points has a productivity rate of 8 Function Points per person month, it will cost about $200,000 or $625 per Function Point. If a project in question is 25% lower in productivity and proceeds at a rate of 6 Function Points per person month, it will cost about $267,000, for a difference of $67,000. The cost per Function Point will rise from $625 to about $833.

There are also indirect costs associated with low productivity, including possible loss of market share and competitive disadvantages if competitors are first to market. However, calculation of the indirect costs requires knowledge of the specific situation.

9. **Methods of prevention**—The most effective preventive technique known to date for low productivity is to displace skilled human development effort with reusable components. Since the most expensive activities associated with software projects are those of finding and fixing bugs, a full software quality control program with defect prevention and defect removal components is, surprisingly, the second most effective technique. Expert-system project estimating tools can provide accurate

early warnings of low software productivity, but unfortunately both managers and clients tend to discount such warnings until it is too late to take effective corrective action. An accurate software measurement program is also an effective, although long-range, preventive measure.

10. **Methods of control**—The most widely advertised productivity control methods today are marketed under the generic name of "Computer Aided Software Engineering" or CASE. The CASE industry has had only a moderate impact on productivity when measured accurately. Many of the claims by CASE vendors for enormous productivity gains (10 to 1 or more) appear to be spurious. However, CASE tool capabilities are rapidly improving. The Information Engineering (IE) tools and methods also have measured performance that lags behind the vendor claims, although the methodology can be effective, and especially so for small and mid-sized projects of up to about 3000 Function Points. A derivative productivity technique termed "Rapid Application Development" or RAD also has claims that may be exaggerated and the measurements limited or suspect, although the RAD method can be useful for small to mid-sized projects of up to 3000 Function Points.

Object-oriented methods are also asserted to be productivity control techniques. For object-oriented languages such as Objective-C, Smalltalk, and C++, the support of reusability via methods and inheritance does lead to productivity improvements during coding. (Other languages which support reuse include Ada, Visual Basic, and Turbo C. Here too, tangible productivity gains during coding are noted). However, there is insufficient data as of 1993 to validate the claims of object-oriented analysis methods, object-oriented data bases, and the front-end object-oriented concepts. The long-range prognosis for the O-O paradigm may be favorable, but through 1993 comparatively few completed, successful, and measured projects have been identified.

The best current productivity results are associated with experienced technical personnel who are supported by adequate levels of capital investment (> $25,000 per staff member); have quiet and private office environments; are trained in and use CASE tools matched to well-structured techniques; use high-level languages, object-oriented languages, or generators; use quality control techniques; and make use of formal reusability approaches at both the design and coding levels.

11. **Product support**—As of 1993, about 50 commercially available tools can estimate software productivity. Examples of such tools include ASSET-R, BYL, BRIDGE, CHECKPOINT®, COCOMO, GECOMO, ESTIMACS, SLIM, SOFTCOST, and SPQR/20. A few tools can deal with rich mixtures of methodology and technical factors, such as all programming languages, and can provide direct estimating support of reuse.

A useful catalog of productivity tools marketed in the United States and published several times a year is *Guide to Software Productivity Aids* (Applied Computer Research, Scottsdale, AZ). The catalog is organized into various sections such as CASE, management tools, etc. and contains short vendor-provided descriptions of the tools. Appendices include vendor directories, tools by platform, and the like.

Many similar catalogs exist, and all give useful surveys of available tools. A few examples include the Auerbach Reports, CASE Outlook Guide, the CASE Trends Products and Industry Guide, the Datapro Reports, the DEC Direct RISK catalog.

However, tools alone are not the solution to the software productivity problem. A combination of cultural, methodological, tool, and even ergonomic improvements are necessary. (DeMarco and Lister's widely quoted statistics indicate that office space and noise levels can influence software productivity as much as tools or methods.)

Further, productivity improvements should be planned carefully over a multiple-year planning horizon and not fall prey to the twin problems of the *silver bullet syndrome* and *short-range improvement planning.*

12. **Consulting support**—Most management consultants deal with productivity-related issues. Only a few collect historical data or have any ability to quantify software productivity. The best-known consultancies for productivity measurement are, in alphabetical order, Computer Power, DMR Group, Howard Rubin Associates, Quantitative Software Management (QSM), Real Decisions, and Software Productivity Research (SPR). The software assessment service offered by the Software Engineering Institute (SEI) has not yet started to collect actual productivity data, although this is planned for the future.

13. **Education support**—Most business schools and software engineering schools offer no courses on software productivity at all. There are many commercial courses which deal with this topic offered by companies such as Digital Consulting Inc., the Technology Transfer Institute, and others. Many vendors offer productivity seminars, and often they are offered for little or no cost. By and large these should be interpreted as marketing events rather than as technical seminars.

A course on Function Point Analysis such as one of the many IFPUG-certified courses is a good precursor, and will deal with a fundamental metric of productivity measurement.

14. **Publication support**—Five other books besides this one by the author Capers Jones deal with software productivity. *Programming Productivity—Issues for the Eighties* (IEEE Press, 1986) includes more than 40 articles on productivity topics. *Programming Productivity* (McGraw-Hill, 1986) deals with the impact of productivity, software costs, and schedules. *Applied Software Measurement* (McGraw-Hill, 1991) deals with measuring software productivity, and also includes current U.S. averages for software productivity for military, systems, and MIS software projects. *Software Productivity and Quality—The World Wide Perspective* (IS Management Group, 1993) compares the productivity rates of various countries for MIS software, systems software, military software, etc. *Critical Problems in Software Measurement* (IS Management Group, 1993) discusses some of the technical problems of measuring the productivity of various occupation groups (quality assurance, technical writing, testing, etc.) as well as overall measurement of full projects.

Dr. Larry Putnam's book, *Measures for Excellence* (Prentice Hall, 1991) is also a recent discussion of measurement practices. Tom DeMarco and Tim Lister's book *Peopleware: Productive Projects and Teams* (Dorset House, 1987) has been very influential, and indeed started several new themes of research dealing with providing good support and office space to software professionals. Tom DeMarco and Tim Lister's *Controlling Software Projects* (Yourdon Press, 1982) is also interesting.

The literature that discusses software productivity is growing quite rapidly, and new books are appearing at what seems to be monthly intervals. Some of the titles that deal with this topic include: James Martin's *Application Development Without Programmers* (Prentice Hall, 1982); Mike Walsh's *Productivity Sand Traps and Tar Pits—How to Detect and Avoid Them* (Dorset House, 1993); Harlan Mills' *Software Productivity* (Dorset House, 1993); John Boddie's *Crunch Mode: Building Effective Systems on a Tight Schedule* (Yourdon Press, 1987); Lowell Jay Arthur's *Programmer Productivity* (John Wiley & Sons, 1983).

There is also an extensive and growing literature on the topics which are known to affect productivity in various ways. There are too many books to cite them individually, but the general topics of Software Measurement, Software Estimating, Software Project Management, Software Reusability, Object-Oriented methods; Information Engineering, CASE, and Software Quality are all relevant as background readings.

15. **Periodical support**—As of 1993, there are no journals or periodicals continuously devoted to the topics of software productivity or the measurement of same. Most of the general purpose software magazines have intermittent anecdotal articles on productivity. Such articles tend to be either "scare" stories about low U.S. productivity, or "blue sky" articles about how some tool or method improved productivity by large amounts. Accurate data and serious statistical analysis is essentially nonexistent for software. American Programmer is serving a useful niche by running articles that contain relatively good quantitative data, such as a recent article by Dr. Jerrold Grochow on the real costs of CASE.

16. **Standards support**—There are no known standards published by ANSI, DoD, IEE, IEEE, or ISO that define what "high productivity" or "low productivity" mean, or set norms for software projects.

17. **Professional associations**—The non-profit International Function Point Users Group (IFPUG) is the most active association that deals with productivity, and publishes the most data by several orders of magnitude. The non-profit International Society of Parametric Analysis (ISPA) is focused on productivity estimation, but obviously deals with productivity measurement too. The Software Cost Estimating and Analysis group (SCEA) is also interested in productivity. The Software Productivity Consortium (SPC) is a non-profit group funded primarily by defense contractors. SPC is doing some interesting work on measurement and productivity methods. Further, the SPC is also exploring functional metrics. The Software Engineering Institute (SEI) is also a non-profit, with funding coming from DARPA and

deals with productivity topics, although in a theoretical fashion. SEI has not published much in the way of quantitative information. The regional Software Process Improvement Network (SPIN) groups have frequent seminars on productivity-related issues.

18. **Effectiveness of known therapies**—Productivity estimation is now easy to perform and surprisingly accurate. Many tools such as Asset-R, CHECKPOINT®, SEER, SLIM, SOFTCOST, ESTIMACS, and even COCOMO versions such as REVIC can estimate requirements, design, coding, documentation, and many other activities and tasks. Such tools also allow "what if" modelling of the impact of alternate languages, tools, methods, and the like. They can also estimate the costs and productivity levels of defect removal activities such as reviews, inspections, and tests.

The best results from leading companies in productivity improvement are impressive: improvement rates of about 15% per year have been achieved for four to five consecutive years for development. In certain situations, maintenance productivity has improved even faster, and has gone up as much as 25% to 30% per year. Military and systems software still lag, and are often less than half as productive as similar MIS projects. In the case of military software, the enormous volume of paperwork required by military specifications such as DoD 2167A make improvement difficult. In the case of systems software, unstable hardware, severe performance constraints, and severe memory constraints tend to affect productivity negatively.

However, the best results come from combined multi-faceted approaches and not from "silver bullets." Rough rules of thumb can be derived of the topics that must be considered to improve software productivity.

For one person projects, tools, programming languages, reusability, and the experience level of the developer are the primary factors to be considered.

For team projects where communication is important, the use of design tools, reviews, and group coordination methods are added to tools, languages, reusability, and experience as factors to be considered.

For large systems involving multiple teams, formal requirements methods, control of creeping requirements, formal estimating methods, formal reviews or inspections, group coordination approaches, various technical specialists, configuration control approaches, and extensive communication facilities are added to tools, languages, reusability, and experience as factors to be considered.

19. **Costs of known therapies**—Expert-system estimation tools with activity-level and task-level productivity prediction capabilities such as SLIM, SPQR/20, and CHECKPOINT® are in the $5,000 to $20,000 range. (Macro estimating tools and COCOMO clones are often of lower cost, but also of lower utility than task-level estimating tools.) Expert-system estimation tools normally return their value in less than a year when used early in the life cycle for projects larger than 1,000 Function Points, or when amortized across 10 or more smaller projects.

Productivity improvement techniques vary too widely in cost for convenient generalization, although capital investment of more than $30,000 per staff member is often observed in enterprises in the upper quartile of U.S. productivity levels. Military, systems, and MIS projects typically use different techniques, as do small programs and large systems. However, since high quality levels tend to correlate with high productivity levels and minimum time to market periods, quality improvement methods are on the critical path to productivity, and are usually cost justified in less than 12 months.

20. **Long-range prognosis**—The technologies for improving software productivity are rapidly improving, and the long-range prognosis is favorable. (However, the current short-range situation is not favorable. The distressing quantity of false productivity claims by tool vendors, and the widespread silver bullet syndrome make it difficult to plot an effective short-term improvement strategy.) There is enough serious research taking place in the United States, Europe, South America, and the Pacific Rim to be moderately optimistic about the long-range prognosis.

CHAPTER 51

Low Quality

1. **Definition**—Software where significant numbers of users are dissatisfied with quality and/or software receiving more than 0.25 user defect reports per Function Point per year.

2. **Severity**—The average severity of incoming bug reports is about 3.5 using the SPR five-point scale. Software products where the average severity is less than three are seriously flawed. The standard SPR definition of software defect severity levels is as follows:

   Severity 1:   Software product is inoperable with serious damage resulting

   Severity 2:   Software product is inoperable and out of service

   Severity 3:   Major functions are inoperable or disabled

   Severity 4:   Minor functions are inoperable or disabled

   Severity 5:   Cosmetic problem such as a typographical error in a manual

3. **Frequency**—Low quality occurs with about 15% of U.S. military software; with about 25% of U.S. commercial and systems software; and with more than 50% of U.S. information systems software. For commercial software, statistics are seldom published but that industry is rife with instances of low quality. The same is true for contract software, unless the contracts explicitly include quality criteria. End-user software is among the worst in terms of poor quality, since it normally lacks reviews, inspections, formal testing, or any other kind of quality control.

4. **Occurrence**—Low quality is often the result of inadequate software development processes. Both errors of omission and errors of commission are common. The sources of software defects can be traced to five origins: 1) Errors in requirements; 2) Errors in design; 3) Errors in coding; 4) Errors in user documentation; 5) "Bad fixes" or fresh errors introduced as a byproduct of fixing prior errors. For large systems of 1000 Function Points or more, total defects will average five bugs per Function Point, and requirements and design bugs may exceed 50% of the total volume of discovered defects.

   The topic of "quality" is somewhat ambiguous for software. One widely-used definition is "conformance to requirements." However, requirements themselves are filled with errors and ambiguity, so that definition leads to an inability to measure requirements quality.

There are a number of attributes for software quality that have been in existence since the 1970's, and seem to derive from the pioneering work of Dr. Barry Boehm. These attributes now occur in various standards, such as the IEE83 or the more recent ISO 9000–9004 standards. The attributes are:

Portability: This is defined as the ease with which software can be transferred from one computer system environment to another.

Reliability: This is defined as the ability of a program to perform without flaw or stoppage for a specific time period.

Efficiency: This is defined as the extent to which software performs its functions without consuming too many computing resources.

Accuracy: This is defined subjectively as freedom from errors, and quantitatively as the magnitude of errors which do occur.

Error: This is defined as a discrepancy between a computed value and the real, correct value.

Robustness: This is defined as the ability of the software to keep working when users or other software packages input incorrect signals or data.

Correctness: This is defined three ways: 1) as the extent to which the software is free from design and coding defects; 2) The extent to which the software meets its requirements; 3) The extent to which the software meets user expectations.

While this list has some merits, it tends to include factors which no other kind of manufactured product would include in a definition of quality, such as portability and efficiency. These are both important topics, but they should not be treated as aspects of quality.

Empirically, the number of bugs or defects is the best overall indicator of software quality in every dimension. A high bug count is more or less equivalent to a high fever in a human patient. If a patient has a temperature of 104 degrees, there is something seriously wrong. Software released with more than about 0.3 bugs per Function Point also has something seriously wrong with it, and is unlikely to be satisfactory under any definition of quality.

5. **Susceptibility and resistance**—Large and complex systems are more susceptible to quality problems than small and simple programs. However, carelessness, excessive schedule pressures, unstable user requirements, or managerial indifference can cause quality problems even in very small software applications.

6. **Root causes**—Eight major causes exist for software quality problems: 1) Lack of a practical working definition for what "quality" means for software; 2) Inadequate defect prevention; 3) Inadequate use of reviews and inspections; 4) Insufficient or careless testing; 5) Lack of quality measurements; 6) Lack of understanding by senior and project management that quality is on the critical path to both time to

market and to market share and user satisfaction; 7) Excessive schedule pressure leading to unwise attempts to shortcut quality control techniques; 8) Unstable and ambiguous user requirements.

7. **Associated problems**—Low quality is a key contributor to the problems of *low user satisfaction* and *friction with users.* Low quality is also a contributing factor to *low market shares* and to *excessive time to market.* Low quality is a causative factor in the problems of *friction with senior management, low staff morale, error-prone modules,* and *high maintenance costs.* It is often associated with *low productivity* and *long schedules* since it shares some of the same root causes.

Low quality itself is often caused by the problems of *inexperienced management, inexperienced staff, creeping user requirements, inadequate estimating, inadequate planning, inadequate defect removal, inadequate measurements,* and *excessive schedule pressure.*

8. **Cost impact**—The costs of low quality are among the most expensive in the entire history of software. The costs of low quality can be divided into four major categories: A) Direct costs of defect repairs; B) Direct costs of litigation and possible damages in the event of law suits; C) Indirect costs due to loss of market potential if a product is late to market because of poor quality; D) Indirect costs from loss of market share and from disgruntled customers switching to competitive products; and a fifth cost element, E) Defect prevention, must also be considered. As a rule of thumb, every dollar spent on defect prevention will reduce defect repair costs by from $3.00 to $10.00.

For an average commercial software product of 1000 Function Points in size developed in a careless manner with minimal use of defect prevention, the defect potential will be about five defects per Function Point. The direct costs of defect removal via reviews, inspections, and testing will be about $500,000 prior to release to customers, but will find and remove less than 75% of the errors, leaving 1.25 defects per Function Point latent in the software at the time of delivery. The defect repair costs of the first two years of customer usage will total to about $750,000. Calculating the indirect costs of lost market potential and lost market share requires knowledge of the competitive situation. Calculating potential litigation costs also requires knowledge of the specific situation.

The true economics of software quality control are subtle, and require an expert system (or a human expert) to assess them accurately. Formal reviews and inspections have the highest measured defect removal efficiencies of any technique, and are very cost effective for large and complex projects with high defect potentials. For smaller and simpler projects, or for those with very effective upstream defect prevention methods, full inspections may become tedious due to the lack of interesting problems, and so lose in both efficiency and cost effectiveness. Testing alone, however, is seldom either efficient or cost effective. Full defect prevention coupled with a carefully planned series of reviews, inspections, and tests can achieve low defect potentials, high defect removal efficiencies, low costs, short schedules, and high user satisfaction simultaneously.

9. **Methods of prevention**—Software defect prevention techniques include formal quality plans; the use of JAD sessions for MIS projects; prototyping; structured analysis and design techniques; reusable designs and code from certified sources; software quality assurance (SQA) teams; total quality management (TQM) methods; quality function deployment (QFD) methods; clean-room development methods; quality measurement programs; reviews and inspections; and the use of defect estimation and measurement tools. Measurement of defect origins, volumes, and removal efficiencies is the best long-term preventive method.

In the United States, a very effective method of prevention is to apply for a Baldrige Award. (This is an annual award for quality named in honor of Malcolm Baldrige, and sponsored by the Department of Commerce.) The Baldrige Award is viewed as highly prestigious, and companies which strive to win one tend to take quality seriously. Those that win it certainly do.

It is interesting to see the different psychological reactions engendered by the Baldrige and by ISO 9000–9004 standards. The Baldrige Award must be sought, and to strive after it requires dedication and enthusiasm. Applying for a Baldrige tends to heighten the enthusiasm for quality within an enterprise, and seems to actually create improvements in quality.

The ISO 9000–9004 standards, on the other hand, are mandated requirements. Achieving ISO certification basically is a lengthy, expensive, and fairly depressing experience.

Compliance to DoD 2167A and the other military standards are also mandated activities, and here too the work is often viewed as burdensome. At least DoD 2167A has a nucleus of common sense and produces some useful deliverables, however. There is enough empirical data to indicate that projects adhering to DoD 2167A are often better than average in terms of software quality.

10. **Methods of control**—The defect removal methods of formal design reviews and code inspections have the highest measured defect removal efficiencies of any technique: they can be more than 60% efficient. Most forms of testing are less than 30% efficient, but a full series of five to nine discrete test stages can achieve a high cumulative defect removal efficiency. Formal testing by trained specialists is the most effective method of test. Test coverage analyzers, complexity analyzers, test case generators, and formal test libraries are useful. Editing documents by professional editors can assist in documentation error detection. Formal configuration control and formal development libraries or repositories are also useful in minimizing "bad fixes" or secondary defects inserted while fixing a primary defect.

There is one special form of testing which compares favorably with inspections in terms of defect removal efficiency. High-volume software producers such as Microsoft, Borland, Symantec, Word Perfect, and the like may use more than 1,000 customers as external Beta testers. Since the defect removal effiency of testing tends to rise with the number of participants, tests by more than 1,000 users concurrently can exceed 75% in cumulative defect removal efficiency.

Software Quality Assurance (SQA) groups have a long history, and are found in most of the leading software quality enterprises. A caveat, however, is that some enterprises give lip service to quality assurance and establish groups that are too small and too underfunded to be effective. Enterprises with active, well-staffed, and well-funded SQA groups are often industry leaders in software quality.

Total quality management (TQM) programs and clean room techniques are intuitively appealing but to date have published fairly little definitive supporting data. For TQM, the enterprises that use the method seriously seem to benefit. Those which only give lip service to the concepts often fail.

Although projects developed under clean-room protocols (mainly those of IBM in Gaithersburg) seem to have high quality levels, it is not clear if the approach will work for projects such as MIS applications with volatile and frequently changing requirements.

The Quality Function Deployment (QFD) approach has worked well for software in Japan, and would seem useful in the United States, although currently there is little empirical data available.

The European ISO 9000–9004 quality standards, implemented across Europe in 1992, are also too new to have created much in the way of tangible results. To date, from contacts with companies that have been certified and similar companies that have not, there is no tangible quality gain from ISO certification. However, this topic is too new and should be revisited on an annual basis. The ISO standards themselves are somewhat obsolete even as they become operational. The ISO software quality standards series fail to even mention defect potential prediction, defect removal efficiency, and other leading quality concepts.

CASE tools have tended to provide little direct support for quality control, although there are some exceptions. However, CASE tool usage does facilitate changing and updating defective specifications and code segments, and hence benefits quality control costs, although hard data on this topic is scarce. Several CASE vendors are now alert to the need for enhanced quality support, so improvements may be forthcoming in the near future.

11. **Product support**—Historical note: the estimating tool SPQR/20 (SPQR stands for "Software Productivity, Quality, and Reliability") which was first marketed in 1985 was the first U.S. estimating tool to feature defect potential and removal efficiency estimates. Several tools since then have replicated these functions. For example, the CHECKPOINT® estimating tool can predict the specific removal efficiencies of more than 20 different kinds of review, inspection, and test activity and hence is widely used among software quality assurance groups.

Many other classes of quality-related tools exist, including: defect measurement tools, testing tools, complexity analysis tools, comparators, and many others. Since these tools tend to operate on various platforms, and to support various kinds of software, it is not easy to generalize.

Large corporations which have achieved high quality levels often build a sophisticated suite of proprietary quality tools: the internal tools available within companies such as AT&T, IBM, Motorola, or Raytheon may have functions superior to those on the commercial markets.

Commercial off the shelf software (COTS) is now available for most SQA functions. Unfortunately, the SQA tool market is dominated by small, independent companies so fully integrated SQA tool suites do not exist as of 1993 on the commercial market place. Examples of various SQA tools that are commercially available include ACT, AdaQuest, Battlemap, CHECKPOINT®, DEC/Test Map, Design Test Tool, Impact, Inspector, MIL/SOFTQUAL, PADS, Pathvu, ProTEAM, Q/Auditor, QualityTEAM, QQA, RA-Metrics, RevuGen, SPQR/20, S-TCAT, SLEUTH, SLIM, SMARTS, SPMT, SOFTQUAL, Software TestWorks, SQAMANAGER, TCAT, TestGen, TestPro, TIE(Q), T-Scope, Verify, VIA/SmartTest, and XRunner.

12. **Consulting support**—Many U.S. consulting organizations have significant practices in the quality domain. Some of them include Andersen Consulting, Bender & Associates, Computer Power, Crosby Associates, Deming, DMR Group, Ernst & Young, Michael Fagan, Hewlett-Packard, IBM, the Quality Assurance Institute (QAI), Quantitative Software Management (QSM), the Software Engineering Institute (SEI), Software Productivity Research (SPR), Software Research Associates, Software Quality Engineering. When considering a quality consultancy, be sure that they have quantitative information as well as opinions about quality.

13. **Education support**—U.S. academic institutions are somewhat behind the state of the art in terms of software quality control. Until recently, few universities included any quality courses or practical subjects such as formal inspection methods. However, there are many commercial courses in topics such as quality control, inspections, Quality Function Deployment (QFD) and Total Quality Control (TQM). In-house courses at major corporations such as AT&T, IBM, and Motorola are usually far more current than academic offerings.

A modern curriculum on software quality should include the following: 1) Quality estimation and measurement; 2) Defect prevention methods (i.e. JAD sessions, prototypes, Quality Function Deployment (QFD) etc.); 3) Pre-test defect removal (i.e. reviews and inspections); 4) Test planning and execution; 5) Post-release defect controls; 6) Sociological and cultural factors in quality control; 7) Advanced quality concepts (i.e. the Baldrige award, Total Quality Management (TQM), etc.).

The Quality Assurance Institute (QAI) features both seminars and conferences on a wide variety of quality topics, and also includes recent work on applying functional metrics to software quality. Computer Power has a full set of quality courses, and a long-standing consultancy in software quality topics. The Software Productivity Research course on Applied Software Measurement (ASM) deals explicitly with the subject of measuring software quality, defect origins, defect volumes, and defect removal efficiency. The Quantitative Software Management course on software quality also includes information on the Baldrige award, and is therefore quite current.

14. **Publication support**—There is a growing library of books on software quality. A sample of titles include Dunn and Ullman's *Quality Assurance for Computer Software* (McGraw-Hill 1982); also by Dunn, *Software Quality Concepts and Plans* (McGraw-Hill, 1990); Gerald Weinberg's excellent *Quality Software Management Volumes 1 and 2* (Dorset House, 1991); and Mary Walton's *The Deming Management Method* (Perigee Books, 1988). J.M. Juran's *Juran on Planning for Quality* (The Free Press, 1989) gives the thoughts of a world-famous quality consultant. By the same author, Juran's *Quality Control Handbook* (McGraw-Hill, 1988) is useful background reading, although not about software per se. H.J. Harrington's *The Improvement Process—How America's Leading Companies Improve Quality* (McGraw-Hill, 1987) is not about software, but is interesting. Robert Glass' *Building Quality Software* (Prentice Hall, 1992) is a fairly recent addition to the software quality library.

Four books by the author, Capers Jones, deal with software quality metrics and economics. *Programming Productivity* (McGraw-Hill, 1986) deals with the impact of quality on software costs and schedules. *Applied Software Measurement* (McGraw-Hill, 1991) deals with the topic of measuring software quality, and also includes current U.S. averages for software defect levels and removal efficiencies. *Software Productivity and Quality—The World Wide Perspective* (IS Management Group, 1993) discusses the quality levels of the 10 most effective countries in quality control. *Critical Problems in Software Measurement* (IS Management Group, 1993) discusses the technical problems of measuring software defect potentials and defect removal efficiency levels.

Christopher Hart and Christopher Bogan's *The Baldrige* (McGraw-Hill, 1992) is of considerable interest, although not devoted to software exclusively. Kaoru Ishikawa's *What is Total Quality Control?—The Japanese Way* (Prentice-Hall, 1985) is also of interest. Michael Deutsch's *Software Verification and Validation* (Prentice Hall, 1982) discusses a well-known military quality approach. A more recent title is William Roetzheim's *Developing Software to Government Standards* (Prentice Hall, 1991) which is a useful guide through the maze of U.S. government quality standards, among others.

One of the finest books on quality ever written, surprisingly, is a quasi-autobiographical novel: Robert Pirsig's *Zen and the Art of Motorcycle Maintenance*. Do not be intimidated by the title. The book deals with a cross-country motorcycle trip by the author and his son, during which the author ruminates on the meaning of quality in many different aspects. A number of Fortune 500 companies use this book as a text to unlock executive minds about what quality is all about.

Another book which has nothing to do with software, but a lot to do with quality, is David Halberstam's *The Reckoning* (Avon Books, 1987). This book deals with how the U.S. automotive industry ignored quality until Japanese quality control had come close to putting them out of business.

Yet another non-software book has also been influential: Phil Crosby's famous *Quality is Free* (Mentor Books, 1979). Crosby was the former ITT Vice President of Quality who started a number of well-known quality approaches. The book, his other and more recent books, and Crosby's method are quite effective in raising executive consciousness to the importance of quality.

Quality has many different subdisciplines, and books on testing, reuse, user satisfaction surveys, reviews, inspections, quality function deployment (QFD), total quality management (TQM), and reliability are also relevant, but there are too many to cite them individually.

15. **Periodical support**—There are no widely distributed commercial software journals devoted to quality, although Software Quality World is known among specialists. Quality Progress also includes occasional articles on software quality. Several newsletters and house organs, such as the ones published by the IEEE and by the Quality Assurance Institute (QAI) deal with quality, but are not widely known. General purpose software magazines cover quality from time to time, but seldom do a really thorough job. Ed Yourdon's American Programmer magazine runs special issues on software quality once a year or so. The military software journal, Crosstalk, published by the Air Force in Ogden, Utah often discusses quality of military software. Software Magazine has recognized the importance of quality, and will be running special articles in 1993. The Swiss-published ISO 9000 News is also a journal dealing with quality topics. However, journalistic coverage of this important topic is rather slight. There are many articles decrying lack of quality, but rather few pragmatic ones which can demonstrate success. Even fewer provide quantitative data. The probable reason is that the accumulated knowledge of the industry to date on software quality is not very deep. House journals by corporations such as AT&T, IBM, and Hewlett-Packard are often very useful in their coverage of software quality topics.

16. **Standards support**—There are a number of DoD, IEE, IEEE, and ISO standards dealing with software quality, and with supplemental topics such as inspections and testing. DoD 2167A is the most widely circulated, and is one of the better examples. Unfortunately, none are really very good. None even discuss the most important dimensions of software quality, i.e. defect potentials and defect removal efficiency. The best that can be said is that the standards provide sample checklists and report layouts that are of some usefulness.

The most significant quality standard in recent years is the ISO 9000 standard (actually ISO 9000 through 9004) which became operational throughout Europe in 1992. This is a most unfortunate standard. The quality concepts which it embodies appear to be somewhat out of date. Worse, the costs and volumes of the paperwork needed to support ISO standards are almost as large as those needed for DoD 2167A. Finally, as this book goes to press, there is no empirical data which indicates that ISO certification actually leads to improved quality (although this situation may change in the future). The ISO situation is so troublesome that a counter reaction is stirring in several industries, which takes the view that the ISO standards are basically a hidden tax or even a trade barrier.

17. **Professional associations**—The non-profit International Function Point Users Group (IFPUG) deals with quality as well as productivity. The ACM, ITAA, AMA, ISO, and many other non-profit associations deal with quality. The IEEE subgroup on Software Quality is also a non-profit association. The non-profit International Society of Parametric Analysis (ISPA) deals with quality estimation from time to time. There is also the Society for Information Systems Quality (SISQ). There are many regional and local software quality groups in such places as San Francisco and Atlanta.

18. **Effectiveness of known therapies**—Quality estimation is now easy to perform and surprisingly accurate. Quality estimating tools (such as SPQR/20 and CHECK-POINT®) can estimate requirement, design, coding, documentation, and bad-fix defect rates. They can also estimate the defect removal efficiencies of standard forms of review, inspection, and test.

  The best results from leading companies and military services in quality improvement are impressive: a full order-of-magnitude reduction in delivered defects per Function Point have been achieved in less than four years. Defect removal efficiencies exceeding 99% are starting to occur for military projects and some commercial systems software projects. Internal information systems still lag, and are often less than 75% efficient in finding defects prior to customer usage.

  Several industries are consistently better than U.S. norms in terms of quality control, and site visits are highly recommended. Among the best industries for software quality have been computer manufacturers such as IBM and Hewlett Packard; telecommunication manufacturers such as AT&T and Motorola; defense contractors such as Raytheon and Hughes, and the military services; medical instrument manufacturers such as GE, Siemens, and Hewlett Packard. Flight control and civilian aircraft manufacturers also do a good job for the navigational and flight instrument software.

19. **Costs of known therapies**—Expert-system estimation tools with quality prediction capabilities such as SPQR/20 and CHECKPOINT® are in the $5,000 to $20,000 range. They normally return their value immediately (i.e. less than six months after purchase) when used early in the life cycle for projects larger than 500 Function Points, or when amortized across ten or more smaller projects.

  Quality improvement techniques vary too widely in cost for convenient generalization. Military, systems, and MIS projects typically use different techniques, as do small programs and large systems. However, since high quality levels correlate with optimum cost levels and minimum time to market periods, quality improvement methods are almost immediately cost justified and can return more than their value in less than 12 months.

  The best empirical results from real companies that have achieved high software quality include the following: 1) A culture that truly supports quality from the top of the company to the bottom; 2) Serious usage of defect prevention methods; 3) Pre-test reviews and inspections; 4) Planned and formal testing; 5) Defect estimation and measurements; 6) Formal and active Software Quality Assurance organizations.

20. **Long-range prognosis**—The technologies for achieving high software quality levels have been improving for many years. The unfortunate lack of knowledge by many software managers, and cultural resistance to change are harder problems. Since high quality is a critical factor for market share, it is hoped that U.S. companies can overcome their cultural resistance and improve their software management capabilities in time to prevent going out of business or losing market share to companies that know what they are doing with software. Hopefully software quality will be under control by the end of 1999, and perhaps by 1997.

CHAPTER 52

Low Status of Software Personnel and Management

1. **Definition**—A) The fairly low ranking of software engineering as a desirable college major versus other forms of engineering; B) The comparatively low regard with which software personnel and management are held by the senior non-software executives of many enterprises and government agencies; C) The comparatively low hierarchical levels of software managers and executives vis a vis other classes of executives in many enterprises and government agencies.

2. **Severity**—The average severity under definition B, above, of the low prestige of software personnel and management vis a vis other high-technology personnel and managers is about a 2.5 on the following five-point scale:

   Severity 1: Software managers and staff viewed as liabilities to the enterprise

   Severity 2: Software personnel viewed as less reliable than other employees

   Severity 3: Outsourcing and downsizing to reduce software staff being considered

   Severity 4: Software executives rank well below others in enterprise hierarchy

   Severity 5: Software executives rank slightly below others in enterprise hierarchy

3. **Frequency**—This sensitive and emotional topic is not universal, but it is common enough to be classed as a major problem. From interviews with senior executives carried out by both SPR and other consulting groups, it would appear that somewhere between one-fourth and one-half of large U.S. enterprises in the Fortune 500 class have senior executives who are less than satisfied with the software managers and personnel employed there. This dissatisfaction manifests itself in four common complaints about software managers and personnel: 1) "Their estimates are always wrong;" 2) "They always miss their schedules;" 3) "They always blow their budgets;" 4) "The quality is usually lousy."

   An article in the July 1, 1992 issue of Datamation entitled "When Non-IS Managers Take Control" encapsulates the perception of software by non-software executives. Speaking of a new billing service concept by U.S. Sprint, the article contained the following passage on page 55: "... The idea would be swallowed by the applications-development monster, driving the cost of the requested system over budget and delayed for years. If and when something ever emerged, the idea's competitive advantage would have been lost."

4. **Occurrence**—This problem tends to be fairly widespread among high-technology enterprises such as aerospace, telecommunications companies, defense contractors, bio-medical companies, and computer manufacturers which employ multiple engineering classes and have fairly diverse technologies deployed. Here the incidence may approach 50%. The problem also occurs among enterprises where software is the only or most common high-technology domain, such as banks and insurance companies. The frequency is lower here, however. On the whole, the frequency and severity of the problem correlates strongly with the size of the enterprise: it is most common among large enterprises with more than 10,000 employees.

When software engineering and other engineering staffing patterns are compared, it can be seen that software often has gaps at the top. The staffing pattern of a typical engineering function more or less resembles the following, assuming that a total of 1000 engineering professionals are employed at the enterprise:

	Software Engineering	Other Engineering
Vice President	0	1
Directors	1	2
3rd line management	8	10
2nd line management	45	50
1st line management	175	175
Professional staff	1000	1000

Software, on the whole, tends to become progressively underrepresented at the higher management levels, vis a vis other forms of engineering. The fundamental reason seems to be that software managers are not regarded as being as dependable or knowledgeable as their colleagues in other engineering disciplines. Thus there is an unwillingness by CEO's and corporate directors to entrust software managers with high levels of authority and responsibility.

5. **Susceptibility and resistance**—The most resistant organizations, which indeed can be considered totally immune, are the pure software companies where the CEO's are themselves software professionals. Microsoft, Lotus, and Borland, for example, can be considered immune to this problem. The most susceptible enterprises are those which share two criteria: 1) Software is on the critical path for new product development; B) The enterprise employed engineers long before software engineering was a recognized profession. These criteria are common in industries such as telecommunications and defense. Enterprises which depend heavily upon software

for corporate operations, such as banking and insurance, can either be susceptible or not based on the number and magnitude of software failures or disasters in the enterprise history.

An interesting phenomenon is that enterprises which have measured software quality and productivity for more than 10 years, and which employ automated estimating and planning tools for software projects, are comparatively resistant. What seems to occur is that when software projects can be expressed quantitatively, the perception by senior management that software is out of control is diminished.

6. **Root causes**—The unfortunate root cause of this problem is that many software managers, and to a lesser extent software engineers, really don't know enough to do their jobs well. A simple quiz which is sometimes used at conferences and seminars reveals a shocking ignorance of basic phenomena:

Question: What are the averages and peak defect removal efficiencies of common software reviews, inspections, and testing methods? (Answers: the average defect removal efficiency is about 30%, and the peak is about 65% and is found with formal inspections.) As of 1992, less than 1% of software managers knew the answers to these questions, when polled at software conferences.

Question: What are the average schedules for civilian systems software projects in the C language for projects of A) 1,000 source code statements, B) 10,000 source code statements, C) 100,000 source code statements, and D) 1,000,000 source code statements? (Answers: A) = 2 months; B) = 9 months, plus or minus 3; C) = 36 months, plus or minus 6; D) = 60 months, plus or minus 12).

As of 1993, less than 10% of software managers knew the answers to these fairly basic questions.

It is interesting and probably significant that most of the occupations ranking higher in perceived status than software engineering are in the class known as the "hard sciences" which have accumulated a large body of empirical knowledge: medicine, electrical engineering, aeronautical engineering, bioengineering, and the like.

7. **Associated problems**—The low relative status of software managers and professional staffs, when it occurs, is strongly associated with *high staff attrition rates, low staff morale*, and *friction with senior management*.

Low status of software professionals is itself caused by *inadequate software engineering curricula, inadequate software management curricula, low quality, low productivity, long schedules, excessive time to market, inadequate measurements, inaccurate cost estimating, inaccurate metrics*, and by both software *management malpractice* and *technical staff malpractice*.

8. **Cost impact**—The direct costs of low status of software managers and staff are those associated with high voluntary attrition rates and the replacement costs of software personnel who moved to other enterprises. Any software group with a

voluntary attrition rate that is higher than about 3% per year probably implies an unhealthy relationship between software staff and the enterprise.

There are also indirect costs in low morale and time wasted on disputes and friction, but these are difficult to generalize.

9. **Methods of prevention**—If indeed the root cause of low status is the fact that software managers and staff do not have adequate knowledge and tools for quality control, cost control and scheduling, then several preventive steps can lead to improvement: 1) Establish targets of ten days of training per year for technical staff members, and 15 days of training per year for software managers using modern curricula; 2) Acquire state-of-the-art software estimating and project planning tools; 3) Establish a software measurement program; 4) Perform a software assessment (or assessments) and use the data to plan specific improvement programs.

10. **Methods of control**—Once the problem of low status becomes embedded in the culture of an enterprise, control is difficult. An approach that is yielding some benefit is to perform one or more software assessments, such as an SEI or SPR assessment, and then use the data to create specific improvement programs. If the assessments do indeed reveal weaknesses in software performance (which senior executives and clients no doubt suspected) then admitting to those problems and striving to eliminate them can at least start a healing process.

11. **Product support**—There are no known products which deal directly with the low status of software managers and technical staffs. However, usage of software estimating, planning, and measurement tools can at least overcome the perception that software has less quantitative data and less ability to control projects than any other operating function within the enterprise.

12. **Consulting support**—Dealing with the low status of software professionals is not a standard consulting practice. Consulting groups that can perform software audits or software assessments can identify problems which might improve status if corrected, but there is no guarantee of immediate or short-term success. There are specialized consulting groups which specialize in personnel and organization topics, such as Dean Meyer Associates. Some personnel search firms also include consulting as an adjunct.

13. **Education support**—The low status of software personnel centers around the problems of low quality, long schedules, and missed commitments. Courses that deal with these problem zones and improve the performance of software personnel may in the long run be of some assistance in solving status-related issues.

14. **Publication support**—The low status of software managers and personnel is dealt with fairly explicitly in Ed Yourdon's *Decline and Fall of the American Programmer* (Prentice-Hall, 1991). Other books which deal with this issue at least peripherally include DeMarco and Lister's *Peopleware* (Dorset House, 1987), Dr. Bill Curtis's *Human Factors in Software Development* (IEEE Press, 1985), and Dr. Gerald Weinberg's *The Psychology of Computer Programming* (Prentice-Hall, 1971).

Dr. Weinberg's *Understanding the Professional Programmer* (Dorset House, 1993) is also relevant. Janet Ruhl's *The Programmer's Survival Guide* (Yourdon Press, 1989) touches upon the status of software personnel. Philip Kraft's *Programmers and Managers: The Routinization of Computer Programming in the United States* (Springer-Verlag, 1977) is dated but interesting. Daniel Cougar and Robert Zawacki's *Motivating and Managing Computer Personnel* (John Wiley & Sons, 1980) is also dated, but remains fairly relevant due to the basic insights. A more recent book is that of Landsbaum and Glass, *Measuring and Motivating Maintenance Programmers* (Prentice Hall, 1992).

Although it has nothing to do with software, Paul Starr's *The Social Transformation of American Medicine* (Basic Books, 1982) is an insightful treatment of the techniques used by medical practitioners to improve their status from one of the least prestigious professions to the highest, and the most lucrative. There is much to consider here on the roles of malpractice monitoring, licensing requirements, mandatory education, and measurement of successful therapies that might be absorbed by the software community.

Isaac Asimov's *Biographical Encyclopedia of Science and Technology* (Avon Books, 1972) is a fascinating chronological treatment of more than 1000 scientists, doctors, and engineers from ancient Greece through the close of the Korean War era. It is fascinating reading, and shows the gradual rise in status of technical knowledge workers over many different eras and cultures. Here too software is not discussed, but there is much food for thought. On a similar theme, Stephen Mason's *A History of the Sciences* (Collier Books, 1962) discusses the rise in status of many scientific and engineering disciplines including medicine, geology, physics, many forms of engineering, mathematics, and the like.

The annual IEEE membership salary and fringe benefit surveys (IEEE Press) provide useful information. Also, the AMA, Massachusetts Software Council, and other professional associations deal with compensation topics, if not status per se.

15. **Periodical support**—Unfortunately, many software periodicals tend to support the concept that software is low in status. Already cited was the July 1992 Datamation article on "When Non-IS Managers Take Over." Other journals tend more often than not to deal with the failure of software personnel, rather than their successes. For example, Fortune Magazine (May 15, 1991) ran an article on "Breaking the Software Logjam" whose title implied that software projects were gridlocked in major companies. American Programmer ran a special issue in early 1993 (March) on whether a number of prominent software engineers and managers would recommend software as an occupation for their children.

16. **Standards support**—There do not appear to be standards that deal with the status of software managers and technical staffs. However, there are formal certification programs that may improve this problem. It is already possible for software personnel to take certification examinations on topics such as cost estimating and analysis, as well as quality control. At present there is no empirical evidence that certified personnel out-perform uncertified personnel, but should such evidence

develop, this topic may become significant. A potential form of standard would be licensing of software professionals. This topic is already under discussion, and indeed a bill was considered in the State of New Jersey to do just this. Licensing might be a potentially powerful step in eliminating the problem of low status, or it could conceivably make the problem worse.

17. **Professional associations**—Most professional software associations are interested in this problem, but few are doing anything positive about it. Certification programs in selected technical areas appear to be of minor benefit, but are still steps in the right direction. Unfortunately, some professional associations are even making the problem worse: for example, the IEEE's continued endorsement of the "lines of code" software metric in the face of overwhelming evidence makes the IEEE seem almost as regressive as the tobacco industry's refusal to recognize the dangers of smoking.

18. **Effectiveness of known therapies**—It is instructive to consider the social history of medicine, which was a very low status occupation 200 years ago and now ranks as the occupation with the highest perceived status in the United States. The approaches used by medicine could also benefit software: 1) Require certification before practice can commence; 2) Establish basic knowledge requirements for various specialties and sub-disciplines; 3) Establish an effective monitoring approach for malpractice; 4) Improve the curricula of academic institutions; 5) Require annual refresher education.

19. **Costs of known therapies**—Unfortunately, all of the costs of solving the low status problem of software managers and professionals have not been worked out. Indeed, it is not even clear if the problem is completely solvable for many enterprises.

20. **Long-range prognosis**—Software is too important an occupation for the economies of the world for it to continue as a seat-of-the-pants occupation with a poor record of success. What may well occur is that the enterprises which first solve the technical problems of improving productivity and quality simultaneously will put their competitors out of business, and the surviving software managers and technical staffs will be of high status indeed.

CHAPTER 53

Low User Satisfaction

1. **Definition**—Software applications where significant numbers of users are dissatisfied with ease of use, training, functionality, quality and reliability, service, or with personnel who are associated with the software product in question.

2. **Severity**—The average severity of low user satisfaction in the United States is about a three on the following five-point scale:

   Severity 1: Very dissatisfied with all aspects of the application and the vendor

   Severity 2: Very dissatisfied with functionality, ease of use, quality, and service

   Severity 3: Somewhat dissatisfied with quality, training, or ease of use

   Severity 4: Somewhat dissatisfied with functionality provided or with service

   Severity 5: Somewhat dissatisfied with minor topics such as screen appearance

3. **Frequency**—Low user satisfaction occurs with about 15% of commercial workstation software applications, 25% to 30% of commercial personal computer applications, and with about 30% to 40% of mini-computer and mainframe applications. For custom software, low user satisfaction approaches 40% across all platforms.

4. **Occurrence**—Low user satisfaction is commonest for batch applications and applications where functions are invoked and controlled by command lines or arcane command structures. Low user satisfaction is reduced somewhat for applications with intuitive and graphically based user interfaces. However, applications that exhibit low quality engender low user satisfaction regardless of surface appearance. Similarly, applications that lack useful functionality will engender low user satisfaction regardless of their appearance and control methods.

5. **Susceptibility and resistance**—Niche applications intended for relatively sophisticated sets of users are often resistant to low user satisfaction. Applications aimed at novice users or the general public are most likely to have low levels of user satisfaction.

6. **Root causes**—The root causes for low user satisfaction include: 1) The state of the art for designing human interfaces for software packages is often fairly crude in 1993 except for special cases such as Macintosh software; 2) Quality control for software is often marginal to deficient in 1993; 3) The great emphasis on short

schedules and reduced time-to-market intervals by software vendors and their clients makes extensive field testing or ergonomic testing difficult; 4) Client or users vary so widely in skills and expectations that it is unlikely that one software package can satisfy all users.

7. **Associated problems**—Low user satisfaction is obviously associated with *low market shares* and sometimes with *high maintenance costs.* There is a strong correlation between *low user satisfaction* and *low quality.* Projects that exhibit low quality will always engender low user satisfaction. The reverse is not always true: the absence of bugs or defects does not guarantee high levels of user satisfaction.

Low user satisfaction itself is often caused by *creeping user requirements, excessive schedule pressure, inexperienced staff, inexperienced users,* and *inexperienced management.*

8. **Cost impact**—The costs of low user satisfaction have direct and indirect components. The direct costs associated with low user satisfaction are those of providing customer service and making any enhancements that appear mandatory. The first release of a typical commercial software package such as a word processor, spreadsheet, or accounting package can expect to run up costs of about $25 to $50 per Function Point in resolving user-satisfaction and quality-control issues (the two are difficult to separate). After a package is released for the third or fourth time, the costs associated with low user satisfaction should drop to less than $10 per Function Point.

The indirect costs of low user satisfaction are more difficult to enumerate and quantify. The worst case would be loss of both market share and market potential due to dissatisfied users seeking other vendors. A hidden indirect cost associated with low user satisfaction is that low user satisfaction is communicable. That is, customers who acquire Product X from a vendor and are not satisfied with it will usually not be satisfied with Products Y or Z from the same vendor.

9. **Methods of prevention**—User satisfaction is a complex and multi-faceted topic. Some of the preventive steps that seem effective include: A) Usability laboratories, or instrumented work areas where experiments in usability can take place; B) Human factors specialists (normally cognitive psychologists); C) Replication or copying of the factors associated with products that have high user satisfaction (i.e. the Xerox, Apple, Microsoft adoption of graphics icons and overlapping windows).

Preventive steps A and B are expensive in their own right. Preventive step C is cheap in its own right, but the most expensive of all if a "look and feel" lawsuit is the result.

Another preventive step, D), is that of Quality Function Deployment (QFD) wherein user quality demands are formally stated, analyzed, and methods put in place to ensure that they are achieved. QFD is applicable to custom software with known users. The QFD approach is harder to utilize for mass-market software applications with perhaps millions of potential users.

Sometimes a Software Quality Assurance (SQA) group can have a beneficial impact on user satisfaction, if the SQA team is chartered to examine interface and user satisfaction topics.

10. **Methods of control**—Annual or semi-annual surveys of user satisfaction is the basic control mechanism for ensuring user satisfaction. It is not impossible for a software product to recover from low user satisfaction, but it is difficult and expensive. Consider the examples of Microsoft Windows and IBM's OS/2. The first few releases of both products engendered such low user satisfaction that smaller companies might have gone out of business. However, both products have evolved into packages with steadily increasing levels of user satisfaction. It is obvious that successful control of low user satisfaction, once a product has been released, has these two components: A) Pay close attention to user complaints and requests; B) Spend a great deal of money and improve your product.

A number of commercial software vendors have established user forums under information utilities such as CompuServe, GEnie, Internet, and Prodigy. These forums are often quite effective in transmitting user opinions to the vendors, and even in transmitting responses back. CompuServe is probably the most widely used forum in the United States for software vendors and clients.

Many commercial software products also have user associations. (Examples include Bachman, CADRE, DB2, the IEF, CHECKPOINT®, etc.). These user associations sometimes perform satisfaction surveys, and then convey the results to the vendors.

Some large vendors have built full-scale "usability labs." These labs are set up like typical offices and fully instrumented, and may even have video recording capabilities. Users can try out software applications and make their likes and dislikes known more or less in real time.

11. **Product support**—Direct product support that deals with user satisfaction is essentially null. This appears to be an unexploited niche as of 1993. However, since the kinds of information dealt with during user surveys is often similar to requirements gathering, it is possible to envision linkages between these two technologies. There may also be future extensions to software estimating tools that could predict the probabilities of low user satisfaction. Finally, there may be extensions to test tools that would deal explicitly with factors that influence user satisfaction.

12. **Consulting support**—Several consulting organizations specialize in user-satisfaction surveys, and can perform such surveys under contract. Individual consultants with a background in cognitive psychology who specialize in human interface design and user satisfaction are also fairly common. Like quality control, the topic of low user satisfaction analysis is becoming a recognized or mainstream consulting discipline.

13. **Education support**—The famous MIT media laboratory has achieved the greatest publicity due to the work on artificial reality and advanced human interfaces. The University of Colorado also carried out some pioneering work in user satisfaction analysis. Many other software engineering schools are starting to offer courses in

human interface design, which is one of the components associated with user satisfaction. At present, there are no courses in either business schools or software engineering schools that deal explicitly with all of the factors which affect user satisfaction—quality, reliability, service, functionality, and ease of use.

14. **Publication support**—Professional books that deal with user satisfaction are normally on one side or the other of a sharp demarcation line: A) books that deal with quality; B) books that deal with human interface design. Books on quality are covered in the chapter "Low Quality." Some of the recent books dealing with human interface design include: Brands' oft-cited book about MIT, *The Media Lab—Inventing the Future* (Penguin Books, 1987); Lauriel's *The Art of Human-Computer Interface Design* (Addison-Wesley, 1991); Thimbleby's *User Interface Design* (Addison-Wesley, 1991); and Rosenbrok's *Designing Human-Centered Technology* (Springer-Verlag, 1991). A classic book in the field is Curtis's dated but still useful *Human Factors in Software Development* (IEEE Press, 1985). Hein van Steenis' *How to Plan, Develop, and Use Information Systems* (Dorset House, 1993) is a recent title that touches upon user satisfaction.

John Guaspari's *The Customer Connection* (AMACOM, 1986) is not about software, but is a thoughtful treatment of exploring customer-related topics. William Perry's *Handbook of Diagnosing and Solving Computer Problems* (TAB Books, 1989) touches upon user satisfaction as one of several problems discussed. Tom Peters' *Thriving on Chaos* (Harper & Row, 1987) is not about software user satisfaction, but puts responsiveness to customers as a central concern for successful managers and companies.

15. **Periodical support**—There are no journals or periodicals that specialize in user satisfaction as an explicit topic on a monthly basis. Several journals carry out intermittent large-scale surveys of user satisfaction: *Datamation, Information Week, CASE Trends, CASE Outlook*, and *Software* are examples. Some of the personal-computer journals such as *BYTE* and *PC Magazine* will occasionally do surveys of user satisfaction, and perform reasonably useful product reviews on a monthly basis. The house journals of the major computer manufacturers, user groups, and software vendors will often report on the results of user satisfaction surveys. As with books, there is a sharp demarcation line. Many journals deal with graphics and human-interface issues, such as the new *Windows* magazine. Other journals deal occasionally with quality or other topics that are associated with user satisfaction.

16. **Standards support**—There are no ANSI, DoD, IEE, IEEE, or ISO standards that deal explicitly with user satisfaction in all its manifestations. There are standards that deal with quality or sub-elements of user satisfaction, however. For example, there is a growing body of standards dealing with ergonomics of computer keyboards and monitors. There are also emerging or de facto standards on topics such as how the left and right mouse buttons should be used by software applications. Nonetheless, it is premature to expect major standards on user satisfaction, since the fundamental research is still being explored.

17. **Professional associations**—The users groups which deal with specific vendors and products are the organizations that are most closely concerned with user satisfaction. Examples of such groups include SHARE, GUIDE, and COMMON in the IBM domain, DECUS in the Digital Equipment domain, the CADRE, BACHMAN, INTERSOLV, and KNOWLEDGEWARE users groups, the IEF users group, and so on. Specific products such as CHECKPOINT® or SLIM may also have users groups. Some vendors and some users groups have on-line forums that are available through CompuServe, Prodigy, or other commercial networks.

18. **Effectiveness of known therapies**—Major companies that have the resources and financial strength to mount a full scale attack on low user satisfaction have been remarkably successful. Microsoft and IBM come immediately to mind. However, solving user satisfaction problems requires a multi-faceted approach. There is no silver bullet.

19. **Costs of known therapies**—A rough rule of thumb is that if a software vendor invests $10 per Function Point in user satisfaction analysis during requirements and design, the vendor can save $75 per Function Point in service expenses after delivery. The components of a user-satisfaction improvement program must be dealt with separately: A) Customer support and service will require one full-time employee for about every 100 customers; B) Customer complaint and fault tracking systems are normally custom-developed for specific vendors at costs in excess of $100,000; C) Human factors specialists as consultants would cost in excess of $3,000 per day, and as employees in excess of $75,000 per year; D) Human factors research laboratories (the physical structure) may cost more than $500,000 to construct and more than $50,000 per year to operate; E) Financial support by vendors to non-profit user organizations vary from nothing to more than $100,000 per year.

20. **Long-range prognosis**—Decade by decade there appears to be an improvement in both the technologies that underlie user satisfaction, and with average levels of user satisfaction. By the end of the 20th century, it is possible that the incidence of low user satisfaction may be significantly reduced. It is encouraging that even direct competitors such as Microsoft, Apple, and Borland are gradually starting to agree on some of the basic factors that affect user satisfaction, such as how to use the right button on a mouse.

The impact of the Apple/Microsoft/Hewlett Packard litigation appears to be somewhat harmful to the user-satisfaction prognosis, and in a larger sense, harmful to the U.S. software industry as well. If "look and feel" litigation becomes common for software, then the prognosis for improving user satisfaction must be curtailed.

Malpractice (Project Management)

1. **Definition**—A) Performing managerial functions so poorly that harm or damage occurs to projects which are under the manager's scope of authority; B) Failure to exert proper authority to prevent harm or damage to projects which are under the manager's scope of authority; C) Repeated and significant errors (more than 35%) in performance of basic software management tasks of schedule planning and cost estimating; E) Repeated delivery of software packages with excessive defect levels (more than 0.25 defects per Function Point in the first year of usage); F) Failure to keep adequate measurement records of projects produced under their authority.

2. **Severity**—The average severity of management malpractice is about a three on the following five-point scale:

   Severity 1: Malpractice causes both project termination and staff attrition
   Severity 2: Malpractice causes project termination
   Severity 3: Malpractice damages project quality or functionality
   Severity 4: Malpractice damages project quality or timeliness
   Severity 5: Malpractice causes significant repair or rework

3. **Frequency**—For licensed professions such as medicine or law, the incidence of malpractice is about 5%. For unlicensed and unregulated professions such as software management, the incidence of malpractice can exceed 15%. The most frequent kinds of software management malpractice are severe schedule errors, severe cost overruns, and inadequate quality control.

4. **Occurrence**—The sociology of software management malpractice is not advanced enough to fully understand the patterns of occurrence. Information systems, systems software, and military software all have instances of malpractice. However, the occurrence of software management malpractice appears not to be homogeneous. Some enterprises appear to have a very low incidence (perhaps less than 5%) while other enterprises appear almost crippled by malpractice (more than 15%). Malpractice appears to operate vertically as well as horizontally. The worst

case situation is where the entire chain of command from the CEO downward exhibits malpractice. Such organizations also have the widest horizontal distribution of malpractice as well, and many operating units can be affected by malpractice. One of the most damaging effects of management malpractice is the impact of poor management on technical staffs. In both the U.S. and Japan, software technical workers with high performance ratings who quite voluntarily cite "bad management" as the commonest reason for leaving.

Management malpractice is most prevalent in project planning, estimating, measurement, and quality control. Failure to use automated planning and estimating tools on projects larger than 5000 Function Points is an example of project management malpractice. Failure to keep adequate measurement records on projects larger than 1000 Function Points is another example. Failure to ensure use of adequate defect prevention and defect removal technologies on software projects is an instance of project management malpractice. Compressing schedules by more than 20% of normal by means of staff overtime is yet another example.

Management malpractice and technical staff malpractice often occur together. On the whole, management malpractice is more widespread. A side-by-side comparison of performance levels of software managers and programmer/analysts on some of the basic activities of their respective occupations is of interest:

Software Management Performance		Software Technical Staff Performance	
Sizing	Fair	Analysis	Fair
Estimating	Poor	Design	Fair
Planning	Fair	Coding	Good
Tracking	Poor	Reviews	Poor
Measuring	Poor	Testing	Good
Overall	Poor	Overall	Fair to Good

5. **Susceptibility and resistance**—The patterns of susceptibility and resistance to malpractice are not fully understood. Enterprises that have formal managerial appraisal programs and reverse appraisal programs appear more resistant than enterprises which lack such programs. Enterprises which have formal management training curricula and which require ten or more days of annual training appear more resistant than enterprises which lack such training. Enterprises where management compensation is below regional or industry averages tend to have high susceptibility to management malpractice.

6. **Root causes**—The root causes for management malpractice are: 1) Lack of standard or objective criteria for judging software management performance; 2) The topics where management malpractice is most common (schedule planning, cost estimating, quality control) are not well covered by standard management curricula; 3) The selection, appraisal, and promotion processes for software managers in

many enterprises may be random and casual; 4) The curricula for software management in most business schools is inadequate; 5) The in-house curricula and on-the-job training provided by many enterprises are not adequate; 6) As of 1993, software management has neither licensing nor certification criteria nor even a basic minimum definition of required knowledge.

7. **Associated problems**—Management malpractice is a significant contributor to many of the major problems of the software industry. For two problems, management malpractice ranks as the commonest cause: *high staff attrition rates* and *low staff morale*. Management malpractice is also strongly associated with *canceled projects, corporate politics, cost overruns, excessive schedule pressure, excessive time to market, friction with users, long schedules, low quality, missed schedules, technical malpractice*, and the *silver bullet syndrome*.

Management malpractice itself is often caused by the problems of *inadequate management training*, and *inadequate career planning*. In some instances, *inadequate compensation plans* can be an indirect cause of management malpractice. In other cases, management malpractice is caused by *excessive schedule pressure* applied by senior managers or clients. The correlation between *executive malpractice* and *management malpractice* is strong enough to hypothesize a causative relationship. The problem of *creeping user requirements* is also a contributor to instances of malpractice. Also *resistance to change* is a common phenomenon.

8. **Cost impact**—The costs associated with management malpractice include both direct and indirect components. The direct costs are those associated with cost overruns and canceled projects attributed to malpractice. It is difficult to quantify management malpractice in dollars and cents. However, the U.S. average for software projects in 1993 is about $1000 per Function Point (from a low of perhaps $600 to more than $2500). For many of the projects where the costs exceeded $1500 per Function Point, management malpractice has been found among the contributing factors (also present were creeping requirements and several other causative factors). Management malpractice may also be associated with more than half of all canceled projects in the U.S., although many other factors such as creeping user requirements are also present.

The indirect costs of management malpractice are those associated with loss of enterprise prestige, loss of long-range business opportunities, and loss of skilled professional staff members who will not work for inept managers. Here too, quantification is difficult. It is significant that enterprises with the highest instances of management malpractice tend to have the highest instances of technical staff malpractice. It is a well-known phenomenon from many human occupations that good technical workers will not work for bad managers.

As of 1993, there have not yet been major law suits or litigation that focused on charges of software management malpractice. Should such litigation occur in the future, and this is likely, then the costs would be extreme as they are for medicine, law, and less commonly for engineers. A corollary expense would probably include malpractice insurance, and as of 1993 there is none available for software.

9. **Methods of prevention**—Methods of prevention are not easy to apply, but they include the following: A) Establishing tangible and reasonable criteria for managerial selection, appraisals, and promotion; B) Establishing annual opinion surveys, and using them as a way of gaining visibility of malpractice; C) Creating an effective human resources or personnel function for the enterprise; D) Establishing a mentorship program, under which senior management will attempt to pass on their knowledge to new managers or those in the mentorship circle; E) Establishing "open-door" policies that allow employees to deal with grievances without the jeopardy of reprisals; F) Establishing a formal management training curriculum that includes both personnel and technical subjects; G) Setting aside a specific number of days per year (from ten to 15 are common) to be used for management training; H) Improving the training in the domains where management malpractice is commonest (i.e planning, estimating, and quality control); I) Establishing a management compensation plan that is not significantly below regional or competitive averages.

10. **Methods of control**—There are three techniques commonly used once management malpractice has become known to higher management: A) Termination of the offending manager; B) Reassignment of the manager to a position within his or her level of competence; C) Attempting corrective action via education, counseling, or mentorship. All of the three have pros and cons. Termination is normally reserved for very serious instances of malpractice. Reassignments are often effective in large companies, but may not be suitable for small enterprises since they lack alternate positions. Counseling, mentorship, or training depend upon the individual personalities involved, but the success rate is less than 50%.

   An unusual but potentially useful control mechanism is to raise the management span of control from an average of eight employees per manager to an average of ten to 12, and use this as a corollary for reassigning less capable managers to staff functions.

11. **Product support**—There are essentially no commercial products that have any impact on managerial malpractice. There are some automated tools available that support skills inventories, and others that deal with personality assessment and other factors such intelligence. None of these have a strong or direct correlation with management malpractice, since the actual skill sets of competent managers is known imperfectly in 1993. Many companies have merit appraisal systems and incentive compensations systems, but most are both manual and highly customized and specific to the organization.

   It is an interesting observation that some of the better software project managers have on tap 10,000 to 20,000 Function Points of project management tools, including sizing, planning, estimating, tracking, measurement, fault or defect tracking, and budget support tools, spreadsheets, word processors, electronic mail and communication packages, presentation packages, and data bases. While usage of such tools does not necessarily mean good management, failure to use any such tools does sometimes seem to correlate with management malpractice.

12. **Consulting support**—Identifying management malpractice is not a standard consulting activity. There are a number of individual management consultants who can assess and identify management malpractice, but this is an extremely delicate topic. Some forms of project audit or project assessment (such as the SEI maturity level assessments) will find instances and report on management malpractice. There are some assessment methods that also deal with corporate issues such as compensation plans, appraisal systems, and opinion surveys that can provide therapy recommendations.

13. **Education support**—None of the business schools or software engineering schools seem to deal with malpractice at all, with the exception of courses on appraisals and personnel issues. Obviously there are other departments and courses such as industrial psychology, psychological profiling, and of course psychiatry that have a bearing on malpractice. However, psychology and software seldom come together to deal with this topic. There are no commercial courses that deal with malpractice either. The American Management Association offers courses in performance appraisals and compensation planning, but nothing that deals explicitly with malpractice.

14. **Publication support**—Software management malpractice is not covered in depth by any current books in print. Several books touch upon the subject in passing. The prime example is Brooks' classic *The Mythical Man-month* (Addison Wesley, 1982). Other examples include DeMarco and Lister's *Peopleware* (Dorset House, 1987); Weinberg's *The Psychology of Computer Programming* (Prentice Hall, 1971); Dr. Weinberg's *Becoming a Technical Leader* (Dorset House, 1986) which says much about *avoiding* management malpractice; Dr. Ben Shneiderman's *Software Psychology* (Winthrop, 1980); and Curtis's *Human Factors in Software Development* (IEEE Press, 1985). Weinberg's *Becoming a Technical Leader* is one of the rare books that deal with overcoming aspects of malpractice. Metzger's *Managing Programming People* (Prentice Hall, 1987) has some interesting observations. Edward Lawler's *High-Involvement Management* (Jossey-Buss Publishers, 1986) is intriguing.

Watts Humphrey's *Managing for Innovation: Leading Technical People* (Prentice Hall, 1987) is not as popular as his more recent work, but is still an interesting treatment based on IBM's management philosophies. Although not dealing specifically with malpractice, Humphrey's *Managing the Software Process* (Addison Wesley, 1991) makes an implied case that malpractice may be present among the lower maturity levels. Somewhat surprisingly, the most explicit discussion of management malpractice is found in the work of W. Edwards Deming, although he does not deal specifically with software. Walton's book *The Deming Management Method* (Perigee Books, 1986) quotes Deming's contention that two-thirds of all quality problems can be attributed to managers, and only one-third to workers. John Adams' (editor) book *Transforming Leadership: From Vision to Results* (Miles River Press, 1986) has relevance, although it does not deal explicitly with software management. Tom Gilb and Suzanna Finzi's *Principles of Software Engineering*

Management (Addison Wesley, 1988) applies some of Tom's eclectic and controversial thinking to managerial topics.

15. **Periodical support**—There are no general software magazines or journals that deal explicitly with the topic of management or technical malpractice. From time to time when a disaster occurs, such as a major outage of telephone or power networks, the near meltdown of a nuclear reactor, or a mid-air collision, there will be intermittent articles that cite management malpractice as a causative factor. From time to time general business journals such as Forbes, Fortune, Business Week, or the Harvard Business Review will touch on malpractice.

16. **Standards support**—There are no known standards by ANSI, DoD, IEE, IEEE, or ISO that establish standard performance criteria for software managers. There are also no mandatory licensing or certification programs. Voluntary certification as a Certified Data Processor has been available through ADAPSO (now ITAA), but comparatively few managers have received certificates.

17. **Professional associations**—There are dozens of professional associations open to software managers, but none of them have any special bearing on management malpractice.

18. **Effectiveness of known therapies**—Prevention of management malpractice by careful, structured hiring practices is sometimes effective. Formal management appraisal systems coupled with opinion surveys appear effective also. Formal training programs in the management domains most subject to malpractice are effective (i.e. project planning, cost estimating, and quality control).

19. **Costs of known therapies**—When software managers are first appointed, they should receive at least ten to 15 days of formal training in both personnel-related topics and technical management (i.e. planning, estimating, budgeting, tracking, quality control, etc.). The cost of this training would vary depending upon many factors, but should be within the range of $5,000 to $20,000.

On an annual basis, management training of about ten to 15 days should be offered to all levels of management and even to senior executives. Such training would normally cost from $3,500 to $25,000 per manager per year, including travel and expenses as well as basic training. Annual refresher training is a standard practice for physicians and attorneys, and should become a standard practice for software professionals.

20. **Long-range prognosis**—Management malpractice is a complex subject, and it is difficult to make a valid long-range estimate. The basic technology of managing software projects is improving rapidly (some 70 project planning tools and 50 software estimating tools are on the U.S. market in 1993). However, the software industry has no effective certification or licensing requirements, no standard performance criteria for software managers, and no professional associations who have been addressing malpractice head-on. It would appear that the negative fac-

tors outweigh the positive factors, and therefore management malpractice may stay a serious problem throughout the twentieth century.

It is interesting that the companies with the best management teams tend to dominate their industries, and therefore often acquire competitors where management malpractice is common. It may be that mergers and acquisitions that are sweeping the software industry will affect malpractice levels, but the prognosis is still uncertain and somewhat pessimistic.

All human occupations are troubled by instances of malpractice, and most professions evolve various techniques for dealing with this endemic problem.

55

Malpractice
(Technical Staff)

1. **Definition**—A) Performing software technical functions so poorly that harm or damage occurs to the projects under development or being modified; B) Performing standard technical tasks (analysis, design, coding, pre-test defect removal, testing, configuration control, integration, and documentation) in ways that are known to be obsolete and ineffective for the projects under development or enhancement.

2. **Severity**—The average severity of technical malpractice is about a three on the following five-point scale:

   Severity 1: Malpractice causes termination of the project

   Severity 2: Malpractice causes poor quality, poor functionality, and lateness

   Severity 3: Malpractice causes poor quality, lateness, and significant rework

   Severity 4: Malpractice causes poor quality and significant rework

   Severity 5: Malpractice causes significant defect repair or rework

3. **Frequency**—For licensed professions such as medicine and law, the incidence of malpractice is about 5%. For unlicensed and unregulated professions such as software development and ancillary occupations, the incidence of malpractice can exceed 10%. The most frequent kinds of technical malpractice are those concerned with software quality, such as failure to inspect key deliverables or failure to use adequate testing and debugging methods.

4. **Occurrence**—The sociology of software technical malpractice is not advanced enough to fully understand the patterns of occurrence. Information systems, systems software, and military software all have instances of technical malpractice. However, the occurrence of technical malpractice is not homogeneous. Some enterprises have little or none (less than 1%), while other enterprises approach catastrophic levels (more than 10%). Technical staff malpractice is strongly associated with management malpractice, and it is a well-known phenomenon for many occupations that good technical staff workers will not voluntarily work for bad managers for very long.

Management malpractice and technical staff malpractice often occur together. On the whole, management malpractice is more widespread. A side-by-side comparison of performance levels of software managers and programmer/analysts on some of the basic activities of their respective occupations is of interest:

Software Management Performance		Software Technical Staff Performance	
Sizing	Fair	Analysis	Fair
Estimating	Poor	Design	Fair
Planning	Fair	Coding	Good
Tracking	Poor	Reviews	Poor
Measuring	Poor	Testing	Good
Overall	Poor	Overall	Fair to Good

5. **Susceptibility and resistance**—The patterns of susceptibility and resistance to malpractice are not well understood. Enterprises that have merit appraisal systems, above average staff compensation plans, technical training programs of ten or more days per year, powerful software tool suites, and benign personnel policies tend to be somewhat more resistant than normal. Conversely, enterprises that are undercapitalized, lack merit appraisals or opinion surveys, offer marginal compensation plans, fail to provide staff training, and utilize marginal software tool suites are more susceptible than normal.

6. **Root causes**—The root causes for technical staff malpractice include some or all of the following: 1) Software engineering ranks in the lower half of knowledge work in the U.S. in terms of professional prestige, so some achievement-oriented college students do not matriculate in software engineering and opt instead for medicine, bio-engineering, or more prestigious technical disciplines; 2) Computer science and software engineering curricula are often woefully deficient (a typical graduate software engineer in the U.S. can seldom produce commercial-grade software during the first three years of employment); 3) The selection, appraisal, and promotion processes for technical staff members in many enterprises are not very good; 4) In-house training programs for software technical staffs are often deficient; 5) Self-improvement is difficult for technical staff members due to lack of time, facilities and on-site libraries, resistance to change, and poor corporate cultures; 6) Excessive schedule pressure on development teams causes haste, carelessness, and malpractice; 7) Many enterprises attempt to use generalists for tasks that are better carried out by specialists.

7. **Associated problems**—Technical malpractice is a significant contributor to the problems of *excessive time to market, canceled projects, cost overruns, friction with users, low quality, missed schedules*. Note than technical malpractice overlaps but

is not the same as having inexperienced staffs. Malpractice often implies the rejection of effective methods as opposed to simple unawareness.

Technical malpractice itself is often caused by *excessive schedule pressure, inadequate software engineering curricula, inadequate staff technical training, resistance to change,* and *inadequate specialization.* Somewhat surprisingly, technical malpractice is often found in enterprises which have *inadequate office environments.* This is probably an associated problem rather than a causative one.

8. **Cost impact**—The costs associated with technical malpractice include both direct and indirect components. The direct costs are associated with cost overruns, repairs, rework, and occasionally canceled projects that result from technical malpractice. As a rule of thumb, projects that are actually completed by staffs with significant levels of malpractice are almost three times as expensive as those produced by staffs with no malpractice: about $3,000 per Function Point as opposed to the 1993 U.S. average of about $1000 per Function Point.

Note: Caution must be used with this kind of cost analysis. Many U.S. military projects exceed $3,000 per Function Point, and technical malpractice may not be present at all. U.S. military specifications cause the production of about 400 English words for every Ada statement, and the cost of paperwork on U.S. military projects is about $1,000 per Function Point for this alone. Coding itself on U.S. military projects using Ada is often less than $500 to $700 per Function Point.

The indirect costs associated with technical malpractice include loss of customer confidence and potential loss of market shares. Another indirect cost is that of replacement of departing staff members: enterprises with significant quantities of technical malpractice tend to have higher turnover rates than other enterprises.

Although not yet a major cost element for software, it is quite likely that litigation expenses involving technical malpractice may occur in the future, and indeed is already occurring. (From time to time, the author has received requests to testify as an expert witness in court cases involving software defect levels.) If so, the expenses associated with malpractice may become astronomical. If malpractice litigation should become common for software, as it has been for medicine, then additional costs for malpractice insurance will occur that are not part of the software industry in 1993.

9. **Methods of prevention**—Methods of prevention are not easy to apply, but they include the following: A) Establishing tangible and reasonable criteria for technical staff selection, appraisals, and promotion; B) Moving away from generalists, and moving toward specialization as enterprises grow larger than about 50 software staff members; C) Creating an effective human resources or personnel function for the enterprise; D) Establishing a mentorship program, under which senior technical staff members will attempt to pass on their knowledge to new staff members or those in the mentorship circle; E) Establishing formal staff training curricula that includes relevant technical subjects; F) Setting aside a specific number of days per year (from ten to 15 are common) to be used for staff training; G) Improving training where malpractice is commonest (i.e. analysis, design, structured coding, and

quality control); H) Establishing a technical staff compensation plan that is not significantly below regional or competitive averages; I) Facilitating methods that allow technical staff to improve, such as Quality Circles or Total Quality Management (TQM) programs.

10. **Methods of control**—There are three techniques commonly used once technical malpractice has become known to management: A) Termination of the offending employee; B) Reassignment of the employee to a position within his or her level of competence; C) Attempting corrective action via education, counseling, or mentorship. All of the three have pros and cons. Termination is normally reserved for very serious instances of malpractice. Reassignments are only effective in large companies, but may not be suitable for small enterprises since they lack alternative positions. Counseling, mentorship, or training depend upon the individual personalities involved, but the success rate is less than 50%.

11. **Product support**—There are essentially no commercial products that have any impact on technical malpractice. There are some automated tools available that support skills inventories, and others that deal with personality assessment and other factors such as intelligence. None of these have a strong or direct correlation with technical staff malpractice, since the actual skill sets of competent software technical staff workers is known imperfectly in 1993. Many companies have merit appraisal systems and incentive compensations systems, but most are both manual and highly customized and specific to the organization.

   It is an interesting observation that some of the better software development personnel have on tap 25,000 to 50,000 Function Points of tools, including compilers and associated environments, design tools, debugging tools, testing tools, screen painters, complexity analyzers, configuration control tools, communication and electronic mail support tools. While usage of such tools does not necessarily mean good technical performance, unavailability of adequate tools does often correlate with projects that are unsuccessful. However, software engineers and programmers are seldom empowered to purchase their own tools so inadequate tooling does not necessarily reflect on the software personnel themselves.

12. **Consulting support**—Identifying technical staff malpractice is not a standard consulting activity. There are a number of individual management consultants who can assess and identify management malpractice, but this is an extremely delicate topic. Some forms of project audit or project assessment (such as the SEI maturity level assessments) may find instances of technical malpractice, but this is not their primary purpose. Some assessment methods that also deal with associated issues such as office space, noise levels, staff compensation plans, appraisal systems, and opinion surveys can sometimes provide therapy recommendations.

13. **Education support**—Unfortunately, computer science and software engineering schools appear to be possible contributors to malpractice. It was observed within ITT that it took three years and substantial in-house training before recent graduates could produce satisfactory commercial-grade software. Basic skills, such as

how to perform a design inspection, how to carry out a code inspection, how to control quality, and how to build common commercial applications were visibly absent from software engineering and computer science curricula.

None of the business schools, computer science, or software engineering schools appear to deal with technical malpractice at all, with the exception of courses on appraisals and personnel issues. Obviously there are other departments and courses such as industrial psychology, psychological profiling, and of course psychiatry that have a bearing on malpractice. However, the psychological domain and the software domain seldom come together. There are no commercial courses that deal with technical malpractice either. The American Management Association offers courses in performance appraisals and compensation planning, but nothing that deals explicitly with malpractice.

14. **Publication support**—Few books deal explicitly with technical malpractice, or any other form of malpractice. A recent title which touches upon the subject is Yourdon's *Decline and Fall of the American Programmer* (Prentice Hall, 1992). DeMarco and Lister's *Peopleware* (Dorset House, 1987) is also relevant. Somewhat older, but insightful, is Curtis's *Human Factors in Software Development* (IEEE Press, 1985). Several books deal with software engineering psychology: Dr. Gerald Weinberg's classic, *The Psychology of Computer Programming* (Prentice-Hall, 1971) is always relevant. Weinberg's more recent *Understanding the Professional Programmer* (Dorset House, 1993) is also of interest. Dr. Ben Shneiderman's *Software Psychology* (Winthrop, 1980) is interesting background information. Metzger's *Managing Programming People* (Prentice Hall, 1987) gives interesting insights from a well-known software manager

15. **Periodical support**—The normal software magazines do not deal with technical staff malpractice at all. Personnel magazines and legal journals deal with various implications of malpractice, but are not widely known among software professionals.

16. **Standards support**—The IEEE standard on software engineering curricula discusses what software engineers should know by the time they graduate, but does not deal explicitly with malpractice. As of 1993, there are no mandatory and only a few voluntary licensing, registration, or certification programs for software engineers. The 1992 debacle by the State of New Jersey in attempting to license software engineers created a major outrage, but the more thoughtful practitioners realize that it may be best for those of us in the profession to establish meaningful professional criteria. If we do not, and state legislatures do it for us, we will probably be seriously at risk.

17. **Professional associations**—There are many professional associations, but not any that have established meaningful criteria for dealing with malpractice. Unlike the American Medical Association and the American Bar Association, none of the software professional associations even have a malpractice review board.

18. **Effectiveness of known therapies**—Prevention of technical malpractice by careful, structured hiring practices is often effective. Formal merit appraisal systems appear effective also. Formal training programs in the technical domains most subject to malpractice are effective (i.e. analysis, design, structured methods, and quality control).

19. **Costs of known therapies**—When entry-level staff members are first hired, they should probably receive at least 20 days of formal training in both company-related topics and technical topics (i.e. analysis, design, inspections, test planning, structured methods, various tools, quality control, etc.). The cost of this training would vary depending upon many factors, but should be within the range of $7,500 to $25,000. This kind of training is standard in major software-producing organizations such as AT&T, EDS, and IBM, that concentrate on entry-level technical employees. The training is necessary because academic computer science and software engineering curricula are not usually capable of graduating students who can produce commercial-grade software without supplemental training.

For experienced technical staff members, training of about ten to 15 days should be offered annually for all grade levels. This training would include both in-house courses, and also attendance at commercial seminars, vendor courses, professional conferences, and the like. This kind of professional staff training will normally cost from $3,500 to $25,000 per employee per year, including travel and expenses, as well as fees for basic training and the costs of student days. This kind of annual education is a normal practice for physicians and attorneys, and should become a normal practice for software engineers as well.

20. **Long-range prognosis**—Technical staff malpractice is a complex subject, and it is difficult to make a valid long-range estimate. The basic technology of developing and maintaining software projects is improving rapidly. However, the software industry has no effective certification or licensing requirements, no standard performance criteria for software practitioners, and no professional associations which have been addressing malpractice head-on. It appears that the negative factors slightly outweigh the positive factors, and therefore technical malpractice may remain a significant problem for some time.

It is interesting that the companies with the best techncial and management teams tend to dominate their industries, and therefore often acquire competitors where malpractice may be more common. It may be that mergers and acquisitions that are sweeping the software industry will affect malpractice levels, but the prognosis is still uncertain and somewhat pessimistic. It is unclear whether performance levels will go up or down as a result of mergers and acquisition. In at least one instance, acquisition of a competitor where malpractice was common caused a sharp increase in voluntary attrition among the better technical staff of the acquiring company, on the grounds their profession was being downgraded by the mass acquisition of marginal performers.

CHAPTER 56

Missed Schedules

1. **Definition**—Anticipated milestones or tangible deliverables that occur significantly after their planned and committed dates.

2. **Severity**—The average severity of missed schedules is about 2.5, but the severity rises later in the life cycle. Following are the standard severities levels:

   Severity 1: Delay causes project cancellation

   Severity 2: Delay exceeds planned date by more than 50%

   Severity 3: Delay exceeds planned date by more than 25%

   Severity 4: Delay exceeds planned date by more than 10%

   Severity 5: Minor delay of less than 10%

3. **Frequency**—Missed schedules are endemic to software, and to date have occurred on more than 50% of all software projects exceeding 1000 Function Points. The probability of severe schedule slips rises with the size of the project.

4. **Occurrence**—Missed schedules tend to accumulate in seriousness and probability as a project moves through its life cycle. They are uncommon at requirements, but grow steadily in frequency during design, coding, user documentation, and especially so during integration, testing and defect removal. Missed schedules during testing are normally the most common and most serious.

5. **Susceptibility and resistance**—Large systems of more than 2500 Function Points that are new in concept and have inexperienced management and staff are the most susceptible to missed schedules. Applications and systems of any size with ambiguous requirements and no ability to control requirements expansion are also highly susceptible. Large systems that attempt manual schedule planning and estimating, without use of proprietary or commercial planning and estimating tools, are highly susceptible to missed schedules. Small, well-understood applications with experienced management supported by estimating and planning tools are most resistant.

6. **Root causes**—Four major causes exist for the problem of missed schedules:
   1) The schedule was not achievable as it was initially established;
   2) The scope of the milestone or deliverable expanded after the schedule was set;

3) The scheduling, estimating, and planning methodologies were inadequate;

4) The enterprise failed to collect useful historical data from past projects.

7. **Associated problems**—Missed schedules are a significant contributor to the problems of *friction with users* and *friction with senior management.* Missed schedules are also causative factors for *canceled projects, excessive time to market, long schedules,* and for *cost overruns.* Missed schedules also contribute to *high staff attrition* and *low staff morale.* Finally, missed schedules also contribute to *low quality.*

Missed schedules themselves are often caused by *inexperienced management, inexperienced staff, creeping requirements, inadequate estimating, inadequate planning, inadequate measurements,* and somewhat surprisingly, *excessive schedule pressure.*

8. **Cost impact**—The costs associated with missed schedules grow in direct proportion to the magnitude of the delay and the size of the project. For projects of 100 Function Points or less, missed schedules tend to add about $2,500 to the final cost of the project. For projects of 1000 Function Points, missed schedules add about $100,000 to the final cost. For projects of 10,000 Function Points, missed schedules add about $3 million to the final cost of the project. For contract software and for commercially marketed software, there may be additional direct costs for nonperformance penalties, and indirect costs for lost market opportunities. Such additional costs require knowledge of the specific situations.

9. **Methods of prevention**—There are four major preventive techniques for eliminating or minimizing the impact of missed schedules: A) Use of commercial-grade software project estimating tools; B) Use of commercial-grade project planning tools; C) Using functional metrics to quantify the changes in the growth of project requirements; D) Full software measurement programs that include activity-level measurements.

10. **Methods of control**—Controlling missed schedules grows progressively harder as the project proceeds. The standard control techniques in frequency of normal occurrence are: A) Voluntary unpaid overtime to attempt to recover the missed schedule; B) Planned and compensated overtime; C) Adding extra staff to the project; D) Reducing project functions or delaying selected functions to a later release; E) Biting the bullet and announcing a delay in final delivery or project completion.

11. **Product support**—Many estimating tools such as SEER, SLIM, COCOMO, REVIC, SPQR/20, and CHECKPOINT® have powerful schedule estimating capabilities. There are also a host of project management tools, which not only deal with schedules but which also handle PERT and critical path calculations. Some estimating and project management tools can be directly interfaced, and many can import and export data from one another. Users can also use the "what if" modeling capabilities to explore the impact of technologies on schedules, such as the use of CASE tools, higher-level languages, inspections, and the like. Many tools also

allow users to specify paid and unpaid overtime, and will deal with the impact of overtime on schedule compression.

12. **Consulting support**—When schedules are suspect on major software projects, the normal reaction is to commission a project audit or a project assessment. Many management consultants can perform these services. Consultants that use automated estimating tools can also predict likely schedules for milestones, phases, and delivery dates. Some assessment consulting services can also identify scheduling issues, including root causes.

13. **Education support**—Most business schools and software engineering schools are not very good in teaching schedule-related topics. However, many commercial courses can deal effectively with schedules. For example, Controlling Software Projects by the Atlantic Systems Guild, and Software Management by QSM deal with schedule-related topics. The course Applied Software Measurement offered by Digital Consulting and SPR includes the current U.S. averages for software schedules, and hence provides a background for comparative purposes.

Schedule prediction is often strongly driven by the sizes of software deliverables. This means that a course in functional metrics is a good prerequisite for software scheduling, since functional metrics are now the most commonly used sizing mechanism for both paperwork and source code sizing. Any of the IFPUG-certified courses in Function Point counting would be useful background.

14. **Publication support**—Larry Putnam's book *Software Cost Estimating and Life-cycle Control* (Prentice Hall, 1991) is a good introduction to the mathematics of software scheduling. Tom DeMarco's earlier book, *Controlling Software Projects* (Dorset House, 1982) also covers schedule-related topics and includes many examples. Barry Boehm's monumental but dated *Software Engineering Economics* (Prentice Hall, 1982) is also a standard text on schedule-related issues. John Boddie's *Crunch Mode: Building Effective Systems on a Tight Schedule* (Yourdon Press, 1987) is highly relevant. William Perry's *Handbook of Diagnosing and Solving Computer Problems* (TAB Books, 1989) discusses many common software problems, including schedule disasters.

The author Capers Jones' book *Programming Productivity* (McGraw-Hill, 1986) deals with the factors that influence schedules. His book *Applied Software Measurement* (McGraw-Hill, 1991) contains current U.S. averages for both planned and actual software project schedules. To date, this is the only book that attempts to quantify the notable gap between actual delivery schedules and the original schedule that was planned or decreed for the project. The book illustrates that the gap grows steadily larger as project size increases, and for major systems the gap between actual delivery and client demands can be several years. The more recent *Critical Problems in Software Measurement* (IS Management Group, 1993) discusses the technical challenge of measuring concurrent and partly overlapping activity schedules.

15. **Periodical support**—There are no software magazines or journals that deal explicitly with schedule-related topics. The general purpose software magazines run articles from time to time on major schedule disasters, but this kind of information is seldom helpful. The journal of the International Society of Parametric Analysis (ISPA) deals with all kinds of predictive parametric models, and schedules are cited from time to time. The newsletters of the Society of Cost Estimating and Analysis (SCEA) and the International Function Point Users Group (IFPUG) also deal with schedules from time to time.

16. **Standards support**—There are no known standards by ANSI, DoD, IEE, IEEE, or ISO that establish normal delivery schedules for software projects of known sizes and technology content. This is both a gap in standards coverage, and a sign that empirical knowledge of software schedules is close to being nonexistent.

17. **Professional associations**—The non-profit International Function Point Users Group (IFPUG) is the most active association for dealing with software schedules. The Society of Cost Estimating and Analysis (SCEA) and the International Society of Parametric Analysis (ISPA) are also concerned with schedule-related topics. (A caution should be noted: software schedule averages based on lines of code are dangerous and unreliable.)

18. **Effectiveness of known therapies**—Schedule estimation is now a standard feature of many commercial-grade software estimation tools including ASSET-R, COCOMO, GECOMO, ESTIMACS, SEER, SLIM, REVIC, SPQR/20, and CHECK-POINT® among others. (Perhaps 50 such tools are marketed in the U.S. as of 1993.) It can be stated that failure to use automated software estimating tools on projects larger than 5000 Function Points is an example of management malpractice, since manual methods are always inadequate for large systems. Several estimating tools are expert systems, and can predict schedules from a basic knowledge of the class, type, and scope of software projects, plus certain skill, method, and tool factors.

Standard project planning or project management tools also support scheduling, and most include Gantt charting, PERT charting, staff-loading, and critical path analysis. About 70 or so project management tools are marketed in the U.S. as of 1993. However, project planning tools are usually not expert systems, and give the best results with the most experienced mangers.

A problem frequently noted during assessments is that when schedule estimates are *longer* than the preconceived notions of clients or senior management, there is a tendency to challenge or overthrow the estimate and seek to establish shorter schedules by decree or fiat. Thus for many "missed schedules" the schedule was not arrived at in a rational fashion.

Schedule recovery from missed schedules and milestones is troublesome. Paid and unpaid overtime can assist recovery up to about a 20% schedule overrun during requirements and design, and perhaps 15% during coding. For missed schedules during testing, overtime cannot usually exert more than a 10% recovery impact. For slips beyond that, either delayed functions or delayed delivery will normally occur. It is obvious from the paucity of controls that prevention is the best solution.

19. **Costs of known therapies**—Expert-system estimation tools such as SLIM, ESTI-MACS, SPQR/20, and CHECKPOINT® are typically in the $5,000 to $20,000 range. They will normally return their value immediately (i.e. in less than six months after purchase) when used on projects larger than 500 Function Points or when amortized across ten or more smaller projects. For major projects of 5000 Function Points or larger, the use of two or three independent schedule estimating methods is recommended.

    Project planning tools are typically lower in price than estimating tools, and run from less than $100 up to perhaps $5,000. In the hands of experienced managers, planning tools return their value almost immediately. In the hands of novice managers, the return period may be longer than the first project for which the tool is used, unless substantial training is also available.

    Schedule recovery techniques vary too widely in costs and effectiveness for generalization. The methods that are used on large systems may not be the same as those on small projects, and there are also variances between military, systems, and MIS applications. Interestingly, there are also international variations, since unpaid overtime is uncommon in parts of Europe.

20. **Long-range prognosis**—The technologies for schedule estimation are now well-formed and already commercially available. The technologies for shortening project schedules are improving rapidly, although some of the better ones are quite expensive. The major problem at the moment is separating what really works from the mass of false productivity claims and ridiculous vendor assertions. In other words, it is poor ethics and culture that is standing in the way. Given the global emphasis on time to market, competitive pressures may bring software scheduling under control in the next few years.

CHAPTER 57

Partial Life-Cycle Definitions

1. **Definition**—A) Descriptions of software development and maintenance life-cycles that omit major and important activities; B) Usage of partial life-cycle definitions rather than full work-breakdown structures as the basis for project planning, and hence incurring unexpected costs and schedule slips as unplanned but necessary activities are encountered; C) The activities omitted by CASE tool vendors who advertise "full life-cycle support" but fail to support major cost elements of software construction such as defect removal and documentation; D) The standard phase structure concept when used as the basis for describing software development activities and tasks.

2. **Severity**—The average severity of partial life-cycle definitions is fairly high: about a two on the following five-point scale:

   Severity 1: Usage of partial life-cycle causes cancellation of project due to overruns

   Severity 2: Usage of partial life-cycle causes major schedule and cost overruns

   Severity 3: Usage of partial life-cycle causes both schedule and cost overruns

   Severity 4: Usage of partial life-cycle causes extra expenses for projects

   Severity 5: Usage of partial life-cycle requires extra time to complete project

3. **Frequency**—The frequency with which partial life-cycle definitions occur and are troublesome varies with the nature of the software, but overall this problem seems to occur on about 50% of all software projects assessed to date. The problem is much more frequent for small projects under 1000 Function Points, but the hazards are lower for small projects. Using some kind of rudimentary, simplistic phase structure as the basis for building large systems (> 5000 Function Points in size) is symptomatic of both managerial and technical malpractice.

4. **Occurrence**—Information systems are the most likely to fall prey to the usage of partial life-cycle definitions and the resulting hazards. Indeed, many MIS projects are scarcely planned at all: they simply commence and run in semi-random patterns until completed or canceled. Commercial "shrink-wrap" software projects are

also likely to fall prey to partial life-cycle definitions and hence encounter work that was not anticipated by senior management. Large military software projects of more than 5000 Function Points are least likely to succumb, since these projects tend to use full work-breakdown structures and automated planning tools as the basis for project planning. Large systems software projects (i.e. operating systems, telecommunications systems, etc.) have been in existence for so many years that partial life-cycle definitions tend to be no longer troublesome. Trial and error methods over many years have accumulated sufficient knowledge to avoid the problems.

5. **Susceptibility and resistance**—The use of expandable work-breakdown structures (WBS) which may begin with phases, but which drop down to the levels of activities, tasks, and sub-tasks tend to immunize against this problem. Planning for a large software project requires thoughtful analysis of scores of activities, hundreds of tasks, and thousands of sub-tasks. Planning at this level of granularity requires automation. While a detailed project plan can be prepared manually, it cannot be updated or modified easily and hence will quickly lose value. This means that careful usage of planning tools which can deal with the complexity of overlapped and partially concurrent activities is necessary to immunize against this problem and create resistance. Anyone using manual planning and estimating methods for a software project is highly susceptible. For unknown reasons, CASE vendors are extraordinarily susceptible to this problem. Advertisements by CASE vendors of "full life-cycle support" are embarrassing when the gaps and omissions which occur are enumerated: i.e. lack of support for defect removal operations; lack of support for user documentation; lack of support for restructuring or geriatric care of aging software; lack of support for configuration control and integration; lack of support for testing; lack of support for project management, etc.

6. **Root causes**—There has long been a tendency to simplify complex problems by developing artificial schema. A traditional phase structure for a software project such as the "waterfall model" is an example of such an artificial simplification (i.e. assuming that software projects will perform only the sequence of requirements, analysis, design, coding, and testing). When the simplified description or schema is merely used for discussion purposes, it is benign. However, if the simplified description is used as the basis for actual project planning, it can be catastrophic, due to the lack of granularity and the critical tasks that are not included.

When confronted with checklists, there is a natural tendency to assume that the lists are complete and that following them exactly is what was intended. Unfortunately, standard phase descriptions are not complete, and often omit critical activities. For example "user documentation" is seldom included in standard phase descriptions because it spans several phases. Therefore if phase descriptions are used as the basis for actual plans, there is a distressing tendency to ignore and leave out necessary work. A multi-level, work-breakdown structure is a better starting point.

As an example, a simple phase structure such as the following is definitely not an adequate starting place for serious project planning:

Phase 1   Requirements
Phase 2   Analysis
Phase 3   Design
Phase 4   Coding/construction
Phase 5   Testing
Phase 6   Installation

7. **Associated problems**—Partial life-cycle descriptions are associated with *cost over-runs, schedule overruns, canceled projects, excessive schedule pressure, false productivity claims, friction with clients, low productivity, low quality,* and often *low morale.*

Partial life-cycles are sometimes caused by *inadequate curricula* for both software managers and engineers; and sometimes by *management malpractice.*

8. **Cost impact**—The costs of using partial life-cycle definitions can be quantified for any specific project, but are difficult to generalize because the impact varies with the size, class, and type of software. The direct costs of partial life-cycle definitions are those associated with performing the activities and tasks which were omitted. The indirect costs are those of lost opportunities, wasted resources, and other somewhat amorphous factors.

9. **Methods of prevention**—There are four primary preventive methods for this problem: 1) Careful measurement of actual software projects down to the levels of activities, tasks, and sub-tasks; 2) Developing planning templates derived from the measurements that go beyond phases, and include activities and tasks; 3) Acquiring and using commercial-grade project planning tools which can support large networks of activities, and which also include critical path calculations, Gantt chart calculations, PERT calculations, and the like; 4) Expanding the definition of "life-cycle" so that it starts on the first day of project initiation and continues until the last day of customer usage, and includes all of the activities which must be included during this time span.

10. **Methods of control**—Once a project is well underway on a plan created from a partial life-cycle description, it is difficult to rectify the situation. Avoiding simple 5-phase to 8-phase schema structures as the basis of development planning can be an effective control method. Following is a more complete 25-activity schema developed by Software Productivity Research (SPR) and derived from the activities of successful projects where plans and actual work coincided closely.

This schema illustrates some of the omissions which occur when normal 5- to 8-phase structures are utilized for project planning. However, these 25 activities are not complete either: each can be exploded down to the level of perhaps half a dozen tasks, and the tasks can be exploded down to the level of a dozen or more sub-tasks. A full work-breakdown structure for a large system may include perhaps 150 tasks, and more than 1000 sub-tasks.

Although the 25 activities in this list are presented sequentially, that does not imply that they will be performed sequentially. Overlap among activities is the normal pattern for software projects. Typically, at least 25% of any given activity is still unfinished when the next activity in sequence commences.

Activity 1: Requirements Gathering

This activity is the normal starting point of both phase structures and more detailed activity and task-based planning methods. An actual plan for a real project would drop below this general activity down to the tasks (i.e. JAD-based or conventional requirements methods) and sub-tasks associated with requirements gathering. An emerging task of some importance is to quantify the preliminary Function Point or Feature Point totals of the software directly from the requirements. Yet another task of considerable importance is to estimate the probable growth in unanticipated requirements which might pop up later.

Activity 2: Build, Outsource, or Buy Analysis

The second activity, once the fundamental requirements have been clarified, is to determine whether the software should be constructed internally, passed over to a contracting organization, or acquired as a commercial package. This second activity is omitted from standard software phase descriptions, which seems to assume that all software will be built internally.

Activity 3: Project Technology Selection

Assuming that the software is going to be built, rather than acquired as a package, the next activity should be to determine the technologies used in construction. Unless this activity is performed carefully, the project will obviously be built using whatever technologies are already in use. These, however, may not be appropriate. Some of the topics to be considered with this activity are those of object-orientation versus conventional methods; client-server or monolithic architectures; various data base choices such as relational versus object-oriented; various design approaches, defect removal methods; programming languages; and the like. Also included in this activity is planning for the repository of project data that will be collected, and selection of project metric and measurement criteria. Test planning, and methods to be used for test data and test case construction are also included here. Technology selection is usually omitted from simplistic phase structure schemas, and the omission is the seed for many subsequent problems.

Activity 4: Reusability Analysis

It is folly to build every program and system as a unique artifact. Therefore the next activity in sequence should be to determine the volume and suitability of reusable materials for the project in question; i.e. reusable designs, code, documents, test cases and data and so forth. This activity has seldom occurred in standard phase descriptions, but is becoming increasingly important. Reusability analysis should be elevated to the stature of a standard activity for all software projects.

Activity 5: Reengineering Analysis

Most standard phase structures and generic development plans such as the waterfall model assume a new application, being developed from scratch. By the end of the century, more than half of all software projects will be enhancements or modifications to legacy systems. Therefore the next activity is to determine if the existing package that is about to be modified requires any kind of geriatric treatment before the new enhancements commence. This activity should also be elevated to the status of a standard. If the work at hand does involve legacy software, then a whole suite of geriatric tasks may be indicated: complexity analyis, restructuring, reverse engineering, and reengineering.

Activity 6: Business Modeling and Value Analysis

Software projects become valuable corporate assets, and therefore it is appropriate to include a formal activity for placing any given software project within the spectrum of corporate needs, and for determining the value of the software to the enterprise. The value can be either tangible value based on savings or revenues, or intangible value based on competitive advantages or enterprise prestige.

Activity 7: Formal Planning and Estimating

This activity, which is seldom included in standard software phase structures, needs to be elevated and treated as an important function. Indeed, for projects larger than 5000 Function Points, or for those with high strategic value, the author recommends the usage of at least two commercial-grade estimation tools and also a commercial-grade project planning tool. Failure to perform formal planning and estimating for projects larger than 5000 Function Points should be considered an example of professional malpractice.

Activity 8: Formal Statute and Standards Review

Every day that passes, new laws and new standards are being drafted which affect software projects. In sheer self-defense, it is important to include a formal activity for reviewing and selecting the standards, statutes, and policy directives which will have an impact on the project. Failure to include this activity, and to do it well, can lead to frustration and delay or even to litigation. This activity seldom occurs in standard phase descriptions.

Activity 9: Prototyping or Mathematical Modeling

For new projects and for some enhancements, it is desirable to create a prototype which covers perhaps 10% of the functionality of the final product. With the advent of new prototyping tools, this activity is becoming easier and easier. Prototyping seldom occurs in standard phase descriptions. For real-time and embedded software with critical performance parameters, mathematical modeling or simulation may also be desirable to ensure that the performance targets are in fact achievable. SPR's assessments have noted several canceled projects which occurred because the performance goals were unachievable, and this was not discovered until the code had actually been written almost 18 months into the project's schedule. That is far too late to discover such a basic flaw.

Activity 10: Data Flow Design

Before the functionality of the software can be determined, it is necessary to come to grips with the data which the software will utilize. Questions such as data sources, validity checking, compatibility with other applications, and data reuse should be determined. This activity seldom occurs in standard phase descriptions, although technologies such as Information Engineering (IE), the Warnier/Orr method, and the Jackson method, have elevated data analysis to the stature of a major activity.

Activity 11: Functional Design

The next activity is to come to grips with the functionality of the software that will be made available to the users or clients. Since functionality often derives from data, this activity normally follows the data flow design. This activity, or the generic topic of "design" is a normal phase in many phase schemas: Design is often cited as Phase 2.

Activity 12: User Information Design

In the past, the development of user documentation was almost universally omitted from standard phase structures, and this omission frequently caused significant cost and schedule problems when it was finally recognized. In the future, now that documentation is no longer pure paper but includes graphical user interfaces (GUI), multi-media representation, hyper-text, and sometimes translation into many different national languages, this activity should not be left to chance. Indeed, user information design and development are about to be elevated into a major software engineering subdiscipline.

Activity 13: Portability and Physical Implementation Design

Not all functions of major systems are located in the software. Hardware and microcode may also be present. This activity deals with the placement of both functions and data. Some of the topics to be considered deal with software versus microcode, software versus hardware, and the nature of the hardware and software platforms for the emerging project. For commercial shrink-wrapped software, this activity also includes planning support for various distribution media including floppy disks, optical disks, PCMIA cards, ROM, or direct downloading. Also, whether the product will run under various operating systems and windowing environments (i.e. DOS, UNIX, OS2, Windows, Windows/NT, Pink, etc.) should be dealt with. Another aspect of this activity is to consider the implications of international distribution. If projects are to be marketed or delivered overseas, translations may be required, the ISO 9000 standards may be relevant, and a host of technical considerations must be acknowledged.

Activity 14: Pre-Development Reviews and Inspections

This activity encompasses all of the design inspections and planning document reviews that occur prior to the main construction tasks of the program or system. Formal reviews and inspections have the highest defect removal efficiencies of any method yet developed, however, these activities have traditionally been ignored in standard phase descriptions. They merit being elevated to formal activities, and used very widely. Failure to use reviews and inspections on systems larger than 5000 Function Points can be taken as an example of professional malpractice.

Activity 15: Code Development and Reusable Component Acquisition

This activity encompasses both conventional programming and the acquisition of reusable components and modules. Code development by itself is much too labor intensive, and reusable materials are starting to be employed in increasing volume. Languages such as object-oriented languages facilitate reuse, but are not mandatory to achieve reusability. Conventional coding has been a standard phase since the 1950's, but reusable material acquisition is a relatively new phenomenon and should be elevated to the status of a formal activity. Coding or "construction" to use a more generic term is often cited as Phase 3 in standard phase descriptions. That it occurs as activity 15 here indicates how much phase descriptions tend to leave out.

Activity 16: User Information Development

Graphical user interfaces, hypertext, and multi-media information are current technologies which are rapidly expanding. They are also having a major impact on software usage information. Within a few years, other major changes may also occur, such as the development of virtual-reality training modules, or the total displacement of paper by low-cost optical media. In any case, the development of user information deserves to be elevated to the status of a formal activity, and must be carried out with skill and professionalism. User information development has long been absent from standard phase descriptions, and creation of good user documentation has been an endemic weakness of the software industry since its beginning.

Activity 17: Inspections, Complexity Analysis, and Testing

Testing occurs in essentially all standard phase structures, and is often cited as Phase 4. However, testing by itself has never been fully sufficient for large systems. The average defect removal efficiency of most forms of testing is less than 30%. The average efficiency of a four-test sequence (unit test, function test, integration test, and system test) is usually less than 75%. The use of code inspections prior to testing can achieve efficiency levels of 60% in their own right, and raise testing efficiency by as much as 10%. All companies and all projects that have approached or exceeded 99% in cumulative defect removal efficiency have used a combination of formal inspections and testing. This topic needs to be elevated to the status of a standard activity. Also, complexity analysis should become a standard task, and utilized on essentially all programs and systems.

Activity 18: Integration and Configuration Control

Keeping track of updates on specifications, documentation, and source codes is a complex task which requires fairly sophisticated automation. The same is true of integrating all components of large systems to ensure that they operate successfully as a complete package. Integration deals with merging all code components, and the configuration control deals with keeping track of changes to either documents or code, and ensuring that all cross-references and affected materials are synchronized. Both activities require support from trained specialists, and from fairly sophisticated automated tools.

Activity 19: Distribution and Installation

This activity is concerned with the ways that software will be put into the hands of its intended users. A host of alternatives exist (optical disks, magnetic disk, tape, direct downloading, ROM, PCMIA cards, etc.). Further, some customized applications personnel employed by the vendor will carry out custom installations of the software on their client's computers. Distribution and installation should be formal activities, and should be carefully planned.

Activity 20: User Training

Quite a lot of modern software is complex enough so that user training is required. The form of the training can either be on-line, by supplemental media such as video or audio disks or cassettes, or by live instructors. In any case, user training should be elevated to the level of a formal activity, and should be carefully planned and prepared if needed.

Activity 21: Formal Project History

Project post-mortems have been used intermittently for perhaps 30 years, and are very useful in collecting historical data that can subsequently be used for estimating similar projects. Collection of a project's historical data should be elevated to the status of a formal activity, and should be performed on all projects over 250 Function Points. Failure to perform such an activity on projects larger than 1000 Function Points might well be considered an aspect of professional malpractice. At this point, the sizes of all deliverables (documents, screens, source code, and test cases) are fully known, and the final total of Function Points in the application can be quantified. Defect levels accumulated during development should also be recorded. All of the influential factors which impacted the final results should also be recorded: i.e. creeping user requirements, attrition of personnel, use of new or questionable tools, or whatever. The effort of putting together a formal project history amounts to only a few days, and the value lasts for years.

Activity 22: Post-Release Defect Repairs

Most standard phase descriptions omit all reference to defect repairs, and seem to assume (naively) that defects don't exist. The accurate recording of bugs or defect reports is one of the major activities of software, and should be performed for all software projects. Failure to do so can be considered as an example of professional malpractice. Accurate recording of defects allows calculations of defect removal efficiency, and can be used to prevent defects from occurring in the future, or to improve various kinds of defect removal operations.

Activity 23: Post-Release Project Enhancements

Once initially deployed, software projects tend to add new functions at a rate of perhaps 5% to 7% per year for as long as the software exists. Further, changes to existing software can trigger modifications of perhaps 2% of the code within a system on an annual basis. Software project histories should be kept from release to release as long as the software has any users at all.

Activity 24: User Satisfaction Survey

Software user satisfaction surveys should become part of the normal culture of software engineering. This means that performing satisfaction surveys should be elevated to the rank of a standard activity.

Activity 25: Project Termination or Withdrawal

About 25% or more of large systems are canceled without being completed. Usually when cancellation occurs, the system is about a year late and spending is at perhaps twice the anticipated amount. For projects that are delivered, it is surprisingly expensive to withdraw a software product from distribution. Sometimes penalties or legal issues may even prevent this from occurring. In any case, canceling projects or removing projects from use are important enough topics so that they need planning and deliberation. Hence, project termination or withdrawal deserved to be elevated to the status of a formal activity.

11. **Product support**—As of 1993, there are some 70 to 75 project planning tools and about 50 commercial software estimating tools on the U.S. market. There are also integrated planning, estimating, and sizing tools in several CASE tool suites, such as those offered by AGS Management Systems, CGI, Texas Instruments, and UNISYS. New tools in both classes have appeared at approximately monthly intervals for the last 18 months, so the market is too dynamic for a full listing. However these tools may be limited by two factors: 1) Their default assumptions may not include a number of important assumptions, or 2) They may not have any default assumptions, and hence all activities must be derived from the user's assumptions.

Examples of some of the more common software management tools include (in alphabetic order): ACCENT VUE, ADW, AGS FullCASE, Andersen FOUNDATION, APECS 8000, Artemis, Asset-R, the Bridge, BYL, CA-Advisor, CA-Estimacs, CA-Planmacs, CA-Superproject, CA-Tellaplan, CHECKPOINT®, COCOMO, CoCoPro,

COSTAR, ESTIMACS, Estimator, Estiplan, GECOMO, Harvard Project Manager, ISTAR, Microman II, MIL/SOFTQUAL, Microsoft Project, MI-Project, MISTER, MULTITRACK, N5500, NES, PADS, PCOC, PLANNER, PMS-II, POWER, Prestige, PRIDE, PROJECT/2, ProjectBASE, ProjectGUIDE, Project Managers Workbench (PMW), PS4, QQA, RA-Metrics, REVIC, SEER, Size Planner, SIZE Plus, SLIM, SOFTCOST, SOFTQUAL, SPQR/20, SPECTRUM, SPMT, STARpro, Sys/PLAN, Time Line, TRAK, UniPress, and VAX Software Project Manager.

12. **Consulting support**—Software life-cycle consulting support is usually offered by product vendors such as Milt Bryce Associates, Andersen Consulting, Ernst & Young, IBM, Quantitative Software Methods (QSM), Reifer Associates, Rubin Associates, Software Productivity Research (SPR), and ABT, and by general management consulting groups such as the DMR Group, Nolan & Norton, or Roger Pressman Associates. Specific consultants may have a bias toward certain life-cycle assumptions.

13. **Education support**—Universities and business schools are slowly modernizing their curricula for dealing with software project management, but it will be many years before most universities are up to speed. Universities that have close ties with business and industry (such as Seattle University, Washington University in St. Louis, or the University of Colorado) are probably the most advanced. Universities which happen to have project management specialists on their faculties, such as DePaul University, George Mason University, MIT, Oakland University in Rochester, Michigan, the University of Minnesota, and the University of Dayton, are also comparatively modern in specific courses taught by these experts. However, from sitting in on classes and from giving seminars sponsored by universities, it appears that very few have yet gone beyond simplistic 5- to 8-phase descriptions of software life-cycles. The concepts of full work-breakdown structures are often introduced, but seldom does a university teach computer science or software engineering at the level of 20 to 40 activities, 100 to 200 tasks, and perhaps 1000 or more subtasks. Courses by consulting groups such as QSM or Andersen, or by commercial education groups such as Digital Consulting or Technology Transfer, may sometimes be more detailed than university courses. In-house training within large corporations such as AT&T, EDS, or IBM is often quite good, but tends to focus on the specific activities and tasks selected by the corporation.

14. **Publication support**—The topic of activity-level and task-level software planning is not very well covered by book publishers as of 1993. However, Dr. Barry Boehms's monumental *Software Engineering Economics* (Prentice Hall, 1981) includes a useful discussion of work-breakdown structures for planning software projects. Tom DeMarco's *Controlling Software Projects* (Yourdon Press, 1982) goes beyond phases, and is a good beginning. Thomas Rullo's *Advances in Computer Programming Management* (Heyden Press, 1980), and Richard H. Thayer's *Software Engineering Project Management* (IEEE Press, 1988) are all interesting too. Phil Metzger's *Managing a Programming Project* (Prentice Hall, 1977 but revised);

T. Gilb and S. Finzi's *Principles of Software Engineering Management* (Addison-Wesley, 1992) are useful. Watts Humphrey's *Managing the Software Process* (Addison Wesley, 1987); and Marciniak, Fry, and Zempolich's *Software Project Management* (John Wiley, 1991) should be considered. All of these, and others too, are interesting and tend to drop below the level of phases.

Specific tool vendors also write books which tend to emphasize how their tools work, but are seldom generalized. Nonetheless, such books are often useful and should not be discounted. Examples of this genre include Milt Bryce and Tim Bryce's *The IRM Revolution: Blueprint for the 21st Century* and the author, Capers Jones' *Applied Software Measurement* (McGraw-Hill, 1991). Both books tend to emphasize the proprietary approaches of the authors, but both contain useful data from industry sources and drop down below the level of phases to activities, tasks, and sub-tasks.

One of the more useful compendiums of automated software management tool information was produced by Captain Kevin Berk, Dean Barrow, and Todd Steadman of the U.S. Air Force's Software Technology Support Center at Ogden Air Force base in Utah (March of 1992). This is a very large catalog of perhaps 150 planning, estimating, and measurement tools. Although this is a good first step toward a complete catalog, even this 200-page effort appears to omit at least 20 of the more recent tools. The rate at which new software management tools appear (approximately monthly) makes it essentially impossible to stay current via normal books and catalogs.

William Roetzheim's *Developing Software to Government Standards* (Prentice Hall, 1991) is a useful overview, since many government standards drop to task-level and sub-task-level requirements.

Brian Dickinson's *Developing Structured Systems* (Yourdon Press, 1980) is an early but still interesting example of dropping below phase levels for planning purposes.

John J. Rakos' *Software Project Management for Small to Medium Sized Projects* (Prentice Hall, 1990) is a useful book for the many managers who are concerned with projects of moderate size and complexity.

An explicit but not totally successful attempt to deal with project management automation is Lois Zell's *Managing Software Projects—Selecting and Using PC-Based Project Management Systems* (QED Press, 1991).

For those interested in acquiring commercial software project management tools, a useful resource is the *Guide to Software Productivity Aids* published by Applied Computer Research, Inc. (ACR) of Scottsdale, Arizona. This is a catalog of various tools, including management tools, which are marketed in the United States. The catalog contains a short section describing each tool (provided by the vendor), the price, vendor's address and phone number, and other useful information. Cross-reference sections and appendices show tools by platform, by type, and other categories.

15. **Periodical support**—As of 1993, a number of periodicals devote significant space to software project management and life-cycle concepts. Intermittent articles appear in the commercial software journals such as American Programmer, Metrics Views, Software Magazine, and Datamation. The IEEE Management Journal, Communications of the ACM, IEEE Software Engineering, and other technical journals may also cover this topic from time to time. The Journal of the International Society of Parametric Analysis (ISPA) and the newsletter of the Society of Cost Estimating and Analysis (SCEA) both discuss project management tools and estimating tools and sometimes cover activity-level estimation. The defense software journal, Crosstalk, produced by the Software Technology Support Center at Ogden Air Force Base has intermittent articles about management tools and methods.

16. **Standards support**—Several DoD standards drop down below activities, and deal with tasks and sub-tasks. For example DoD 2167A does this. IEEE and ISO standards fluctuate between being very high level and very low level, but seem to lack a mid range that discusses activities.

17. **Professional associations**—Several interesting associations deal with software project management topics: SCEA (Society of Cost Estimating and Analysis) is a non-profit association which centers on military software estimation and cost analysis (and on military hardware too). ISPA (the International Society of Parametric Analysis) is a world-wide non-profit association of companies and individuals which build and use parametric models. The large professional associations often have sub-groups interested in project planning: Check with the IEEE, ACM, ITAA, or other groups for local special-interest groups. SPIN, the new "Software Process Improvement Network" is also interested in project management methods and activity-level planning.

18. **Effectiveness of known therapies**—The effectiveness of software project management planning methods is improving fairly rapidly. Planning tools have long been effective in the hands of experienced managers; but are still only marginally effective for novices and amateurs who may not even be aware of some of the activities that may be needed. Estimating tools add rigor and precision to software cost modeling, but such tools should be carefully calibrated and validated before accepting their output without question. One advantage of estimating tools is that several of them include activity and task level estimates and include as many as 25 activities and 150 tasks. Be cautious of simplistic estimating tools which cover only phase levels.

19. **Costs of known therapies**—*Planning tools* range in cost from less than $100 to more than $10,000. Here too most operating systems and many hardware platforms have such tools available. As of 1993, personal computer versions under DOS or Windows tend to outsell other kinds of planning tools, with UNIX being in second place. Planning or project management tools are most valuable for the most experienced managers. These tools tend to grow in value in direct proportion to the size of the project being planned. Indeed, for projects over 5000 Func-

tion Points, failure to use such tools should be considered to be malpractice. They normally return their value almost at once (less than 3 months) when used on projects larger than 1000 Function Points.

Estimating tools range in cost from less than $1000 to more than $25,000. Tools are available under DOS, Windows, UNIX, and for some mainframe systems. These tools are valuable for both novice managers and for experienced managers. The value tends to rise in direct proportion to the size of the project being estimated. They normally return their value in less than 12 months for projects larger than 1000 Function Points. Failure to use such tools on projects above 5000 Function Points should be considered to be malpractice, since manual estimating methods have proven to be grossly inadequate for large systems.

Measurement tools range in price from $10,000 to $20,000. These tools will typically return their value in less than 18 months when used on projects larger than 1000 Function Points in size. They can return their value in less than 12 months when used on ten or more small projects. The absolute value of measurement tends to rise with both the size of software projects and the number of projects measured. A strong case can be made that failure to measure projects larger than 1000 Function Points in size should be considered to be malpractice.

20. **Long-range prognosis**—By the end of the century, software project managers in leading corporations and government agencies should have access to powerful, integrated management methods and associated tool suites which are closely coupled to CASE tools. On the whole, the long-range prognosis for software project management is quite favorable, except for the natural human tendency to resist new ways of doing things until the evidence becomes overwhelming. Even in 1993, the leading companies are utilizing expandable work-breakdown structures that encompass complete projects, phases, activities, tasks, and sub-tasks. These multiple levels are starting to be supported by integrated planning, estimating, and measurement tools. On the whole, the prognosis is favorable.

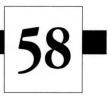

Poor Organization Structures

1. **Definition**—A) Placement of software organizations at inappropriate locations within a corporation or government agency; B) Cumbersome or ineffective departmental structures within a software organization; C) Software project organization structures that impede or slow the process of software construction and/or maintenance.

2. **Severity**—The average severity of poor organization structures in the U.S. is quite high, and ranks about a 1.5 on the following five-point scale:

   Severity 1: Poor software placement, departmentation, and project organizations
   Severity 2: Poor software departmentation and poor project organizations
   Severity 3: Poor departmentation within the software function
   Severity 4: Poor project organization structures for all multi-person projects
   Severity 5: Poor project organization structures for some multi-person projects

3. **Frequency**—Software is a comparatively new occupation, and effective organizational principles for software are still in evolution. Placement of software organizations at inappropriate locations within the corporation is endemic, and occurs in perhaps 70% of all large software-producing organizations. Cumbersome and ineffective departmental structures are also endemic, and occur in perhaps 50% of all large software-producing organizations. Poor structures for individual projects are fairly common, but not as widespread as the other two problems: the frequency here is that about 35% of multi-person software projects will be organized in ineffective ways.

4. **Occurrence**—There appear to be patterns of effective and ineffective organization structures that vary by industry and by the size or the enterprise. Unfortunately, large-scale empirical studies of software organizational effectiveness do not seem to exist. The commoner forms of observed organizational problems include:

Inappropriate Subordination of the Software Function

For many companies, software professionals have become the largest occupation group within the company, and software is often critical to the effectiveness and time to market of the company's products. It would be appropriate, therefore, for the software function to report directly to senior corporate management. However, in many organizations where software is the critical product component, software is often subordinate to the engineering function. It is a significant phenomenon that although the number of software engineers outnumbers electrical engineers and most other forms of engineering in U.S. companies, software executives at the vice-presidential level do not occur with similar frequency.

Artificial Fragmentation of the Software Function Among Operating Units

A very common phenomenon in the U.S. is to break up software production into comparatively small groups, each of which reports in to a functional executive such as sales, marketing, manufacturing, engineering, finance, personnel, and so forth. The rationale for this structure is to optimize the rapport between software personnel and the clients whom they serve. However, such fragmented groups have a number of disadvantages, including: 1) Lack of opportunity for professional advancement; 2) Slow technology transfer between groups; 3) Lack of a "critical mass" among the small groups, which prevents serious software engineering technology research; 4) Redundancy and duplication of effort among the small groups; 5) Lack of standardization among methods, tools, and approaches used by the various small groups.

(In another context, the deployment of tanks and armored military units, it was discovered that fragmenting armored units into small companies and deploying them in support of infantry units was much less effective than consolidated armored divisions.)

Excessive Layers in the Management Hierarchy

An interesting but unanswered question is, "what is the optimal number of layers in the corporate hierarchy for a company or government agency of any given size?" A colleague who visited Russia reported some 32 layers of management between Boris Yeltsin and the operating units of the Russian government—that explains quite a bit about the difficulty of making changes and modernizing the country. Any organization with more than about 12 layers of management between the CEO and the operating units should evaluate its organization structure. Of course, management in the middle layers who might be displaced will obviously resist any restructuring.

Although the data is incomplete, a maximum of about eight layers of management seems feasible.

Arbitrary and Artificial Spans of Control

The span of control concept originated more than a hundred years ago, as a by-product of studies on the distance which troop units of various sizes could march in one day. Smaller units of eight or less could march much further than larger units of several hundred, primarily because of the difficulty of getting larger groups moving and stopped. Without really thinking about the principles involved, U.S. companies tend to consider a staff of no more than eight workers reporting to one manager as being optimal. Indeed, there is some literature which suggests that staff sizes of four to six may be optimal for moderately sized projects. However, a study carried out by the author in IBM in the 1970's raised some doubts that a staff of eight was truly optimal for all software systems. Software projects where the span of control was 12 actually tended to outperform smaller staffs when building really large projects such as operating systems where many hundreds of personnel were engaged. The reason was interesting: software components tended to be divided artificially to fit the size of the available departments. Small departments could not handle a complete component such as the scheduler or supervisor of the operating system, so the components were subdivided among two or more small departments. This is a topic which needs much more research, and many more empirical observations to draw definite conclusions.

Failure to Establish a Formal Maintenance Function

For small software staffs of up to about 25 personnel, development and maintenance are normally carried out by the same people, with maintenance (defect repairs and minor updates) being performed on an "as needed" basis. For larger groups, and especially so when the software function exceeds a staff of 100, a separate maintenance group becomes desirable. Maintenance work tends to be intrusive, and get in the way of development. Thus organizations where maintenance and development are done by the same people typically have trouble with making their development schedules.

Failure to Establish a Formal Testing Function

For small software staffs up to about 25 personnel, testing is normally carried out by development personnel. However, for larger groups and larger projects, a number of specialized kinds of tests may be needed, such as stress tests, system tests, and regression tests. Also, formal test libraries are needed, and care must be exercised to ensure that test cases themselves are adequately prepared. Testing of large systems is a specialized discipline, which benefits from having specialists assigned to it.

Failure to Establish a Formal Quality Assurance Function

Software quality control techniques are not very well covered by academic curricula, so many software engineers and managers do not even know the measured efficiencies of various kinds of review, inspection, and testing. Not only do many software professionals lack adequate knowledge of software quality approaches, but schedule pressures are often so intense that there is no way to learn or to apply the knowledge if it is learned. Formal quality assurance groups tend to be effective in both transmitting knowledge of quality approaches, and in ensuring that such knowledge will actually be applied to software projects. All software organizations with a total staff size of over 35 professionals should consider the establishment of a formal quality assurance function.

Failure to Establish a Software Engineering Research Function

Software engineering is a rapidly evolving discipline. In the past five years, a host of new technologies have emerged that need serious consideration: CASE, object-oriented methods, Total Quality Management (TQM), Quality Function Deployment (QFD), viral protection, client-server architectures, and graphical user interfaces (GUI) to name but a few. Small software organizations usually cannot afford the luxury of formal research on these emerging concepts, but all large organizations with more than about 100 software professionals should consider establishing a formal software engineering research laboratory to explore, evaluate, and assist in teaching advanced methods and approaches. For organizations with 1000 software professionals, a software research laboratory with about 50 personnel divided into advanced technology and applied technologies wings would be worth consideration The advanced technology group would consider topics at the extreme limits of the state of the art, and possible future technologies. The applied technology group would consider current technologies that might benefit the organization.

Inappropriate Usage of "Matrix Management" Organization Structures

For software projects, productivity tends to decline as the number of managers associated with a project goes up. Projects with more than eight managers engaged have an alarming tendency toward cost and schedule overruns, and a significant tendency toward being canceled. Unfortunately, the matrix management approach tends to deploy almost 50% more managers on a given project than the conventional hierarchical approach. Thus the probability of cost overruns, schedule slippages, and canceled projects is much higher with matrix structures than with hierarchical.

5. **Susceptibility and resistance**—Small enterprises that employ less than 30 software professionals are normally fairly immune to organizational problems since small organizations tend to have fairly fluid structures that evolve to meet needs. Enterprises that employ between 100 and 1000 software professionals appear to be most susceptible to organizational problems. Very large enterprises with many thousands of software professionals tend to be heterogeneous: some locations have severe organizational problems, while others appear to have resolved the issues.

There are surprising patterns of susceptibility and resistance by industry, and by class of software as well. High-technology companies that produce systems software such as computer manufacturers, defense contractors, and telecommunications manufacturers appear more resistant to organizational problems than many other industries. Banks, insurance companies, and information-system software-producing organizations appear fairly susceptible. Commercial software producers also appear fairly susceptible. Why these patterns occur, or even if the patterns are real and not based on insufficient samples, are currently unknown.

6. **Root causes**—The root cause of poor software organization structures is the lack of empirical data on which organization structures are effective and which are ineffective for software. Lack of empirical data is fairly common for new sciences and new engineering fields, and although software is approaching 50 years as a recognized discipline, that is still young compared to other forms of engineering.

7. **Associated problems**—Poor organization structures are strongly associated with *canceled projects, cost overruns, excessive time to market, high attrition rates, long schedules, low productivity, low quality, morale problems, poor technology investments,* and *poor technology transfer.*

    Poor organization structures are often caused by the problems of *inadequate management curricula, friction with senior management,* and occasionally with *management malpractice.*

8. **Cost impact**—The direct costs of poor organization structures are difficult to quantify. However, assessments and consulting engagements within the same industry and on similar projects in various companies reveal variances of more than 50% in the number of people required to do the same kind of work, and variances of more than 30% in schedule durations for similar projects. Although the data is incomplete and may be incorrect, the well-organized enterprises and projects tend to be much better than average, and the poorly-organized enterprises tend to be much worse than average.

9. **Methods of prevention**—The most effective preventive step would be a large-scale assessment study involving perhaps 200 software-producing organizations, which would examine the impact of organization structures on overall performance, including productivity, quality, user satisfaction, technology transfer, and attrition rates. It is technically possible to do such a study, but large-scale studies involving hundreds of groups and interviews with thousands of personnel are necessarily expensive.

    A preventive approach at the level of small individual companies is to establish an organization planning committee that reports annually to the president or CEO. The duties of the committee would be to review the current organization structures and make recommendations for improvement. A similar approach used by large companies is to establish an organization planning department, normally reporting to the vice president of personnel.

10. **Methods of control**—Once poor organization structures come into existence, it has been difficult to control them in the past. In many companies, organization planning appears to be chaotic and unstructured. Organizations come and go without apparent reason, except the subjective notions of senior executives. It is

an interesting observation that large companies in the U.S. appear to go through waves of either centralizing their operating functions or decentralizing them at three- to seven-year periods. In the year of transition, when the company is changing policy from centralized to decentralized or vice versa, organizations are particularly chaotic.

Several technologies are moving into widespread deployment that may help in controlling software organizational problems: software assessments using the SEI or SPR approach (or both), business process reengineering, and Total Quality Management (TQM). All three of these technologies have the effect of "unfreezing" organizations, and introducing changes that may be beneficial. The approaches are synergistic when used together.

A control method that is sometimes effective is to bring in organization consulting groups, which may be able to add rationality to the organization restructuring process.

11. **Product support**—As of 1993, there appear to be no commercial products available that are aimed at software organization planning. It would seem technically possible to build an expert system that could predict the effectiveness of various organization placements, department structures, and decentralized or centralized structures, and the use of matrix or hierarchical organization styles.

12. **Consulting support**—Quite a number of management consulting companies deal with organizational issues, as do many individual consultants. Examples of such consulting groups include A.D. Little, Andersen Consulting, DMR Group, the Atlantic Systems Guild, Index Consulting, N. Dean Meyer Associates, Nolan, Norton & Company, and Software Productivity Research.

Formal audits or assessments using either the SEI or SPR approach will examine organizational issues. The SEI assessment technique is more prescriptive in the need for certain organizations such as formal quality assurance.

13. **Education support**—Courses in organization design and organization placement are part of the standard curricula of most business schools. However, courses dealing with optimal organization principles for software are almost non-existent or at least hard to find. Private courses such as "Controlling Software Projects" by the Atlantic Systems Guild seem to come closer to the mark than do most university courses. As of 1993, management science has not actually reached clear and definitive levels of understanding optimal software organization structures.

14. **Publication support**—The well-known book by Tom DeMarco and Tim Lister, *Peopleware*, (Dorset House, 1987) is a good introduction. Dr. Gerald Weinberg's classic *Psychology of Computer Programming* (Prentice Hall, 1971) is still valuable after more than 20 years. Another useful book is *Human Factors in Software Development* (IEEE Press, 1981) by Dr. Bill Curtis. A more recent book that touches organizational topics is Watts Humphrey's *Managing the Software Process* (Addison-Wesley, 1987). N. Dean Meyer's *Structural Cybernetics* (N. Dean Meyer, Ridgefield, CT, 1993) is relevant.

Robert Brill's eclectic collection of numerous articles, *Techniques of EDP Project Management—A Book of Readings* (Yourdon Press, 1984) discusses organizational topics. Dean Meyer and Mary Boone's *The Information Edge* (Gage Publishing Company, 1989) touches upon organizational topics. Mary Boone's *Leadership and the Computer* (Prima Publishing, 1991) is a fascinating look at how CEO's use information and computers. The book is not directly about software organizations, but contains much thought-provoking information.

A new topic, Business Process Realignment, has started to become popular in recent months. The thesis is that software applications and the groups that produce them may be lagging modern business needs. This topic is quite new, but several books are known to be planned for late 1993 and 1994 publication. Tom Peters' *Thriving on Chaos* (Harper & Row, 1987) is not about software, but does discuss some highly unusual organization concepts that may have relevance. This book was one of the pioneering efforts on business realignment.

15. **Periodical support**—Personnel journals are the most likely to have articles on organization planning, but they are seldom found in software engineering or programming departments. From time to time the IEEE Transactions on Engineering Management will have topics on organization. The standard business journals cover many aspects of organization in almost every issue: Business Week, Harvard Business Review, Forbes, The Economist, and so forth. The conventional software periodicals deal with organizational issues only as anecdotes, such as reporting a major restructuring by Microsoft, IBM, DEC, etc.

16. **Standards support**—There are no known standards published by ANSI, ITAA DoD, IEEE, ISO, or other standards organizations that deal explicitly with organizational topics. There may be specific functional areas such as Software Quality Assurance required by various standards, but nothing on generic organization planning. Given the state of the art, it is probably best not to have standards on this topic as of 1993.

17. **Professional associations**—The major professional groups such as ACM, AMA, ASM, IEEE, and so forth are obviously interested in organizational issues, but normally do not have any explicit programs or subgroups that deal with these topics.

18. **Effectiveness of known therapies**—It is reasonably clear and convincing that good organization structures benefit morale, productivity, and quality. It is also convincing that bad organization structures damage morale, productivity, and quality. However, the exact determination of "good" or "bad" organizations is still too uncertain. A periodic review of organization structures on an annual basis appears beneficial. Use of management consultants who specialize in organizational issues appears beneficial. However, the available data on organizational effectiveness for software is rather sparse. Audits or assessments are usually effective in finding organizational problems; less so in curing them. Business re-engineering and Total Quality Management (TQM) facilitate the culture and climate for dealing with organizational problems, but are not cures in and of themselves.

19. **Costs of known therapies**—Software audits and assessments, which cover organizational issues as one of the their topics, tend to run from $25,000 to $100,000. Specific consulting studies on organizational issues can start as low as $5,000 and run as high as $250,000 for a major Fortune 500 class enterprise. The actual costs of changing organizations within major corporations can easily run to millions of dollars annually.

20. **Long-range prognosis**—As software reaches its 50th year as an industry, trial and error methods have begun to reveal organizations that work, and organizations that are harmful. Now that software assessments, business re-engineering, and Total Quality Management (TQM) are starting widespread deployment, improvements in organization planning should start to occur. Although the prognosis may be overly optimistic, it is likely that organizational effectiveness will be under full control by the end of the century.

59

Poor Technology Investments

1. **Definition**—A) Investment in software tools, methodologies, or services that do not return the value anticipated; B) Investment in software tools, methodologies, or services that degrade or make worse the problems the investment was made to alleviate.

2. **Severity**—The average severity of poor technology investments is about a three on the following five-point scale:

   Severity 1: The investment creates more serious problems than existed before

   Severity 2: The investment returns no positive value, and the situation may be worse

   Severity 3: The investment returns null value, and the situation is unchanged

   Severity 4: The investment returns marginal and less than anticipated value

   Severity 5: The investment returns positive value, but over a very long time span

3. **Frequency**—Under definition (A), more than 50% of all dollars spent on software productivity tools appear to be poor investments. Under definition (B), perhaps 5% of all dollars spent on software productivity tools appear to be poor investments.

4. **Occurrence**—Poor technology investments are endemic in the industry and affect all sizes and kinds of enterprises with distressing frequency. MIS, systems, and military software producers are equally prone to this problem.

5. **Susceptibility and resistance**—The entire software industry and all users are somewhat susceptible to poor technology investments, given the lack of definitive productivity and quality benchmarks prior to 1991. Even large and rather sophisticated companies are not immune to poor technology investments. Enterprises that have accurate quality and productivity measurement programs are most resistant to poor technology investments. Unfortunately, enterprises that are in economic distress and losing money are highly susceptible.

6. **Root causes**—The root causes of poor technology investments are diverse: 1) The lack of any quantitative knowledge of U.S. productivity and quality levels prior to 1991; 2) The chronic lack of measurement programs, which prevent software managers from knowing how effective or ineffective various tools and methods are; 3) The long historical usage of LOC metrics, which tend to conceal the values of several important technologies; 4) The failure of U.S. software engineering and management schools to deal with complex problems that require multi-faceted solutions; 5) The lack of independent, non-commercial evaluation services (similar in concept to the Consumers Union and *Consumer Reports*) for the software industry; 6) The unregulated nature of the software industry, and the lack of any legal or ethical guidelines preventing false advertising.

7. **Associated problems**—Poor technology investments contribute significantly to *friction with users* and *friction with senior management.* Poor technology investments are also causative factors for *canceled projects, excessive time to market, long schedules,* and *cost overruns.* Poor technology investments also contribute to *high staff attrition* and *low staff morale.* Poor technology investments also contribute to *low productivity* and *low quality.*

   Poor technology investments themselves are often caused by *false productivity claims, inadequate software management curricula, inexperienced management, inexperienced staff, inadequate package evaluation plans, inadequate package acquisition policies, inadequate estimating, inadequate planning, inadequate measurements, inaccurate metrics, management malpractice,* and *excessive schedule pressure.*

8. **Cost impact**—The cost impact of poor technology investments can be divided into direct and indirect components. The direct costs of poor technology investments are the sums of all dollars spent on tools or methods that are ineffective. The indirect costs of poor technology investments are even more significant: lost opportunities, long schedules, and reduced amounts of discretionary capital to spend on tools and methods that are effective. Unfortunately, approximately 50% of the money spent in the U.S. on software productivity tools and methods can be classified as poor technology investments under the definitions used here.

9. **Methods of prevention**—Accurate software measurement is the best long-range preventive method for poor technology investments. Commercial software estimation tools are also useful preventive methods when used to assess the impact of new languages, methods, and tools (Caution must be exercised to ensure that the estimating tools can accurately deal with the technologies in question). For software vendors themselves, careful analysis, controlled studies, and careful measurement of Beta Test results are effective preventive approaches.

   Some vendors, such as IBM, also have screening by Quality Assurance and corporate attorneys of all advertising claims to ensure that false advertising claims are not being made. Some vendors have user associations, which often serve as an effective preventive method for poor technology investments, by letting potential clients discuss the pros and cons of a given technology with experienced users of the technology.

For investment in tools, methods, and technologies, the most effective control mechanism is to carry out broad economic studies on the return on investment (ROI) actually experienced by users.

What would be desirable is a really thorough long-term study of the effects of various tools, methods, and approaches on software performance. Such a study could either be a longitudinal study of the evolution of software practices within one organization, or a statistical study that looked at many different organizations in various stages of evolution.

The methodology of such a study would be to capture the costs, schedules, and other quantitative and qualitative factors associated with various technologies, and then work out the impacts using multiple regression analysis.

For some technologies, such as formal inspections, there is a continuous stream of data which dates back to the late 1970's. Thus many projects have been analyzed which: A) Did not use inspections at all; B) Were starting to use inspections; C) Had been using inspections for one or more years.

When the results of 50 A-style projects, 50 B-style projects, and 50 C-style projects are compared, the value or ROI of inspections is clearly evident.

Following is a simplified example of the kind of analysis that comprises ROI calculations. Assume that the total development costs of a software project, Case A, that does not use inspections are $1000 per Function Point. (The testing costs for a project without inspections amount to $400 per Function Point.) Assume that the development schedule for the project was 18 months. The maintenance costs for defect repairs and customer support total $2,000 per Function Point.

Assume that the total development costs for a similar project, Case B, that did use inspections, were $900 per Function Point. The inspections themselves cost $100 per Function Point, but testing costs were reduced to $200 per Function Point. The development schedule for the project was 12 months. The maintenance costs for defect repairs and support total $500 per Function Point.

When comparing Case A and Case B, it can be seen that an investment of $100 per Function Point for inspections generated savings of $200 per Function Point in testing costs. Further, the savings in maintenance costs were $1,500 per Function Point.

Thus in this simple example, an investment of $1.00 for inspections created a direct return or ROI of $17.00 in value for every $1.00 invested.

When the impact of shorter development schedules are considered, which might result in additional revenues or more savings, the ultimate value could obviously be even higher. This kind of ROI analysis is crude and imperfect, but at least it is now possible to carry out preliminary value studies of software tools, methods, and approaches.

Since the entire field of quantifying return on investment (ROI) for software technologies is both new and uncertain, there is not yet any definitive data on what constitutes a "good" or a "bad" investment. The preliminary data suggests that a five-level classification may be useful:

Excellent ROI	=	> $15.00 returned for every $1.00 invested
Good ROI	=	> $10.00 returned for every $1.00 invested
Fair ROI	=	> $ 5.00 returned for every $1.00 invested
Marginal ROI	=	> $ 2.50 returned for every $1.00 invested
Poor ROI	=	< $ 2.50 returned for every $1.00 invested

The values shown above are based on both observation and modelling. They are quite preliminary, and future data may change the results substantially. Indeed, the data which follows has a very high margin of error, and should not be used for any purpose other than preliminary discussions and informal analysis. The data is definitely not rigorous enough for making serious business or technical decisions. Even so, it is encouraging that the software industry has reached a level where ROI studies are technically feasible.

The ROI data is sorted in order of the maximum return after 48 months of usage, and shows the approximate return each year for an initial investment of $1.00.

Technologies
(Approximate return for each $1.00 invested)

	12 Months	24 Months	36 Months	48 Months
Full Software Reusability	$1.00	$3.00	$15.00	$30.00
Reusable architectures	$0.00	$0.20	$0.75	$1.50
Reusable estimates	$0.20	$0.30	$2.00	$3.00
Reusable plans	$0.15	$0.25	$1.00	$2.00
Reusable requirements	$0.10	$0.40	$1.50	$3.00
Reusable designs	$0.10	$0.40	$2.50	$5.00
Reusable source code	$0.15	$0.50	$2.50	$6.00
Reusable user documents	$0.05	$0.10	$0.75	$1.50
Reusable human interfaces	$0.00	$0.15	$0.50	$1.00
Reusable data	$0.20	$0.30	$1.75	$3.50
Reusable test cases	$0.05	$0.40	$1.75	$3.50

Technologies
(Approximate return for each $1.00 invested)

	12 Months	24 Months	36 Months	48 Months
I-CASE (full integration)	$1.50	$2.50	$10.50	$25.00
Project management support	$0.30	$0.40	$2.00	$3.50
Sizing				
Estimating				
Planning				
Budgeting				
Tracking				
Assessment				
Data modelling support	$0.05	$0.10	$0.50	$1.00
Requirements support	$0.00	$0.05	$0.25	$0.70
Analysis support	$0.10	$0.15	$0.25	$1.00
Design support	$0.25	$0.45	$1.50	$4.00
Development support	$0.25	$0.45	$1.50	$5.00
Documentation support	$0.00	$0.05	$0.30	$1.00
Quality support	$0.25	$0.30	$1.50	$3.50
Maintenance support	$0.05	$0.10	$0.50	$1.00
Rework support	$0.10	$0.20	$0.50	$1.50
Usage analysis support	$0.00	$0.00	$0.10	$0.30
Repository support	$0.10	$0.15	$0.50	$1.50
Communication support	$0.05	$0.10	$0.75	$1.00

Technologies
(Approximate return for each $1.00 invested)

	12 Months	24 Months	36 Months	48 Months
Baldrige Award (Winning)	$4.50	$7.00	$12.00	$20.00
Software quality measurements	$1.15	$3.50	$10.00	$17.50
Cost and quality estimation tools	$2.50	$5.00	$12.00	$17.50
Formal design inspections	$3.50	$6.00	$10.00	$15.00
Formal code inspections	$2.50	$6.00	$12.00	$15.00
Long-range technology planning	$1.00	$5.00	$10.00	$15.00
High volume Beta testing	$4.00	$8.00	$10.00	$15.00
Client-Server Architectures	$0.50	$2.00	$8.00	$13.50
Reengineering tools	$1.50	$2.50	$10.00	$12.50
Object-Oriented languages	$1.15	$3.00	$7.50	$12.50
Project management tools	$1.50	$4.00	$8.00	$12.50
User satisfaction surveys	$3.00	$5.00	$8.00	$11.00
Joint Application Design (JAD)	$2.25	$4.00	$7.50	$10.00
Productivity measurements	$1.50	$4.50	$6.00	$10.00
Process assessments	$1.50	$3.00	$6.00	$10.00
Full prototyping	$2.00	$3.50	$5.00	$10.00
Improved management training	$1.15	$3.00	$5.50	$9.50
Baldrige Award (Applying)	$1.10	$2.00	$6.00	$9.00
Total Quality Management (TQM)	$0.85	$1.50	$4.50	$8.50
Functional metrics	$1.75	$3.00	$4.50	$8.00
Executive briefings (software)	$1.75	$2.50	$5.00	$7.50
Quality Function Deployment (QFD)	$1.75	$3.00	$6.50	$7.50
On-line reference/research	$1.50	$3.00	$5.00	$7.50
Structured coding	$1.50	$3.50	$6.00	$7.50
Reverse engineering tools	$1.25	$2.50	$4.50	$7.50
Improved staff training	$0.90	$2.00	$5.00	$7.50
Structured design	$1.25	$2.00	$4.50	$6.50
Code restructuring tools	$1.75	$3.50	$5.00	$6.50

Technologies
(Approximate return for each $1.00 invested)

	12 Months	24 Months	36 Months	48 Months
I-CASE tools (1993 level)	$0.75	$1.25	$3.50	$6.50
4GLS/Generators	$1.25	$2.00	$4.00	$6.00
Partial Prototyping	$1.75	$2.50	$4.00	$6.00
Staff morale surveys	$1.75	$2.50	$4.00	$6.00
Information Engineering (IE)	$0.75	$1.50	$3.50	$6.00
Groupware/network tools	$1.25	$2.00	$3.00	$6.00
Inter-company technical exchange	$1.75	$2.50	$4.00	$5.50
Expert system shells	$0.75	$1.00	$2.50	$5.50
Staff specialization	$0.75	$1.75	$3.00	$5.50
Improved hiring practices	$0.95	$2.00	$3.00	$5.00
Standard development methods	$1.25	$2.00	$3.00	$5.00
Improved communication	$1.25	$2.00	$3.00	$5.00
Ada programming language	$0.75	$1.00	$2.00	$5.00
Clean room development	$1.25	$1.75	$2.50	$4.50
Complexity analysis tools	$1.30	$2.00	$3.00	$4.50
Improved office space	$0.25	$1.00	$1.50	$4.00
Improved staff compensation	$0.40	$1.25	$2.50	$4.00
Outsourcing (Domestic)	$1.00	$2.00	$3.00	$4.00
Informal reviews	$1.50	$2.50	$3.00	$4.00
3GLS (COBOL, FORTRAN)	$1.25	$1.50	$2.50	$3.50
ISO Certification (International)	$0.75	$1.25	$1.75	$3.50
Formal standards	$1.00	$1.15	$1.75	$3.00
Outsourcing (International)	$1.50	$4.00	$3.50	$3.00
Business process reeningeering	$1.50	$4.00	$3.50	$3.00
Low-volume Beta Testing	$1.25	$1.50	$2.00	$3.00
CASE tools (partial)	$0.80	$1.10	$1.50	$2.50
Object-Oriented analysis	$0.90	$1.05	$1.35	$2.50
RAD	$2.50	$2.00	$1.75	$1.25
LOC-based estimation tools	$1.50	$1.00	$0.90	$0.80

Technologies
(Approximate return for each $1.00 invested)

	12 Months	24 Months	36 Months	48 Months
ISO Certification (Domestic)	$0.85	$0.65	$0.60	$0.55
End-user software development	$2.00	$1.25	$0.75	$0.50
Software science metrics	$0.75	$0.65	$0.55	$0.45
LOC metrics	$0.70	$0.50	$0.40	$0.30

Once again, this information has a high margin of error and should be used only for preliminary discussion. It might be asked why such data is published if its accuracy is suspect. Unfortunately, by the time this kind of information is both available and accurate, it may be the next century. It seems best to publish preliminary findings, under the assumption that major errors will be noted by reviewers, readers, or other researchers.

10. **Methods of control**—Methods of control vary based upon whether the technology in question is new, or has current users. If the technology is new, then pilot studies accompanied by modeling or estimating the impact of the technology prior to wide-spread adoption can be an effective control. If the technology in question has current users, then contacting them and finding out how well or poorly the technology actually works is a very effective control method. Joining user groups, or participating in user conferences can be effective. For technology researchers with access to electronic bulletin boards, networks, and multi-company electronic mail, a broadcast query can often result in surprisingly good insights into the effectiveness of technologies.

11. **Product support**—A number of commercial estimating tools can be used as simulation models to explore the impact of new methods, tools, languages, and organization structures on software performance. Some of the commercial tools with these capabilities include the newer COCOMO versions such as REVIC, SEER, SLIM, Softcost, SPQR/20, and CHECKPOINT®. Such tools have powerful productivity and cost estimation capabilities and can model the effect of technologies to be utilized on the projects being estimated. These capabilities can be used to model the impact of tools, methodologies, languages, and even office space. Some tools have a built-in knowledge base and a comparison mode, so any project can be compared against U.S. norms derived from similar projects in terms of class, type, size, and methods. There is also a class of software simulation modeling tools which are not conventional estimators, but allow users to work through projects where various kinds of known problems might occur.

12. **Consulting support**—The consulting group at American Management Systems have built an interesting consulting practice centering around return on investment

analysis. The British OVUM consultancy also deals with this topic from time to time, and publishes many monographs and case studies. Also in the United Kingdom, consultancies such as the Macleod Group deal with return on investment in various software methods and approaches. Obviously Software Productivity Research (SPR) also deals with return on investment studies.

Many management consulting organizations also market tools, and hence are likely to find themselves in conflict of interest situations. (Note that the author's company, Software Productivity Research, markets both tools and consulting, and hence must frequently think carefully about conflict of interest.) Other consulting organizations may be locked in to a specific approach, such as the Object-Oriented paradigm or Information Engineering. Here too, conflict of interest can result. On the other hand, consultants without a knowledge of how specific methods work and at least a moderate belief in their effectiveness may have little to offer. The Software Engineering Institute (SEI), Software Productivity Research (SPR), and Hewlett-Packard have project assessment services (as do several other consulting groups) that deal with the impact of various tools and investments on software performance. However, SPR and HP also market tools. Consulting services to look for are those that can also assist client companies by helping them select the combination of tools, methods, and environmental factors that will give optimize high quality, high productivity, lowest cost, and shortest schedules with minimum wastage. (However, potential clients should treat consulting claims with the same caution that they treat any other vendor's claims.)

13. **Education support**—So far as can be determined, few of the computer science or software engineering or business curricula in the U.S. offer courses on software ROI evaluation, tool selection and value analysis, or technology investments. Exceptions to this rule include the Naval Post-Graduate school in Monterey and MIT's Sloan school. Several commercial courses include coverage of these topics. SPR's course on Applied Software Measurement (ASM) deals with the subject of measuring Return on Investment in software technologies and tools. Courses by QSM and the Atlantic Systems Guild also touch on this subject. A simulation modeling approach using methods developed by Dr. Tarik Abdel Hamid and S. Madnick has been offered commercially by Tom DeMarco and Ed Yourdon, and this model deals with the impact of various methods and approaches on software performance. These workshops are known as "War Games."

14. **Publication support**—Two books by the author, Capers Jones, deal with software productivity, quality, and the impact which various tools and methods have on these factors. *Programming Productivity* (McGraw-Hill, 1986) deals with the impact of productivity, software costs, and schedules. *Applied Software Measurement* (McGraw-Hill, 1991) deals with the topic of measuring software productivity, and also includes current U.S. averages for software productivity for military, systems, and MIS software projects and so provides useful background data. A book by T. Abdel-Hamid and S. Madnick on *Software Project Dynamics* is also quite relevant, and discusses modelling the impact or value of selected approaches.

However, on the topic of the value of the whole computing and software complex within enterprises, Paul Strassman's *The Business Value of Computers* (Information Economics Press, 1990) is widely cited. Also Weil's *Do Computers Pay Off* (ICIT Press, 1990) covers this topic. A book edited by Thierry Noyelle of the United Nations also discusses relevant value data: *Skills, Wages, and Productivity in the Service Sector* (Westview Press, 1990).

15. Periodical support—There are no journals that deal dispassionately and accurately with the results of investing X dollars in Y technologies for software. However, many journals do publish very useful reviews and comparisons of product groups. Journals such as BYTE, PC Magazine, Information Week, and the like often publish very interesting and useful comparative evaluations for hardware products, software tools, and utilities. Unfortunately, many articles in the general software journals and even the more scholarly journals are embarrassingly incomplete and anecdotal. In the "hard" science journals dealing with physics, chemistry, and medicine, about 50% of the page space is devoted to a discussion of how the measurements were taken and how the study was controlled, so other researchers can replicate the findings. The contents of software articles devoted to how measurements were taken and how the study was controlled is somewhere between 0% and 3% of the page space. This illustrates how amateurish software is in 1992. The exceptions are the product evaluations by some of the personal computer magazines such as BYTE and PC Magazine, where descriptions of how the products were evaluated approaches standard engineering practices.

A related topic is starting to attract considerable research attention. Many companies have invested enormous sums in computers and software since the 1960's. Often these investments were made with the assumption that overall enterprise productivity would improve, or at least the productivity directly affected by computers. Current data indicates, however, that each dollar invested in computers has generated a return of only $0.80. The preliminary data is suspect, but the results are shocking enough for this topic to be called "the productivity paradox" and to accumulate quite a lot of recent research.

Some of the studies on this topic are those of Erik Brynjolfsson of MIT's Sloan School (in Communications of the ACM), Richard T. Due the Canadian economist who publishes with Auerbach (Due's "The Productivity Paradox" in the winter 1993 issue of Information Systems Management discusses this topic quite succinctly), Michael Hammer who published in the Harvard Business Review, and many other authors.

16. Standards support—ANSI, the IEE, IEEE, and ISO have no meaningful standards that deal with either "proof of claims" by vendors, or with technology investments by clients and consumers. The DoD standards of the U.S. Department of Defense at least touch on proof of claims.

17. Professional associations—The non-profit vertical industry associations such as LOMA for insurance and the managed health care groups are the most likely to deal effectively with poor technology investments. Local groups such as the Boston Computer Society and the regional CASE User Groups are effective in dealing with false claims and minimizing the chances for poor investments. Curiously, some of the user groups associated with both computer manufacturers (such as SHARE, GUIDE, or COMMON in the IBM world, and DECUS in the DEC world) are fairly effective in dealing with poor technology investments. There are even on-line forums using services such as CompuServe that are helpful in avoiding poor investments. Organizations that deal with metrics, measurement, and estimation are often interested in value and ROI: the International Function Point Users Group (IFPUG), the International Society of Parametric Analysis (ISPA), and the Society of Cost Estimating and Analysis (SCEA) are examples. The various regional Software Process Improvement Network (SPIN) groups are interested in ROI too, with particular emphasis on process matters.

18. **Effectiveness of known therapies**—Software measurement is a very effective therapy against poor technology investments, but takes several years for the effectiveness to reach full potency. Software estimating tools such as SLIM, SPQR/20, CHECKPOINT®, and others in the industry are also effective when used to assess technology impacts. However, care must be exercised in ensuring that the estimating tool can deal with the technology in question. For products and methods with user associations, contacting experienced users is a very effective therapy against poor investments.

One problem should be discussed. So long as exaggerated claims are common among tool and methodology vendors, any company that does not make such claims may be at a competitive disadvantage. Thus vendor claims, including those of SPR, should always be carefully evaluated and confirmed, if possible, by contacting actual users of the products or services under consideration.

19. **Costs of known therapies**—Contacting current users of tools and methods and finding out how well they work is the least expensive therapy. (Never take vendor claims at face value.) Calculating standard return on investment (ROI) rates is a fairly inexpensive therapy, although collecting sufficient data can take from several days to a month. Using commercial software estimating tools is also a possible therapy. Establishing a full and formal software measurement program for productivity and quality is the most effective long-range therapy, but a fairly expensive one.

20. **Long-range prognosis**—Unless the software industry sets voluntary ethical standards and eliminates false advertising, poor technology investments cannot be eliminated. Whenever consumers are bombarded with false or questionable claims, it is easy to make mistakes. Therefore, false claims are likely to continue indefinitely, and it will be surprising if they are eliminated prior to the end of the twentieth century. The industry would also benefit from a standard method for calculating return on investment.

CHAPTER 60

Severe Layoffs and Cutbacks of Staff

1. **Definition**—Elimination of more than 10% of software personnel (among others) by means of early retirements, transfers to other work, incentives for resignation, or outright layoffs, or other forms of involuntary termination.

2. **Severity**—The average severity of layoffs, when they occur, is difficult to predict because it tends to be based on the financial condition of each separate company. Following is an attempt to rank severity levels in terms of percentages of staff affected:

   Severity 1: Layoffs affect from 50% to 100% of software personnel

   Severity 2: Layoffs affect more than 50% of software personnel

   Severity 3: Layoffs affect from 25% to 50% of software personnel

   Severity 4: Layoffs affect from 10% to 25% of software personnel

   Severity 5: Layoffs affect less than 10% of software personnel

3. **Frequency**—Both the frequency of layoffs and their magnitude have increased since SPR began performing assessments in 1985. From the 1960's through about 1989, the software staffs within many companies grew about 10% annually.

   Although layoffs and cutbacks occurred for many individual companies and some industries, such as automobile and steel production, software professionals were often buffered and were not as heavily impacted as personnel in mechanical or electrical engineering, administrative personnel, or other classes of employees. Indeed, from 1984 through 1989, more than 90% of SPR's clients were expanding their software staffs by various amounts.

   From 1989 forward, waves of significant layoffs began to sweep through industries that were producers of, and heavy users of, mainframe and minicomputer software (i.e. computer manufacturers, telecommunication manufacturers, airlines, defense contractors, oil companies, etc.). These more recent layoffs are affecting software personnel nationally, and are particularly severe in the regions that previously had the fastest growth rates of software professionals: California and New England. Not every industry is shrinking, of course, and pure software companies are often continuing to expand. Even so, the five-year period from 1989 through 1993 has been one of profound change and redirection for the computer and software industries. From 1989 through the time of publication of this book (mid 1993) about 30% of SPR's clients have been engaged in downsizing their software staffs, about 40% are remaining constant, and only 30% are continuing to expand in terms of personnel.

As this book was being prepared, a local radio station in Boston ran a program on job losses in New England. About one third of the lost jobs since 1989 could be attributed to down-sizings and reductions within the computer industry, for companies such as DEC, IBM, Wang, Prime and Data General. Unlike earlier downsizings, software personnel have been vulnerable to job losses under the current weak economy. The future is difficult to see, and the long-range impact of continued downsizing among computer and software groups makes predicting future trends difficult and uncertain.

4. **Occurrence**—All classes of software tend to be affected: information systems, systems software, military software, and commercial software. What is interesting is the nature of the response by each class of software. For information systems, either voluntary attrition, layoffs, or outsourcing to a domestic contractor have the highest occurrence. For systems software, on the other hand, overseas outsourcing is becoming a significant topic. For military software, outright layoffs are the most common occurrence. For commercial software houses, layoffs and financial failure tend to occur rather close together.

5. **Susceptibility and resistance**—For large civilian companies, layoffs and cutbacks correlate almost exactly with the financial condition of an enterprise. Companies that are losing money and experiencing sagging cash flows tend to have layoffs. Companies that are making money and have positive cash flows tend to hire. For venture-funded start-ups of course, the enterprises run at a loss for the first 12 to 18 months, but if losses continue too long, either additional rounds of capital or layoffs will occur. For government software groups, the patterns of expansion and contraction are linked to budgeting cycles. Sectors that are popular with voters and elected officials tend to grow, while sectors that are out of favor tend to shrink. In 1993, for example, defense is shrinking at the national level

6. **Root causes**—The most generalized root cause for layoffs and cutbacks appears to be the following: an enterprise markets one or more successful products and begins to grow rapidly. Based on this growth, suppliers and related industries also grow in turn. As sales continue upward, the company's planning group recommends expansion to meet anticipated future demand. However, after a period of time, which can range from less than five years to more than 20 years, one or more alternatives to the successful product also enters the market and begins to gain market share. As additional competitors enter the market, prices decline and margins shrink. Since the original company's growth plans cannot be switched off like a light, the company continues to expand personnel for several more years in the face of declining

sales. Eventually the company becomes overstaffed relative to its income and the demand for its products, begins to lose notable amounts of money, and then starts to lay off personnel. This appears to be the pattern observed in New England, for enterprises such as Prime, Data General, Wang, DEC and IBM.

The essential root cause may be that successful products begin to create myths of invincibility, so that executives and personnel in the companies which create them have trouble in recognizing viable alternatives until too late.

For reasons that may be rooted in the human psyche, success seems to prevent innovation. In both military history and the history of many businesses, a successful innovation tends to slow down further innovation. The original idea, no doubt brilliant at the time, becomes enshrined and sanctified so that alternatives are dismissed or even suppressed. For example, both DEC and IBM have been chided in the press for not realizing the impact of personal computers and workstations on the market for mini-computers and mainframes. This is no different than the failure of military strategists to perceive the profound changes in warfare that airplanes and tanks might create.

7. **Associated problems**—Layoffs and cutbacks are associated with most of the problems in this book. Some of the more visible associations include *canceled projects, excessive time to market, friction between clients and contractors, friction between software management and enterprise executives, poor organization structures*, and *low user satisfaction*. A problem not explicitly discussed in this book, *litigation expenses*, is also often associated with layoffs and cutbacks.

Layoffs and cutbacks themselves may be caused by *ambiguous improvement targets, artificial maturity levels, poor quality, excessive time to market, inadequate risk analysis, inadequate value analysis, management malpractice*, and two problems not explicitly discussed in this book: *inadequate competitive analysis*, and *suppression of innovation*.

8. **Cost impact**—What is surprising about layoffs and cutbacks is that they often result in a company spending more money than if staffing continued to be level. In addition to one-time costs or charges, it often happens that the enterprise cannot function without some of the personnel who retired or were released, so they often return as consultants and may even add to the company's expense levels. Further, there are many disturbing tendencies about layoffs that can degrade a company's performance afterward, such as the fact that the best people tend to leave in the largest numbers. Also, when massive layoffs are in progress the morale of the staff is always quite low, and confidence by clients is reduced as well. SPR has not been commissioned to perform a formal study of the economics of layoffs and downsizing, but from observations among clients who are in the midst of such events, costs tend to go up before they come down.

9. **Methods of prevention**—There seem to be no effective methods of prevention that are accessible to the ordinary employees and managers of an enterprise. Developing a string of new, innovative, and profitable products is obviously a pre-

ventive measure, but it is not one that a company can simply turn on when needed.

10. **Methods of control**—In the course of its assessments of enterprises that are downsizing and laying off personnel, SPR has observed a number of hazardous practices which are potentially controllable. Following are short discussions of some of the more visible problems associated with staff reductions.

Consider Rebirth in a New Business

Several companies were versatile enough to change business strategies and become successful in new directions after downsizing or failing in their original business plans. Franklin and Wang, for example, come to mind as companies that successfully changed directions. Franklin, indeed, became a pioneer in small hand-held electronic dictionaries, encyclopedia's and the like after stumbling as a personal computer company. Wang is now moving into software services.

Consider Staff Reactions to Rumors of Layoffs

Staff morale in enterprises where rumors of layoffs are occurring plummets, and performance sags as well. It is an interesting observation that in both the United States and in Japan, the employees with the highest appraisal scores tend to be the quickest to leave voluntarily when a company is facing layoffs. Obviously such employees have the easiest time in finding new jobs. The employees who typically do not commence active job searches are those who may be nearing retirement, are waiting for vested rights to accrue, or who may not have skills that are immediately marketable. Sometimes employees stay because of a loyalty to the enterprise, or because they truly enjoy their work. Also, in today's economy, equivalent jobs may not be readily available.

Consider Compensation Reduction Rather than Cutbacks

Some companies may opt to reduce compensation levels by various percentages rather than lay off permanent personnel. This strategy is normally selected as a temporary expedient, with the assumption that portions of salary payments are being deferred until the immediate problem with cash flow is overcome.

Consider Early Retirements and Departure Benefits

One of the common inducements of large companies is to offer early retirement packages, as an inducement to have employees leave before the normal retirement age. Quite a large number of both DEC and IBM personnel, for example, took advantage of the packages offered by these companies. Unfortunately, not every company can afford to do this, and many small companies do not even have retirement plans. The down side from the point of view of departing employees who want to work elsewhere is that they may have to relocate to other cities. If large numbers of employees are departing more or less simultaneously in a small geographic area (such as Maynard, Massachusetts, where DEC is headquartered, or Poughkeepsie, New York, where IBM has it largest plants) the local real estate market may plunge so steeply that moving becomes difficult.

Consider Retraining of Employees

From time to time, companies experience a surplus of one job skill, while experiencing shortages of others. For example, a few years ago many telecommunication manufacturers had a surplus of electrical engineers and mechanical engineers, and a shortage of software engineers, when switching systems migrated from being electro-mechanical to fully digital. The success rate of offering retraining is good enough so that companies seem to benefit from it, although obviously not everyone wants to change careers and some who wish to do so may not be successful. Unfortunately, retraining is normally restricted to very large corporations since smaller ones usually lack both the cash and the educational facilities to make retraining feasible.

Minimize Cuts in External Training and Education

Some of the first activities to be cut when cash flow is negative are the expenses of external training and education such as seminars and conferences. These costs are perceived as discretionary, and so usually eliminated as soon as the economic picture becomes clear. Unfortunately, the long-range impact of such cuts can degrade the performance of the staff and management if the cuts are anything other than temporary (say six months or so).

Minimize Cuts in Administrative Support

There is a natural tendency by technical managers to want to preserve technical workers, so administrative and support personnel may be released before technical workers and in larger numbers. This means, of course, that the administrative work will fall upon the shoulders of the remaining technologists, hence interfering with their primary technical tasks and lowering their performance levels. If possible, a balance of technical and administrative workers should be preserved.

Minimize Cuts in Specialist Occupations

Large software groups tend to have many specialists: Quality assurance, testing, technical writers, maintenance, network operations, data base administration, integration, configuration control, human factors and the like. It often happens that these specialists may be released in larger volumes than the general software engineering population. This policy appears unwise for several reasons: A) The general software engineering population probably cannot do the work as well as the specialists; B) Critical specialists will probably be rehired as consultants, with additional costs accruing.

Avoid Artificial Preservation of Management

In most enterprises, the people who are responsible for creating the sequence of layoffs in the enterprise are managers, and they seldom include their own names on the list. It has been observed in several companies that after layoffs have stabilized, the final ratio of management to staff had dropped from about 1 manager for every 8 workers to 1 manager for every 5 workers. Obviously, management had been somewhat buffered from the layoffs and cutbacks affecting technical workers. The ratio of senior managers and executives was even more skewed. Since the problems of the enterprise usually start at the top, or with senior management, the artificial preservation of the very group that could not prevent the financial losses from occurring does not bode well for corporate survival.

Replacement of Corporate Officers and Executives

Unless the senior executives of an enterprise are the owners or the major shareholders, it is a common practice by boards of directors to replace the top ranks of an enterprise with new incumbents, often from outside the corporation. This has recently occurred with both DEC and IBM, for example. There is no guarantee that the new arrivals can turn around the situation which caused the layoffs in the first place, but at least they do not have the psychological handicap of having built the organization and its products using a pattern that no longer works. In other words, the new incumbents are not emotionally attached to the past successes of the enterprise, and hence may be in a better position to make profound but necessary change. What is interesting is that sometimes the displaced executives end up doing outstanding work within other companies.

Consider the Impact of Closure of Buildings and Facilities

Several of SPR's clients have closed office buildings or manufacturing plants and consolidated the workers at other locations. Unfortunately, this has tended to result in overcrowding: three or more personnel sharing a cubicle or small office; lack of facilities for holding reviews and inspections; and a general increase in noise levels. In the United States (as opposed to Japan) productivity and quality tend to sag in noisy, crowded facilities. While one can easily recognize the lease and facilities cost savings associated with overcrowding, it is fair to balance these savings against the known reduction of staff performance levels.

Evaluate Harsh Versus Benign Layoff Policies

While available cash determines what is possible, the author has observed wide variances in the way layoffs are handled. The best is when the company offers out-placement support, resume creation support, and even permits employees to utilize office services such as copiers and telephones. The worst are simple termination notices with minimal benefits for the departing staff.

Be Cautious of Delayed Payments

When companies are in financial distress, one of the first actions usually taken is to delay accounts payable and stretch out the average payment time from 30 days or less to 45 or even 90 days. Small suppliers and consultants who work with companies that are in financial distress may find themselves in trouble too, if they anticipate prompt payments.

Avoid Artificial Funding Criteria for New Projects

In one of SPR's client organizations that was downsizing staff, the corporate controller issued a directive that any new software project would be required to reduce operating costs in order to be funded. One software project in the early planning stages was a very innovative tool that was to be given to the company's clients to aid in planning their usage of the company's primary product. In other words, it was a software project intended to increase revenues rather than to cut costs. Initially, funding for the project was denied, since it violated the controller's directive on cost reduction. However, when apprised of the situation, the controller amended the directive to include software projects that might increase revenues, as well as those that might lower operating costs.

Pros and Cons of Across the Board Versus Selective Staffing Reductions

The two most common forms of staffing reduction are the following: A) Arbitrary reductions across the board, such as closing an entire facility; B) Selective reductions under which the enterprise tries to preserve what it thinks to be its most valuable assets. Surprisingly, the former is sometimes better than the latter. When an entire facility is shut down, there is no disgrace among the employees who are let go, since all are equally affected. On the other hand, when employees are let go selectively, there is sometimes a perception that those released are less capable than those retained. Further, selective staffing reductions are clearly fraught with subjective opinions, and may not actually select the right people to stay behind.

Explore Concurrent Downsizing and Hiring Within the Same Enterprise

Even while enterprises are downsizing and laying people off, they may not stop all hiring. In large companies, conglomerates, and government groups there may be substantial growth in some sectors at the same time that substantial shrinkage is occurring elsewhere. The enterprises that have fairly cohesive personnel departments which are aware of all locations can often point employees toward new jobs within the enterprise. However, conglomerates and some government agencies may not be aware of other opportunities. One large corporation was observed to be laying off software personnel in one division, and hiring them in another division in a particular city. Ironically, the two divisions had not been in contact and were acting independently even though the two personnel offices were less than one mile apart.

11. **Product support**—There appear to be no commercial products which have a direct bearing on staffing reductions, layoffs, early retirements, and the like. Several companies have built proprietary tools that can deal with such topics, but they are often closely guarded and not widely available even within the company to say nothing of the outside world.

Software Productivity Research (SPR) has built an experimental tool for dealing with downsizing of staff, although it is a research project and not commercially available. To illustrate the concept of what such tools do, the tool is initialized with the staff sizes of various specialist, generalist, administrative, and management job categories; mix of contract and regular employees; current annual software costs; current productivity and quality levels; and the current size of the corporate software portfolio. The user can specify various levels of shrinkage (or growth) in software staffing levels. The tool will analyze the mix of job categories, generate the most likely reductions in each job category, and then calculate the resulting one-time costs, annual costs, and the productivity levels and quality levels that might result.

12. **Consulting support**—Dealing with layoffs and cutbacks in an optimal fashion is a specialized form of consulting. The consulting groups that are most likely to deal with this situation are those which integrate out-placement counseling and out-placement services for departing employees. However, these consulting groups are seldom qualified to deal with the software productivity, quality, and cost implications of severe downsizing. Therefore it may be desirable to seek advice as well from management consulting groups such as Andersen, A.D. Little, Deloitte, Peat Marwick, McKinsey, DMR, or the like. A final point: due to the variety of litigation potentials associated with layoffs, cutbacks, and downsizing, legal counsel can be viewed as essentially mandatory.

13. **Education support**—There is almost a total shortage of both academic and private educational offerings on how to deal with severe layoffs. Most business schools cover this topic and have case studies available, however. Some of the management consulting groups may have worked with clients that were downsizing or laying off personnel, and hence may have private education to offer. It is hard to imagine a public course being offered on "laying off software personnel" since anyone who attended would be immediately suspected of planning a layoff. On the other hand, there are a number of local seminars dealing with the topic of "surviving layoffs and cutbacks" or "careers in transition."

14. **Publication support**—The software and computing industries have both been growing until quite recently, so books on layoffs and declines are not yet common. No doubt, many future authors will discuss the problems of IBM, DEC, Wang, and other once glamorous manufacturers. Ed Yourdon's *Decline and Fall of the American Programmer* (Prentice Hall, 1992) is beginning to look highly relevant. Books on the decline of other industries provide much food for thought. Brock Yate's *The Decline and Fall of the American Automobile Industry* (Vintage Books, 1983) is also useful. Also dealing with automotive decline, David Halberstam's *The Reckoning* (Avon Books, 1987) contains many thoughtful insights. (Readers might also find Gibbons' multi-volume *Decline and Fall of the Roman Empire* useful too, at least to see the origin of so many books that use "Decline and Fall . . ." as part of their titles.)

Rand Araskog's *The ITT Wars* (Henry Holt and Company, 1989) discusses the various takeover attempts that led to ITT's downsizing. A more recent book,

Richard B. Miller's *CITICORP: The Story of a Bank in Crisis* (McGraw-Hill, 1993) also shows the factors leading to downsizing.

Robert Levering, Michael Katz, and Milton Moskowitz's *The Computer Entrepreneurs* (New American Library, 1984) is interesting, since in 1993 many of the companies cited in 1984 as fast-growing have failed, downsized, or changed business strategies. The author Capers Jones' monograph *Software Productivity and Quality Today—The Worldwide Perspective* (IS Management Group, 1993) discusses the number of software professionals in about 60 countries, and points out the United States is facing ever-increasing software competition.

Susan Rosegrant and David Lampe's *Route 128* (Basic Books, 1992) discusses the ups and downs of the high technology companies surrounding Boston. (There is a technical bookstore within walking distance of the author's office: the Softpro computer and software bookstore in Burlington, Massachusetts. It provides an interesting way of judging the health of the local economy. Since 1990, the Softpro computer bookstore has added the equivalent of a complete shelf of books dealing with resume preparation, job searches, and career changes.)

15. **Periodical support**—As this book is being written, essentially all magazines that discuss software and computers are running article after article on the changes in the industry associated with IBM, DEC, and the others. Most business journals are also covering the topics. Since about 1991, almost every issue of every relevant journal has included editorials, articles, or various studies on what the authors think is happening.

16. **Standards support**—So far as can be determined as of 1993, there are no standards at all that deal with layoffs and downsizing published by any major standards group such as ANSI, ISO, IEEE, etc. Interestingly, there are laws and government mandates on letting people go, and these are particularly stringent in Europe.

17. **Professional associations**—All of the professional associations are interested in the increasing numbers of layoffs and cutbacks among computer and software workers. None are in a position to do very much about it, except keep statistics and occasionally offer help to members who are seeking work.

18. **Effectiveness of known therapies**—So far as can be determined, the only technique that can cure cutbacks and layoffs is to keep making reasonably high profit levels. All companies would like to do this, but few are able to do so forever. Indeed, the average life expectancy of a U.S. corporation is shorter (less than 50 years) than it is for a U.S. citizen (more than 72 years).

19. **Costs of known therapies**—It is extremely difficult to quantify the costs of layoffs in general, although this can be done for any specific company or government agency with fairly good precision.

20. **Long-range prognosis**—It is difficult to judge the future of this particular topic. If the U.S. software and computing industries follow the trends of U.S. automotive

and aircraft manufacturers, then the peak of U.S. software dominance may already be behind us. On the other hand, the pure software companies such as Microsoft, Borland, Computer Associates, and the like are continuing to grow and thrive. What may be occurring is a change from a hardware dominated industry to a software dominated industry. If so, the U.S. technology base and the number of trained professionals are both arguably the best in the world. However, the U.S., Europe, and Pacific Rim countries still build software largely by hand, and this makes them vulnerable to countries with low labor costs such as India, Poland, or Mexico. The prognosis is guarded: by the end of the century there is better than a 70/30 chance that the United States will remain the world's largest software producer. But by 2025 A.D., the odds may have declined substantially.

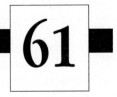

CHAPTER

Short-Range Improvement Planning

1. **Definition**—A) The common assumption that large and complex problems dealing with software can be resolved in less than one year; B) Failure to create software technology improvement plans that span more than one year to 18 months; C) The widespread failure to create long-range (three or more years) operational or strategic plans among U.S. software groups.

2. **Severity**—The average severity of the problem of short-range planning is quite high: about a 2.5 on the following five-point scale:

   Severity 1: No serious or formal technical planning at all

   Severity 2: No planning or follow-up beyond the current fiscal or calendar year

   Severity 3: Little planning beyond the current year; and little follow-up of plans

   Severity 4: Long range plans produced, but few are implemented

   Severity 5: Long-range planning, but few plans followed to completion

3. **Frequency**—Lack of long-range planning and the corollary problems of failing to implement plans once they are created, and failure to follow-up and see if anticipated results were actually achieved, appear to be endemic among U.S. businesses and government groups. More than 70% of the enterprises assessed by SPR to date have lacked long-range plans, others have no methods in place to follow such plans even if they existed. (Note: Since SPR is often commissioned by enterprises that want to create long-range plans, there may be bias in SPR's observations about this problem.)

4. **Occurrence**—Civilian MIS producers, civilian systems software, commercial software producers, and military and defense software producers all exhibit this problem. Military and defense organizations are somewhat more likely to produce long-range plans than are civilian groups, but seem no better in follow-up or implementation. Large high-tech companies such as computer manufacturers and

telecommunication manufacturers are the most likely to create long-range plans, but are no more likely than other companies to implement the plans or to follow-up on results. No industry stands out as being much better or worse than others, although some companies are clearly superior to others. For reasons beyond the scope of this book, companies in countries of the Pacific Rim such as South Korea, Japan, Singapore, Hong Kong, and Taiwan are somewhat more likely to create long-range plans than U.S. or European equivalents.

5. **Susceptibility and resistance**—The patterns of susceptibility and resistance are not clearly known. Somewhat surprisingly, small U.S. companies with less than 50 software personnel are more likely to create long-range plans than are large enterprises with more than 1000 software personnel. This phenomenon appears to be related to funding: venture capitalists and other funding sources for small businesses usually require a business plan as a pre-condition for funding approval. Among larger enterprises, those which have a vision of becoming "best in class" or of being industry leaders are more likely to produce long-range plans than other companies. Indeed, companies whose vision of themselves is "best in class" tend to create improvement targets, and then create plans for achieving those targets. Such companies are also likely to apply for Baldrige Awards, or take other actions such as commissioning SEI or SPR assessments in order to validate their progress.

6. **Root causes**—The root causes for lack of long-range planning are uncertain, but several hypotheses have been put forward that may shed light on this problem:

Financial reporting frequency

U.S. companies normally report financial results to shareholders every quarter. This tends to create a pattern of short-range thinking, since many managers and executives will be held responsible for the results of the current quarter. By contrast, Japanese companies report financial results once a year.

Management tenure

American managers seldom hold the same position for more than about 18 months. There is little incentive to create long-range plans if the incumbent will not be present to carry the plan through to completion. A corollary to this situation, which may derive from the U.S. political system, is that the new incumbent of any managerial position routinely discards the plans of the previous incumbent.

Lack of baselines and periodic measurement programs

Plans are normally created to resolve a problem, or to improve some aspect of corporate performance. Unless there is a quantified baseline, and periodic measurements to judge improvements, there is little incentive to create long-range plans. Hence the widespread lack of measurement of software may trigger a malaise in lack of effective planning too.

False Claims and Lack of Return on Investment Data

Software managers and engineers are bombarded by advertisements from software tool and methodology vendors which include fanciful claims of "10 to 1," "100 to 1" or even "1000 to 1" productivity improvements. Often these claims have no empirical support of any kind. Such claims tend to make technology planning difficult, because they shift the burden of proof on to the manager creating the plan.

7. **Associated problems**—Lack of long-range planning is frequently associated with the *silver bullet syndrome, poor technology investments, inadequate measurement, inaccurate metrics* and also with *corporate politics.* Lack of long-range planning is often found in the same companies which experience *canceled projects, cost overruns,* and *excessive time to market.*

   Lack of long-range planning itself can be caused by *inadequate tools and methods for project management* and *inadequate curricula for management.*

8. **Cost impact**—The costs of lack of long-range planning do not lend themselves to easy or direct calculation. In the long run, companies which have this problem can expect to lose market shares, and to lag behind their competitors who do plan effectively.

9. **Methods of prevention**—Companies and government agencies might consider establishing three tiers of planning horizons: tactical, operational, and strategic. The layer of tactical plans deals with what is going to be accomplished over the next 12 months. The layer of operational plans deals with what is going to be accomplished over the next three years. The layer of strategic planning deals with what is going to be accomplished over the indefinite future, ranging from more than three years to as many as ten years out.

   For improving software, operational planning for a three-year period fills a useful gap. Three-year plans are short enough so that many of the personnel who create the plan will be present to observe the results. Three-year plans also fall within the horizon of many value-analysis approaches such as dealing with the internal rate of return and the accounting rate of return. Thus three-year operational plans have a better chance of being funded than would five-year plans, or long range strategic plans. Following is an example of a six-stage, three-year operational plan for software improvements to illustrate the concept:

Stage 1: Focus on Management (Months 1 through 6)

All SPR assessments and most of the serious studies on software problems carried out by other management consulting groups have noted that, as a class, managerial problems are more common and more serious than any other kind.

This observation is also true of other fields beside software. Indeed, the well-known management consultants W. Edwards Deming and Jospeh M. Juran have both observed that two-thirds of the manufacturing problems can be traced to management; only one-third to the workers.

Therefore, the work of the first six months should concentrate on bringing software managers up to speed on the topics in which they must be experts if their enterprises are to achieve "best in class" status.

Since all human beings are more or less blind to their own shortcomings, the first item on the agenda for moving toward software excellence would be a formal assessment by an outside group. As of 1993, there are at least a half a dozen different assessment methods available.

The first six months should also include a quantitative baseline, so that you know your current portfolio size and its state of decay, and so you know your productivity and quality levels and ranges.

Some of the key accomplishments of the first six months will be to bring all managers up to speed in the technologies of project planning, project estimating, productivity measurements, and quality measurements. These are the skills they need to evaluate the impact of the technologies that will be introduced later.

After the first six months, a software management team should be fully equipped with modern project estimating and planning tools. As a result of assessments, they will know exactly what their software strengths and weaknesses are, and they will know your current productivity and quality baselines, and they will have started both quality and productivity measurement programs, as well as user-satisfaction measurements.

The approximate costs for the first six months will range from about $3,500 to $20,000 per project manager in one-time expenses for estimation and project management tools. The consulting fees for assessments, baselining, and establishing measurement programs will run from $25,000 to more than $100,000 depending upon the size of the enterprise.

The first stage will have a minimal direct impact on productivity, but quality might go up by as much as 10%. Once software quality is measured, it usually improves.

Stage 2: Focus on Structured Methods (Months 6 through 12)

The second six-month period focuses on methodologies. Methods need to be selected before too many tools are acquired because tools support methodologies rather than the other way around.

All software professional should understand the basics of structured analysis and design, Data analysis, structured coding, reviews and inspections, Joint Application Design (JAD), and the other fundamentals. Surprisingly, not everyone does. Therefore a suite of courses in standard software engineering methods is often utilized by leading companies.

This period also begins to focus on two powerful quality control techniques: *defect prevention methods,* and *defect removal methods.* Formal design and code inspections have the highest removal efficiency of any technique yet noted, and are about twice as efficient in finding bugs as most forms of testing. Note that inspections are used by all of the companies which are in the upper 10% of SPR's quality ranges, such as AT&T, Motorola, IBM, Raytheon, etc.

This is also the period when the high costs of maintenance begin to be addressed via complexity analysis, restructuring, and other geriatric-care methods and approaches. Note that high maintenance costs are much more common and also more serious for large companies than small, so the need for geriatric software care rises with the size of the enterprise.

After this six-month period, a software engineering community will be trained in using some of the most effective development methods yet created. Aging legacy software will also be starting to come under geriatric care.

The costs accrued during this six-month period can range from about $1,000 to $3,000 per technical staff member for geriatric-tool acquisition. Training in the various technologies may run from $1,500 to about $3,500 per staff member. Expect each member of the technical staff to receive about ten days of training during this six-month interval.

By the end of Stage 2, quality may have improved by perhaps 25% compared to the initial baseline, and productivity by 10% to 15%. The pattern of having quality improve faster than productivity is the most effective and by far the safest. (If productivity went up faster than quality, then maintenance costs would rise steeply and user satisfaction might decline.)

Stage 3: Focus on New Tools and Methods (Months 12 to 18)

Substantial investment in new tools before management is trained in estimating and measurement, and before methodologies firm, is often a serious waste of corporate funds. Too often, software managers and executives fall prey to "silver bullet" advertising by CASE vendors or other tool vendors, and naively purchase tools with the expectation of achieving large productivity or quality gains in a short time.

Further, most long-range studies on the effectiveness of CASE and other software tools reach two similar conclusions: 1) Unless as much is invested in training as in the tool, the results will be marginal; 2) Experienced, well-trained software professionals get more value from tools than do inexperienced personnel.

The object-oriented paradigm is on a very steep growth curve. Object-oriented languages such as Smalltalk, Objective-C, and C++ have been in existence for more than ten years, and have substantial empirical data available. The newer aspects of the O-O paradigm, such as object-oriented analysis and design and object-oriented data bases lack substantial empirical data in 1993 as to their value, their impact on quality or productivity, or any other significant topic. Therefore, caution should be used when approaching the O-O domain: it is being advertised as a new kind of "silver bullet" and some of the claims appear to be exaggerated. One of the tasks managers can perform as a result of their Stage 1 training and estimating tool acquisition is to model the impact of new technologies, such as the O-O paradigm, on upcoming projects.

Client-server architectures and application downsizing are also on a steep growth curve. Here too, caution is indicated since not every application lends itself to downsizing. Further, the technology base for client-server projects is still evolving, and currently lacks much in the way of rigorous quality assurance approaches. Here too, managers can model the pros and cons of this technology using the skills they acquired in Stage 1.

By the end of this period, software groups will have experimented with some of the major technologies that have emerged within the last ten years. A software measurement program, created during Stage 1, can demonstrate the effectiveness or lack of effectiveness of any of the approaches selected. Both software staff and managers will be experienced enough so that they can make definitive evaluations of any tools and technologies that seem useful.

This is the most expensive period in terms of one-time expenses, which is why tool acquisition is offset by 12 to 18 months. It will take that long to enable you to get adequate value from the tools you acquire, since tools give the greatest value to the best and most experienced managers and technical staff members.

A fully Integrated CASE tool suite which supports the entire life cycle with no major gaps will require in excess of 50,000 Function Points of processing power. The acquisition cost for such an I-CASE tool suite can exceed $1.00 per Function Point, and is not likely to be below about $0.25 per Function Point. Thus a full I-CASE tool suite can run from about $15,000 to perhaps $50,000 per seat. This is not a small investment, nor one to make without substantial analysis dealing with return on investment (ROI).

In addition, both managers and technical staff members will need extensive training in the tools you are acquiring. Expect to devote ten to 15 days per staff member for training during this period, and to pay from $5,000 to $7,500 per staff member for courses and instruction.

When tools and training are summed together, the total expenses for this time period can range from about $20,000 to almost $60,000 per technical staff member for large enterprises moving into Integrated or I-CASE, and from $5,000 to $20,000 per staff member for small enterprises moving into partial CASE.

By the end of Stage 4, quality can be 30% to 50% better than the initial baseline, and productivity can be better by perhaps 25% to 35%. Here too, note that quality levels should go up faster than productivity levels to avoid catastrophic maintenance increases.

Stage 4: Focus on Infrastructure (Months 18 through 24)

Software excellence is not a one-time exercise. It requires sustained, continued effort. Therefore the fourth six-month period focuses on infrastructure, or the continuing effort needed to keep a software group healthy and at the leading edge of the state of the art. In Stages 1, 2, and 3 both management and staff learned so many new things that time is required to absorb and internalize the new concepts. This is particularly true of technologies which require a new mind-set, such as the object-oriented paradigm or moving to client-server architectures. Therefore Stage 4 is devoted to using the new methods, tools, and skills acquired in the earlier stages to ensure that they work successfully and meet both cultural and technological needs.

Another of the critical accomplishments of this period is establishing annual education policies for both management and technical staff, with ten to 15 days of training provided every year.

Yet another critical accomplishment is to begin to recognize the need for specialization, and to start formalizing the hiring practices needed to bring special skills into the organization. In all human activities, including software, specialists tend to out-perform generalists. For software as of 1993, more than 50 kinds of software specialists are found in leading software organizations, including quality assurance, testing, technical communication, integration and configuration control specialists, estimating and measurement specialists, and many others.

By the completion of this period, any software organization should be able to pass ISO certification for marketing software in Europe. The larger software organizations should also be at or rapidly approaching level 3 on the SEI capability model series.

The expenses during this period vary too widely for convenient summarization. Expect to spend from $1,000 to more than $2,000 in continued training for every manager and technical staff member for topics such as learning the Baldrige criteria and moving into total quality management (TQM). The communication and office space expenses are the most uncertain during this time period.

By the completion of Stage 4, software quality levels can exceed the initial baseline by as much as 50% to 75%, and productivity levels by 35% to 50%. This is not yet "best in class" status, but it should be very good compared to U.S. norms. Unless a company can move into Stage 5 and begin to utilize reusable materials, Stage 4 is the normal upper limit of progress given the technologies that are currently available to the software industry.

Stage 5: Focus on Reusability (Months 24 through 30)

Full software reusability programs tend to have the highest return on investment of any technology since software began (about $30.00 returned for every $1.00 invested). A total of some ten software artifacts are potentially reusable, and value will increase for each of the artifacts that are encompassed in a software reuse program.

However, a strong caution is indicated: successful reuse demands zero-defect materials. It is unsafe and uneconomical to reuse materials that are filled with bugs. It is also unreliable. This is why reusability is offset by two years from the start of the program. It can take that long before an enterprise is good enough to develop anything that is worth reusing!

By the end of this period, an enterprise should be able to exceed 50% reusable materials in every application that the enterprise develops. The greater the volume of reusable, certified material, the greater productivity and quality levels will become.

As of 1993, full reusability programs are new enough so that the costs are uncertain and can only be addressed with a high margin of error. The costs for creating reusable plans and estimates are the best known, and are comparatively inexpensive: less than $100 per project, assuming that you already own estimating tools that can support template creation.

Since reusable materials must be certified to very high levels of reliability and quality, you can probably expect to pay from $3,000 to $5,000 per technical staff member to create your initial library of reusable artifacts. You will also have training costs of perhaps $1,000 per staff member and manager. This training will bring them up to speed on the fundamental principles of reusability and the mechanics of using your library.

The successful deployment of reusable material has the highest payoffs of any technologies yet identified. Not every enterprise will be able to implement the full Stage 5 reuse technologies, but those who do can achieve impressive results (as demonstrated by mathematical modeling): software defect levels better by 70% to 90% than the initial baseline, productivity levels up by 100% to 200%, and schedule reductions of perhaps 30% to 50% or more compared to the Stage 1 baseline.

Stage 6: Focus on Industry Leadership (Months 30 to 36)

By the end of three years of concentrated effort, an enterprise should be good enough to be considered as "best in class." When this level is achieved, both quality and productivity rates will be in the upper 10% of all industries.

It is often useful for enterprises to commission or perform surveys of what their competitors are doing, or to take part in various "best in class" assessments to ensure that their progress is as advanced as anticipated.

Specific numeric goals associated with such leading-edge enterprises include defect potentials of less than one defect per Function Point; defect removal efficiency levels that are consistently higher than 95% and may exceed 99%; and average productivity rates that are above 25 Function Points per staff month and may exceed 100 Function Points per staff month for projects with the greatest volumes of reusable materials.

For organizations with these accomplishments, software will no longer be regarded as a troublesome, uncontrolled technology. Schedules will be much shorter than today's norms, and predictable within a margin of about plus or minus 3%. Costs will be much lower than today, and here too predictable within very small margins. Quality will be high enough so that post-release defects seldom occur, and this in turn will raise user satisfaction levels to very high levels.

Since working on successful projects in well-managed enterprises is a pleasant experience, staff morale should be very high also. There are enormous benefits to be gained from bringing software under full control, and severe hazards for the enterprises who cannot accomplish this.

However, all software managers and technical staff members will have experienced three years of very hard work. The range of expenses over this three-year period run from a low of about $30,000 to a high of about $80,000 per staff member when equipment, tools, and training are all included and summed together. These amounts *exclude* improvements in office space and office ergonomics, which could easily double the costs.

Software excellence is not easy to achieve, and it is not inexpensive to achieve. But if an enterprise depends upon software for competitive advantages, for the products that it builds, and for efficiency in operations, it may not be safe to move into the 21st century with anything less than a world-class software organization.

10. **Methods of control**—Methods of control and methods of prevention are essentially the same: select a planning horizon (i.e. two, three, four, or five years) and develop an initial plan. Then implement the plan, and update the plan as the need arises.

11. **Product support**—Although there are many project planning and estimating tools available, there are comparatively few tools aimed at longer range operational or strategic planning. For small companies, there are several tools available which can facilitate the production of business plans. For dealing with longer range operational and strategic improvements over entire corporations which may have hundreds of projects and thousands of staff, there are no specific tools available.

Software Productivity Research (SPR) has produced an experimental tool aimed at corporate software planning, but it is a research project and not available on the commercial market. To illustrate the concept, the experimental SPR tool is initialized with the current software population of an enterprise, and current average productivity and quality levels. Users then input the current capabilities of the enterprise in terms of methods available, tools, etc. Various levels of improvement targets can be specified, culminating with "best in class." The SPR planning tool then considers and selects an assortment of new tools and methodologies over and above those currently deployed, calculates the acquisition costs, calculates the training costs, generates management and staff curricula, and predicts the improvements that would result compared to the initial baseline, and the time period needed to achieve the final goal. This experimental tool is called an "Enterprise Software Planner" or ESP for short. A variant of the basic tool deals with SEI maturity levels, and can quantify the time and costs required for an enterprise to move from any initial or starting level up to any higher level, through SEI Level 4 (Level 5 is too uncertain as of 1993).

12. **Consulting support**—Operational and strategic consulting support is available from a variety of consulting groups and also from product vendors. Among the product vendors, Quantitative Software Methods (QSM), Reifer Associates, Rubin Associates, Software Productivity Research (SPR), and ABT deal with operational and strategic topics. Among general management consulting groups, Andersen Consulting, McKinsey & Company, the DMR Group, Dean Meyer Associates, Nolan & Norton, or Roger Pressman Associates cover operational and strategic topics. The well-known Software Engineering Instituite (SEI) is moving into the domain of strategic planning, although their work on this topic is not yet very far along.

13. **Education support**—Universities and business schools tend to be more effective with operational and strategic planning than they are with the specifics of software project planning. Essentially any good university, college, or business school will have courses available on intermediate and long-range planning. However, very

few have courses on intermediate and long-range planning for software organizations.. Universities that have close ties with business and industry (such as Seattle University, Washington University in St. Louis, or the University of California at various locations) are probably the most advanced. Universities which happen to have project management specialists on their faculties, such as George Mason University, MIT, Oakland University in Rochester, Michigan, the University of Minnesota, and the University of Dayton, are also comparatively modern in specific courses taught by these experts.

14. **Publication support**—The topic of long-range planning for software is not very well covered by book publishers as of 1993. However, Robert B. Grady's *Practical Software Metrics for Project Management and Process Improvement* (Prentice Hall, 1992) gives some insight into Hewlett-Packards' five-year software plans. Keki R. Bhote's monograph on *Next Operation as Customer (NOAC)* (American Management Association, 1991) gives some interesting insights into process improvements used by Motorola, including their widely-cited "5-Up" programs. Tom DeMarco's *Controlling Software Projects* (Yourdon Press, 1982), Thomas Rullo's *Advances in Computer Programming Management* (Heyden Press, 1980), and Richard H. Thayer's *Software Engineering Project Management* (IEEE Press, 1988) are all interesting and cover aspects of longer range planning. Phil Metzger's *Managing a Programming Project* (Prentice Hall, 1977 but since revised); T. Gilb and S. Finzi's *Principles of Software Engineering Management* (Addison-Wesley, 1992); Watts Humphrey's *Managing the Software Process* (Addison Wesley, 1987); and Marciniak, Fry, and Zempolich's *Software Project Management* (John Wiley, 1991), all of these, and others too, are interesting, but deal only peripherally with longer range enterprise planning for software.

   Specific tool vendors also write books which tend to emphasize how their tools work, but are sometimes more general. An example of this genre includes the author Capers Jones' *Applied Software Measurement* (McGraw-Hill, 1991). This book deals with corporate-level improvements as well as specific project improvements.

15. **Periodical support**—As of 1993, the most useful sources of information about corporate-level planning for software are the well known business journals such as Business Week, Fortune, Forbes, Harvard Business Review, and The Economist. Among the software journals, those which have a business slant such as Information Week and Computer World are more likely to discuss such topics than the more technical journals. Sometimes house journals by vendors of software project management tools may contain relevant articles, such as Knowledge Base which is published quarterly by Software Productivity Research, or the Rubin monthly newsletter. Intermittent articles on corporate topics may appear in software journals such as American Programmer, Software Magazine, and Datamation.

16. **Standards support**—As of 1993, there are no standards by ANSI, DoD, IEE, IEEE or ISO that cover the longer ranges of operational and strategic planning. Most standards stop at project planning or short-range tactical planning, such as the IEEE standard on project management plans.

17. Professional associations—There are individual members and occasional special interest groups in many associations that are concerned with operational and strategic planning. However, no major organizations have been identified that deal with long-range planning and improvement strategies for software-intensive companies. The older and traditional professional associations, such as the IEEE and the ACM, are interested in strategic topics, and will often have discussions on such topics during their conferences. The International Society of Parametric Analysis (ISPA) covers long-range software planning models in its journal and at conferences, but not frequently.

18. Effectiveness of known therapies—It is difficult to judge the effectiveness of long-range software planning, since the data is sparse to date. Those few long-range plans that have been developed and then implemented seem to have returned positive value. An example would be Hewlett-Packard's five-year software quality improvement plan, which was both implemented and followed up. Also, Hartford Insurance was successful in developing a long-range maintenance improvement plan. However, many other long-range plans were simply not implemented, or if portions were implemented, there was little follow up.

19. Costs of known therapies—*Project Planning tools* range in cost from less than $100 to more than $10,000. However, such tools have only peripheral value when dealing with entire corporations, since many hundreds of projects in various stages of completion may be on-going at any given date.

Project Estimating tools range in cost from less than $1,000 to more than $25,000. Some estimating tools feature the ability to aggregate data from multiple projects, and to express results for an entire corporate portfolio. Tools with these capabilities are more relevant to long-range operational and strategic plans than single-project estimators. Also starting to become available are estimating "templates" that are derived from various classes of software project. Some of these templates may be relevant, since "best in class" templates are obviously an interesting concept.

Measurement tools range in price from $10,000 to $20,000. These tools will be critical in the follow-up phase of a long-range improvement plan, to measure the rate at which progress is occurring. In this capacity, measurement tools typically return their value in less than 12 months when enterprises are actively pursuing corporate improvement targets.

Assessment tools range in price from about $2,500 to $20,000. These tools are normally intended to be used across many projects, where they can be extremely helpful in identifying patterns of strength and weakness that form the basis of operational and strategic improvement plans. Assessment tools will normally return their value in less than 12 months, if used on a portfolio of at least ten projects.

20. Long-range prognosis—The long-range prognosis is guardedly favorable. Long-range operational and strategic planning is not extremely difficult to carry out from a technical viewpoint. However, the culture of the U.S. software industry has not yet demonstrated much commitment to long-range planning or even medium-range planning. Even so, by the end of the century, software managers in leading corporations and government agencies should have access to operational and strategic planning tools which can integrate the results of dozens or even hundreds of separate projects. As reliable data on the return on investments in various tools and methods becomes plentiful, software improvement planning will become more effective.

62

Silver Bullet Syndrome

1. **Definition**—The concept, derived from Dr. Fred Brooks' famous article, that a single tool or methodology will be the "silver bullet" that cures software productivity or quality problems. (The original derivation is the Folklore notion that werewolves can only be killed by a silver bullet.)

2. **Severity**—The average severity of the silver bullet syndrome in the U.S. averages about a 2.5 on the following five-point scale:

   Severity 1: The product or service in question is irrelevant or harmful

   Severity 2: The product or service in question produces no visible improvement

   Severity 3: The product or service in question makes marginal improvement

   Severity 4: The product or service in question is useful, but insufficient alone

   Severity 5: The product or service in question is useful, but difficult to learn

3. **Frequency**—The silver bullet syndrome is endemic to the software industry. More than 70% of U.S. software managers seem to be afflicted by the belief that one tool or method will solve many serious problems. More than 50% of U.S. software productivity tool companies slant their advertisements to imply that their offerings are "silver bullets" that will cure serious problems.

4. **Occurrence**—The silver bullet syndrome affects MIS, systems, and military software personnel with equal severity, although the "silver bullets" differ. For MIS software 4GL's, CASE, Information Engineering (IE), Client-Server architectures, downsizing, and RAD are the current silver bullets. For systems software, object-oriented methods or "the O-O paradigm" comprises the current silver bullet, with SEI maturity levels and CASE occurring too from time to time. For military software personnel, SEI assessments and Ada are the current silver bullets.

   The advertisements for CASE tools, Information Engineering (IE) methods, Rapid Application Development (RAD), and 4th Generation Languages are all likely to be phrased in silver bullet terms by the vendors themselves. The Object-Oriented paradigm is also beginning to use silver bullet slogans. The SEI maturity level concept is also becoming another silver bullet: it is interesting to see how many enterprises believe that moving up a notch or two on the SEI maturity scale will solve their software problems.

The tools and methods which are perceived by vendors or clients to be "silver bullets" may be useful and may generate valuable results, and indeed many of them do. The fundamental point is that there is no single tool, methodology, or concept that by itself can create large improvements in software productivity, quality, or any other tangible aspect of software performance.

Consider the analogy of medicine. An antibiotic such as penicillin is certainly a useful and valuable therapy for many bacterial infections. But antibiotics are not effective against viral infections or many other diseases. Physicians do not automatically prescribe antibiotics for all patients, nor will such drugs cure all conditions.

This rudimentary analogy simply suggests that software practitioners should understand the nature of the problems which confront software projects, and carefully evaluate a combination of technical and social approaches which match the conditions that need correction.

5. **Susceptibility and resistance**—Both software vendors and clients are highly susceptible to silver bullet syndromes. Indeed, the entire software industry and all users are somewhat susceptible to silver bullet thinking, given the lack of definitive productivity and quality benchmarks prior to 1991. Enterprises with accurate measurement programs are most resistant to the silver bullet syndrome.

6. **Root causes**—The root causes of the silver bullet syndrome are diverse: 1) The lack of any quantitative knowledge of U.S. productivity and quality levels prior to 1991; 2) The chronic lack of measurement programs, which prevent software managers from knowing how effective or ineffective various tools and methods are; 3) The failure of U.S. software engineering and management schools to deal with complex problems that require multi-faceted solutions; 4) The lack of independent, non-commercial evaluation services (similar in concept to the Consumers Union and *Consumer Reports*) for the software industry; 5) The unregulated nature of the software industry, and the lack of any legal or ethical guidelines preventing false advertising; 6) The tendency of software vendors to make assertions based on "apples or oranges" comparisons, such as comparing coding productivity rates using a 4th-generation language against the effort required to build a complete system, including all specifications and documentation.

7. **Associated problems**—The silver bullet syndrome is a significant contributor to *friction with users* and *friction with senior management*. The silver bullet syndrome is also a causative factor for *canceled projects, excessive time to market, long schedules,* and *cost overruns.* Silver bullet thinking also contributes to *high staff attrition* and *low staff morale.* Silver bullet syndrome also contributes to *low productivity,* and to *low quality* as well as *short-range improvement planning.*

527

The silver bullet syndrome is often caused by *inadequate management curricula* and is associated with *poor technology investments*. Some aspects of the silver bullet syndrome may derive from *management malpractice*.

The most pernicious problem created by the silver bullet syndrome is that it serializes improvements that should take place in parallel, and slows down tangible progress to a zero, or even to a negative amount. Since it normally takes from six months to a year to judge the effectiveness of any change in tools or methods, enterprises that do only one thing at a time can take years to improve, if they ever do. This is one of the reasons why enterprises that rank low on the SPR or SEI software effectiveness level scales usually are slow as molasses to move upward.

The silver bullet syndrome itself seems to be caused by *false productivity claims, inadequate software management curricula, management malpractice, inexperienced management, inexperienced staff, inadequate package evaluation plans, inadequate package acquisition policies, inadequate estimating, inadequate planning, inadequate measurements,* and *excessive schedule pressure.*

8. **Cost impact**—The cost impact of the silver bullet syndrome can be divided into direct and indirect components. The direct costs are those of the silver bullets purchased by clients, and they equal the sums of all dollars spent on tools or methods that are ineffective. The indirect costs of silver bullets are even more significant: lost opportunities, long schedules, and reduced amounts of discretionary capital to spend on tools and methods that are effective. Even vendors and those who market silver bullets are damaged. In the case of vendors, the direct revenues resulting from sales must be balanced against the indirect costs of lost business due to customer dissatisfaction. In some instances, silver bullets can also lead to litigation expenses if clients file suit for fraudulent advertising.

9. **Methods of prevention**—Recognition that software problems are diverse and need multiple approaches is a good preventive method. Accurate software measurement is the best long-range preventive method for silver bullet syndrome. Commercial software estimation tools are also useful preventive methods when used to assess the impact of new languages, methods, and tools. Caution must be exercised to ensure that the estimating tools can accurately deal with the silver bullet in question. For software vendors themselves, careful analysis, controlled studies, and careful measurement of Beta Test results are effective preventive approaches. Some vendors, such as IBM, Bachman, and UNISYS also have screening by Quality Assurance and corporate attorneys of all advertising claims to ensure that silver bullet-type claims are not being made. Some vendors have user associations, which often serve as an effective preventive method for the silver bullet syndrome.

10. **Methods of control**—The software industry, unlike many other industries such as the pharmaceutical industry, does not have governmental regulation or prohibition of false "silver bullet" productivity claims. There are as yet no published ethical guidelines for software advertising claims, and no independent consumer or gov-

ernmental organizations that can validate or challenge productivity or quality claims. For software, the phrase Caveat Emptor, or let the buyer beware, is the current mode.

As of 1993, software is essentially an unregulated industry with no effective canons of ethical conduct. In the future, one or all of the software industry associations such as ADAPSO, ITAA, the IEEE, ACM, or ASM, may establish canons of ethical conduct that are actually adhered to. Such canons have been promulgated from time to time, but are not enforced nor do they have any legal status. Specific companies such as IBM, Bachman, UNISYS, and CADRE have established internal controls to eliminate false productivity claims.

Other companies, such as a CASE vendor who recently cited productivity improvements of "up to 1000 to 1" based on the observations of a nominal "world's most famous productivity expert" are taking the silver bullet syndrome to new heights of exaggeration.

Software clients are not powerless to deal with the silver bullet syndrome, however. A measurement program for productivity and quality can gradually immunize companies from this affliction. Also, the mathematics of calculating return on investment (ROI) are starting to be widely known, even if the raw data for software tools and methods is suspect.

The analogy of medical practice is worthy of consideration. Physicians do not depend on a single medicine to treat all diseases, and software managers should not expect a single tool or methodology to be effective against all problems.

11. **Product support**—Tools for modeling the impact of various methods, languages, tools, and approaches if used thoughtfully can be effective against the silver bullet syndrome. Indeed, leading organizations may utilize as many as three or four different estimating tools and check for convergence or divergence in the way they react to a given situation. Some of the tools frequently employed for such analysis include, COCOMO, SEER, ESTIMACS, SLIM, SOFTCOST, SPQR/20, CHECKPOINT®, and many others, since these tools have productivity and cost estimation capabilities. About 50 such tools are on the commercial market as of 1993, and one new tool per month is entering this market. Users should of course be cautious, since estimating tools themselves may be viewed as "silver bullets" in their own right.

12. **Consulting support**—Many consulting organizations are locked into a specific methodology, which can itself be considered a silver bullet. For example, the Software Engineering Institute (SEI) and its licencees are obviously locked into its assessment approach and its five-stage capability model. These approaches have obviously become silver bullets to many DoD and military groups. Other specialized consulting niches include client-server development, downsizing, CASE, information-engineering, and object-oriented methods. While all of these are useful, none by itself is truly sufficient to deal with the broad range of issues surrounding software development and maintenance.

Clients should be sure that consultants, like medical doctors, know about more than a single therapy. Multi-client consortia, such as those offered by Index

Systems, Nolan & Norton, the Software Productivity Consortium (SPC) and Software Productivity Research (SPR) often consider a broad spectrum of solutions. Potential clients should also be as cautious of consulting groups' claims, as they would for any other vendor of products or services.

13. Education support—Software engineering and business schools seldom offer any courses that touch upon the silver bullet syndrome (other than courses in pathological psychology which are not part of software curricula). One exception would probably be Dr. Fred Brooks' graduate courses at the University of North Carolina. Only a few commercial courses are broadly based, and cover many possible approaches. The "War Games" simulations offered via DCI with Tom DeMarco and Ed Yourdon as instructors cover many topics. SPR's course on Applied Software Measurement (ASM) deals with the subject of measuring software productivity and costs, as a way to avoid the silver bullet syndrome. Similar courses also deal with technology evaluation, and quantifying the return on investment for combinations of various tools and methodologies.

The in-house training of major corporations such as AT&T, IBM, and Motorola are also effective in avoiding the silver bullet syndrome. These large organizations have built complex systems for many years, and they know from first-hand experience that signficant progress requires a multi-faceted approach that encompasses tools, methods, training, culture, and even the physical office environment.

14. Publication support—Tom Gilb's *Principles of Software Engineering Management* (Addison Wesley, 1988) advocates multiple approaches for complex issues. So does Meiler Page-Jones' *Practical Software Management* (Dorset House, 1985).

Watts Humphrey's book *Managing the Software Process* (Prentice Hall, 1987) has become a kind of a silver bullet by accident, but the book itself recommends a broad-scale, multi-faceted approach to evolutionary improvement in software processes and methods. The book *Peopleware* by Tom DeMarco and Tim Lister (Dorset House, 1987) is an excellent antidote for those who have been poisoned by the notion that tools can solve software problems. Roger Pressman's *Software Engineering: A Practitioner's Approach* (McGraw-Hill, 1982) is broad-based in its coverage, as is Richard Fairley's *Software Engineering Concepts* (McGraw-Hill, 1985). Tarik Abdel Hamid and S.E. Madnick's *Software Project Management* (Prentice Hall, 1988) recommends a multi-faceted approach to software management, and discusses many trade-offs that should be considered.

Three books by the author deal with software productivity, quality, and the impact which various tools and methods have on these factors. *Programming Productivity* (McGraw-Hill, 1986) deals with the impact of productivity, software costs, and schedules. *Applied Software Measurement* (McGraw-Hill, 1991) deals with the topic of measuring software productivity, and also includes current U.S. averages for software productivity for military, systems, and MIS software. *Critical Problems in Software Measurement* (IS Management Group, 1993) deals with the kind of data which must be collected to carry out multiple regression studies of software tools, languages, or methods.

Dr. Gerald Weinberg's *Introduction to General Systems Thinking* (John Wiley & Sons, 1975) is an excellent antidote to the silver bullet syndrome, since it deals explicitly with the interconnectedness of multiple factors. Dr. Weinberg's more recent books on *Software Quality Management: Volume 1 Systems Thinking* (Dorset House, 1992) and *Software Quality Management: Volume 2 First-Order Measurement* (Dorset House, 1993) have much to recommend in them also. The same author's *The Secrets of Consulting* (Dorset House, 1985) has a great deal of practical advice about avoiding various mind-traps that might lead to erroneous conclusions or bad advice. Dr. Weinberg and Donald Gause's *Are Your Lights On?* (Winthrop Publishers, 1982) also tackles the silver bullet syndrome by means of a discussion of how to ferret out real problems from surface manifestations.

Kenichi Ohmae's *The Mind of the Strategist—The Art of Japanese Business* (McKinsey & Company, 1982) is not about software per se, but definitely makes a case for multi-faceted analysis of complex real-world problems. Olga Crocker, Syril Charney, and Johnny Sik Leung Chiu's *Quality Circles* (Methuen Publications, 1984) examines one of the most successful industrial approaches yet conceived for approaching difficult problems in a realistic, multi-faceted way.

Software is not the only occupation to face the silver bullet syndrome. Thomas Kuhn's widely-cited *The Structure of Scientific Revolutions* (University of Chicago Press, 1970) examines the nature of abrupt paradigm shifts. Bernard Cohen's *Revolution in Science* (Harvard University Press, 1985) is a more recent treatment of a similar theme. G.N. Parkinson's *Parkinsons' Law and Other Studies in Administration* (Houghton Mifflin, 1957) is a classic management book, which should be read by all managers in every industry.

Many disciplines outside of software have developed various doctrines about overcoming their silver bullet syndromes. Military history is particularly rich in discussions of unsuccessful generals and disastrous campaigns due to simplistic ideas on the part of senior officers. The field of operations research is also fruitful for exploring the need for multi-faceted approaches to complex problem domains. Physics, chemistry, medicine, mathematics, and essentially all forms of engineering have their own silver bullets from time to time.

15. **Periodical support**—Most of the general software magazines have occasional articles on silver bullet thinking, but just as often they move in the opposite direction and print unvalidated articles about how a single tool or method can make order-of-magnitude improvements. On the whole, the software periodicals are immature and very unprofessional when it comes to topics like fact checking and validation of contents. For software, even referred journals are not very good, since the referrees themselves may be prone to silver bullet thinking. Dr. Fred Brooks' famous article, "No Silver Bullet: Essence and Accidents of Software Engineering" was published twice. The first publication was in *Information Processing '86* edited by H.J. Kugle and published by North Holland. The most widely cited

publication, however, was in IEEE Computer, Volume 20, Number 4 in April of 1987. It is well worth reading.

16. **Standards support**—There are no effective standards by ANSI, DoD, IEE, IEEE, or ISO that deal with silver bullet problems. It is unlikely that there will be such standards during the twentieth century.

17. **Professional associations**—The non-profit International Function Point Users Group (IFPUG) deals with a broad range of methods and tools. The International Society of Parametric Analysis (ISPA) has a broad membership of people interested in parametric models, some of which can be used to depict the impact of potential "silver bullets." Several local associations such as the Boston Computer Association and the Massachusetts Software Council are mildly helpful antidotes to the silver bullet syndrome. Some of the regional non-profit CASE User Groups are also helpful. Surprisingly effective are some of the on-line user groups that communicate via CompuServe, Internet, Prodigy or similar services. The regional Software Process Improvement Network (SPIN) groups are also interested in this topic.

18. **Effectiveness of known therapies**—Software measurement is a very effective therapy against silver bullet syndrome, but takes several years for the effectiveness to reach full potency. Software estimating tools such as COCOMO, SLIM, SPQR/20, CHECKPOINT®, and others in the industry are also effective when used to assess silver bullet claims. However, care must be exercised in ensuring that the estimating tool can deal with the silver bullet in question. For products and methods with user associations, contacting experienced users is a very effective preventive method against silver bullet syndrome.

   One problem should be discussed. So long as silver bullet claims are common among tool and methodology vendors, any company that does not make such claims may be at a competitive disadvantage.

19. **Costs of known therapies**—Contacting current users of tools and methods and finding out how well they work is the least expensive therapy. (Never take vendor claims at face value.) Calculating standard return on investment rates is a fairly inexpensive therapy, although collecting sufficient data can take from several days to a month. Using commercial software estimating tools such as SLIM, SPQR/20 and CHECKPOINT®, which are in the $5,000 to $20,000 range, is also a possible therapy. Establishing a full and formal software measurement program for productivity and quality is the most effective long-range therapy, but a fairly expensive one. A full measurement program for productivity normally requires about 2% of the total software staff time, and a quality measurement program also requires about 2%. However, given the fact that wastage and poor investments in silver bullets may approach 50% of all productivity tool purchases, the costs of measurement can normally be recovered in 24 to 36 months.

   Both surprisingly effective and fairly inexpensive are the on-line network services such as Internet or CompuServe. It is possible to query actual users of tools and methods to gain their experiences. The author seldom receives less than a dozen responses to queries about tools and method effectiveness. From time to time on a particularly controversial approach, the responses may push 100 and substantial technical information may be made available.

Software vendors are aware of how on-line information can be used for or against them. The more astute are supporting their own bulletin boards or assigning technical experts to respond to questions that float across the networks.

20. **Long-range prognosis**—The long-range prognosis for the silver bullet syndrome is not favorable. Throughout history and for all human endeavors, people tend to look for silver bullets. Software is no exception. Therefore the silver bullet syndrome should stay a common problem for the rest of the twentieth century, and perhaps forever.

Slow Technology Transfer

1. **Definition**—A) An unusually long time span required for training personnel in, and their adoption of, a new but proven and beneficial technology; B) Technology transfer intervals that exceed normal intervals by substantial amounts, such as more than 50%.

2. **Severity**—The severity of slow technology transfer in the U.S. should be judged against a normative baseline derived from the population size of the group to which the technology is aimed. The average severity is about a three on the following five-point scale:

Severity 1: Technology transfer exceeds normal range by more than 100%

Severity 2: Technology transfer exceeds normal range by more than 75%

Severity 3: Technology transfer exceeds normal range by more than 50%

Severity 4: Technology transfer exceeds normal range by more than 30%

Severity 5: Technology transfer exceeds normal range by more than 20%

Population	Normal Time Range
1	1– 6 months
10	6– 12 months
100	12– 24 months
1000	36– 60 months
10000	60– 96 months
100000	96–144 months

From a survey of several hundred inventions and scientific discoveries from 1800 through 1992, it appears that the average time span for a civilian invention to move from initial creation to widespread deployment is about 14 years. Military inventions take about 17 years. It is an intriguing consideration that these time spans are about the same as the protection provided by U.S. patents.

3. **Frequency**—Slow adoption of new technologies is a normal human condition, and has been observed in many human activities. Examples of slow technology transfer include adoption of new weapons (i.e. rifles versus muskets) and new scientific theories (i.e. plate tectonics). Technology transfer is slower for concepts that require paradigm shifts (i.e the Object-Oriented paradigm or the use of Function Point metrics) than for incremental improvements that do not require a paradigm shift (i.e. using C++ instead of C). The software industry seems to be no slower than any other industry or human occupation in technology transfer. The observed incidence of slow technology transfer in the U.S. indicates that about one-third of U.S. enterprises are laggards in technology transfer, about one-third are within the normal range, and about one-third are moving faster than expected.

4. **Occurrence**—There is no doubt a pattern to the occurrence of slow technology transfer, but there is insufficient data in 1993 to fully derive it. Some of the partial observations about slow technology transfer include the following: A) Technology transfer is slower among governmental and military organizations than among civilian; B) Technology transfer is slower among decentralized organizations than among centralized; C) Technology transfer is slower among software managers than among technical staffs; D) Technology transfer is slower among software groups that lack library or reference facilities than those which have such facilities; E) Technology transfer is slower among organizations that lack training facilities and training targets than among those which have both.

5. **Susceptibility and resistance**—Enterprises that are losing money and downsizing are most susceptible to this problem. Enterprises that are benign in their treatment of personnel, which have targets of at least ten days of training per year, and which encourage employees to participate in professional activities (i.e. conferences, writing books and articles) are most resistant.

6. **Root causes**—The root cause of slow technology transfer appears to be based in the normal human psychology. The human mind establishes a set of paradigms about methods, tools, and technologies. Once such a paradigm is established, all evidence to the contrary tends to be discarded. Only when the evidence becomes overwhelming is there likely to be a paradigm shift, and then it may be quite abrupt.

The normal human reaction to a new technology is interesting. Most people do not evaluate the actual merits of the technology. Instead, they ask "who is using this technology?" If indeed it is a new technology with few users, most people will initially reject the concept and refuse to try it until bolder spirits have pioneered the concept. Only the most innovative 10% or 15% of humans will try new concepts without some form of social endorsement. This phenomenon is endemic to the human condition, as the following four anecdotes might illustrate.

The British Admiralty initially rejected self-leveling naval guns for the stated reason that, "if the idea had any merit, some of the navies of the world would already have built such weapons."

The process of Xerography was rejected by investment bankers for many years on the grounds that "few companies seem to produce plain-paper copies today, so the market is not large enough justify investment."

The first spreadsheet, Visicalc, had trouble getting venture funding or financial backing for the stated reason that, "not very many business people use spread sheets today, so the market is not large enough to justify investment."

The obsolete "LOC" metric is still widely used in spite of formidable proof that the metric is ineffective and harmful. The commonest reasons cited by users of LOC when questioned as to why they use this metric is, "Well the XYZ corporation uses lines of code" or "Dr. John Doe uses lines of code in his book." Note that the metric itself is not analyzed objectively, but only the fact that other people use it. Indeed, when the company or the authority cited are queried, they also point to other users. Computer company A recently justified usage of LOC because competitor B used that metric. Company B justified usage because company A used the metric. Neither company had evaluated LOC objectively. Both assumed incorrectly that the other company had validated the metric. This kind of circular loop is very common.

In all four cases, there was essentially zero analysis of the underlying merits of the technology in question. In the first three cases, the *only* consideration given to the technology was to note that current usage did not exist or was not widespread, and that was justification enough for not using it.

In the LOC case, the same reasoning prevails, but in the opposite direction. For LOC, continued usage is justified because other people and other enterprises also use LOC. The fact that the technology itself is obsolete and even harmful to economic understanding is not evaluated.

It may easily be seen that the normal human mind is prey to a significant logical fallacy in two parts: Part 1 of the fallacy is the notion that good ideas will transfer rapidly and widely because of their intrinsic merits. Part 2 of the fallacy is the corollary notion that ideas which have not yet been transferred widely or rapidly must be bad ones. The second part of the fallacy is the true root cause for slow technology transfer.

The psychological domain of human reactions to belief systems is known by the name of *cognitive dissonance*.

7. **Associated problems**—Slow technology transfer is so widespread that it is a background contributor to many problems including *excessive time to market, canceled projects, cost overruns, long schedules, low productivity, low quality*, and *missed schedules*.

Slow technology transfer itself is often caused by *inadequate software engineering curricula,* and *inadequate staff technical training. Resistance to change* is a fundamental but subtle cause of slow technology transfer.

8. **Cost impact**—The cost impact of slow technology transfer has both direct and indirect components. The direct components can now be quantified fairly accurately by means of functional metrics. For example, suppose a technology choice

is to be made between writing a military application in the new Ada language or in the older Assembly language. The cost per Function Point for U.S. military software using Assembly language is more than $3,000. The cost per Function Point for Ada applications is only about $1,750. Even a rudimentary economic analysis can show the advantages of this technology shift.

The indirect costs of slow technology transfer are more difficult to quantify. However, an informal study carried out some years ago at the Mayo Clinic noted that software organizations which provided ten or more days of annual training to their technical staffs were significantly better in two parameters than similar organizations that provided no training at all: 1) The voluntary attrition rates were lower; 2) Annual productivity rates were higher. This study is not sufficient to make general conclusions, however.

9. **Methods of prevention**—Prevention of slow technology transfer requires substantial investment and serious commitment by senior management, and a multifaceted approach. In the early 1980's, the ITT Corporation attempted a serious push on speeding up software technology transfer among the 8,000 or so software professionals scattered throughout the world. The direct costs of the technology transfer and improvement program ran to perhaps $3 million per year, and included these components: A) ITT initiated two major software conferences per year (one in Europe and one in the U.S.) with attendance of about 400 ITT software professionals at each; B) ITT set targets of ten days of training annually for software managers and technical staff; C) ITT built a training organization and a training center in Connecticut and established several teams of traveling instructors to introduce advanced software topics at all locations; D) ITT established both a software newsletter, and created a new house magazine, *Programming;* E) ITT built an expert-system curriculum planner that could assist in long-range career training; F) ITT offered a tuition refund program for employees wishing to pursue academic education; G) ITT offered on-site television instruction in conjunction with major universities; H) ITT established an Applied Technology directorate to evaluate tools, methods, and approaches that might benefit software; I) ITT arranged preferential corporate licensing and purchasing arrangements with vendors of tools that were selected as being useful to the ITT software community; J) ITT nominated several technologies as "key" technologies (i.e. formal inspections, object-oriented languages, etc.) and offered accelerated on-site training to all ITT software laboratories; K) ITT encouraged employees to publish in professional journals and to write books by allowing them to keep any royalties that might accrue, and even provided production support for text and graphics.

10. **Methods of control**—Before slow technology transfer can be controlled, it must first be identified. A project audit or a project assessment using one of the standard assessment techniques such as those of SEI or SPR will usually identify slow technology transfer. Once identified, then some or all of the steps mentioned under "Methods of prevention" should be implemented.

An emerging way of speeding up technology transfer is to perform a formal return on investment (ROI) analysis, and then attempt to accelerate the technologies with the greatest yield. However, given the wide lack of historical measurement data, ROI analysis for software has been a troublesome topic. (Refer to the section of this book dealing with Poor Technology Investments for preliminary data.)

11. **Product support**—Products that directly alleviate slow technology transfer are increasing in number and capabililties. The early work in computer-aided instruction (CAI) is now being joined by multi-media approaches, expert systems, neural-nets, hypertext, virtual reality, optical storage, and small portable viewers. It is premature to judge their effectiveness, but conceivably the methods of technology transfer may be on the edge of profound changes. Indeed, it is now possible to carry the equivalent of a small to medium library on optical disks, and have access to the information from portable optical drives which weigh less than a pound.

    A method of surprising power in facilitating technology transfer are the networks and electronic mail connections which now link companies and researchers literally all over the world. Almost any new or emerging technology will trigger a burst of queries and responses using Internet, CompuServe, Prodigy, or the like. These networks not only facilitate queries of static resources such as journals and data bases, but also allow dynamic exchanges of information among researchers globally. As a minor example, as this book was in preparation the author was able to query researchers in more than a dozen countries via Internet and CompuServe about topics that were to be discussed. For countries where time changes make live phone or Fax exchanges inconvenient (i.e. Australia, Japan, South Korea, etc.) electronic messaging has become the most popular form of technology transfer, and one where software and computing personnel may be significantly in advance of other scientific and engineering disciplines.

12. **Consulting support**—Many consulting organizations and many individual consultants deal with the topic of slow technology transfer, but there is a sharp dichotomy in the consulting arena. Consulting groups that can identify slow technology transfer are not necessarily the same as the consulting groups that can provide courses or improvement therapies. Some can do both, of course, but many are specialized.

13. **Education support**—Academic institutions that have established direct ties to the business or industrial community are the most effective. Examples of such universities include the University of Colorado in Boulder, UCLA, Washington University in St. Louis, MIT's Sloan School, the Harvard Business School, and many others. Universities, unfortunately, tend to run from three to five years behind the state of the art. The reason is that it takes at least that long to write and publish text books and generate standard academic teaching materials.

    In-house training within the larger software producing corporations can also be effective, and is often more current than academia. Lyman Hamilton, former

Chairman of ITT, once remarked that the U.S. Fortune 500 companies had more in-house instructors than all American universities put together. Examples of companies that have effective in-house training include AT&T, EDS, IBM, ITT, Hewlett-Packard, Motorola, and many others. These companies may also offer training to their clients as well. Some even support universities by providing part-time faculty or financial grants.

The major software vendors offer many practical courses that center around the products marketed by the vendors themselves. Examples of software vendors with reasonably large curricula include Andersen, Bachman, Borland, CADRE, Computer Associates, Lotus, and Microsoft.

For software, both non-profit and profit-making educational companies offer many state-of-the-art courses. Indeed, for brand new technologies that are only just coming into prominence, the commercial educational services are often far superior to academia. Examples of non-profit education are those offered by the American Management Association, the IEEE, and IFPUG. Examples of profit-making education are those offered by Computer Power, Inc.; Digital Consulting , Inc.; Extended Intelligence, Inc.; the Quality Assurance Institute, Inc.; QSM, Inc.; SPR, Inc.; James Martin Associates; and Yourdon, Inc.

14. **Publication support**—There are thousands of books on specific technologies, but books dealing with the process of technology transfer are smaller in number. A selection of titles where technology transfer is the main theme would include Humphrey's *Managing the Software Process* (Addison Wesley, 1987); Yourdon's *Decline and Fall of the American Programmer* (Prentice Hall, 1992); Pressman's *Making Software Engineering Happen* (Prentice Hall, 1990); DeMarco's *Peopleware* (Dorset House, 1987); Barbara Bouldin's *Agents of Change* (Yourdon Press, 1989); and Dr. Gerald Weinberg's *Quality Software Management* (Dorset House, 1991). Dr. Weinberg has been a student of technology transfer for many years, and has written almost an entire library of excellent software volumes. Other books by Dr. Weinberg include *The Psychology of Computer Programming* (Van Nostrand); *An Introduction to General Systems Thinking* (John Wiley & Sons); and *Becoming a Technical Leader* (Dorset House).

Peter DeGrace and Leslie Stahl's *The Olduvai Imperative: CASE and the State of Software Engineering Practice* (Yourdon Press, 1993) discusses the differences between the reality and the claims of various approaches. Robert Block's *The Politics of Projects* (Yourdon Press, 1983) takes an interesing look at some of the political barriers to software progress.

Several classic books on technology transfer have nothing to do with software, but are fascinating reading. Kuhn's widely-cited *The Structure of Scientific Revolutions* (The University of Chicago Press, 1962) has been among the most widely cited. Cohen's *Revolution in Science* (Harvard University Press, 1985) is also widely quoted. Perhaps the most intriguing and also somber is the late Isaac Asimov's *Biographical Encyclopedia of Science and Technology* (Avon Books, 1964). Asimov's book is somber because of the distressingly high percentage of scientific innovators who were imprisoned, executed, or otherwise mistreated for seeking to advance human knowledge in the face of social and cultural resistance.

The domain of psychology known as *cognitive dissonance* deals with conflicts between belief systems, and the barriers to changing opinions. There is a huge literature on this topic, which was made popular in the 1960's by the psychologist Leon Festinger.

15. **Periodical support**—Periodicals that discuss technology transfer directly are mostly specialized educational journals that don't get much circulation among the ordinary software engineering community. Of course, *all* journals are themselves vehicles for technology transfer, and one of the most successful methods for conveying ideas from person to person in all human history. A visit to a good-sized book store with a magazine section can reveal more than 200 periodicals on every conceivable topic of human experience. For software technology transfer, the various professional journals such as those by the ACM, IEEE, Yourdon's *American Programmer*, or the CASE journals comes about as close as any to the core issues dealing with technology transfer in their respective topics.

16. **Standards support**—Several standards organizations including the IEEE, ISO, and SEI have worked on draft or actual software engineering curricula. SPR has prepared a draft curricula for software managers. None of the standards organizations can react quickly enough to stay current: the "average" lag for a standard is more than three years. Nonetheless, the standards are a good starting place.

17. **Professional associations**—The Association of Computer Training and Support (ACTS) is a non-profit organization that deals with technology transfer (although not necessarily with the rate of change.) The IEEE, ADAPSO (now ITAA), ACM, and ASM non-profit associations are also concerned with professional training. The Software Engineering Institute (SEI) has also done work on technology transfer.

Several specific technologies have non-profit groups centering around them, which are often involved with technology transfer. The International Function Point Users Group (IFPUG) offers courses and facilitates technology transfer of functional metric approaches. Several regional CASE user groups also exist. In some industries, non-profit industry associations facilitate technology transfer. For example LOMA assists in technology transfer among software executives within the insurance industry.

18. **Effectiveness of known therapies**—Slow technology transfer is perhaps endemic to the human condition. It is not clear if any of the available therapies are consistently effective, given normal human reactions to new facts and concepts. However, companies that encourage innovation are often rewarded for such encouragement by successful projects and higher morale. Companies that discourage innovation tend to have a disproportionate number of canceled or disastrous projects, lower morale, and higher voluntary attrition rates among top performers. But such observations and information are only anecdotal and not verified by controlled study.

19. **Costs of known therapies**—A leading company with a ten-day target for annual professional education will probably pay around $5,000 per year in basic fees for training, and another $3,000 per year for the time required for each student while they are away from their normal jobs. In round numbers, companies can anticipate expenses of about $10,000 per year per software professional

Note that annual refresher training is the normal practice for physicians and attorneys. It would be desirable to institute the same concept for software professionals. Indeed, unless an occupation has continuous access to new findings, it is arguable that the word "profession" is inappropriate. Without access to a continuous stream of new information, software "craft" would be closer to the truth than software "profession."

On-line information services are already a growing business. Multi-media education is about to become a major sub-industry, and these technologies are hypothesized to reduce training costs and elevate effectiveness simultaneously. However, it will be four or five more years before the economic situation can be worked out in detail.

20. **Long-range prognosis**—Slow technology transfer has been part of the human condition for thousands of years, but there is now some reason to assume that the future will be perhaps better than the past. As a class, software professionals appear marginally more ready to accept new technologies than several other professions. However, this might just be due to bias in the samples or due to extrinsic factors.

The advent of networks, on-line information services, and multi-media computing with optical storage may change the equation on technology transfer. It can categorically be asserted that the basic tools for facilitating technology transfer are about to reach unprecedented levels of effectiveness. Whether humans will make optimum usage of these new capabilities is an unanswered question. However, the technical capability for reducing technology transfer time should improve by an order of magnitude before the year 2000 AD. There is no guarantee that average human beings will take advantage of these new technologies, however.

Software Assessment and Management Terms

INTRODUCTION

One of the most common problems encountered when performing both SPR and SEI assessments is inconsistent usage of terminology. Even fairly widely used terms such as "productivity," "quality," "inspection," and "unit test" vary widely from company to company, and even department to department within a company.

When SPR consultants and assessors are collecting information by interviewing project teams, more time is spent on explaining terms and dealing with terminology issues than on any other aspect of the assessment. In a typical three-hour assessment session, from 30 to 60 minutes will usually be devoted to terminology issues.

Most sciences and engineering disciplines that are growing rapidly go through periods of rapidly expanding terminology. Software engineering is no exception. What follows from this expansion of the basic vocabulary of a discipline is a period of confusion and ambiguity that can last from ten to more than 50 years! Eventually, the inconsistencies will be resolved and standard dictionaries of terms will become widely utilized. Unfortunately, that time is still in the future for software.

There is no shortage of software engineering dictionaries or glossaries in 1993, but they are often inconsistent among themselves and sometimes woefully inadequate. For example, the IEEE standard glossary of software engineering (Std 610.12.–1990) lacks all references to functional metrics, in spite of the fact that IFPUG is the largest measurement association in the United States. The IEEE glossary also has very few management terms, or those connected with assessments and risk management.

In software as in other disciplines, advances in fundamental technologies bring expansion in the vocabulary associated with the discipline. New concepts and terms go hand in hand. Indeed, the rate of growth of this glossary has been

542

surprising. When SPR began performing its assessments in 1985, it soon became obvious that many terms were being questioned and discussed in every session. The first glossary produced in support of SPR assessments was only about 20 pages, and defined only about 100 terms. If the software industry continues to generate new terms and concepts at the current rate of terminology, then by the end of the century, a software engineering and management dictionary will approach the size of *Dorlands' Medical Dictionary,* which is to say almost 2000 pages. This will probably be necessary, since software is rapidly developing its own argot of special terms, or standard words used in special ways.

When assessments take place, or even when productivity and measurement consultants meet with clients to discuss their studies, it can be noted that they spend quite a bit of the conversation ensuring that the terms and measurements under discussion mean the same thing to all parties.

This glossary is not a complete compendium of all software engineering terms, but rather deals with the terminology issues most often encountered in performing software process assessments using the SPR methodology. It is intended as a practical source of terminology information when dealing with the topics that are discussed in the general domains of productivity, quality, assessment, and other managerial topics.

Software assessors and measurement specialists quickly learn some of the hazards that can result from inconsistent terminology. For example software productivity has been measured with source code metrics for almost 50 years. Yet this basic term can mean either physical source code lines or delimited source code statements. The apparent difference in the size of program can vary by 500% depending upon which choice is made. Much of the literature that uses source code metrics does not even state which choice the author made. Plainly, to become a true engineering discipline, software engineering needs to adopt standard definitions for its basic terminology.

Like any advancing science, the vocabulary of software engineering is rapidly expanding. Glossaries must be updated at least annually to stay current. Considering how recently measurement of software has been a technology, the progress is in terminology is impressive.

Abeyant defect—A user or field-reported defect which cannot be replicated at the system maintenance center, and so defect repairs cannot begin until additional information is received from the user site. Defects temporarily in suspense pending new information are termed "abeyant" by IBM. This is an example of a term which varies locally from company to company.

Acceptance criteria—The list of requirements which a program or system must accomplish before customers take delivery. Late changes in acceptance criteria, or hidden criteria derived from explicit criteria have been chronic problems for software projects.

Acceptance test—This is a form of testing in which users exercise software prior to formally adopting it for production runs. This form of testing occurs often with MIS projects. It is one of the more elusive activities for both measurement and estimation due to the fact that users seldom charge their time or record the effort involved. See also "Field test." The IEEE definition assumes that acceptance testing will be formal, but many such tests are quite casual.

Account—This denotes a discrete and unique data collection point for financial or measurement data. Accounts are normally identified by unique numbers. For example, the IBM software accounting structure consisted of a five-digit major account number (i.e. identifying a specific system such as the MVS operating system), a four-digit project number (i.e. identifying a specific project, such as modifying an access method), a two-digit lab identifier (i.e. a location such as San Jose or Poughkeepsie), and a three-digit minor account number for specific tasks (i.e. activities such as design, coding testing, etc.).

Accounting Rate of Return—This is one of the several figures of merit used to determine whether an investment is potentially good or bad. There are a number of ways of calculating the accounting rate of return, and they tend to yield widely varied results. The Internal Rate of Return gives a more standardized figure of merit.

ACM—This is the acronym for the Association of Computing Machinery, one of the earliest and largest professional organizations of the computing industry, and one which sponsors a number of major software engineering conferences, and also publishes a well-known journal, Communications of the ACM.

Acquisition—This term is becoming a generic for software that is acquired from an outside vendor or contractor. The term is also breeding supplemental terms such as Acquisition Quality or Acquisition Metrics.

ACR—"Applied Computer Research," which is a private family-owned seminar and consulting business headed by Phil Howard. ACR publishes a number of guides to productivity tools, software executives, and the like.

Active Quality Assurance—This term denotes a Quality Assurance group that is an active participant in reviews and testing. The opposite definition is "Passive Quality Assurance" which implies a QA group whose job is merely to monitor the performance of reviews and tests.

Actuals—This term denotes the accumulated expenses or effort that have really occurred as a software project is developed. Unfortunately, the term "actuals" implies much greater precision than usually exists. The error rate observed in what most companies think of as their actual costs for software have often been from 30% to 50%, with most of the errors being omissions of activities such as user documents, management, and overhead functions.

Accuracy—A vaguely defined term dealing with the required precision for calculations and outputs. Also used in conjunction with estimating and measurement tools, with no standard meaning or numerical precision. It is often asserted that a good estimating tool is "accurate to within 5%" but exactly what that might mean is ambiguous. The IEEE definition is more restrictive, and deals with magnitudes of errors or freedom from error.

Activity—This term is the third level in the normal five-level sequence of cost collection points: i.e. 1) project; 2) phase; 3) activity; 4) task; 5) subtask. An "activity" is a bounded collection of tasks and subtasks aimed at accomplishing a discrete function or producing a discrete deliverable. For example, during the testing phase, the performance of unit test would be classed as an "activity." The tasks of unit testing would include test case preparation, text case execution, and defect repairs. A subtask of test case execution would be to record any bugs that were found. See also "account" and "work breakdown structure."

ADAPSO—The acronym for the "Association of Data Processing Service Organizations" which is one of the larger professional associations dealing with software. However, the organization recently changed its name to "Information Technology Association of America" or ITAA for short.

Adaptive maintenance—Modifications performed in order to migrate an application to another platform or allow it to work with another operating system. See also "Corrective maintenance," "Mandatory maintenance," and "Perfective maintenance."

AEA—The acronym for the "American Electronics Association," which is one of the larger professional associations dealing with computers, peripherals, and software. The AEA publishes information on executive and technical compensation, and so their data is often used for comparative purposes. The AEA is also active in the venture capital community, and the AEA conferences are a frequent contact point between software entrepreneurs and the financial world.

Algorithm—The sequence of instructions that must be encoded to in order for a computer to solve a particular problem. Algorithms have definite starting and stopping places. The term algorithm can apply to both finite, bounded problems such as square root extraction routines and calendar management routines and it can apply to major problems such as defect prediction. The inclusion of the "algorithm" parameter is one of the attributes which separates Feature Points from Function Points.

Alpha Test—This somewhat dated term derives from engineering, and means the first test of a product when it is still in a very unfinished condition. Alpha testing is normally internal to an organization. Alpha Tests are normally followed by Beta Tests when products are actually ready for customer usage.

American Productivity Institute—This is the name of a U.S. based association that explores aspects of productivity. Software has not been a particular strength of the association, but doubtless that will change in the future.

American Programmer—This is the name of a software engineering and management journal owned by Cutter Publishing, and edited by Ed Yourdon and Toni Nash. This journal has become a well-regarded source of current information on measurement, estimation, CASE, risk assessment, and many other software topics.

ANOVA—The acronym for "Analysis of Variance" which is a statistical method for ascertaining ranges of parameters.

Annual Productivity Report—The natural reporting frequency for productivity in large enterprises is annually, which is also the natural reporting frequency for profit and loss. Several major software producers have adopted the policy of creating a productivity report in the first quarter of each year which includes all projects that were finished and went into production during the previous year.

Application—This is the generic term for a program or system that handles a specific business area. Examples include accounting applications, manufacturing applications, and insurance applications. The term is used most often for information systems, but is a generic term that can be applied to systems and real-time software also.

Application Generator—This term denotes a tool that will nominally create a full software application with little or no programming. Such generators appear to be reasonably effective in specific niches such as banking and accounting. An application generator differs from a program generator in that some of the run-time services are provided by the generator itself, which must be present when the application runs.

Applications Software—Software developed primarily for a business or managerial purpose. The term overlaps MIS and information systems, and is often used in contrast to systems software or software necessary to operate a computer.

Applied Software Measurement (ASM)—The practical set of "soft" factors, "hard" productivity and quality data, and supporting project size, value, and risk information needed to manage software projects, and software businesses, with accuracy and success. ASM is a new term, and a major advance over the irrational and incomplete measures and metrics that characterized the first 45 years of the software business. The term "applied" denotes realism, high accuracy, and practical business value.

Appraisal—This term denotes a periodic review of an employee's job performance by management. Annual appraisals are the norm in the U.S. The relationship between appraisal scores and productivity and quality is important, but seldom discussed in the literature due to the confidential nature of the appraisal data. See also "Reverse Appraisal".

Approval Cycle—This important term refers to the process of gaining funding or management approval to introduce a new tool or method into an organization. The approval cycle can sometimes slow progress if it is allowed to grow into bureaucratic excess. Normally the approval cycle is based on the magnitude of expense. For example first line managers may have spending approval for up to $1000; second line managers may spend up to $5000; and so on. The approval cycle concept is intrusive when the cost of approval is greater than the cost of the acquisition, such as eight signatures being required to purchase a $50 book for a library.

Architecture—This is one of the more troublesome concepts for both measurement and estimation, due to the ambiguity and vague definitions for the term. It is generally defined as some intermediate stage between the initial requirements and the specifications during which the entire complex of hardware, software, and design considerations will be viewed as a whole. Sometimes but not always a deliverable termed an Architecture Specification is an output. There is a second and more specific definition, which refers to the starting point for designing and specifying software. The two major architectural methods are "function analytic" and "data analytic" architectures.

ASM (concept)—This is the abbreviation for "Applied Software Measurement" which is the new and emerging set of practical quality and productivity data, and supporting factors needed to manage software projects and software enterprises with high accuracy and success.

This is a new term for an emerging and important new concept.

ASM (organization)—This acronym stands for the "Associations of Systems Management," which is one of several professional organizations open to qualified managers of systems and software.

Assessment—A general term for a review of the processes used in developing and maintaining software. Sometimes used more narrowly to mean the status of a project in the context of how closely it comes to its planned rate of progress. Also used more restrictively in context with other terms, such as "stage assessment" or "quality assessment." The term is also used in a special or restricted sense by the consulting groups that carry out assessments, such as DMR, Hewlett-Packard, Nolan & Norton, Roger Pressman Associates, SEI, and SPR.

Asset—For software, this term is used to mean a particular tool or set of functional capabilities which an organization owns or needs, such as a project planning tool. The term is also used to define a specific feature of a CASE tool.

Asset Inventory—A study of the full set of the software tools and capabilities owned by an organization.

Assignment scope—The amount of work for which one person will normally be responsible. This useful concept can be evaluated for any reasonable unit of work, including source code, KLOC, Function Points, Feature Points, pages, and many others. Assignment scopes can be calculated directly by dividing the quantity of any deliverable by the staff that produced the deliverable. When used in conjunction with Production Rates, the Assignment scope concept is a key part of estimating.

Attrition—The departure of staff members. There are two primary forms of attrition: voluntary, where the departure is initiated by the employee; and invol-untary where the departure is initiated by the enterprise. For many years the software industry was troubled by abnormal attrition rates that sometimes exceeded 30% a year, and in extreme cases exceeded 60% a year. With this much flux, it was very difficult to achieve any kind of stable project organization or make long-range productivity improvements. In the 1980's, software attrition has been lower, but it still remains a problem. Leading edge enterprises such as AT&T may achieve less than a 3% annual voluntary attrition rate. There is generally an inverse relationship between attrition rates and enterprise productivity.

Audit—The fundamental definition of this term is from cost accounting and denotes an impartial review of a set of financial records by an independent accountant or team of accountants. For software however a second and less rigorous definition occurs in which the term means a more or less critical review of a project to determine whether it should be continued or canceled. In some corporations, software audits are common events.

Auerbach Publishers—This publishing company specializes in computing and software management books, magazines, articles, reviews, and monographs.

Availability—The time when a consultant or worker is not actually on a job, and hence can be assigned. This term also is applied to computers, where it refers to the amount of time that the computer is up, running, and capable of being used. Computer availability is normally expressed as a percentage.

Average—This term can of course define either the arithmetic, geometric harmonic, or weighted mean, the mode, or the median values of a range of data points. For software, it is often restricted to the arithmetic mean and used quite naively and inappropriately. The basic problem is the mistaken assumption that once an average value has been determined, it can be used for predictive purposes. Unfortunately the standard deviation for many software tasks is so broad that the average is almost useless.

Average productivity—This is a semi-mythical concept since the United States does not have either a national data base for productivity nor a standard metric for productivity measurement. The Rome Air Development Center (RADC) data base maintained by the U.S. Air Force is often used as a surrogate, and a ten-year history of productivity from this data base yields rates of about 3100 source statements per staff year, which would be roughly equivalent to 25 Function Points per staff year. The Software Productivity Research (SPR) data indicated a 1990 average of about 5 Function Points per staff month, overall. However, a true national average for a country the size of the U.S. would need data from some 75,000 projects and more than 5000 enterprises. This is more than twice as large as the sum of all known productivity data bases added together.

Average Work Day, Week, Year—This is an important concept for productivity purposes, and one which must be considered for international studies. In the U.S., the normal work week for accounting purposes is five 8-hour days, or 40 hours in all. In the course of an average year, there will be about 220 working days. In Canada, however, the normal work day is 7.5 hours and the normal work week is 35 hours. In Japan the normal work day is 8 hours but there are 5.5 working days, or 44 hours. Over and above these accounting norms, the actual effective amount of time when people really work must be considered. In the U.S. the effective work day is between 5 and 6 hours, with between 2 and 3 hours devoted to slack time, coffee, and other non-productive pursuits.

Backfire Function Point Calculations—A method developed by Software Productivity Research, Inc. for generating Function Point totals directly from counts of source code statements. The backfire method is based on the observed correlations between Function Points and source code size (procedural and data definition statements, without comments or blank lines) for many languages. COBOL, for example, has been found to average 105 source code statements per Function Point. Ada 83 averages about 71 statements per Function Point. The C language averages about 128 statements per Function Point. Therefore it is straightforward to retrofit Function Points to aging software if the language(s) and source code counts are known. The primary use of the backfire method is to fit Function Points to aging software for historical productivity studies. About 355 languages and dialects can now be sized using the backfire method.

Backwards Loading—This term means setting the delivery date for a software project and then trying to force the development schedule to meet the predetermined end point. This is a common but not satisfactory way of scheduling many software projects. It is the source of many assertions that "software is always late." The complete phrase for this term is "backwards loading to infinite capacity."

Bad Fix—When fixing bugs or making updates to existing software, it is very common to accidentally inject a fresh bug at the same time that the previous bug was repaired. The observed volume of bad fixes range up to 20% for large unstructured software programs and systems. As systems age, the bad fix rate tends to go up over time due to increasing entropy and elevated levels of complexity. Bad fixes are one of the five standard defect categories on which statistics should be kept (requirements, design, code, documents, and bad fixes).

Baldrige Award—This is an award for achieving high levels of quality that is named in honor of the economist Malcolm Baldrige, and sponsored by the U.S. Department of Commerce. In general, the Baldrige (as it is known) tends to focus executive, staff, and enterprise attention on quality. Those enterprises who have achieved this award (AT&T, Motorola, etc.) report that their efforts toward the Baldrige have indeed focused all levels on quality improvement. In general, the Baldrige has served as a national focal point on quality improvement. See also ISO 9000.

Bang Metric—This is multi-valued software productivity metric developed by Tom DeMarco. The Bang Metric overlaps certain aspects of the IBM Function Point technique, but includes many more parameters. Like Function Points, the Bang Metric is intended to be applied early in the life cycle and to give productivity results free from the error and ambiguity of source code metrics. The Bang Metric and Function Points were both developed during the mid to late 1970's, and appear to be independent inventions.

Batch—This term, one of the older terms of software, means a form of processing where all transactions are accumulated for various periods and then processed at once. For example, accumulating pay data for a month and then producing all pay checks at the same time. The opposite term to Batch is "On-Line."

Base Code—This term originated within IBM, and originally was derived from the mathematical concepts of Base and Delta functions. It has now taken a software meaning as the quantity of source code in an existing program or system. This term is usually used in reference to updating or enhancing the original version of the software. (See also "New Code," "Changed Code," "Delta Code," "Reused code", and "Deleted Code.")

Baseline—For software, this term denotes the starting point against which progress will be judged. When enterprises first begin to measure software productivity and quality, their first complete report is considered to be the baseline and serves as the origin point for improvement.

Before You Leap (BYL)—This is one of several entry-level cost estimating tools that originated as COCOMO clones. Many of the functions of this model appear to be derivative from either COCOMO, or other models.

Bench Mark—This term, originally from carpentry, has come to mean a standard figure of merit against which projects or enterprises may be judged. The term is semi-mythical for software, due to the lack of either a national data base or standard measurements.

Best and Final Offer—This term is used primarily for military and defense software, and refers to the final cost estimate and the final business arrangements offered by a vendor to the contracting agency.

Best in class—This is an ambiguous term, whose meaning is essentially that of seeking out the better or best enterprises within a set of competitors, so that they can be used as models. Normally the phrase implies the leading enterprises within an industry, such as the telecommunications or computer industry. Another way of approaching this topic would be to consider enterprises in the top 10% in terms of quality, productivity, or other tangible dimensions. This approach would lead to any enterprises, for example, with average productivity rates in excess of 25 Function Points per month or average defect removal efficiencies in excess of 95%. See also "world class."

Beta Test—This term normally refers to the first test of a product by its actual customers. However, this is a highly ambiguous term. Sometimes Beta Test is used merely to denote the second test in a series, which may be an internal test. Beta Test normally follows Alpha Test by a considerable time period. The Alpha/Beta terms have been replaced to some degree by more descriptive terms such as Unit Test, Function Test, Stress Test, Acceptance Test, and the like.

Billable Hours—Normally defined as the work effort for a consultant will bill a client. Surprising variations occur. For commercial and management consultants, the billable time normally includes work at the client site and consultant's own office, but not travel time. For DoD and military consultants, travel time is sometimes included. In any case, many consultants work a great many more hours than are actually billed.

Black Box Testing—A form of testing that validates the external features of a design and ignores the internal structure of the program or system. See also "White Box Testing."

Blueprint—A reusable design. The term is exactly analogous to a blueprint for a house or physical structure. After almost 50 years of software development, it is gradually becoming possible to extract the salient features from frequently developed applications and encapsulate them in standard design sets, starting to be called blueprints. Unfortunately, Texas Instruments uses the word "template" for exactly the same concept as used here for "blueprint." SPR uses the word "template" for

a standard, reusable software plan and estimate.

Borrowed code—Code that is taken, more or less intact, from some other application or from some other component of the current application. Borrowed code is not the same as reused code, and the two terms should be kept separate. Borrowed code may require substantial modification, whereas reused code can be utilized with close to zero change. Borrowed code may or may not have bugs in it, and if bugs should occur in the original version, the users of the borrowed code may not even be informed. See also "reused code." and "partially reusable code."

Boston Computer Society—This is one of the larger regional non-profit organizations which deal with computing, hacking, software development, and other topics of interest to the high-technology computer. The Boston Computer Society also sponsors an on-line bulletin board, and hosts many special-interest meetings.

Bottom Up Estimate—Synonymous with micro estimate, and refers to the method of producing a software estimate by dealing with each activity separately and then summing the results. It is the opposite concept from top down estimating or macro estimating which generates an entire estimate from a single equation and then divides the estimate into small components via ratios or percentages.

Bridge—This is an awkwardly named cost estimating model acquired by ABT corporation, which "bridges" a gap in their well-known Project Managers Workbench (PMW) planning tool. Close coupling of planning and estimating, plus support for Function Points, are features of this combination.

Budget—A planned sequence of expenditures over time with costs assigned to specific tasks or jobs. (See "Variance Report.") Budgets are normally departmental functions, rather than project functions. If a budget is set for a department, it may include planned expenditures for multiple projects. One of the classic difficulties of historical cost data analysis for software is in trying to separate out project expenses from departmental expenses.

Bugs—This term is one of the oldest in the software profession. It originated in the 1950's when the late Admiral Grace Hopper found an actual insect jamming the contacts of an electromechanical switch. The term now refers to errors or defects that find their way into programs and systems. Some software quality researchers find it desirable to replace the pejorative term "bugs" with other terms such as errors, defects, faults, and failures. The most rigorous go so far as to assert that a "failure" is the visible manifestation of an "error" and that errors in turn can be subdivided into errors of omission and errors of commission. Such nuances would seem to be hair splitting.

Build—A functionally independent piece of software that supports a well-defined subset of a system. Large projects are often constructed as a series of builds, each of which can be tested and used independently.

Build Plan—The specific tasks and the sequence or concurrency with which those tasks will be performed, together with the anticipated start and stop dates. A build plan is a normal deliverable for large systems.

Bundled—A form of product pricing for hybrid products that have both hardware and software components in which the price is set for the hardware only, and the software is essentially given away with the product. See also "unbundled." Bundling is starting to fall into some disfavor for mainframe systems, but is still quite common for mini computers and micro computers.

Business Process Reengineering—A concept, originating circa 1991, which puts forth the reasonable concept that software should closely support business functions, and that in addition, business functions themselves need to be reevaluated and modified as external conditions change. This topic is becoming a new subdiscipline of management consulting.

Business Systems Planning (BSP)—This term denotes a major form of strategic study that was developed by IBM in the 1970's. The purpose of the study is to match overall business goals and strategies with the probable kinds of information systems necessary to support them. The costs of BSP and similar strategic studies are fairly high, although the value is high too. The costs of such studies is one of the reasons why enterprise level productivity is much lower than project level productivity.

Burden rate—This is defined as the amount of money which must be added to the monthly salary of employees to include rent, utility bills, interest, and certain other cost elements. If the average salary for employees is $4000 a month, then a typical burden rate might be $1000 a month, leading to a fully burdened salary rate of $5000 a month. The fully burdened rate would normally be used for cost estimating.

Calibration—A technical term that means tuning a software estimating model so that it matches either actual historical data or a user's subjective view of what projects should cost. Due to the low accuracy and high error rate of historical data, calibration is not an exact science. In studies of estimating models versus historical data, the natural tendency is to explain wide variations as being due to errors on the part of the estimating models. In fact, it often happens that the estimating models are cor-

551

rect, and the error lies in the historical data itself, which may omit from 30% to 50% of the real costs of software.

Canceled projects—Software projects that are canceled and never completed are one of the major unexplored domains of software productivity. Major corporations such as IBM may cancel up to 25% of their large software projects. The costs of these projects are one of the key reasons why enterprise productivity rates are so much lower than project productivity rates. Canceled projects also explain why companies with large R&D efforts may have lower productivity than those which lack such exploratory work.

Capital expenditure—A form of spending in which an enterprise trades money (capital) for acquisition of tangible objects such as furniture, computers, and the like. Capital expenditures and expenses are significant for accounting and taxation purposes.

CASE (Computer Aided Software Engineering)—This comparatively new term defines systems that attempt to automate some or all of the tasks of managing, designing, developing, and maintaining software. Although the CASE vendors make assertions of "10 to 1" or even "20 to 1" improvements in productivity, these assertions are not yet supported by empirical data. A full CASE environment that supports management, development, enhancement, maintenance, package acquisition, defect removal, and documentation would have about 110 separate tools. Most CASE products today include from six to about 25 tools, and appear to omit many important features. Few or none give adequate support to management, defect removal, user documentation and other major cost drivers outside the mainline design/coding set. See also "I-CASE."

CASE Outlook—This is one of several journals dealing with computer aided software engineering. See also CASE Trends and CASE Strategies. This journal is published in Lake Osewgo, Oregon and edited by Gene Forte. This journal also publishes a companion catalog of CASE tools, and performs surveys related to CASE usage.

CASE Strategies—This is one of several journals dealing with computer aided software engineering. This journal is published in Arlington, MA and edited by Mickey Williamson. This journal has both news topics, and in-depth technical topics.

Case study—A more or less complete description of what transpired in a particular business or technical situation. The term is often used by business schools to focus attention on the relevant factors associated with marketing decisions, strategic decisions, and so forth.

CASE Trends—This is a journal published in Shrewsbury, MA and edited by Eliot Weinman and Daniel Kara. This journal is one of several which deal with Computer Aided Software Engineering. This journal also has a companion catalog of CASE tools and services. The publishers also sponsors various conferences and seminars, such as the Re-engineering Conference via DCI.

CASE user groups—There are many regional non-profit groups which meet and discuss topics of common interest. The CASE domain has been rather fruitful in this regard, and there are regional CASE groups in New England, New York, the Bay Area (around San Francisco), Atlanta, Kansas City, Raleigh-Durham, and many other locales.

Cash-flow problems—One of the commonest problems for small businesses is that they tend to spend more than they earn, from time to time, which means that their reserves of cash for payrolls and mandatory expenses may turn negative. Lines of credit or borrowing can help, but this problem is endemic among small software and consulting organizations. Cash flow problems explain, among other things, why small companies have trouble ascending the SEI maturity ladder above Level 2: they can't afford the infrastructure. From assessments of small companies, many times their productivity is higher than larger companies at SEI level 3 or higher; and occasionally their quality will be better also.

Catastrophe Theory—This is a new area of research only just starting to be applied to software projects. It deals with events that trigger abrupt departures from previous trend lines, such as for example earthquakes and major volcanic eruptions. When applied to software, catastrophe theory attempts to come to grips with events, such as canceled projects, that cause trend lines like Rayleigh Curves to be inaccurate indicators.

Chaos—An emerging area of scientific research that is just starting to be applied to software projects. Chaos is the term applied to the non-linear mathematics that must be used to define irregular phenomena such as the flow of turbulent fluids. Fractal geometry is a sub-discipline of the new science of chaos. Given the irregular nature of large software projects, it is quite possible that the new mathematical techniques being developed will be suitable for software estimating and measurement.

Changed code—Modifications to portions of the source code in an existing program or system. Changed code usually occurs when an existing application is being enhanced or modified. Changed code differs slightly from "Delta Code" which is the sum of both new plus changed code. However, Changed Code and "Modified Code" are synonymous.

Charge back—A billing structure under which users of a service must pay for its use. This term is also fraught with troublesome overtones. Most enterprises began the computer era with software development and the usage of computers provided as a service to users and clients. At some point, most enterprises decide the time has come to begin charging for these services, and so introduce some form of charge back systems. User dissatisfaction and considerable heat is the normal reaction when charge back systems are first started.

Chart of accounts—A standard list of activities or tasks to be used for cost estimating, tracking, and measurement purposes. No U.S. or world standards exist for software charts of accounts. The smallest development chart of accounts that can be used for systems software, information systems, and military projects includes about 25 activities: 1) Requirements; 2) Prototyping; 3) Architecture; 4) Formal project planning; 5) Initial analysis and design; 6) Detail design; 7) Formal design reviews; 8) Coding; 9) Reusable code acquisition; 10) Purchased code acquisition; 11) Formal code inspections; 12) Independent verification and validation; 13) Formal configuration management; 14) Formal integration; 15) User documentation; 16) Unit testing; 17) Function testing; 18) Integration testing; 19) System testing; 20) Field testing; 21) Acceptance testing; 22) Independent testing; 23) Formal quality assurance; 24) Installation and training; 25) Project management. Supplemental charts of accounts for user costs, maintenance, and package acquisition also occur. Also, any given chart of accounts can be exploded into the tasks and subtasks which constitute a full work breakown structure. A coarse chart of accounts, dealing only with phases, such as requirements, design, coding, and testing, is not sufficient for serious productivity and economic research.

CHECKPOINT® AND CHECKMARK®— These are the U.S. and British trade names for a full life-cycle integrated measurement and estimation tool developed by SPR, Inc. All development and up to 20 years of maintenance, plus quality, are included in the estimates.

Chief programming team—A form of project organization in which a lead technical person, the chief programmer, has some supervisory and technical responsibilities over other programmers and over the direction of a project. This method was popular in the 1970's and is still used intermittently.

CEO—This term is the shorthand way of stating "Chief Executive Officer." Normally the CEO is either the chairman or the president of a corporation. The CEO usually reports directly to the board of directors, and has various important fiduciary responsibilities. The CEO is normally charged with the long-range strategy of the corporation. Often in large companies, the CEO will be assisted by a "Chief Operating Officer" or COO who is responsible for day to day running of the enterprise. See also CIO, CFO, and COO.

CFO—This term stands for "Chief Financial Officer." The CFO is normally an executive vice president (or the equivalent) responsible for the accounting and finance functions. The CFO may also be the treasurer of a corporation, but not always. See also CEO, CIO, and COO.

CIO—This comparatively new term stands for "Chief Information Officer" which is a new title associated with an executive responsible for all corporate information and the people who control both its storage and the development of systems to utilize it.

CIO (magazine)—This is a magazine aimed primarily at senior software managers and chief information officers. It is one of a suite of magazines published in Framingham, MA and edited by Bill McBride.

Class library—This is one of the terms associated with the object-oriented paradigm. It refers to collections of defined classes, which can be browsed, examined and have their salient features passed on via inheritance, so that derivative classes can be easily created. See also "Inheritance."

Clean room development—This is a new term that is derived from the manufacture of microelectronic components that would be contaminated by dust and hence require special sealed locations with filtered air. For software the term means developing a program or system in such a way that defect prevention and removal steps occur for each deliverable as is created, before it is passed down the line for the next step in the overall software process.

Client/server applications—A hybrid application involving two separate components, and often two processors as well. The "client" portion of the application handles the user interface and basic processing functions. The client portions are usually developed for personal computers, work-stations, or end-user devices. The "server" portion of the application handles data base management functions. The server portions are usually developed on mini-computers, mainframes, or other fairly robust and powerful personal computers. Client/server applications offer an alternative to traditional mainframe software, and are also an alternative to pure personal computer applications. Client/server is a fairly new technology as of 1993, with some hazy concepts, incomplete tool suites, and rather uncertain quantification in terms of quality and productivity. The overall concept is architecturally interesting.

COCOMO (COnstructive COst MOdel)— A closely related family of software cost estimating models developed by Dr. Barry Boehm of TRW. The COCOMO equations originally applied primarily to avionics projects, and covered only the kernel activities of design and coding. Upstream activities such as requirements and peripheral activities such as user documentation were not included. As the COCOMO models evolve, they are starting to cover more tasks. The COCOMO algorithms are in the public domain, and hence have contributed to a number of software estimating models such as BYL, GECOMO, and WICOMO, or the Wang Institute Cost Model.

Code complexity—This term denotes one of several different kinds of complexity that can be associated with software projects. The other kinds of complexity are logic or problem complexity and data complexity. Only code complexity can actually be measured objectively, but the McCabe essential and cyclomatic metrics and the NPATH complexity metric do an adequate job. Problem or logical complexity is the most abstruse, since even psychologists have no precise metric for that topic.

Code of ethics standard—A standard that describes an acceptable pattern of behavior in terms of honesty, diligence, etc. for software personnel. Refer to IEEE standards 1002–1987.

Coding—This basic term is highly ambiguous, and has been defined at various levels of granularity. At the most granular, coding is defined as only the physical task of writing source code statements. A more common definition however includes the tasks performed by individual programmers; i.e. low-level design, actual writing of source code, desk checking, and unit testing. The most expansive definition for coding includes all of the prior tasks, plus the acquisition of any reusable code that might be included. Since productivity rates will vary dramatically with the definition, care should be exercised when using this term. No matter how coding is defined, it is not always the major cost element of software. For large systems, defect removal costs and paperwork costs usually exceed coding costs, which drops to third place overall.

Commercial off the shelf software (COTS)—This term, often used by the military, denotes software that will be leased or sold to other companies or individuals. As a class, commercial software is distinguished by better than average defect removal and better than average user documentation, although this latter point is debatable. Because of packaging, formal training, user documentation, and the like the productivity rates for commercial software are about half of that of similar internal software projects.

Commentary lines—Source code consists of three broad categories of statements: executable statements, data declarations, and commentary statements. The relative proportions of these three vary, but 40% executable statements, 40% data declarations, and 20% comments would not be unusual in typical programs. There is general agreement that the first two should count for productivity measurement purposes, but comments have been subject to debate. Opponents say that comments are "easy" and might be written artificially just to raise productivity while proponents say that comments are important and should be counted. IBM normally does not count commentary statements, and hence companies that follow IBM's lead do not count comments either.

Committee—This term denotes a group made up of members from various departments or units that is formed to explore a particular subject such as measurement, compensation, or the like. Committees are usually formed to make recommendations that management can implement.

Common systems—This term denotes a system that will be used simultaneously by more than one unit of an enterprise. For example, a payroll system that is used by every major corporate location. Common systems have very high requirements and design costs associated with them, but overall can be quite economical.

Competitive analysis—This term denotes a thorough study of how and why a company's competitors are doing well. Competitive analyses in major corporations are often supported by very sophisticated economic and strategic planning models. There is an enormous amount of public domain information available on products, companies, and company executives from commercial and public data bases which lends itself to competitive analysis.

Complexity estimate—A numerical prediction of the probable number of inter-related factors that cause projects to be viewed as complex by human observers. The commonest software complexity estimates include the McCabe cyclomatic and essential complexity metrics, the NPATH complexity metric, and the SPQR and CHECK-POINT® triple complexity factors of logic, code, and data complexity.

Component—This term is often used for systems and real-time software, and is defined as the collection of programs and modules that perform a single identified technical or business function. Examples of components include the scheduler of an operating system, or the parser of a compiler. This term is used infrequently for information systems. The size ranges of components are usu-

ally 25,000 to 250,000 source code statements, or 200 to 2000 Function Points.

CompuServe—This is one of several on-line information services. It is included herein because CompuServe is the host for a number of software tool user forums and bulletin boards. Examples of software companies where users communicate via Compuserve include Borland, Microsoft, IBM, and Symantec. This information utility also includes forums for computer languages, CASE, computer consultants, and other software-related study groups.

Configuration management—This term means the methodical storage and recording of all software components and deliverables as projects are under development. The term also implies cross referencing among deliverables, and the ability to trace backwards to the original requirement for any function. Configuration management is both a requirement and a major cost element of military software.

Consultants—This term has several definitions. The most widespread definition meant a contract programmer who worked for a standard rate. The curious change in tax law in 1987 by Senator Patrick Moynihan that caused such consultants to be considered employees of either their client or a consulting company has thrown this definition into chaos. Another definition of "consultant" is applied to management consultants who perform various strategic and analytical services for clients.

Constraints—This term denotes limits or conditions on a project. Very few project managers can actually select the target delivery date for a project, choose any set of useful tools, or select any and all staffing that they feel the project might require. Most projects begin with at least some constraints on delivery date, costs, staffing level, and other factors. Although constrained projects are the norm, unreasonable constraints is one of the major reasons for disasters.

Continuous integration—A form of system building in which new features are added as a stream, instead of being batched into discrete builds.

Contract software—A program or system developed under some form of contractual arrangement by an outside organization rather than by employees of the enterprise that lets the contract. This is a fairly common way of load balancing and reducing a backlog. It is interesting that studies of productivity rates have noted that contract software is often twice as productive as similar programs or systems developed by employees rather than contractors. There seem to be three reasons: clients are more precise in their requirements when dealing with contractors; the contractors are fairly expert or they would not have received the contract; the contractors work many more hours than they actually bill to the clients.

Contingency factor—This term applies to a reserve amount which companies add to cost estimates and budgets to cover unanticipated expenses and to act as a buffer against estimating errors. Normal contingency factors would be 35% added to cost estimates produced during requirements, 25% if produced during design, 15% if produced during coding, and 5% if produced during testing. Sometimes this term is replaced by pejorative terms such as "fat" or "fudge factor."

Conversion—The migration of software from one platform to another, such as moving from IBM to DEC computers, or changing from a flat file to a relational data base. The term has practical significance for software measurement and estimation since conversions occur often enough to require their own estimating algorithms. See also "Re-engineering" and "Reverse engineering".

COO—This term is shorthand for "Chief Operating Officer." The COO is normally either the president of a company, or an executive vice president. The COO is usually responsible for day to day operational decisions. Often the COO position is subordinate to the CEO position, although both may report directly to the board. The COO is usually named by the board. See also CEO, CFO, and CIO.

Corporate culture—The overall spirit and intangible aura of an enterprise. Enough assessments have been carried out to assert that the corporate culture is one of the stronger determinants of success or failure. The better corporate cultures tend to stress fairness, individual responsibility, and respect for both employees and customers. The more harmful corporate cultures tend to stress schedule adherence, pecking order in the corporate hierarchy, and absolute subordination of employees to management.

Corporate measurement program—A fully staffed team of measurement specialists who produce both quality and productivity measurement reports covering an entire enterprise. Only a small number of leading edge enterprises such as IBM have full corporate measurement programs. The sum of the productivity measurement and quality assurance measurement staffing and costs can amount to 3% to 4% of the total software population and budget for an enterprise. The normal staffing of a corporate measurement team would include several statisticians, several systems analysts, programmers to build the corporate measurement software, a data administration specialist, and data entry personnel. Such a team would normally report into a Vice President, and would be managed by a Director or Assistant Director. In addition, major operating units of the corporation would have satellite measurement teams for local studies.

Corporate politics—This is the normal phrase used to define the cliques and power struggles which take place within most human organizations, and almost all medium to large companies. Corporate politics can be severe enough to jeapordize corporate survival, and therefore should be noted in assessments.

Corrective maintenance—Modifications to a software program or system to repair defects. See also "adaptive maintenance" "mandatory maintenance," and "perfective maintenance."

Correctness proofs—A mathematical technique for validating algorithms. In practice, this method is expensive and is itself prone to error. There is currently no empirical data which can demonstrate that software which has been "proved correct" actually has lower error rates in production than software using ordinary defect removal methods. There is empirical data, however, that errors in the correctness proofs themselves are very common.

Cost analyst—A specialist who performs or assists line management in the reviewing internal and vendor of software cost estimates. In military and defense industries, this position is quite common as it is in the computer industry itself. The position is quite rare outside of these domains. See also "Cost estimator."

Cost avoidance—One of the ways of justifying new tools or new systems is the assertion that they will result in savings. The term cost avoidance implies reduction in expenses such as defect removal costs as a result of taking some explicit action.

Costs/Benefits Analysis—A study in which the development, execution, and maintenance costs for an application are matched against the anticipated value of the application. Cost/benefit analysis is still a crude and unscientific activity for many software projects.

Cost bucket—This term is used informally almost as slang, and means one of the tasks or activities against which costs will be accumulated. See also "Account."

Cost center—This term denotes a business function, such as software development, which charges users for its services. Whether software should be offered as a service within companies or should charge clients or users is not a clear cut topic. What is clear is that when enterprises switch and convert any service from an overhead function to a cost center, there will be sharp debate and temporary dissatisfaction by users. See also "Overhead" and "Profit center."

Cost driver—A factor that exerts a strong influence on software productivity. The term is derived from Dr. Barry Boehm's COCOMO model. The capability of software team members was the most significant cost driver noted by Dr. Boehm.

Cost estimate—A predicted total of the expenditures required to develop a software application. Several cost estimates are normally produced for large systems: the initial cost estimate is produced during the requirement phase; there will be a second cost estimate during the design phase; and a third will often be produced during development. Cost estimates can be produced manually, but manual estimates are difficult to update. As of 1993, some 50 commercial cost estimating tools for software projects are marketed in the United States.

Cost estimating department—A formally chartered group of software estimating specialists. Cost estimating departments are often found in defense industries and the computer industry itself, but are rarely found in enterprises that do not produce commercial grade software.

Cost estimator—A specialist who performs or assists line management in the creation of software cost estimates. In military and defense industries, this position is quite common as it is in the computer industry itself. The position is quite rare outside of these domains. See also "Cost analyst."

Cost of capital—This term is used in net present value calculations, and is equivalent to the interest rate paid for money. The term is also equivalent to "discount rate."

Cost of measurement—A full corporate productivity measurement program will require one full time professional measurement specialist for every 100 technical staff members, and hence amount to about 1% of software budgets. Quality measurements will require about 2%, and so a fully populated measurement program can amount to 3% to 4% of the total software budget for an enterprise.

Cost of quality—A unit of measure for software quality that includes the sum of the costs of finding defects, fixing defects, preventing defects from occurring, and warranty costs. This is a most unfortunate choice of names. "Cost of Quality" gives a misleading impression that quality improvement tends to require abnormal expenditures above a baseline in order to improve. The reverse is true. In studies by major companies such as IBM, the projects with the highest quality always had the shortest development schedules and the lowest costs. A name such as "Cost of Error" would come closer to highlighting the real cost driver. The cost of quality concept divides costs into three buckets of appraisal, prevention, and repair. The whole concept is in need of modernization for software engineering purposes.

Cost of sales—The marketing, advertising, and selling expenses associated with commercial software products.

Cost per defect—A unit of measure for software quality that is normally calculated by dividing the total costs for a defect removal activity such as testing by the total number of defects found. Cost per defect is dramatically misleading since the normal calculations tend to penalize quality and achieve the lowest values for the most defective software. The most serious misconception based on cost per defect is the widely quoted but incorrect assertion that "it costs 100 times as much to fix a bug during production as it does during design." See also "Defect removal costs."

Cost plus incentive—This phrase means one of the ways government and military contracts are handled, in which the contracting company is able to recover their costs and in addition, receive an agreed to profit or incentive.

Council—A more or less permanent group or committee that meets on a regular basis to offer advice and guidance on topics within the competence of the group. Councils are often formed by companies to deal with interdisciplinary and interdivisional topics, such as quality, productivity and engineering technology.

Counting rules—The local standards (there are no U.S. national standards) which enterprises adopt for counting source code. For example the IBM counting rules for systems software counted executable statements and data declarations but not comments. Source lines were counted by enumerating delimiters, rather than counting physical lines of a screen. Included code was counted once for a program rather than having each replication counted separately. Variations in apparent size of more than 500% have been observed that are not real, but are due to the fact that there are no U.S. standards for counting source code. One of the reasons for the wide and seemingly random variances in reported productivity rates for similar projects is counting variations. Several sets of counting rules have been published, including those of the IEEE, SEI, and SPR. There are also local counting rules used within many major corporations such as AT&T, Siemens, IBM and Motorola. A comparison of these multiple rules reveal very little consistency. Multiple incompatible counting rules are essentially the same as having none. There are also counting rules for Function Points, which are published by the International Function Point Users Group (IFPUG). The IFPUG rules are equivalent the de facto standards for U.S. function point counting.

Coupling—One of the fundamental concepts of structured programming. It denotes the way parts of a program or system interface. Some forms of coupling, such as branching directly via "go to" statements are considered harmful.

Creeping user requirements—In a study of several hundred software projects, approximately 35% of the functions delivered to the users could not be found in the requirements at all. The maximum observed growth in creeping user requirements exceeds 200%. It is not uncommon for developers and users to add functionality and features very late in the development cycle. See also "Noise" and "Transmission loss."

Critical Design Review (CDR)—This is one of several standard design reviews associated with military standard DoD 2167A. The CDR is the most significant of the suite of military design reviews.

Critical path—This term, derived from the PERT method, implies the set of activities that must be completed in sequence and on time if the entire project is to be completed on time. Critical path calculations are present in all of the 70 or so commercial software planning tools.

Critical success factors (CSF)—A small number of topics that are influential in determining the outcome of a business activity, and then monitoring those factors for change. Critical success factors for software are normally viewed as completing certain milestones, and by more sophisticated enterprises as achieving quality targets as well.

Crosstalk—This is the name of a military software engineering journal published by the Software Technology Support Center (STSC) at the U.S. Air Force's Ogden facility in Utah. Crosstalk has become a widely-cited journal that is also used as a distribution point for policy statements by the Department of Defense. On the whole, the journal does a commendable job of editorial coverage given declining budgets and reduced work hours by the staff.

Cumulative defect removal efficiency—This important term is one of the key metrics for both quality and productivity purposes. It means the percentage of software defects found by all reviews, inspections, and tests prior to handing the software to its users. In order to measure cumulative efficiency, all bugs found prior to delivery are added to the bugs found by users in a fixed time interval, such as the first year of production. Leading edge commercial software producers such as AT&T and IBM routinely exceed 95% in cumulative defect removal efficiency. Ordinary MIS projects in average companies seldom exceed 75%. Since the methods that raise defect removal efficiency also improve productivity, this is a very significant metric indeed.

Customer satisfaction survey—Many large software producers perform annual or periodic formal surveys of how well their customers like the products and support offered by the vendor. Some publishers of journals and some commercial market research firms also carry out formal studies on this topic.

Customer support—Answering user questions and helping software clients learn to use the product. Customer support is a major cost factor for commercial software, but of less importance for internal software that is not marketed. A rough rule of thumb indicates that one customer support person is needed for about every 100 customers or users.

Cyclomatic complexity—This is one aspect of the McCabe complexity metrics, with essential complexity being the second. This metric is a measure of control flow complexity, and approximates the number of regions on a standard control-flow graph. The cyclomatic complexity metric is normally an integer value, and can be calculated by taking the number of edges in the control-flow graph, minus the number of nodes, plus two. Empirically, perfectly structured code has a cyclomatic complexity of "1." As the number of branches in the module or program rises, the cyclomatic complexity metric rises too. Empirically, numbers less than ten imply reasonable structure, numbers higher than 30 are of questionable structure. Very high cyclomatic numbers of more than 50 imply the application cannot be tested, while even higher numbers of more than 75 imply that every change may trigger a "bad fix." This metric is widely used for Quality Assurance and test planning purposes. See also "Essential Complexity." The metric is also used to judge the results of "before and after" restructuring of applications.

DARPA—The acronym for Defense Advanced Research Project Agency. It refers to an organization that is part of the Department of Defense which funds various research programs. DARPA has been funding the Software Engineering Institute (SEI), for example.

Data—This major term is surprisingly ambiguous. Its basic definition means the raw facts that are collected about entities, activities, businesses, and the like. Before raw data can be utilized, it must be processed and converted into information.

Data administration—Refers to a group, department, or person that is assigned responsibility for the overall control of the data and information required to run an enterprise. See also "Data base administration."

Data analysis—This is one of the two major architectural methods that has evolved for software. The data analytic method starts with the exploration of the data structure and data flow for the program or system being designed. Examples of data analytic methods include the Warnier-Orr technique termed "data structured system design," the Jackson technique, and several others. Data analysis is the younger of the two major architectural methods, having originated in the 1970s. The older function analytic architecture originated in early days of the industry in the 1950's. The data analytic architecture is used most often for MIS projects, and seldom for systems software.

Data base—This term has come to mean a specific kind of software tool built to hold large amounts of information. More than 250 data base tools are on the current market. Many of them are mutually incompatible and mutually antagonistic, to the detriment of the entire industry. The concept of a data base has many sub-varieties within it, include hierarchical data bases, relational data bases, object-oriented data bases. These are outside the scope of this glossary.

Data base administration (DBA)—This term refers to a group, department, or person that is responsible for maintaining the integrity of corporate data bases.

The term overlaps data administration, but differs in that the DBA function often controls the physical storage of data as opposed to its ultimate usage.

Data complexity —Denotes the subjective complexity of the data elements and file structure of an application. This is the most difficult form of complexity to measure. Some progress is being made by evaluating the number of entities and the number of relationships which connect the entities.

Data definitions—One of the three major divisions of source code, with executable statements and comments being the other two. One of the sources of ambiguity with LOC metrics centers around variances in whether data definition statements should or should not be counted for productivity purposes. The SPR protocols do include data definitions.

Data element—This term is roughly analogous to a "field" in a tape file. It is also one of the supplemental counting elements of IBM's Function Point technique, and has been adopted by IFPUG as a counting element.

Data files—This term has been becoming progressively more ambiguous as data technology matures. It used to mean a specific, physical storage place such as a card deck or a reel of tape. With data base technology, the definition changed from a physical to a logical view. It can now mean a flat file, a leg in a hierarchical data base, a table in a relational data base, or a path in a network data base. A count of logical data files is one of the major input parameters for the IBM Function Point method. Indeed, this is the single most heavily weighted parameter.

Defect—A bug or problem which if not removed could cause a program to either fail or to produce incorrect results. Although the term is widely used, and the meaning is clear enough in ordinary conversation, this term lacks a truly satisfactory and rigorous definition. Many bugs or errors should be viewed as defects. For many others, it is uncertain and perhaps the problem might be viewed as a potential enhancement rather than an overt error.

Defect origins—Specifies the deliverable in which a defect first entered a program or system. Five common origins exist: requirements, design, code, user documentation, and bad fixes. Direct measurement of the numbers of defects found in each origin point is one of the most successful forms of quality measurement. For a new variation on this approach, refer to "Orthogonal defect classification."

Defect potential—This term implies the probable number of defects from all causes that will be encountered during the development and production of a program or system. The defect potential is enumerated as the sum of five defect categories: requirements defects, design defects, coding defects, documentation defects, and "bad fixes" or secondary defects. Defect potentials are surprisingly high. Some large real-time systems have achieved total defect potentials of more than 150 defects per KLOC, which is roughly 20 defects per Function Point.

Defect prevention—This important term defines the sets of technologies that minimize the risk of human error by software staffs. Defect prevention technologies include structured analysis and design, high-level languages, participation in joint application design (JAD) sessions, and even reviews and inspections since these activities help in the prevention of defects as well as removal. The quantified results of defect prevention can be significant. One major corporation averaged six defects per Function Point as the sum of errors from all sources (requirements, design, code, documentation, and bad fix defect classes) prior to a multi-year improvement program. Within three years the defect potential had dropped to three defects per Function Point. A synergistic combination of defect prevention and defect removal can yield dramatic improvements in the quality of delivered software. For example at six defects per Function Point and 80% cumulative defect removal efficiency, some 1.2 defects per Function Point would be delivered to users. At three defects per Function Point and 90% efficiency, only 0.3 defects per Function Point would be delivered: a four to one improvement.

Defect removal—The sum of all activities that are aimed at removing defects from software: desk checking, reviews, inspections, editing, and all forms of testing. This is a major concept because the sum of defect removal costs are usually the first or second most expensive aspect of software. For large systems projects such as operating systems and switching systems, defect removal is the most expensive known activity. For military projects, defect removal is usually the second most expensive activity, with paperwork being the most expensive. (Coding is often in third or fourth place.)

Defect removal costs—The sum of all forms of defect removal (private desk checks, reviews, inspections, and all forms of testing) is often the most expensive single cost element of software, and is always in the top three most expensive activities (paperwork and coding are the other two). For large systems, defect removal will routinely absorb 30% or more of all development costs. However, defect removal costs have a granular structure that only leading-edge enterprises measure. The three basic cost elements of defect removal are preparation costs for writing test cases and preparing for inspections; execution costs for running test

cases and holding inspections; and repair costs for fixing any bugs that occur. Preparation costs act like fixed costs since they will stay constant regardless of how many bugs occur; execution costs are variable but rather inelastic; defect repair is the only true variable cost that is directly related to the number of defects. Failure to track defect removal costs in terms of these three elements is why "cost per defect" is so frequently misleading.

Defect removal efficiency—This important term specifies the percentage of defects that are removed by any given operation such as a code inspection, review, or test stage. The measured defect removal efficiencies of most forms of testing is less than 35%, while formal code inspections can sometimes exceed 65%. The direct measurement of defect removal efficiency is a long-term operation. Normally, defect totals are accumulated from requirements throughout development, and on into customer usage. After one year of customer usage, all of the bugs reported by customers are considered together with the pre-release bugs, and this is the basis of the removal efficiency calculation. If users report ten bugs in the first year, and 90 bugs were found before release via inspections and testing, then it is obvious that the removal efficiency approximated 90%.

Defect severity—The relative impact of defects on the use of a program or system. IBM uses a four-level coding scheme for defect severities. Severity 1 means that the software cannot be used at all. Severity 2 means that it can be used, but major functions are disabled. Severity 3 means that minor functions are disabled. Severity 4 means a cosmetic problem such as a spelling or typographic error. Commercial software normally has very few Severity 1 bugs but a great many (40%–45%) Severity 2 bugs, due in part to the fact that companies fix high severity bugs faster.

Deleted code—Source code removed from an existing program or system. Code deletion often occurs when a program is being enhanced or modified. Deleted code is notoriously difficult to measure, since the effort of physically deleting code and then testing the product to be sure it has not regressed can be a significant cost. These costs must be applied somewhere, and that is the crux of the problem. Should deletion costs be assigned to new code or functions added at the same time, or should they be assigned to a separate deletion cost bucket? A separate deletion cost bucket seems reasonable.

Deliverable—A tangible, physical object that is the output of a software development task. Examples of deliverables includes pages of requirements, specifications, test cases, and source code. There are also synthetic deliverables, such as Function Points or Feature Points.

Delivery productivity—This important term denotes measuring the output productivity or a software team, by using the delivered product as the basis of measurement. The term "delivery productivity" is in opposition to "development productivity" which is the term used for measuring what a team builds rather than what it delivers. The difference between the two can be enormous. Delivery productivity includes reused code, while development productivity usually excludes it. Hence for projects with substantial volumes of reusable code, delivery productivity rates can be high: 27,000 source statements per staff year, which is more than 200 Function Points per staff year. Such rates are almost 10 times higher than would be normal for development productivity for the same project. Expressed in Function Points, the cur-

rent U.S. norm for development productivity is about 5 Function Points per staff month. When reused code, packages, borrowed code and other aspects of partial reuse are considered, delivery productivity can exceed 100 Function Points per staff month.

Delta code—The sum of new and changed code that occurs when an existing program or system is being modified. This term originated within IBM, and is derived from the concept of Base and Delta functions used in mathematics. See also "Changed code."

Demographic study—This is a full corporate-wide study of the number of software staff employed by the enterprise, usually by job category. Demographic studies often indicate that software employees comprise the largest technical occupation group within many companies or government agencies.

Department—The commonest meaning of this term is a group of staff members that averages about eight employees, all working on a more or less common project. Under this context, U.S. department sizes range from two up to about 30 staff members. However, the term also has a larger meaning as a major organization such as "Department of Defense."

Department management tasks—In many corporations, managers are primarily responsible for departments. This is the organization (normally with from three to 12 people) for which budgets are produced, and which is the unit around which space and facilities are planned. A department may be responsible for a single project, for several small projects, or for only a portion of a large project. See also "project management tasks" and "people management tasks."

Depreciation—The reduction in value of capital equipment, buildings, and other property over time. Depreciation is a factor in the measurement and estimation of hybrid products that include both software and hardware components.

Design—The tasks associated with specifying and sketching out the features and functions of a new application prior to formal coding.

Design of experiments (DOE)—The design of experiments is a recognized topic in the "hard" sciences such as physics. It concerns ensuring reliability in instrumentation, data collection, and avoiding false signals and polluted results. This topic is just beginning to move into software engineering, where its rigor will be greatly appreciated.

Design to cost—This term originated in the U.S. government and means a deliberate attempt to match the technical capabilities of a system to a predetermined cost range.

Desk checking—The private review and debugging that individual programmers and analysts carry out. Desk checking is seldom studied and hence the empirical data on its costs and efficiency is sparse.

Development—The broadest definition implies the sum of all tasks and activities necessary to build a software product. A more restricted definition implies only the central tasks of designing and coding the software product, omitting the tasks of requirements, user documentation, and the like. Unfortunately, both the broad and restricted definitions are used in software engineering literature. This is a major source of ambiguity. The same ambiguity shows up in CASE and productivity adds. Whenever claims of "10 to 1" productivity (or more) appear, it is usually because the costs of some tiny portion of a development cycle are being compared to a full development cycle.

Development center—A research group established to explore improved software techniques, and then transmit the most successful of those techniques to other members of the software function. Development centers will normally have one staff member for perhaps 25 programmers and analysts.

Development productivity—Measuring what a software team builds as the basis for productivity rates. The term is used in opposition to "delivery productivity" where the unit of measure is what the team delivers to clients. There are often enormous differences between the two. Development productivity measures usually exclude reused code and reusable components, since the staff plainly does not have to develop them. Delivery productivity usually does include reusable components, since the emphasis is on the output to clients rather than the process of development. Development productivity rates are usually 4000 source statements per year or less, which would be perhaps 32 Function Points per staff year. Delivery productivity rates have been measured at more than 27,000 source statements per staff year, which is about 200 Function Points per staff year.

Direct (costs, labor, staff)—The word "direct" means the mainline activities of building a software project as carried out by the primary development personnel. The opposite of direct is "indirect" which is sometimes synonymous with the term "overhead" and means activities and staff that often work on many other projects simultaneously, such as integration specialists, configuration specialists, secretarial support, and the like.

Director—A senior software manager that is responsible for a number of projects, a laboratory, or some other major aggregation of staff and effort. A second meaning refers to the directors of a company, which means the board formally charged with setting policy and providing overall business guidance.

Discount rate—This term is equivalent to "interest rate" and means the percentage that will be compounded in net present value calculations. See also "Cost of Capital."

Division—A major organization within an enterprise, such as "Field Engineering Division." Some companies, however, use the term for a smaller group of perhaps eight employees which would normally be termed a department.

Documentation—The printed and displayed materials which explain an application to its users. Traditional examples of software documentation consist of printed users guides, reference manuals, programmers guides, and operator guides. Modern software is accompanied by on-line documentation such as HELP screens, and on-line tutorials. Some applications even utilize multi-media information that can include graphics, sound, animation, and the like. The concept of documentation is rapidly evolving, and major changes should occur before the end of the century. Most forms of documentation can now be sized by means of functional metrics. For examples, standard User's Guides such as the Microsoft Word for Windows User's Guide average about 0.5 pages per Function Point.

DoD 2167A—This is one of a large suite of U.S. military standards issued by the Department of Defense. This one is particularly significant, since it encompasses many requirements for software quality. Without perhaps intending to, DoD 2167A calls for the production of such enormous volumes of paperwork that about 400 English words are produced for every Ada statement created by projects which follow this standard. Paperwork constitutes about 52% of the total costs of software when this standard is closely adhered to.

Downsizing—This term has two meanings: A) Moving software from mainframes onto smaller platforms such as work stations, personal computers, or networked computers; B) Laying off staff and shrinking the size of enterprise employment. For various reasons, definitions A and B often occur at the same time. See also "client/server."

Dual salary plan—A salary plan in which technical staff such as programmers and managerial staff can receive equal compensation. This is a surprisingly important topic in terms of the impact on both morale and on software productivity. A full dual salary plan will keep technical and managerial salaries equivalent up to about the level of a director or fourth-line manager.

Duplicate defect—This term means the 2nd, 3rd, or Nth report of a bug that has already been reported. Duplicate defects are recorded of course, but normal quality metrics are based on valid unique defects.

Dynamic analysis—A form of defect removal in which the code is executed; i.e. testing. The opposite term is "static analysis" where the code is reviewed or inspected but not run. Both forms of defect removal are useful.

Early warning system—A deliberate policy and support system for identifying potential problems far ahead, so that they can be avoided. Unfortunately, most corporate early warning systems (and many military ones as well) tend to be less than optimally effective. This seems to be due less to measuring the wrong parameters than it is to a natural human tendency to see hazards only when they are close and unavoidable.

Economic productivity—The standard economic definition of productivity is "goods or services delivered per unit of labor or expense." Prior to the invention of Function Points, economic productivity was not a factor that could readily be applied to software due to the lack of a suitable metric for the goods or services which software comprise. Function Points per Staff Month is the best current approximation of economic productivity for software. Alternate forms of functional metrics, such as Feature Points and the British Mark II Function Points are economically valid, but need to be translated back and forth between IFPUG standard Function Points.

Education—The training provided to staff and to management by an enterprise. Sometimes "education" is used to mean technical or managerial courses, while the term "training" is used to mean craft or skill related courses.

Education targets—The number of days per year which an enterprise sets aside for staff training purposes. Leading edge enterprises set aside from 10 to 15 days per staff and management year for educational purposes. Productivity rates are usually higher at enterprises with education targets than at enterprises that provide little or no education.

Effectiveness—This term denotes whether a method or software deliverable is useful for its intended purpose. Effectiveness and efficiency are often used as contrasting terms. Efficiency is defined as how fast a product is developed and effectiveness suggests how well it works.

Efficiency—The common meaning of this term simply denotes performing a task with the least amount of wasted motion. Several special definitions occur with software. The most important of the special definitions is "defect removal efficiency" or the percentage of errors that are present which are actually found. A second special definition contrasts efficiency with effectiveness, where efficiency implies the speed of software development and effectiveness implies the usefulness of the deliverables to the enterprise.

Effort—This important term denotes the amount of human work that is associated with a software project. Effort is normally measured with work units, such as person hours, person days, person months, or person years.

Embedded software—Software that is inside a physical object and controls its behavior. This is a more or less specialized term for software inside navigational devices, radar sets, oscilloscopes, and other instruments. Embedded software has its own characteristic productivity and quality profiles.

Empirical data—Information drawn from field trials and actual projects, as opposed to data taken from artificial experiments and small controlled studies. A shortage of good empirical data has been a chronic problem for software engineering since the industry began. Much of this shortage can be traced to irrational metrics such as "lines of source code."

Enhancement—The modification of an existing program or system in order to add new functions that were not present before the enhancement took place. Enhancement is becoming the major task of software as the industry matures. Neither the productivity rates nor the shape of the productivity curve for enhancement projects are the same as for new development. Enhancement productivity peaks when the size of the update is roughly 2% to 5% of the size of the original application. For smaller changes, the overhead costs of recompiling and regression testing yield low productivity, while for larger changes the original product usually has heavy internal modification which also lowers productivity. Although common usage tends to blur together the terms "maintenance" and "enhancements" the two concepts are actually quite distinct. Enhancements deal with augmented functionality, while maintenance deals with defect repairs. See also "maintenance."

Enterprise—A corporation, government agency, or other major assemblage of workers under a common charter, management team, and set of policies.

Enterprise analysis—This rather ambiguous term refers to studying the data and software needs of an entire enterprise. Some forms of enterprise analysis are associated with IBM's Business System Planning (BSP) method; others are associated with the Information Engineering (IE) paradigm; and some are informal or proprietary.

Enterprise computing—This term, fairly new in 1992, is coming to mean the kinds of software and data that can be widely utilized across multiple locations and business units. The topic encompasses the evaluation of data base and repository, strategies, wide area networks (WAN) and local area networks (LAN). The term is still amorphous and undergoing evolution.

Enterprise productivity—This unit is defined as the annual total of Function Points or Feature Points delivered to users, divided by the total staff of the software organization. Since this unit includes the effort for canceled projects, and indirect staff such as management and secretarial support, enterprise productivity rates are normally only about one-third as high as project productivity rates. In the United States, enterprise productivity averages about 30 Feature Points per staff year, while project productivity averages about 96 Feature Points per staff year.

Enterprise Software Planning (ESP)—A consortium of companies licensed to use the tools and methods developed by Software Productivity Research, Inc. of Burlington, MA, from 1985 forward. The ESP groups utilize a concept of developing internal consultants who are employees of the enterprises study-ing productivity, rather than having external consultants perform the measurements and collect data. Both diagnosis and improvement methods are studied.

Entity—A thing, such as a person or an object about which data will be collected and stored in a data base. This term is starting to be significant for software measurement and estimating, since the British Mark II method for calculating Function Points uses entity counts. Both entities and relationships among entities are a significant aspect of information systems design. See also "Relationship."

Entropy—The concept of entropy derives from physics, and is a basic property of all systems. Entropy means the gradual tendency of a system to move toward disorder and random processes. Dr. Laszlo Belady and Dr. Meier Lehman of IBM discovered that large software systems also seemed to be subject to entropy, in that the accumulation of small changes and updates over time gradually eroded the original structure of the systems so that they became progressively harder to modify. The reversal of entropy is one of the major claims of software restructuring tools.

Entry criteria—The tasks that must have been performed prior to starting a given activity such as an inspection, integration, or a test step.

Entry level staffing—A hiring practice of bringing in staff who are recent college graduates, and then usually following up with some form of internal training and education. The opposite form of hiring would be Experienced Staffing. Entry level staffing often leads to a low stable attrition rate and a shared culture. The computing industry itself tends to use entry level staffing, while other industries such as defense tend to use experienced staffing.

Environment—The set of tools and the physical surroundings in which software is developed is one definition of "environment." A more restricted definition also occurs, in which the environment is taken to mean only the tool set which is available. See also "Physical environment."

Error—A mistake made by a programmer or software team member that caused some problem to occur. See also "Defect."

Error-prone module—Bugs or defects are seldom randomly distributed through the modules of programs and systems. Instead, they tend to clump in a very small number of places termed "error prone modules." Studies of this phenomenon started in the 1960's and continue to verify the existence of such modules in large systems. As a rule of thumb, 3% of the modules in a system will receive about 50% of the total volume of bugs or defect reports. The factors that cause error-prone modules include complexity and individual human variation. Surprisingly however, many error prone modules are not poorly structured or intrinsically bad; many become error prone due to never having been tested. Error prone modules are a completely treatable condition and companies such as IBM have been able to eliminate them completely.

ESPRIT—The acronym for "European Software Program for Research in Information Technologies." This defines a relatively wide-ranging research consortium that spans many European companies and countries. See also PYRAMID.

ESTIMACS—This is a software cost estimating tool developed by Dr. Howard Rubin of Hunter College, and marketed commercially since 1983. In 1986, Computer Associates acquired the MACS corporation, and with it the rights to ESTIMACS. ESTIMACS is based on MIS projects, and is partly derived from an earlier IBM technique for MIS estimating.

Essential complexity—This is one of the two McCabe complexity metrics, with Cyclomatic Complexity being the other. This metric is a measure of the control flow of an application, and differs from Cyclomatic Complexity in that the actual graph of the control flow of the application is simplified by removal of redundant branches and paths. See also "Cyclomatic Complexity."

Estimate—Predicting the future outcome of a project in terms of various factors including sizes, schedules, effort, costs, quality, value, and risk.

Estimating model—This term implies an automated tool that can perform cost estimating, quality estimating, or some other major predictive function. More than 45 commercial estimating models are on sale in the U.S., and many companies such as IBM have proprietary estimating models as well. Estimating models or tools are normally expert systems, derived from the analysis of many thousands of historical projects. Expert systems are normally value priced, and as a result the costs are notably higher for estimating tools than for Project Management tools, which is a related but different tool category. Estimating tools and project management tools are beginning to coalesce and include direct technical links. Indeed, actual mergers and acquisitions of estimating and project management tool companies are escalating rapidly.

Exception reporting—A form of management early warning system in which managers are informed only of unusual situations that are beyond normal safe ranges. Exception reporting cuts down the volume of information which managers must understand.

Executive—A senior management position with certain legal and corporate obligations. Executives are liable for their actions, and are subject to suits should they fail in their responsbilities.

The normal population of executives starts at the director and vice presidental level in most companies, and typically comprises less than 1% of total work force of an enterprise.

Executive performance targets—Corporate executives are legally responsible for software quality (the executives, not programmers will be sued if systems fail) and are by position responsible for software productivity. Therefore when enterprises set explicit targets for quality and productivity, they should be set for executives. When IBM established software quality and productivity targets, only management and executives were included. This has a pragmatic basis. If individual staff members do not meet corporate targets, they have very little ability to improve since they are not authorized to buy better tools or methods. If executives do not meet corporate targets, they have considerable abilities to improve since they are authorized to buy better tools or methods.

Executive sponsorship—Since the normal reaction to measurement by software staffs and management alike is distrust and resistance, it is quite important to have high level support when corporate software measurement programs begin. Vice presidential or CEO support can be very helpful during the early stages of starting a measurement program.

Exempt—This term is used by the U.S. Bureau of Labor Statistics and the Department of Commerce to mean an employee who does not automatically get overtime; i.e. one who is exempt from overtime. To be exempt normally implies being part of management or in a senior capacity. The opposite term is "non-exempt" which means that such employees get paid overtime when their work demands such. Most U.S. software professionals are exempt, and do not receive overtime payments. They also work an average of 46 hours a week, so that something approaching 15% of the total effort on software projects may be in the form of unpaid overtime and hence invisible.

Exit criteria—Conditions that must be met before an application can be considered qualified to complete an inspection, test, or phase. See also "Entry Criteria."

Expansion factor—This term has several different meanings that are not very closely related. The oldest definition was the amount of storage which an instruction required in a computer. For example an IBM 1401 assembly language instruction required about four bytes of storage. A second definition used the term to mean the number of executable machine instructions required to execute one statement in a source language. Thus for COBOL, an average COBOL source instruction required perhaps three machine instructions when the program was being executed. The most recent definition means the number of source statements required to implement one IBM Function Point. For example, COBOL requires an average of about 105 source statements to code one Function Point.

Expense—The periodic outlay of cash for services and salaries which are required to run a business is one definition. Expenses are treated differently from capital expenditures for taxation and financial reporting purposes. A second and less restrictive definition for expense is merely the outlay of money.

Experienced staffing—A hiring practice that seeks out staff that already have job experience, as opposed to entry-level staffing of personnel right out of college. Experienced staffing is the norm in the defense industries, where once a contract is received work must begin almost at once.

Expert system—This can be defined as either a software package that performs a difficult intellectual task or a human

570

expert. There are many estimating systems that can meet this definition, although few project planning systems can. The prevalence of expert systems derived from thousands of software projects is one of the differentiating factors between the planning and estimating tool market.

Export license—In an attempt to prevent ex-Soviet block countries from gaining access to U.S. technologies, the Departments of Commerce and Defense are requiring formal licenses before exporting software or computers outside the U.S. For software at least, this seems to be having the primary effect of making the U.S. less competitive without actually augmenting protection. The costs and effort to get an export license must be factored in, as must the schedule.

External input—This is one of the factors used in calculating Function Points. The term denotes data or control that crosses an application's boundary in an incoming direction. This term is abbreviated IT (for input type) in the 1984 IBM method, and EI (external input) in the 1990 IFPUG method. The 1990 Albrecht and SPR methods use the abbreviation IT (input type).

External inquiry—This is one of the factors used in calculating Function Points. The term denotes a query/response pair. This term is abbreviated QT (for query type) in the 1984 IBM method, and EIF in the 1990 IFPUG method. The 1990 Albrecht and SPR methods use the abbreviation QT (query type).

External interface—This is one of the factors used on calculating Function Points. The term denotes data or control information that passes the application's boundary. The term is abbreviated EI (for external interface) in the 1984 IBM method, and EIF (external interface file) in the 1990 IFPUG method. It is also termed "external user data group" in the 1990 Albrecht and SPR methods.

External output—This is one of the factors used in calculating Function Points. The term denotes data or control that crosses an application's boundary in an outgoing direction. The term is abbreviated OT (for output type) in the 1984 IBM method, and EO (external output) in the 1990 IFPUG method. The 1990 Albrecht and SPR methods use the abbreviation OT (output type).

External software—Denotes software that will be built by one company or enterprise and marketed or delivered to others. This class of software normally has more complete documentation and better defect removal than internal software which enterprises build for their own consumption.

External user data group—This is one of the factors used in calculating Function Points. The term denotes a file or collection of data maintained outside an application's boundary. This term is equivalent in concept to the 1984 IBM "external interface type" and the 1990 IFPUG "external interface file." The 1990 Albrecht and SPR abbreviation for this term is EU.

False advertising—A very common problem for CASE and software tool vendors. More than 50% of CASE ads exhibit false or incorrect claims of dramatic improvements in productivity. Whenever claims such as "10 to 1" or "20 to 1" or even "1000 to 1" occur, look carefully at the ad and you will discover: A) The measurement method is not defined; B) the baseline against which the claim is being made is not defined; C) the number of projects measured is not stated; D) how the measurements were taken is not defined; E) What other factors may have been present in the comparison (differing skill levels, project sizes, etc.) are not defined. The software industry should begin to police itself and avoid such harmful claims.

Fault—This term is one of the many nearly synonymous words for a bug or software defect. A fault is defined as the manifestation of an error. See also "bugs," "defect," "error," and "error prone module."

Fault report—A written description of a software bug or defect. Fault reports are normally written by someone other than the programming staff themselves, and so the usual meaning of this term denotes bugs found by external staff such as test or quality assurance, or users. Terms with similar meanings include "Trouble Report" or TR which is widely used by many companies and government agencies. IBM used "Program Trouble Memorandum" or PTM for internal fault reports, and "Authorized Program Analysis Report" or APAR for bugs reported by clients.

Fault tolerant—The ability of software to keep running even when it contains errors. This is obviously a difficult accomplishment, and to do it at all requires care and often redundancy in key functions.

Feature—A function or capability of a software application. The term usually applies to capabilities that are significant enough to be used in advertising or which demonstrate some competitive advantage. Within some industries, such as telecommunications, the term "feature" is often used in special or restrictive ways.

Feature points—A unit of measure of software projects developed by Capers Jones of SPR, with the advice of Allan Albrecht. Feature Points are an extended form of Function Points intended to be used by real-time and systems software as well as by information systems. Feature Points are derived by a formula that uses the five Function Point parameters (inputs, outputs,

inquiries, logical files, and interfaces) plus an additional sixth parameter for the number of algorithms which must be developed for the program or system. Feature Points have the interesting property of yielding counts that are almost equal to Function Points when applied to information systems, but much larger totals for realtime and systems software.

Feedback—The basic term means taking the output from an amplifier and connecting it to the input, so that signal strength is increased. In business, feedback means monitoring a process and noting any deviations from plans, so that corrections can be made if needed. Another and casual definition is simply giving information to someone.

Field service—This term means sending enterprise software maintenance staff out to customer sites to help with defect analysis and repairs. Field service is offered by major computer and software vendors for main frame software, and when it occurs, is a major expense category. Indeed, the cumulative costs of field service are often greater than the costs of developing an application. Field service is also why commercial software maintenance costs are so much higher than internal software maintenance costs.

Field test—A form of testing often used by commercial software vendors and computer manufacturers. The term means a special arrangement with early users of a product to try out the product in their own enterprises. Field tests are usually covered by special non-disclosure and contractual arrangements. See also "Acceptance test."

File type—This means the kind of data file used by an application. It is one of the supplemental factors considered by the IBM Function Point technique.

First line manager—The bottom rung in a management rank. By definition, first line managers have only staff and technical employees reporting to them since they are the lowest level of formal management. There also exists a title of "supervisor" which may or may not overlap the concept of first-line management.

Fiscal year—The business year for accounting purposes used by an enterprise. Fiscal years are important for budgeting, financial reporting, and tax purposes.

Fixed costs—This term is normally applied to repeating expenses such as rent on office space and equipment. It has a more subtle application for software projects, however. Many of the actual costs of software development are not related to coding at all. For example, requirements and user documentation are independent of coding. These non-coding tasks are not fixed costs in the standard meaning of the term, but they act like fixed costs in that they will stay constant regardless of source language. This is the origin and explanation of the LOC Paradox. As software is written in higher level languages, the coding or variable cost declines but the fixed costs stay at a constant level.

Fixed price—Usually a contract to produce a program or system in which the price is determined before development. Fixed price contracts obviously need very accurate cost estimates to avoid overruns.

Fifth-generation language—This concept is even more amorphous and poorly defined than fourth-generation language. The vendors who utilize the phrase "fifth generation language" are often concerned with screen painting, graphical user interface, or pictorial methods for software development. The whole concept is essentially undefined.

Fog index—This is but one of several indicators of the readability of text passages. Many complexity and readability

tools are automated, and when used on specifications and user documents perform valuable service in augmenting clarity. Unfortunately, this class of tool is not widely known or utilized by the software engineering and mangement community.

Fourth-generation language—This is a troublesome term which has no adequate definition. The problem lies in the word "generation" which is quite subjective and ambiguous. Roughly speaking, the first generation of languages comprised basic assemblers. The second generation comprised ALGOL, FORTRAN, COBOL and some others. The third generation becomes murky, but includes PASCAL, BASIC, report generations, query languages, and a mixed bag of other things. The vendors of fourth generation languages are selling random products that include program generators, query languages, and data base languages. James Martin attempted to bring order to this chaos by defining a fourth generation language as being one that was "ten times as powerful as COBOL." However, the concept of "power" was not defined. Function Points provide a useful approximation. Using the number of statements used to encode one Function Point, the following ratios apply: 1st = > 200 statements; 2nd = 100 to 199 statements; 3rd = 50 to 99 statements; 4th = 15 to 49 statements; 5th = < 15 statements.

Function—This term derives from mathematics. For software, it has come to mean one of the capabilities which an application provide to its users. It also has a somewhat restricted meaning closer to the mathematical origins of the term, where a function means a single algorithm, such as a "square root extraction function."

Function Analysis—The oldest of the two major software architectural methods. The other is data analysis. Function analysis is used for both systems and information systems. Examples of function analytic architectures include the Yourdon design technique, the Gane and Sarson design technique, and many others.

Functional Capability Review (FCR)—Refers to a special review used for military and defense software, in which a defense contractor must demonstrate much of the target system before a contract can actually be received. The cost of functional capability reviews can be millions of dollars. This is one of a suite of special military process steps which are seldom performed (for good reason) by civilians.

Function Point Analysis (FPA)—The generic term for counting Function Points in the normal mode, using detailed requirements or functional specifications. It is also the name of a well-known book by Dr. Brian Dreger, which is published by Prentice Hall.

Function Points—A unit of measure for software projects developed by A.J. Albrecht of IBM. Function Points were put into the public domain by IBM, and are now controlled by the non-profit International Function Point Users Group (IFPUG). Function Points are derived by a formula that multiplies the number of inputs, outputs, inquiries, logical files, and interfaces by empirically derived weights and then adjusts these values by a complexity multiplier. Function Points were used initially for information systems, and have the useful attribute of remaining constant regardless of the source language or languages used for an application. Function Points and derivatives such as Feature Points provide the best fit for economic productivity since the software industry began. See also "Feature Points," "Mark II Function Points," "SPQR Function Points," and "Backfire function point calculations."

Gantt Chart—A method of displaying overlapped and partially concurrent activities by using horizontal lines to reflect the time required by each activity. Gantt charts are very useful for software projects due to the high degree of overlap and concurrency that typically occurs.

GECOMO—This is a software estimating tool marketed by GE Marconi. GECOMO started as a COCOMO clone, but has subsequently added functions from other tools. For example, GECOMO attempts to replicate the sizing functions contained within SPQR/20 and CHECK-POINT® using Function Points as the basis.

Generally Accepted Accounting Principles—While not widely realized by non-accountants, the basic methods of accounting are not frozen but evolve rather frequently. This term means the set of general concepts which are sanctioned by the American Institute of Certified Public Accountants. There is a strong need for a similar set of principles for dealing with software measurement.

General Ledger—An account book containing summaries of all financial data and transactions, such as accounts payable and receivable.

Generalist—This term, the opposite of "specialist," denotes staff that have multiple skills and can perform many tasks such as design, coding, testing and documentation. Small enterprises usually have generalists, but as companies and projects grow larger, they begin to require specialists. As a rule of thumb, the generalist approach works well for projects that require from one to ten total staff members. For large systems such as operating and defense systems, with hundreds of staff members, the generalist approach is counter productive and such projects need a full range of specialists.

Generation—This term nominally defines a set of products or concepts that share basic similarities and originated at more or less the same time. This term has no precise meaning, and therefore is difficult to pin down. Both languages and computers are segmented by generation in the software press and literature. As of 1988, "Fifth Generation Languages" and "Fifth Generation Computer" appears to be the upper limit. However, neither the years of origin nor the similarities of the objects are sufficiently well known to be sure what the term "generation" really means.

Geriatric Care for Aging Software—This phrase has come to mean restructuring, remodularizing, and otherwise reversing the entropy of aging software.

Goals—Denotes a target toward which an enterprise is moving. Unfortunately, many enterprises tend to set their goals in ambiguous and abstract ways, with one very common technique being to use percentages against an unknown base; i.e. "improve productivity by 50%" without actually defining what that means. For goals to be workable, they must be concrete rather than abstract. Examples of workable goals might be "achieving more than 95% cumulative defect removal efficiency" or "achieving more than 15 Function Points per staff month on development projects."

Goal seeking—Denotes a special kind of expert system which is capable of working backward from a goal and explicating what steps must be taken to achieve the goal. Goal seeking is being actively researched by software estimating companies.

Graph theory—The mathematical study of graphs. Graph theory provides some of the fundamental mathematics for the restructuring process. An unstructured program is converted into a graph, the graph is mathematically simplified, and then the new and structured version of the program is created from the new graph.

Guideline—A procedure or policy statement where acceptance is optional and can be decided by the project manager. The term also denotes a generally accepted practice.

Halstead metrics—A set of metrics developed by the late Maurice Halstead of Purdue University. The Halstead metrics are also termed "Software Science." These metrics divide lines of source code into two smaller atomic units: the verbal portions which are termed "operators" and the noun or data portions which are termed "operands." From this basic dichotomy, the Halstead metrics go on to encompass length, volume, vocabulary, and supplemental concepts such as difficulty and complexity. The Halstead metrics have many sources of error, and it is seldom possible to validate claims and assertions derived from them.

Hard data—The quantifiable facts about a project that can be observed and measured with minimal ambiguity or subjectivity. The primary hard data for computer programs and systems consists of the costs expended, the times required to complete tasks, the staff assigned to tasks, and the sizes of deliverables. The opposite term to hard data is soft data, which refers to subjective factors such as the skill of the staff and the usefulness of tools and methods.

Hardware—This term means a physical computer and its peripherals such a disk drives and printers.

Hardware dragalong—This term is used by computer manufacturers, and defines sales in hardware products that directly result from software. For example, the sales of Apple II computers that were caused by VisiCalc would be an example of this term.

Headcount—A quasi-slang term that means the staff assigned to a software department or project.

Headhunter—A slang term for a person or group that does personnel recruiting for managers, technical staff, or executives.

Hierarchical management—A form of project organization in which the project staff report in a chain of command similar to a military organization. This form of organization contends with the more recent Matrix Management organization, and usually the hierarchical form has better results for software projects.

Historical data—The normal definition of this term means the accumulated cost, schedule, and effort data derived from actual completed projects. Unfortunately that definition implies much greater accuracy than usually exists. In exploring the validity of historical data in many enterprises, errors of 30% to 50% were not uncommon, and in extreme cases the errors reach about 70%. The commonest errors are failure to record unpaid overtime, failure to record user costs, failure to start tracking until late in the requirements phase, failure to record management costs, and failure to record overhead activities such as integration and user documentation.

Human factors—This term has no exact meaning, but generally denotes the ease or difficulty of using a system. Considerable research and much trial and error surrounds the human factors area. Empirical evidence suggests that iconographic interfaces such as those used by the Apple Macintosh are easier to use than command or menu driven interfaces.

I-CASE—The acronym for "Integrated Computer Aided Software Engineering." The term was perhaps originated, and certainly made popular, by James Martin, the international lecturer. The phrase implies a higher level of integra-

tion than stand-alone CASE tools. See also "IPSE."

Icon—This term, which originally meant a religious image or statue, has now come to mean a visual image used as part of a computer interface. Icons are more succinct than text, but sometimes obscure.

IDC—This is the abbreviation for "International Data Corporation" which is a company that performs large scale statistical and demographic surveys of computing and software marketing information.

IEEE—The Institute of Electrical and Electronics Engineers, the largest professional group in existence. The IEEE has been one of the major pioneers for both software measurement and estimation, and the IEEE standards committees perform very useful service.

IEEE Standards—This term denotes an accepted way of dealing with a topic that has been endorsed by the Institute of Electrical and Electronics Engineers. There are many dozen such standards, and the numbers increase annually. Currently the IEEE is working on both software quality and productivity measurement standards, and on many other useful standards as well.

IFPUG—This term stands for the International Function Point Users Group. Formed in 1986, this non-profit organization consists of several hundred companies that are using Function Points for measurement and estimation. The annual growth rate of this organization was 46% over the last few years. As of 1993, IFPUG had become the largest measurement association in the United States.

Impossible region—Denotes a project where the desired schedule or the available staff are not sufficient to complete the project as specified. The term itself is derived from graphing effort versus time from actual projects, and noting the region of the graph where no successful projects have ever been completed.

Inch pebble—A pejorative term used when project management has established too many milestones for convenience.

Included code—Denotes code, such as a subroutine or a utility, that can be appended to a program by a simple invocation without requiring much in the way of coding. Included code, borrowed code, and reusable code are similar in concept but differ in nuance.

Independent testing—A formal test conducted by a company or enterprise other than the one developing the software that is to be tested. Independent testing is required by military specifications and is one of several unique military software cost factors that seldom or never occur outside of the defense business.

Independent Verification and Validation (IV& V)—A formal review of software project deliverables (specifications, documents, etc.) that is carried out by a company or enterprise other than the one developing the software that is to be reviewed. IV&V is one of several unique military software cost factors that seldom or never occur outside of the defense business.

Indirect (costs, effort, staff)—The opposite of "direct" and means the work that supports a project but is not actually part of mainline development. Indirect staff include secretarial and administrative staff, and sometimes staff or tasks that simultaneously support many projects at once, such as configuration control or integration.

Individual productivity—This term is defined as the productivity level of actual staff members. Individual productivity has the widest range of uncertainty of any measure. In controlled experiments where eight programmers were given the same specification, the range was 26 to 1 between the fastest and the slowest. Individual productivity is also a touchy topic. Indeed, it is illegal to measure individual productivity in several European countries. Because of the implications and constraints on measuring individual productivity, some major corporations do not measure projects of less than two person years of total effort. The smaller projects are simply lumped together and dealt with as a set. Individual productivity can be quite high for outstanding contributors: rates in excess of 25,000 source code statements per person year have been observed, which is about 200 Function Points per staff year. It is definitely a mistake to confuse individual productivity with either project or enterprise productivity.

Industry—This term was once well understood, but is now quite ambiguous. Formerly an industry was a reasonably well-defined collection of enterprises devoted to specific kinds of products and services. More recently, the term has become ambiguous because of all of the mergers, acquisitions, and conglomeration of enterprises. For example, the tobacco industry has been moving into foods and services. The computer hardware companies have been moving into software, and the major software houses have been buying up consulting groups.

Industry productivity—The productivity differentials that are associated with various segments of U.S. industry, and with specific industries such as banking or insurance. Prior to development of Function Points and Feature Points, there was no suitable metric that could be used to explore this topic. Early data indicates that the computer companies, contract developers and outsourcers, insurance companies and software vendors average more than 36 Feature Points per staff year, while at the opposite extreme some government agencies, academic institutions, and defense contractors average less than 12 Feature Points per staff year.

Inflation rate—Defines the progressive increase in real costs over time. It is normally discussed in terms of percent, such as 10% per year. Inflation rate is usually ignored for small projects, but must be dealt with for large multi-year software systems. This can be a major topic for international software studies. Some countries in South America have inflation rates that have run to 1000% in a single year.

Influential factors—In the IBM Function Point method, a set of 14 influential factors are defined that are evaluated to create a final complexity multiplier. This complexity multiplier is then used to calculate the Adjusted Function Point Total. The 14 factors are: 1) data communication; 2) distributed functions; 3) high performance objectives; 4) heavily used configuration; 5) transaction rate; 6) on-line data entry; 7) end-user efficiency; 8) on-line update; 9) complex processing; 10) reusability; 11) installation ease; 12) operational ease; 13) multiple site; 14) facilitate change.

Information—For software, this term has come to mean the user oriented output of a data processing system after the raw data has been converted into hopefully useful information. The term also has a more formal definition under Shannon's' Information Theory where it means an intelligible message.

Information center—A group of personal computer and software application specialists who are placed together in a department that is chartered to assist end users such as accountants and sales people in learning to use computers, terminals, and software. The normal ratio of information center staff to users would be about 1 to 100.

Information engineering (IE)—This is a major sub-speciality within the methodologies used to develop information systems. As of 1992, perhaps 15% of all MIS projects are built using the information engineering paradigm, and the percentage is rising annually. The IE paradigm begins with corporate information modelling prior to the commencement of any specific software project. The projects themselves derive more or less natually from the needs discovered via the corporate modelling. The IE paradigm is supported by a rich variety of tools and methods.

Information system—This surprisingly ambiguous term roughly means software that provides some kind of data or reports to the staff and management of an enterprise. Examples of information systems include general ledger systems, sales lead systems, accounting systems, and benefits tracking systems.

Information theory—The mathematical analysis of communication developed by Dr. Claude Shannon of Bell Laboratories. The concept has been extended far beyond its original domain, and some of the terms and concepts from information theory are now widely used. See also "Noise" and "Transmission loss."

Inheritance—This is an aspect of the object-oriented paradigm. The term refers to the ability to create new classes which share some of the characteristics of classes that already exist. This augments the ability to reuse components. To illustrate the logic of inheritance, the classes "Ford" and "Chrysler" would obviously inherit some of the aspects of a general class, "automobile."

Inputs—The screens, reports, or forms that present data to an application. A count of inputs is one of the basic parameters for the IBM Function Point method.

IPSE—This is the acronym for "Integrated Programming Support Environment." This phrase is roughly equivalent to CASE or I-CASE, and means the collection of tightly coupled tools needed by software engineers and managers. IPSE is more common in Europe than in the United States, where I-CASE tends to stand for the same suite of related topics.

Inquiries—This term means the questions or explanatory information that users can request from an application. A count of inquiries is one of the basic parameters of the IBM Function Point method.

Inspection—This term defines a rigorous technique developed by Michael Fagan of the IBM Corporation. Inspections imply training of the inspection team, well-defined roles that include a moderator and recorder, and the complete measurement of defects encountered. Inspections cover requirements, design, code, user documentation, and even test plans and test cases. Inspections have the highest measured efficiency of any known form of defect removal, and are the only technique to achieve efficiencies of 75% or more in field conditions. See also "Structured walkthrough," "Review," "Static analysis," and "Defect removal."

Institute for Defense Analysis (IDA)— This is a non-profit organization which does various research projects for the Department of Defence. In 1992 IDA carried out a study of various software process assessment methods (SEI, SPR, Hewlett-Packard, etc.) which has not been published, apparently because it pointed out flaws in the SEI method with perhaps too much candor.

Integration—This term denotes the process of fitting together the various components of a system so that the entire system works as a whole. Integration is a formal task for large systems, and computer manufacturers and other large system producers often have integration departments staffed by professional integration specialists. For MIS producers and smaller enterprises, integration is usually informal. Many small programs do not require integration at all. When formal integration occurs, it is a major expense. However, this topic is seldom measured accurately, so empirical data is scarce.

Integration test—This term means a test carried out on a system after it has been integrated into a working whole, as opposed to the earlier unit and component tests carried out on pieces.

Integrity—This term has several meanings. The commonest meaning denotes the soundness of the overall architecture of a system. A second meaning denotes the extent to which unauthorized access to a system can be prevented.

Interface—This term, originally from sewing, has become a major term for software. It is defined as the coupling between two or more parts of a program or system, or the coupling between two or more systems. Errors and bugs associated with this coupling are a major source of trouble for software. The number of interfaces is also a parameter in the IBM Function Point technique.

Internal software—Software which an enterprise creates for its own use, as opposed to software which will be marketed or delivered to another enterprise. See also "External software."

Internal rate of return—This is one of the key financial measures used to determine if an investment is potentially good or bad. It is defined as the discount rate which equalizes the present values of expected cash outflows and inflows. It is normally found by trial and error methods, which with a computer is easily carried out. Many companies set Internal Rates of Return targets, such as 30%, and will invest in projects whose yield exceeds the target.

579

International development—A system or application that is being developed jointly by several companies. Large multi-national corporations such as IBM and ITT sometimes have as many as 15 different laboratories all over the world working on components of the same system. As a general rule, international development is subject to high travel costs and low productivity. One major international system required more than 3000 trans-Atlantic trips, and the actual costs of travel were greater than the costs of the code for the system.

International Standards Organization (ISO)—This is one of the important standards associations. ISO is located in Switzerland, but members represent all countries. ISO standards catapulted into prominence in 1992, when for the first time they were required throughout much of Europe. See also ISO 9000.

Internet—This terms denotes a massive (more than 150,000 users) global net connecting universities, companies, government agencies, and private individuals. Internet has grown to become an information exchange utility powerful enough to actually impact human history and military operations. For example, during the failed Soviet coup attempt, Internet contacts made the real story available to the West, even though television and radio transmissions were censored. Earlier, U.S. citizens were warned via Internet of possible bloodshed in China before the shooting in Tienanmen Square. The normal usage of Internet is to allow scholars and researchers to communicate ideas, and so far as can be determined, no other approach in human history has linked so many scholars so closely.

Interoperability—A highly ambiguous term, with countless definitions. The sense of the term is allowing users to access enterprise-wide data with some degree of ease, and without resorting to elaborate conversion and extraction protocols. Other definitions overlap data reusability and data conversion ease.

Interval—This term denotes the duration or length of an activity such as coding, testing, and the like. It is equivalent to the schedule for the activity, which is a more common term than interval. Interval is used in the telecommunications industry by companies such as AT&T.

Invalid defect—This important term stands for a bug report which, upon analysis, is either not a bug at all or if it is a bug is one in some other software product rather than the one to whom the bug report was sent. Commercial software vendors routinely receive in excess of 15% invalid defect reports from their clients, with user errors, hardware errors, and errors in some other product being the largest contributors to the load. Note that even though invalid defects are not the fault of the product in question, substantial costs accrue to software vendors in exploring the invalid defect reports and explaining to possibly indignant users where the true fault resides.

ISO 9000—The generic name given to a suite of related standards (ISO 9000 through 9004) which set out quality requirements. The ISO 9000 standards have been mandated for Europe starting in 1992, so many companies are now going through a protracted ISO certification process. As of late 1993, there is no empirical evidence that organizations which follow ISO 9000 and have received ISO certification actually have higher quality than companies which do not use this standard. Indeed, there is a school of thought which asserts that the ISO 9000 standards are not legitimate quality standards at all, but merely a hidden tax.

ISPA—This stands for the International Society of Parametric Analysis. ISPA includes all forms of parametric analysis but has a relatively large and sophisticated membership that specializes in software. Most of the commercial software estimating companies have members. The ISPA conferences are useful sources of new ideas in modeling and estimating.

Job category—A specific classification established by management and personnel which has a formal title associated with it, such as "programmer" or "systems analyst." This topic is surprisingly ambiguous, and more than 100 discrete job categories have been noted. The ambiguity makes software measurement and estimating difficult between companies, or even within large companies, since it is not always certain which tasks will be performed by whom. Some corporations have no formal job categories, or use only a single generic category such as "member of the technical staff." Serious demographic and productivity studies are very difficult in such enterprises.

JS-1, JS-2, JS-3, JS-4—A series of software cost estimating models developed by Randall Jensen of Hughes Aircraft.

K—The normal abbreviation for 1000 when used to discuss software. Strictly defined, K means 2 raised to the 10th power and hence should mean 1,024. In ordinary usage, K means 1000.

KLOC or KSLOC—The normal abbreviation for "K lines of code" which is a rough approximation for 1000 source code statements. When KSLOC is used, the "S" stands for "source." In normal usage, KLOC stands for exactly 1000 source code statements rather than the 1024 statements which would be used if "K" were strictly defined as 2 raised to the 10th power. KLOC and KSLOC have been impediments to progress for many years, when used as productivity or quality metrics. See the "LOC paradox."

Kiviat Graph—A multi-faceted graphic representation technique named after Phil Kiviat (but actually used long before he was even born). Kiviat graphs are used to display the results of many changing variables simultaneously. For software, Kiviat graphs are often used to display productivity, quality, and other targets on the same graph. The form of a Kiviat graph is a star-like set of lines radiating from a central point. This central point provides the zero point or origin of the lines, each of which stands for a particular metric. It is normal to draw connecting lines between each end point on the radiating lines, to produce an irregular shape that reflects progress against all goals at once. Normally Kiviat graphs have an even number of radiating lines, with four and eight being the most common.

Knowledge base—The sum of all information about a particular topic. A knowledge base is different from a data base in that much of the knowledge may be on paper or in forms which are not immediately accessible to computers.

Knowledge engineering—When building expert systems, this phrase refers to the interviews and methods used to extract knowledge and information from domain experts.

KSLOC—The normal abbreviation for "K lines of source code" which is a rough approximation for 1000 source code statements. KSLOC and KLOC are identically defined. Neither are acceptable for productivity or quality studies. See also the "LOC paradox."

Language—The specific assembled, compiled or interpreted language used for a program or system. If individual dialects are counted as languages (i.e. if True Basic, Turbo Basic, Quick Basic, are considered separate languages) then almost 600 languages exist today.

Languages exert a strong but often exaggerated influence on software productivity. See also "Mixed languages."

Language level—The concept of "high" and "low" level languages has been in existence since the early days of the computer era. Surprisingly, an actual numerical expression for the level of a language was not developed until 1973 when IBM's San Jose lab created a mathematical technique for converting the size of a program in any arbitrary language into the equivalent size in some other language. The IBM method used basic assembly language as the starting point, and this language was by definition Level 1. Higher level languages were evaluated on the basis of how many basic assembly language statements were required to create the functionality of one statement in the target language. Thus COBOL was assigned a level of 3 because it required, on the average, three assembly statements to create the functionality of one COBOL statement.

Leading indicator—This term, taken from economics, means a metric that is helpful in assessing the probable trend or outcome of a software project. Examples of leading indicators include the number of defects found versus the predicted number anticipated, and the variance between budgeted and actual expenditures.

Learning curve—The gradual improvement in performing a task that occurs as workers become more expert over time. It is a significant phenomenon in real life. It has been empirically validated for software projects.

Library—For software, this term has two meanings. The first is the traditional usage of the term as a repository of books and journals. The second is a more restricted term, as the set of materials which support a software project. In this second form, the phrase "project library" or "program library" may occur.

Legacy system—This fairly recent term (first noted circa 1989) has come to mean an aging software application. The phrase has a slightly humorous connotation, and implies that maintenance for the application has been handed down to a younger generation of software staff, and that the originators of the application have moved to other work or retired.

Life-cycle—This is a very widely used term, but it has been troubled by totally inconsistent definitions. The earliest known definition circa the 1960's meant the sequence of events in building and maintaining software from requirements to retirement. This was a reasonable choice. More recently CASE vendors have started advertising "full life cycle support" but have not included defect removal, maintenance, user documentation, and many other tasks. Exactly what any given assertion of "full life cycle support" means is now seriously flawed.

Line and staff—This term is derived from military terminology, and means that there are two kinds of general work in enterprises. Line work is defined as actual work on the products or services the enterprise creates for customers. Staff work is defined as support for the line workers. Coding, for example, is usually a line task while accounting is usually a staff task.

Line of balance—A way of graphing actual versus anticipated results. Line of balance is often used for software cost tracking, and takes the form of a graph where the horizontal axis is the time dimension and the vertical axis is the cumulative total of dollars expended. The budget for the project is drawn on the graph, and as time passes, the actual expenditure line is superimposed on the budget line. If actual costs are above the budget line, then cost overruns might occur. If actual costs are below the budget line, then progress may be slow.

Litigation—The generic term for various kinds of law suits and legal actions which require court appearances. The term deserves inclusion in a software glossary, since software is one of the most litigious of all U.S. industries. Litigation for copyright infringement, "look and feel" violations, theft of intellectual property, and many other topics are absorbing increasing amounts of effort and funds within the software domain.

LOC Paradox—A mathematical anomaly first published by the author, Capers Jones, of IBM in 1978 in the IBM Systems Journal. When programs are written in higher level languages, their apparent productivity expressed in terms of "source code per time unit" is lower than for similar applications written in low level languages. This is due to a paradoxical flaw in the unit of measure, since real economic productivity goes up in accordance with language level. Although the discovery of the paradox was a surprise for software, the fundamental mathematics which cause it had been known for more than 200 years. It is a fundamental law of manufacture that if a product manufacturing cycle has a large quantity of fixed costs and the number of units manufactured goes down, then the cost per unit must go up. When software migrates from low level to high level languages, the non-coding tasks act as though they were fixed costs (i.e. specifications, documentation) while the number of source code "units" goes down. Hence the cost per unit must go up.

Logical complexity—This term denotes one of the three major forms of complexity that are associated with software. It means how hard are the actual problems facing the design and development team. There are no effective

metrics for this topic, and it is usually dealt with by asking the team to evaluate difficulty on a scale of 1 to 5 with 1 being easy and 5 being hard. Logical complexity, code complexity, and data complexity are the set of complexity topics used by the SPR Function Point technique.

Logical files—The storage of information in some form. The specific form can be a flat file, a leg in a hierarchical data base, a table in a relational data base, or a path in a network data base. A count of logical files is one of the key parameters in the IBM Function Point technique, and has the highest weighting factor.

Logical internal files—This is one of the factors used in calculating Function Points. The term denotes a file or data group for user purposes that is maintained within an application. The 1984 IBM method uses FT (for file type) as the abbreviation for this term. The 1990 IFPUG method used ILF (internal logical files). The 1990 Albrecht and SPR methods use IU (for internal user data group) for the same concept.

Lower CASE—A slang expression, originating circa 1989, with the general meaning of CASE tools which support the latter end of a software development cycle; i.e. coding, integration, testing, and the like. See also "Middle CASE" and "Upper CASE."

Machine independence—This term denotes software that can run on multiple computer types. Certain operating systems such as MS-DOS and UNIX and certain languages such as C facilitate machine independence. See also "Portability."

Macro estimate—An estimating technique that attempts to predict the entire costs for a software project via a single equation. The resulting total estimate is then decomposed into individual task estimates using ratios and percentages.

Macro estimating has a high margin of error compared to micro estimating.

Macro instructions—An artificial assembly language instruction that is a shorthand way of invoking a substantial set of actual assembly language instructions that perform some technical or business function. Macro instructions cause measurement and estimation confusion because of uncertainty regarding whether to count only the invocation of the macro, or to count the entire expanded form. Development productivity measures usually count only the invocation, while delivery productivity measures would count both.

Maintainability—The relative ease or difficulty of modifying an existing program or system. This term can be evaluated either subjectively by asking the programmers or numerically, by using the McCabe or NPATH complexity metrics. Maintainability is directly proportional to structure. In a series of interviews with 26 maintenance programmers, half of whom were adding enhancements and half of whom were fixing bugs, the effort to maintain well structured software was considered to about one fourth that of poorly structured software. That is, any given update could be made in one fourth the time. The bad fix rate was asserted to be lower by 50% as well.

Maintenance—This term has been ambiguous and troublesome since the computing era began in the 1940's. The commonest definition of maintenance is "any change made to an existing program or system once it enters production." This definition lumps enhancements and defect repairs into the same group, which is unwise from both a business and technical standpoint. A more precise definition of maintenance used by IBM is "defect repairs made to an existing program or system after it is delivered to users." This term restricts the

word "maintenance" to repair, which is a reasonable limitation. See also "Re-engineering," "Restructure," and "Conversion."

Maintenance assignment scope—This is one of the most important metrics for enterprises with libraries of aging, legacy systems. The maintenance assignment scope is defined as the number of full-time staff required to keep a portfolio of applications running. This metric is normally expressed in Function Points, and the current U.S. average is approximately 500 Function Points in the portfolio per staff member. The largest maintenance assignment scopes can exceed 1500 Function Points. For poorly structured, low-level languages such as aging assembler, the maintenance assignment scope may drop below 300 Function Points. A full suite of geriatric services (complexity analyzers, restructuring tools, reverse engineering tools, and re-engineering tools) have been observed to triple the maintenance assignment scope of a major insurance company over about a five-year period.

Maintenance department—This term denotes a formal group that is responsible for small enhancements, defect repairs, and routine updates of software. Such departments are often quite efficient, and companies whose total software staffs exceed 200 employees often create maintenance departments.

Maintenance specialist—This term means a programmer or analyst whose full time responsibility is defect repairs and enhancement to existing software. In large corporations this is a fully recognized job description. See also "Maintenance assignment scope."

Major defect—Denotes a high severity (Severity 1 or 2) bug that often causes total product failure or serious disruption. See also "Minor defect and "Defect severity."

Malpractice—In licensed professions such as law, medicine, and some forms of engineering, this means performance of harmful actions which were avoidable if normal professional caution had been used. The concept is seldom applied to software, but in fact is a major problem and especially so among software management. Examples of professional malpractice in a software context would include: A) Failure to use estimating tools on large systems of 5000 Function Points or more; B) Using LOC metrics for productivity and quality studies involving multiple languages, without compensating for the well-known LOC paradox.

Man-month—This is an ancient term that dates to the 19th century. It was made famous by Fred Brooks' book "The Mythical Man-Month." Man-Month is considered to be a sexist term, and has recently been replaced by the neutral "Person-Month" which has the same basic definition. The basic definition is the normal working period of a typical employee, i.e. a value that ranges from 140 to 180 hours per calendar month depending upon country, overtime, holidays, and the like.

Management consultant—Denotes a consultant who specializes in advice to executives and managers. Management consulting groups are moving rapidly into measurement and estimation as these technologies become more scientific.

Manager—This important term is surprisingly ambiguous. The standard definition is someone entrusted by an enterprise with both staff supervision and project responsibilities. However, the term can be used interchangeably with "supervisor" at the low end of its definition, and with "director" or "executive" at the high end.

Mandatory maintenance—Updates or changes to a program or system due to changes in law, government regulations, standards, corporate policies, or some other external authority. See also "Adaptive maintenance," "Corrective maintenance," and "Perfective maintenance."

Mark II Function Points—Denotes a variation to IBM's Function Point method that was developed by the British consultant Charles Symons of Nolan, Norton & Company in London. The Mark II method adds the use of entity counts as a key addition to the IBM technique. It also ups the number of complexity factors from 14 to 19. Mark II usage is generally confined to the United Kingdom.

Matrix management—Defines a project organization structure in which employees actually report to a technical manager rather than a project manager, but are assigned to work under the general guidance of the project manager. Matrix management is common for software, but does not seem to produce very good results. Matrix management requires lateral cooperation among technical and project managers. The opposite concept to matrix management is the older "hierarchical management."

Maturity level—This ambiguous term originated with Watts Humphrey of the Software Engineering Institute (SEI). It denotes an arbitrary and artificial five-level set of plateaus of increasing sophistication in the treatment and understanding of software. The SEI maturity metric runs from low (1) to high (5) and is an absolute rather than relative metric. The middle value (3) is not actually the U.S. average, but instead one of the plateaus of increasing sophistication. Interestingly, the set of enterprises to attempt the SEI evaluation averaged only about 1.5, which is a low and depressing data point. The SEI scale and the SPR scale of software effectiveness are both five points in range, but run in opposite directions. The SPR scale, which pre-dates the SEI scale by several years, uses 1 for "excellent," 2 for "good," 3 for "average" and so on. The SPR scale is a relative scale, and is adjusted annually to match changing national conditions. Artificial and arbitrary categorization schemes sweep the industry from time to time, and then fade away. See "Stages Hypothesis" for an earlier example.

McCabe complexity metrics—A set of metrics derived from graph theory that assign numeric values to program control flow. Essential complexity and cyclomatic complexity are both aspects of the McCabe complexity view.

Mean Time Between Failures (MTBF)—This is one of the standard reliability metrics, and is defined as the clock time between observed software problems.

Mean Time To Failure (MTTF)—This is one of the standard reliability metrics, and is defined as the clock time from the moment a user starts a program until a problem occurs.

Mean Time to Interrupt (MTTI)—This term is not part of reliability theory, but instead denotes how long a typical programmer can work without being interrupted by a phone call or visitor. One study of this phenomenon noted that with shared or open office environments, the MTTI averaged only 11 minutes.

Mean Time to Repair (MTTR)—This term denotes how long from the moment a bug is reported until the fix is safely installed on a user's system and the bug has been closed. For commercial software, MTTR is a constant source of management concern. Sometimes the MTTR can stretch out into months, with continued customer grief as an attribute. IBM attempts to fix Severity 1 bugs within two weeks and Severity 2 bugs within a month, as a rough guideline.

Measurement—This term is surprisingly ambiguous. Fully defined, it means collecting both hard and soft data for projects. Hard data consists of tangible,

quantitative things such as schedules, staffing, resources, and sizes of various deliverables. Soft data consists of the opinions of the staff and managers on topics such as the usefulness of tools, arbitrary constraints levied against the project, creeping requirements, and the like. Measurement also includes analyzing the specific combinations of soft factors that caused the hard data to be higher or lower than normal. The term "measurement" implies environmental, skill, and methodology factors as well as costs, effort, staffing, and deliverables.

Measurement specialist—This term denotes a full-time professional staff member whose job is working on the measurement of software. Measurement specialists are a new job title and still comparatively rare except in very large companies such as IBM.

Meeting and communication costs—This is one of the hidden but very costly aspects of large software development organizations. A study by a major insurance company with more than 1000 people in their software function discovered than about 12% of the total monthly time was devoted to meetings and communication, while coding itself amounted to just over 8%.

Merise—This term refers to a structured methodology that is a French national standard, and also widely used in other European countries. Merise is not well known in the U.S. but deserves greater recognition.

Method—In a general sense, this term refers to a way of carrying out some activity using a standard, predetermined approach. This is also one of the terms used in a special sense by the object-oriented paradigm. A method is roughly equivalent to a procedure or module in conventional programming terminology.

Methods analyst—This term, originating before the computer era, denotes a technical staff member who studies manual techniques for carrying out manufacturing or clerical tasks.

Methodology—The general meaning of this term is a set of formal protocols followed when performing a task, such as an inspection. A somewhat more restrictive definition refers to a recognized and sometimes commercially marketed complex of tasks and deliverables which, it is asserted, will give better results for software development than random techniques. See also "System Development Methodology."

Metric—A unit of measure for expressing quantified information in such a way that comparisons are possible. Examples of software metrics include Function Points, Feature Points, McCabe complexity metrics, cost per defect, cost per KLOC, and many others.

Micro estimating—An estimating technique that deals separately with each task or activity that must be performed for a software project, and then accumulates the total cost for the project by summing all of the individual task estimates. Micro estimating is intrinsically more accurate than macro estimating, but more difficult to perform. Micro estimating is derived from the concepts of work breakdown structures. See also "Parametric analysis" and "Macro estimating."

Middle CASE—A slang expression, originating circa 1991, and roughly meaning CASE tools which support activities in the middle of a software development cycle, such as technical documentation and perhaps detailed design. There is no exact break point between lower CASE, middle CASE, and upper CASE.

Milestone—This term implies a major checkpoint in the activities being carried out on a software project. Normal milestones include completion of requirements, completion of high level and detail design, completion of coding, com

pletion of testing, and delivery or handover to clients. (See also "inch pebble".)

Military software—Software that follows U.S. military specifications such as the DoD new 2167A quality assurance specification have unique cost and productivity implications. As a rule of thumb, military projects will spend more money on paperwork and create more pages of specifications and documentation than any other kind of software. Sometimes military projects generate more than 400 English words for every line of delivered source code. Military projects also have a set of unique activities that only occur when military standards are required, such as independent testing and independent verification and validation. As a class, military software projects require more work on more tasks and have the lowest productivity of all forms of software. Military software has developed its own argot, and glossaries of military software terminology are approximately as large as this glossary.

Military standards—This is the generic name for a host of detailed procedures and guidelines produced by the uniformed services and the U.S. Department of Defense. Military standards are precise and careful, but they tend to lead to paperwork of astounding volume and verbosity. About 52% of the costs of military software is tied up in the production of specifications and other paper deliverables.

Minor defect—This term means a comparatively trivial bug such as a spelling error. Generally speaking, Severity 3 and Severity 4 defects would be classed as minor. See also "Major Defect" and "Defect Severity."

MIPS—This is the acronym for "Million Instructions per second." The term has been used to measure hardware computing performance. It is now falling out of favor and being replaced by standard tests of certain tasks.

MIS—This term stands for "management information system" and means a program or system developed primarily for internal use in operating a business. The term is often used in contrast to systems software. MIS and information system are more or less synonymous.

MITI—This is the acronym for the Japanese "Ministry of International Trade and Industry." MITI is a major force in international competition, and the dominant source of Japanese competitiveness in software and computing.

Mixed language projects—Many software projects (about one third of all that have been observed) are written in more than a single language. Combinations of C and Assembler, COBOL and SQL, are very common. A few projects may include as many as 15 different languages. Mixed language projects add confusion to source code metrics and are difficult but not impossible to evaluate. It is easily possible with minor computer assistance to evaluate the contributions of each language to both the size and functionality of the final application.

Modified code—When a program or system is updated, some of the existing code is usually changed. This is termed modified or changed code.

Module—This term means the smallest collection of source code that collectively performs a technical or business function. A module is a sub-element of a program, and often consists of about 50 source code statements in a well-structured application. There are of course enormous modules that were created either before structured programming was invented or without regard to its conventions that may exceed 5000 source code statements. These gigantic modules are often error-prone. From time to time the word "module" and "program" are used synonymously. The word program actually implies a stand-alone unit which is complete in itself, while the word module implies a only a partial solution. A program can consist of several modules, but a module itself is an atomic unit.

Monthly quality report—Bug reports can come in at any time, including around the clock. However, for the purposes of management review and corrective actions, the natural reporting frequency is monthly, unlike productivity where the natural reporting frequency is annually. Monthly quality reports usually include data on both customer reported and internal bugs. An annual summary of quality data would be normal also.

Monthly status report—For large software projects (or any other kind), it is normal to report progress and problems on a monthly basis.

Monthly variance report—In many enterprises, the cost tracking systems for projects and departments generate a monthly report that shows budgeted versus actual expenditures. Such reports are normally called "variance" reports.

Multiple regression analysis—This is a statistical technique for exploring the impact of combinations of parameters on the outcome of a project or model. This powerful approach can be used to identify the influence of soft factors on hard data such as schedules, resources, quality, and costs.

Natural metric—This term denotes a simple, tangible metric which can normally be expressed in integer values such as "a dozen eggs." When the LOC metric originated in the days of tab cards and coding sheets, it was also a natural metric. Natural metrics are easy to use, but very limited in applicability and also prone to other errors if miscounted. See also "synthetic metric."

Net present value—This is a technique for comparing inflows and outflows of cash given some discount or interest rate that management employs as a standard return on investment. This method is often used to judge the attractiveness of investments.

New code—This is code that must be created specifically for a new program or system. The term "new code" implies the task of coding, and excludes reused code.

Non-commentary source statements (NCSS)—This term is used for both estimating and measurement, and refers to the executable and data definition portions of program or system, but not to comments. Except for pure coding and activities closely tied to coding (such as code inspections) all code related metrics are hazardous for productivity and quality measures. See also "LOC Paradox" and "KLOC."

Non-exempt—This cumbersome term defines project staff members that are "not exempt from overtime" and hence must be paid overtime if they go beyond the normal work day or work week. The U.S. Department of Commerce and the Bureau of Labor Statistics are the originators of the term.

Noise—This term, derived from Information Theory, means random or unwanted signals added to a message. For software projects, the term can also mean functions added by the development staff but not requested by the users. This is a surprisingly common occurrence, and one study found about 15% of the delivered functionality consisted of noise-level functions which the developers thought "might be useful." See also "Creeping Improvements" and "Transmission Loss."

Noise-level problem—This term denotes a minor problem which does impact the basic functioning of an application. A spelling error in a message is an example of a noise-level problem. The term is borrowed, perhaps incorrectly, from Information Theory. See also "Severity level."

Normal form—This term is taken from mathematics but has become wide spread in software in the context of relational data base technology, where it refers to the several ways of ordering information, such as first normal form, second normal form, etc.

Normalization—This term defines the mathematical conversion of raw data to a standard form. The purpose of normalization is to allow comparisons between projects. The usual form of normalization for software is to convert cost and effort data into "cost per Function Point," "Cost per KLOC" or a similar basic metric.

NPATH complexity metric—This is one of the emerging techniques for exploring the structural and control flow complexity of software. The NPATH metric deals not only with basic control flow, but with iterations of loops and total execution.

Object—This is a term used in a special way under the object-oriented paradigm. Its definition there in is roughly equivalent to a module. However, an object is a collection of both data and functionality, which latter is termed "method."

Object-oriented paradigm (OO)—This is an emerging and significantly different form of programming which deals with encapsulated functional and data units termed "objects." The advantage of objects is that once defined, they can share certain aspects with similar objects via a technique called inheritance. This facilitates reusability and enhances both quality and reliability. The OO domain started with programming languages such as Smalltalk, Actor, Objective C, and C++. It is rapidly expanding, and now includes OO analysis and design, and OO data bases. The OO paradigm is growing fast enough to have formed its own magazines, conferences, created its own gurus, and is rapidly becoming a major sub-industry in its own right.

On-line software—Denotes software that is used interactively and provides immediate or nearly immediate responses. An example of on-line software would be an airline reservation system. See also "Batch Software."

Open office environment—Denotes a physical office arrangement in which desks and workers are placed in large areas without any walls or partitions. So far as can be determined, this is the least effective and efficient arrangement for software of all possibilities. See also "physical office environment."

Operational plan—An intermediate planning interval, in the range of perhaps three years. The term derives from military science, and is similar in concept to the three levels of military planning; i.e tactical, operational, and strategic.

Operations research—This term, originating during World War II, denotes a formal mathematical discipline dealing with the study of large and complex activity chains. Operations research has useful applications than span the range from military planning to the distribution of consumer products.

Opinion survey—Since enterprises where the staff morale is good often have better productivity than enterprises where staff morale is bad, annual or semi-annual opinion surveys are a natural adjunct of a full productivity improvement program.

Opportunity—For software projects, this term has come to mean a problem that someone has found. Rather than use the negative term "problem," the term "opportunity" has become a euphemism.

Order of magnitude—This term is defined as a ten-fold increment or decrement compared to a base value. For software, the term is often misused in advertising by statements of "order of magnitude improvements in productivity" without any tangible evidence at all.

Organization structure—This term denotes the functional departments and the network of reporting hierarchies that make up an enterprise. This is an important term due to the impact that organizations have on software productivity and quality. As a rule of thumb, centralized organizations are more productive than decentralized. Specialist groups such as maintenance and testing departments are more productive than generalist organizations where everyone does everything. Hierarchical management structures are more productive than matrix management structures. The data that supports these assertions is fragmented, but reasonably believable.

Orthogonal Defect Classification—This term, new in 1992, denotes a new categorization scheme for defects created at IBM's T.J. Watson Research Laboratory. This scheme associates defects with the major deliverables which must be repaired in order to correct the defect. There is much merit in this approach, and its publication may well resolve some ambiguities with more traditional taxonomies for defects. See also "Defect Origins."

Outsource—A fairly new term, originating circa 1990, meaning contracting with a vendor for all of the work of an entire software and data processing function. Outsourcing is often perceived (and often truly is) as more cost effective than internal software and data processing groups. Domestic outsourcing deals with companies in the same country. International outsourcing deals with companies in other countries.

Output—A generic term defining one of the physical or logical creations of an application that leaves the application's boundary in an outgoing direction. Also, a term used in the calculation of Function Points, with a similar meaning. In the context of Function Points, an output is abbreviated to OT (for output type) in the 1984 IBM method. The 1990 IFPUG method used EO (external outputs), while the 1990 Albrecht and SPR methods use OT (output type) for the same concept.

Overhead—This term has a number of widely different meanings. One basic meaning is a service that is given to users, such as developing software. This definition is used in opposition to "cost center" which implies payment for a service. A second definition means the rent, utility bills, etc. necessary to house an enterprise. A third use of overhead is as the set of staff and activities that are necessary to run an enterprise, but who are not direct contributors to the projects or products which the enterprise creates. Corporate management, purchasing departments, etc. comprise overhead functions.

Overlap—It is very common for software activities such as coding to start before previous activities such as design are complete. The general term for this phenomenon is overlap and it can be defined as the percentage of a previous activity still unfinished when the successor activity begins. For example if Task A requires 4 calendar months to complete and Task B starts when Task A is finished with the third month, then Task B overlaps Task A by 25%. Both schedule and resource overlap exist.

Overtime—This term means work carried out beyond the normal working period of the enterprise, such as late in the evening, weekends, and holidays. Overtime can be either paid or unpaid. Unpaid overtime is one of the major sources of error for both measurement and estimation of software.

Package acquisition—This term means the purchase or lease of software from an outside source, rather than development. This is a major cost element, and one large international company discovered that their production library had more packages than any single class of software developed by the enterprise itself.

Package evaluation—This term denotes the more or less careful examination of one or more programs before deciding to acquire it. Some large corporations have full-time package evaluation groups staffed by package evaluation specialists.

Package modification—This term means enhancing or modifying purchased or leased software to customize it to local requirements. This task is one of the most hazardous and risk-prone activities in all of software. If the vendor provides support and help then package modification is acceptable. If the vendor will not assist, the package modification is very often not economical.

Paperwork—This term means the sum of all paper deliverables which support and surround a software project; i.e. requirements, plans, specifications, user documentation, fault reports, correspondence, and the like. Collectively paperwork is the first or second most expensive activity in software. For military projects, paperwork costs usually exceed all others, and for large non-military projects the total paperwork costs are usually in second place. MIS projects tend to produce some 20 different document types containing an aggregate of 30 English words for every source code statement. Commercial software that is to be marketed usually produces some 50 different document types containing about 80 English words for every source code statement. Military and defense projects following military specifications may produce up to 100 different documents containing an aggregate of almost 400 English words for every Ada source code statement.

Paradigm—This word is borrowed from other sciences, and means a general synthesis of the concepts of a science. For example, the concept of plate tectonics is a paradigm from geology. For software, several paradigms seem to exist at any given time. For example, the waterfall and spiral models are paradigms of alternate development approaches.

Parameter—This term denotes a single factor or variable that can influence the outcome of model or equation. More than 300 parameters have been identified that can influence software productivity by at least 1%. There are more parameters than percentage points because military, commercial, and MIS projects are not influenced by the same set of parameters, nor are development and enhancement projects. There are about 80 parameters that can create a 5% shift, 30 parameters that can create a 10% shift, and about a dozen that can create a shift of 15% or more.

Parametric analysis—This term denotes the study of the relative importance of parameters on the outcome of a model or equation, often by means of multiple regression techniques. Parametric analysis is one of the fundamental underpinnings of software estimating. See also "Macro estimating" and "Micro estimating."

Pareto analysis—This is one of the mathematical techniques used to evaluate the sources and distribution of errors. It is often used by Quality Circles and during training in Total Quality Management (TQM). Pareto analysis may also be part of Quality Function Deployment (QFD).

Partially reusable code—This term implies existing modules that can be linked or added to a new program or system, but these partially reusable modules require some customization prior to being usable. Partially reusable code is an intermediate step on the path to reusable code. The modifications raise the defect potentials of the partially reusable code to perhaps unsafe levels. See also "Borrowed code" and "Reusable code."

Participative management—This term denotes a formal approach to running projects in which managers and staff more or less equally contribute to the setting of goals.

Passive quality assurance—This is a semi-pejorative term applied to Quality Assurance groups whose task is not to review or test software, but to monitor and ensure that reviews and tests are carried out to corporate standards. The opposite term is "Active Quality Assurance."

Penetration team—This term, usually restricted to military projects, defines a special group of expert programmers who attempt to break through the protective devices of a computer or software system as part of its test cycle.

People management tasks—This term refers to the personnel and human oriented tasks which are a normal part of software management. The people management tasks include interviewing, hiring, motivating, appraising, promoting, transferring, and terminating. See also "Project management tasks."

Percentages—This term implies the use of percentages for displaying the findings of a study. Although this is a common technique, it is fraught with error and is the source of many serious misunderstandings for software. One of the oldest uses of percentages has been to illustrate the overall magnitude of costs by phase, such as the traditional "design took 40%, coding took 20%, and testing took 40%" assertions. The problem with the use of percentages is that there are no stable relationships that will stay constant from project to project. Using percentages for estimating is as unprofessional as would be a medical doctor diagnosing flu for a patient simply because 60% of other doctor's patients have the flu.

Perfective maintenance—Modifications to a software program or system in order to improve performance, appearance, elegance, or some other attribute. See also "adaptive maintenance," "corrective maintenance," and "mandatory maintenance."

Person-month—This is the modern and non-sexist equivalent to the older term "man-month." The definition is the same, and means the normal working period of hours or days associated with average calendar months. This factor is intrinsically troublesome for large-scale studies involving multiple companies and multiple countries. Not only are there major variations in holidays and vacation periods, but also in corporate culture and work ethic. See also "Work hours" which is a more reliable unit of measure.

PERT—This is the acronym for "Program Evaluation and Review Technique." The concepts of PERT originated in the 1950's as an aid to building large naval military systems. The PERT method uses the concepts of milestones, activities, and slack time. Via liner programming, the PERT method can calculate the critical path, or the sequence of development steps that must be completed on time in order for the entire projected to be completed on time. See also "Critical Path."

Petri nets—This term denotes a special form of network analysis often used for dealing with information and control flow through software. Petri nets are often automated, and are useful in dynamic analysis and solution of timing problems.

Phases—This is the second stage in a normal five-level cost-collection sequence of project, phase, activity, task, and subtask. The term "phase" means the fairly gross divisions of a software development cycle into discrete stages. The normal phases for a software project include: 1) requirements; 2) top level or initial design; 3) detailed design; 4) coding or construction; 5) integration and test, ; 6) installation and training; 7) maintenance. It is not uncommon to conclude each phase with a formal review prior to funding or moving on into the next phase. Unfortunately, the phase concept is an artificial simplification that is often harmful. The harm occurs when phases are used as the final cost collection accounts for resources and costs. Many activities such as user documentation and project management span multiple phases. Therefore phase-related cost data tends to conceal vital information. A full Work-Breakdown Structure (WBS) is more difficult to administer, but much more valuable in the long run. Cost collection to the level of activities is much more useful than cost collection to the level of phases. See also "account," "activity," and "task."

Phase review—This term means a formal review at the completion of a major milestone such as completion of requirements or completion of top level design. Computer manufacturers and military software projects often have formal phase reviews, while MIS projects and internal software often omit this event. Phase reviews seldom live up to expectations in terms of rigor. Too often they are perfunctory, and projects sail through them only to be canceled as a result of an audit or some more thorough investigation of progress.

Physical environment—This term means the office space, furniture, and basic surroundings available for software staffs. The physical environment was shown to be a major productivity factor in the study by Tom DeMarco and Tim Lister, where programmers in the high quartile had over 78 square feet of office space, as opposed to less than 44 square feet for those in the low quartile.

PIER—This is the acronym for "Productivity Information Exchange Roundtable." PIER groups were started in the New England area in the late 1970's as an informal way of sharing software productivity information among interested companies. The concept has spread to the midwest, west, and Canada.

Piracy—This term denotes the unauthorized copying of licensed software without the permission or authorization of the vendor. Piracy is an unfortunate although common problem, and is endemic across many software-using organizations.

Planning—The prediction of the sequence of activities and the resources that must be used for a software project. A variety (more than 70) of automated planning tools are available on both micro computers and main frame computers that can assist in software project planning. Most of them require expert human planners to be used effectively though. See also "estimating" and "project management." See also "account" and "activity."

Planning horizon—This term denotes the normal period for which an enterprise prepares statements of profit and loss. The U.S. planning horizon is quarterly, as opposed to the Japanese planning horizon, which is annual. A secondary meaning denotes the distance into the future for long-range plans; i.e. three years, five years, or whatever. The United States is somewhat at a disadvantage for strategic planning, since a five-year plan exceeds the tenure during which many managers are in a single position.

Platform—This fairly new term defines the hardware and support software with which any given program is intended to operate. Some generic platforms include mainframes, minicomputers, or microcomputers. More specific platforms might get down to the level of specific chips and vendors.

Poisson distribution—This term denotes a form of statistical scattering often associated with software fault densities.

Politics—This term denotes the more or less secret management disputes and disagreements that are common in all large organizations. Politics have a surprising and major impact on software, and more than a few large projects have been disasters or even canceled because the various managers and executives involved disliked one another and refused to cooperate. See also "Corporate politics."

Portability—This term denotes software that can be moved from computer to computer with little or no modification. Some languages such as C and some operating systems such as UNIX and even MS-DOS facilitate portability. See also "Machine Independence." For inexplicable reasons, portability was defined as a quality attribute in a report by Dr. Barry Boehm. Portability is important, but actually has nothing to do with quality. Unfortunately, this misalignment of the concept as a quality parameter has continued under various quality standards such as ISO 9000.

Portfolio—This term means the entire set of programs and systems owned by an enterprise at any point in time. Major corporations have enormous portfolios that sometimes exceed 100 million source code statements or 8 million Function Points divided among 25,000 or more small programs and more than 500 medium to large systems. The economic and productivity implications of portfolios is becoming a major new measurement and estimating topic. See also "production library" which is essentially a synonym.

Post mortem—This term denotes a meeting of management and staff held after completion of a software project to discuss what went right, what went wrong, and what might be done in the future to improve development. Post mortems are often useful. During a post mortem, the sizes of all deliverables (Function Points, source code, pages, and test cases) should be confirmed. All resources expended, schedules, and influential soft factors should also be noted, so that the post mortem data can be used to estimate future similar projects. Post mortems normally take about 4 hours, and are well worth the investment.

PRICE-S—This was the first commercial software cost estimating program in the United States. It was developed by the RCA corporation, and has been marketed since 1974. In its original form, PRICE-S was calibrated for large military projects only. It has evolved over time to handle a wider range of projects and smaller sizes as well.

Private defect—This term denotes bugs found by the developers themselves, as opposed to bugs found by quality assurance, test groups, or users. Since most enterprises do not require staff to report on their own bugs (nor should they), very little empirical data exists as to the volume of private defects. A few studies using volunteers indicate that private defects comprise about 15% to 30% of the total defect volumes for software projects. See also "Public Defects."

Proactive—This recently-coined term is the opposite of "reactive" and denotes trying to solve problems before they occur, as opposed to merely waiting passively.

Process—This term means the step by step sequence of activities that must be carried out to complete a project. There is a more specialized meaning also, in the form of "process control" which defines a type of software used to deal with continuous flows of materials, such a pulp paper or oil.

Production library—This term means the complete set of programs and systems which an enterprise has available for use. A large scale study of IBM's production libraries by Bob Kendall and Charles Lamb revealed some surprising findings. The average life expectancy of an application in the production library was less than 16 months before it disappeared, with infant mortality being quite astonishing. Less than 5% of the applications used more than 50% of the total MIPS available. See also "portfolio." See also MIPS.

Production rate—This important term defines the amount of a deliverable that can be produced by a single worker in a standard time period, such as a month. The unit of production can be any reasonable deliverable, such as Function Points, Source Code or pages of specifications. The production rate and assignment scope concepts form a powerful set for estimating purposes.

Productive work—This term roughly means the amount of actual employee working time in the course of a day or week. Due to lunch, coffee breaks, and the like, the amount of productive work during a normal 8 hour day will be just over 5 hours in the United States. There are major differences in this factor from among companies and from country to country.

Productivity—This widespread and important term had no precise definition for software from the inception of the industry until October of 1979, when Albrecht published the Function Point metric. The normal economic definition of productivity has been "Goods or services produced per unit of labor and expense." Until the invention of Function Points, the economic definition could not be used due to the lack of precision in defining software's goods or services. Since "lines of code" are not economic commodities, and coding is not the primary activity of large system development, LOC metrics could not be used for productivity measurement. Several informal and alternate definitions for productivity were usually ambiguous and imprecise, such as the very common "finishing a project on time and within budget." See also "LOC paradox."

Productivity analysis—This term is roughly equivalent in meaning to "process assessment." It was used by Software Productivity Research in the years 1985–1988 as the definition for the kind of assessment which SPR carried out. See also "Baseline."

Productivity improvement plan—This term denotes a formal plan that encompasses the steps on the path to improving software productivity. Such plans are normally established for as long as five years in the future, with very detailed planning assumptions for the next year.

Productivity improvement rate—This term denotes the annual increase in productivity which is anticipated by an enterprise. For large corporations, 10% annual improvement is a normal upper limit while more than 15% a year would be quite remarkable. Long range studies of companies over several years indicates that productivity improvement correlates strongly with the starting position. Companies that were well below U.S. norms tend to improve slowly. Companies that were already ahead of U.S. norms tend to improve more quickly. For the software industry as a whole, productivity tends to double at

about ten year intervals. Of course individual projects can be improved faster, but entire corporations usually cannot. It is important to also consider quality. See "Quality Improvement Rate."

Productivity paradox—This term originated circa 1992, and is related to observations by economists that the return on investment in software, computing, and related services by many enterprises appears to be negative; i.e. only about $0.80 returned for every $1.00 invested. However, the data on which these claims are made is uncertain. The topic is generating a number of articles, and some interesting new research among academic institutions and business schools.

Profit center—This term denotes a part of an enterprise that actually generates revenue by marketing its services to outside companies and clients. There is an evolution that occurs when companies become sophisticated with software and computing. They usually start by providing software services to internal clients for free, as an overhead function. Then a point is reached when the company decides to charge for these services, and the software function becomes a cost center. If this is successful, then the company may decide to generate new revenues and the software organization can become a profit center. For some companies such as Boeing and McDonnell Douglas, this evolution has been quite successful.

Program—This term defines a unified collection of code, often segmented into modules, that performs a specific business or technical task. Programs are usually considered to be smaller than systems, and are often the product of a single programmer. The average size of programs in industry in the U.S. is approximately 1200 source code statements or 10 Function Points. The term "program" also has other meanings. In the military, the term sometimes means a massive interweaved set of hardware and software activities associated with a weapons system, such as "the Aegis program." In casual and informal discussions, the word "program" can mean a plan.

Program generator—This term denotes a short-hand way of creating software by means of a descriptive mechanism that describes inputs, outputs, and processing steps without using a procedural programming language. The output of a program generator is usually an executable program, and often source code in a recognizable language such as COBOL. Program generation is a rapidly evolving technology with a reasonably impressive track record. Program generators differ from Application Generators in that the output of a program generator is usually a program that can actually be executed. Output from an application generator normally requires some form of run-time servicing from the generator in order to execute. However in day to day parlance, application and program generators overlap. For productivity measurement purposes, the input to the program generator is the normal unit of measure, not the output from it.

Program trouble report (PTR)—This term denotes a written description of a specific bug or defect. Variations such as "program trouble memorandum" or PTM also occur (IBM, for example, uses PTM). For most efficient statistical analysis, each PTR should contain only one problem description, and it should contain codes for the severity and probable origin of the problem.

Programming—This term originated for software in the 1940's when the computer era began. In those early days, programming and coding were more or less synonymous. Today programming has an expanded definition and includes

all of the tasks needed to develop and maintain software: design, specifications, coding, testing, documentation, and so forth.

Project—This term defines a contiguous set of programs and deliverables that will be created using more or less consistent methods by a team that is assigned to the task more or less from beginning to end. It is perhaps easier to give examples of the term "project" than to define it. A new compiler created by a software house, an order entry system created for a manufacturing company, and a personnel benefits tracking system for a bank are all examples of projects. Other examples include the software for a PBX by a telecommunications company, and an integrated software design tool by a CASE vendor. This term also refers to the top level in a five-layer system for accumulating software costs: 1) project; 2) phase; 3) activity; 4) task; 5) subtask.

Project class—This term is used by the SPR estimating models to denote the business or contractual arrangement governing a software project. Fifteen classes are used, which range from a Class 1 personal project to a Class 15 military project. In real life as well as in the SPR models, the class concept affects the paperwork and production methods in significant ways. See also "Project Type."

Project management system—This term denotes software packages that provide aid for one or more of the project management tasks. Surprisingly, most project management systems only do a single task, such as plan. Unfortunately, the artificial restriction of the phrase "project management" to tools which primarily created PERT charts, GANTT charts, and leveled resources is a serious terminology flaw. A new generation of integrated project management systems that aid all six project management tasks (sizing, planning, estimating, tracking, measuring, and assessing) is currently emerging.

Project management tasks—This term denotes the tasks for which managers are normally responsible when in charge of software. The usual set of project management tasks includes planning, estimating, sizing, tracking, and measurement. More recently, assessment has been added to the set. See also "Department management tasks" and "People management tasks."

Project manager—This term denotes the senior executive in charge of a software project. This occupation is so well defined that there are conferences, newsletters, and other communications that circulate among project managers. The term is much broader than software, and also is used for hardware, weapons systems, and many other categories. See also "Project Supervisor" and "Project management functions."

Project nature—This term is used in the SPR estimating models to denote whether a project is new, an enhancement, a conversion, a maintenance project, or a package acquisition project.

Project office—This term denotes a special department associated with large systems that contains specialists whose job is planning, estimating, and monitoring the progress of the system itself. For systems in excess of 1 million source statements or 8000 Function Points, project offices are not uncommon.

Project scope—This term is used by the SPR estimating models to provide generic size definitions. Eight scope levels are currently used: 1) disposable prototype; 2) evolutionary prototype; 3) module or sub-element of a program; 4) reusable module or macro; 5) complete stand-alone program; 6) program within a system; 7) major system; 8) follow-on release of a system. Each scope implies various activities. For example,

systems and follow-on releases normally imply the need for integration, configuration control, formal testing, and the like. Such activities are not assumed for prototypes, for example.

Project supervisor—This term denotes a lower-level manager who is usually responsible for a single department or team. See also "Project Manager."

Project type—This term is used by the SPR estimating models to denote the technical nature of a software project. Fourteen types are used, which range from a Type 1 nonprocedural application to a Type 13 Artificial Intelligence program. Type 14 is reserved for hybrid projects containing multiple types. In real life as well as in the SPR models the type concept affects productivity. See also "Project Class."

Project productivity—This is the most widely discussed productivity measure in the United States. The normal definition of project productivity is the sum of the direct effort devoted to the development of a successfully completed project. For MIS projects, it is becoming the standard to use Function Points for project productivity measures, and rates of about five to 20 delivered Function Points per staff month would not be uncommon. Note that canceled projects, indirect effort, and many other elements are outside the scope of project productivity as it is commonly defined. See also "Enterprise Productivity" and "Individual Productivity."

Proposal—This term means a formal assertion to a contracting office that an enterprise can build a program or system that meets the specifications of the contracting group. Proposals vary in formality and contents. The proposal itself often follows a "Request for Proposal" by the contracting office. For military and DoD contractors, the proposal process is both extensive and expensive.

Prototype—This term denotes a partial version of a program done as an aid to designing the final product. Two forms of prototypes are common: disposable and evolutionary. A disposable prototype is created as a temporary object to aid in clarifying certain features, and then discarded when its purpose is complete. An evolutionary prototype is built as a skeleton of the complete program, and the additional functions are appended later. Disposable prototypes have been demonstrated to be successful as aids for software, but the evolutionary prototypes often lead to problems later. The short cuts that are normal when prototyping often cause less than optimal structure and less than careful defect removal. Prototypes range in features, but tend to mirror from 5% to 15% of the functionality of completed projects. See also "Time-box prototype."

Public defects—This term denotes bugs found by someone other than the original programmer or author, such as bugs found by a quality assurance group, test group, or the users of a software project. See also "Private Defects."

PYRAMID—At one time this was an acronym, but the meaning seems to have disappeared. In any case, the term refers to a European research project in software measurement and metrics. The PYRAMID project has involved many companies and countries, and has done innovative work. However, there has been an unfortunate tendency for PYRAMID research to stay with LOC metrics and avoid functional metrics. PYRAMID is a part of a larger European effort in software research termed ESPRIT.

QAI—This term stands for the "Quality Assurance Institute" which is a private family-owned seminar and consulting organization headed by Bill Perry.

Quality—This term is extremely ambiguous for software. It has been variously defined to mean conformance to user requirements, high levels of customer satisfaction, reliability, and a low number of bugs found in a given program or system. Most of the common definitions are subjective and semi-unmeasurable, except for treating quality as the number of bugs found. It is notable that software with a high bug count is almost never satisfactory under any of the other definitions of quality.

Quality assurance—This term has several meanings that cover a broad range of possible work. The oldest meaning defined a group of specialists who were responsible for testing software and were termed the Quality Assurance group. Presently this concept changed, so that some Quality Assurance groups did not test software themselves, but only monitored the tests. It is also possible to assign Quality Assurance responsibility to the developers themselves, without having a formal independent group at all. The overall meaning of the word is some type of formally assigned responsibility for ensuring that quality is not ignored. A fully staffed active Quality Assurance group in a modern high technology corporation may account for perhaps 5% of the total software professionals. If the QA staff falls below 3%, there is a chance that they will be overstressed. See also "Active Quality Assurance" and "Passive Quality Assurance."

Quality circle—This term denotes an organized set of employees trained in the mathematics of quality who meet on a voluntary basis to focus on improving the quality of products, processes, and methodologies. The concept is an outgrowth of the work of J. Edwards Deming and has been pragmatically successful in many industries and for many kinds of work. For software in the

599

U.S., the technique has not been widely utilized. The fact that U.S. programmers have been found to be low in the need for social interaction may be part of the reason. Japan currently has more quality circles per capita than any other nation.

Quality function deployment (QFD)— This term denotes a fairly new method, long used in Japan for engineered products. Under QFD protocols, users and software developers meet during the requirements phase to explore the kinds of quality factors which the users care about. The system or application is then built with these factors as integral parts. QFD is new in the United States, and the preliminary results are useful. QFD and JAD have some similarities, but with QFD the focus is primarily on quality.

Quality improvement plan—This term denotes a year by year description of the methods and steps an enterprise will go through in order to improve software quality. Normally the introduction of full design and code inspections, front-end process improvements such as Joint Application Design (JAD), and better test control are included, as are restructuring, error-prone module removal, and so forth.

Quality improvement rate—This term denotes the speed with which an enterprise can improve quality. Due to inspections, error-prone module removal, and other techniques that have an almost immediate impact, quality can be improved by as much as 25% to 40% a year even for large corporations. At this rate, quality can compound to six-sigma levels within five years. It is important to improve quality at a faster rate than productivity, or else the cost of maintenance will go up as more and more mediocre code is added to a production library.

Quarterly profit and loss report—This is a normal U.S. reporting interval for financial data. Quarterly reports are usually more condensed and less elegant in physical appearance than annual reports. Some enterprises report on software productivity at the quarterly intervals, although quarterly fluctuations are often semi-random. It is interesting that Japanese profit and loss statements are only prepared on an annual basis, which gives Japanese managers a longer planning horizon than their U.S. counterparts.

Queuing theory—This is a mathematical subdiscipline which deals with the arrival at and departure from queues. Queuing theory is part of the fundamental mathematics of the service business, and also used for computer design.

Ratios—Many common rules of thumb are expressed in terms of ratios, or the quantity of one kind of work related to some other kind of work. Common ratios include such topics as a 1 to 1 ratio between programmers and terminals, a 1 to 8 ratio between managers and staff, a 1 to 10 ratio between technical writers and programmers and so forth. The ratio concept is frequently misused and often leads to erroneous conclusions.

Raw data—This term defines the unvalidated information that might be collected by a tracking system during the course of a software project. The accuracy of raw data is so low that it can seldom be used for serious studies of productivity or quality. The usual problems with raw data are the omission of many activities, such as requirements, user documentation, management, and overhead tasks such as integration. Secondary problems with raw data include accidental charges to the wrong accounts, unpaid overtime, and reporting errors. The error content of raw data may range from 30% to 50%.

Rayleigh curve—Lord Rayleigh was a British physicist of the late 1800's and early 1900's. He discovered a family of curves that often approximated natural phenomena such as the spread of epidemics. These curves were explored by Peter Norden of IBM as a possible way of representing the growth of staff and effort for software projects. Colonel Larry Putnam of the U.S. Air Force developed the SLIM estimating model around the concept of Rayleigh curves. One very notable aspect of Rayleigh curves is the relationship between the time and effort axes. Time and effort are not interchangeable, and with Rayleigh curve mathematics, attempts to compress a schedule closer than its natural end point will drive up effort in a dramatic fashion.

Real-time software—This term has two fairly distinct definitions. The oldest definition meant software that was required to execute almost instantly, such as air traffic control systems or missile detection systems or radar software. A more recent evolution of the term has broadened the definition so that it includes various interactive systems that give answers while the user is logged on and waiting, even though several seconds or even minutes might go by, such as airline reservation systems.

Red flag item—This term denotes a serious problem that requires management attention. The term is used in context with monthly status reporting.

Reengineering—This is an emerging term that is defined as extracting the latent information contained in the source code of an aging existing program or system in order to develop a new and improved version of the existing software. The technical idea of re-engineering is that much of the missing design information that is normally lost as software ages is actually present but hidden in the code itself. By sophisticated expert systems methods, this hidden information can be reconstructed. See also "Reverse engineering," "remodularizig," and "restructuring."

Reference library—A collection of books, journals, and other materials which an enterprise maintains for use of its technical staff members. The existence or absence of a good reference library is a surprisingly significant factor. U.S. leaders in both quality and productivity, and a statistically significant percentage of Baldrige Award winners, tend to have on-site reference libraries in excess of 5000 volumes. It is not certain if the existence of such reference libraries is a causal factor, or merely coincidental. Due to the significance of this topic, the present or absence of a reference library is a strategic factor analyzed when SPR assessments are performed.

Regression analysis—This term defines a statistical technique used to quantify the impact of a parameter on the outcome of a model.

Regression testing—This is a special form of testing used when software is updated or enhanced. In this case the word "regression" means to move backwards, and regression testing is carried out to ensure that the current updates have not degraded or damaged any previous functions.

Relationship—This term is often used in the phrase "entity-relationship." It denotes the associations and linkages which might occur among various entities. For example, the entities "parent" and "child" denote a relationship between the two.

Reliability—This term is defined as the failure interval associated with a program or system in actual usage. Reliability is normally measured in terms of mean time to failure (MTTF) or mean time between failures (MTBF).

Reliability models—This term defines a set of mathematical and sometimes computerized models that attempt to predict the probable reliability of software under operational conditions. Most reliability models differ from reality in two major areas: they are insensitive to the clumping effect of error-prone modules; they do not adequately address the correlation between defect levels and failure rates, which may be due to the lack of empirical data available to the reliability modellers.

Remodularizing—This term is defined as breaking up large and unmanageable modules (more than 500 source code statements) into smaller and more intuitive segments. Remodularization is often carried out at the same time that aging software is restructured. Note that remodularization is a manual task and is not usually offered by restructuring software. See also "re-engineering" and "reverse engineering."

Repository—This term was made popular by IBM in the late 1980's when it was featured as the central storage mechanism for the AD/Cycle suite of integrated CASE tools. In principle, a repository should be able to contain all of the information associated with software projects: text, numeric information, graphics, images, and perhaps voice data and multi-media information as well. The quantity of all information for a major software house is so enormous that optical storage and an object-oriented data base would seem the only viable host for a full repository. The concept is evolving over time at a rapid rate.

Requirements—This term is defined as the statement of needs by a user that triggers the development of a program or system. In addition to this basic definition, there are many other implications that surround requirements. Although Phil Crosby, the former ITT Vice President of Quality, makes a case that "quality means conformance to requirements," it has been observed for software that the requirements themselves are among the chief sources of

error. It is very common that requirements for software projects are incomplete, ambiguous, and frequently changing.

Request for proposal (RFP)—This common term means a formal statement by a contracting office that they are soliciting enterprises to bid on a contract for a program or system. This is the normal way that military and government software often begins, as do many other large systems.

Research—This term denotes an exploratory mode of searching for new and improved methods, tools, and approaches. Many large corporations such as IBM and ITT have established actual software research laboratories. The normal size of these laboratories is a total of about 125 to 150 staff members.

Research and development—This is a general concept used by businesses for the essentially exploratory work of bringing out new systems and new products. There are a number of general rules or correlations about the relationship between R & D expenses as a percentage of sales, or about the impact of R & D on long-term corporate success. One of the negative aspects of venture financing is the tendency to reduce R & D expenses and drive up marketing expenses.

Resource—This term is used to mean a worker or staff member by many project management tools. Resource can also have a more general meaning as a repository of useful data or help.

Resource leveling—This term means balancing the available staff hours or days against the tasks to be accomplished, and either slipping or readjusting tasks to match the available staff time. Resource leveling is complex when performed by hand or with a calculator, but is a standard function of most project planning tools.

Resource overlap—It is not uncommon for any given staff member to work on several tasks during the same day, such as design and coding. Unless a very precise tracking system is used, these mixed tasks become blurred together and make it difficult to measure the true costs of either.

Response time—This term, usually measured in seconds, means the delay after striking the enter key before a terminal or work-station can accept the next command. Empirical studies by IBM indicate that if the response time is above one second, a worker's mind will drift off onto other topics so that the effective lost time is actually much greater than the response time itself. In a survey of more than 100 enterprises, average U.S. response time is somewhere between one and five seconds for mainframe and minicomputer terminal users. One of the notable advantages of fast personal computers and work stations is that they routinely offer sub-second response time for many tasks which formerly tool more than five seconds.

Restructuring—This term is defined as the restoration of an existing program or system so that it adheres to the formal structured programming conventions, without degrading the functions of the existing software or destroying its usefulness. Restructuring is a fairly new technical area which originated in the early 1980's. The more sophisticated restructuring tools are based on graph theory and operate by first graphing the existing structure, then simplifying the graph, then restructuring the code itself. The pragmatic results of restructuring usually reduce complexity and simplify maintenance, although the size and performance of the restructured code may be slightly less than optimal. COBOL, FORTRAN, and PL/I are the languages that currently have some form of restructuring tools available.

Retirement rate—This term has a technical definition that means the frequency with which applications are dropped from a production library. Typically, more than 15% of the applications in a production library will disappear on an annual basis.

Return on investment (ROI) —This term is the general definition of a whole set of various methods for calculating whether an investment would be good or bad. See also "Accounting rate of return" and "Internal rate of return."

Reverse appraisal—This term denotes a review of managerial performance by employees who report to the manager. This concept is usually implemented via annual morale and opinion surveys. It has a practical utility, since bad management is one of the factors most strongly associated with poor productivity, poor quality, and high attrition rates.

Reverse engineering—This term has several meanings. One of them is sinister, and implies taking apart a competitive product to copy it. A second definition is benign, and means studying an aging program or system in order to build a new and improved version.

Review—This term denotes a more or less formal examination of the specifications, code, or other deliverable from a software project. Reviews are similar in concept to both Inspections and to Structured Walkthroughs. In practice, reviews are often less formal and usually lack the rigor of measuring discovered defects.

Review cycle—This term denotes the normal chain of approvals which specifications, plans, and other project deliverables must go through. For large systems in geographically dispersed enterprises, the review cycle can be quite protracted.

Sometimes more than a dozen signatures may be needed.

Reusability—This is an important concept that means the ability to make subsequent use of standard parts and concepts. The idea of reusability more or less started with Eli Whitney, and has been of tremendous importance to manufacturing and industry. Reusability in software is only starting to be a serious research topic. The possibly reusable artifacts for software include reusable architectures, reusable designs, reusable specifications, reusable code or reusable modules, reusable test case, reusable data, and reusable documentation. Some companies and projects are already developing new applications with more than 75% reusable components by volume.

Reused code—This is code that is linked into a program or added to the program without actually being coded on a line by line basis. The concept of reused code implies a library of existing modules that can be accessed at will. Reusability also implies stability, in the sense that reusable code should not require modification before it can be used. If reused code does require any modification, then it becomes "borrowed code" or "Partially Reusable Code" and many of the economic advantages of full reusability disappear. Most experienced programmers have private libraries which allow them to develop software with about 30% reused code by volume. Reusability at the corporate level aims for 75% reused code by volume, and requires special library and administrative support. Corporate reusable code also implies changes in project accounting and measurement practices to give credit for reusability.

Risk—This term means the probability that a software project will experience undesirable events, such as schedule delays, cost overruns, or outright cancellation.

Risk is proportional to size and inversely proportional to skill and technology levels. In considering aspects of risk for large systems, the risk of schedule slippage approaches 100% since most such systems are late. The risk of cost overruns is greater than 50%. The risk of outright failure and cancellation is about 10%, since one out of every ten large systems begun in the U.S. will not be finished and delivered.

Risk analysis—This term denotes a more or less formal study of the potential hazards that might be encountered in the course of developing a new software system. Risk analysis is usually formal for military projects; informal for other classes of software.

Root cause analysis—This phrase, often used in both Quality Function Deployment (QFD), Total Quality Management (TQM), and process assesments denotes a formal backwards exploration from an instance of a problem to the ultimate reason why the problem occurred. For example, a root cause analysis of a particular bug or defect might trace it back to a coding error, a design error, or a requirements error, or even something else. The techniques and protocols of root cause analysis are important, and should be part of all software engineering and management curricula.

Scaffold code—This term denotes temporary code created to assist in testing or running part of an unfinished program or system. Usually the scaffold code is thrown away when the project is finished. Scaffold code is seldom studied empirically, so data on its volume and cost is sparse.

Schedule—This important term is defined as interval from the first day of requirements or the receipt of a project request until the day of delivery of the finished application. The difficulty with schedules is not the basic definition, but the

604

fact that dozens or even hundreds of overlapped and semi-overlapped activities must be considered.

Schedule overlap—This term denoted the fact that many software activities are still unfinished when follow-on activities begin. For example, requirements are still in flux when design commences. Design is still underway when coding begins. One way of measuring this overlap is a simple percentage; i.e. 25% of the requirements were added after design began. See also "spiral model" and "waterfall model."

Schedule pressure—This term means the implied or explicit threats which enterprise management levies upon software project managers in order to ensure that schedules are not slipped. Schedule pressure is among the chief sources of software cancellations and project disasters, since it leads to hazardous short cuts. European and U.S. companies are driven more by schedule pressure than by any other visible phenomenon.

Schedule slippage—This term means the deviation from an announced date of delivery for a project or some other deliverable. Analysis of software projects indicates a surprising rule: raise the initial schedule in months to the 1.05 power and the result will approximate the actual delivery schedule for a software project. Thus if the initial schedule is 18 calendar months, the actual schedule would be about 21 months.

Second-line management—This term denotes a manager to whom a layer of subordinate managers reports.

Security—This term denotes a host of important and widely diverse topics including physical security, data security, network security, military security, and many others. Projects with stringent security requirements normally pay a cost for this with extra effort, and hence have lower productivity.

SEER—This is one of several software cost estimating models aimed primarily at military and defense software. See also COCOMO, CHECKPOINT®, PRICE-S, REVIC, SoftCost, and SLIM.

Show stopper—This term denotes a problem severe enough to cause a project or deliverable to be canceled.

Silver bullet—This term originated in the lore than only a silver bullet could kill a werewolf. It became famous in software when Dr. Fred Brooks published a famous article entitled "No Silver Bullet" which contained the idea that it took more than one tool or method to make notable improvements in software productivity. Dr. Brooks' assertion remains true, but many vendors of tools have started calling their wares "silver bullets."

Silver bullet syndrome—The naive belief, often fostered by CASE and tool vendors, that a single tool or approach can make notable improvements in productivity. From SPR assessments, it can be stated that enterprises which succumb to the silver bullet syndrome not only fail to improve productivity by significant amounts, but many of them end up going backwards instead, due to the steep learning curves of some of the tools acquired.

Site—This term denotes a single physical location consisting of one or more buildings that are present on a tract of land under one ownership. Typical sites consist of office buildings, or research laboratories that may have multiple buildings on a single tract.

Site license—This term denotes a form of contractual arrangement for software in which the vendor allows multiple copies of the software to be used at a client site. This term is highly ambiguous because of variances in what a "site" truly means.

Six-sigma quality level—This phrase refers to a concept made famous by Motorola of achieving a defect rate of 1 error per million (i.e. .0000001). A similar concept is to express the defect removal efficiency as 99.999999%. As of 1993, six-sigma quality has seldom been achieved by large software projects. It is not intrinsically impossible, but it is not an easy task.

Size—This important term has many differing definitions. The overall concept is one of magnitude, but the exact unit is often ambiguous. Empirical data indicates that as size goes up, productivity comes down. Such data exists for size in terms of Function Points, Feature Points, source code, staff, and managers. It is interesting that the productivity reduction attributable to the managerial population seems greater than many other size factors. A still more surprising finding is that software productivity is related to the overall size of an enterprise, measured in terms of total employment. What is surprising here is that project productivity is highest at the extreme ends of the spectrum: companies with less than ten total employees and companies with more than 100,000 total employees. In the middle, there is a notable sag in productivity rates.

Sizing—This term is evolving rapidly. Its original definition was prediction of the amount of source code it would take to implement a program or system. Since 1985 it has been possible to size or predict not only source code, but also other deliverables such as specifications, documentation, test cases, and the like. A secondary definition used by some enterprises means a rough estimate of the resources needed to develop a program or system. Two diverse sizing techniques exist. The oldest was sizing by analogy, in which the deliverables for a new project were assumed to be roughly the same size as those of a similar older project. Since Function Points were publicized in 1979, a newer sizing technique has evolved by extrapolation from Function Points. The SPQR/20 software estimating model has included sizing of source code and major documents via Function Points since it originated in 1985, and was the first commercial software estimating tool to adopt Function Points as its standard sizing method.

Size/power formula—This term denotes a simplistic set of relationships that were originally discovered in the 1960's, and continue to be used although their intrinsic accuracy is not high. For COBOL, if the size of the application in KLOC is raised to the 0.6 power, the result will be the approximate calendar month from requirements to delivery. If the size of the application in KLOC is raised to the 1.4th power, the result will be the approximate amount of person months for the tasks of requirements, design, coding, testing, documentation, and management. For example, a 10 KLOC COBOL program would be 3.9 calendar months and 25 person-months using the above formula. The size/power formula is not very accurate even for COBOL and would be dramatically in error for languages that were of higher or lower level than COBOL. These simplistic formulas have a limited value only in doing reasonableness checks of estimates created by more formal techniques. Similar size/power formulae have been developed for Function Points and Feature Points, but here too, accuracy is not good enough for such formulae to be useful for serious estimating.

Skills inventory—This term denotes an organized data base that shows the academic and job experiences required for successfully occupying an employment position. Although skills inventories are often useful, they sometimes suffer from several problems, including misdefinition of skills, and excessive or artificial skill requirements. The whole concept is subject to trial and error methods.

Slack time—This has both a common and a technical definition. The common definition is time spent waiting to begin an assignment, or time spent between assignments, or time spent thinking on miscellaneous non-project tasks. The formal definition, taken from PERT, is the time spent waiting for a required predecessor task to be finished.

SLIM—This is the abbreviation for the Software Life Cycle Management estimating model developed by Larry Putnam and marketed by his company, Quantitative Software Management. SLIM was originally developed for large military projects, but has evolved over time to handle other types of software and smaller projects as well. SLIM was the first commercial software estimating tool to use the well-known concept of Rayleigh curves as explicit software predictors. See also BYL, BRIDGE, COCOMO, CHECKPOINT®, GECOMO, PRICE-S, REVIC, SPQR/20, and SoftCost.

SoftCost—This is a parametric software cost estimating model marketed since 1986. See also BYL, BRIDGE, COCOMO, CHECKPOINT®, GECOMO, PRICE-S, REVIC, SPQR/20. About 50 such models exist.

Soft data—This term signifies factors that are intrinsically subjective and prone to human interpretation. Examples of soft factors include the skills of programmers and analysts, the clarity of the requirements, and the completeness of the design. Although the soft data is subject to wide ranges of human error, it is important to collect such information because the soft data is the cause of variations in productivity and quality. With multiple-choice questions and reasonable care, the soft data can be both useful and meaningful. A total of more than 500 individual soft factors have

been identified that can cause productivity and quality variations, including skill factors, environmental factors, constraint factors, and many others.

Software—This term denotes computer programs and systems and the associated documentation that describe them, when the term is used in the context of the computer industry. (The recording industry also uses the term, but with a definition outside the scope of this glossary.)

Software effectiveness level (SEL)—This term denotes a five-point weighting scale developed and copyrighted by Software Productivity Research, Inc. The SEL scale is a five-point scale intended to show the usefulness of tools, methods, and environmental factors in such a way that statisticians can use the data for regression analysis. The SEL scale uses 1 for a rating of excellent, 2 for good, 3 for average, 4 for deficient, and 5 for poor. The SEL scale is a relative scale that is adjusted annually to match changing technologies. The SEL scale evaluates more than 400 items. The SEL scale is often compared to the SEI maturity scale, but the SEL scale is for statistical analysis while the SEI scale is only an overall umbrella of abstract concepts. It should be noted that the ranges are reversed between the SEI and SEL scales, with 1's and 5's having the opposite meanings between the two. The SEL scale is older than the SEI scale by several years.

Software engineer—This term denotes a formal job description used by some computer and high-technology corporations for staff that concentrate on systems and product software.

Software engineering—This term means the application of accepted canons of professional knowledge to the tasks of software development and maintenance. In reality, what is called software engineering is often very far from the ideal.

Software Engineering Institute (SEI)—This is a research and consulting organization funded by DARPA and located in Pittsburgh, Pennsylvania and associated with Carnegie Mellon University. See also "Maturity level" and "Software effectiveness level."

Software factory—This term denotes a form of software development first popularized by Japanese companies such as Hitachi. The software factory concept envisions software being produced like a manufactured product more or less following the assembly line technique.

Software physics—This term denotes a set of measurement techniques developed or described by Kenneth Kolence for measuring throughput and computer performance.

Software productivity analysis—This term is used by Software Productivity Research, Inc. to denote a rigorous study of all of the factors that impact software productivity and quality by as much as 1%. See also "Assessment."

Software Productivity Consortium (SPC)—This is a research and consulting company located in the Washington D.C. area that is sponsored by a number of military and defense companies. The Software Productivity Consortium (SPC), Software Engineering Institute (SEI), and Software Productivity Research, Inc. have similar names, but are not connected. SPR was incorporated in 1984, and is probably the oldest of the three groups.

Software Productivity Research (SPR)—This is a research, consulting, and product company located in Burlington, Massachusetts. Software Productivity Research and the Software Productivity Consortium and the Software Engineering Institute have similar names, but are not connected.

Software quality assurance (SQA)—This phrase denotes a special organization of personnel responsible for quality-related activities. SQA groups range in size from less than 1% of the general software population (which is too small to be effective) up to about 10%. An average SQA group runs to about 3%. See also "Active quality assurance" and "Passive quality assurance."

Software science—This term means the metrics developed by the late Dr. Maurice Halstead of Purdue University, and also known as Halstead Metrics. The term "software science is an unfortunate misnomer since many aspects are more mystical than scientific in the usual meaning of the word science. See also "Halstead Metrics" and "Zipf's Law."

Source code management system—This term denotes a library tool for keeping track of source code, and for protecting source code from unauthorized modification. Source code management systems record all updates, and assist in version control. See also "Configuration control" and "Repository."

Source code metrics—From the start of software in the 1940's until October of 1979, source code metrics were the only units of measure for software. In October of 1979 A.J. Albrecht of IBM gave a public lecture on Function Points and so provided the first alternative. Although source code metrics have been the norm for 45 years and are still the most widespread, they have a number of serious and permanent deficiencies. The lack of any standard definition is the first problem (See "Source line" and "Source statement"). This problem could be solved by a standards organization such as the IEEE, but the next problem cannot. The second and much more serious problem is the fact that source code metrics go the wrong way when measuring the productivity of high level languages. Both cost per source line and source lines per time period are worse for high level languages than for low level languages. This problem is due to the mathematics of the metric itself, and cannot be corrected. (See the "LOC Paradox.")

Source lines—This is one of the two major variations associated with counting source code. Source lines are defined as physical lines on a terminal or coding pad. The other major counting method is that of source statements. For languages such as COBOL that support multi-line conditional expressions, there may be twice as many source lines as source statements in a program. On the other hand, for languages such as BASIC with multiple statements per physical line, there may be four or five times as many statements as there are physical lines. Widespread failure by software authors to state whether their productivity data was based on lines or statements is one of the major embarrassments of software measurement and causes errors of several hundred percent.

Source statements—This is one of the two major variations associated with counting source code. Source statements are defined as statements terminated by a delimiter such as semi-colons that notifies the compiler that an expression has ended. For languages such as COBOL that support multi-line conditional expressions, there may be twice as many source lines as source statements in a program. On the other hand, for languages such as BASIC with multiple statements per physical line, there may be four or five times as many statements as there are physical lines. Widespread failure by software authors to state whether their productivity data was based on lines or statements is one of the major embarrassments of soft-

ware measurement and causes errors of several hundred percent.

Span of control—This term denotes the number of subordinates that report to a manager; normally eight in the United States. The term itself predates the computer era and originated in the 1880's when the U.S. Army studied the efficiency of troop movements of various sized units, and as a result, introduced squads and platoons. The span of control concept is usually only applied to the number of workers reporting to a manager, but there are related applications that are equally significant. For example, when seven or eight managers have to cooperate, or when groups of any occupation must work together the time spent communicating goes up more rapidly than the amount of tangible work performed. It is interesting that for software projects, the reduction in productivity as team size increases tends to correlate more closely to the number of managers than to the number of programmers. Projects with multiple managers are usually significantly lower in productivity than projects with only one manager, leading to the possible conclusion that a larger span of control with fewer managers and more workers might be a good choice for software.

Specialists—This term means a worker who has optimal skills and abilities for particular tasks. As the software and computer era mature, more and more identifiable types of specialists are starting to occur. The set today includes human factors specialists, estimating and measurement specialists, testing specialists, planning specialists, and some 35 more. In large corporations with more than 1000 total professionals employed in software, the population of specialists may be larger than the population of coding programmers. The number and types of software specialists is roughly proportional to the total number of software employees. Enterprises with less than 100 total software staff usually have few if any specialists. When the total staff rises above 500, then maintenance specialists and data base specialists, for example, usually appear. See also "generalists."

Specifications—This is the general term for a wide variety of paper-based descriptions of a program or systems. The full set of specifications can include any or all of the following: Functional specifications, Program logic specifications, detailed module specifications, requirements specifications, architecture specifications, and many more. The sum of the specifications for civilian projects can sometimes exceed 100 English words for every source code statement in COBOL, although the normal quantity is closer to 30 English words for every source code statement. For military software, up to 400 words per Ada statement have been noted. The specifications range broadly from totally non-existent to the largest contributor to overall systems costs. Military and DoD projects that follow military specifications will have formal and extensive specifications while internal MIS projects often have perfunctory specifications.

Spiral model—This is a newer depiction of a typical software development cycle than the traditional Waterfall Model. The Spiral Model assumes feedback and concurrency among tasks, which is more realistic than the linear organization of the Waterfall Model.

SPQR—This is the abbreviation for "Software Productivity, Quality, and Reliability" used as a trade mark by Software Productivity Research for its line of estimating and measurement tools, including SPQR/20. SPQR is also the ancient Latin abbreviation for "Senatus Populus Que Romanus" which translates to "the Senate and the People of Rome." SPQR was used on the banners of the Roman legions, and is still used commemoratively even today.

SPQR/20—This is the abbreviation for the Software Productivity, Quality, and Reliability estimating model developed by Software Productivity Research and marketed since 1985. The "20" stands for the approximate number of parameters involved in typical estimates. SPQR/20 deals interchangeably with MIS, systems, and military projects. This tool was the first commercial estimating for software to feature sizing logic based on Function Points. See also BYL, BRIDGE, CHECKPOINT®, COCOMO, ESTIMACS, GECOMO, PRICE-S, SEER, SLIM, SoftCost.

SPR Function Point method—This term refers to an alternative way of calculating Function Points developed by Capers Jones of Software Productivity Research, Inc. The SPR method gives results that in side-by-side trials on over 100 projects has matched the IBM method within 1.5%. However, the SPR method uses only three complexity parameters (Logical complexity, code complexity, and data complexity) and is significantly faster in usage. The SPR Function Point method is automated and is part of the SPR measurement and estimating product line (CHECKPOINT®, CHECKMARK®, and SPQR/20™).

Staff—This term has several alternative definitions. A basic definition is simply the people who work for an enterprise. A second definition is in opposition to "line" and means tasks that support product development but are not actually part of development; such as accounting and administration. A third definition means the direct reports to an executive; i.e. the staff that reports directly to a CEO or vice president. The word can also be used as a verb, where it means to hire or acquire new personnel.

Staffing buildup—This term denotes the rate at which a team or company can grow its staff. The software industry has a whole has grown at a rate of perhaps 12% a year since the 1960's. Empirical data suggests, but is not yet certain, that there is a maximum safe limit for building up a staff beyond which problems of control and communication become rampant. About 15% a year would be the maximum safe corporate growth rate for medium and large enterprises.

Stages hypothesis—This term denotes a concept that originated at Harvard with Warren MacFarland and Dick Nolan. The concept is that companies go through discrete plateaus or stages as they move through time. The specific domain of the stages hypothesis is the use of computers and software, and the assertion is that each stage has a characteristic spending profile and set of technical attributes. The stages hypothesis originated in the 1970's and is still in use, although it has been challenged. Artificial and arbitrary categorization schemes sweep through the software industry from time to time. See also "Maturity level."

Standard—This term defines a set of protocols that should be followed unless a formal deviation is approved. Standards may be local to a department, corporate-wide, industry-wide and developed by a standards organization such as the IEEE or the National Bureau of Standards. They may also be international and endorsed by the ISO or International Standards Organization. Standards for software engineering and for software management are being developed at all levels, and are in a state of flux. There are currently no national software quality or productivity measurement standards in the U.S. although the IEEE is preparing drafts of both. See also "Guideline."

Standard industry classification (SIC)—This term denotes a variable length code developed by the U.S. Department of Commerce that is used to identify several thousand industries and sub-industries for economic and statistical studies. A two-digit basic code identifies overall major industries, such as 48 for the communications industry. The third and fourth digits give finer breakdowns. The SIC concept is useful for software measurement and estimating, since it allows data to be organized in a meaningful way without actually revealing the names of specific companies.

Start date—This basic term is one of the hardest items of information to pin down for measurement or estimation purposes. The term itself means the point in time when development of a program or system begins. But for many programs and systems, a long period (maybe even a year or more) can go by before the need for and nature of an application becomes clear. The most effective way of setting the start date is simply an arbitrary decision by the senior management.

Static analysis—This term refers to defect removal steps that do not require execution of the software, such as inspections. The term "static analysis" is widely used by the defense contracting and military communities; is seldom used elsewhere.

Stein's paradox—This is an interesting statistical observation that the average of a set of averages may be a better indicator of performance than any given average.

Strategic factors—This term means those aspects of an enterprise that affect software, but which are global in scope. For example, the existence or absence of an overall business strategy will affect software. In a similar manner, factors such as dual salary plans, the physical office environments, and training for software staff members are strategic factors because they apply more or less globally throughout an enterprise. See also "Tactical factors."

Strategic plan—This term denotes a long range plan where the horizon is usually at least three and perhaps five years to ten years out. See also "Tactical plan" and "Operational plan."

Strange attractor—This term, derived from Chaos theory, defines the locations of stable patterns in turbulent phenomena. Strange attractors differ from the attractors of linear systems such as swinging pendulums in that their graphs are usually non-repeating curves. This concept is just starting to be explored for software, and may have utility in software cost and reliability estimating.

Strength report—This is an output from a Software Productivity Analysis that describes the areas where projects are better than U.S. norms. See also "Weakness report."

Stress testing—This term denotes a special kind of testing to see how a software product will operate under full load, or with maximum numbers of users.

Stroud number—This term denotes the questionable assertion that the human mind can make about 18 decisions a second. The Stroud number hypothesis is one of the less rigorous concepts associated with Halstead or Software Science metrics.

Structure—This term is used in both adjectival and adverbial form to describe almost any possible object or action connected with software; i.e. structured analysis, structured coding, structured design, structured documentation, and so forth. The definition of the term implies some sort of rigor and perhaps even a set of rules. The term is often used without any rigor at all, however. For sub-elements of this term, such as structured coding, there are rules and here the evidence suggests that adherence to the rules is advantageous for both quality and productivity.

Structured walk through—This term denotes a set of protocols for examining the specifications, code, and other deliverables. The concept is similar to that of an inspection, although formal design and code inspections have a more rigorous preparation and more careful tracking of the outcome. Historically, structured walkthroughs were invented by IBM Poughkeepsie while inspections were invented by IBM Kingston.

Stub—A temporary set of program statements created to allow a module to be tested.

Supervisor—This term denotes perhaps the lowest level of management, and implies a quasi-managerial responsibility for some technical staff members. The term also applies to the management of clerical and hourly rate craft personnel.

Support code—This term denotes the code that would be used in building tools that would in turn be used to build a software product. For example, if an enterprise built a test library as a precursor to building a large system, the code for the test library would be termed support code. This effort should be measured as a distinct project from the final application.

Synthetic metric—A metric that is derived from calculated information, rather than from direct observation. Examples of synthetic metrics include amperes, volts, joules, ohms, farads, and henrys from electricity; barometric pressure; horsepower, cholesterol levels, caloric contents, the Celsius and Fahrenheit temperature scales, and many others. Function points are an example of synthetic metrics associated with software. Synthetic metrics are far more pervasive in science and engineering than natual metrics, and often far more useful. The synthetic metric "horsepower" can be applied to electric motors and gasoline engines, for example. The synthetic metric Function Points can be used to measure requirements, design, coding, testing, and even management. As a class, synthetic metrics are far more powerful and useful than natural metrics such as LOC.

System—A system is a linked collection of programs or components that performs a generic business of technical function. Examples of systems range from accounting systems through operating systems. This is the largest size unit that is used for software. Some systems, such as IBM's MVS are larger than 8 million source code statements. The military "Star Wars" system may approach 30 million source code statements in size. Expressed in Function Points, systems may grow to 250,000 Function Points. The average size of a typical MIS system such as accounts payable is much smaller, however, being in the vicinity of 1000 to 10,000 Function Points.

System test—This term denotes the final stage of testing on a completed project, when all hardware and software components are put together as a whole.

Systems analysis—This term denotes the exploration and study of user needs, often by means of interviews and/or review of current methods.

Systems analyst—This term denotes a technical staff member occupying a job description that encompasses the task of systems analysis.

Systems assurance—Denotes a form of Quality Assurance that is aimed at ensuring that all parts of a system meet corporate goals and standards.

Systems development methodology (SDM)—Refers to a complex of tasks and deliverables that are organized toward developing software systems. The SDM concept originated in the 1960's as a response to the problems of building large software systems. SDM's

predefine the steps that must be taken, the progress reports, the format and content of specifications, the stages of testing, and so forth. SDM's are often effective for large systems, which is their forte. For small projects and enhancements they may be cumbersome and excessive. Many companies built their own SDM's in the late 1970's. Unless SDM's are refreshed and updated at frequent intervals such as annually, they tend to rapidly fall behind the state of the art.

Systems engineer—This term does not connote formal engineering degree, but means a technical staff member who is working on both hardware and software aspects of a system.

Systems software—This term is used in opposition to applications software, and is defined as software which is required to operate a computer or a physical device such as a switching system. The term includes operating systems, telephone switching systems, access methods, compilers, assemblers, and several others.

Tactical factors—This term denotes the specific aspects of a project that can cause it to vary from other projects. Tactical factors include the skills of the team, the specific tools available, and the methodologies used. See also "Strategic factors."

Tactical plan—This term denotes the specific improvements or changes in tools or methods that an enterprise will carry out in a fairly short time. Tactical Plans usually cover a 12-month period. See also "Strategic plan."

Targets—This term means quality, productivity, or schedule goals toward which a given project is aiming. Targets can be set with various metrics, and typical targets might include "Development productivity rates of more than 15 Function Points per staff month" or

"Cumulative defect removal efficiency higher than 95%." Targets can also be set amorphously, such as "improve quality by 50%" or "Achieve SEI level 3 within two years."

Task force—This term, originating in World War I, means a temporary grouping of technical and managerial staff chartered to explore a major issue. Task Forces are often useful for studying and bounding problems, but they are notably ineffective in actually solving problems. Excessive creation and use of task forces is a sign that the fundamental organization structure of an enterprise is defective and needs to be updated.

Technical writer—This term means a staff member occupying a formal job description, and responsible for documenting hardware, software, or systems. Not all software companies have technical writers, but those who do usually find that a ratio of one writer to every ten or 12 programmers would be the minimum useful number.

Template—This term unfortunately has two contradictory meanings: A) Since 1985, SPR has used this term means a set of estimating parameters derived from one or more completed projects. B) Since about 1990, Texas Instruments has used this term to mean a design derived from prior applications. SPR uses the term "blueprint" for this concept, which term is much closer to other forms of engineering than the TI usage of template.

Test case—This important term is surprisingly ambiguous, and has come to mean a set of protocols or test scripts that can validate one function of an application.

Testing—This term is defined as the set of defect removal tasks that include executing all or part of the application on a computer. There are more than 12 common forms of testing including unit test, function test, stress test, regression test, independent test, field test, etc.

When measured, testing has not been found to be either efficient or effective. Most forms of testing are under 35% in measured efficiency, and even a string of four or five different kinds of testing in a series can often yield results that are less than 50% efficient; i.e. less than one bug out of two will be removed.

Test library—This term means a formal collection of the test cases that are owned by an enterprise.

Third-line manager—This term means a manager with two lower layers of managers reporting in. This is normally the highest management group where the word "line" is used. There are some Fourth Line managers, but the normal title for an executive with three or more levels of subordinate management would be "Director" or "Vice President."

Throughput—This coined term is both important and ambiguous. The basic definition is the amount of work a computer system or software system can process in a given time period. The ambiguity resides in the fact that there are no standard benchmarks for measuring throughput. Empirical data is also surprising. If throughput includes outages and lost time while a system is in failure mode, measured over a long period of perhaps a month, then certain types of reliable software can outperform other modules that execute more rapidly but fail at frequent intervals.

Time-box prototype—This term denotes a special kind of prototype which was originated with the DuPont software organization. A specific time period is established (from three weeks to six weeks are the norm) and the entire prototype is completed within that period. This tends to give a sharp urgency to the work, and also a definite sense of closure. The time-box method has been fairly successful.

Time and materials—This term denotes a contractual arrangement in which the provider bills the client for the actual time spent on work, plus fees for producing any deliverables such as printing costs for reports, slides, and the like. This is a common form of contract for management consulting; less common for contract programming.

Time and motion study—This term means a set of formal observations and measures of how workers go about their tasks. The concept originated during World War I and has often been applied to various manufacturing operations. The concept is sometimes used for software studies as well.

Top down estimate—This term means estimating a complete project with a single equation, and then decomposing the estimating via ratios or percentages to calculate individual tasks. The term is roughly synonymous with macro estimating, and shares that methods intrinsic lack of accuracy. The opposite of top down estimating would be bottom up or micro estimating.

Total Quality Management (TQM)—This is a comparatively recent term which became current circa 1989. It refers to attempts to control quality by more all-pervasive means than simple inspections and standard QA practices. A TQM program also examines human behavior, all processes, acquisition, and so forth. Whether TQM will actually be effective, or merely be a temporary phenomenon such as the "zero defects" programs of the 1950's, is premature to assess. Preliminary observations indicate that when TQM is taken seriously, the results are impressive. When TQM is given lip service and used only as a slogan, the results are harmful.

Tracking—This term defines the accumulation of costs and resources over time, with the costs being assigned to specific tasks or a specific chart of accounts. Unfortunately, tracking is seldom accurate, and errors of omission occur that

total 30% to 50% of the real costs of a software project.

Training—This term means providing some form of tutorial or education to staff members. Although the distinction is often missing, "training" usually refers to courses dealing with a specific product or tool, while "education" usually refers to courses dealing with general concepts.

Transmission loss—This term, originally from Information Theory, has come to be applied to software with a slightly different set of meanings. For software projects, transmission loss refers to the functions that users requested that are accidentally omitted by the development staff. In empirical studies, about 10% of the requested functions of large systems are omitted more or less accidentally. See also "Noise" and "Creeping requirements"

Travel costs—For large international corporations, travel costs can be in the top five expense elements for software. One large multinational developed a system that needed more than 3000 trips back and forth across the Atlantic. The costs of travel on this system exceeded coding costs, although such enormous travel costs are rare.

Unbundled—This term denotes software that is priced separately from the hardware on which it resides. See also "Bundled."

Unit test—This is defined as testing carried out personally by individual programmers on their own code. This form of testing is by nature difficult to measure, since customarily employees are not asked to report their own errors. From time to time, volunteers do report their own errors for experimental studies, and the results of these experiments indicate that Unit Test is about 25% efficient, or will find 1 bug out of every 4 that is present.

Unpaid overtime—This term means work performed outside the normal working hours, where the employee is exempt or not paid for the work. Unpaid overtime is a major source of error for both software measurement and estimation. Several large systems have been examined where the staff hours approached 60 hours a week, but the unpaid overtime was not recorded. This is a major source of error for both measurement and estimation purposes.

Upper CASE—An ambiguous term which roughly means the set of tools available to support front-end activities in a software development cycle, such as requirements and high-level design. See also "lower CASE" and "middle CASE."

Unstable hardware—This term means a computer or platform for a developing program or system that is itself being built at the same time. This situation occurs in the computer business itself and in the telecommunications business. When it does occur, it causes serious problems and delays because software problems and hardware problems interact.

Usability—This term denotes the overall effort required to learn, operate, and utilize software or hardware.

User—The human being in whose behalf a program or system is being written. For measurement and estimating purposes, users have a significant impact. Software written for users who are knowledgeable and who participate actively during requirements and design has a much better success rate than software written for users who are inexperienced or who do not participate fully.

User association—This term means a more or less formally organized group of customers who use a vendor's products or services. User associations range from ad hoc groups to major corporations. The IBM user associations, COMMON, GUIDE, and SHARE have thousands of members and are important enough to sometimes cause IBM to change policies. Some user associations

have bulletin boards or forums using on-line services such as Compuserve.

User costs—In many companies, the users of software perform quite a substantial amount of work during the development cycles of major projects. For example, users are participants in requirements, they assist during prototyping, they may write their own user documents, they perform acceptance testing, and in some cases users may actually manage software projects. However users seldom charge their time to standard project cost buckets, and many do not record their time at all. The result is a sizable gap in the normal cost and productivity data available for research purposes.

User documentation—This term denotes the printed and on-screen text and tutorial materials which inform clients how to turn a program on or off and utilize its functions. User documentation is a major cost element for commercial software. User documentation is also a weak link in the software engineering chain: in five years of observation, user documentation was evaluated as poor to mediocre in almost half of commercial microcomputer software, and almost 25% of mainframe software. Finally, user document costs are a partly unexplored area of measurements for MIS projects, due to the fact that the users themselves often produce the documents, but do not charge their time to the project chart of accounts.

User friendly—This very unsatisfactory term has no standard definitions at all. At best it is a subjective term that denotes an application that is not excessively difficult to learn and use. Software vendors tend to apply the term erroneously to applications that are in fact quite difficult to use. Hence, the ambiguity of the term.

User satisfaction—This term means whether users are or are not happy with a delivered application. The factors promoting high user satisfaction are ease of learning, ease of use, error handling, quality of documentation, product quality, and service. The factors that diminish user satisfaction are poor quality, incorrect or misleading documentation, poor service, and cumbersome or inadequate functionality.

Validated data—This term defines information that has been examined and corrected. Only validated data is safe for serious studies of productivity and quality, since the error rate of raw data is often 30% to 50%.

Valid unique defects—This cumbersome term is very important for software quality purposes. It is defined as real defects (as opposed to invalid defects) that are reported initially (as opposed to duplicate reports). Valid unique defects comprise the basic figure of merit used by companies such as IBM for software quality measures.

Value—This term can mean several different things. The basic definition for software means business value, or why a program or system is being developed in the first place. A second meaning is replacement value, or how much it would take to recover from the loss of a program or system. A third meaning is strategic value, or what advantages a program or system might give versus competition. The concept of value and the task of value analysis is fairly primitive for software.

Vaporware—This term, formed by analogy with hardware and software, is a slang expression for software announced too long before its delivery to be believable.

Variance report—This term means a periodic analysis of the difference between what was budgeted for a project and what is actually being spent. Variance reports are often created monthly.

Variable costs—This term means the cost elements of a software project that change elastically in response to changes in scope or technology. Coding costs, for example, will vary in response to language or to the size of the program or system.

Venture capital—This fairly recent term defines a major new sub-industry of organizations that invest money in start-up or early stage companies. The concept is not very old, and the Digital Equipment Corporation (DEC) is perhaps the most significant example of venture funding in the computer arena. Entrepreneurs should be aware that the failure rate of venture-funded companies is actually quite high, and that venture funding is no guarantee of success. It is also interesting that the first or primary company to develop a new technology almost always has trouble receiving venture capital, due to the nature of the investment process. The 2nd through the 50th company to enter a field usually find it easy to get venture capital, which is why so many technical areas quickly become saturated and overcrowded.

Virus—This is a new term for an alarming phenomena: Software that is deliberately written to invade operating systems, replicate itself, and sometimes kill its host. Viruses have been created both as pranks and as deliberate sabotage.

Warranty—A guarantee from a vendor to a client that a product will behave as advertised. Warranties may be explicit or implied. Software has been notable for resistance to offering warranties. Look closely at the warranty description of any software package and you are likely to find more disclaimers than commitments.

Warranty costs—This term denotes the specific costs for making repairs or replacing a product under some form

617

of explicit or implicit warranty. Most U.S. software has no warranties and so warranty costs are seldom tracked. This is an emerging topic of some importance, since Japanese software vendors have started supplying warranties with software exported to the U.S.

Waterfall model—This term defines one of the standard, but inaccurate, views of how software projects are built. A waterfall model envisions a series of tasks, with the output of each task becoming an input to the successor task. This concept ignored overlap and concurrency, and is not very useful. An alternate and more useful concept is the Spiral Model, which envisions feedback loops and high concurrency between tasks.

Weakness report—This term denotes an output report from an assessment or a Software Productivity Analysis that shows the areas where the projects studied were worse than U.S. norms. See also "Opportunity" and "Strength report"

Weighting factor—This term denotes a mathematical technique for adding to the effect of a parameter or variable. For example in the IBM Function Point technique, weighting factors are used to adjust the impact of inputs, outputs, inquiries, data files, and interfaces. The original weighting factors multiplied inputs by 4, outputs by 5, inquiries by 4, data files by 10, and interfaces by 7.

Withdrawal—This term means the removal of a software product from the market place. Withdrawalis a complex business issue with a number of legal and warranty implications that surround it.

World class—An enterprise whose software performance is deemed good enough to compete successfully in global markets. See also "Best in class." This term was originally used to describe sporting events which could be or were held at the international level.

Work breakdown structure—This term means a formal analysis of the activities, tasks, and sub tasks that must be carried out to build a software project. Work breakdown structures are difficult to carry out by hand, but are easily performed with automated project management tools.

Work (day, month, year)—The term denotes the normal working periods for accounting purposes. This is a surprisingly inconsistent parameter and is responsible for significant errors in productivity studies. A normal U.S. work day is eight hours, the work week is 40 hours, and a working year in the vicinity of 1760 hours or 220 days. European, Canadian, and Japanese norms are quite different, and these must be factored in when doing productivity measurements or estimation. The Canadian work week, for example, is normally 35 hours while the Japanese work week is normally 44 hours. This is too big a difference to ignore.

Work bench—This term, originally from carpentry, has come to mean the collection of software tools available to professional staff. The best known is the Unix Programmers Work Bench.

Work effort—This important term is defined as the accumulated human time devoted to the tasks of developing or maintaining software. This basic definition conceals a myriad of possibilities, and one of the major problems of software has been the random and inconsistent activities considered as part of work effort. Some enterprises measure only coding; others measure design, code, and unit test; still others measure all of the tasks needed to put software into the hands of clients, both direct and indirect. About 25 discrete activities should be measured to capture enough data for meaningful statistical analysis of software development. The 1984 IBM Function Point method considers 20 discrete activities as part of its standard work effort calculations. This is one of the reasons why IBM's Function Point method is primarily used only for MIS projects, since the 20 activities exclude some major tasks that occur on systems and military projects, such as formal Quality Assurance, IV&V, etc. IFPUG should consider this problem, and amend the chart of accounts associated with Function Point data collection.

Work group—This somewhat ambiguous term has come to mean the set of people who must communicate and share materials while working on a common project. The concept is often associated with local area networks and tools intended to be used by several personnel concurrently. The term also has relevance to software license agreements.

Work station—This term is ambiguous, but generally means a high-end personal computer that at least in theory is optimized for certain kinds of programming tasks. The most visible difference between work stations and high-end personal computers is that work stations cost more, and software that operates on them may cost more as well.

Work unit—This term defines the time period which enterprises use for expressing cost and productivity data. The range of possible units includes work hours, work days, work weeks, work months, and work years. Larger companies and large systems usually deal in terms of work months or work years, while smaller companies and smaller projects usually deal in terms of work hours or work days.

Zipf's law—The linguist George Zipf discovered that the vocabulary of a text passage was proportional to its length. That is, long novels usually had a wider variety of words than short stories. Benoit Mandelbrot, the discoverer of fractals, noted that this law would be true even for random symbols divided at random intervals. Zipf's Law was published in 1935, and has been known by linguists for more than 50 years. This law was rediscovered and found to be true for programs as part of Halstead's Software Science research. That is, long programs and large systems will use a greater variety of instructions than small programs. This is not a surprising fact, but Software Science made a number of exaggerated claims based on this phenomenon.

Zero defects—This term denotes the deliberate corporate goal of commitment to strive toward perfect quality. Zero defect programs originated in the 1950's and were quite popular in the 1960's. The concepts are still laudable, but the idea is no longer at the forefront of corporate actions.